ANGER
Management

ALEPH

An independent publishing firm
promoted by *Rupa Publications India*

First published in India in 2024
by Aleph Book Company
7/16 Ansari Road, Daryaganj
New Delhi 110 002

ISBN: 978-93-93852-75-5

1 3 5 7 9 10 8 6 4 2

Printed in India

ANGER
MANAGEMENT

THE TROUBLED DIPLOMATIC
RELATIONSHIP BETWEEN
INDIA AND PAKISTAN

AJAY BISARIA

ALEPH

For my parents,
Priyamvada and Jagat Narayan Bisaria,
who were witness to Partition,
and had many stories to tell
of the times before and after.

CONTENTS

PROLOGUE: THE EXIT

I was expelled from Pakistan in 2019.

I had been stationed in Islamabad as India's high commissioner for twenty months at that time. It was August, the month that cooled Islamabad, when evenings turned pleasant, leaves turned golden to drift aimlessly on sidewalks. To the city's many expats, it felt more like early fall in Europe than late summer in Asia.

A gorgeous orange sun dipped into the horizon as I gazed out of the window of the armoured black BMW driving me to the Islamabad International Airport, a hurriedly inaugurated new facility, still leaking from recent rains. I felt short-changed by my unusual diplomatic departure. No fancy farewell reception preceded it, no series of dinners with special Balochi meats and Punjabi hospitality, no goodbye speeches, no jhappi-pappis, no media interviews to summarize my tenure, no witty recalls of my adventures in Islamabad mansions, not even a hurried shopping trip to Jinnah Super for mementos. I had a gnawing sense of leaving behind an unfinished agenda, something I had forgotten to do but could not quite recall what. It felt more interruption than closure, as if I had been plucked mid-stride on my way to work on a pleasant, unremarkable day.

I boarded a flight to Abu Dhabi on that breezy, almost autumn evening, after the unannounced drive on the Srinagar Highway. I wondered if I would ever return, as I tried to process the events of the past week that had altered my neat plans for the month and jolted the already troubled ties between South Asia's sibling nations.

The diplomatic euphemism for my exit was somewhat kinder than its characterization by the media—my host country had decided to downgrade the bilateral relationship with India and hence the post of high commissioner had become redundant. Therefore, Pakistan would no longer be sending its designated high commissioner to New Delhi. And could the Indian high commissioner in Islamabad please leave? The banner headlines were, of course, gleefully announcing that I had been expelled.

My position was not the only casualty. Pakistan had also announced a ban on trade with India, potentially inflicting much damage to its own pharmaceutical and textile industries. These were its first fuming reactions to the Indian parliament's decision to revoke Article 370 of the Constitution, extinguishing the special status of Jammu and Kashmir (J&K) and bifurcating it into two union territories.

Even as I quietly boarded the Etihad flight to Abu Dhabi, media vigils awaited me at Wagah and at Attari, on both sides of the Punjab land—crossing between the two distrustful neighbours. My impending departure had become a subject of shrill speculation over the previous three days, from the moment my marching orders became public. Electronic media channels on both sides of the border had cameras trained on the crossing's large clanging iron gates, expecting me to arrive by road at Wagah, cross over to Amritsar, and catch the evening flight to Delhi. We had led them on; a dummy booking in my name had been in place on Air India since the previous day. The channels were playing up each micro-step of my exit; the tickers were breathlessly breaking the news, 'Expelled Indian HC on way to Wagah'.

It would have been only right to cross back at Wagah. Zero Point, the white border marker was the parting gift of the British in 1947. It was where Wagah touched Attari on the Indian side, it was what I had gingerly stepped over as I walked into Pakistan to kick off my assignment less than two years earlier.

This was a border point defined by spectacle. As the only road-crossing between the two countries till 1999, it had a colourful past. It inhabited popular imagination as a tourist site where a piece of martial theatre had been performed by two adversarial forces every evening since 1959. Only an eruption of conflict or some particularly ugly rupture in the relationship interrupted the proceedings. Pakistan was even fonder of the performance than its bigger neighbour, having just seven months earlier converted the return across that border of captured Indian pilot Abhinandan Varthaman into a televised drama, after an aerial dogfight downed the pilot in Pakistan. Varthaman's bloodied, mustachioed face, gloatingly released on WhatsApp videos, became for India a marker of the Pakistan army's vulgar machismo; and when Pakistan was compelled to return him, he was made to cross over on foot at Wagah, after an achingly long wait into the night.

Going by this batting style, we thought there would be much temptation to position me for Pakistani television as a chastened Indian diplomat compelled to return home. Not to be outdone in countering this narrative, the Indian TV crews were waiting a few hundred metres from Zero Point to paint me the returning hero.

I disappointed them both with an unglamorous aerial exit.

I left Islamabad with mixed feelings—much lightness and some regret. I was relieved to exit the surreal bouts of hostility that marked my professional life, but missed being in the thick of the hard talk, missed being able to bid farewell to many personal friends and diplomatic colleagues.

～

Five days earlier, as shrill birdsong pierced the dawn on 5 August, hours before India's parliament dismantled Article 370, I had walked briskly on the little lawn within India House in the tony F6 sector of the geometrical cityscape of Islamabad—a town created in the 1960s, modelled after the ancient city of Taxila next door—with the foreboding that something dramatic would happen. Yet, I had nary a suspicion that rapidly unfolding events in the next few hours would precipitate my exit from the country within the week.

In conversations days earlier, some Western diplomats had alerted me that Pakistan's leadership was repeatedly and nervously summoning them, complaining of India's military build-up in Kashmir. The American envoy had suggested to the foreign office mandarins that Pakistan should convey its strong feelings directly to the Indian high commissioner.

And so, at 6 p.m. on 5 August, I was summoned to Pakistan's foreign office. I had conferred with India's foreign secretary, Vijay Gokhale, before the meeting, since it was plain what my hosts would say. I was to meet my primary interlocutor, Foreign Secretary Sohail Mahmood, with whom I had struck up a comfortable working relationship; we were on first name terms. We had candidly discussed some difficult issues in the past during my visits to India when he was Pakistan's high commissioner in New Delhi and also in Islamabad over his past few months as the foreign secretary, where we had together untied some knots. But this was different. It was serious. I did not know it then, but it would be my last meeting with him, and the toughest conversation we were to have.

As I was led into the plush corner room, defined by its oversized bottle-green chesterfield chairs, I quipped to lighten the mood, 'Looks like we've kept you busy.' Mahmood nodded unsmilingly, 'I wish you hadn't.' We shook hands. I hoped to keep the tone friendly; we were, after all, professionals doing a job. 'High Commissioner, we have a statement from the highest levels of our government, which I will read out,' he began stiffly. This was clearly not the day for first names. He droned gently through strong words of outrage at India's decision, a prepared script that I assumed would be out in the media minutes after I left his office.

In fact, that statement was to become the party line that would in subsequent days be repeated as Pakistan's official narrative at every conceivable forum and would soon be embellished with harsher, more abusive words. I was wondering what exclusive message would be delivered for India in this special démarche I was summoned for. I nodded at the young second secretary, Vipul Dev, who had accompanied me to this meeting. He took furious notes. These were not really necessary, given that the text of Pakistan's outrage was soon made available to the world:

> The Foreign Secretary summoned the Indian high commissioner to the foreign office and conveyed a strong démarche on the announcements made and actions taken by the Government of India with regard to Indian Occupied Jammu and Kashmir (IOK) today.
>
> The Foreign Secretary conveyed Pakistan's unequivocal rejection

of these illegal actions as they are in breach of international law and several UN Security Council resolutions. Pakistan's resolute condemnation of the unlawful actions aimed at further consolidating the illegal occupation of Indian Occupied Jammu and Kashmir was underscored....

The Foreign Secretary called upon India to halt and reverse its unlawful and destabilizing actions, ensure full compliance with UN Security Council resolutions, and refrain from any further action that could entail serious implications.

The Foreign Secretary reiterated that Pakistan will continue to extend political, diplomatic and moral support to the indigenous legitimate Kashmiri people's struggle for realization of their inalienable right to self-determination.[1]

This level of rhetoric was pretty much par for the course for India–Pakistan squabbles. But this time, it was only the take-off point for more to come. After the foreign secretary had sombrely delivered this tough message in his elegant corner room, I said I had a few points to make. This seemed to puzzle my host. A démarche by the foreign office of Pakistan to an Indian diplomat, howsoever harsh, normally meant you hear out a tirade, mostly delivered politely, say you'll pass it on back home, exchange pleasantries on some unconnected subjects, shake hands and leave. The script that evening was altered.

I said that while I would, of course, pass on the contents of Pakistan's statement to my government, I was under instructions to reject this take on events and in turn explain India's position to Pakistan. What had transpired in our parliament was an internal matter for us—India had made amendments to its Constitution through due process in its legislature, and we believed Pakistan had no locus standi in this matter. We presumed Pakistan had read India's Constitution, particularly Article 370,[2] which was a temporary and transitional provision that India's government and legislature was entitled to change. Due procedure had been followed in broad daylight after a nationally televised debate. This issue did not change the status quo on the border; the sanctity of the Line of Control (LoC) had not been disturbed in any way. Besides, one of the factors that had complicated the J&K situation for India was Pakistan's export of terrorism across the border for over three decades. The last bit was not strictly part of the script for the occasion, but I had improvised the talking point, to offer a more rounded appreciation of India's take on events.

The foreign secretary, while not surprised by the thrust of my argument, did appear taken aback by this kind of pushback. He was not about to give me the last word. He countered that Pakistan completely rejected India's posture and went on to explain how cross-border events had nothing to do with India's 'siege' of Kashmir.

I walked out after a grim handshake. The TV channels were breaking the story on Pakistan's démarche even before I ended my five-minute drive from the imposing Ministry of Foreign Affairs (MOFA) building in Islamabad's red zone to the Indian high commission in the adjoining diplomatic enclave. After some consultations with Delhi, we decided not to publicly share our version of my posture at the meeting that day. In any case, Pakistan's démarche did not get much play in the Indian media. Far too much was going on within the country.

On 7 August, the official outrage crystallized further. In a special session of Pakistan's parliament, the mood was of high indignation, often masking high panic; the decibel levels were matching the anger. Pakistan's leadership was floundering for the right response. Foreign Minister Shah Mahmood Qureshi fulminating in parliament and in media interviews against India's agenda to 'bury the issue of Kashmir',[3] warned that diplomatic ties were under stress and hinted that the Indian high commissioner might be asked to leave.

At the high commission, we went on high alert. I asked all diplomats to stay back in the chancery and work on contingency options. Pakistan could choose from a menu of angry expressions—snapping diplomatic ties, closing down the mission, reducing the strength of diplomats by half, or just expelling the Indian high commissioner. We could all be leaving our station in the next days, or even hours. Would we need to kick in war protocols like the destruction of records? Would we need to leave in a convoy of cars for Amritsar the next day?

In the event, Pakistan decided to exercise the least disruptive choice. I was given seventy-two hours to leave the country.

The director general for South Asia, Mohammad Faisal, called in Second Secretary Akhilesh Singh, whom we had hurriedly designated the acting deputy high commissioner—since the regular deputy, Gaurav Ahluwalia, was away in India—and passed on Pakistan's 'request' for India to withdraw its high commissioner.

Pakistan's spokesman made it public the next morning:

> Pursuant to the decision of the National Security Committee yesterday, the Government of India has been told to withdraw its High Commissioner to Pakistan. The Indian Government has also been informed that Pakistan will not be sending its High Commissioner-designate to India.[4]

No deadline for India to 'withdraw' me was revealed to the media. India's response the same day was calm but unusually expansive:

We have seen reports that Pakistan has decided to take certain unilateral actions in respect to its bilateral relations with India. This includes the downgrading of our diplomatic relations. The intention behind these measures is obviously to present an alarming picture to the world of our bilateral ties. The reasons cited by Pakistan are not supported by facts on the ground. Recent decisions by the Government and Parliament of India are driven by a commitment to extend to J&K opportunities for development that were earlier denied by a temporary provision in the Constitution. Its impact would also result in the removal of gender and socio-economic discrimination. It is also expected to result in an upswing of economic activity and improvement in the livelihood prospects of all people of J&K. It is not surprising that such developmental initiatives that could address any disaffection in J&K should be negatively perceived in Pakistan, which has utilized such sentiments to justify its cross-border terrorism.

The recent developments pertaining to Article 370 are entirely the internal affair of India. The Constitution of India was, is and will always be a sovereign matter. Seeking to interfere in that jurisdiction by invoking an alarmist vision of the region will never succeed.

The Government of India regrets the steps announced by Pakistan yesterday and would urge that country to review them so that normal channels for diplomatic communications are preserved.[5]

Expressing 'regret' rather than condemnation was in Indo–Pak diplomatese a pretty gentle protest. But Pakistan was in no mood for a review. Two days later, I was headed home.

⁀

History is replete with stories of diplomats who have met darker fates than an expulsion. Envoys have been lynched by angry mobs, downed by assassins' bullets, beheaded by enemy forces, even eaten in cannibalistic rituals. But such gory ends to diplomatic assignments have mercifully been rarer in recent times, since the United Nations and its Vienna Convention started regulating the behaviour of host countries towards accredited diplomats.

In several troubled relationships, diplomats have often been the first casualties when trouble started, easy pickings when angry hosts were examining more complex policy options. And particularly in the turbulent history of Indo–Pak ties, diplomats have faced a spectrum of churlish actions by their hosts: robustly abused in the foreign office, accused of activities unbecoming of diplomatic status, pilloried in the media, even harassed and beaten on the streets.

And, of course, expelled.

To be sure, such diplomatic downgrades have been as much in evidence in other troubled diplomatic relationships across the globe, between hostile neighbours or between major adversarial powers. But the degree of volatility has perhaps been especially heightened in the case of the two troubled South Asian neighbours.

When I reflected on my situation, I wondered how many of my predecessors or counterparts in the seven decades of the tortuous history of this relationship had faced similar fates.

In the turbulent days leading up to my departure, even as I assured family back home that I was in no physical danger, I sent reports and assessments to headquarters on the evolving situation. I called up two of my predecessors, to get the context straight in my head. The first was T. C. A. Raghavan my go-to colleague, a historian, and a veritable encyclopedia on the relationship, who had handled Pakistan multiple times in his career and written extensively on it. He said he had hoped it would not come to this, but told me reassuringly that I would still continue to be the high commissioner to Pakistan, but based in India 'on temporary duty'.

I then rang up Vijay Nambiar, who had faced a similar fate two decades ago. I wanted to get some insights from the turn of the century. He told me cheerily that he had not been removed at Pakistan's instance, but *withdrawn* by India, as a reaction to the terror attack on India's parliament in 2001. He had even played some golf before his departure. Now that was a thought. I could follow this precedent and exit on a swinging note with a farewell round at the Islamabad Golf Course. But I decided against this option. I might ruffle feathers on either side of the border and, worse, overload the already crowded agenda in a seventy-two-hour notice period.

The last expulsion by Pakistan before mine was not of an ambassador but of the chargé d'affaires (CdA) at India's mission in 2003. Sudhir Vyas had been asked to leave in tit for tat moves, after Pakistan's CdA (who later became foreign secretary and caretaker foreign minister in 2023), Jalil Abbas Jalani, was asked by India to leave, having been caught handing over cash to Kashmiri separatists.[6] The countries had behaved unpredictably even during wars: in 1971, diplomatic relations had snapped the moment war was declared and the high commissioner arrested; but in 1947, 1965, and 1999, diplomatic missions operated with no official bugle sounded on war. So, I had the dubious distinction of being, technically at least, the first Indian high commissioner in the history of the relationship to have actually been expelled by Pakistan.

With my own marching orders in hand, I was curious to discover why some diplomats had to leave their official perch, and how they reacted to the imminence of exiting prematurely from their host country. What caused that departure and what followed it? More importantly, were there any 'normal' times in this chequered diplomatic history?

The questions were many. What leads to a diplomat being booted out by a host country? How bad does the relationship need to get to reach this pass? Does it go through a familiar and repetitive trajectory? In other words, are all premature exits the same or do they each have a unique historical fingerprint attached to them? Each story of diplomatic exit would capture the dynamics of ties and some of the currents of the deteriorating relationship. Each expulsion, or recall, marked the end point of a process of diplomatic engagement getting strained to breaking point. Sometimes, the diplomatic tiff was only leading up to the next stage in the escalation ladder, the snapping of diplomatic ties, or armed conflict. Sometimes the two processes worked in parallel.

And what made for good times in the relationship? Were they only short aberrations in a turbulent, bitter relationship?

As I pondered all this, I wondered if the story of Indo–Pak diplomacy might not be told from the point of view of its practitioners, those who exited early and those who stayed long in the trenches? What sort of narrative might result if we plucked out the diplomatic players, the footnotes of history, and placed them centre stage, with the larger events playing in the background?

Thus was born the idea of this book.

INTRODUCTION: A QUEST FOR IDENTITY

The Partition of 1947 has sometimes been seen as a failure of India's pre-independence diplomacy. The departing British had dictated the terms of their exit to their colonial subjects, driven by their own strategic interests and from a position of asymmetric strength. The leaders of India's freedom struggle had little wiggle room in the negotiations, their own differences emphasized, widened, and exploited by their wily masters. They stood accused of rejecting power-sharing arrangements and the loose confederation the British had proposed in 1946. They lacked the leverage or experience to extract from the powerful colonials any more favourable deal than the creation of two hastily carved out successor countries from the undivided mainland of the subcontinent, each disappointed by borders suddenly thrust upon them. That it would spawn sustained hostility and decades of angry, distrustful interaction between them, was a tragic—but mostly unforeseen—consequence of the seminal partition moment.

In fact, Pakistan's promoters had insisted that the opposite would happen. The two-nation theory[1] held the implicit promise that the creation of a separate Muslim country would do away with the acrimony between the two nations, as delineated by the two major religious faiths of colonial India. And so, amity would ultimately prevail between the neighbours, since their new borders would keep them out of each other's hair.

Across the more than three quarters of a century since then, the siblings have been unable to overcome the foundational animosity that has permeated their relationship and have, in fact, added several more layers of mutual suspicion. In deconstructing this epic subcontinental rivalry, scholars have teased out complex etiologies, ranging from congenital distrust to religious schisms to geopolitical imperatives. But looking in the rear-view mirror of history, the diplomatic ties between India and Pakistan, as indeed the contours of the broader relationship, appear to be determined by one overarching factor: Pakistan's quest for identity. This quest has played out, most visibly, along two axes of contestation: territory and security. These ideas of identity, territory, and security have populated scholarship on the subcontinent and recur in the narrative of this book.

With Independence, national identity had to be redefined and reimagined in both countries, but Pakistan took on the additional burden of determining, even inventing, an identity distinct from India's. The first Pakistani, in the official narrative, was thus not Pakistan's founder, Mohammed Ali Jinnah, but Mir Qasim, the first Muslim to set foot in this region in 712 CE. In its quest for identity, Pakistan was not just seeking parity with India, but mostly emphasizing the differences with its larger twin. While the countries continued to share 'cultural intimacy', the state-building process in independent Pakistan stressed the 'differences' to gain legitimacy, and self-worth, for itself—a nation distinct from India. This idea of Pakistan, premised on irreconcilable differences between Hindus and Muslims, formed the core of Pakistani nationalism. This notion, in fact, shaped Pakistan's foreign and national security policy and thus informed its diplomacy with India.

In many ways, the two-nation theory was defying the traditional understanding of nationhood that had been prevalent in the Western world since the seventeenth century, and reinforced in the twentieth by the United Nations, a multinational institution created in 1945, just two years before Partition. The post-colonial Indian nation could have been constituted according to Western benchmarks: of a community with shared history, ethnicity, culture, and, of course, territory. But the British had now effectively endorsed the proposition that religion-based entities, 'nations', could reside in such a state. This was a convenient strategic recourse for the former colonials, even though clearly at odds with most twentieth century political beliefs.

Once matters moved from theory to reality, the 'imagined' communities of the Indian and Pakistani nations needed to rapidly define their postcolonial national identities. While India, like most postcolonial states of the twentieth century, set out to define and accept, through an intensely debated Constitution, an identity distinct from that of the colonial British, Pakistan saw the creation of a national identity as a task of building a sense of self as the Other of India. For India, the robust debates in the Constituent Assembly were as much about defining identity as crafting a Constitution to guide its destiny. Soon, India was on a constitutional path that embraced a secularism hard to reverse. But Jinnah and his successors started a process of constructing a new national identity for Pakistan, rather than tweaking an existing one, based on post-1947 realities. It was a national identity that would, apart from distancing itself from India's, submerge Pakistan's regional identities: those of Bengalis, Balochis, Sindhis, Pashtuns, and others. In fact, the non-Punjabi ethnic groups still don't accept the imposed construct. The Pashtuns, for instance, say they have been Muslims for 1,400 years, Pakistani for just seventy-five years, but Pashtun for 4,000.[2] Similarly, the linguistic identity of Bengalis was challenged with the imposition of Urdu, as the state went about creating a Punjab-centred identity. A common identity as India's Other, Pakistan's security apparatus hoped, could also serve to keep Pakistan's provinces united by a common hostility to India.

Over the years, Pakistan has struggled with this imagined community, this invented identity. Latter-day allusions to Riyasat-e-Medina as the ideal welfare state of fourteen centuries ago have pointedly been made in political discourse, reinforcing the identity confusion. It serves Pakistan's leaders not only to define a new national identity, but also to underscore that their nation's imagination of itself is more West Asian than South Asian. When the greeting Khuda Hafiz is changed to Allah Hafiz, the debate resurfaces over whether Pakistan's identity is Muslim or Arab, more akin to Islamic national identities of the western deserts where the faith originated. Since Partition, this identity debate has been a source of contestation within Pakistan as well. It was a religious identity that required Pakistan to insist it was both a Muslim and an Islamic state. A secular identity was not an option. As Pakistan's strongest dictator, General Zia ul-Haq, put it: if we are not Islamic, we should have stayed in India.[3] Some academics have been harsher on Pakistan, accusing it of claiming nationalism, while in fact lacking a nation.[4]

Providing more grist to Pakistan's internal debate was the political rise of a Hindu nationalist movement in India, with the proponents of this movement emphasizing India's Hindu past, traditions, and customs as the basis of Indian identity. This slant on Indian identity remained a politically charged and complex debate in India, with critics arguing that the movement's emphasis on Hindu identity and culture undermined India's pluralistic values and promoted a narrow worldview. But India's internal debates, harking back to a pre-Islamic past, led Pakistan to create a straw man of a non-secular and majoritarian Hindu civilizational state, discriminatory towards minority communities, particularly Muslims, and by extension hostile to Islamic Pakistan. The official Pakistani posture of stridently calling out any perceived discrimination against Indian Muslims, not just in the Muslim-majority state of J&K, influenced both the rhetoric and substance of the relationship.

Minority relations, within both India and Pakistan, have remained contentious since Independence and continue to be a testing topic for their diplomacy to this day. The idea of Pakistan was in a sense one aimed at resolving the fears of a minority in colonial India, a Muslim population of around 100 million in 1947, forming a fourth of a mainly Hindu nation. At Pakistan's creation, with 70 million citizens, an estimated fifth of them Hindus, a bizarre theory gained ground characterizing the minorities on both sides of the border as 'hostage populations' that would not be persecuted beyond a point, for fear of reprisals against their counterparts across the border.[5] Minorities would thus become groups that governments could intimidate, defend, or use as a negotiating tool. This theory did not retain much traction after the migrations triggered by Partition, but was occasionally evoked in the discourse of both countries. In subsequent years, however, India's constitutional secularism stood in contrast to Pakistan's lurch towards theocratism, further frightening the minorities in the Islamic state.

IDEOLOGY MATTERS

Pakistan felt obliged to describe a formal 'ideology' to define its national identity. It did so on the basis of the two-nation theory, as also by redefining its Islamic history and by reimagining the partition moment. The ideology travelled across the decades, to be frequently revisited and tweaked, but never abandoned.

Adherence to this national ideology, whether in the form of values, principles, beliefs, or mythologies, became a highly politicized state-driven process in Pakistan. Once the army became predominant, the political reality of the national security driven 'garrison state' was established. That garrison state arrogated to itself the role of being the defender not just of territory, but also of the ideological frontiers of Pakistan. The dictator Yahya Khan first used this formulation during his brief, ill-fated reign in the late 1960s.[6] During the civil–military debates in Pakistan in the 1990s, the civilian prime minister Benazir Bhutto bravely argued that the army should protect Pakistan's physical rather than its ideological borders, leaving the political class to determine ideology. However, military rulers—Ayub Khan in the 1960s and Zia ul-Haq in the 1980s—immersed Pakistan's security state into the business of defining its doctrine, co-opting the religious right in the process. Even civilian leaders like Zulfikar Ali Bhutto were compelled, in the 1970s, to use this playbook to consolidate power, making the state a radical entity intolerant of both its own minorities and of its non-Islamic neighbour.

For Ayub, Yahya, and Zulfikar, defining a national religion-based ideology was a tactical necessity; but for Zia, who made the process irreversible, it stemmed from deep personal religiosity. Even as Zia's security state arrogated to itself the role of defending the ideological boundaries of Pakistan, it stamped out pretences of civilian democracy, as it decreed civilians incapable of the task of defending ideological frontiers. And it did so in concert with the religious right, accommodating the jihadi mindset, hostile to domestic minorities and neighbours.

The ideological debate seeped into Pakistan's foreign policy and was applied over the decades most often to India, not only in terms of the rhetoric but also in the practice of its diplomacy. The strong use of ideological symbols and vocabulary in political discourse made it harder for Pakistan to practise a more pragmatic and flexible foreign policy.

The ideology of Islam was reinforced in the 1970s and 1980s, essentially to provide legitimacy to Pakistan's leadership. Some scholars have argued that Pakistan had by the 1980s established an Islamic identity that transcended the political, economic, and social realms from which ideology is often drawn. In the persistent public debates within the country, the argument is often made that a gulf had grown between Jinnah's idea of Pakistan and the one his successors shaped in later years.

India, meanwhile, was resiliently drawing its identity from its Constitution, laboriously worked out in its defining years, even though this identity was periodically challenged by left-wing movements since the early decades, or by right-wing movements that got greater political traction from the 1980s onwards. The ideology and the idea of India has been a robustly contested space for decades. But it has arguably not had a major influence on the country's foreign policy. A broad political consensus evolved in the country: for a secular, realist, and interest-driven foreign policy. A pragmatic approach to the rest of the world was the overtly stated and generally observed norm.

LOST TERRITORY

The unrequited quest for territory for Pakistan has been the most painful aspect of its search for an identity, especially when this clashes with India's idea of territory. Beyond the question of who we are, this quest raises fundamental issues that define nationhood: what belongs to us; where are the limits of our land and sea borders; how much of the rivers are ours? For both countries, the borders of Kashmir and the Indus system waters have been flashpoints of disagreement since the lines were drawn. But other areas contiguous to their common borders have also produced friction. The two countries have disputed each other's claims on land and maritime borders of the western Indian state of Gujarat, on Bengal in the east till 1971, and also on the waters of Punjab's Indus River and its tributaries. Specific negotiations have taken place on contested points like Siachen, Sir Creek, and Tulbul. Pakistan's official narrative has consistently promoted the irredentist notion of a state incomplete without incorporating the territory of Kashmir. The quest for territory thus became central to a search for identity, with the slogan 'Kashmir Banega Pakistan' or its description as Pakistan's jugular vein. A Pakistani writer and diplomat in fact likened the bilateral relationship to one of a joint family with first cousins, who are close in every way, till the matter of dividing the family inheritance comes up.[7] One viewpoint has it that if the issue of J&K had been addressed in the 1960s with the same diplomatic dexterity as the division of the Indus waters, we would have averted several conflicts of later years. Not everyone buys this reasoning. To many, the core divergence between India and Pakistan lies elsewhere, in the mind: in unsettled notions of identity, in concerns of security.

India's nationalism tends to be predominantly territorial, rather than religious, ethnic, or ideological. A territorial construct of Akhand Bharat (Undivided India) was a strand of thought popular in the run-up to Partition, partly to counter the move to divide the land. The construct survives to this day, as a fringe notion that asserts that the expanse of territory of all of modern-day South Asia is a common civilizational and cultural space and therefore one nation. Defending every inch of independent India's territory is often seen as the role not just of the armed forces, but a civic duty of every Indian. This brand of nationalism is seen as a foundational principle, with Partition itself seen as an unfair carving out of territory, followed by wars where Pakistan and then China occupied lands that belonged to India. To some modern writers, even this is a dangerous form of nationalism since it could discriminate against those seen as outside the territorial community, 'whether they be foreigners, immigrants, or minorities'.[8]

SECURITY: AN IMAGINED ENEMY

The search for security has been another defining feature of Pakistan's national quest. This search drove Pakistan to become a 'security state', also dubbed a garrison state, with an over-securitized foreign policy run by an unelected security establishment. Pakistan's institutional paranoia, its perception of India as its primary existential threat, has been the underlying factor in many of its interactions, and is indeed the main driver for the structural primacy of the army within its polity. With four major conflicts behind them, not just defending, but changing borders became a key goal for the Pakistani state. Moreover, irredentism on Kashmir, as noted earlier, became a matter of faith of Pakistan's foundational ideology.

Pakistan's search for security has taken several ideological turns. In a fundamental sense, Pakistan's struggle to safeguard the security of its nation state was seen in the initial years as an easier process: privileging hard power over diplomacy. With military force the instrument of choice, diplomacy was seen as a less reliable tool. Even in contemporary times, Pakistan tried to revisit its security paradigms. It defined a new security policy giving primacy to economic security or to geo-economics. This was a policy designed to overcome the infirmities of its economy, which, in turn, limit its political, military, and diplomatic power.

In its pursuit to define its identity with an ideology, in its quest for an imagined lost territory, in its search for security, Pakistan's approach has been to change the territorial status quo as a revisionist power, even while India has been content to be the status quoist power. Pakistan has over the decades adopted different means of trying to change the status quo on Kashmir. The first two decades meant using hard power and military power, when bilateral and global diplomacy seemed not to be bearing fruit. This expressed itself in the wars of 1947 and 1965 (reprised also in 1999) when the Pakistani state deployed a civilian cover to seize territory in Kashmir. Or the proxy war it initiated from 1989 onwards. For India, the territorial question was only one of the several diplomatic issues that would come up between unfriendly neighbours.

While territorial ambitions drove the wars between the countries, issues of security and identity were also at play. In the first quarter century of their existence, the countries fought three wars. These wars were fought overtly, when the power differential was not perceived to be large. But covert warfare became essential for Pakistan from the 1980s when the differential grew. The next quarter century saw proxy wars in Punjab and Kashmir. The relationship in the last quarter century has been transacted under a nuclear umbrella that gave Pakistan a perception of parity; but from India's point of view, it also gave the Pakistani state greater gumption to attempt proxy terrorism.

A thesis that has gained traction within Pakistan's official narrative is that while Pakistan's elections are about tabdeeli (change), Indian political parties seek popularity at the hustings showcasing hostility with a villainous neighbour. In the last three decades, it is in fact acts of terrorism, rather than bilateral ties, that have drawn headlines during Indian elections. Often, the two become indistinguishable in the Indian electoral discourse.

GLOBAL IMPACTS

Global currents have also had a strong impact on bilateral diplomacy. In other words, the rest of the world, and particularly the play of the major powers, has significantly influenced the India–Pakistan relationship. The British influenced matters in the region during the early years of Independence. By the mid-1950s, the Americans were seeking partners for influence in the subcontinent. China played a significant role with its 1960s strategic defence alliance with Pakistan, driven by the need to contain a common adversary, India; this intimate Sino–Pak alliance, strengthened by Pakistan's abject economic dependence on its northern neighbour, heightened for India the threat of a 'combined front' war.

The Soviet Union and the United States turned the region into a Cold War battleground in the 1970s; in fact, the four-decade superpower rivalry overlapped with and impacted the formative years of India–Pakistan bilateral ties. To many observers, Pakistan's close alliance with the United States provided it the confidence to launch two of its three major wars with India. Pakistan had, in fact, effectively leveraged its geostrategic location to emphasize its relevance to the major powers. The US Cold War reliance on Pakistan from the 1950s was followed by it seeking Pakistan's support in its war on terror in Afghanistan from 2001. It was critical for Pakistan to use global geopolitics to its advantage and to seek alliances with the major powers. It needed to counter the perceived India threat, and to seek 'geopolitical rents' to run its economy. When these rents began to dry up with the US withdrawal from Afghanistan in 2021, Pakistan required a newer strategy to shore up its dysfunctional economy. A preference for 'geo-economics', in essence a euphemism for fixing the Pakistani economy, became the stated goal for establishing a viable state.

DIPLOMATS AND LEADERS

In the tortured history of India–Pakistan ties, the agency of diplomats has mattered in tweaking the trajectory of the relationship. The early Indian and Pakistani diplomats, serving in the shadow of a traumatic Partition, deserve special credit for practising their craft with conviction. While the decade after independence saw contestation over the territory of Kashmir, it also saw a state-building process that deployed the nuts and bolts of diplomacy. Territorial compromises—for instance, defining a LoC in Kashmir in the aftermath of conflict, or sharing the waters of the Indus rivers—were the early fruits of the diplomacy. But the countries also discussed initiatives to resolve more immediate challenges like minority matters and economic decoupling.

Diplomats were often conflicted about raising minority matters. Dealing with issues of minority welfare across the border was part of the initial diplomacy, mostly policy overreach. This approach became cause for routine reciprocal accusations of anti-minority policies. For Pakistan, critical commentary on the treatment of Indian minorities was additionally a tool to assure its citizens that the equivalent Muslim population on the Indian side was somehow worse off than those within the Pakistani state. This was especially important after 1971, when the two-nation theory was effectively jettisoned by the creation of Bangladesh.

Economic issues were discussed at length in the early years, to achieve a rational decoupling of two nations born of one unit. Later, economic diplomacy needed to be innovative. Pakistan became wary of Indian efforts at encouraging trade, because they could dilute the Kashmir 'cause'. When India granted most favoured nation (MFN) status to Pakistan in 1996, Pakistan was placed in a quandary. For India, particularly after the 1990s, trade with Pakistan was more a confidence-building measure (CBM) than an element of its global economic policy, given the size of the Indian economy and its robust relations with the rest of the world. One strand of discourse within the country suggested that if India could continuously expand trade with one adversarial neighbour with differing perceptions on borders (China), could Pakistan not learn from that experience? Trade could create constituencies for peace and also equities within the system. However, trade and economic relations could never take off because they were overcome by sentiment and an instinct of not wanting an adversary to profit.

Some diplomats became personally associated with major initiatives, where they could persuade leaders to move in a particular direction. Indian diplomats dealing with Pakistan's military dictators persuaded successive governments to engage in the 1960s and 1980s. In the late 1980s, high commissioners in both countries were credited with averting nuclear escalation by engineering cricket diplomacy. In the twenty-first century,

Pakistan's ambassador played a critical role in facilitating a summit meeting in Agra in 2001, while a backchannel led by an Indian diplomat came close to a territorial 'resolution' in 2007.

The main drivers in the diplomacy between India and Pakistan, however, have been the leaders of the countries. Still, structural factors that defined the nature of the two states have also played an important role. For historians, this has often meant a debate between the 'great men' theory and the 'historical inevitability' hypothesis. Pakistani scholar-diplomat Husain Haqqani has argued that there have been many false dawns in India–Pakistan relations due to an over-reliance on the great men theory. Duos of leaders had held great promise of breakthroughs in their times: Zia and Rajiv, Benazir and Rajiv, Sharif and Gujral, Sharif and Vajpayee, even Sharif and Modi, seemed to signal new phases of constructive engagement. But the hopes were belied each time by the structural flaws in the relationship, the primary one being the dominance in Pakistan's polity of an army paranoid about India.

⌣

A more fundamental question could be raised about interstate relationships: does diplomacy even matter? Its practitioners have, through time, tried to elevate diplomacy to the level of an esoteric science, sometimes even a dark art. When the newly communist China established its foreign office in 1949, its first diplomat, Foreign Minister Zhou Enlai, paraphrased the Prussian general and military strategist Carl von Clausewitz, defining his craft as 'the continuation of warfare by other means'. For this brand of warfare, Zhou recruited diplomats to serve as a 'civilian army', a parallel made more real by contemporary Chinese 'wolf warrior' diplomacy. In Washington, state department mandarins and scholars use the acronym DIME (diplomatic, information, military, and economic) to remind themselves of the 'instruments that must be orchestrated in making foreign policy: diplomacy, information, military, and economic', with a studied primacy given to diplomacy.[9] In the decades of Cold War diplomacy between the US and the Soviet Union, diplomats took pride in not allowing a hot war in their territories, with conflicts confined under the containment paradigm in other theatres and fought mostly through proxies.

In troubled relationships, diplomats have sometimes found themselves standing between peace and war, deploying their craft to influence decisions as also the behaviour of foreign governments and peoples, through instruments such as dialogue, and negotiations, or other non-violent measures. The relatively modern Western notion of diplomacy as a 'complex art combining relationships, advocacy, inducements, threats, coercion', approximates to the classical tools advocated by Chanakya in the third century BCE: saam, daam, dand, bhed (suasion, inducement, punishment, manipulation). In fact, formal diplomacy, as old as the nation state,[10] is not always the weapon of choice for neighbours; hard power tactics and covert actions remain options on the table to conquer territories or to coerce counterparts.

While Indian diplomats were often seen by their Pakistani counterparts as wily and insincere, Pakistani diplomats of times past were thought of as urbane and suave, polished by their elite feudal upbringing, playing a weak hand well, charming the world with better articulation, if not credible narratives. This seemed to change in the current century, when the personalities of the diplomats seemed to matter less than the substantive postures of their countries and leaders.

Another enduring debate in India–Pakistan ties is about the credibility of the diplomatic actors themselves. Diplomacy in closed rooms sometimes perpetuates the self-interest of diplomatic elites, excluding impacted groups like the common people. Political leaders in India have often been pitted against military elites in Pakistan, as primary negotiators in the relationship. This asymmetric contest has not always led to the best outcomes.

Some scholars argue that in most societies, power is diffusing away from states to a much broader range of actors. This has created a 'diplomatic deficit' in the old structures of international relations, when non-state actors—civil society groups, academics, and private sector leaders—are excluded from conversations where they could champion positive change. So, the political, military, and diplomatic elites, a more exclusive club in Pakistan than in India, need to make space for conversations between civil societies: youth, academia, think tanks.

Within these constraints, diplomats have played a critical role in both the formulation and implementation of foreign policy. At several points, diplomats on either side were able to persuade political leaders to make choices against their judgement or beyond the confines of their vision and play along with what the officials were suggesting. Track II diplomacy or deniable backchannel communication deploying non-diplomats has been another aspect of bilateral diplomacy. It has often been successful when public glare can kill initiatives before they can reach any degree of maturity.

A PAINFUL JOURNEY

This book explores the journey of Indo–Pak diplomacy since Independence, examining the seminal events of each decade, the military actions, the diplomatic highs and lows. The pattern that emerges is of attempts at constructive conversations periodically interrupted by conflict and violence, of several false dawns and dashed hopes.

The first decade was marked by Partition and the war over Kashmir that broke out soon after. The state-building diplomacy of the decade saw a pact on minorities and a robust conversation on a 'no-war' peace deal. The second decade saw the beginning of Pakistan's military rule and the eruption of the war of 1965 over Kashmir. Yet the high point of the diplomacy of the time was the Indus Water Treaty that Nehru signed in 1960 with Ayub Khan. The third saw the 1971 war that broke Pakistan in two, with the creation of Bangladesh. A conference at Simla in 1972 defined the peace-making diplomacy. In the fourth, Punjab came into focus with a proxy war. The Siachen action of 1984 was another example of a contest over territory, and a consequence of undefined borders in J&K. The fifth decade from 1987 saw a proxy war begin in Kashmir, for which India had little answer. Yet diplomats managed to conjure up a mechanism of a comprehensive dialogue to address these issues. The sixth decade was when both countries went nuclear; but Pakistan still tried covert action in Kashmir in Kargil, under the nuclear umbrella. Proxy terror groups also became more active under that umbrella, yet diplomacy continued with Prime Minister Vajpayee's Lahore visit of 1999, the Agra summit of 2001, the Islamabad Summit of 2004, and a robust backchannel conversation that went on till 2007, until the Musharraf dictatorship collapsed. The seventh decade, starting 2007, was defined by the Mumbai terror attacks of 2008. A structured dialogue was resumed in the wake of the Mumbai terrorism, supplementing a continuing backchannel engagement, even as India's global diplomacy was stepped up. A new government in India tried 'swearing in diplomacy' in 2014, with sincere follow-up conversations; but in 2016, when terror struck in Uri, India seemed to finally craft an effective response to sub-conventional warfare. India declared there would be no talks with terror, keeping diplomacy on a low key from 2016. The eighth decade, starting 2017, has already seen a terror attack in Pulwama, India's air strikes in Balakot and the administrative restructuring of Jammu and Kashmir: all in a single year, 2019. The relationship plummeted, but quiet conversations did yield some results, like a ceasefire in early 2021, and hopes for a modus vivendi even with Pakistan's apparent economic collapse.

৵

A word about the periodization. Several books on India–Pakistan relations prefer an organic periodization around major events, like wars and coups and military rule. I discovered that a periodization in terms of decades after Independence lent itself to a surprisingly neat way to dwell on the story. Each decade followed a pattern of defining moments or crises, use of hard power to deal with these and some efforts at resolution.

Decade	Defining Events	Military Action	Diplomacy
1947–1957	Partition	1947–49 war	Nehru–Liaquat Pact, 1950; Decoupling
1957–1967	Ayub Khan's Coup, 1958	1965 war	Indus Waters Treaty, 1960; Tashkent Agreement, 1966
1967–1977	Creation of Bangladesh	1971 war	Simla Agreement, 1972
1977–1987	Punjab terrorism	Proxy war in Punjab, 1984; Siachen action	Zia's visits to India
1987–1997	Kashmir terrorism; Mumbai serial blasts, 1993	Proxy war in Kashmir	Composite Dialogue
1997–2007	Nuclear Tests 1998; Mumbai train attacks, 2006	Kargil; Mumbai train attacks 2006	Lahore, 1999; Agra, 2001; Islamabad, 2004; backchannels
2007–2017	Mumbai Terror Attack, 2008	Uri Surgical Strikes, 2016	Resumed Dialogue; Summits; Modi's Lahore trip, 2015
2017–2023	Pulwama, 2019; Article 370 revocation	Balakot Strikes, 2019	No talks with terror; Ceasefire, 2021

The diplomatic structures to deal with this troubled relationship have not evolved significantly. Over seventy-five years and more, twenty-five Indian heads of mission have served in Pakistan, giving each an average tenure of three years. They have been based in India's diplomatic mission in Karachi from 1947 to 1968 and then in Islamabad. Diplomatic ties were snapped for five years after the 1971 war, and had remained downgraded to CdA levels for another five, owing to India's anger over terror attacks or Pakistan's over administrative rearrangements in Kashmir. Both countries did invest their best diplomatic resources in each other. Pakistan's twenty-three heads of mission posted in Delhi have been the most senior members of Pakistan's foreign service; several have gone on to become foreign secretaries or foreign ministers. Pakistan has had its embassy in New Delhi all along with the consulate in Mumbai that paralleled the Indian consulate in Karachi operational from 1979 to 1996. High commissioners were periodically rechristened ambassadors whenever Pakistan quit the Commonwealth (as it did between 1972 and 1989) or was suspended for a slide back on democracy (as in 1999, 2007).

As stated, Pakistan's identity crisis has severely impacted its relationship with India, as have precepts of ideology, territory, and security. At the same time, global factors have been at play, apart from the choices made by leaders and, on the margins, the agency exercised by diplomats on the ground. Over the last three quarters of a century, military actions, violence, and hostility have been balanced by attempts to stabilize the relationship through diplomatic innovations and often, peace efforts. These have not always succeeded, but have been relentlessly attempted by both leaders and diplomats. The turbulent journey of India–Pakistan diplomacy has seen more lows than highs, more pessimism than hope.

What follows is a practitioner's account, one more interpretation of a relationship much too important for the world not to be examined periodically from newer perpectives. It mostly represents an Indian view, with Indian diplomats often providing a vantage to critical events. Other observers and actors, like Pakistani diplomats and analysts, add their voices often enough. In this narrative, I have mostly stayed clear of details of military and covert actions and intelligence operations, fascinating as they can be, since several shelves in libraries are dedicated to these. The principal aim of this book is to examine the tempestuous relationship between India and Pakistan through the lens of diplomacy.

A Note on Style

Names of people and places have been spelled as per conventions that were in use at the time of the events in this narrative.

1947–1957: BUILDING STATES

MIDNIGHT'S NATIONS

Swelling with pride, the portly freedom fighter in a Gandhi cap rigged up a tricoloured cloth onto a makeshift flagpole at the Palace Hotel in Karachi. It was barely a few hours after South Asia's seminal moment: that fateful midnight when a departing colonial empire allowed a fifth of humanity to take control of its own destiny, that instant when India shook off two centuries of subjugation, to wake to light and freedom.[1] The man hoisting the Indian flag in Pakistan was Sri Prakasa, a Congress Party activist who had spent the past decades agitating for India's freedom. He was now also free India's first high commissioner to its newly born neighbour, his hotel room his home country's embassy, and he its sole employee. The envoy was also the solitary vocalist that morning of 15 August 1947, as he delivered a rendition of the patriotic Bengali song 'Vande Mataram' for his audience of sundry hotel staff and guests. He was gamely covering for a missing choir of Sindhi girls, scheduled to perform at this momentous event. When the day's festivities were done, the eager hotel management would illuminate the flag that night and every night of his stay, to humour their first diplomatic guest.

Producing the singing choir had been the responsibility of the envoy's fellow Congress leader and comrade of several years, Choithram Gidwani, who had petulantly rejected the invitation to join the event 'for freedom was no freedom for which Sindh had been sacrificed'. Gidwani was based in Karachi with the imposing title of president of the Provincial Congress Committee, a post he had held continuously for a quarter century. Bewildered to find the ground beneath his feet abruptly belong to a new country, Gidwani was now bitter, in equal measure, about this pointless Partition and about the end of the road for the Sindh Congress. He seemed as surprised by the new diplomatic position the Congress leadership had conjured up in Karachi as he was upset at being overlooked for it. More fundamentally, Gidwani grasped neither the permanence of the new boundaries of the two newly-created nations nor their new external obligations. Since he was available, why would any other Congressman have any business showing up to represent India? A nonplussed Prakasa had no good answer. He suggested to his colleague that this query was best addressed to the party's president and the designated prime minister of India, Jawaharlal Nehru.

Like several of his comrades in the Indian National Congress, Prakasa had been viscerally against the idea of a partition. He hoped that the proposal was somehow reversible. He had gone to jail during the Quit India agitation against British colonialism in 1942 and remained passionate about fostering communal harmony between Hindus and Muslims. Many in his host country, however, did not associate that sentiment with the party to which Prakasa belonged, seeing the Indian National Congress as a majoritarian Hindu behemoth. Still, a large number of Indian politicians in late 1947 wished—as their counterparts on the other side of the border feared—that the two countries would somehow come together again within months of the departure of the British. Through the next eighteen months of his tenure, the Indian envoy would go on to make his views annoyingly clear to his Pakistani hosts.[2]

It was still unclear at their independence where the border between the twin nations would appear. But Karachi, the sleepy capital of the Sindh province, nestling on the Arabian Sea, hometown of Pakistan's founding father, Mohammed Ali Jinnah, was quite emphatically the seat of the new government.

The previous day, Prakasa, as India's chief representative to the 'new sovereign state'—he could still not get himself to call it a separate country— had attended an independence ceremony in Pakistan's new constituent and legislative assembly in Karachi; Lord Louis Mountbatten was in town on his last day as the last British viceroy to India—to formally transfer power to the government of the new state of Pakistan and to inaugurate Jinnah as its first head of state. Jinnah had, of course, chosen to become Pakistan's governor general, refusing to cede that role, even temporarily, to Mountbatten, as the Indian leaders had done. Mountbatten's schedule, packed with events that day, determined the timing of the function: he would do the honours in Pakistan on the eve of the designated Independence Day, and then rush back to join the midnight ceremony in Delhi. Prakasa sat sullenly, discomfited by the proceedings at the government house in Karachi, underwhelmed by the 'mutually complimentary and felicitous' speeches by Mountbatten and Jinnah.

In contrast, freedom at midnight in neighbouring India had been greeted with soaring rhetoric from its first prime minister, Nehru, who spoke poetically of the soul of a nation long suppressed finding utterance. The fateful date was chosen by Mountbatten to commemorate the second anniversary of an event he was proud to have played a role in: the Japanese surrender to the Allied Forces in World War II. The date met with resistance from Vedic astrologers who found it inauspicious. Midnight between the two dates thus became the acceptable compromise, satisfying both the vanity of the world's largest, albeit dying, empire and the alignment of the planets above it.

That it was an auspicious time was one issue the devout on both sides agreed upon: the month of Ramzan was on. 15 August fell on the privileged twenty-seventh 'night of destiny', the last Friday of the holy month. Many in Pakistan saw this as 'the divine imprint on the birth of Pakistan' and would question the cabinet's decision, in June 1948, to designate 14 August as the future date for celebrating Pakistan's Independence Day. The British parliament's Indian Independence Act, 1947, of July, they pointed out, mentioned 15 August as the appointed day of the birth of the two dominions. Besides, Jinnah and Pakistan's cabinet had been sworn in on that day. But Pakistan's young government wanted to distinguish its identity as well as birth hour from India's midnight moment.[3]

The midnight hour was to become a striking metaphor for India's destiny. It was a moment of awakening. Midnight's children would be born to a brighter future even though the darkness of the night would cloak 'midnight's furies' that led to mass communal killings. Even Nehru's paean to the joy of freedom was tempered with references to the pain of Partition, the loss of vast swathes of territory to a sibling nation. Nehru spoke of a 'tryst with destiny' and a pledge taken long years ago at the Karachi session of the Congress that declared 26 January 1930 as the purna swaraj or 'total independence' day for India. He also spoke of redeeming that pledge 'not wholly or in full measure', which was seen as a gentle lament about the loss of territory. But Nehru had ended his midnight poetry with heady hope for the future.

It was this hope that infused the population the next day, as newly freed citizens of India fervently raised hundreds of saffron, white, and green flags across the country in a blissful dawn of celebration, to the accompaniment of passionately sung patriotic songs. India's envoy in Pakistan plugged into this heady moment as he raised the revered tricolour in territory that had ceased to be part of his motherland.

While Pakistan needed urgently to create new state mechanisms to write its fresh destiny, India had a headstart, with functioning governance structures vacated by the departing British in Delhi. Nehru had clear ideas of the mission ahead, the Congress had been preparing for this moment for decades. India would resolutely be born as a parliamentary democracy, every one of its adult citizens would be allowed to vote. Nehru would be his own foreign minister, with a powerful vision of India's unique role in the world. He would display a progressive approach to governance in putting together a cabinet team of ideological rivals, including Law Minister Bhimrao Ramji Ambedkar, a leader of the backward castes, and Industry Minister Syama Prasad Mookerjee of the right-wing Hindu Mahasabha, apart from the steely home minister, Vallabhbhai Patel, a Congress colleague with views that often diverged from Nehru's own. These worthies held mostly conflicting views on dealing with the severed territory of Pakistan.

Meanwhile, the tallest leader of the subcontinent was deeply distraught. He had marked 15 August with a solemn fast of protest in Calcutta, which had seen an orgy of communal violence. To that great soul, Mahatma Gandhi, the freedom for which he had long struggled, had come at an unacceptable price. Independence had also meant Partition and heart-wrenching bloodshed.

Jinnah himself had been in Delhi, before he flew into Karachi on 7 August, barely a week before he was sworn in as the first executive head of a new nation. He had been caught up in working out the modalities of Pakistan's birth: from the boundaries of the new Pakistani state to its Constituent Assembly to the minutiae of the independence ceremony to the logistics for the import of the shiny Rolls-Royce he would receive as a gift from Mountbatten. As he left his home on 10, Aurangzeb Road, in New Delhi, Jinnah suspected he would never return to India. He had tried to become the sole spokesman[4] of India's hundred million Muslims, but although he hadn't quite achieved that, he had accomplished the incredible feat of wresting a nation from the departing Raj. Only a few months earlier, a new Muslim nation had seemed a distant dream and Jinnah had voiced the fear that he might not live long enough to see Pakistan.[5]

Ten days before the creation of the twin nations, Prakasa, just turned fifty-seven, was at home in Benares on the banks of the Ganga. He was sorting through some papers when the phone rang. On the line was Congress president and prime minister-designate Nehru, requesting him to take over as India's high commissioner to a country that, to Prakasa, 'was being created by the vivisection of the living body of our dear motherland'[6]. Prakasa, whose feelings about this offer were distinctly mixed, conveyed to Nehru that he would think the offer over and respond in a day. Prakasa had no indication of this offer a couple of days previously in Delhi, where he served as member of the Constituent Assembly. He surmised that Nehru had made his decision just before the phone rang.

Sri Prakasa had been a freedom fighter and Congress Party leader, an activist for Hindu–Muslim amity with no aspiration for high office. He pointedly did not wish to be a 'symbol of the partition' that he 'totally abhorred'. His scholar and theosophist father, Bhagwan Das, was even more uncomfortable with his son's assignment; the Partition, acquiesced in by the Congress leadership, militated against his own life-long goal of communal harmony. Das was eventually persuaded to bless his son's assignment, but Prakasa's own misgivings persisted about 'duties and responsibilities to which I was a total stranger'.[7]

Earlier in the year, the British decision to exit India had been accompanied by the creation of a partition committee to work out the nuts and bolts of the division. After the arrival in Delhi of Mountbatten in March, the committee evolved into a council in June 1947. The viceroy chaired the body, with two representatives each for India (Sardar Patel and Rajendra Prasad) and Pakistan (Liaquat Ali Khan and Abdur Rab Nishtar). Prakasa had heard that the Partition Council had recommended an early exchange of high commissioners, as part of a mandate that addressed 'all matters connected with the partition'.[8] The council faced an array of immediate decisions that included 'the final demarcation of boundaries, the division of the armed forces, division of the staff of the various branches of government, the division of assets, the jurisdiction of courts, the economic relations between the two dominions, as well as methods of deciding how domicile should be determined'.[9] The setting up of diplomatic missions was just one of the many tasks the two countries faced as they decoupled.

Two days after Sri Prakasa received the call from Nehru, the designated envoy had with trepidation hastened to Delhi, to meet with his mentor. Nehru saw the hesitation and 'obvious lack of self-confidence' of his envoy pick and offered him a deal: he should represent India at the inauguration of Pakistan and on his return, take a final call on whether to, in fact, take up the assignment.

Thus, the newly minted diplomat found himself on a plane to Karachi on 12 August, three days before either the sending or the receiving country found an independent place on the world map, and five before they knew where their borders lay. On landing, he checked into the Palace Hotel that was to serve for several years as the de facto diplomatic enclave of Pakistan's new capital. The Indian diplomat's arrival was devoid of all ceremony. Since both countries were to remain in the British Commonwealth headed by King George VI, no credentials were to be presented to local leaders. Instead, the envoy carried a formal letter of introduction with India's greetings to the designated prime minister of Pakistan, Nawabzada Liaquat Ali Khan, well-known to Prakasa as a former Muslim League leader from the United Provinces and the finance minister in India's interim government from 1946.

Prakasa had known Nehru and Jinnah, but had been equally familiar with several other Congress and Muslim League leaders, many now relocated in Pakistan. He realized that this was why he had been chosen as India's first envoy. In a 'loose informal dress', Prakasa, met with a warm reception at the home of Pakistan's prime minister designate, who was also to serve as its foreign minister for the first few months of the Indian envoy's tenure.[10] Liaquat dispensed with formalities and sat his old acquaintance down for a friendly chat, establishing an easy working relationship that was to serve them both well.

Prakasa settled down quickly to revive his network of connections with several key actors in Karachi from times past, working from his office in his hotel room where he was himself 'both secretary and clerk'.[11] An early diplomatic engagement he had was with his British counterpart, also camping in the same hotel, an experienced diplomat and crafty player of the geopolitical Great Game, Sir Lawrence Grafftey-Smith. The English diplomat was later credited with coercing Prime Minister Liaquat Ali to cancel a trip to Britain's feared post-war rival, Russia. The exchange between the envoys, however, was not quite brimming with rare insights into high strategy. Prakasa's takeaway was a practical gem of bureaucratic wisdom that the Englishman imparted: 'Don't invite the work; let the work come to you.'[12] A flood of work, complex and challenging, would nevertheless inundate Sri Prakasa in the months he spent in Karachi. He would spend much of his tenure dealing with Partition's pains: migration, refugees, massacres, bloodshed, as also the complex processes of consolidation of the two sibling states as they tried to integrate princely dominions and fought over the territory of the most contested kingdom of them all—Kashmir. These themes reverberated not just during Prakasa's brief tenure in Pakistan and for his successors in the years after Independence, but were to cast long shadows over Indo–Pak diplomacy of the next several decades.

THE BOUNDARY AWARD

High Commissioner Sri Prakasa returned to India soon after the independence rituals in Pakistan. His doubts about the assignment were lessening; the excitement about his job in Karachi was mounting. He had decided to accept his new mission. He now packed his bags for a longer stay across the border. By the time he went back to Pakistan at the end of August, events had moved with bewildering speed: his home and host country now had a line firmly dividing them. The much-anticipated and feared boundary award came on 17 August, setting in motion a train of events that none seemed able to control or even fathom. These events would reverberate intensely across the decade and beyond, their ripples felt to this day.

A London judge on his first visit to India, Cyril Radcliffe had created two Muslim-majority regions in the east and north-west of India, carved out of Punjab and Bengal. Radcliffe had drawn up borders over six weeks, despite poor maps, squabbling deputies, and bouts of dysentery. The boundary award, based on multiple opaque and largely subjective principles—some determined in secret British confabulations well before Radcliffe's arrival—had been announced on 17 August, leaving millions stranded on the wrong side of the new lines, triggering unforeseen chaos. Those hastily drawn borders also provided cause for four wars and decades of aggravating animosity between two neighbours.

Radcliffe's lines disappointed Jinnah. His was a 'truncated, moth–eaten and mutilated' Pakistan.[13] The two Muslim majority provinces of Punjab and Bengal, which Jinnah had hoped to acquire in their full glory, were now carved and divided by a jagged line in blue pencil. The city of Lahore had fallen within Pakistan while Amritsar and the strategically located district of Gurdaspur in Punjab remained in India.

Pakistan was now a 'country divided into two Wings a thousand miles apart, that fantasic bird of a place, two Wings without a body' with two wings, separated by a thousand miles of Indian territory.[14] The western wing consisted of the newly delineated West Punjab (with Lahore as its capital), merged with the North-West Frontier Province (Peshawar), Sindh (Karachi), Baluchistan (Quetta), and thirteen undecided princely states. East Bengal (with Dacca as its capital) now became East Pakistan.

Prakasa had returned to a grimmer reality in Lahore—the former capital of undivided Punjab, now the Pakistani city just across Radcliffe's line. He watched another tragedy unfold as he camped 'in a small corner' in a 'hospitable house full of refugees',[15] with his colleague, deputy high commissioner for West Punjab, Sampuran Singh, in what used to be the Punjabi freedom fighter Lala Lajpat Rai's home. The events of the next few days would horrify the high commissioner—bloodshed, butchery and rage would accompany the unplanned movement of vast populations.

∽

India's independence had seemed increasingly inescapable since the end of World War II, as a devastated Britain emerged from the ravages of war with a dwindling appetite for empire. Scholars still debate when the Partition of the country became inevitable, but the definitive declaration of Pakistan's impending birth came only in 1947. The exit from India had been officially announced by Britain's prime minister Clement Atlee in February 1947, formalized in June with the Mountbatten Plan, and then given legal force by the Indian Independence Act, 1947, passed by the British parliament in July. The Act allowed for the creation of the 'Dominions of India and Pakistan' on 15 August and for their immediate secession from the British Commonwealth. Mountbatten had crunched the timeline for independence by ten months, advancing the original target date of 30 June 1948. Imperial fatigue was the likeliest cause. But the British spun it as a signal of the sincerity of the Raj in departing India swiftly and as an attempt to stem riots and bloodshed that had accompanied rising communal tensions since August 1946. Whether this new timeline in fact averted violence or added to it, is a historical counter-factual that still engages scholars.

The boundary award was published on 17 August, two days after Partition, though it was meant to precede it. Mountbatten had hoped to time the announcement to a few days before Independence. If it came too early, communal violence could escalate. Too late would mean a chaotic

Partition. But Radcliffe and his Boundary Commission presented a fait accompli to the governor general when they eventually got the job done only after Independence. Mountbatten released the maps two days after presiding over two Independence events. The impact was worse than he had feared. Political leaders felt swindled of territory. Jinnah felt his Pakistan was truncated. People on both sides of the new border felt cheated. Muslims in Punjab were enraged because they expected Gurdaspur district—now in India—to have gone to Pakistan because of its ethnic composition—a 51 per cent Muslim majority—but also because the city of Qadian, sacred to the Ahmadiyya sect, was located there. This would later be seen as ironic, given that the minority would not be considered Muslim in Pakistan in the coming years.[16] Pakistan perceived another conspiracy in Gurdaspur being awarded to India: it would enable land access to Kashmir that India could use to establish a hold on the princely state that had yet to make up its mind on which way to go.

Many Sikhs were upset that their revered Nankana Sahib—where the first Sikh guru was born—and Kartarpur Sahib—where he spent his last days—had been handed over to Pakistan. Sikhs were now being ruthlessly massacred in western Punjab by bloodthirsty mobs, which included their own neighbours, often with the aim of stealing property. In eastern Punjab, angry Sikhs were on the loose, killing Muslims. These Muslims were in turn trying to escape to West Punjab. Those who succeeded further contributed to the cycle of retribution and revenge. In the month of August, 15,000 were killed in Punjab alone. Partition's genocidal violence would eventually leave more than 1 million dead.[17]

Several Partition tales reveal the profound uncertainty of those times. The former capital of the Raj in the east, Calcutta, had remained in India while the city of Lahore had gone to Pakistan. Radcliffe later revealed to Indian journalist Kuldip Nayar: 'I nearly gave you Lahore...but then I realised that Pakistan would not have any large city. I had already earmarked Calcutta for India.'[18] Lahore had Hindus and Sikhs in the majority but Radcliffe saw no option because of the paucity of big towns in Pakistan. Nayar found to his horror that 'Radcliffe had no fixed rules to go by when he drew the boundaries between India and Pakistan.'[19] Some scholars question this version, ascribing it to Radcliffe's fading memory. The dividing lines of Partition, they argue, had been drawn in London to suit the British interest of creating a viable state to India's west, beholden to Britain; so Radcliffe's role was perfunctory.[20]

THE GREAT INDIA GAME

Narendra Singh Sarila was an aide-de-camp (ADC) to Governor General Mountbatten before he joined the 1948 batch of India's foreign service and went on to serve for thirty-seven years as an Indian diplomat. In his book on the 'untold story' of India's Partition, Sarila emphasized a thesis that has since gathered wider support based on archival evidence. He argued that the Partition of India was firmly connected to the geopolitical 'Great Game' that was being played from the nineteenth century, between the British Raj and the Czarist empire, for control over Central Asia and Afghanistan. He thus laid the blame for 'Divide and Quit' at the door of the departing British Raj, rather than on either Jinnah or Nehru.

The nineteenth-century Great Game was being played out in Afghanistan and Central Asia. The British had fought wars in Afghanistan, built railway networks to the Khyber Pass, and helped the rulers of Kashmir extend their influence into Chinese Xinjiang: all to keep the areas of India's western approaches from slipping into Russian influence.[21]

Sarila demonstrated the British conviction in the 1940s that if they withdrew from India, Congress leaders would be unsympathetic to British military interests. He pointed out that Lord Wavell, who was the viceroy from 1943 to 1947, was among the first to be persuaded that while the Congress was unlikely to further British military interests, the Muslim League would be willing to do so. Hence, if the League were to succeed in separating India's strategic north-west from the rest of the country, British interests would be better served by a military deal with this new state, particularly in defending the oil wells in the Middle East. As 1946 went by, Wavell's point of view became acceptable in British military circles. Nehru's oath in the Constituent Assembly to declare India a sovereign independent republic free from the Commonwealth, reinforced the assessment that a pliant western splinter state was more in the British interest.

Sarila has argued that midway through World War II, the British realized that they would have to quit India sooner than later, and in the process abandon a military base that had served them well for over fifty years. Their strategic thoughts then turned to closing the gap that would result in tying up a Commonwealth defence against the Soviet move to the south, towards the 'wells of power in the Indian Ocean'.[22] To find a solution, they looked for manoeuvres in India through what was described by Churchill as 'opportunism and improvisation'.

Decades later, a brilliant Indian scholar-diplomat, Chandrashekhar Dasgupta, delved deep into freshly declassified archives to decipher the colonial strategy of that period and came to similar conclusions as Sarila. He pointed out that after the Mountbatten Plan on the transfer of power to the dominions was finalized in June 1947, the British army, navy, and air chiefs met in July to reiterate that the 'main and overriding consideration should be to retain both India and Pakistan within the British Commonwealth, or at any rate ensure that they will cooperate (militarily) with us'.[23] The British strategic tilt towards Pakistan had become a strong factor in the India policy now being rolled out: the chiefs of staff concluded that 'while the ideal outcome would be to secure the cooperation of both India and Pakistan, on the other hand, the area of Pakistan is strategically the most important in the continent of India and the majority of our strategic requirements could be met, though with considerably greater difficulty, by an agreement with Pakistan alone.'[24]

Based on archival evidence, Dasgupta inferred that 'by August 1947, the British authorities had determined that their strategic interests in the subcontinent lay primarily in Pakistan, though the hopes of a defence treaty with India as well had not yet been given up. The decisive consideration was the proximity of airbases in West Pakistan to the Gulf region.'[25]

While British military officers were warmly welcomed in Pakistan, their reception in independent India was cooler. Nehru wanted complete nationalization of the armed forces by June 1948—the date originally determined for the transfer of power. When the date was abruptly advanced, the Indian leader had to reluctantly accept the persisting British presence, even as Partition changed priorities, but he continued to lament the structural anomaly. 'It is incongruous for the army of a free country not to have its own officers in the highest ranks', he wrote to Mountbatten in July 1947.[26]

A crucial meeting of the provisional Joint Defence Council was held a fortnight before Independence, on 29 July 1947. Chairing the meeting attended by Jinnah, Liaquat Ali Khan, and Sardar Patel, Mountbatten remarked that the forces of the two dominions would not fight each other, since 'under no circumstances could British officers be ranged on opposite sides'.[27] Later events would suggest that neither Patel nor Jinnah then fully registered the viceroy's hint: the British would work against any national security choices made by the new countries they served if these choices would endanger their own officers. So, '...immediately after the transfer of power, secret orders were issued by Auchinleck to British officers, requiring them to "Stand Down" in the event of a conflict between the two dominions.'[28] In other words, if either India or Pakistan were to attack the other, British officers in both armies were under orders to sabotage these plans.

A different point of view was also initially in currency, suggesting that British interest lay in leaving behind a united India. Its primary proponent was Field Marshal Claude Auchinleck, who felt that a united Indian Army— with British, Hindu, Sikh, and Muslim soldiers—could succeed in a united India and defend its overseas interests. But Lord Wavell's argument was winning. He had a long discussion with Churchill in 1945 where he seems to have persuaded the British prime minister of the advisability of a partition.[29]

The strategic calculation in the empire's twilight was simple: Britain's true Pakistan policy was to keep a part of its old Indian empire—that which jutted into Central Asia and lay along Afghanistan, Soviet Russia, and China—in the hands of the successor dominion that had promised defence collaboration. Britain openly supported Pakistan at the UN. In fact, US telegrams documented Britain's pro-Pakistani tilt in Kashmir.[30]

The agreement to partition India was announced in Delhi on 3 June 1947. Krishna Menon, who was then head of the India League in the UK, wrote a letter to Mountbatten on 14 June, while staying with Nehru in Delhi, which raised concerns on the British strategy. Did they intend to use West Pakistan and the princely state of Kashmir, asked the diplomat, as bases to contain the perceived Soviet desire to expand their influence in the Indian Ocean, Afghanistan, and the Persian Gulf?[31]

British internal reports in 1947 were clearly emphasizing that British strategic interests in the subcontinent should be focused on Pakistan. There was also some hope that some large princely states may remain independent and even provide the right for military aircraft to use bases in Hindustan.

The geopolitics of the period marked the intersection of a nineteenth-century contest with a twentieth-century dynamic. The post-war compulsions of the Cold War were still evolving, even as the nineteenth-century contestations were playing out their endgame. Pakistan was being used by the British as a bulwark against Russia and the colonial idea of Russia coveting the jewel in the imperial crown. There was a time right after the world war ended, when the Great Game and the Cold War overlapped in the subcontinent, from 1945 to 1947, to provide an additional impulse for the birth of Pakistan.

Some scholars however argue that the colonial role in Partition is overstated. After all, the British Cabinet Mission Plan of 1946 proposed keeping India intact as a loose confederation with a centralized defence and foreign policy. But Partition, whatever its etiology, served British post-colonial goals well.

The subcontinent was also impacted by the larger geopolitics of a world emerging from a crippling war. The incipient Cold War after 1945 meant that former world war allies were turning adversaries, and a tired Britain was passing on the baton to the United States for leading the emerging post-war West.

The post-war era was geopolitically less complicated for India. The US had not quite started playing a role in South Asia; it was just beginning to pick up its Cold War interests from the British. The Cold War strategy of containment of the USSR was still evolving, even though a US diplomat George Kennan had sent a long telegram from Moscow in 1946, advising his government to check the rise of the Soviet Union. Communist China was defining its relationship with the brotherly communists next door in the USSR and was still half a century away from its assertive rise. The only external force of consequence was the departing colonial empire with residual interests in the region.

Yet, India decided not to exit the British Commonwealth with Independence, privileging continuity over anger against colonial oppression. This showed great sagacity and restraint on the part of India, given the numerous provocations by the British. For instance, the British had earlier even refused to grant India 'dominion' status, as they had done for Canada. Consequently, the Indian National Congress had hardened its demand in 1930 for complete independence. By 1947, the unifocal attention of India's leadership was on independence, rather than on questioning the colonial depredations of the past century, the famines, the killings. On the part of the British, the Commonwealth was being fashioned as a 'third force' in a world becoming bipolar. The decolonization project itself was only a tactical retreat: the British were keen to continue exercising influence over the strategic affairs of the subcontinent.[32] The leaders of India, and even more those of Pakistan, saw some national interest being furthered by remaining plugged into Britain-led structures.

PERSUADING PRINCESTAN

Shahryar Khan was thirteen when the princely state of Bhopal, located deep in India's belly, decided in 1947 to remain an independent entity. Shahryar's grandfather and Bhopal's ruler, Nawab Hamidullah Khan, kept his options open. He would merge the state with India only in 1949, when the writing on the wall was clear. The nawab's eldest daughter and heir apparent, fell out with her father over a second marriage and opted for Pakistan in 1950, going on to settle there with her son. In 1960, when the nawab passed away, Pakistan's dictator Ayub Khan offered Begum Abida Sultan and Shahryar the option to return to Bhopal to claim their heritage. Both Abida—who had proudly claimed a lineage of women rulers of Bhopal—and her twenty-six-year-old son, declined. Fate kept Shahryar Khan away from his royal title, or perhaps a role as an Indian diplomat, as he joined Pakistan's Foreign Service and rose to become a cricket- and peace-loving foreign secretary. Shahryar's was only one tale of the destinies of India's royals taking peculiar and accidental turns after Independence.[33]

Bhopal's dilemmas were replicated across the canvas of the subcontinent in 1947. As the two sibling nations built their states and national identities, they needed to confront this peculiar territorial challenge: of a third and more complicated sibling that the departing Raj was leaving behind. This was 'Princestan', a collection of 565 princely states scattered across the expanse of the empire, imbued now with enough legal agency to decide which way to go. The princely states had been tied to the East India Company and later to the British Crown by a complex scheme of 'subsidiary alliances', an edifice of indirect rule that created a 'network of collaborators', a motley collection of maharajas and nawabs—Hindu, Muslim, and Sikh—'who in return for their allegiance were permitted by the British to run their fiefdoms more or less as they chose'.[34] With India, Pakistan, and the princely states being treated with legal equivalence by most in the departing British establishment, the Balkanization of India stood as a very real possibility in 1946. It was only the vision and resolve of India's leaders, and particularly some deft internal diplomacy by Home Minister Sardar Patel, which prevented chaos.

Merging the princely states with the Indian state was one of the most 'structurally monumental tasks' that India's administration faced after Independence. Patel, who engineered this process (assisted by the resourceful civil servant and secretary in the Ministry of States, V. P. Menon) did most of the heavy lifting in folding the bulk of Princestan into India. Mountbatten was quick to grasp and then articulate the reality that while the states could exercise a choice in theory, 'geographic compulsions' implied that most of them must choose India. This effectively meant that the departing empire was advising only the states that shared a border with Pakistan to accede to it. It was one more reason for Jinnah to suspect Mountbatten of a bias in India's favour.

A conspiracy theory, which has seen several avatars, suggests that in the run-up to independence, a 'vile plan' was devised by a handful of powerful princes 'to join neither India nor Pakistan'. By one account, the plan was led by the chancellor of the chamber of princes, the nawab of Bhopal, operating under the patronage of Jinnah and Viceroy Wavell, with the blessings of Churchill himself. The idea was to create a third dominion called Princestan where the 565 princely states would stay outside the ambit of the two free states and retain paramountcy under the aegis of the departing British. The success of such a malevolent plan would have made newly independent India unstable and vulnerable. However, three persons stood in the way of the nefarious British plan to Balkanize India: Nehru, Mountbatten, and Patel battled the rulers of the princely states at every twist and turn to foil that cunning plan, even as the process of decolonization had begun.[35]

Between May and August 1947, the vast majority of states signed simple instruments of accession devised by V. P. Menon. The instruments provided for a princely state's ruler to accede to the dominion of India or Pakistan. That meant giving up jurisdiction on three subjects: defence, external affairs, and communications. These documents derived legal force from two pieces of British legislation: the Government of India Act, 1935, that allowed princely rulers to join the 'Federation of India'; and the Indian Independence Act, 1947, that provided for British suzerainty over the princely states to end on 15 August 1947.

Eventually, while most princely states were absorbed readily into India or—where they were contiguous only to it—into Pakistan, the issue remained of the aspirations of a few major states: Junagadh, Hyderabad, and Kashmir. Holding out also—to a lesser extent—were Kalat in the west and Sylhet in the east; both would eventually fold into Pakistan. India had to demonstrate a great deal of resolve and tenacity in consolidating territories: negotiations with the princes required extraordinary patience and skill, and a fair degree of guile.

Still, a handful of states held out. Some simply delayed the decision to watch unfolding developments. For instance, Piploda, a small state in central India, did not accede until March 1948. The bigger problems arose with a few states, mostly those that found themselves on the border. Jodhpur tried to play both suitors, liaising with Pakistan to negotiate better deals with India. It was finally Junagadh, Hyderabad, and Kashmir that the two dominions had to negotiate in their early diplomacy. Eventually, each of these territorial issues saw the use of strong state force to precipitate outcomes. The trajectory of developments in Kashmir in particular would haunt the neighbours and poison their ties.

JOSTLING WITH JINNAH

Karachi was not wholly unfamiliar to Sri Prakasa. He had first visited the city in 1931 as general secretary of the Indian National Congress, to attend a party session under then president Sardar Patel. This had been a heady moment for the Congress: the independence movement was celebrating the political victory of Gandhi's Dandi March (April 1930) against British salt laws and the subsequent invitation by the British government to Congress leaders to come to the Round Table Conferences in London (1930–32). Just two years earlier, in the 1929 session in Lahore, Nehru, as Congress president, had declared total independence as the party's goal. By the time of Prakasa's first visit to Karachi, Jinnah had parted ways with the Congress and now was with the Muslim League, a political formation getting ideological direction from the radical poet Mohammad Iqbal. Both Lahore and Karachi were thus closely tied to the freedom movement for India.[36]

One of the factors that landed Sri Prakasa his diplomatic assignment in Pakistan was his longstanding association with Jinnah. The two men had rubbed shoulders for a decade (1935–45) in the central legislative assembly of British India, a faux parliamentary structure created after limited franchise elections in 1934 to take the pressure off the Raj from pesky demands for Indian independence. Jinnah had by then formed an independent party with Muslim members, which was to merge later into the Muslim League. Sri Prakasa had been deeply suspicious of Jinnah. He had seen the Muslim leader change his position from nationalist to 'rabidly communal leader'.[37] Sri Prakasa claimed in his memoirs that Jinnah was among those who had a 'hearty laugh' in 1935 over a pamphlet that proposed a separate state of Pakistan,[38] when the paper was distributed to assembly members at its very first session.

In 1939, after a riot in his native Uttar Pradesh, Sri Prakasa had debated communal relations with Jinnah. He argued for a syncretic Hindu–Muslim culture, while Jinnah seemed determined to establish his new state, even as he assured the future high commissioner that as soon as Pakistan was established, all possible problems would be immediately solved.[39] Jinnah was by now treating the Congress as a purely Hindu body. He had the support and even active encouragement of the British. They allowed him to spread communal poison with impunity while for much less, Prakasa felt, Hindus were put in jail.

Eight years later, as India's envoy to Pakistan, Sri Prakasa made no secret of his ideological differences with his former political colleague, now the all-powerful leader of his host country. To Prakasa, Jinnah's ideological predilection was to view all citizens of the two new countries as generic 'Indians', who were simply inhabitants of separate dominions or 'nations': Hindustan and Pakistan.

Prakasa was among the guests at the banquet for Mountbatten in Karachi on 13 August 1947, when Jinnah, as governor general-designate of the dominion of Pakistan, espoused his two-nation thesis, of religion defining nationhood. He referred to the two upcoming countries as Hindustan and Pakistan and expressed the hope that inhabitants of these countries could live in peace with one another. Two days earlier, in his 11 August speech to Pakistan's Constituent Assembly, Jinnah had famously advocated a secular Pakistan, when he said that all non-Muslims living in Pakistan should regard themselves as Pakistani, regardless of race or religion. Prakasa saw glaring contradictions between Jinnah's declaration of a progressive vision and the situation on the ground; he surmised that Jinnah was keen that the Muslims who had stayed behind in India should regard themselves as 'Hindustanis' and not interest themselves too much in Pakistan. In its early years, Pakistan continued to use for India the terms Hindustan or Bharat. (Ayub Khan in the 1960s decreed that Pakistanis resume using 'India'.)

Issues of nationalism and its symbols remained a persistent theme in Prakasa's engagement with his hosts. In one conversation, the chief minister of Sindh, Mohammed Ayub Khuhro, told Prakasa that the Muslim League had only used the idea of Pakistan as a 'bargaining chip' and that its promoters never really wanted a partition or a separate Pakistan. This resonated with Prakasa's own convictions. He had thus heard the thesis two decades before historian Ayesha Jalal made the argument more coherently.

On another occasion, Prakasa discussed this issue with the founder of Pakistan himself. As an infirm Jinnah sat on a sofa in Karachi at a reception, Prakasa got a chance to buttonhole him. Jinnah started the conversation politely enough. 'How are you, Mr Sri Prakasa,' he began. 'I see you after a long time.' They discussed Prakasa's recent tour of Mohenjo-daro, the iconic Indus Valley site in Sindh's Larkana district. The envoy asked the head of state why there was an emphasis on calling Pakistan an Islamic state. When Jinnah insisted he never had personally used the term 'Islamic', Prakasa pointed out that his prime minister, Liaquat Ali, had. Jinnah was upset: have it out with Liaquat, why quarrel with me? At this point, an irritated Jinnah ended the chat.

It turned out that Jinnah was right about not having ever deployed the term Islamic, as Sri Prakasa confirmed from the record with the *Dawn* newspaper. He wrote a polite letter to Jinnah explaining his error in conflating 'Muslim' with 'Islamic'. He never got a response. Prakasa inferred from this episode that Jinnah wanted Pakistan to be a Muslim state, not an Islamic one, but was unable to rein in his political successors in altering the nature of the Pakistan state, remodelling it as an 'Islamic' theocratic state.

In fact, the first draft for the new Pakistan came while Jinnah was alive. Liaquat Ali Khan had brought to Jinnah's sickbed in Quetta the draft of an 'objectives resolution' for Pakistan that would draw divine authority for an essentially theocratic nation. This upset Jinnah and, in one telling, he flung the paper in anger and frustration. The document was nevertheless used by Liaquat Ali as Pakistan's guiding light a few months after Jinnah's death. For the first time, religion was formally inserted into the charter for the state of Pakistan. Pakistan's Constituent Assembly adopted the resolution on 12 March 1949, and it has since formed part of Pakistan's successive constitutions. Jinnah's Muslim nation would formally become an Islamic republic in 1956, when the idea of a theocratic Pakistan would triumph, as promoted by Maulana Maududi, the founder of the Islamic party, Jamaat-e-Islami (JeI).

Sri Prakasa was convinced that just as Partition was a matter of 'perpetual sorrow' for him, Jinnah in his final days also regretted his decision to create Pakistan. The Indian high commissioner had heard stories of Colonel Ilahi Baksh, the doctor who attended on Jinnah during the last phase of his illness in August–September 1948 at Ziarat near Quetta. In his memoirs, the doctor claimed he heard Jinnah say that he had created Pakistan but was now convinced he had 'committed the greatest blunder of my life'.[40] He also claimed he heard Liaquat Ali Khan mutter after emerging from a sick Jinnah's room, 'the old man has now discovered his mistake'.[41] An earlier edition of the doctor's book was censored and banned. This claim remains controversial to this day.

PUBLIC MEN AND PERMANENT OFFICIALS

As a freedom fighter and politician, India's first high commissioner to Pakistan was innocent of the ways of the bureaucracy his country had inherited from its erstwhile rulers. Prakasa did not belong to the elite Indian Civil Service (ICS), which was soon to send some of its members into the diplomatic service for the two new countries. He stood in sharp contrast to the suave Girija Shankar Bajpai, who was pre-independence India's first 'Agent-General' to the US and also to the United Nations, the latter born just two years before India. Bajpai returned to India to head the foreign office as India's first secretary general, with PM Nehru retaining the ministerial portfolio for External Affairs.

The Indian Foreign Service (IFS) had been created in 1946 with an executive order. It was too new and too stretched to place professional diplomats in every important post. Bajpai had been tasked by Nehru to cobble together a professional foreign service for the new nation to claim its place in the world. Since the IFS had been formally set up by Nehru's interim government in 1946, and started recruiting fresh talent from 1948, the prime minister got personally involved in strengthening this cadre with a group of envoys from among his friends, relatives, and even the rulers of princely states. Nehru had at Independence sent his sister, Vijaya Lakshmi Pandit, as ambassador to Moscow; his friend Krishna Menon to London; and in 1950, would despatch the eminent historian, Sardar K. M. Panikkar, to China.

Putting together a diplomatic service to represent a new nation was no easy task. Bajpai faced the challenges of ignorance about world affairs in the political system and a strong prejudice against the civil services, seen as a colonial legacy. Some nationalists were demanding 'a new approach and a new type of public servant'. But without ever going as far as Sardar Patel in willingly relying on the services, Nehru did accept the need for a foreign service cadre. The first crop of diplomats came by poaching some 150 officers from the ranks of the ICS and allied services. One such ICS officer was Kewal Singh, later high commissioner of India in Pakistan; he was among those who received a telegram one day in 1948, asking him to join the IFS.[42]

But the ICS was also depleted; a number of its potential recruits had been pulled in for short spells of military service during World War II. Academia became the next port of call; a few like P. N. Haksar were recruited from there, just as a few journalists were picked up. Another natural catchment for diplomats seemed to be the princely houses of India, where 'sophisticated youngsters'[43] were available, with bleak princely futures; some six princes were persuaded to join the diplomatic corps. Some more were recruited from the national movement and, of course, Nehru picked some from among his former colleagues in the Congress Party.[44]

Sri Prakasa seemed to lack the panache of Nehru's other choices, but enjoyed his trust. Some scholars have suggested that Nehru erred in picking Prakasa, someone neither familiar with the nuts and bolts of diplomacy nor with the big picture of the new geopolitics of the region. He was not from the ICS, nor was he royalty nor an urban sophisticate. Prakasa was in that sense a political appointee. He felt like an outlier in the new diplomatic service. While he was gone from Pakistan's capital to Delhi for his first consultations, the ministry had despatched a high-ranking ICS officer as his deputy high commissioner (DHC). In his memoirs two decades later, Prakasa still referred bitterly to this new colleague sprung on him as his 'so-called deputy'.[45] Such officials, he was convinced, resented his appointment and were suspicious of 'public men'. In terms of organizational hierarchy, apart from a deputy in Karachi, he had one each in Lahore and in Dacca, all ICS men. Their work ethic did not particularly impress him; they played bureaucratic games, he was convinced, to trip up their seniors.

After a point, it was clear that the mandarins in Delhi were running policy, and the high commissioner (HC) had little control over the DHCs in Lahore and Dacca. His request for copies of their reports was turned down by headquarters; he felt he did not have a real picture of what was transpiring in East Bengal or even in West Punjab. He felt bitter that he was reduced to being a sort of a 'joint DHC' in Sindh, for there was always a joint DHC from the ICS drawing a higher salary than he did.[46] He felt that permanent officers could not help 'having a narrow outlook and working in accordance with the prescribed routine', trained as they were to follow their earlier British masters in 'donning and doffing their hats and behaving exactly as their European superiors did'.[47]

He felt these officers, unlike freedom fighters such as him, had loyally served the British and had not opposed independence only because it helped them rise to the positions vacated by the departing colonials. So, the civil servants were now compelled to serve 'those very people whom they were suppressing in the course of the political movement and sending to jail'. When holders of political office in India were being drawn from public life, the freedom fighter felt, the Indian officers of the British regime resented serving under them.[48]

The high commissioner did complain to the prime minister and even asked, on one occasion, to be relieved of his office. Nehru assuaged the feelings of his friend and shared his own grouse: high-ranking ICS officers thought that the government should be run according to their directions and he himself had a tough time keeping them in check and getting his policies implemented. Interestingly, Nehru eventually came to the conclusion that ambassadors from public life sent to foreign countries had not been successful.[49]

2

PARTITION PAINS

The horrors of Partition were staggering in scale. The new borders had triggered the migration of some 15 million people and the massacre of at least 1 million. Muslims had constituted a quarter of the 400 million Indians in 1947, concentrated though they were in colonial India's north-west and north-east, in Punjab and Bengal. While the new state of Pakistan now was home to some 75 million in its two wings, close to 40 million Muslims chose to stay back in India. Hindus and Sikhs, on the other hand, were ethnically 'cleansed', almost down to the last person, from West Punjab and the North-West Frontier Province, just as Muslims were killed in East Punjab. Up to a quarter million Sikhs—a distinctly identifiable minority—lost their lives at the hands of Muslim marauders in West Punjab. It was only in interior Sindh and in East Pakistan that a Hindu community of some significance stayed on, dropping the percentage of Hindus in the territory that became Pakistan from 15 per cent in the 1941 census to 1.5 per cent in 1951.[1] In post-Partition India, of the population of 330 million, 7 million were Hindu and Sikh refugees who had fled from Punjab and Bengal.[2]

With the massacres and migrations, the newly arrived refugees began giving voice to the trauma inflicted upon them. They would soon dominate the diplomatic discourse between the two countries, infecting it with the bitter and bloody legacy of fear and hatred. And anger.

For the new-born Pakistan, the murders and the mass migrations were an unanticipated shock. For both countries, it rubbished the British argument that a fast-tracked independence and partition would save lives. Pakistan was overwhelmed by the refugee crisis, even though Jinnah and the rulers in Sindh seemed relatively untouched by it. Refugees—and the burdens they bore—became a major headache for the new state.

Pakistan's 1951 census would show that about 10 per cent of its population of 75 million was of refugee origin. The west of the country was home to about 34 million people and the east some 42 million. More than 6.5 million Muslims had migrated into Pakistan from India, the bulk of them between August and November 1947. 4.6 million of these had evacuated from East Punjab alone.[3] The numbers hid the larger story of unspeakable human tragedy that had begun to poison attitudes in both countries.

Jinnah had said, six years before Partition, that he was willing to sacrifice the Muslims in the Muslim-minority provinces of India to create a state of Pakistan for those 60 million in the Muslim-majority provinces of north-west and eastern India.[4] In his 11 August 1947 speech, however, Jinnah had made a distinctly secular assertion; a recent political biography[5] confirms it was an opportunist one, not reflecting his larger world view. While Jinnah was assuring Pakistan's minorities of protection, he was perhaps compelled to do so in the face of communal killings threatening the Pakistan project. Jinnah knew that his new state was not equipped to manage the influx of up to 35 million Muslim refugees from India.

With the migrations, minority proportions that were a fifth (21 per cent) of the people in the territory of Pakistan in March 1947 had plunged to 1.6 per cent by December. But voices had also risen in the first decade for separate nations: for the Bengalis in the east and for the Majithia Sikhs[6] in West Pakistan.

India did better in preserving its minority proportions. The number of Muslims stood at about an eighth (12 per cent) of the total at Independence and continued to remain in that region after decades. (In contemporary times, both countries have comparable Muslim populations of over 200 million.)

The new Pakistan government was mostly unprepared for the migration and violence of 1947. The demand for a separate Muslim homeland had never really been accompanied by any serious one for a transfer of populations. Besides, some had been lulled into complacence by the bizarre 'hostage populations' theory: that large minority populations in both India and Pakistan could serve as guarantors of communal stability.

Historians have not quite fixed the responsibility for Partition-related violence because of the complex and controversial manner of its unfolding. Scholars have debated whether Mountbatten should be at least partially held culpable for the chaotic Partition process. The West Punjab government blamed the Sikhs, while the non-Muslims blamed the Muslim national guards, a quasi-military organization associated with the Muslim League, for its role in initiating the violence.

The late boundary demarcation added to the chaos. The loss of Nankana Sahib and Kartarpur Sahib had created great anguish among the Sikhs and talk began of shahidi jathas (martyrs' military detachments) that would seek to reverse the losses. The chaos reached such a height that Master Tara Singh, Akali leader and chief minister of East Punjab, said he could not guarantee Muslim refugees safe passage through Amritsar. Refugee trains laden with corpses were creating cycles of revenge killings. Bouts of communal violence in East Pakistan had caused a similar, though not total, exodus of Hindus.

The migration of refugees from Punjab, Bengal, Delhi, and UP to Pakistan was not the final chapter in the exit of Muslim refugees. The Indian police action to take over Hyderabad in September 1948 would lead to a further influx of Muslim refugees into Pakistan. The 1951 Pakistan census would record 95,000 refugees from the Deccan state of Hyderabad. This phenomenon of refugees escaping persecution played into the politics of both countries, and would get exacerbated at different points of history, particularly after communal riots and wars, as in 1965 and 1971. Every bout of communal violence in East Pakistan similarly caused an exodus of Hindus.[7]

BORDERS AND BUTCHERY
Scholars have unearthed evidence of more of than 70,000 gruesome rapes on both sides of the border. Each statistic hid a story of horror, brutality, and trauma that defined the times. Memories of the pain passed through generations. Anger was too mild a descriptor of the emotional upheaval. Madness became the more accepted metaphor for the paroxysms of violence and revenge. While rage has often accompanied memories of Partition, they are also dealt with by silences of denial of the unspeakable horrors that gripped those times.

These stories weighed heavy on the diplomats of the times. The office of Sampuran Singh, deputy high commissioner in Lahore, was overrun by both traumatized returnees from across the border and those desperate to cross over into India. Singh's problem was mirrored in Delhi at Pakistan's high commission.

Yet, these civil servants needed to focus on immediate, more complex tasks at hand. The early diplomacy between the neighbours needed to be executed against the backdrop of the greatest mass migration ever. Never in known history till then had the transfer of so many millions taken place in such a short period. The civil servants were seeking instructions from leaders trying to make sense of the chaotic events. Nehru was deeply disturbed by the unfolding horrors in Punjab. He visited the province thrice in August 1947, making aerial sorties, spending time at the sites of communal clashes, talking to angry refugees in camps.[8] It hardly occurred to him that he was effectively negotiating migration with a foreign country. He visited places on both sides of the border scarred by barbaric acts. For Sampuran Singh and Sri Prakasa, these were visits by the head of their home government visiting a country where they were accredited, but they had the feel of internal tours by Nehru to calm a domestic crisis.

On one occasion, Nehru flew over a convoy of refugees: 10 miles of 'scared, miserable Muslims', perhaps a hundred thousand of them, travelling from Jalandhar to Lahore. The convoy had to pass through Amritsar, where 70,000 agitated refugees from West Punjab had just come in, from the opposite direction, having seen killings of their kin. The danger loomed of massacres triggered by intersecting convoys. Nehru suggested bulldozing a road around the town so that the two convoys would not meet.[9] On another trip, he crossed into Lahore along with Lady Edwina Mountbatten to visit a refugee hub, the Lajpat Bhavan in Lahore. He then teamed up with Pakistan's Prime Minister Liaquat Ali to tour by air various districts of East and West Punjab to see the horrors first hand, and attempt to check them.

High Commissioner Prakasa himself toured the border districts by road, along with a young major in Pakistan's army, Ayub Khan—later to become Pakistan's military ruler—and Sardar Baldev Singh, India's first defence minister. The sights of overcrowded trains and stories of butchery left a strong imprint on the diplomat. He saw the 'self-arranged and self-managed transfer' of millions of human beings from one side to the other of the Punjab in August and September 1947. He saw things that would have made 'even the devil weep'.[10]

The communal riots had wrenched Gandhi's soul. He told Sri Prakasa only twenty-seven days before his assassination that his lifetime's labour had 'gone down the drain'.[11]

While politicians on both sides were trying, often jointly, to quell the communal fires, diplomats and officials needed to start working on more complex administrative arrangements related to the refugees.

STUCK IN SINDH

Partition was a profoundly perplexing human tragedy for Sri Prakasa, not only because of the murders and rapes that shocked the world, but also for the plight of the refugees who survived.

Until 1952, no passports were needed for travel between India and Pakistan; Muslims from India could easily move back and forth. But the Indian high commission's job was to issue travel permits, given the need to modulate the flow of evacuees. Not too many permits needed to be issued in Punjab. The riots had ethnically cleansed all Hindus and Sikhs from western Punjab, just as Muslims in East Punjab had been killed or had migrated, except from the enclave of Malerkotla. In Sindh, the story was a little different. Of its 4 million people, about 1.5 million were Hindus living in urban areas. But there were also about 200,000 relatively poor Hindus who could not be easily evacuated, since they were in an inaccessible rural hinterland, mainly in the Tharparkar district.[12]

Partition had savaged the province of Punjab the most. In Bengal, leaders on both sides had managed to persuade populations to stay where they were. But the horrors were now beginning to touch Sindh, where the high commission was located. A 'holocaust' unfolded in January 1948 in Karachi, with violence against Sindhi Hindus, which hastened their terrified flight to India. Over a million Sindhis fled in the first half of 1948 and this exodus continued till 1951, when only about 200,000 remained in the province.[13] Several voyages had to be undertaken by sea, given that the land route through the Punjab border had become unviable due to the violence, while air journeys were expensive and did not allow household goods to be carried. The high commission had even set up a camp in an open space in town for people who were coming from the interiors of Sindh towards Karachi to escape to the new India.

The high commissioner recorded three waves of exodus of the Hindus of Sindh from Karachi. The first was of Hindu government employees, the second of Sindhi Hindus, and the third of Muhajirs, settlers who had escaped from India, but were now changing their minds and returning to their homes in India. Several of these were the Muslims who had migrated from Prakasa's native eastern Uttar Pradesh, only to be rapidly disappointed by the Pakistan they saw. They clamoured to return to their native lands, given the hostility in Sindh. Prakasa noted that he did not receive requests from any Punjabi Muslims for facilitating a return to India. It was mainly the UP Muslims who had come to Karachi with belied hopes and were anxious to go back.[14]

The Hindus with means to return were doing so with increasing urgency. And the Indian diplomats were willing to help. A group of wealthy Hindus approached Sri Prakasa in panic one midnight, afraid of being arrested the next day, pleading for permits to leave by dawn. The high commissioner did them the favour. He was now armed with stamps and seals at home to deal with such emergencies.[15]

The traditional deployment of Hindus and Christians for menial jobs in Pakistan created a peculiar dynamic of compulsions for its administration. While Prakasa tried hard to get the Hindu migrant labour from Uttar Pradesh to return to their homes for their annual leave, or simply because they wanted to return, the Pakistani authorities invoked the essential services act to say that 'labourers, domestic servants of government officers and such others' could not go away. This deeply offended the high commissioner. He took up this sectarian affront with Prime Minister Liaquat Ali, appealing to his origins in UP. Pakistan's prime minister shocked the high commissioner with his reflexive response: who would clean the streets and latrines of Karachi? An outraged Prakasa reported this remark to Nehru who did raise this matter with his opposite number, to no avail. Several other fires were raging. The plight of migrant labour, or casteist slurs against them, were hardly a priority.

On one occasion, Prakasa privileged a pregnant woman with a permit, a scarce resource on account of the constraints of transport. The next day, he was amused to find a large number of allegedly pregnant young women appealing for early departure. He gave them the benefit of the doubt and armed them all with exit permits without the mandatory medical exam.

Tension over refugees mounted within the Indian camp. The high commissioner felt that his second in command had a direct line to Delhi and was bypassing him to seek directions from the ministry. Prakasa once wanted to grant return permits to some Muslim weavers from Benares who had arrived as refugees in Karachi; but his deputy, driven perhaps by his resentment of some biased acts of Muslim officers in Delhi, had consulted headquarters and obtained instructions to overrule the envoy and refuse the permits.

KEEP THEM THERE!

During his tenure in Pakistan, Prakasa frequently returned to India for consultations, mainly on the refugee crisis he faced. Mahatma Gandhi, in one meeting, exhorted Prakasa to try to take care of the Hindus who were left behind, particularly in the rural areas. A companion of Gandhi, Pandit Sunderlal, who was working for Hindu–Muslim amity, was concerned that the Indian diplomat was tasked with removing all Hindus from Pakistan. 'Do try that they may remain there,' he pleaded. On another occasion, Gandhi gave Prakasa an earful on the atrocities in Pakistan against Hindus. Gandhi himself had been facing mounting criticism for his stout defence of Muslims in India and his alleged neglect of the plight of the Hindus being massacred or expelled from Pakistan. The envoy was still smarting from the Mahatma's outburst on his way out, unfairly directed at him he thought, when he bumped into another Congress stalwart, Sardar Patel, then home minister. Patel similarly addressed Prakasa sharply as a proxy for Pakistan, 'in words of biting sarcasm', causing the envoy 'deep anguish'.[16]

Prakasa immediately rushed to Prime Minister Nehru and offered to resign. He felt he no longer enjoyed the confidence of Gandhi and Patel. The month-old high commissioner then learnt a lesson all Indian envoys to Pakistan since learn at some point or the other: Pakistan policy in India is driven personally by India's prime minister and it is best to seek direct instructions from the PM. Nehru told Prakasa that since he enjoyed his prime minister's full confidence, he should proceed to Pakistan without hesitation. Prakasa did enjoy Nehru's trust almost through the entire period of Nehru's premiership, as he went on to become governor of Assam, Madras, and Bombay provinces, serving in these high offices until a year before Nehru's death.

But on his visits home in the months after Independence, Prakasa was feeling the heat of the complex refugee crisis that Partition had triggered. It weighed on his mind even during his last meeting with Gandhi. Prakasa had returned to Delhi after a trip to Dacca in January 1948 to call on Gandhi. He wanted to clarify his position since he felt 'some returning Hindus of Sindh had poisoned Gandhi's ears'[17]. But he could not find time alone with the Mahatma. Gandhi was assassinated later that month. To his regret, the high commissioner did not get a chance to make his case.

FATHERS OF THEIR NATIONS

1948 was a tragic year for both India and Pakistan, as the respective fathers of their nations passed away, barely a year into Independence. Mahatma Gandhi, who had remained away from any government role, fell to an assassin's bullets just five months after Partition in January 1948, while Jinnah, Pakistan's larger than life founder, succumbed to tuberculosis eight months later. India's first diplomat in Pakistan recorded the passing of both from Karachi. He looked at their legacies from a unique vantage point in his memoirs.

Gandhi and Jinnah had been colleagues in the Congress Party, friendly at first and rivals later. Jinnah had welcomed Gandhi's return to India from South Africa in 1915 and had even been hailed by Gandhi, in a 1916 Congress meeting, as an 'ambassador of Hindu-Muslim unity'. But Gandhi's revolutionary new tactics had upset and upstaged Jinnah. When Jinnah resigned from Gandhi's Congress in 1920, and joined the Muslim League a few years later, their paths diverged. But their trajectories still intersected.

Gandhi had anointed Nehru as his political successor; a strong relationship of mutual trust had evolved between the two men. Jinnah, on the other hand, trusted nobody. Liaquat Ali became a political heir of sorts, but did not enjoy Jinnah's trust and himself passed away three years after Independence. Both Gandhi and Jinnah had their dreams only partially fulfilled. Gandhi's India came with a Pakistan-sized hole and, worse, with the pain and horrors of the communal riots. Jinnah got a moth-eaten version of his imagined homeland, and had to leave behind his coreligionists in Muslim-minority provinces (with the partition of Muslim-majority provinces of Punjab and Bengal) like UP and Bihar.

Gandhi was by far the tallest leader the Congress had produced. He had been president of the Congress in 1924 and had visited Karachi multiple times. In 1931, some Karachi residents commissioned a bronze statue of Gandhi and placed it in a prominent city square. The bronze figure underlined Gandhi's stature in undivided India.

When Gandhi was murdered in 1948, Sri Prakasa decided to honour his memory with a ritual dip in the nearest waters. En route to the Arabian Sea that lapped Karachi's Clifton Beach, he went barefoot to bow before the statue prominently positioned near the Sindh High Court, on Cantonment Road, later called Court Road.[18]

Gandhi was keen to visit Pakistan after Independence. His agenda would have included engaging with the traumatized Hindu minority in Sindh. Sri Prakasa recalls that two Parsi envoys visited Karachi with a message from Gandhi expressing a desire to meet Jinnah and suggesting that Gandhi 'was willing and anxious to come to Karachi'[19]. But Jinnah's resentment of Gandhi had not diminished. These envoys read a clear signal from people close to Jinnah that Pakistan's leader was not prepared to meet India's most important leader unless he picked up an equivalent position in protocol, like that of the governor general of India. Thus, the quest for parity became an important concern for Pakistan since Independence. Prakasa felt that at some level, Jinnah envied Gandhi not having taken a formal position in India. Gandhi's Parsi friends were still in Karachi, trying to break the ice with Jinnah's team, when the shocking news came of Gandhi's assassination. 'Sad and sick at heart, they left for home'.[20]

Jinnah's death months later was a turning point for Pakistan. He was leaving behind an inchoate Pakistan and no real successor to take his legacy forward. The funeral was a sombre affair in Karachi. While others were dressed fashionably in black, the Indian high commissioner went, as an 'old-fashioned Hindu from Kashi', in a simple white kurta and dhoti.[21] He respectfully circumambulated the body, but later reflected on the irony that a man as proud as Jinnah who 'gave the impression to others that the earth was not good enough for him to tread on', should also 'lie thus stretched on its back'. Jinnah's daughter, Dina, with her husband, Neville Wadia, came for the funeral. Jinnah had bequeathed his house in Karachi, as well as the one in Bombay, to his sister Fatima. The high commissioner assessed that Jinnah had died an unhappy, lonely man. Pakistan's founder, the envoy felt, had perhaps never dreamt that such exoduses would take place and had 'evidently hoped for a peaceful division of the country'[22].

Pakistan had lost its founder Jinnah much before he could explain his idea of Pakistan or even work out its details. India in contrast had a Constituent Assembly furiously at work. The loss of Gandhi and Patel was not as deeply felt as Jinnah's in Pakistan, for India had the continuity and weight of Jawaharlal Nehru for the first sixteen years.

DEBATING PARTITION

Partition's memories and legacies have remained contested, even after three quarters of a century, engaging scholars and journalists, often seeping into the politics of both countries. They are unlikely to be laid to rest even with the passing of the generation that saw the division of their lands.

Several scholars have suggested that the movement to create Pakistan that inexorably led to the tragedy of Partition was essentially one led by the Muslim elites in India's Muslim-minority provinces (UP, Bihar, Bombay), driven by an impulse to compensate for the loss of power and to counter the prospect of being governed by a brute Hindu majority once the British left. Some key ideologues and influencers of the day drove the process: it required, one analyst argued, 'a Syed Ahmed Khan to plant the seeds, an Iqbal to imagine and especially a Jinnah to grasp the opportunity to convert the Muslim insecurity at having lost an empire into the demand for a separate homeland.'[23]

Thus, Partition became South Asia's major turning point in the twentieth century and a lightning rod for debates on a range of issues like identity, territory, security, nationalism, minority rights, and migration. Some saw it as an answer to past wrongs and others as a cause of the crises it caused, from riots to wars to nuclear weapons to minority fears. It also became a continuing debate in the diplomatic discourse between the two nations, on whether the unfinished agenda of Partition had to be addressed before any other meaningful conversation could take place.

State-driven narratives of Partition in Pakistan for decades extolled Jinnah as the masterful planner of the immaculate conception of Pakistan, until a Pakistani historian challenged the received wisdom a couple of decades later. In her influential academic work, *The Sole Spokesman: Jinnah, the Muslim League and the Demand for Pakistan*, Pakistan's best-known historian, Ayesha Jalal, argued in 1985 that Jinnah had used Pakistan in the 1940s as a bargaining chip to get a better deal in the share of power for the Muslims of India, for whom he had become the 'sole spokesman'. In this argument, Partition was more the responsibility of Nehru and the Congress leadership, too ambitious to accept the last British attempt at unity that Jinnah was willing to go along with: a loose confederation proposed by the Cabinet Mission Plan of 1946. For the Congress, this narrative suggested, Bengal and Punjab were politically crucial: these undivided Muslim-majority states would have thrown up the most seats for the Lok Sabha. Thus, in any voting along communal lines, these provinces would have dwarfed the role of the Congress Party in an undivided democratic India. So, Partition was politically the preferred outcome for the Congress Party, as it was for Jinnah, even though what he got was a 'moth–eaten' avatar of the Pakistan he dreamt up.

Jalal's fresh take on the birth of the nation challenged not just the dominant narrative—of Jinnah having conceptualized Pakistan perfectly—but also implicitly questioned the two-nation theory—of religion as Pakistan's sole raison d'être—that Zia's Pakistan was trying to reinforce in the 1980s. Jalal's argument was strengthened by pointing to the birth of Bangladesh in 1971, which had struck a decisive blow to the two-nation thesis.

This interpretation also challenged histories written till then, mostly driven by the study of the causes of Partition. In Jalal's telling, Partition was neither the only possible outcome being negotiated in the run-up to Independence, nor even its most likely result. Jalal's persuasive thesis itself became the dominant orthodoxy, until newer narratives challenged it three decades later. Recent scholarship[24] suggests that while Jalal's theory was a startling one at that point, it did not tell the entire story of the Pakistan movement, which in fact predated Jinnah's demand articulated in March 1940. This scholarship bases itself on a reading of documents from across

India to point out that Jinnah knew exactly what he was fighting for, did so with tenacity, but did not live long enough to follow up with a coherent vision for Pakistan's future.[25]

The Partition process was chaotic. It set in motion a train of events, pointed out scholar Yasmin Khan, unforeseen by every single person who had advocated and argued for the division.[26] Khan argued that the fledgling countries had to undertake the complex governmental business of teasing out two new states, with full administrative and military apparatus, at a time of social uncertainty, loss of trained manpower and paucity of resources. Moreover, their diplomatic capacity of dealing with each other had not quite evolved.

While the Kashmir issue is often cited as the cause of several foundational problems, it was Partition that caused many of the ongoing conflicts in South Asia, not least because it was the 'source of the suspicions and national myths that are deeply rooted in the definition of one state against the other'.[27] But not all of South Asia's current problems can be laid at the feet of Partition. Events have moved on from 1947 and difficulties created by the Radcliffe Line 'instead of being salved by the balm of diplomacy, have become running sores'.[28]

The interest in the Partition moment continues to animate the work of newer generations of scholars. Among, looking at Partition from fresher angles is a Pakistani granddaughter of a Partition survivor Anam Zakaria, who argued that memories of Partition have often been repackaged through state narratives; rather than slowly dissipating, these memories have only hardened over the years. On the Indian side, Aanchal Malhotra, another granddaughter of Partition refugees, has derived insights from the physical objects and memories of Partition.

And so the scholarly[29] as well as political debate[30] rages to this day, with no clear judgement on the why of Partition. But while Partition was the original sin, it was by no means the only one that spawned the flawed diplomacy of the next seventy-five years and more.

In the early days of the formation of the two countries and their interaction with each other, there were many different turns that events could have taken. These what ifs, these counterfactuals of history, engage scholars and politicians to this day. Surely, having Mountbatten as India's first governor general and allowing British army generals to continue was a flawed choice. If India's objective was to retain every bit of territory of the Himalayan princely state, Kashmir, then a homespun head of state would have served India better. Had Pakistan not made the grave misjudgement of encouraging a tribal invasion in 1947, Kashmir may have remained an independent country, another Himalayan nation to the north of India, like Nepal and Bhutan, to be wooed or suppressed not just by India and Pakistan, but also by China. If Nehru had chosen to be governor general,

Indian generals could have ensured that Pakistani troops were beaten back into their own territory in 1948 and India perhaps would have never needed to make any reference to the UN.

Or going further to pre-Independence choices, would the death toll have been greater if the British had left with no Partition, leaving the Indians—Hindus and Muslims and Sikhs—to sort out their differences and negotiate the evolution of the new nation? A future high commissioner to Pakistan landed at the doorstep of the last viceroy to find some of the answers. Kewal Singh, then posted as deputy high commissioner in London, used the opportunity of his posting to meet with Mountbatten and ask him the questions that had troubled most observers of Partition and its aftermath. Why did Mountbatten advance the date of Partition to 1947? Mountbatten replied that in his assessment the point of no return had been reached in March 1947 after which the butchery had to be prevented. He had hoped that the army would remain united for another year to prevent any conflict. He had expected to be the common governor general for a year for both dominions, to settle matters amicably, but Jinnah had been adamant and wanted sovereign Pakistan to have her own army; and himself wanted to be governor general.[31]

What is unquestionable is that if the subcontinent had not been partitioned, it might have been possible to avoid four Indo–Pak conflicts, and even perhaps the 1962 Sino–India clash. The what ifs of history can be endlessly fascinating, but historical actors of the times need to grapple with contemporary realities. One such reality in 1947 was a beautiful valley in the lap of the Himalaya that would present the most vexing challenge for the sibling nations.

3

THE KASHMIR CONUNDRUM

Less than a week after Partition, Colonel Akbar Khan, director of weapons and equipment at the Pakistan Army headquarters in Rawalpindi, started planning an ingress into Kashmir, to pre-empt its accession to India.[1] Khan and his band of military strategists had good reason to be proactive. Soon after the boundary commission had carved up Punjab and Bengal, unfairly in their view, the Pakistan Army was looking to merge Kashmir with Pakistan to compensate for lost territory and consolidate the new nation. The Pakistan Army had just inherited Rawalpindi—the largest garrison town of the British in the subcontinent—established to defend the sensitive north-western periphery of the empire. Holding a third of the military assets of the British Indian Army, Pakistan's army was disproportionately large, compared to Pakistan's population of about a sixth of British India.[2]

Colonel Khan was seeing worrying signs. Maharaja Hari Singh, Dogra ruler of the princely state of Kashmir, was professing neutrality but appeared to favour India. His vision of retaining Kashmir, as a 'Switzerland of the East' with a doctrine of 'positive neutrality', might not withstand, Pakistani military officers feared, a militarily powerful India. Gandhi and Mountbatten had already visited the maharaja in Srinagar in the summer of 1947, from all accounts, to persuade him to join India. This would not only endanger Pakistan's borders, but also its nascent ideology; the foundational two-nation theory would itself be challenged, given that the Hindu king's subjects mostly followed the Muslim faith.

It would thus be critical to force the hand of Kashmir's ruler to change the balance of power and geography in Pakistan's favour. This idea would quickly translate into the top secret 'Operation Gulmarg', a tribal invasion of Kashmir. Akbar Khan knew the territory well. He had already been involved in providing arms to demobilized soldiers of World War II, in the Poonch region on the western fringes of the princely state, to foment a rebellion against the maharaja and build momentum for the accession to Pakistan. The scheme now was to mobilize some 20,000 Pashtun tribesmen from the north-west and launch them into Kashmir by October.[3]

But these audacious plans needed to be hidden from the British officers commanding the Pakistan Army. They were soon approved, bypassing the white military commanders, by Prime Minister Liaquat Ali—to whom Akbar Khan reported as military adviser—and almost certainly by Jinnah himself. Pakistan's army was thus all set to implement a brazen battle plan for a foreign invasion, within seventy days of Independence, keeping its own army chief in the dark.[4]

The tribal invaders, guided by 'experienced military men', equipped with modern arms, carried in a fleet of 300 trucks, and driven by a lust for loot and rape, swarmed into the princely state on 21 October. They could well have succeeded in capturing the princely state's capital, Srinagar, had they not been distracted by an orgy of pillage. The raiders first captured Muzaffarabad, near the border of the princely state, terrorizing local Hindus and Sikhs. They then rapidly advanced towards the heart of the valley, capturing Baramulla, a major town to the north of the valley. They were 20 miles by road from Srinagar on 24 October, with hardly any resistance from the forces of the princely state, when the maharaja sent an SOS to Delhi, asking for forces. Governor General Mountbatten effectively vetoed the idea of sending forces from the Indian dominion to defend Kashmir, without first securing the accession of the state to India. Without that document, India would be invading foreign territory.

On 26 October, the maharaja was woken up in Jammu, where he had fled for safety from Srinagar, to sign the accession agreement that State Secretary Menon flew down from Delhi with. On 27 October, even as Governor General Mountbatten formally signed off on the document, Indian Army troops were airlifted to Srinagar, where they were welcomed by Sheikh Abdullah's National Conference leaders and soon engaged the raiders on the outskirts of the capital. Thus began the first Kashmir war between India and Pakistan.

By 14 November, Indian troops had retaken Baramulla and Uri and driven the raiders to the peripheries of the valley, as winter set in. What prevented Indian troops from pursuing the raiders to the border, to have them vacate a third of the state that they still occupied? Both military and political factors were at play. The transitional British structures played a major role in preventing that outcome.

Akbar Khan was proud of his military ingenuity. But his memoirs suggest he did not quite imagine he was setting a precedent. He could not have foreseen that he was creating a template for Pakistan's military tactics in the next decades that would eventually visit tragedy not just on its neighbours, but its own citizens as well. The unfolding events in Kashmir were also driven by the larger strategic calculations and tactical manoeuvres of the departing British Raj.

STAND STILL AND STAND DOWN

The slow state-building process in India had given the colonial empire much residual influence in the free dominions. As India and Pakistan struggled to consolidate their security systems, as we have seen, British officers continued to helm their armed forces. India had moreover

entrusted to its British head of state a critical executive role of presiding
over the defence committee of the cabinet, effectively giving him a veto
on military decisions. Pakistan had a freer military hand, with Jinnah as
governor general, and only British officers, not a head of state, to be kept
out of the loop when necessary.

The British had engineered 'standstill' agreements at Independence, that
obliged India, Pakistan, and the princely states not to upset the status quo.
They provided that all the administrative arrangements would continue
unaltered until new arrangements were put in place by 1948. Akbar Khan's
adventure in Kashmir had clearly violated this standstill agreement between
Pakistan and Kashmir.

Worse, well before the Kashmir crisis erupted, Field Marshal Auchinleck
had, as noted, issued secret 'stand down' instructions to British commanders
in the Indian and Pakistani armed forces. Nehru and Patel were not
aware of these instructions issued on 30 September,[5] but it had become
abundantly clear to them they could not rely on the British officers, who
were taking orders from London, rather than from the Indian government.
More importantly, Mountbatten, on the strength of his military experience,
now chaired a vitally important cabinet committee that could not be easily
bypassed for any major military choices.

These factors played a crucial role in staying India's hand during the
Kashmir crisis. Auchinleck's instructions were reinforced by London, when
the British cabinet decided on the issue on 13 October, a week before the
raiders landed in Kashmir. Prime Minister Attlee conveyed his approval of
the stand down instructions in a telegram to Auchinleck on 15 October.
The reinforced instructions had a major impact on decisions and the course
of events in Kashmir at the end of the month.

Crucially, Mountbatten ensured that India did not extend operations
up to the Pakistan border in the Poonch and Mirpur districts in November
1947. He even sabotaged his own government's plans for creating a 'cordon
sanitaire' along the border through aerial action against the raiders of
Kashmir. 'He foiled his government's instructions for preparing contingency
plans for a counter-strike across the Pakistani border, while prevailing upon
Nehru to take the Kashmir issue to the UN.'[6]

In India's first war, Mountbatten was not just a figurehead but in fact
the executive head of India's military decision-making. He was party to
the secret order for a stand-down, clearly an act of betrayal by the British.
Political morality would have required Mountbatten to resign his post
rather than work against the interest of the government he was serving.
But those were extraordinary times.

When tensions arose over Junagadh, Mountbatten and Army
Commander-in-chief General Rob Lockhart did their best to restrain India
from taking the military route. Lockhart's role was particularly egregious

in the case of Kashmir. He had refrained, on Auchinleck's advice, from implementing the Indian government's order to send military supplies to the maharaja. Likewise, he did not share the indication he received from his counterparts across the border about the movement of armed tribesmen into Kashmir. India's leaders had to jump through other hoops to exercise their security choices: they needed to satisfy Mountbatten's insistent demand that they secure the maharaja's accession before giving him military help with an airlift to counter that invasion from Pakistan.[7]

In his multiple contortions to balance competing interests, the governor general tried to slip into another role: of becoming a mediator between India and Pakistan. These were times before concepts like 'conflict of interest' came into vogue. 'This must be the only case in the annals of diplomacy where a holder of the highest office in the country has attempted mediation between that country and another,' observes Dasgupta.[8] Mountbatten had little doubt that the tribal invasion was a deliberate proxy attack mounted by Pakistan on a territory that had acceded to India. Yet, the governor general did his utmost to prevent India from extending military operations up to Jammu and Kashmir's border with Pakistan. Dasgupta argues that thanks to this British betrayal, India could not summon the speed, secrecy, and surprise, essential elements of an effective military response. And soon, international intervention pre-empted the option of Indian troops going across the Kashmir border.[9]

The archives point to several more layers of British misdemeanour. London was aware of the invasion plan, as Pakistan's acting army chief, General Douglas Gracey, stated categorically. The evidence also suggests that the British foreign secretary Noel Baker had, without consulting the cabinet, given the nod for the Pakistani move into Kashmir.[10] Most Indian scholars see this as an act of colonial perfidy. Ironically, Pakistani writers, with equal rancour, tend to lay the blame for their military failure in Kashmir at the British doorstep. On 27 October, Jinnah had ordered General Gracey to send regular troops to counter the Indian action, but Gracey refused, and instead asked for approval from the supreme commander of all British forces, Auchinleck, in New Delhi.[11]

Dasgupta credibly argues that India's contingency planning for a counter-attack across the Pakistani border could not have been executed without the 'Indianization' of the military leadership. This plan would be put in place only five years after Pakistan's attack in Kashmir. In August 1952, Nehru could inform parliament that 'any further aggression or attack or military operations in regard to Kashmir, if such takes place on the other side, that would mean all-out war not in Kashmir only but elsewhere too'. This was the policy that was finally implemented in 1965.[12]

JUNAGADH SIDESHOW

The stand-down instructions had been first tested in a princely state in India's west. The eccentric nawab of Junagadh, famous for his 800 pet dogs, unexpectedly announced on 15 August 1947 that he was acceding to Pakistan. Adding layers of complexity to the situation was the fact that the Muslim nawab's subjects were mostly Hindu and that Junagadh was surrounded by neighbours who had acceded to India. To make matters more convoluted, the nawab claimed overlordship of both these neighbours now in India: the princely states of Babariawad and Mangrol.

The nawab's decision to accede to Pakistan was met with a bewildered silence from the new nation he had decided to throw in his lot with. On 21 August, V. P. Menon wrote formally to the Pakistan high commissioner in Delhi, asking for an indication of Karachi's policy on Junagadh's proclamation of accession. Since the state was not geographically contiguous to Pakistan and a large majority of its population was non-Muslim, wrote the civil servant, it was important to ascertain the views of Junagadh's people on accession. The high commission in Delhi did not respond to this ticklish issue, nor did Karachi. On 12 September, Nehru followed up with a telegram to Pakistan conveying India's readiness to accept the verdict of the people of Junagadh. The message was carried personally to Karachi by Mountbatten's chief of staff, Lord Ismay.

A suspicious Pakistan played for time. In a sloppy opening diplomatic gambit, Pakistan's foreign office refused to take cognizance of India's telegram on the grounds that 'it bore no number or signature to show that its issue had been authorised'. On 13 September, nearly a month after the nawab's offer, Pakistan finally conveyed that it accepted Junagadh's accession.

This left the British in a peculiar quandary. Armed action by India in Junagadh now looked inevitable. But Mountbatten, as head of one British dominion, could not acquiesce in action that could lead to war with the adjacent dominion. Mountbatten did his best to dissuade Nehru and Patel from armed action, but the show of force became inescapable by the end of September.

Mountbatten even suggested lodging a complaint with the nascent United Nations against Junagadh, questioning its act of aggression in the Kathiawar region. Patel and Nehru rejected the proposal. Patel sagely observed that possession was nine-tenths of the law and he would in no circumstances lower India's position by going to any court as a plaintiff. Nehru proposed on 30 September to India's Defence Committee that the matter should be decided by a referendum or plebiscite of the people concerned. He added that 'we shall accept the result of the referendum whatever it may be, as it is a desire that a decision should be made in accordance with the wishes of the people concerned'. The implications were clear for the remaining major princely states whose fate was under negotiation: a referendum in the Muslim-majority Kashmir was expected to favour Pakistan while one in Hindu-majority Hyderabad would tilt in favour of India.[13]

This was a dramatic new initiative and Pakistan's prime minister heard of it soon enough. When Liaquat Ali happened to visit Delhi on 30 September for a meeting of the Joint Defence Council, Mountbatten engineered a conversation between the two prime ministers. Nehru declared India's faith in a strong democratic principle that the will of the people should be ascertained in all difficult cases and that India would always be willing to abide by a 'decision obtained by a general election, plebiscite or referendum conducted in a fair and impartial manner'. Mountbatten intervened to emphasize 'that this policy would apply not only to Junagadh but also to any other state'. Mountbatten later recalled that Liaquat's eyes sparkled, 'he was, no doubt, thinking of Kashmir'.[14]

Significantly, Liaquat Ali did not respond then to Mountbatten's offer, possibly because he wanted to consult Jinnah. Pakistan's archives have never been opened to provide this answer on why Pakistan chose to ignore the Indian offer of settling all cases of disputed accession by a reference to the will of the people, a principle that would have helped its case for Kashmir. Pakistan chose instead to 'insist on the ruler's prerogative in the case of Junagadh and Hyderabad, while, in the case of Kashmir, she made secret preparations to obtain a decision by the force of arms'.[15] The mirror opposite of Pakistan's preference suited India: going by the ruler's discretion in Kashmir, but factoring in popular sentiment in Junagadh and Hyderabad, two states that in any case had no land borders with Pakistan.

Just as the first moves were being made on the crisis in Kashmir, the Junagadh affair was reaching its endgame. By 27 October, the nawab had already fled to Karachi, taking with him the entire cash balances of the treasury and most of his beloved dogs. On 1 November, Indian civil administrators, accompanied by a small armed force, took over the administration of both Babariawad and Mangrol. On 8 November, the Indian government accepted the administration of Junagadh after the dewan, Sir Shah Nawaz Bhutto, father of the future leader of Pakistan, Zulfikar Ali Bhutto, saw the writing on the wall and requested the Indian government to take over.

GILGIT BALTISTAN
Another sideshow to the central Kashmir drama was being played out in the northern mountains of the Himalayan state. The maharaja's accession to India implied that the high Himalayan territory of Gilgit Baltistan would also integrate into India. But this move did not suit British interests. An effective coup was mounted by a British officer of the Gilgit Scouts, to

prevent this outcome. While Indian writers have seen this as a conspiracy or worse, another example of British perfidy, Pakistani commentators have portrayed it as a popularly backed rebellion.

The revolution in Gilgit took place on the night of 31 October 1947. Gilgit, together with Baltistan, Hansa, and Nagar, formed the 'northern areas' of the princely state of J&K. Major William Brown, the maharaja's commander of the Gilgit Scouts, positioned by the British on 1 August 1947 when they handed over the 'Gilgit agency' to the maharaja, 'mutinied' on 1 November 1947, overthrowing the maharaja's governor of the region, Brigadier Ghansara Singh. Brown had secretly invited his Pakistani friends in, even before the bloodless coup. The Pakistani political agent arrived on cue on 16 November to take over the administration of Gilgit. The Scouts also managed to subsequently capture Dras and Kargil in the Ladakh region and cut off Indian communications to Leh. Only in the autumn of 1948 did India manage to recapture all of the Kargil district, leaving Baltistan under Gilgit control. Military historians underline these events as the tactical genesis of the Kargil conflict of 1999 that we will encounter in Chapter 6.

THE HYDERABAD ACCESSION

Even as the countries were at war in Kashmir, another large princely state was still holding out a year after Independence. To Patel and Nehru, Hyderabad's integration into India was non-negotiable. After a Pakistan had been carved out in the west and one in the east, India did not want yet another one in its heart. The preparations for the use of force were on. Indian and Pakistani diplomats of the day were already scrambling for overseas weapons for the ongoing war effort in Kashmir. Pakistani trade commissioners were asked to get arms from France and Germany, playing off one European against the other. In the fog of that war, a conflict entrepreneur called Sidney Cotton got involved in transporting weapons from Europe via Pakistan into Hyderabad, supporting the pro-nizam militia of Razakars.

The endgame in Hyderabad came relatively rapidly with 'police action' while India and Pakistan were technically at war over Kashmir. Under the fiction of civilian action, it was in fact military action at play with 'Operation Polo', involving an army division backed by air power. The action compelled the eccentric nizam to abandon his ambitious hope of running an independent enclave deep within India. When Hyderabad was finally liberated on 16 September 1948, Cotton escaped to Pakistan taking several Razakars along. In the bloody aftermath of the liberation, up to 40,000 were killed as the Razakars resisted the army and civilian militants. To calm matters, Nehru even considered making the nizam an ambassador overseas, but was advised that the former ruler's miserly habits and odd sartorial choices would not make him an ideal diplomat. He was instead made governor, a non-executive head of the province. From a strategic perspective, the integration of Hyderabad was India's 'first successful attempt at coercion'.[16]

A CASE FOR THE UN

Sri Prakasa in Karachi was not in any way involved in negotiating the Kashmir situation; it seemed a crisis far away from Pakistan's capital. He had little feedback or briefings on the diplomatic and military developments that were taking place. The war seemed like his prime minister's job, even though it was being fought with the country he was accredited to. But like all worthy envoys, he had his personal, if completely naive, take on the imbroglio and weighed in on how the issue could be resolved. Exasperated by Pakistan's Kashmir obsession and dismayed by the violence, the high commissioner advocated a simple solution: hand over the territory to Pakistan. He shared this view with Mountbatten when he called on him in New Delhi. The governor general relayed the sentiment to Nehru in a meeting on 25 November 1947. An alarmed Nehru dashed off a letter to Prakasa the same afternoon:

> I was amazed to learn from Mountbatten that you hinted at Kashmir being handed over to Pakistan for the sake of peace all round. If we did anything of the kind our government would not last many days and there would be no peace at all anywhere in India. Probably it would lead to war with Pakistan because of public opinion here and of war-like elements coming in control of our policy. We cannot and we will not leave Kashmir to its fate.... All of us realize that this Kashmir venture is no easy matter. We did not undertake it light heartedly and we are not pursuing it with any easy confidence. We know the difficulties perhaps more than you do. Nevertheless, we are going to go through it and it is desirable that you should make this perfectly clear in your private talks whenever this question arises.[17]

This was an extraordinary but perhaps richly deserved reprimand from the prime minister to his maverick envoy.

With the lull in the fighting in the winter of 1947, the Kashmir dispute went to the United Nations. As we have seen, Mountbatten had been pushing Nehru to make a reference to the UN to end the conflict. He finally had his way, when, on 1 January 1948, India filed a complaint with the Security Council against Pakistan, under Article 35 of Chapter 6 of the UN Charter. It asked the council to call upon Pakistan to stop giving assistance to the invaders. On 5 January 1948, the UN announced the imminent formation of a plebiscite administration.

The day India complained to the UN, it also acquired a new British commander-in-chief, General Roy Bucher, who followed the glorious tradition of his predecessor, General Lockhart, in deceiving India's civilian leaders. Bucher reached a private understanding with his counterpart in Pakistan, General Gracey, to turn a blind eye to the induction of Pakistan regulars into parts of J&K, in return for an informal truce between the dominions. Bucher informed his Pakistani colleagues of his military plans, promising not to move beyond certain positions. He even offered to send a covert signal to Rawalpindi if the Indian government changed his plan.[18]

With a war still in progress on the borders in the summer of 1948, Sri Prakasa got a chance to visit the Kashmir Valley, at the invitation of his friend, the prime minister of Kashmir, Sheikh Abdullah. The Sheikh had himself been appointed to his role as prime minister of the emergency administration of Kashmir in March 1948. Prakasa was in Delhi and made his trip to Kashmir to get a sense of the mood in the valley. Sheikh Abdullah seemed confident of popular support and shared his conviction with the envoy that if he got two more years 'you may have your plebiscite or anything else, the whole lot of the people will go for India and no one will think of Pakistan then'.[19]

That assertion was never tested. By the last week of December 1948, the United Nations Commission for India and Pakistan (UNCIP) succeeded in laying down the basis of a ceasefire agreement. British high commissioner in Delhi, Sir Archibald Nye, through Bucher, approached Nehru with the suggestion of an immediate ceasefire in anticipation of the formal adoption of the UNCIP resolution. With Nehru's approval, Bucher conveyed the offer to Gracey who accepted it on behalf of Pakistan. At midnight of 31 December 1948, the ceasefire between the two dominions came into force, thus ending the first India–Pakistan war.

When the UNCIP arrived in Karachi in 1949, to work out the implementation of the ceasefire, Sri Prakasa felt that both India and Pakistan were displeased by its 'slow and ponderous proceedings'. In fact, an asymmetry was developing in the way the two countries treated the UNCIP: Pakistan was welcoming the group as a saviour while India was increasingly sceptical of its role. The UN resolutions of 1948 (Nos. 39 and 47) detailed by the UNCIP in August 1948 laid out a contentious three-step sequential process that included the withdrawal of Pakistani nationals from western J&K, demilitarization and eventually, a plebiscite. With Pakistan's refusal to remove its nationals, matters were deadlocked on the first step. The ministry in Delhi had asked the high commission not to deal with the UNCIP. However, the envoy ignored the instruction and received the secretary of the commission in his office. He was also testing his own brand of diplomacy for Kashmir.

He dreamt up a three-point formula: common citizenship; freedom of movement between the two states; and a neutral Kashmir under the guarantee of the surrounding powers, viz., Afghanistan, Russia, China,

Pakistan, and India. Expectedly, this formula did not find many takers in Delhi. In fact, Prakasa advocated this solution yet again in his memoirs in 1965, revealing that it annoyed Nehru whenever he proffered this unsolicited peace plan. But the envoy saw no other way forward, even as he, in later years, ruled out Kashmir going to Pakistan. This scheme—or the part advocating free mobility of people between the countries—resembled the four-point formula ascribed to Musharraf, which would be discussed on a backchannel forty years later, as we shall see in Chapter 6.[20]

Sri Prakasa wondered, in his innocence, why his country was treating the marauders of Kashmir as Pakistan's regular forces. He found no reason to disbelieve Pakistan's UN representative (and later foreign minister) Muhammad Zafarullah Khan, who eloquently claimed that Pakistan had nothing to do with the tribal invaders. The war at the border went on for more than a year, through two seasons in 1947 and 1948, until the sides ceased fire. Clearly, Prakasa was not willing to admit, even to himself, that he was not aware of much that was taking place at the borders, where other actors, military and political, were playing complex games.

On 29 July, Indian and Pakistani representatives formally signed, under the supervision of the UNCIP, a 'Karachi Agreement'. This established a ceasefire line, 830 kilometres long, from Jammu to the map coordinates NJ98432 near the Siachen Glacier. The line would later morph into the Line of Control. By 1950, Jammu and Kashmir was in India's administrative control, barring a third of its territory to the west and north, now under Pakistan's control. But the differences with Pakistan had been referred to the United Nations. In Pakistan's subsequent narrative, India had defied the UN resolutions on Kashmir that required a plebiscite in the contested territory. The Indian retort was that Pakistan failed to vacate the parts of J&K in its control, thus violating the first in the sequence of steps prescribed by the UN for a plebiscite.

Article 370 was in place in the new Indian Constitution giving the state a temporary special status within the Indian union. (This status would only be rescinded seven decades later, as we shall see in Section 8.) The politics within Kashmir was also getting muddied in the 1950s. Sheikh Abdullah, under increasing suspicion of working towards independence for Kashmir, had a rift with Nehru in 1953. He was arrested. The Sheikh, all-powerful in the Srinagar valley, had also fallen out with Maharaja Hari Singh, now exiled in nearby Jammu. The maharaja's son, Karan Singh, was made regent and then the nominal ruler, sardar-e-riyasat. The Sheikh's arrest was seen by many as Nehru's grave and impetuous miscalculation. It would impact the political destiny of Kashmir over the next few decades.

Global diplomacy on Kashmir had started soon after the conflict. The United Nations, under the mandate of its resolutions on Kashmir, was keen to mediate the dispute. It continued to rapidly churn out peace proposals through its appointed mediators. In December 1949, a Canadian general, Andrew McNaughton, came up with several proposals on truce, demilitarization, and plebiscite. India rejected these. Another mediator, Owen Dixon, a judge of the Australian High Court, appointed in April 1950, failed to please either country when he recommended a more radical plan—the partition of Kashmir.

This UN-prodded diplomacy continued through the 1950s. The next mediator appointed in April 1951 was the American educator and political activist, Frank Graham, who recommended in 1953 that the best course would be for the parties to have direct negotiations. Graham was reflecting a sensibly realistic assessment six years after Partition and four years after the UN-brokered ceasefire had become effective in Kashmir—the solution would come either by mutual accommodation or military contest between the two countries. Hence, since the military solution appeared off the table, direct negotiations would be the way forward, even if Pakistan chose not to rule out the second option. Thanks to some efficient diplomacy or sheer fatigue, both countries decided to give direct talks a go.

The events in Kashmir from 1947 to 1949 had created a special bitterness between the neighbours in their early years, dashing any hope of building economic and military interdependence. For Pakistan, as the weaker of the adversaries, the existential threat from India loomed larger than life, soon seeping into its foundational strategic thought. The priority of building up the armed forces became an issue initially of survival and later of convenience, to justify disproportionately large defence expenditure. Prime Minister Liaquat Ali Khan underlined this concern in a broadcast to the nation on 8 October 1948: 'The defence of the state is a foremost consideration...and has dominated all other governmental activities. We will not grudge any amount in the defence over our country.' Pakistan thus embarked on the establishment of a 'political economy of defence', diverting resources away from critical nation-building requirements. The early years (1947–1950) saw up to 70 per cent of the national budget being allocated for defence.[21]

This conflict also informed Pakistan's thinking on the need for outside alliances. The Americans now appeared a better bet than the fading British, especially in the light of the US need for regional Cold War allies as part of the policy of containment towards the Soviet Union and China. When external US military and economic assistance eventually arrived for Pakistan in 1954, the strings were firmly attached of membership of regional US-led alliances—the Southeast Asia Treaty Organization (SEATO) and the Baghdad Pact.[22]

4

DECOUPLING

'There are no parallels anywhere to the nature of the diplomatic relations subsisting between India and Pakistan, or to the type of system evolved for conducting these relations'—concluded a 1948 fortnightly report to headquarters from the deputy high commissioner of India in Lahore, M. K. Kirpalani.[1] The diplomat was referring to tasks that 'related not only to defence, or security or intelligence gathering, but covered rather just about all aspects of life—who lived where, who could marry whom, where they could travel, what they could own, and how they could meet their parents.' Nowhere else in the world, the overwhelmed diplomat noted, would diplomatic staff 'be called upon to perform as many different sets of tasks, as those in the offices of the Indian High Commission in Karachi and Lahore'.[2]

Kirpalani's despatch struck historian Pallavi Raghavan as curious. Why should an Indian diplomat in Lahore be 'lamenting the burden of... administrative responsibilities' rather than addressing, say, the preparedness for the war in Kashmir or the bloodshed of Partition? More broadly, why were diplomats of the time preoccupied with such mundane matters, rather than being consumed by larger concerns of war and peace and massacres of their citizens? Were they consciously privileging nation-building over ideology, pragmatism over emotion? Were they drawing solace from the minutiae of daily diplomacy, a defence mechanism to block out a bloody past, to keep animosity at bay?

Kirpalani's predecessor in Lahore, Deputy High Commissioner Sampuran Singh, as we have seen, had been swamped in 1947 by refugees. One thousand eight hundred kilometres to the east of Lahore, across central India's expanse, in Dacca, India's representatives were initially spared a refugee crisis, but were soon tackling a similar set of issues in eastern Pakistan. B. K. Acharya, India's deputy high commissioner in Dacca from 1952 to 1956, was cabling his trauma to Delhi as he started his tenure. The challenge was whether to prioritize refugee issues above all else. Or to deal simultaneously with a portfolio of equally pressing problems, while ensuring that conflict did not break out again.

In Delhi and in Calcutta, Pakistan's diplomats had no easier task as they dealt with the partition and war. Pakistan's first envoy in Delhi, Zahid Hussain,[3] an economist who spent six months in India before going on to found the central bank of Pakistan, was inundated with similar issues. Hussain, and his successors in the 1950s, were being repeatedly summoned by the Indian government to discuss problems of refugees and minorities.

Matters of war and peace and border disputes were no doubt addressed as well, but not, apparently, with as much immediacy. Informed by the experience of 1947–48, India was pushing the idea of a 'no-war pact' in its early diplomacy. Pakistan would push back for primacy being given to territorial disputes. In 1950, when India's first secretary general of the Ministry of External Affairs (MEA), Sir Girija Shankar Bajpai, summoned the Pakistani high commissioner in Delhi to discuss a 'No War declaration', the diplomat replied that 'existing disputes relating to Kashmir, Junagadh, the canal waters, and evacuee property ought to be settled first'. But he promised to explore the matter further with his government.[4]

These newly minted diplomats of two newly born nations were addressing common themes of state-building, in the backdrop of a tangle of other complications arising from the disruptions of Partition—murder, mayhem, ethnic cleansing, and a war in the Himalaya. In the beginning, it did seem that there was no clear way forward.

MANAGING MINORITIES

Towards the end of 1947, the diplomatic lines were still being drawn on what minority issues would be appropriate for Indian and Pakistani envoys to raise with their hosts, in the larger context of assertions of sovereignty and surging nationalism. The decoupling of two independent nations was an accepted principle but its practice was proving hard. Sri Prakasa fielded endless complaints from India, of ill treatment of Hindus in Pakistan; and of similar mistreatment of Muslims in India. The envoy felt it was part of his mandate to convey concerns to both governments on the (mis)treatment of minorities. The first Indian and Pakistani envoys were addressing particularly vexed issues related to minorities that would occupy their successors, to a lesser or higher degree, across the next decades.

When he heard of Hindus being mistreated in Sindh in late 1947, an agitated Sri Prakasa had dashed off a diplomatic note to the Pakistani foreign office, asking for an enquiry into the incident. He received a sharp response that this was Pakistan's domestic issue, effectively asking him, the envoy recalled, not to 'poke my nose in the affair'. Prakasa wrote back that he agreed with that constitutional position entirely, but would still like the Pakistan foreign office never to hesitate to enquire of him about 'any complaints of mistreatment of Muslims in India'. He would 'make the fullest enquiries' and let them know the facts. The Indian diplomat believed this deft move calmed his prickly hosts and enabled him to subsequently discuss minority issues more frequently and frankly with Pakistan's prime minister, Liaquat Ali. Prakasa even occupied himself with helping in the 'negotiation of some marriage alliance between families that had migrated to Pakistan and others that have remained back in India'. His passion for playing matchmaker even earned the envoy a flattering compliment from his Pakistani counterpart in Delhi, who told Prakasa he was working as an ambassador for both countries.

Even in the early years, while the countries remained in a state of war, their diplomats doggedly grappled with the minority question. They set up two India–Pakistan conferences in 1948, focused primarily on minority issues: one in Calcutta and the other in Karachi. Finance Minister Ghulam Mohammad led the Pakistan delegation for the first, Sri Prakasa accompanying him. At the second conference in Karachi, Foreign Minister Zafarullah Khan headed the Pakistan team. Prakasa rated both these conferences as entirely futile, even as he got his first taste of the tough negotiations between the two countries, where hardened positions frustrated progress. He felt that both countries only made identical allegations in tense, infructuous meets.

For Sri Prakasa, while Zafarullah Khan had taken inflexible positions on minority issues in the foreign ministry and United Nations, even threatening 'direct action' against India for infringement of minority rights, other interlocutors were proving much more sympathetic. Pakistan's Minority Affairs minister, Chaudhry Khaliquzzaman, pitched for more sober negotiations on minority issues, keeping in mind the interests of India's Muslims.

Another dynamic struck India's high commissioner during the bilateral negotiations. While on a visit to Delhi, Prakasa saw officials in the Delhi Secretariat welcoming Pakistani secretaries like long-lost brothers. Watching the warmth of interaction between officials of both sides, Prakasa wondered why the country had been partitioned at all. Several of his successors on both sides of the border observed this paradox of personal warmth and official hostility, at least in the twentieth century. Cultural intimacy frequently overcame irreconcilable talking points.

NEGOTIATING STATES

The logjams of the first couple of years of diplomacy had seemed impossible to break. The early disputes included the control and occupation of Kashmir, settling the question of control over the Indus Waters canals, evacuee property, division of assets, and the financial settlement to be completed between two countries. Indeed, by January 1950, relations between the two were mired in deadlock. The two new armies had already been in conflict in Kashmir by December 1947. The question of the accession of Hyderabad had come to a head by September 1948. The evacuee property conferences had largely failed in terms of securing concrete compensation for either government. Inter-dominion trade had come to a halt entirely following the currency devaluation crisis of 1949.[5]

But matters turned soon enough. Diplomacy in the 1950s saw better outcomes, seemingly blocking out the rancour of the first three years. A factor driving the pragmatism was the fact that the early bilateral diplomacy was led and even conducted at the apex level. After Independence, both prime ministers continued to hold the foreign portfolios, dealing primarily with each other. Pakistan had appointed Zafarullah Khan, a jurist, as foreign minister in December, while Nehru retained that portfolio in all seventeen years he was prime minister. Nehru in fact began corresponding with Liaquat Ali on minority issues soon after Jinnah passed away in 1948. The Nehru–Liaquat Pact of 1950 was a fruit of these early conversations. The diplomats then continued to work towards a no-war pact that became another milestone to reach, as they went about building the new nations. For India, such a deal was more critical, to quell Pakistan's temptations for military revisionism. Conversations also started on resolving water disputes, to move towards an Indus Water Treaty that was finally cobbled together in 1960 after nine years of tough negotiations.

The decoupling process had begun soon after Partition. Gandhi himself, along with Mountbatten, had facilitated the first division of assets in 1947. The Mahatma's moral pressure and the governor general's legal argument had persuaded a reluctant Indian leadership to transfer to Pakistan 550 million rupees as balance of the partition payments, despite Pakistan's aggression in Kashmir. A double taxation avoidance agreement was in place by December 1947. Discussions started on a no-war pact in 1949, almost as soon as the ceasefire came into effect at the Kashmir border.

But these were halting steps in an overall climate of hostility. It was only in the 1950s that the diplomatic processes picked up pace. The initial frustrating bouts of conversation transitioned soon into more serious negotiations, ending with concrete outcomes. This made the 1950s a most productive period of diplomacy, bucking the trend of later decades in terms of sustained diplomatic efforts and outcomes at all levels. In the 1950s, Nehru had at least five summit meetings with Pakistani prime ministers on Kashmir.[6] And by the late 1950s, negotiations gathered steam for an ambitious treaty to divide the Indus waters.

The three key outcomes of the first decade of diplomacy were: the Nehru–Liaquat Pact of 1950, focused on minority rights mainly in Bengal; the Indus Waters Treaty that was finally concluded in 1960; and discussions on a 'no-war pact', more optics for the world than substance, but important for replacing war with talks about peace. The no-war pact, a diplomatic indulgence, drew from the inter-war pacts of Europe, which followed the principle of surrendering some sovereignty for peace.[7]

Some have argued that it was the trauma of Partition that triggered the cooperation of the early years. The shock should have led to mounting animosity, but did the opposite. The diplomats went about their jobs with greater commitment. Conversely, some attribute the accumulating baggage of hostility of subsequent decades, to the absence of a trauma comparable to Partition, that precipitated the constructive diplomacy of the 1950s. While the diplomatic infrastructure being created included mechanisms for joint solutions, at least the bureaucratic engagement did 'arrest the pace of the slide towards hostility'.[8]

DISPOSSESSED

A key issue for diplomatic negotiation between the two fledgling nations was of the abandoned possessions of the refugees. The 15 million displaced left behind a complex challenge for diplomats—of dealing with abandoned property—as much as 2.7 million hectares of land, almost the size of Belgium, was abandoned by Hindus and Sikhs in West Punjab alone, with 1.9 million hectares left behind by Muslims in East Punjab.[9] This was later variously described as 'evacuee property' or 'enemy property', signalling the intention of both states and the remote possibility of compensation.

India's high commissioner had a few property matters of his own to deal with. After he had spent an initial month at the Palace Hotel in 1947, Sri Prakasa received an offer from Pakistan's fledgling government to occupy a half-built house in Karachi, that could double as India's embassy and the high commissioner's residence. Prakasa surmised that his good friend, Liaquat Ali, would have known that the Indian was a 'widower of simple tastes' and would make do with this building for both his office and residence. He noted wryly that the Saudi ambassador had been offered four houses in the same neighbourhood, reportedly to house each of his three wives separately, with the fourth one kept vacant for a possible addition.

Another man worried about property was Liaquat's boss, Governor General Jinnah. In effect the most prominent evacuee with property issues back in India was the founder of Pakistan himself. Jinnah had not entirely broken up with his former home in India. His heart, according to Sri Prakasa, was very much in his two houses in Bombay and Delhi, perhaps the only bond that held with his old country of residence. When Prakasa met him on one occasion in Karachi, Jinnah had already successfully negotiated the sale of the historic Delhi house. Only some minor formalities remained. The house at 10, Aurangzeb Road, where Partition was decided upon, went to Jinnah's friend Ramkrishna Dalmia, who rented it out to the Dutch ambassador for a princely sum of five thousand rupees a month and eventually sold it to the Dutch government in 1951 for five lakh rupees.

Jinnah loved his Bombay house even more. He was keen that it be left untouched after Partition, for his return one day. The pressure was however mounting on the Indian government to take over that property. Sri Prakasa got a call from Nehru in 1948 saying that the situation was becoming embarrassing for the government and it must requisition the house. Nehru asked his envoy to check with Jinnah what rent he wanted for the house and what he planned to do with it. Prakasa sought an interview and was granted one soon.

Jinnah received the envoy in a sitting room with 'heaps of files' around him. Pakistan's governor general was taken aback by the Indian prime minister's message and 'almost pleadingly' said: 'Sri Prakasa, don't break my heart. Tell Jawaharlal not to break my heart. I have built it brick by brick. Who can live in a house like that? What fine verandahs! It is a small house fit only for a small European family or a refined Indian prince. You do not know how I love Bombay. I still look forward to going back there'. The surprised envoy asked Jinnah if he really wanted to go back to Bombay and whether he could report this to his prime minister. Jinnah was emphatic: 'Yes, you may.'[10]

Sri Prakasa immediately relayed this conversation to Nehru, who later also received a letter from Jinnah, repeating his wishes for the house. The house remained undisturbed, until pressure again built up after a few months. Nehru instructed Prakasa to say that the house this time must be requisitioned and Jinnah be asked to specify the rent. Prakasa wrote to Jinnah, who was by then sick with tuberculosis and recuperating in the mountain town of Ziarat on the North-West Frontier. The envoy got a reply saying that Jinnah wanted three thousand rupees a month and hoped his wishes on the nature of the tenant would be respected. It had not occurred to Jinnah to ask if the property could be earmarked for a Pakistani diplomat. The house eventually went to the British deputy high commissioner. The episode left India's envoy to wonder if Jinnah's heart belonged not in the government house in Karachi but in his house in Malabar Hill, Bombay.

This extraordinary exchange between the two subcontinental leaders took place at a time their countries were at war. An envoy was brokering the price of real estate, not peace between warring forces in the state of Kashmir. In his telling, Prakasa suggests that Jinnah at some level still hoped for a scenario where Pakistan's founder could visit India and stay in his Bombay house. Other biographers of Jinnah have argued that he may have just been having a weak moment.[11]

What this episode does support is the thesis that Jinnah had been so consumed by his efforts to create Pakistan that he had never got around to seriously plotting its future. His months in power, beset with a host of crises of nation-building, aggravated by debilitating disease, made it harder for him to define a long-term vision for Pakistan, let alone planning its relations with its largest neighbour. His distrust of India's leaders, his former Congress colleagues, was accompanied by an often benign, if simplistic, vision of India–Pakistan relations, even when the countries were at war.

On one occasion, he observed to the first US ambassador to Pakistan, Paul Alling, that India and Pakistan could be like USA and Canada. The parallels were striking—the two North American countries shared the longest border either possessed, traded with each other and shared bonds of history. Besides the US was separated from a non-contiguous wing, Alaska, by the vast expanse of Canada. The difference of course was that the expanse between East and West Pakistan belonged to an adversarial neighbour with a recent history of bitter conflict.

When Jinnah died, his will bestowed Jinnah House to his sister Fatima. The story continued in the twenty-first century, when Vajpayee first accepted and then rejected in 2002 the contention of Jinnah's grandson (Nusli Wadia) that the house belonged to him. The house was eventually taken over by the MEA.

SHARING THE SKIES

After the land was divided, the skies had to be split too. Overflights over each other's territories became an issue for both countries then and later. Bans on overflights became accepted instruments of political play and diplomacy. This was even more so when Pakistan was 'that country divided into two Wings without a body' with an eastern and western wing. In March 1948, when Jinnah wanted to fly from Karachi to Dacca, to visit the eastern wing of his new nation, he was keen not to land on Indian territory, with the countries at war in Kashmir. Prakasa phoned Prime Minister Nehru and got the overflight authorization. The envoy subsequently signed an air services agreement on behalf of India in Karachi in June 1948; it ambitiously envisaged flights by designated airlines of both countries on multiple routes including Delhi–Karachi and Calcutta–Dacca. Overflights went smoothly through the 1950s and 1960s and became an issue only in 1971. They then continued to be contested for India's westward flights over the territory of Pakistan and Pakistan's eastward flights to Southeast Asia.

EXPULSIONS

The fine tradition of expelling high commission staff had got off to an early start, within a year of the setting up of the embassies. In 1948, India accused four Pakistani air force officers of spying.[12] It amused Prakasa that Pakistan discovered the identical number of officers of identical status on the Indian side who were doing the 'self-same work of spying'. Later, when a second secretary of the Pakistan high commission in Delhi was asked to leave on allegations of spying—to be subsequently rebranded as 'conduct unbecoming of status as a diplomat'—the Pakistan government found an Indian second secretary in Karachi also to be guilty of a similar offence and required him to be withdrawn. A robust tradition of expulsions grew, not quite matching the Cold War dynamic of detection and expulsion of spies between the two superpower blocs, but becoming an indicator of the state of the relationship.

TRADING WITH THE ENEMY

Under the British empire, South Asia was perhaps the most integrated region in the world. Till 1947, goods and people could transit freely from Rangoon to Kabul. This changed with Partition. The barriers that came up make this one of the least economically integrated regions on the planet over seventy-five years later. The early diplomats kept the economic decoupling going despite heavy odds—an agreement to avoid double taxation had been put in place in December 1947 even as a conflict raged in Kashmir, while the first banking and trade agreements were in place by June 1949.

The statist economic models of the early days ensured that trade also pitted economic liberalism against the forces of nationalism. Both countries were in the grip of nationalist economic fervour that favoured state intervention rather than the free movements of goods and commodities.[13] The early economic arrangements were particularly shaken by a burst of Pakistani nationalism. Prime Minister Liaquat Ali was completing the Pakistanization of the armed forces, appointing the future dictator Ayub Khan in January 1949 to replace the British officer Bucher. In the same vein, Liaquat in September 1949 refused to join India and other members of the sterling currency area in devaluing their currencies against the US dollar. As the Indian rupee plunged in value against Pakistan's, India retaliated by ceasing trade, thus ending the effective common market that had existed between the two dominions since 1947.

While the non-devaluation by Pakistan of the pound sterling created trouble for India, it had another unforeseen consequence for West Pakistan's leaders. The decision impacted strongly on the eastern wing of Pakistan. The jute trade, tied with India till 1949, suffered a body blow. The resulting recession in East Pakistan fed into existing political discontent and further strained relations between the two wings.[14] Effectively, in parallel to the decoupling between the two sovereign nations, the decoupling of the two wings of Pakistan had also begun soon after Independence.

5

THE FORMATIVE FIFTIES

Three years after Independence, the sibling nations had managed to survive the disruptions of Partition, refugees, the Kashmir conflict, and a befuddling start to a decoupling process. Their domestic political trajectories—as also rapid global realignments—were now influencing their diplomacy. India had rapidly written its new Constitution, after its Constituent Assembly robustly debated its expansive provisions, drawing from the best global experiences in democracy. The 1950 Constitution, envisaging a republic empowering the Indian people with electoral democracy, became the greatest political venture since the one in Philadelphia in 1787—as important a victory for freedom as America's two centuries earlier.[1] Historians have since made persuasive parallels of the Constitution's adoption with the American and French revolutions. The document that would define India's democracy, itself a gigantic step for a people previously 'dedicated largely to irrational means of achieving otherworldly goals', established both national ideals and institutional mechanisms to achieve them.[2]

Even as the Constitution set India up for a decade of consolidating the republic, the country was blessed with strong leaders to guide the political process. The team of Nehru and Patel had given India steady hands at the wheel in the foundational three years of the new nation. Across the border, Pakistan had a tougher start, aggravated by the passing of Jinnah barely a year after Partition. The country still struggled to define its identity, failing to give itself effective governance structures or a foundational document.

During this period, diplomatic exchanges between the neighbours intensified despite the deep divide of Kashmir. Sri Prakasa left Karachi for Assam after eighteen months of his diplomatic innings, to start a new gubernatorial career. Nehru continued the tradition of Indian high commissioners arriving in Karachi brandishing pre-Partition connections with Pakistani leaders. Prakasa was succeeded by Sita Ram, who had been the president of the provincial UP legislative assembly before Partition, where Liaquat Ali was his deputy. The third high commissioner, Mohan Singh Mehta, a well-connected London barrister and incidentally the father of 1970s foreign secretary Jagat Mehta was personally roped in by Nehru for the job. The fourth, C. C. Desai, had been a friend at Cambridge of Iskander Mirza, Pakistan's prime minister during the envoy's term.

The diplomats faced newer challenges. While the partition of Punjab at Independence was the biggest crisis faced by the diplomats, civil servants and leaders of the day, the other partition in the east had been less bloody. It had not caused a massacre or mass transfer of populations in 1947, but was still a problem on a slower fuse. India's diplomats in Dacca then had feared a continuing exodus of refugees that would threaten India's economy. Three years later, long after the dust had settled on the chaotic mass migrations in the west, their worst fears were coming true.

Soon after India became a republic in 1950, Sukumar Sen, the chief secretary of West Bengal, travelled to Dacca for one of his periodic meetings with his East Pakistani counterpart, Aziz Ahmed. On 10 February, around mid-morning, while the talks were in progress in the secretariat building, the Pakistani side sprang a surprise: they paraded a woman in blood-stained clothes—allegedly a Muslim rape victim from Calcutta.[3] This story was played up in the media, provoking anger and eventually violence—a bloodbath of revenge against Hindus across East Pakistan.

For B. K. Acharya, India's deputy high commissioner in Dacca in 1950, the problem was real and immediate. Soon after the secretariat drama, he was cabling home blood-curdling stories of Muslim mobs killing Hindus. In February 1950, Bengal was facing its communal catastrophe much the way Punjab encountered its holocaust in 1947 and Sindh in 1948. Acharya was on the frontlines of this challenge, as he reported massacres, rapes, and the forced expulsion of more than 5 million Hindus by Muslim mobs. Prime Minister Nehru publicly accused Pakistan of sustained 'anti-India and anti-Hindu' propaganda in East Bengal.[4]

NEGOTIATING MINORITIES

Eruptions of communal violence in Bengal and Sindh in 1950 engaged India's diplomats. Sri Prakasa remained deeply involved in calling out the violence, provoking Ghulam Muhammad, Pakistan's minister for minorities, to remark: 'Mr. Sri Prakasa looks after the interests of Hindus in Sind. My government gives him every facility to do so.... Ask him if his house is not the beehive of lots of people.'[5] Pakistan was claiming similar rights in India. K. Shahbuddin, a member of the Pakistan delegation on minority matters, contended that his own government had every right to raise the issue of the treatment of Muslims throughout India, since it was also 'a question of principle', involving both the governments' concerns with minority welfare across the border.[6]

While politicians on both sides were playing up minority politics, the mandarins were acutely conscious of the pitfalls of this activism. Nehru himself had not made up his mind as to 'what the Government of India could do to assist those who were nationals of Pakistan and were still living in East Bengal'.[7] Subimal Dutt, secretary in India's Ministry of External Affairs, advised the first deputy high commissioner at Dacca, Surjit Bose, that 'in strict theory, minorities must seek the protection of their government, and not of the government of the neighbouring Dominion'. Chief Secretary Sen pointed out in Calcutta: 'If we want our High Commissioner or Deputy High Commissioner to pursue complaints from Hindus in East Bengal, a similar request from Pakistan is sure to come.' Too close a relationship between the minority populations and the diplomatic missions would also lead to 'Muslims in India coming to regard the Government of Pakistan as their protector' and which would 'be taken advantage of by Pakistan and will lead to embarrassing results in actual practice.' Moreover, the consequence of such a policy would also require the granting of facilities to the Pakistan deputy high commissioners to 'visit all parts of the Indian Union, since it is their contention that that Muslim migration has been taking place from all across the Indian Union'.[8]

Delegations from both countries started meeting in 1950 to negotiate these pressing minority issues. The failure of the 1948 agreement to quell anti-minority actions was obvious, so not much hope was pinned on a fresh understanding. But what was different now was that both Nehru and Liaquat Ali felt impelled to put out the communal fires in Bengal and were informed by the experience in Punjab and Sindh. The anger at atrocities against minorities was manifesting in curious ways—some talk began of exercising the military option both to visit revenge and to resolve the minority problem. An alarmed president of India, Rajendra Prasad, wrote to Nehru on 18 March urging that war be avoided.[9]

To the surprise of observers, the Nehru–Liaquat Pact was inked in April 1950, despite widely divergent views on the subject of minorities. It was a strong political signal on the security of minorities. Apart from providing for safe passage to refugees wishing to return to dispose of property, it envisaged retrieval of looted property and rescue of abducted women, with a special focus on Bengal. The document superseded the 1948 pact that had given greater political weight to structures and mechanisms. What struck some observers of the day was that while attempting decoupling, the countries were surrendering some sovereignty. They had endorsed an entirely new principle: that the representative of India in Pakistan would have certain responsibilities towards Pakistani Hindus while his Pakistani counterpart in India would similarly bear some responsibility towards the Muslims living in India.[10]

Despite its infirmities, the Nehru–Liaquat Pact did quell the violence and answer the immediate needs of minorities in the partitioned east. It also stood the hostage population theory on its head, advocating the need of mutual ownership of minorities in Bengal, with promises of their welfare rather than reciprocal threats of harm. But the significance of the pact went deeper, into issues of identity and nationalism. For Pallavi Raghavan, this agreement would extend the jurisdiction of their high commissions into the welfare of minority citizens across the border. To states as notoriously prickly about their sovereignty and jurisdiction as India and Pakistan, the signing of such an agreement by their prime ministers did represent a significant moment.

The pact was also 'an example of how, in the aftermath of partition, the necessity of solidifying the fact of the partition further, could also enable acts of greater cooperation between both states'.[11]

The document represented a pragmatic understanding of the reality of minority politics but was at the same time an awkward, even dangerous, formulation, compromising sovereignty for dealing with domestic minorities.

Not everyone agreed with the radical provisions of the pact. Syama Prasad Mookerjee, India's first minister for Industry and Supply, resigned from Nehru's cabinet, questioning the agreement, as also the special status for Kashmir. He went on to found the Bharatiya Jana Sangh, the predecessor to the Bharatiya Janata Party, in 1951.

TRUST AND TRADE

Trade between the neighbours appeared essential, despite the animosity, to replace the internal trade that had prevailed till 1947. By February 1951, as the first trade agreement lapsed, India and Pakistan signed a more efficient one in Karachi, despite the erosion of trust and Pakistan's refusal to devalue its currency. So, the countries agreed that India would export coal, steel, pig iron, cement, timber, and textiles to Pakistan, and import from Pakistan jute, cotton, food grains, hides, and skins. The trade agreement of February 1951 was seen all over the world as a triumph of economic commonsense over politics. The terms of these agreements were fractiously negotiated, but were, nonetheless, carried out.[12]

In later years, trade would be seen both an argument for promoting peaceful interdependence and building confidence on the one hand and a ban on it as an instrument for expressing anger, on the other.

Despite these positive developments, Pakistan's army remained bitter about its government's handling of the Kashmir war. The acceptance of UN mediation and ceasefire was seen as weakness and a squandered opportunity to capture the valley of Kashmir. On 23 February 1951, rebel officers led by Major General Akbar Khan, who was smarting from his failed adventure of 1947, met with leftist revolutionaries like poet Faiz Ahmed Faiz, to force out the Liaquat government. The failed coup, dubbed the Rawalpindi Conspiracy, became the first of several such coup attempts in Pakistan's history, their success rate climbing from Pakistan's second decade.

A few months after the failed coup attempt, Liaquat Ali fell to an assassin's bullet. This murder mystery would never be solved, but the needle of suspicion pointed in the direction of the army. Speculation has swirled since that Liaquat was punished for his attempts to work out a no-war pact with India.[13] The hardliners saw any pact foreclosing the option of military action as abandoning the Kashmir cause. With Liaquat's assassination, Pakistan's national politics entered a chaotic period of 'destruction of democracy', during which bureaucrats were increasingly transformed from the 'state's servants to its masters'.[14] Liaquat was posthumously seen as the only other politician who could have taken the baton from Jinnah. But history would damn Liaquat Ali Khan with faint praise, as a 'respected if uncharismatic prime minister, who was to stand head and shoulders above most of his successors'.[15] Pakistan's fledgling democracy floundered in the 1950s, but in India Nehru remained the unquestioned leader through the decade.

CHOOSING BETWEEN MOTHERS

India held its first general elections by early 1952. This exciting experiment was following up on the Constitution that had uniquely empowered India's masses with universal franchise. A newly independent country had chosen to move straight into universal adult franchise, rather than at first reserve the right to vote to men of property, with the working class and women granted the right much later.[16] Nehru received a resounding mandate from the people of India to consolidate the new nation.

Across the border, Pakistan's leaders showed neither the will nor the vision to hold elections or to give its people a constitution. But they were trying to catch up with India's bureaucratic structures. An executive cabinet decision had given administrative basis to cobble together a diplomatic service in June 1948. Much of it was improvised by inviting Muslim officers serving in India, particularly from the ICS, to take charge on an ad hoc basis. Pakistan's foreign service was finally created with a formal resolution in October 1952, five years after the birth of the country. The structure pretty much mirrored the British and Indian foreign services, and many of the basic political instincts were similar, emanating from the same DNA.

As a side note to the making of the Pakistani diplomatic corps, it should be mentioned that not all diplomats in Pakistan were personally convinced that religion was a sufficient basis for statehood or even for choosing the state they served. One of them was Ansar Khan, one of Pakistan's first diplomats at the UN headquarters in the 1950s. Khan identified more with India's view of the world. Indian politician, writer, and former UN diplomat Shashi Tharoor tells his story.

> The positions taken by Indian diplomats at the United Nations, their leadership in challenging apartheid, Nehru's role on the Suez crisis, and the policy of non-alignment, all struck (Khan) as speaking to his own sensibilities, articulating his own soul...why did he now have to be Pakistani when every fibre of his moral and intellectual being rejected the two-nation theory and abhorred what had become of his

land? ....Ansar Hussain Khan finally received his wish. He surrendered
his Pakistani passport and ....became an Indian. Ansar bhai was living
in retirement in Geneva...when he snapped. He...shot (his wife) dead...
and succumbed himself to a heart attack...to most Indian officials
it was his astonishing choice that defined him; he was always the
Pakistani who switched sides, just as he would always remain, in
Pakistani eyes, the traitor who crossed over to the enemy.[17]

Ansar Khan's stark dilemma and his crisis of identity was also Pakistan's.
But the diplomat made a more wrenching, and ultimately tragic, personal
choice.

JOINT DEFENCE AGAINST WHOM?
The Pakistan Army, under the leadership of General Ayub Khan from
1951, was spoiling for a larger role in the polity as the only efficiently
functioning public institution in Pakistan. In fact, the seeds of Ayub's
rule were planted in 1953, when the Pakistan Army stepped in to quell
a rebellion in Punjab against the Ahmaddiyas, a sect seen as not being
Muslim enough. The army, it was contended, saved the state from chaos.
The myth these events bred of the infallibility and clinical efficiency of the
army, and it being the only institution in Pakistan that worked had now
taken root.[18]

Pakistan's army was watching other curious political developments
that year. Prime Minister Khawaja Nazimuddin was ousted as a result of
internal turmoil, including the anti-Ahmaddiya riots and other incidents,
leaving a leadership vacuum. Pakistan's ambassador to the United States
got a pleasant surprise soon after, when, on a visit to Karachi, he found
himself elevated as prime minister of his country. Mohammad Ali Bogra,
a Muslim League political activist from East Bengal, had joined Pakistan's
diplomatic service in 1947, and served as envoy in Burma and Canada
before he was appointed Pakistan's ambassador to the US. Bogra was an
outsider and political lightweight and therefore acceptable to the powerful
Governor General Ghulam Mohammad. Bogra also happened to be an anti-
communist believer in a strong US relationship for Pakistan. He went about
strengthening the US alliance, earning the appreciation of the secretary of
state John Foster Dulles, President Eisenhower's aggressive Cold War hound.

At the same time, Dulles was deeply suspicious of Nehru. The feeling
was mutual. The American claim was that Nehru's fidelity to the concept
of non-alignment was 'obsolete, immoral and short-sighted'. Nehru did
not take kindly to this interpretation. The US was clearly privileging anti-
communist postures to ones of democratic solidarity, at the height of the
containment policy against communism.[19] When he would fall out of favour
in domestic power struggles two years later in August 1955, and had to

step down as prime minister, Bogra would simply manage a deal to be appointed again as ambassador to the US, provoking commentators of the day to dismiss him as more suited to being a diplomat than a politician. He would later bounce back as Pakistan's foreign minister in 1962.

But Bogra's years as prime minister were also years of frenetic diplomacy between India and Pakistan. He met Nehru thrice in 1953 alone and would visit India multiple times during his tenure. In the first phase of the direct negotiations in 1953, Nehru and Bogra met in London on 5 June, in Karachi on 25 July, and in New Delhi on 16 August. The atmospherics seemed favourable. Nehru received an ecstatic welcome in Karachi. Bogra, in turn, got a rousing reception in New Delhi. Badruddin Tyabji, who accompanied Nehru to Karachi in 1953, called this a golden period of India–Pakistan relations, which saw an upsurge of emotional longing for reconciliation and an open conversation on Kashmir.[20]

Both men talked up their meetings as productive. But Bogra was aiming for the sky and blamed Nehru for throwing cold water on his proposal for a 'joint defence policy'.[21] This was a bizarre ambition under any circumstances—of rival countries emerging from war and a bitter partition to discuss a joint defence pact or a military alliance. Against whom? The Russians? The Chinese? Nehru was restrained in not dismissing this absurd proposal out of hand. He diplomatically pointed out that such an agreement must be based on a common foreign policy of the two countries; otherwise, it could easily lead to India being involved in military pacts contrary to her non-alignment policy.[22]

Kashmir, still the central contentious issue between the countries, was seeing dramatic developments in 1953. In June, Syama Prasad Mookerjee was arrested by the Jammu and Kashmir Police when he tried to cross the border of the state demanding the abolition of its special status. He was provisionally diagnosed with a heart attack and shifted to a hospital but died a day later. A young journalist who accompanied him, Atal Bihari Vajpayee, would return from the border to continue the campaign across the decades. Nehru had not abandoned a commitment to 'ascertain the people's wishes', squeezed as he was between the maximalist demands such as those of Mookerjee—full integration—and Sheikh Abdullah—full autonomy.[23] In July, Nehru was in Karachi, for a visit that involved tough negotiations on Kashmir. In August, in what was seen as Nehru's massive error of judgement, he had Sheikh Abdullah dismissed and arrested. For Pakistan, Abdullah changed 'from quisling to poster boy of Kashmir freedom'.[24]

Much of the bilateral conversation focused on Kashmir. Nehru seemed to have reluctantly agreed to the demand for a plebiscite in the state. But differences remained. Pakistan was clearly seeking to challenge India through an alliance with the US, and Bogra was himself the channel for the US outreach. Nehru was concerned that the US was no longer neutral, its pointed overtures to Pakistan bringing the Cold War to South Asia. Bogra was unhappy when Nehru suggested a plebiscite administrator from a small country, instead of Fleet Admiral Chester W. Nimitz of the US. The superpower play in the region gave Nehru additional reason to walk out of the plebiscite deal.

A SEAT IN SEATO

In May 1954, Pakistan entered into a military pact with the emerging superpower and Britain's closest post-war ally, the US. The 'Mutual Defence Agreement', finalized in Karachi, had been designed by the Eisenhower regime to pull Pakistan firmly into the American orbit. The US continued to push a pliable Bogra on defence pacts, as it searched for allies against the growing threat of communist expansion. Dulles was delighted at Bogra delivering Pakistan's concurrence in joining the US in the anti-communist SEATO alliance in September.

With its entry into a key alliance mirroring the North Atlantic Treaty Organization (NATO), Pakistan had walked firmly into the US camp. It would soon also enter the Baghdad Pact, later rechristened Central Treaty Organization (CENTO), a UK-and US-designed alliance in West Asia, another Cold War defence barrier against the Soviets. For Pakistan, these alliances served to cement its partnership with the West and turn on the taps for US military and economic aid to counter India. Many in Pakistan saw the largesse as reward for Prime Minister Liaquat Ali's refusal to be seduced by Stalin's invitation to Moscow and instead show up in the US in 1950. Pakistan's moves, later seen as a strategy to 'extract geopolitical rents', was perhaps Pakistan's original foreign policy blunder that 'securitized' its polity—putting the army into the driving seat—and put its economy on crutches. The Soviets under Stalin continued to be suspicious not just of Pakistan as a British proxy, but even of India as a 'Commonwealth lackey', rather than a country seeking strategic autonomy through a Nehruvian vision and the invention of the political idea of non-alignment.

The Cold War was intensifying and the US was replacing the UK as the predominant Western global power. Pakistan's dalliance with the US was not going down too well with Nehru. On one occasion, Bogra gave away Pakistan's internal thinking to a US magazine: 'US aid might help Pakistan in solving the Kashmir problem by augmenting her military power'.[25] This outraged Nehru. With the US having now become a party in the India–Pakistan problem, Nehru hardened his position on Kashmir and demanded the withdrawal of American personnel from the UN Observer group.

Pakistan's anti-communist thinking ruled out China as a partner at this stage. China was not yet an important power and the communist country was consolidating itself with a stronger embrace of the Soviet

Union. It had also apparently come closer to Pakistan's arch-rival India, through 'Panchsheel'—the five principles that spoke of non-aggression and non-interference. These had been emphasized in a joint statement in Delhi on 18 June 1954 by Nehru and Chinese Premier Zhou Enlai in what was later seen by India as the 'Panchsheel deception'. Neither side then touched upon the long, ambiguously-defined boundary between them.[26]

Within India, Kashmir was being more firmly integrated into the country. In May 1954, a presidential order effectively curtailed the special status and statutory autonomy given to Kashmir in 1950. The federal government now had legislative jurisdiction in a majority of subjects of the Union List, beyond the three matters—defence, foreign affairs, and communication—listed in the 1947 Instrument of Accession. This was seen as the 'beginning of the end' of Article 370 of the Constitution that had granted temporary autonomy to the Muslim-majority state.[27]

By September, it was apparent that direct negotiations had stalled. Pakistan's establishment, empowered by the US, was opposing a peaceful bilateral settlement on Kashmir, while India was strongly opposing US military assistance to Pakistan. But the atmospherics again changed abruptly by the end of October 1954, after political changes in Pakistan led to the dissolution of the Constituent Assembly and a stronger grip by the Pakistan Army on the cabinet—General Iskander Mirza became minister of the interior and General Ayub Khan became the minister of defence.

A SOVIET AFFAIR

This soft coup in Pakistan that catapulted Ayub Khan to the cabinet, and promised some political coherence within, provided an unexpected boost to relations with India. It led to a situation that would become unthinkable from the next decade: India invited Pakistan's head of state as guest of honour for its Republic Day military parade in January 1955. Governor General Ghulam Mohammad of the Dominion of Pakistan responded enthusiastically and came with his prime minister and two other senior cabinet ministers in tow. His words at a state banquet seemed to signal the start of a new era:

> I think this dark period of strain has now lasted too long and the time has now come to end it completely.... Let us put an end to our disputes. We owe this as a duty to posterity not to leave them a legacy of misunderstandings and bitterness.[28]

The dark period would, of course, not end even in the next several decades. But the visit created enough goodwill to trigger the resumption of direct talks. These began in May 1955, when Prime Minister Mohammad Ali Bogra showed up in Delhi again. The leaders seemed to be keen to try 'new ideas' and a new approach, implicitly giving up on the old idea of a plebiscite in Kashmir. Nehru later revealed that he had even offered his Pakistani counterpart a permanent and formal division of the state along the 1949 ceasefire line.[29]

The fresh diplomatic initiatives came in for international acclaim. The *New York Times* commented: 'Both Pakistan and India were talking about plans which would be variations of the status quo of a divided state and would not involve a plebiscite in the entire state.'[30] Bogra, in his enthusiasm, now annoyed his own side when he went further than the traditional Pakistani position in his public remarks. Speaking of new ideas, he suggested that either a referendum or elections would be as acceptable like a plebiscite to Pakistan in ascertaining the wishes of the people of Kashmir. On his return to Pakistan on 19 May, the prime minister faced blistering media attacks for his folly. He was compelled to rapidly climb down, as critics demanded that there should be no more bilateral talks with India. He was obliged to clarify that the Kashmir issue had not been withdrawn from the UN. Pakistan's media played up this about-face—while he had returned from Delhi satisfied with the results of his meeting with Pandit Nehru, Mr Muhammad Ali Bogra now says that no satisfactory progress was made in Delhi.[31] In 1955, Nehru's policy of non-alignment still had a virtuous glow about it. But India was beginning to show some realism and flexibility in choosing partners. Watching the moves in South Asia by its rival, the US, a de-Stalinizing Soviet Union made a friendly overture to India, the first partnership it was attempting with a 'third world' nation. Prime Minister Nehru travelled to a warm reception in Moscow in June 1955, where Soviet Premier Nikolai Bulganin even proposed 'suggesting at a later stage India's inclusion as the sixth member of the Security Council.' In a lapse of judgement, Nehru felt this was not a serious possibility and preferred to wait till mainland China was admitted.[32] A few months later, Bulganin accompanied the first secretary of the Communist Party, Nikita Khrushchev, on a return visit to India. The duo also spent a weekend in Srinagar where Khrushchev won over his Indian hosts by stating that the whole of Kashmir was part of India.[33] Khrushchev made it abundantly clear that the Soviet Union would be a reliable partner, sensitive to India's core interests. The USSR supported Indian sovereignty over Kashmir and the Portuguese coastal enclave of Goa. Multiple Soviet vetoes in the Security Council in subsequent years gave India a great deal of diplomatic comfort.

India's growing geopolitical weight based on support from a superpower was not however matched by economic muscle. It was emerging from the depredations of empire with a struggling economy, growing moderately at just over 3 per cent. Nehru had set up an economic experiment of state-driven growth with the state occupying the commanding heights of the economy. He had launched the first Five-Year Plan in 1951, focusing on industrializing the country and building infrastructure in key sectors like energy and transportation. Large river dams and power projects like the Bhakra Nangal were being seen as the 'temples of modern India'. India was struggling with poverty and underdevelopment, even while punching above its weight in global affairs as Nehru took a leadership position in the developing world. But in October 1956, with the Soviet invasion of Hungary and India's silence on the issue, the halo of non-alignment was dulling and the West was beginning to get disillusioned with Nehru.[34]

AN INTEGRAL PART

In November 1956, the Constituent Assembly of Jammu and Kashmir adopted a resolution making the state an integral part of the Indian union and accepting the affiliation of the state to India. In a reaction akin to the one in August 2019, when Article 370 was amended by India, a flustered Pakistan raised the matter strongly with the United Nations Security Council (UNSC), protesting this move to reorganize the state internally. India argued that the UN had failed to settle the question of aggression by Pakistan and that India's promise of plebiscite was to the people of Kashmir and not to the Government of Pakistan. It did not occur to anyone to try and expel diplomats. On its part, Pakistan finally worked out its constitution, six years after India's, to graduate from a British dominion to the Islamic Republic of Pakistan.

In the first decade of Independence, the UN provided the platform for India and Pakistan to parry over Kashmir. And diplomacy over the ex-princely state at the UN acquired a life and dynamic of its own. On 23 January 1957, the head of the Indian delegation to the UN, Krishna Menon, delivered an eight-hour speech in New York, defending India's stand on Kashmir. India's diplomat had scored a point, beating the record of Pakistan's foreign minister, Zafarullah Khan, who had famously spoken on Kashmir for five hours in 1948, soon after India took the matter to the UN.[35] To date, Menon's speech is the longest ever delivered in the United Nations, covering five hours of the 762nd meeting of the UN Security Council on 23 January, and two hours and forty-eight minutes the next day. Between the two parts, India's star diplomat collapsed from exhaustion and had to be hospitalized. Menon's passionate defence of Indian sovereignty in Kashmir enlarged his base of support in India, and led to the Indian press dubbing him the 'Hero of Kashmir', a few years before he became the villain of China for his role as defence minister during the Chinese aggression of 1962.

The filibuster at the UN was accompanied by Nehru's moves to consolidate the federal hold on Kashmir. The Constituent Assembly of Jammu and Kashmir, now adopted the new Constitution for the state that declared it an integral part of the union of India. The final move came symbolically on India's seventh Republic Day on 26 January 1957. The Constituent Assembly then dissolved itself to make way for an elected legislative assembly.

Menon's efforts did not prevent the Security Council from passing a resolution on 24 January, criticizing the resolution passed by the Constituent Assembly of Kashmir and insisting that the future of the state could be decided only by plebiscite. This was the last time the Security Council was to intervene in the Kashmir dispute. Another draft resolution on 14 February was vetoed by the Soviet Union. This was the first Soviet veto, and was to be followed by several more.

Soon after, the next mediator appointed by the UN, the Swedish diplomat Gunnar Jarring, visited both India and Pakistan in the spring of 1957, but failed to resolve their differences. He concluded that the changes in political, economic, and strategic factors surrounding the Kashmir question, together with the changing pattern of the relations of the major powers with Pakistan and India, had created a situation where a peaceful plebiscite could not be held.

Meanwhile India's second general elections in 1957 reaffirmed its democratic credentials and the argument that the people of Kashmir were expressing their views by voting both federally and provincially. Nehru received a fresh mandate to govern an India he was consolidating. At the peak of his power, Nehru quipped that Pakistan had one army chief and six prime ministers in this period while it was the other way round for India.

It was not just Nehru and the leaders of the day that were passionate about Kashmir and its future. The issue evoked much fervour among Indian and Pakistani diplomats for the decade, with another military solution attempted by Pakistan in the next. Both military action and diplomacy have remained tools on the table ever since.

The first decade was also unique for the scale of challenges and the counter-intuitively constructive responses. The pains of Partition, its brutal massacres, its teeming refugees, served not just to scar psyches and poison ties, but also to present huge logistical challenges to the fledgling nations. The territorial challenge was of integrating the princely states. The principal problem was the status of Kashmir, over which the sibling nations had their first war that started a few weeks after Independence and ended with the ceasefire of 1949.

Though both countries lost their founding fathers, Gandhi and Jinnah, in 1948, just about within a year of Independence, their trajectories differed. While Pakistan's polity floundered, India recovered, with its first prime minister, Nehru, consolidating the polity and economy, accepting the reality of Pakistan. Yet, surprisingly, the diplomacy between the countries remained sincere, professional, and constructive, as the new nations tried to decouple themselves as independent states and negotiate the minutiae of their new diplomatic ties, the building of their states.

The first decade was not just setting the basis for the future relationship between the two young nations. According to Pallavi Raghavan, the period in fact 'witnessed the height of the sense of possibility in the capacity of the state, and the capabilities, responsibilities, and accommodativeness of its institutions'. The 'hectic cooperation and dialogue' of the 1950s had a deeper significance, Raghavan argues, 'since that generation had witnessed the very worst of the traumas of sub-continental politics.' Yet, they concluded that the 'best remedy for the situation called for a series of detailed negotiations.'[36] Both the traumas and the fruit of the negotiations were passed on to succeeding generations of diplomats.

If Nehru found it tedious to deal with the unimaginative 'daftaries' (bureaucrats) of Pakistan in his first decade as PM, dealing with the 'vardis' (uniforms) in the next decade would be simpler. But a miscalculation in the second decade would lead to war and squander many of the surprising victories of the early years.

1957–1967: DICTATORS AND DEMOCRATS

6

THE GARRISON STATE

Rajeshwar Dayal, India's designated high commissioner to Pakistan, felt some trepidation as he prepared to present his credentials to General Ayub Khan, his host country's first military dictator. He had arrived in an ornate horse-drawn carriage at the president's house in Karachi and waited in the 'durbar hall' that reminded Dayal of the Rashtrapati Bhavan back home in Delhi. It was November 1958, a month after Ayub had dislodged his country's president, Iskander Mirza, in a bloodless coup, to crown himself Pakistan's head of state. A mythology of clinical, even brutal, efficiency was being spun around Ayub—here was the strongman Pakistan needed to pull itself out of a stagnating quagmire spawned by years of ineffective leadership; here was the man for the moment, the patriot who headed Pakistan's only effective functioning institution, the army; here was the ruthless leader who would remove the scum and arrest the decay for the good of the people. Pakistan, the argument went, had been done in by poor rulers in its formative decade, while India had progressed under statesmen of stature; so finally, here was a Pakistani leader in the second decade who would usher in an era of better governance.

On 27 October 1958, a few weeks before Dayal landed in Karachi, President Iskander Mirza had been lounging at home in his dressing gown, when a delegation of three army generals barged in and calmly instructed him to dress and leave Pakistan 'in the interests of the country'. The shocked president was given just over an hour to pack up and depart. He and his Iranian wife, Khanum Naheed, were asked to 'buy their own airline tickets and pay for their passports'. Mirza was essentially ordered to surrender his role as Pakistan's head of state, since his chief martial law administrator, Ayub Khan, now had his job.[1] The president was escorted out of his home and thence into oblivion, to eventually die in England in humble exile.

A few months before his own unceremonious exit, Mirza had opined to the US ambassador in Karachi that only a dictatorship would work in Pakistan. He had seen himself as that benign dictator when he imposed martial law on 7 October 1958, after dismissing the last of a succession of colourless prime ministers—Feroz Khan Noon—abrogating the Constitution of 1956, dissolving parliament, and appointing his trusted army chief Ayub Khan as his martial law administrator. Ayub would, of course, go on to deftly dismiss his boss within three weeks and take more effective control of power, cementing the martial law that Mirza had proclaimed.

Ayub's rise had begun seven years earlier. He had taken over in 1951 as the first Pakistani army chief, picking up the baton from General Douglas Gracey, the last Englishman to hold the job. Ayub was elevated as Pakistan's defence minister in 1953 in what is now seen as a soft coup. But to Ayub, he was only leading to fruition a revolution initiated by Pakistan's 'last capable civilian politician', Iskander Mirza, who had eventually lacked courage and was 'too stupid' to take this revolution to completion[2]. So, Ayub had reluctantly stepped in to fulfil Pakistan's destiny. He recalled in his memoirs that he was most unhappy making this decision.

> I was unhappy for him (Mirza) too. How unfortunate that he could not be loyal to anybody.... All the politicians had been tried and found wanting; there was no one else left on the civil side.... Even if Iskander Mirza had wanted to play straight, he would not have had the courage to stand up and face the consequences of the reforms which were being introduced.[3]

Across the border, Nehru had not been impressed by the arrival of a Pakistani strongman; he dismissed the new political dispensation as a 'naked military dictatorship'. To Dayal, an ICS officer who had been picked up for the foreign service by Nehru, 'there could hardly have been a more inauspicious moment for a new envoy to take charge of the Indian mission in Pakistan'.[4]

When Dayal landed in Karachi after the coup, he was also continuing the tradition of Indian high commissioners arriving in Karachi brandishing pre-Partition connections with Pakistani leaders. Sri Prakasa had known Jinnah and Liaquat Ali as his political contemporaries in India. His successors—Sita Ram, Mohan Singh Mehta, and C. C. Desai—had all built on their pre-Partition connections with Pakistan's leaders. Dayal was the fifth in this series of Nehru's elite picks for Pakistan. While not the first to claim close acquaintance with Pakistan's rulers, he was perhaps the one to leverage the connections most effectively. He saw the challenges in the relationship as largely a legacy of the Partition. His brief was to take smaller steps towards reducing the tension, a not unfamiliar mandate for most of his successors. In his initial assessment

> the main problems dividing India and Pakistan were part of the unfinished business of Partition. These were the undemarcated border, the division of the waters of the Indus basin, the question of evacuee property, the settlement of the public debt of undivided India, and the disposition of the India Office Library in London. There was also the hardy annual of the Kashmir question, over which wordy battles had

been fought for years at the United Nations and which was straining the rhetoric of vituperation on both sides. Overhanging all these problems, a poisonous psychological atmosphere prevailed, the result of which was an almost total stoppage of trade, severe restrictions on travel, and unbridled press propaganda. My instructions from the Prime Minister, as indeed were my own predilections, were to try and work towards the reduction of the state of tension between the two countries and to promote the solution of the more manageable problems. The question, however, was how and where to start.[5]

While Dayal was troubled by the prospect of interacting with an untested military dictator at the helm of a hostile government, another more immediate concern was also gnawing at him—that Ayub Khan may not acknowledge their past association. Eighteen years earlier, Ayub and he had served together in Mathura in the United Provinces: Dayal as a district official and Khan as a captain in the Indian Army. The envoy was painfully aware that past associations with Pakistan's rulers had not empowered any of his predecessors in transforming bilateral ties.

When it came time to meet with General Ayub Khan, Dayal worked with Pakistan's chief of protocol, with schoolboyish diligence, to familiarize himself with the choreography of the colonial-era credentials ceremony. The high commissioner and his retinue of embassy officers were to slowly approach the head of state, bowing every few paces. The president was to appear with fanfare from the far end and await the envoy, who would make a formal speech and present his letters of credence. The president would respond with his own words of welcome and then invite the envoy to an antechamber for a private audience.

Dayal was in for a surprise. As he entered the hall where the meeting was to take place, the president advanced rapidly towards the diplomat, brushing protocol aside, with outstretched hand and broad smile. As the two men stood, Ayub Khan began an animated conversation with Dayal, making solicitous enquiries about his family. The envoy awkwardly reminded the president of the formal agenda and proceeded to step back to deliver his scripted speech. Ayub hurriedly went through the motions and then sat Dayal down for a chat. Soon, it was two colleagues swapping news of common acquaintances and family, not quite envoy and head of state exchanging curated talking points.

This interaction set the tone for a relationship of easy informality that continued throughout the tenure of the high commissioner. Dayal was quite taken in by Ayub's charm and soon became a strong advocate for him with Nehru and the Indian establishment. Dayal even managed to have the president tweak protocol again, this time to join him at the embassy residence in Karachi for a Republic Day function on 26 January

1959. A beaming Ayub Khan spent considerable time at the soirée, seated between the high commissioner and his wife, the easy bonhomie pointedly on public display. 'Word quickly spread around', the diplomat recalled, 'that the President and we were close friends of long standing'.[6] This opened several doors for the Indian envoy in Karachi.

The diplomat and the dictator developed a strong personal bond that deepened when Ayub, in a later private meeting, disarmingly asked the envoy if he had his trust. Dayal reassured the dictator he did, and ventured to ask if 'he too felt the same about me'. They then went on to candidly discuss the stalemate in bilateral relations. The mutual affirmation of confidence was to serve Ayub well. Dayal pushed the Indian system to set up a visit by Ayub to India and then spent considerable effort in persuading a sceptical Nehru to visit Pakistan.

Dayal was originally scheduled to arrive in Karachi half a year earlier. The prime minister of Pakistan, Feroz Khan Noon, had even sent him a warm letter of welcome advising him to come early. But a UN mission kept the designated envoy away. Those were times when India's newly-minted diplomats, mostly ICS officers, played multiple roles, abandoning bilateral assignments—even critical ones as in Pakistan—to take on lengthy UN gigs in global hotspots, self-importantly bringing peace to the post-colonial world.

A NO-WAR PROPOSAL
In April 1959, Pakistan signed a bilateral defence cooperation agreement with the US, which obliged the superpower to take 'appropriate action', in case of aggression against Pakistan, including through the use of armed forces. While the interests of the two countries had converged, the goals were different—the US was deploying Pakistan against communist adversaries, while Ayub was banking on American backing in dealing with India.

Pakistan's status as a US Cold War ally in South Asia had strengthened steadily after it joined the Western alliances in the mid-1950s. In July 1957, Pakistan's prime minister Huseyn Shaheed Suhrawardy, on army chief Ayub Khan's prodding, had offered the US a secret intelligence base at Badaber near Peshawar in north-west Pakistan. This base added to the growing strategic value of Pakistan for the US; the CIA's U2 planes could now keep an easy eye on military preparations in the Soviet Union.

Pakistan could not however play both sides in the Cold War. When Pakistan's eager embrace of the US was outed, it angered the Soviet Union. Moscow was outraged by Pakistan's decision to allow its territory to be used for spying on its territory. When it shot down a U2 plane on 7 May 1960 and arrested its pilot Gary Powers, the Soviet Union warned Pakistan 'not to play with fire'.[7] But Ayub had irreversibly hitched his wagon to the West. The Americans would go on to operate the base for a decade, with 1,200 military and technical personnel. The secret facility would lead to greater confidence in the US in their new ally, located strategically on the periphery of an enemy empire.

Pakistan, on its part, needed to monetize this growing trust; its fidelity opened the gates for generous US military and economic aid that had begun flowing, eventually totting up to $5 billion till 1962. The assistance would be frequently calibrated in the next decades—increased to reward good behaviour and, more often, suspended to punish choices not in the American interest.

Around the time he worked out a defence agreement with the US, and perhaps at its nudging, in April 1959, Ayub Khan dusted off the old proposal for a 'joint defence' pact with India. When Nehru questioned the familiar gambit and again asked the obvious question, which he had asked six years earlier—joint defence against whom—Ayub darkly pointed north and forecast that in the following five years, South Asia would be vulnerable to major invasions from that direction. Ayub was hinting at the dangers from both communist empires—China and the Soviet Union. A Pakistani diplomat later speculated that Ayub may have been trying to humour Washington, Pakistan's new military partner; or genuinely believed in the communist threat; or was using a tactical gambit to pressure Nehru into addressing the Kashmir issue, before dealing jointly with an external threat.[8] Pakistan's new dictator was likely doing all three.

Pakistani concerns about the Chinese seemed genuine enough, even for Indian observers of the times. In the early stages of Chinese muscle flexing in 1959, when the Dalai Lama fled to India, some Pakistani leaders severely criticized the Chinese suppression of the revolt in Tibet, which they compared to the Soviet action in Hungary in 1956. Chinese claims against India across the McMahon Line (the boundary between Tibet and British India as agreed in 1914) had provoked concerns of similar demands China might register against territory under the occupation of Pakistan.[9] In fact, Ayub Khan's offer of joint defence with India seemed to have been driven at least in part by genuine concerns about China's expansionist policies. On their part, the Chinese saw, in Ayub's joint defence proposal, American designs to create hostility against China in its backyard.

Ayub's joint defence pact would also have bound both countries not to go to war. The notion of joint defence was a diplomatic riposte from Pakistan to the idea of a non-aggression pact that India had been promoting since the 1950s, to prevent a reprise of the war of 1947–48.

But Nehru had seen through Pakistan's new game. Ayub reacted with injured innocence to Nehru's cynicism about this latest gambit. The dictator was hurt that India had deliberately misinterpreted and rejected his proposal by attributing 'false motives' to Pakistan. He insisted in his memoirs that he was only repeating a proposal made by two of his predecessors and that

> there was nothing sinister in the proposal, nor was I the first one to have made it. The Quaid-e-Azam (in 1948) thought that it was of vital importance to Pakistan and India, as independent sovereign States, to collaborate in a friendly way jointly to defend their frontiers both on land and sea against any aggression.... In April 1953 Mohammad Ali Bogra, who was then Prime Minister of Pakistan, declared that, once outstanding disputes between the two countries had been settled and a suitable climate created, joint defence of India and Pakistan could be advantageously considered by the two countries.[10]

Ayub revealed his central motive when he laid out a grandiose vision of friendship with the caveat that the prerequisite for such an understanding was the solution of big problems like Kashmir and the canal waters. Once these were resolved, the armies of the two countries could disengage and move to their respective vulnerable frontiers. This would give us the substance of joint defence; that is, freedom from fear of each other and freedom to protect our respective frontiers.

He complained that his Indian counterpart Nehru deliberately chose to misunderstand the proposal and declared in the Lok Sabha on 4 May 1959:

> We do not propose to have a military alliance with any country, come what may.... I am all for settling our troubles with Pakistan and living normal, friendly and neighborly lives—but we do not want to have a common defence policy which is almost some kind of a military alliance—I do not understand against whom people talk about common defence policies.[11]

Internally, Ayub was consolidating what would become an eleven-year tenure that did end Pakistan's instability of the 1950s, but firmly established the 'garrison state', a permanent structural infirmity in Pakistan's polity that would impact India at multiple levels.[12]

In Indian strategic thinking at that point, the sole challenge for India in the region was the bilateral confrontation between India and Pakistan, posing the constant danger of war. A no-war pact, therefore, seemed more relevant. The proposal for a joint defence agreement in the absence of an external threat thus seemed unnecessary, if not a political ruse.

Hindsight showed that India had overblown the threat from Pakistan, just as it had underestimated the one from China. Some observers of the day disagreed with India's policy of the times. Surely, India could have benefited from making common cause with Pakistan against Chinese aggression. In fact, the argument went, if Jinnah had survived another five or six years, he may have pursued his vision of a common security concept for two sovereign and friendly states. This thesis was supported by Iskander Mirza, Pakistan's exiled president, who averred that if he were still Pakistan's leader, he would have flown to Delhi and assured Nehru that Pakistan would solidly stand by India in her defence.[13] But soon enough, all of this would cease to matter, when Pakistan would again see India as its principal adversary. The strategic benefits of embracing India's hostile northern neighbour were getting clearer to Ayub.

When he assessed the situation within Pakistan, Dayal shared Ayub's contempt for Pakistan's past leaders. In the envoy's eyes, Pakistani leaders of the 1950s were essentially officials, 'daftaries' as Nehru had called them, who leapfrogged over Muslim League politicians to occupy high offices. They had been a 'scheming, self-serving'[14] lot, Dayal felt, while Ayub, with his sweeping powers, was a more promising bet for India. Dayal talked up Ayub's capacity to deliver better bilateral ties, given the dictator's unchallenged power and refreshing pragmatism. The envoy's assessment was that 'whatever may have been the change in Ayub Khan's perceptions since his transformation from an Indian patriot during our Mathura days in 1940 to a Pakistani zealot, he took an encouragingly pragmatic view of the situation and saw the advantage of coming to political settlements with India, starting with the more immediate problems.'[15]

The diplomat made it his mission to mend fences, cabling back upbeat assessments of the new Pakistan dispensation under Ayub. Buoyed by his personal access to Pakistan's dictator, Dayal pushed his home establishment to accept a visit by Ayub to India. With his briefings and recommendations back home, Dayal chipped away at his prime minister's distrust of Pakistan's military dictator. Against his original instincts, Nehru, who had been underwhelmed by the overpromoted civil servants who ruled Pakistan, had begun to veer towards Dayal's view that a dictator running Pakistan might somehow turn out to be a better bet for India, giving more coherence and stability to Pakistan's policy. Dayal had begun taking matters directly to Nehru, bypassing some hardliner foreign ministry colleagues and particularly staying clear of Defence Minister Krishna Menon, a known hawk, completely opposed to trusting Pakistan. Ayub Khan finally did stop by for a transit visit to Delhi in September 1959, which helped clear the path for Nehru's own visit to Karachi.

Despite the high-level engagement with India, Pakistan's dictator was concerned that his Western benefactors were now beginning to see India as a more credible bulwark against the other communists, the Chinese, who were now a decade-old power demonstrating larger global ambitions. US arms and equipment were also trickling in as military aid to India, albeit with similar conditions as applied to Pakistan—American weapons were to be used only to repel Chinese aggression. Pakistan protested initially but muted its criticism by the end of 1959, when the Sino–Pak alliance became a clearer objective for the military regime of Ayub Khan.

In the debate for a no-war pact vis-à-vis a joint defence agreement, it was now clear to India that Pakistan was still not willing to give up on its demand of resolving the 'core' Kashmir dispute before addressing any other matter. Many in India believed that Ayub had proposed the carrot of a no-war pact only to soften up India on the Kashmir issue and on the division of the river waters. Ayub's military mind told him that he had only a small window of opportunity to get the better of Pakistan's permanent enemy before the power differential between them became wider, making India impossible to challenge militarily.[16] While Dayal was upbeat about the positive turn the relationship could take with Nehru's proposed visit, he had in his exuberance failed to read the ingrained distrust of India and the revisionist ideas swirling in Ayub's shallow mind. These were to be revealed to the world a few years later when Pakistan attempted a stealthy military conquest of Kashmir.

In Delhi, Nehru who remained his own foreign minister, also had a channel of communication open with Pakistan's high commissioner A. K. Brohi, a prominent Sindhi politician and lawyer whom Ayub had sent in February 1960. Brohi, who would go on to become Pakistan's law minister, and an ideological adviser to Pakistan's dictator Zia, was also a mentor of the famous Sindhi Indian lawyer, Ram Jethmalani. Brohi was well-connected in the upper reaches of Indian society; in the year he spent in Delhi, he frequently met Nehru for breakfast, as India's leader planned his approach for his visit to Pakistan.[17]

PARTITIONING THE WATERS

In September 1960, Pakistan and India defied expectations to sign the Indus Waters Treaty, agreeing to the division of the six rivers that flowed through the Punjab. In its final shape, the treaty allocated the waters of the western rivers (Indus, Jhelum, and Chenab) to Pakistan, giving it four-fifths of the waters of the system. Limited use of the waters of the western rivers was also permitted to India, which was allocated all the waters of the eastern rivers (Ravi, Beas, and Sutlej). Since Pakistan had been receiving water from these eastern rivers till Partition, India agreed to pay £62 million as compensation to Pakistan, to build replacement canals from the western rivers. The treaty did not require India to deliver any specific quantities of water to Pakistan, but the upper riparian country was obliged to let flow the water of the western rivers to the lower riparian, after drawing a limited amount for activities like 'run of the river' projects.[18]

The treaty had been long in the works. It was a culmination of more than a decade of assiduous technical negotiations. Nehru's visit to Karachi to sign the document was seen at once as a path-breaking resolution of a vexing water dispute and a lost opportunity to resolve the larger disagreement on land in Kashmir.

The discussion on the Indus deal had begun soon after Partition, in 1948. As the countries battled over the land of Kashmir, India had threatened to cut off water supplies of the canals, since Partition gave it an upper riparian hold over the rivers winding south into Pakistan. In May 1948, a water agreement had been finalized, only to be denounced in Pakistan as one signed under duress. Observers had been troubled by a very real concern of a water war between the countries.

Pakistan had been disquieted since 1948 by the construction of the massive Bhakra Dam on the Sutlej, an eastern river that flowed into the Chenab in Pakistan, before emptying into the Arabian Sea. In 1950, Pakistan proposed arbitration to deal with the issue of sharing waters, but India did not agree. In 1951, both governments agreed to involve the World Bank. The next year, the bank's president, Eugene Black, had offered his good offices for a solution of the dispute, which both countries agreed to. By 1954, the World Bank was suggesting dividing the waters into eastern and western rivers. Eight years of quiet technical negotiations ensued before the deal was finally struck.

Both sides were unhappy with the eventual shape of the water treaty of 1960. For many Pakistanis, the treaty was a sell-out to the crafty Indians. For others, it was a pragmatic arrangement. Ayub Khan recalled in his memoirs that 'the only sensible thing to do was to try and get a settlement, even though it might be second best, because if we did not, we stood to lose everything...while there was no cause for rejoicing at the signing of the treaty, there was certainly cause for satisfaction that a possibly very ugly situation had been averted'.[19] Most Pakistani observers were more optimistic than the president. This was a win-win solution that would unlock World Bank funding for a 'decade of development', cutting dependence on India. Some out of the box ideas were in play too. Ayub Khan had generously offered to construct a barrage in the lower sections of the Indus River to direct water to parched Rajasthan as well as to feed the Bombay region with Sui natural gas from Balochistan.[20]

For some in India, it was an overly generous arrangement for an upper riparian country. For the idealists and some US experts, the treaty missed out on the optimal development of the Indus basin for hydro-electric projects (like in the Tennessee valley) that could have benefited both poor nations. Notwithstanding the critiques, the treaty was largely hailed for decades as a successful model for dividing river waters between adversarial neighbours. Pakistan gained funds from the World Bank for the construction of two large dams (Mangla on the Jhelum and Tarbela on the Indus), apart from multiple link canals from the western rivers to Pakistan, to replace the loss due to the diversion of the eastern rivers. Both countries would go on to construct hydel projects in the 1970s and 1980s. The treaty also stood out as a 'unique achievement of the professional diplomacy of the 1950s', and one of the 'innovations of partition'.[21]

Over decades, the treaty has been tested by tough times in bilateral ties. The debate periodically crops up in the twenty-first century, on India's upper riparian generosity for Pakistan, compared to the absence of any such sentiment in China for India, where the Brahmaputra waters are 'weaponized'.[22] Each time India encounters terror, or after a meeting of the Permanent Indus Commission (PIC), the debate is rekindled on whether to abrogate the Indus treaty. The river waters would continue to be an emotive issue, with mutual suspicions rising whenever relations hit a low point, and dispute resolution mechanisms increasingly invoked in the twenty-first century.

↺

Nehru's 1960 visit was not all about water. It was also about land. While the talks on dividing the river waters had continued quietly under the auspices of the World Bank, the negotiations on the Punjab land boundary had taken on a higher bilateral profile. In September 1958, Nehru had signed an agreement with Prime Minister Feroze Khan Noon on resolving the border issue of land enclaves in Bengal. A year later, in 1959, by which time Ayub Khan was in power, Nehru designated Swaran Singh, a trusted Punjab hand and then minister for steel in his cabinet, to talk to the dictator's nominee: Pakistan's railway minister, General Khalid Sheikh. Swaran Singh's nomination came as a result, at least partially, of the pressure brought to bear by High Commissioner Dayal. The two men were mandated to discuss the Punjab boundary. This conversation progressed well during Nehru's visit. Dayal felt that it should have been broadened in scope to include the Gujarat boundary as well. This turned out to be sound, if unheeded, advice given that this border would become a source of conflict over the Rann of Kutch in 1965. The most contentious issue of the land border in Kashmir was gingerly placed in a separate box, given the involvement of the UN and the bigger chasm in the positions of the two countries.

To the diplomats of the day, Nehru's visit to Pakistan at the height of his powers, in September 1960, spelled a great opportunity to come to terms with Radcliffe's Line in Punjab. The Indian deputy high commissioner in Karachi, K. V. Padmanabhan, recalled that the ambitions of the summit meeting went beyond the division of waters to a hope of delineating land borders south of Kashmir. He found the discussions remarkably constructive, helped by the fact that

> the leaders of the respective teams were old friends and college mates from pre-Partition Lahore.... Once these two men [Swaran Singh and

Khalid Shaikh] established their rapport, they left the details to their principal advisors: on the Indian side, M. J. Desai, and on the other side Sikander Ali Baig. Once it was established that the main purpose of the exercise was to achieve maximum agreement and that neither side was out to steal an unfair advantage, it was easier to work out a solution. It was found that neither India nor Pakistan had an overwhelming case to be made on its stand on a particular dispute. One side gracefully conceded the other's claim were valid, and that was that.[23]

Bizarrely, Dayal took off on a UN mission to the Congo just before Nehru's visit to Pakistan in September. The UN secretary general, Dag Hammarskjöld likely pressed Nehru to release Dayal to be deployed as the UNSG's special representative, given that Dayal had helped Hammarskjöld broker peace in 1958 in Lebanon, and an Indian face was required in the context of a large Indian peacekeeping contingent managing the sudden Belgian withdrawal from the Congo. But as the key architect of the Indo–Pak détente, Dayal would have been expected to be working night and day to convert a major visit of his prime minister into a success, to tease out lasting deliverables, and to prevent any mishaps in its conduct. The high commissioner's glaring absence was noted by the hosts. Ayub later bitterly told Dayal that the Indian government considered the Congo more important than Pakistan.

In the week Nehru spent in Pakistan on the visit, which was largely pegged to the Indus Waters Treaty, he also discussed a number of other issues: the Punjab boundary, taxation, customs, evacuee properties, even defence matters. Kashmir was not formally on the agenda but was clearly the elephant in the room. It was here that India's prime minister had decided to draw a line. Playing on Nehru's mind was the vast gap in positions on the Kashmir issue and the errors in judgement he had made in Kashmir policy after his previous visit to Karachi in 1953. Ayub Khan, instigated by trusted cabinet minister Zulfikar Ali Bhutto, was ready with his maximalist position—demanding a plebiscite—while Nehru favoured going with the status quo with minor adjustments. Nevertheless, Nehru erred again in not having a full discussion on Kashmir. Arguably, a conversation between India's democratic leader, and Pakistan's military dictator, both domestically strong, may have averted a war five years later.

Both Ayub and the Indian high commissioner interpreted the deadlock on Kashmir as the visit's failure. Dayal was crestfallen when he learnt of the outcomes of Nehru's visit. Dayal got a debrief of the 'Murree encounter' from Foreign Minister Manzur Qadir, who sat in the front seat for the ride where the president and the prime minister drove up to Murree in an open car. There was 'no conversation' between the two leaders during the hour-long drive. Qadir's attempts to start a conversation were met with 'deafening silence'. When Qadir probed the president on the meeting, all that Ayub Khan revealed was that when he tried to open a conversation about Kashmir, Nehru simply stared out of the window at the scenery and 'shut up like a clam'. From that time, Dayal felt, the 'relations between the two countries, which had been built up brick by brick, suddenly collapsed in rubble'.[24]

Dayal realized that his prime minister's visit was not the crowning moment of his tenure, as he had hoped it would be. It ended his smooth run with Ayub's government, though his social capital remained intact. He recalled that while attitudes at governmental level began to harden, 'our personal relations with the President and his family continued to be cordial enough. Our social relations generally also continued as before. We took our daily walks, unaccompanied by securitymen, both in Karachi and in Murree', he recalled.[25]

A major factor limiting the success of the Nehru–Ayub summit was that little preparation preceded it. No active diplomacy or backchannels were used to leverage the positivity of the Indus treaty and Nehru's visit at the crest of his popularity. Everything had been left to the leaders to sort out at the last moment. The absence of the envoy was perhaps a key factor in getting it wrong.

Nehru was to eventually meet Ayub five times, but their chemistry remained inert. Ayub's attitude was typical of the overreach on Kashmir that characterized Pakistan's negotiating posture even decades later in the times of other dictators.

The conversation during Nehru's visit did touch on Kashmir in the context of China. As the deputy high commissioner K. V. Padmanabhan recalled.

India expressed concern about Chinese activities on the northern border of Kashmir and emphasised the concern they felt about a possible threat to Pakistan also from them. Ayub Khan, without batting an eyelid, shook his head gravely and promised to study the question with his military advisors. Little did the Indian side suspect that Pakistan would be handing over to the Chinese sizeable chunks of the territory in the northern part of Kashmir in return for China's support of Pakistan's claim for the annexation of Jammu and Kashmir. In fact, all our bilateral discussions and grandiose schemes came to practically nothing because of Pakistan's insistence that India should make substantial concessions with regard to Kashmir. Thereby ended another chapter in the unfulfilled agenda of cooperation between India and Pakistan.[26]

Nehru later confirmed that he discussed the China factor during his visit. He revealed that in his discussions with Ayub, he shared 'our confidential maps as to where we thought the Chinese were and where we were, and asked what (the) position of the Chinese was on their side of the border.' Pakistan's foreign secretary 'said he knew nothing about those matters at all'. [27] Nehru later elaborated: 'Whatever our differences were on Kashmir, I thought it would be advantageous to have a uniform policy with regard to the Chinese aggression....'[28]

TROUBLE FROM THE NORTH

During this period, the sporadic surface cordiality aside, Pakistan's hostility towards India and Ayub's obsession over Kashmir did not diminish. This unremitting focus also informed Pakistan's approach to China and its diplomacy in Delhi. One note of dissent to Ayub Khan's policies came from his high commissioner in India, A. K. Brohi, the popular diplomat in Delhi's political and social circles. Brohi abruptly resigned in Delhi in March 1961, just over a year into his assignment, since he could not accept the 'patently wrong' instructions sent by Ayub. He chose to go straight to his home in Karachi, rather than debrief the president and others in Rawalpindi. He genuinely believed that the 'community of interests between India and Pakistan and the enormous fund of goodwill between the two peoples far outweighed the grievances and the irritants so exaggerated for political reasons'. [29]

Soon after Nehru had revealed in India's parliament his exchanges with Ayub on China, the bad news came from Peking. On 4 May 1962, Pakistan and China declared they had decided to hold negotiations to settle their border dispute along the part of Kashmir in Pakistan's possession. India was just beginning then to get the measure of the growing Sino–Pakistan axis. An exasperated Nehru said: 'It is very surprising that Pakistan which is a champion standard-bearer against Communism should now try to club with China.'[30]

A couple of months later, Gopalaswami Parthasarathi, often simply called GP, was posted as India's ambassador to Pakistan. GP was an unusual diplomat, with a penchant for landing in history's hotspots. He had just finished a trying tenure in China, and would watch in dismay as a Sino–Indian conflict unfolded in October 1962, just as he began his diplomatic innings in Karachi. GP did not quite fit the profile of the standard ICS diplomat of the times. Nehru had handpicked the young journalist writing for the Press Trust of India (PTI), to catapult him into diplomacy. GP had turned to journalism from sport, he was a Ranji Trophy level cricketer for Madras, as also a double university blue in cricket and hockey at Oxford. He had apprenticed with the *The Times* of London in the 1930s and had written for *The Hindu* in the 1940s, before he became the first London correspondent for PTI in 1949, churning out incisive commentary on foreign affairs for an independent India. He returned to Bombay as PTI's chief editor in 1952. He caught Nehru's eye with his writings, defined by a clear-eyed analysis of global affairs. He also happened to be the son of Nehru's political associate and minister in his first cabinet, N. Gopalaswami Ayyangar. After his induction into India's diplomatic service in 1954, the forty-two-year-old star journalist, then known for his expertise on Southeast Asia, was sent off to serve initially in Cambodia, Vietnam, and Indonesia.

GP's next three assignments would propel him to the frontline of India's high-voltage diplomatic action of the 1960s. He was sent as ambassador in China in 1958, where he watched the gathering war clouds and came away in 1962 feeling betrayed by the Chinese aggression on India. It was now his turn to spend three years in Pakistan as India's envoy, from October 1962, just as the war with China began.

India's Himalayan War of 1962 had been building up for at least five years. In September 1957, a major turning point had come in India's relationship with China, surprising both Nehru and Defence Minister Krishna Menon. China brazenly announced that it had completed the Aksai Chin Road, linking two restive parts of its periphery—Sinkiang and Tibet. The road passed through a hundred miles of Ladakh, in territory that belonged to India. China was now openly warning India of its strength and hegemony in Asia. By January 1959, Premier Zhou Enlai informed Nehru that the McMahon Line was not acceptable as a boundary since no formal delimitation of the Sino–Indian border had ever taken place. China simply said that it had not been ready in 1954—when it had signed up for the principles of good neighbourly Panchsheel—to discuss this question, but had now decided to take a position. China was further embittered by the Tibetan rebellion and India's decision to grant asylum to the Dalai Lama in March 1959.[31] All these matters came up for discussion when Zhou visited India in April 1959.

Nehru tried hard to retrieve the situation. In February and again in April 1960, he met Zhou Enlai in Delhi for some tough discussions on the boundary. Zhou offered to accept the McMahon line as the boundary in the eastern sector, abutting India's north-east, provided India was willing to pay the price by accepting the Chinese occupation of Ladakh. This was totally unacceptable to India. Official meetings in 1960 and 1961 produced no results, while Chinese intrusions into India continued unabated.[32] In the middle of July 1962, Chinese troops launched an attack on the Galwan Valley in Ladakh. India's forces repulsed the assault. China watchers would recall this painful episode six decades later in 2020, when Chinese troops again moved aggressively forward in Galwan.

Pakistan was watching closely. In its official narrative, the 1962 conflict was a result of 'India's aggression' against China. To Ayub, both Cold War adversaries—the US and USSR—had come together to side with India against China: Soviet military supplies and the Kennedy administration's stepped up economic assistance, in Pakistan's view, had egged India on to maintain a 'forward policy' against China, in order to negotiate the boundary question from a position of strength. In Pakistan's perception, India sought military aid from the US, in letters facilitated by John Kenneth Galbraith, then US ambassador in India, who had coordinated closely with Nehru.[33]

On 8 September, the Chinese finally crossed the Thagla Ridge in the eastern sector, to mount attacks on India. A series of skirmishes led up to a harsh mountain war from 20 October to 21 November. Chinese and Indian troops fought bitterly, causing major losses for India both in the Western Sector of Ladakh and the Eastern Sector of Assam. India's humiliating defeat caused an internal political churn, even as Nehru was personally devastated and politically weakened. Defence Minister Menon was relieved of his duties.[34]

The geopolitical currents were also shifting. The war in the high Himalaya was coming at a time of a great Sino-Soviet split, that itself got accentuated by this Asian conflict. It was also playing out in the backdrop of an unfolding Cuban missile crisis that almost brought the superpowers—the US and the USSR—to nuclear blows.[35] The US and Britain expressed much sympathy for India against the Chinese aggression but did not actually join the conflict. Nehru wrote to Kennedy on 25 October, at the height of the crisis. As a result, US arms, mainly infantry weapons, arrived in India and further supplies were speeded up. In Pakistan's official telling, Nehru had in 1962 written 'a hysterical letter, a silly letter asking [the] US to bomb China'.[36]

On 20 December, as the dust settled on the war, US president John F. Kennedy and British prime minister Harold Wilson announced a decision to provide military aid of $1.2 million to India. Pakistan's official version of events holds US Ambassador Galbraith responsible for this largesse: he was opting, in Abdul Sattar's account, for 'transitory personal success'—he was trying to win Nehru over for the US 'since the US believed that India could successfully compete with China for leadership of Asia.' It was soon after India's devastating war with China, but Galbraith seemed to be ahead of his times by six decades in assessing the geopolitical future. His view was echoed in Washington. Months before his assassination, Kennedy would repeat to Pakistan Ambassador G. Ahmed, on 11 August 1963, that he wanted Pakistan and India to join in 'common defence' against China.[37]

To many observers, a surprise during India's border war with China in 1962 was that Pakistan let go of the strategic opportunity to jump into the fray to settle the Kashmir issue in its favour. To his minister Bhutto, this was because Ayub Khan was weak and indecisive. Ayub seemed to regret his decision soon and said so in public. Nehru was shocked by Ayub's admission and made his views clear in an interview to a US journalist in 1964. Pakistan's mentality, Nehru said, was based on 'fear and hatred' of India. That did not make for good policy. 'Ayub Khan,' he noted with a sigh, 'said he was sorry he did not take advantage of the invasion of India by China to intervene.'[38] It was only three years later that Ayub was to fully buy into and act upon Bhutto's advice, with more direct revanchist aggression.

Pakistani leaders were, in this period, pleading with the US and Britain to influence India on the Kashmir question, or at least to prevent the use of Western weapons against Pakistan. The real concern seems to have been that a growing power differential with India would in the future make it harder for Pakistan to wrest Kashmir by force.

7

DIALOGUES OF THE DEAF

The chasm between Indian and Pakistani positions on Kashmir had further widened by 1963. Pakistan was not going to be satisfied with any adjustment to the ceasefire line that failed to satisfy its claim to large chunks of the northern state, particularly the valley of Kashmir. India, on its part, was not about to agree to calling into question the legal accession to India of the state of J&K. It had 'ascertained the wishes of the Kashmiri people' through provincial elections in 1957 and did not favour a referendum to second guess that choice. India was now opposing the idea of a general or regional plebiscite for another reason—the communal propaganda accompanying such a plebiscite could lead to religious riots, not just in Kashmir, but all over India and in East Pakistan. The partition of the valley—proposed by some UN mediators—was also increasingly unacceptable. The experience of the partition of Punjab and the bloodshed it entailed was sobering enough. Nehru was arguing that the Kashmir Valley was a unit, economically and psychologically, and its partition would 'create more problems than it would solve'.[1]

Pakistan was meanwhile trying to strengthen its new external alliance in exchange for Kashmiri territory. In October 1962, even as India was at war with China, Pakistan started border talks with the Chinese and soon decided to give up a strategic chunk of north-eastern Kashmir under its occupation—the Shaksgam Valley—to China.

Bolstered by the deal with China, Pakistan decided to up the ante with India on the Kashmir issue. Pakistan's tendency across the decades has been to talk to India either when it senses acute weakness or its opposite—overwhelming strength. The Pakistan army's tactical instinct was to gain military advantage on the 'core' Kashmir issue when India was relatively weak or to prevent a dilution of the Kashmir cause when India was relatively strong. After the war with China, Pakistan felt India was wounded and incapacitated. This perception was the catalyst for six rounds of talks (from December 1962 to May 1963) between Zulfikar Ali Bhutto, Pakistan's minister for industries, at the time, and Swaran Singh, India's minister of railways at the time.

The first meeting in Rawalpindi in December 1962 did not go well. It was held a day after China and Pakistan had announced their boundary agreement, seen as illegal by an angry India. Pakistan thought 'India wasted much time' protesting the deal. The talks focused on various plebiscite options put in place by UN mediators, which India rejected. At the second round in New Delhi in January 1963, Pakistan felt India had come up with a new excuse to reject a plebiscite, viz., that if Kashmiri Muslims voted in Pakistan's favour, the Hindus of India would consider this disloyalty. In Pakistan's reading, India was proposing a political settlement implying the partition of Kashmir. The Pakistan side indicated a willingness to consider a division along the Pir Panjal watershed in northern Jammu, giving Pakistan a strategic sliver of territory—the districts of Reasi, Mirpur, and Poonch.[2]

This political settlement idea was further discussed at the third round in February and the fourth round in March. The Indian side was suggesting division of the state along the boundary broadly corresponding to the ceasefire line, with minor adjustments and modifications. Pakistan was galled that India remained 'adamant' on the Kashmir Valley.

On 2 March 1963, Pakistan and China sealed the deal on the Shaksgam Valley, with foreign minister Chen Yi and industries minister Bhutto signing on the dotted line. For India, this was an unacceptable trade in territory that belonged to it. But in Pakistan's telling, it gave nothing away and in fact gained moderately from an 'exchange of territories'.

No progress was achieved in the fifth and sixth rounds of talks in April and May. The positions were diverging further. In Pakistan's assessment, as the danger of a further flare-up on the border with China receded, Nehru had no incentive to give in to a settlement with Pakistan. Also, the India–US relationship was entering a new phase after the 1962 war. From Pakistan's vantage point, the US was now attempting a Cold War play, seeking to wean India away from neutrality, from the Soviet orbit into the embrace of the West.[3]

The Kashmir talks finally broke down on 16 May 1963. While Nehru may have been trying to reach some closure on Kashmir as his legacy, Ayub was playing for time to plan for his attempt at forcing a military solution. The 'six round charade' thus ended with little to show for it.[4]

MAJOR POWER PLAY

The Sino–Pak deal on Himalayan territory was playing out against the backdrop of another geopolitical development—the Sino-Soviet split that began to surface in the 1960s—this would have a major impact on the subcontinent. China's hostility towards India and its standoff over issues of territory with its communist brother, the USSR, meant the Chinese needed other regional friends—Pakistan was the geo-strategically convenient candidate. On its part, it was clear to Pakistan following the 1962 war, which way it should turn; its relationship with China had taken off on a new trajectory.

A critical foreign policy goal for the Beijing-based People's Republic of China (PRC) in the 1950s and 1960s was to be recognized by the UN, instead of the Taiwan-based Republic of China (ROC) government.

In the annual UN motions from 1962, Pakistan voted to grant China a seat in the United Nations. In return, the Chinese had withdrawn disputed maps that showed them occupying territory claimed by Pakistan. The two countries had rapidly concluded border talks begun in October 1962. Foreign Minister Bhutto dropped a hint in Pakistan's National Assembly on 19 July 1963,[5] that reshaping Pakistan's foreign policy would entail a closer relationship with China.

The shifting sands of relations between major powers had significantly influenced the course of the war India faced in 1962 and would impact other gathering conflicts. These were also troubled times for Nehru's India. Hobbled by the disastrous war of 1962, Nehru faced a Kashmir on the boil. In 1963, a holy relic, a hair of the Prophet, went missing from the Hazratbal Mosque in Srinagar, causing an upheaval in the valley. Though the relic soon mysteriously reappeared, Pakistan was widely believed to be behind the mischief. At the very least, it was seen to have drawn the wrong lesson from the incident—that Kashmir was ripe for an uprising, all it needed was a nudge from across the border.

A RIPE FRUIT

A few months later, Pakistan appealed to the UN Security Council on the Kashmir matter, triggering council debates in February, and again in May 1964. It was however blocked from pushing any binding 'resolutions' on the matter by the threat of a veto by the Soviet Union, now solidly behind India. Pakistan was now ardently wooing China; the country effusively welcomed Zhou Enlai in Karachi in February 1964. An unkind cut for Pakistan came later that year, when the US ambassador to the UN, Adlai Stevenson, told Bhutto to his face that Pakistan was bringing the Kashmir issue to the Security Council for internal propaganda.[6] Seeing a dead end at the UN, Pakistan was trying to persuade the Chinese to back it for a military solution.

Events within Kashmir were also moving rapidly. The state was convulsed by violence and agitation. The release from prison of the lion of Kashmir, Sheikh Abdullah, in April 1964, had the immediate effect of quelling the turbulence. It raised hopes that the Sheikh's uncaging after eleven long years would alter the situation on the ground. Nehru, now unwell, seemed to grope for some finality in his lifetime on the Kashmir matter. He even sent Abdullah to Pakistan to invite Ayub to visit India.

But Nehru died while the Sheikh was still in Pakistan. With that was extinguished this latest Indian initiative on Pakistan. Nehru's death, which engendered a genuine fear of instability in India, also became Pakistan's excuse to cancel Ayub's visit to Delhi.

On the growing Pakistan–China collusion, a young Opposition member, Atal Bihari Vajpayee, spoke out in India's parliament in 1964 to play down the China threat. He pointed out that the two-front challenge was not an issue that bothered Nehru:

> I remember I once saw him very angry during the days of the Chinese aggression when our Western friends were trying to prevail upon us to arrive at some compromise with Pakistan on Kashmir. When he was told we would have to fight on two fronts if there was no compromise on the Kashmir problem, he flared up and said we would fight on both fronts if necessary. He was against negotiating under any pressure.[7]

Once Ayub cancelled his visit, High Commissioner Dayal and other Ministry of External Affairs mandarins persuaded the new Congress prime minister, Lal Bahadur Shastri, to visit Pakistan instead. On 12 October 1964, Shastri stopped by in Karachi on a transit visit. The diminutive Indian prime minister reinforced the impression in Ayub's and Bhutto's minds that they were dealing with a weakened India led by a debilitated post-Nehru leadership. Ayub had complained to Dayal in 1960 that Nehru had looked down on him in contempt. He in turn seemed to be repaying the compliment four years later to Shastri, looking at the soft-spoken Indian prime minister with matching condescension. K. S. Bajpai, who was involved in the visit as a young diplomat, later recalled that the summit's 'superficial cordiality could not conceal Pakistan's increasing disdain'.[8]

A DRY RANN IN KUTCH

Another bizarre twist for Pakistan came when Shastri invited Ayub Khan as the chief guest to India's Republic Day parade three months later. In January 1965, the parade was being held for the first time at Rajpath, the former Kingsway of imperial times. But Ayub did not show up. He chose to duck the invitation and sent his agriculture minister instead. The reason would be clear before the end of the year—Ayub was in the throes of planning a military solution to the Kashmir issue. India's move reinforced his assessment that it was going through a period of weakness.

Ayub was also busy consolidating power at home. He won rigged presidential elections on 2 January 1965, as the Pakistan Muslim League (PML) candidate, beating the popular sister of Pakistan's founder, Fatima Jinnah. It was a sham election based on limited voting by an electoral college of 'basic democrats' that his 1962 Constitution permitted. He was facing allegations of widespread rigging, political murders in Karachi, and a brazen campaign of disinformation against his main rival.

For India, it was time to consolidate the federal hold in Kashmir and to revisit the initiative that had begun with the release of Sheikh Abdullah before Nehru's death. In March 1965, the legislative assembly of Jammu and Kashmir amended the Jammu and Kashmir Constitution of 1957. The title and post of the ceremonial head of state was abolished and the state received the post of governor in line with arrangements in other Indian states. Direct election from the state for the Lok Sabha was now decreed, replacing the practice of nomination of members by the state assembly. These moves represented a dilution of the special status of J&K and further 'hollowed out' Article 370 that had conferred the special status to the state. Article 370 would progressively be eroded across the decades but would survive in that residual, weakened form till 2019, as we shall see in Section 8.[9] These events again inflamed the valley as well as Sheikh Abdullah, whose fiery speeches led to him being arrested again in May 1965. They also strengthened Pakistan's determination to go to war over Kashmir.

But Pakistan wanted to first strengthen its global alliances. With the US ambivalent, Pakistan reached out to both communist neighbours, China and the Soviet Union. Ayub Khan got a hero's welcome in March 1965. This further emboldened him for his upcoming irredentist adventure that year, where he hoped the Chinese would gang up with Pakistan in an attempt to wrest Kashmir from India. Ayub also visited the Soviet Union in April 1965—the first visit of a Pakistani leader to that country. Ayub was persuaded that the Soviets would not intervene in case of a Pakistani military confrontation with India, despite growing Indo–Soviet ties. As the weaker power, Pakistan's search for alliances was driven by its perception that India's conventional military superiority could be countered by Pakistan's smart alliances, weapons, and soldiers, apart from the element of surprise. Pakistan's strategic thinkers had convinced themselves that their Pathan soldiers were more martial than their Indian counterparts ('one Muslim equals ten Hindu soldiers') and that a weakened India would not have the will or resolve to fight Pakistan.

᷒

A clash in the Rann of Kutch in Gujarat was, in retrospect, a dry run for the bigger war of 1965. The border in the Kutch had not been delineated at Partition, and Pakistan decided to test India's resolve there. Pakistan had provoked the clashes. But in its official telling, it only reacted to Indian forces advancing to the north in January 1965 to establish new posts; this forced Pakistan to send in troops to stop India from resolving the dispute unilaterally.

As fighting flared in April, and the armies skirmished several times, India chose not to escalate the hostilities but instead tried diplomacy. On 29 April, Prime Minister Shastri signalled India's intentions, when he said it would fight Pakistan at a time and place of its choosing. The former colonial masters stepped in. A ceasefire arrangement was hammered out on

1 May, not through negotiations between Indian and Pakistani diplomats, but by British envoys Sir Morrice James in Islamabad and John Freeman in New Delhi, leading up to an agreement that was signed finally on 30 June 1965.

The ceasefire pact envisaged resolving the matter bilaterally or through appeal to a three-member international tribunal. Prime Minister Shastri welcomed the agreement and renewed the offer of a no-war treaty. But Pakistan insisted on invoking the tribunal process; it would continue for three years and 170 sittings in Geneva and its award would come only in February 1968. This left only a residual matter of the Sir Creek area, the disputed strip of water in the Rann marshlands. This was an easy enough dispute to resolve, even though neither side has had the will to close the matter in the over five decades that have passed since.[10]

Pakistan's official account admits that the Kutch affair made Pakistan overconfident. It also made India 'want to settle a score', and proved to be one more stumble towards a war that came within five months of the clash. To Ayub, the episode reinforced the assessment that in Shastri, India had a weak leader who lacked the appetite to challenge Pakistan seriously. Pakistan drew another wrong lesson from the face-off—if India had agreed to an international tribunal after the war in Kutch, then it might agree on one for Kashmir too. The Kashmir dispute had remained dormant, particularly since UN mediator Gunnar Jarrings' report in 1959. And the Kutch affair encouraged Pakistan to attempt having this frozen issue thawed out and internationalized.

In June 1965, Ayub Khan and Shastri touched on the matter in London, on the sidelines of a jamboree of Commonwealth heads of government. Shastri also introduced a diplomat to Ayub he would soon send to Karachi as his envoy: India's deputy high commissioner in London, Kewal Singh. Ayub said he would welcome Singh in Pakistan. Singh had little inkling of how extraordinary that welcome would be.

8

A GRAB AT KASHMIR

Kewal Singh arrived in Karachi on 5 August 1965, riding on hope and confidence in a relationship that on balance seemed headed in a positive direction, despite the difficult years since the 1962 war. The Kutch run-in of April seemed to have reached a fair diplomatic resolution. Unusually, the designated high commissioner in Karachi got an appointment for his credentials ceremony the day after his arrival in the new capital of Islamabad. The seat of the federal government had already moved to Islamabad, while the Indian high commission and other diplomatic missions were gearing up to move into new premises over the next few years. Singh was pleasantly surprised by this alacrity in Pakistan's response; it was a good sign, this goodwill from his hosts. At the ceremony for which he flew in from Karachi, Singh spoke with emotion and nostalgia: he had spent the first thirty years of his life in what was now Pakistan. Ayub struck a similar high note—he pledged to reciprocate every move from India for better understanding.

The bonhomie would last exactly three days.

While the president and the envoy had been exchanging pleasant sentiments of peace and reciprocal goodwill, a war was building up at the border. A day earlier, as the high commissioner had landed in Karachi, 2,000 armed infiltrators, dressed as tribesmen, had walked stealthily from Muzaffarabad into the Indian part of Kashmir, to begin a campaign of arson and violence. 5 August was to become a day marked in red in Kashmir's calendar, more than half a century before the abrogation of its special status on that very date.

Kewal Singh morphed rapidly into a wartime diplomat. He had received troubling reports from Delhi—of several batches of well-armed Pakistani military personnel in civilian clothes perpetrating a well-planned agenda of violence and sabotage in Kashmir. Indian forces were engaging these outsiders, arresting scores of them and killing many in skirmishes. But more kept coming. On 8 August, India's home minister, Gulzari Lal Nanda, revealed to the media after an emergency cabinet meeting that armed men from Pakistan had infiltrated India and were fomenting 'disturbances'. On 9 August, Prime Minister Shastri instructed the envoy in Karachi to lodge a strong protest with Ayub Khan against Pakistan's aggression and to warn its leadership that unless the infiltrations were stopped immediately, the consequences for bilateral relations would be grave.[1]

Singh worked the phones but failed to get a meeting with Ayub.

At 7 p.m. on 10 August, however, Singh was granted an audience with Foreign Minister Bhutto. The young minister, identified later as a key driver of Pakistan's 1965 gambit, was dismissive of India's démarche. He was belligerent and aggressive through the meeting, insisting that what was happening was an open revolt by Kashmiris against 'India's military occupation'.

In Pakistan, Foreign Secretary Aziz Ahmed was in the dark. He later revealed[2] that he was taken aback by reports in the press on 9 August. He did not know of the operation; the number of armed men who were reported to have crossed the ceasefire line particularly surprised him. Once again, this demonstrated that the civilians were only reacting to decisions already taken by the military, even though Bhutto played a key role.

The briefing messages from Delhi told the envoy that more than a hundred raiders were killed in the first five days of the operation and scores arrested. He also learnt that 'most of the raiders belonged to the Pakistan Army and were well-equipped with Sten guns, rifles and explosives'. The raiders of Kashmir were soon making international headlines. The *Washington Post* was explaining to its readers that this event was Pakistan's Bay of Pigs, referring to the failed landing operation of Cuban exiles that had been launched by the CIA less than five years earlier in April 1961. The implication was that this Pakistani attempt to grab territory in Kashmir would fail, as had the US attempt to reverse Cuba's Castro revolution.[3]

GIBRALTAR TO LAHORE

In Karachi, Bhutto was pleased at this turn of events. As an ambitious young politician within a military regime, an India hawk, and foreign minister since 1963, he had been pushing Ayub for a while for a military solution in Kashmir. He had been arguing with the full force of his Berkeley law degree that Pakistan's ingress into the disputed territory would not invite an Indian response on the international boundary (as indeed it did not in 1947–48) simply because it would be illegal; while a war in disputed territory was kosher, an attack across the international boundary, Bhutto felt, would invite international opprobrium. This argument had weighed heavy in Ayub's war calculus.[4]

Pakistan's despatch of raiders into Kashmir was code-named Operation Gibraltar—named after the Muslim conquest of Spain from the Strait of Gibraltar. The plan had been developed in the 1950s, drawing inspiration from the first Kashmir war of 1947–48. It was now executed by Ayub's army as an 'attack by infiltration' by an irregular force that would eventually grow to 40,000 highly motivated and heavily armed men. It was preceded by a meticulous 'Operation Nusrat', launched to find gaps in the ceasefire line that the mujahideen could use as entry points to assess the response of the Indian Army and locals in Kashmir. The fighting was to be confined to

Kashmir in order 'to defreeze the Kashmir problem, weaken Indian resolve, and bring India to the conference table without provoking general war'.[5]

The August incursion, denied at the time, later had a glib official explanation. This was Pakistan's reluctant recourse to the military option, its spokesmen said, given the popular uprising in Indian Kashmir and the dashed hopes for a peaceful settlement. Major General Akhtar Hussain Malik, who prepared the scheme, had called for incursions by 'Kashmiri volunteers into India-held Kashmir'.[6] The move was based on three assumptions: the people in Kashmir would rise in support of the guerrillas, a large-scale Indian offensive against Pakistan-occupied Kashmir (POK) was unlikely, and the possibility of attacks across the international border could be ruled out. All three, in Pakistan's own official account, turned out to be wrong.[7]

International alarm bells were ringing soon enough. In the second week of August, UN Secretary General U Thant visited India and Pakistan. These were innocent times, when India still would allow conversations with eager external peacemakers. The major world powers were not in a hurry to jump in directly. They had seen the slanging matches between India and Pakistan on Kashmir over the previous couple of decades and were already 'bored stiff'.[8]

Within India, the outrage was mounting. Even in the midst of the crisis, Prime Minister Shastri read the situation clearly. He said in a broadcast to the nation on 13 August 1965:

> ...there is no doubt that this is a thinly disguised armed attack on our country organised by Pakistan and it has been made as such.... the world will recall that Pakistan created a similar situation in 1947, and then also she initially pleaded innocence. Later, she had to admit that her regular forces were involved in the fighting.

Pakistan's line was one of stout denial. Bhutto was now pushing the public spin he had used privately with the Indian envoy: that since India had closed all doors to a peaceful solution of J&K, the people of the state had been driven to rebellion and Pakistan's sympathies were with them.

↗

Diplomatic relations had not been severed in August but this now seemed imminent. High Commissioner Kewal Singh in Karachi was worried about the classified records and documents at his mission falling into enemy hands. He had already worked out a deal with Delhi to have officers carry trunks by successive flights over two months to deliver these secret records to New Delhi. An attaché, Bhaumik, had already been dispatched on 27 August with the first instalment of documents; Bhaumik had volunteered for the assignment since he wanted to bring back his mother to take care of his pregnant wife, but eventually could not make it back for a couple of months. Singh was bracing for a raid on the mission and seizure of these secret documents, which, in his dark fantasy, would be published daily in *Dawn* with provocative headlines.

On the battlefront, India's counteroffensive was on. By the end of August, Indian forces had occupied large chunks of territory in the Kargil area in the north of Kashmir and around the Haji Pir pass between Uri and Poonch. On 1 September, Pakistan struck again, launching Operation Grand Slam, deploying tanks in Chhamb in the Jammu area, to cut off Kashmir from Indian Punjab. Pakistan's diplomatic script remained to argue that India was forcing a war on it. President Ayub in his broadcast on 1 September alleged that the Kashmiris had risen in open revolt, that Pakistan had only offered sympathy and support to these valiant fighters against Indian tyranny.

Given the communications of those times, the high commissioner and his team in Karachi were oblivious to the details of the action on the borders. Very little information was trickling in from headquarters. Media reporting was unreliable and biased. The Pakistan media hardly mentioned the all-out attack that had been launched by the Pakistan Army supported by the Pakistan Air Force and some 70 Patton tanks in the Chhamb area.

Kewal Singh recalled in his memoirs that he would have acted differently had he known even a fraction of the reality on the ground that evening. Thanks to his ignorance, and driven by personal goodwill towards his host, Singh even set out on 3 September to attend a marriage reception in Rawalpindi, hosted by Pakistan's finance minister Mohammed Shoaib for his son. Singh overruled the advice of the Indian liaison officer in Islamabad, the Lahore-born G. L. Puri, who was worried about the impending outbreak of war. He realized 'the folly of my decision' when he walked into the Rawalpindi club, a representative of an enemy country in the midst of war, to attend an event where the eyes of Pakistan's military and civilian elites were upon him. Singh saw the surprise of his hosts and rapidly left the soiree.[9] He would later get a measure of the level of hostility when he saw a newspaper item that said that the sari gifted by the Indian high commission for the wedding was sold by his hosts to raise funds for Pakistan's war effort.[10]

The international community was getting increasingly alarmed by the hostilities. On 4 September, the UNSC passed the first resolution on the conflict, calling for a ceasefire. But the situation on the ground was evolving rapidly. When High Commissioner Singh returned to Karachi from his social misadventure in Rawalpindi on 5 September, he got into a huddle with his colleagues to take stock of the conflict. The rapid descent towards full-blown war seemed imminent. But if the situation was fast drifting in that direction, he should have received from headquarters 'a number of warning signals required by the war book of any foreign office'. What he had instead was radio silence from Delhi. For an India at war, that post in Karachi, deep within enemy territory, was either forgotten or not a priority.

On the border, India was acting decisively. The substantive Indian response to Pakistan's Kashmir offensive came with speed and surprise. India launched a counteroffensive action in the shape of a march towards Lahore on 6 September. India's action in Punjab, to open another front, showed Shastri's leadership, and also that India's war-fighting capability—the systemic strength of its army and the collective wisdom of its cabinet—was intact, implying that decisions of war and peace could be made with institutional efficiency even in the post-Nehru era.

As Indian troops marched towards Lahore, the Indian high commission team in Karachi, oblivious to battlefield reports, scrambled to hear President Ayub Khan's special broadcast to the nation. They learnt from Ayub that the Indian Army had attacked the Lahore front, a sequel to India's 'aggression of the past five months'. Ayub informed his nation that Pakistan was at war and declared an emergency. He chose not to refer to the infiltrators of Kashmir but spoke of the familiar trope of those times, of India having never reconciled to the establishment of an independent Pakistan where Muslims could build a homeland of their own.

Pakistani war hero and politician, Air Marshal Asghar Khan, later assessed that even as late as 4 September, Ayub did not feel that the Indians would react so strongly.[11] He was misled by false assurances and a misreading of the situation by his foreign minister, Bhutto, who was forcefully making the legal argument, as we have noted, that since Kashmir was a disputed territory, the Indians would not dare to move on the settled international border. Bhutto had shouted down the military view that an adversary attacked on the throat may choose to retaliate with a knife to the gut.

Later accounts from Pakistan admit that the official propaganda during the war had built up an impression of Pakistani forces having gained a great advantage, if not victory, over India. Not for the first time, Pakistan's state propaganda deluded its own people and even its leaders.[12]

The high commission staff in Karachi were now in 'lockdown' mode—all personnel had been asked to remain in the chancery office or in the two India-owned residential buildings, Shivaji Court and Hindustan Court. With all his staff in virtual house arrest, the HC needed to take a critical wartime decision about when to destroy classified papers. Political counsellor K. S. Bajpai, in charge of burning the records, piped up with a pertinent question. (Bajpai would later be appointed high commissioner in Islamabad after the 1971 war.) Were the two countries really at war? Did Ayub's broadcast to the nation amount to a declaration of war? The argument was that a technical declaration of war was essential before the countries went about the business of dealing with their diplomatic missions, property, and personnel as warring countries should. After debating this issue without conclusion, the good bureaucrats decided to ask their host country for a clarification—were the countries indeed at war? Deputy High Commissioner Prakash Kaul was rushed to the foreign office. He politely asked his interlocutors in Karachi if their countries were at war, and if so, whether steps would be taken to protect the diplomatic missions under the Vienna Convention. He received a prompt bureaucratic reply that the matter would be referred to the appropriate authorities: 'We cannot answer such questions without reference to Islamabad and shall get in touch with the High Commission later.' Effectively, in the midst of a major border war, Pakistan's officials were telling Indian diplomats that they were unsure whether their countries were really at war. As it turned out, neither government formally declared war or thought of closing down diplomatic missions.

Nevertheless, fearing a sudden attack on India's premises, the high commissioner and his team started a bonfire on 7 September to burn the classified documents and cipher codes. They also gathered most staff and families into the chancery premises to forestall angry mobs attacking the residences. Sentiment against India was ratcheting up in Karachi and the enemy's diplomatic representation suddenly was a vulnerable target.

On 8 September, a contingent of armed police descended upon the home of Frank Dewars, first secretary at the high commission. Some ten policemen and an officer, armed with guns and bayonets, barged in to begin ransacking the family's belongings and throwing things out. The police officer on duty said that he had orders from his superiors to search for a secret transmitter sending messages to India from within the building, Hindustan Court. Kewal Singh and his deputy Kaul pushed back against the police team. The excitable Kaul was livid and demanded the cops leave immediately. He yelled at the bearded superintendent, 'O, Darhiwale... are you not ashamed of yourself? How dare you enter these diplomatic premises, without our permission and frighten women and children in this barbaric manner? Will you and your men get out of the premises immediately!' The superintendent grinned provocatively and said he had orders to look for a secret transmitter.[13]

Kaul burst out, 'That is a stupid pretext to harass and insult the families of the high commission. What the Pakistan government is doing has not happened in the 200 years of diplomatic history of the world. You will pay for this.' Kewal Singh tried to calm down his deputy and asked him

to contact the foreign office. Kaul did so and was assured that a 'protocol officer' would arrive immediately. Kaul also telephoned the foreign media, representatives of AFP and the *New York Times*. He was still speaking to the *New York Times* correspondent when his phone went dead. When the protocol officer arrived, Kaul protested strongly and the officer in turn protested to the superintendent of police. The policeman snarled at the civilian, 'just vanish unless you want trouble.' The orders were clearly coming from authorities other than the foreign office.

Similar scenes were repeated in Shivaji Court, where gun-toting policemen were ransacking boxes and cupboards while the officials and their wives and children were made to sit along the corridors. To Kewal Singh the whole exercise seemed intended to frighten and humiliate the families. 'So sad, so crude and so utterly meaningless.' This, he felt, did not represent Pakistani culture and stemmed from minds that were poisoned by consuming hatred.

More was to follow. As the high commissioner drove to his residence in Clifton in the late evening, he saw soldiers surrounding his own residence. He asked his driver to take a detour to the residence of the Sri Lankan high commissioner. General Wickrama Wijyekhoon received his Indian counterpart warmly and the two diplomats discussed the conflict, the destruction of records and the police searches. The Indian high commissioner requested Wijyekhoon to send a message to his government to be conveyed to our high commissioner in Colombo about the conversation they had. He agreed to do so. But Singh later discovered that he never did act upon the request.

The Sri Lankan diplomat's decision, the Indian diplomat realized, was correct according to international convention. A diplomat was not supposed to send messages on behalf of a country that was at war with his host government. Kewal Singh's Pakistani counterpart in Delhi was more fortunate, though. For the Pakistani high commission in New Delhi, Singh later learnt, two embassies continued to act as a channel to send detailed communications to Islamabad. But Singh was disappointed in his Sri Lankan counterpart: he should have at least sent a situation report, which the Indian mission had no means of sending.[14]

When Kewal Singh reached home, he found about two dozen soldiers guarding each gate. Some police officers had been all over the house in his absence for a perfunctory inspection. They took away a radio set, a revolver, and a visitors' book. Also, at Hindustan Court and Shivaji Court, radios, transistors, and firearms had been taken away by the police. The radio sets were missed most by the high commission since they were the only means to access information of the war.

The high commissioner tried to catch some sleep after a harrowing day, spent visiting the scenes of the searches and meeting frightened families. But he never got that well-deserved rest. First Secretary Amar Singh knocked on his door at 2.30 a.m. with grim news.

The chancery had now been occupied by hundreds of Pakistani policemen and officers, who had sent a police jeep to summon the HC to the office. Kewal Singh bristled at the 'stupidity' of the Pakistani officers in calling for him and officiously declared he would be available only to the president, the foreign minister, and the foreign secretary. But he soon changed his mind—concerned at the trouble at the office—and followed the police jeep in his own car. At the chancery, the policemen appeared 'sullen', having found only empty cupboards since secret documents had been incinerated already. They were still ostensibly looking for the mysterious transmitter. They left soon.

The next night, the Indian high commissioner was summoned by Foreign Secretary Aziz Ahmed at 1.30 in the morning. Knowing Ahmed's aggressive style, Singh anticipated a stormy session and kept reminding himself to be calm even if provoked or insulted. When he arrived, Singh smiled as he greeted the foreign secretary, who 'scowled grimmer than usual' and curtly asked him to sit down for a meeting that would be forty minutes long, 'the most unpleasant I have ever faced'. Ahmed started by shouting about the treacherous aggression launched by the 'rabid Hindu leaders' who had evil designs against Pakistan for a long time. He fulminated, increasingly incoherent, about Kashmir and Indian tyranny and aggression. Singh intervened with a smile to say that he had already sent a note to the foreign office saying that the armed raiders from Pakistan should be stopped forthwith from entering Kashmir, as otherwise it could lead to grave consequences. The foreign secretary interrupted him rudely and spoke of the 'Hindu fascists in New Delhi who should be made to realise that instead of their evil designs to undo Pakistan, this misadventure by India would lead to its own disintegration'.[15]

Kewal Singh remained pointedly polite, saying that he would convey these serious warnings and threats to his government 'provided you open my communication channels with New Delhi'. He would then report not just these messages but also of the 'raid on the Chancery, the police searches of all the houses and personal possessions including my own and the police harassment and humiliation of the Indian families'.[16] This further infuriated the foreign secretary who 'kept up his rant'. At this point, the high commissioner rose to say that unless the foreign secretary had something more worthwhile to say, he would leave. He left without a handshake or a goodbye.

The next weeks for the high commissioner were spent in an information vacuum. He was virtually under house arrest, completely cut off from the outside world—without radio or telephone communications or visitors. After four days, his butler was finally allowed to go out once a day, with a military escort, to buy foodstuffs or tinned provisions. The high commissioner remained unaware of what was happening on the war front or to some 300 members of the Indian diplomatic staff and families in Karachi. It was only on 28 September that an army officer of the rank of brigadier arrived in a jeep to announce that the high commissioner was now permitted to go from the residence to the chancery building with a military escort. This told Kewal Singh that the war may have ended.

꙳

While Kewal Singh was incommunicado, the border war and global diplomacy had taken several twists and turns. Amidst the battles on the ground, China had stayed its military hand but rushed to the diplomatic aid of its new partner. On 16 September, China delivered an ultimatum, asking India to dismantle its 'military structures on the Chinese side of the border' within three days. For India, the danger of a second military front opening to the north seemed real. But the Chinese threat later proved to be a hollow one. The USSR and the US also stayed aside pointedly, preferring global diplomacy at the UN. The perils of the expansion of the war triggered a UN Security Council resolution on 20 September that went beyond past texts to call for a 'settlement of the political problems underlying the present conflict'. The ceasefire was finally announced on 23 September.

Getting out of his four weeks of enforced seclusion, the high commissioner also learnt of the travails that his staff had gone through. A baby had been delivered at the chancery with no outside medical assistance. A mob had attacked the chancery premises on 21 September, with 200 people shouting obscene slogans; an hour later, another fierce group, a thousand-strong this time, arrived at the scene with a truckload of stones, which they tossed into India's premises, with improvised explosives and kerosene bombs. Fortunately, the building survived this orchestrated attack. The Indian staff was enraged, not just at the mobs and at Pakistan, but also at their own government, which had abandoned them in the heart of enemy territory during the war. Deputy High Commissioner Kaul was vocally critical of his own government and leadership that had failed them.

High Commissioner Kewal Singh and his political counsellor K. S. Bajpai tried gamely to soothe the distraught staff and explain that the leadership in the ministry and the country was perhaps too preoccupied with the war to be able to attend to their situation in the high commission. Kaul was unrelenting in his rage against the abandoning of the mission by the ministry and India's leadership. Singh reflected in his memoirs that while he understood Prime Minister Shastri's preoccupations, things might have been different if Nehru were still alive. He would probably have checked on the welfare of the mission through his foreign secretary, asked him to get reports on how diplomatic staff and their families were faring in Karachi and Dacca through friendly diplomatic missions or by approaching the UN or the International Red Cross.

Trying as the situation was, Kewal Singh later felt it could have been a lot worse. His heart missed a beat when he read about what happened to the US embassy in Iran when the Revolutionary Guards took over its premises in November 1979, and kept over sixty diplomatic staff captive for 444 days.[17] The Iranians had painstakingly put together all shredded records and published them over the next few months, to the considerable embarrassment of the US administration, and jeopardized many high placed Iranians who were mentioned in these records. At the US embassy in Tehran in 1979, several barriers had to be overcome before the armed militia got their hands on the classified material. But at the Indian high commission in Karachi in 1965, only a glass door had separated the records from the intruders.

All through the crisis of 1965, it did not occur to either country to withdraw its envoy from the enemy nation or expel theirs. War was not formally declared, diplomatic ties were not cut, the high commissions remained operational. This was an undeclared war; diplomatic communication, however shrill, was maintained. This diplomatic situation paralleled the one of 1947 to 1949, where despite bloodshed on the border, the conflict barely made it to the formal bilateral agenda.

The post-mortem of the war has extended across several decades. Later writings confirm that Pakistan's strategic objectives were to 'defreeze' the Kashmir problem and weaken Indian resolve, forcing India to negotiate on the Kashmir issue, without provoking a general war. About two decades earlier, Pakistan had used similar tactics in its attempt to capture Kashmir. Once again, in 1965, Pakistan had made a critical error of assuming that Kashmir was a 'ripe fruit' about to fall into its lap. And thirty-four years later, Pakistan would make the same miscalculation in Kargil—of launching a 'deniable' infiltration led by irregulars, hoping to capture some border territory in a conflict limited to Kashmir, and to bring India to the negotiating table through renewed international attention.

The 1965 war infused deep distrust into the bilateral relationship. This distrust would deepen with another war in six years. More broadly, India's wars of the 1960s, starting with 1962, became decisive factors in ending the trust generated by the diplomacy of the 1950s. India had to grapple with its security vulnerabilities both to its north and to the west. The trauma and horrors of Partition had perhaps generated an impulse for constructive state-building and trustful diplomacy, but the wars of the 1960s ended India's period of strategic naiveté, as they underlined the need for a strong security sensibility to protect the state from adversarial neighbours.

Most analysts of the time saw the war as a military stalemate. Some others felt that while India did not win the war, Pakistan in fact lost it since it failed as the aggressor to secure its objectives of conquering Kashmir or even of 'defreezing' the Kashmir issue.

In Pakistan's internal assessment, the war was soon interpreted as the culmination of the rise and fall of expectations of a peaceful settlement of the Kashmir dispute. Pakistan had been agitated over India's legal manoeuvres since October 1963 to erode the disputed and even the 'special' status of Kashmir. Nehru had made it clear in November 1963 that a gradual erosion of the special status of Kashmir was in progress, even as Bakshi Ghulam Mohammed had been installed in power through rigged elections. Pakistan's planners were also deluded into believing that the inflamed sentiment in Kashmir following the theft of the holy relic in 1963 was a pro-Pakistan movement. India's march towards greater military strength was seen in Pakistan as interrupted by a post-Nehru transition. In a strategic sense, Pakistan assessed that the window was closing on its opportunity to precipitate a military solution in Kashmir.

Pakistani writers refer to the hubris of the Kutch victory, but a deeper attitude problem defined the Pakistani military makeup at that point. Ayub Khan held the bigoted notion that Hindu morale would not stand more than a couple of hard blows at the right time and place.[18]

While Ayub blamed Bhutto and some of his generals for their flawed counsel, the ruling dictator could not escape the lion's share of the blame; even the failure of the talks between Swaran Singh and Bhutto after the 1962 war was later pinned on Ayub. He was seen as having missed the opportunity for diplomacy to achieve a breakthrough towards a settlement of the Kashmir issue, in conformity with the aspirations of the people. He had then fallen into a military trap with a war that did nothing to further the Kashmir cause. Reinforcing the assessment of his reluctance to own the conflict, Ayub was silent on the 1965 war in his memoirs published in 1967.[19] Some Pakistani writers hold him responsible for both wars—1965 and the one to follow in 1971.

Pakistani analysts also rue the fact that while China did support Pakistan diplomatically, the US failed to do so. The cold US reaction became a matter of deep disappointment in Pakistan. There was no meeting of SEATO or CENTO, the US remained pointedly neutral, the UK was unresponsive. Pakistan was getting increasingly disillusioned with the US and arguing that they were 'power drunk' and that Pakistan was seeking friends, not new masters.

As we've seen, Pakistan had tried through the 1960s to garner from the US some political support for its core interest—the Kashmir cause. It also sought arms to realize a military solution. The US did back Pakistan on the global stage, pushing a UN resolution on Kashmir in 1962 that aggressively called for direct negotiations to resolve the dispute. But this was blocked by the hundredth Soviet veto at the UN on 22 June 1962, thanks to India's warming ties with the Soviet Union. Pakistan did try to invoke the 1959 agreement during its war in 1965 but the US argued that the action clause could only be triggered exclusively by aggression by a communist state. This is cited by Pakistani analysts as one of the first in a series of acts of American perfidy towards Pakistan.

However, US arms supplies had continued, with Pakistan initiating its military adventure against India in 1965, armed with Patton tanks and fighter aircraft of US manufacture. Nevertheless, US support was tempered, as we will see, by larger geopolitical concerns—the need to balance communist China with democratic India that translated into lukewarm political support for Pakistan in 1962 and a hands-off posture in 1965. Disappointed by the failure of its Western alliances in 1965, Pakistan attempted to cobble together another short-lived foreign policy precept of 'bilateralism', distinguished from non-alignment, which was a policy that in effect sought to distance Pakistan from the west and open windows to the east. Bhutto later tried to convert this into a doctrine of international relations but this hasty innovation did not survive beyond Bhutto's tenure as foreign minister.[20]

K. S. Shankar Bajpai, a thoughtful young Indian diplomat at the chancery in wartime Karachi, felt disappointed by India's approach. India, he felt, should have prolonged the war and not surrendered the advantage. Reflecting on the conflict decades later, Bajpai noted that Bhutto had long been contemplating an 'Algeria-type situation' for Kashmir, inspired by the referendum in Algeria that got it independence from the colonial French in 1961. But Pakistan had finally decided on a military solution since 'the hawks won Ayub over when Washington's fitful disenchantments with Pakistan started strangling vital American aid'. Pakistan's logistical problems were sharper than India's; neither side could fight a long war, but a 'briefly longer war was feasible'. Bajpai pointed out that even the army chief Sam Manekshaw 'openly regretted that we missed our chance'. Bajpai argued that 'a state accustomed to handling power might at least have considered the intriguing political consequences of delaying the ceasefire.' On the long-term meaning of 1965, Bajpai felt that it demonstrated Pakistan's obsession with Kashmir. Pithily summarizing ties in the twentieth century, Bajpai observed that

> the 1965 war was born of 1962, which left us looking like bumblers....
> We foiled Pakistan's resulting adventure, doubtless an achievement,

albeit limited, but it turned Pakistan to other means: fomenting dissidence in our Punjab, feeding subversion elsewhere, developing terror as an instrument of policy, apart from making life difficult in J&K, while scheming its way to nuclear power. All comprehensively demonstrating an undying obsession—doing India down, wresting J&K.[21]

On 20 October, almost a month after the declaration of the ceasefire, Kewal Singh was called in for consultations to India. The high commissioner hoped that his summons by his home country would be noted by his Pakistani hosts as a demand that they should make amends for the 'outrageous violations by the Pakistani government'[22] of diplomatic immunities and privileges of the Indian high commission in Karachi. The Indian government had in September lodged a strong protest with Pakistan's government on the invasion and ransacking of houses of diplomatic personnel and the mission. The permanent Indian representative at the UN, G. Parthasarathy, had launched a similar protest with the secretary general of the UN. But the Pakistani government flatly rejected the protests and in turn accused India of breaches of diplomatic practices in dealing with its diplomats in Delhi. Pakistan's diplomats in India never had much of a rough time during the conflict, but knee-jerk counter-accusations were the norm, and would remain the practice over the next decades.

Pakistan also called in its high commissioner Mian Arshad Hussain from New Delhi for consultations. The mistrust between the two countries had now deepened. The Indian high commissioner was not allowed to board the plane for Delhi for more than twenty-four hours, awaiting the departure of the Pakistan high commissioner for Karachi. The Indian side was insisting upon its high commissioner leaving Karachi before it could agree on Hussain's departure. In the end, both high commissioners left for their countries simultaneously, on the evening of 25 October, more hostages than diplomats accredited to neighbouring countries.

As the Indian high commissioner returned home to Delhi on 25 October, the next act of the drama began in New York at the UN Security Council. In yet another abortive meeting, the Security Council was trying to cobble together terms of the ceasefire and of withdrawal of the adversarial forces to their pre-5 August positions. Despite admonitions by the president of the Security Council, Bhutto insisted on raising the discussion on the internal situation in Kashmir after sharp exchanges with the Indian delegation. As Bhutto persisted, the Indian delegation led by Foreign Minister Swaran Singh decided to walk out of the council. Flying into yet another tantrum, Bhutto shouted, 'the Indian dogs have gone home'.[23] Bhutto's anger and frustration at the unravelling of his 1965 design was getting the better of his diplomacy.

A TRUCE IN TASHKENT

Security Council resolutions adopted on 4 and 6 September 1965 asked both countries to withdraw all military personnel to pre-5 August positions. On 9 September, UN Secretary General U Thant paid a visit to Pakistan and India. Pakistani diplomats were particularly displeased that, despite numerous attempts, he made no mention of the earlier UN resolutions of 1949–50.

The US, still beset by internal turmoil after after President John F. Kennedy's assassination a couple of years earlier on 22 November 1963, showed some reluctance in jumping in to mediate this latest South Asian conflict. But the Soviets now engaged with both parties with equal zeal. On 18 September, Prime Minister Shastri told parliament that Premier Kosygin had sent him a note offering Soviet good offices to settle the differences between India and Pakistan. He revealed four days later that India had accepted the offer. Pakistan accepted the same offer in the middle of November, and a meeting was set for 4 January 1966 in Tashkent. The main concern for India was the withdrawal of forces from the Haji Pir Pass, Poonch–Uri, and Kargil positions. These were strategic heights along the LoC that Indian troops had acquired during the conflict. These were also bases from which Pakistani invaders had launched past incursions into India. Surrendering these critical territorial gains, acquired at great human cost, would not go down well with India's military.

High-level delegations from both sides arrived in Tashkent on 3 January 1966. Prime Minister Shastri repeated the need for a no-war pact or at least an agreement that the armed forces of the two countries would not in future bear arms against each other. Pakistan was still insisting that such a peace agreement would work only if 'basic disputes' were addressed, a standard euphemism for the primacy of the Kashmir issue. In Tashkent, drafts flew fast and furious between the two sides and were just as summarily rejected. The Soviets kept a studied distance from the negotiation but Alexei Kosygin and Andrei Gromyko tried hard in separate discussions with the delegations to push for common ground. On 6 January, Kosygin spent nearly ten hours with both delegations trying to bridge the gaps. On 7 January, Ayub and Shastri met for two hours without aides and their 'exchanges confirmed that their positions were quite irreconcilable'.

High Commissioner Kewal Singh decided to try his own diplomacy that evening. At the end of a lavish cultural performance by the Bahor ensemble at the Ali Sher Nawai Theatre, attended by both delegations,

Singh walked across to his Pakistani counterpart, high commissioner to India, Arshad Hussain, and greeted him warmly. Hussain looked the other way and did not even respond to the greeting. Singh walked out of the hall, surprised and crestfallen at the snub, blaming himself for the indiscretion. But Hussain accosted Singh in the corridor later and told him that he had acted cool since his leaders were 'glaring' at him. The two high commissioners agreed to meet discreetly the next day to see if they could find common ground. They pretended to go shopping opposite the Tashkent Hotel, at the state departmental store. Hussain explained to Singh that it would be hard for the Pakistani delegation to go home with a document that did not refer to Kashmir. Singh then helped trigger 'an honourable compromise' in a formulation that said that both sides explained their respective positions on J&K.

The more important issue for India was the future of Haji Pir and other strategic heights. Shastri had publicly committed that these vital posts would not be vacated, but the Security Council resolution supported by the Soviet government, and which India had accepted, required that forces of the two countries be withdrawn to pre-5 August positions. The Indian side finally decided to give up these claims and withdrew to the 5 August levels in the larger interest of the joint declaration. After two more days of aggressive mediation by the Soviets, Shastri and Ayub signed the Tashkent Declaration at 4.30 p.m. on 10 January. The signing ceremony was followed by a reception, after which the two delegations were to depart on the morning of 11 January.

Watching the proceedings, Bajpai felt India had given away too much. Bajpai was the designated protocol officer who dropped off the prime minister to his room after the reception. Shastri had looked tired 'but no one thought he would succumb to a heart attack the same night'. Bajpai's shock at Shastri's passing that midnight was matched by his disappointment with the outcomes in Tashkent. Fifty years after India had signed on the dotted line, Bajpai recalled that the agreement

would be forever questioned for returning heroically captured J&K areas. We went determined not to return them, unless Pakistan agreed to renounce force and accept the ceasefire line as a frontier. How we could interpret what we signed as achieving those objectives is anyone's guess. We did face unexpected difficulties: Russia's skilful diplomacy turned from pro-Indian to even-handed, seeing possibilities of weaning Pakistan away from its then bugbear China. Originally urging the Tashkent meet not for a final settlement but to start a process, Moscow pressed for an agreement there and then, with messages sent through our ambassador warning of a return to the UN Security Council, and without the benefit of a Soviet veto.[24]

While many have held the dilemma of surrendering the heights or abandoning the Tashkent deal to have taken its toll on Shastri, to Kewal Singh, Shastri did not seem unduly concerned about this issue. In their last meeting, the prime minister asked Singh to quickly get back to his duties in Pakistan, since the declaration called for high commissioners to resume their posts quickly and India needed to signal the importance it attached to the Tashkent Agreement.

Bajpai in his later years was willing to concede that India's national capacity was limited in 1965, but he rued that the lessons had not been learnt even five decades later. 'All too often,' he reflected, 'there are no solutions. Problems can only be managed until circumstances change.... Pakistan's 1965 gamble failed, but we only scotched the snake, not killed it.... In 1965, we were economically floundering, militarily weak, politically bickering, and still diplomatically inexperienced. The lessons of 1965—not to be any of those things—are obvious. So too is our refusal to learn.'[25]

AN UNCERTAIN PEACE DEAL

The Tashkent Declaration provided for the withdrawal of forces to restore the status quo ante of 5 August 1965 and the return of the high commissioners to their posts. Strong criticism was voiced within both countries, of their leaders squandering at the negotiating table what the armed forces had won on the battlefield. In India, Shastri's passing somewhat muted the censure. In Pakistan, the agreement flew in the face of the manufactured narrative that Pakistan had won the war by repulsing India's attempts to capture Lahore. Ayub Khan's position became increasingly untenable, particularly since the wily Bhutto was slowly distancing himself from the Tashkent outcomes. Facing mounting anger on Pakistan's 'capitulation', Ayub launched a spirited campaign to 'educate the people' on the Tashkent Declaration, travelling across Pakistan for frank discussions with opinion shapers.

An optimistic Kewal Singh himself tried to make the most of the Tashkent spirit when he resumed duties in Karachi in mid-January 1966. When Ayub arrived in Karachi from a tour of Lahore, he asked Kewal Singh to see him. At 8.30 a.m., on 20 January, Singh arrived at the president's house where he saw 'scores of cars' bringing in an audience of public intellectuals for another session with the president on Tashkent. It was a smiling, relaxed and confident Ayub that greeted the Indian HC. The president explained to the diplomat how he had gone against military and political advice to sign the Tashkent Agreement in the larger interest of peace between the countries. He apologized for the behaviour of Pakistani officials who had harassed staff of the Indian mission and said that high commission members in future would be shown every courtesy. Singh agreed with Ayub that it was important to normalize relations and build goodwill before addressing differences.

The high commissioner came away convinced of Ayub's sincerity in trying to resume ties. He recommended to Delhi that permission for overflights be resumed immediately; the wartime ban was hurting Pakistan in sustaining links with its eastern wing. The proposal was rejected on the grounds that the issue could be discussed along with others, when ministers of the two governments would meet. Singh sent a stronger telegram to Delhi arguing that lifting the ban was a critical first step towards reconciliation and went so far as to suggest it was 'short-sighted political policy' to use it as 'some kind of bargaining counter'. Even as a bargain, the resumption of overflights was of 'equal importance to us'[26] given the longer routes Indian flights were taking. He asked his views to be placed before the prime minister. Four days later, he got a cable saying that Prime Minister Indira Gandhi had agreed with President Ayub's proposal to resume overflights.

But the goodwill was not seeping down to the ground. At a Republic Day reception on 26 January, at the residence of Uma Shankar Bajpai, deputy high commissioner and elder sibling of political counsellor K. S. Bajpai, the atmosphere was festive at 7 p.m. Uma Shankar had arrived recently from London, and was expecting several diplomats to join the party that evening. An 'underlying message' was the celebration of India's success in the war and also the success in smuggling out First Secretary Frank Dewars, the police officer posted at the mission, whom the Pakistani agencies had linked to espionage. Naval Attaché Jack Shea had arranged a daring escape from Karachi for Dewars and his family just a few weeks earlier. Shea, along with his wife, Dorothy, was among the first guests at the reception. Shea had just had a whisky as he chatted with a guest, when he felt dizzy. He suspected his drink had been spiked, excused himself and made it to a washroom on the first floor, where he was struck on the head with a heavy object. Soon, three men, hiding in the toilet, mercilessly beat up the naval attaché, tossed his battered body over the terrace into bushes, and disappeared. Shea spent weeks in a Karachi hospital in a coma and months recovering from the battering. India complained in Pakistan as also in New Delhi. Pakistan denied any hand in the assault. But the incident demonstrated a new aggression in the diplomatic relationship, not seen before.[27]

As part of his post-Tashkent outreach, Kewal Singh again met with the dreaded Foreign Secretary Aziz Ahmed. If the previous midnight encounter had been the worst meeting of his life, the current one was 'distressing' even in the aftermath of India's gesture of permitting overflights. Ahmed expressed no regret on the harassment and violence against Indian diplomats and said that all allegations made by the Indian high commission were 'fabrications' to malign Pakistan. Once again, the exasperated high commissioner walked out of the meeting without a handshake.

When he received the letter from Mrs Gandhi on overflights, Kewal
Singh went to meet with President Ayub and Bhutto at the latter's residence
in Larkana in Sindh. Bhutto was clearly setting policy on India; Ayub
seemed increasingly reluctant to overrule him. Bhutto again insisted that
Kashmir was the main issue and seemed ready to repudiate the Tashkent
agreement. Nevertheless, they agreed to a meeting of ministerial delegations,
which finally came about in Rawalpindi on 2 March 1966. India sent a
high-powered delegation led by Foreign Minister Swaran Singh, hoping to
take forward the 'Tashkent spirit'. But within thirty minutes of the start
of the meeting, Bhutto dashed all hopes by invoking Kashmir and harking
back to the UN resolutions of 1949–50. The meeting ended with a clumsy
formulation that Pakistan requested for 'special importance of reaching a
settlement of the Jammu and Kashmir dispute', while the Indian side joined
only in the statement that 'all disputes' should be resolved.

High Commissioner Kewal Singh felt personally responsible for the
volte-face by Ayub and for the failure of the talks. As he saw off the Indian
delegation, one of the officials reminded Singh: 'This is the result of your
ill-conceived insistence on the resumption of overflights. Pakistan is no
longer interested in any dialogue.' This barb added to Singh's dejection.
Soon after the talks failed, anti-India rhetoric and propaganda rose, with
Bhutto accusing India of treachery. Worse, both Bhutto and Ayub were
making scathing attacks on India. The events of March 1966 had sealed
the fate of the Tashkent declaration and Bhutto was leading the charge
for its quick burial. Ayub Khan, pressed by Bhutto, was now distancing
himself from the 'unfair' Tashkent deal.

But Bhutto had a longer game plan. It would soon become clear that
he was carving out his political future founded on a posture of vitriolic
attacks on India and an unwavering commitment to the Kashmir cause.
Ayub's favoured politician had sensed that the military dictator was about
to complete his long run as Pakistan's ruler. Driven ostensibly by his
opposition to the peace with India after the Tashkent fiasco, and sensing
the collapse of Ayub, Bhutto quit as foreign minister in June 1966, aiming
at a more exalted political future. This ended the Sindh politician's tenure
as cabinet minister of eight years, three of which were spent as foreign
minister, where he guided Pakistan's destiny, developed close ties with
China, and became the major driver of the war with India. But he had
also annoyed the US and the UK, and caused American aid to be ended.

In the midst of rising political turmoil, High Commissioner Kewal Singh
left Pakistan in October 1966 to take over as Indian envoy in Moscow. He
was soon replaced by the Dacca-born Samarendra Sen, a veteran ICS officer
who understood Pakistan well. Sen took over an Indian high commission
poised to move to Pakistan's gleaming new capital of Islamabad.

⌐

By 1967, the ethnic divide between Pakistan's west and east had widened. This also impacted relations between India and eastern Pakistan. Sectarian riots in 1964 that killed over a thousand people in Dacca had exacerbated this long-standing problem. Hindu refugees flooded north-east India. The 1950 Nehru–Liaquat Pact was unravelling. East Pakistan was also upset that the west had left that region undefended during the 1965 war; some in the west had even suggested, implausibly, that China would step in if India invaded the east. More fundamentally Dacca University economists mocked the two-nation theory with a 'two-economies theory', pointing to the brazen reallocation of funds to the west, despite the economy of the east contributing most of Pakistan's export revenues. At a 1966 Opposition party conference in Lahore, the charismatic grassroots politician and leader of the Awami League, Mujibur Rahman, had proposed a six-point plan of autonomy, challenging Ayub Khan's sham 'Basic Democracy' scheme. All this would be the run-up to another painful partition in South Asia, and the creation of a new nation to India's east.

1967–1977: A SUBCONTINENT REDRAWN

9

JOI BANGLA

On the twentieth anniversary of its independence, 14 August 1967, Pakistan officially moved its capital to Islamabad. This had been Ayub Khan's pet project, launched in the beginning of his reign. Islamabad had already been declared the capital city in 1960 and Rawalpindi, close to the army headquarters, served as the interim capital, where the seat of government initially shifted from Karachi. The Indian high commission had a new address in Islamabad from 1967. High Commissioner Samarendra Sen rented a modest building in the F6 sector for the office and moved into a neighbouring bungalow that served as his residence. Sen was in good company. Other diplomatic reidences surrounded his. And about a hundred yards away, at the foot of the Margalla Hills, was the residence of Pakistan's ruler Ayub Khan. The high commission left a subsidiary office—now a consulate—in Karachi and continued to operate one in an increasingly restive Dacca.

Sen watched with special interest the mounting anger in East Pakistan towards the western wing. The bond between the two wings had been an uneasy one since Partition in 1947. Religion had long been deployed to divide the Bengali people. Some writers suggest that the genesis of the divisions in the subcontinent should be traced to earlier in the century, to the first partition of Bengal in 1905 (when the British rejigged the Bengal Presidency, dividing it into a largely Muslim west and Hindu east) or even earlier, to the divisive politics following the Revolt of 1857 (when Indian troops rebelled against the British East India Company), or even before that, to the Battle of Plassey of 1757, which first divided Bengal and allowed the East India Company to establish its empire.

In negotiating Pakistan, Jinnah had successfully played up religion as the primary marker of identity to join the eastern and western wings into one nation. In March 1948, Jinnah had flown down to the eastern wing of the country he had created on his maiden visit as Pakistan's powerful ruler. Indian HC Sri Prakasa in Karachi had pushed New Delhi for the overflight permissions for Jinnah, for a visit meant to consolidate support in the eastern wing. Little did the Quaid know that he was sowing the seeds of its partition within the next quarter century. Jinnah's speech at Dacca University in March 1948 was tone deaf in declaring in English to his shocked audience that Urdu would be Pakistan's national language. This was seen as an arrogant put-down of the Bengali language, and a failure to read the cultural, as against religious, basis for Bengali nationalism.

The speech was met with dismay and heckling. Jinnah compounded his indiscretion later in the same month in a radio address, where he repeated that Urdu would not just be the link language, but the only language for Pakistan. This did not go down well in a region where language was central to identity; it led to the first signs of resentment at 'West Pakistani racism'. Jinnah was then at the peak of his powers as Pakistan's governor general, combining an autocratic executive role with that of a ceremonial head of state, almost like a British viceroy. He was the unchallenged authority of a country he had created 'with his typewriter'[1], but the core of his creation lay in Punjab, with Bengal on the distant periphery.

Punjabi Pakistanis added insult to hurt Bengali pride by ignoring the historical Bengali contribution to Pakistan's creation—the Muslim League had begun operations in Bengal, and the Pakistan movement got much of its strength from the eastern wing, making partition inevitable by 1947.

The language movement had exploded when police killed student protestors of Dacca University on 21 February 1952, as they rallied against the language policy. The killings led to wider civil unrest in the east. In the first elections to provincial assemblies in 1954, the Awami League-led United Front trounced the Muslim League comprehensively. The twenty-one-point manifesto of the front demanded autonomy for East Pakistan as envisaged in the 1940 Lahore resolution. The Karachi government was compelled to grant official status to the Bengali language in 1956. But the protests on language now evolved into strident voices for parity in economic development. East Pakistan had woken to the fact of discrimination at all levels. The foreign exchange earned by the East's exports was seen as being usurped by the west. The east seemed to be subsidizing a Punjabi army. Young Bengali economists were asking for a course correction, if not a systemic overhaul.

In March 1966, the Awami League led by Sheikh Mujibur Rahman had first put forward the six-point programme that demanded a 'federation of Pakistan in the true sense of the Lahore resolution'. It demanded that the federal government should deal with only two subjects: defence and foreign affairs, while all residual subjects be vested in the federating states. This was reminiscent also of the Cabinet Mission Plan of 1946 (envisaging a loose confederation of India and Pakistan) that had been accepted by Jinnah but rejected by Indian leaders. From early 1968, the protestors had a new reason to intensify the agitation—the 'Agartala conspiracy' case was slapped on Mujib and thirty-four Bengali military officers, accusing them of colluding with 'Indian government agents' in a scheme to 'divide Pakistan'. Mujib was arrested in the case in May 1968 and a trial began.[2] East Pakistan remained disturbed by agitations related to language, economic exploitation and, in the late 1960s, the six-point programme and the Agartala case. Bengal had been instrumental in creating Pakistan in 1947, but in twenty-three years, the project seemed to be unravelling because of disaffection in the east.

ᵔ

In the west, Bhutto cashed in on Ayub's falling stock and his own growing popularity to found the Pakistan People's Party (PPP) in Lahore on 30 November 1967. The party sought 'egalitarian democracy' and 'application of socialistic ideas to realise economic and social justice'. Challenging General Ayub Khan was the immediate priority. People were already questioning Ayub's self-serving democracy, where 80,000 partyless 'basic democrats', had been indirectly elected in 1962.[3] These sham democrats, claiming to represent 125 million Pakistanis, had elected Ayub as president, where, as has been noted, he rigged elections to beat the opposition candidate, the sister of Pakistan's founder, Fatima Jinnah. But people in Pakistan, particularly politicians and the intelligentsia, were now yearning for the sort of real electoral democracy that seemed to be thriving in India and in other postcolonial nations.

On the bilateral front, the Tashkent spirit had evaporated and newer irritants were creeping into the relationship. Pakistan tried to confiscate more property of pre-1965 Indian companies that had stayed behind, declaring it enemy property. India protested. India was expressing outrage at the building of the Karakoram Highway, linking the northern Gilgit region of Kashmir with Xinjiang province of China.

In early 1968, as Ayub Khan began celebrating ten years of his reign as the 'Decade of Development', outraged citizens erupted into agitations. While much has been made in Pakistan of the economic prosperity of the 1960s, with Western economists invited in to mentor Ayub's enlightened economic policy, the reality was not as rosy. Modest economic growth came with aggravating inequity. While Harvard's advisory services were guiding development, with growth hovering around 6 per cent, economists, both in Pakistan and the US, were also assessing that Pakistan suffered from 'extreme elite capture', with twenty-two families controlling vast swathes of the economy, and more than 85 per cent of resources.[4] Corruption was rampant. Ayub's son, Gauhar, was alleged to have profited and built an industrial empire with this nepotism.

The global students' movement had brought a new element of young hope in Pakistan, along with widespread disturbance and demonstrations. Ayub was losing his ability to effectively contain dissent through his security forces.[5] In the east, additional problems were caused by brewing resentment against the political domination of the Punjabis, particularly the sustained economic exploitation of East Pakistan for markets and raw material. The new capital city of Islamabad, for the Punjabi elites, was being built, it was claimed, with Bengali blood and taxes.

Bhutto was detained for breaching the peace in November 1968, while Mujib was already in jail for colluding with India to divide the country. Other political dissidents were arrested as well. Bhutto made a legal appeal, contending that he had been arbitrarily arrested for 'differences I developed with the regime over the ceasefire and the Tashkent Declaration'. But disturbances persisted. War hero Air Marshal Asghar Khan joined the opposition movement in November. By the end of 1968, revolutionary zeal and collapsing governance threatened the military regime. Ayub tried to stem the dissent in the only way he knew. He dispatched the army to major towns in both wings and raised the bogey of the existential threat from India. In a 29 December speech in Lahore, he warned that the enemy, 'with its well-organised 30 divisions', would 'invade Pakistan and can do so in a week's time.'[6]

A DEMOCRATIC DICTATOR

By January 1969, the Opposition parties were demanding that emergency conditions imposed by Ayub be lifted, elections be held, and political prisoners released. Ayub, physically ailing by now, and with his back to the wall, did release Bhutto and other Opposition leaders in the west. He invited them to negotiate Pakistan's political future. He also withdrew the Agartala case—none of the charges of the alleged secessionist conspiracy had been proved in a year—against Mujib and other arrested leaders. This set Mujib free to agitate in the east and to be feted as 'Bangabandhu'— friend of Bengal. In February, Ayub announced that he would not be a candidate for the next election and gave some vague assurances on direct elections. This was not enough. Ayub's own basic democrats and other supporters had begun to turn on him. He was compelled by the army to resign on 25 March 1969, handing over the reins to his army chief, General Yahya Khan, and paving the way for another bout of martial law.

Yahya started his tenure by saying what several dictators had done soon after takeovers—that he had no ambition other than the 'creation of conditions conducive to the establishment of a constitutional government'[7]. He almost meant it.

Kewal Singh, India's envoy in Pakistan during the 1965 war, was watching the situation closely. He had returned from diplomatic stints in Moscow and Bonn, as secretary in the ministry in New Delhi. His portfolio included India–Pakistan relations. He was back in Pakistan in July 1969, on a visit to sign boundary maps for the Kutch boundary (over which the two countries had gone to war in April 1965), in accordance with the Kutch tribunal's awards. Prior to the visit, Singh met Prime Minister Indira Gandhi to discuss his brief for his meeting with Yahya Khan. She concurred in his proposal to focus on resuming trade and air services. He was keen to revive the fabled Tashkent spirit that had visibly flagged since his departure from Pakistan. For his meeting with Yahya, Singh had managed a letter from PM Indira Gandhi, suggesting the resumption of contacts to restore relations in various fields.

When Kewal Singh called on Yahya in July, he started with a relatively minor diplomatic issue that he had also raised with President Ayub in 1966. This was a pet project: to cooperate in the United Nations and other international organizations and not put up rival candidates for the same post. Yahya, yet unschooled by his establishment on diplomatic postures with India, willingly agreed. But he soon made a U-turn in the meeting, when one of his aides reminded him that 'basic issues need to need to be settled first', a euphemism for the primacy of the Kashmir issue.

Along with B. K. Acharya, the high commissioner (who had replaced Samarendra Sen when he retired in December 1968—he had earlier been India's deputy high commissioner in Dacca), Kewal Singh met several key personalities at a reception hosted by Acharya and came away feeling that public opinion in Pakistan favoured better understanding and goodwill between the two countries. He concluded that Yahya's fickle take on India–Pakistan relations did not reflect either popular or elite opinion in Pakistan.

Yahya soon sent a response to Indira Gandhi's letter, saying that Pakistan was ready for a dialogue for normalization and improvement of relations provided India was willing to find answers to 'all outstanding issues'[8]. Clearly, the foreign office had drafted the letter persuading the president to place the issue of Kashmir before *peripheral* ones like trade, communications, and the movement of peoples. Kewal Singh knew that Kashmir had not been discussed during his visit but the formulation had been inserted by the foreign office to ensure that their obsessively promoted Kashmir cause was not diluted even for a moment. This was to become Pakistan's reflexive response to, and the default position on, most Indian peace initiatives. Exceptions would be made only occasionally when a confident and pragmatic leader overruled the establishment.

Under the sway of his bureaucrats, Yahya acted hawkishly again, when he opposed India's entry into the Organisation of Islamic countries (OIC), at its first summit in Rabat in September 1969. After initially appearing to accept India's inclusion, Pakistan threatened to walk out of the OIC if India was admitted. Other Islamic countries did not counter Yahya's tantrum. This embarrassed India greatly. India withdrew its ambassador in Rabat, Sardar Gurcharan Singh, as a mark of protest.

Events in the eastern wing were soon to take matters in a different direction. Yahya remained true to his word and announced general elections in Pakistan in a broadcast to the nation on 28 November 1969. He also declared that the 'one unit'—in which all West Pakistani provinces had been integrated since 1955—would be dissolved and each province would have its own autonomy with its own legislative assembly and government.

This was widely welcomed by other provinces in West Pakistan that had seen the one-unit system for what it was—a ruse for Punjabi dominance. Yahya had also promised universal franchise that had been a distant dream for Pakistan for all these years. These announcements were met with great optimism in India. Pakistan would finally follow India's path of the past two decades—of democracy based on universal adult franchise. A segue into genuine democracy was expected to reduce hostility and confrontation, otherwise assumed to be natural corollaries of military dictatorships.

The promise of a free election triggered robust poll campaigns within Pakistan from January 1970. The Awami League positioned elections as a referendum for the six-point autonomy programme for the 75 million people of East Pakistan. Bhutto countered with a promise of economic and social reforms and preserving the unity of the country. But his message was focused on the 55 million people in West Pakistan. On these two diverse manifestos, the two major parties from Pakistan's two disparate wings were seeking their first truly democratic mandate from the people, almost two decades after India had taken that path.

Relations between the two wings of Pakistan sank further in 1970, as a major disaster struck East Pakistan on 12 November. A devastating cyclone swept over the offshore islands and coastal districts of East Pakistan. This was one of the worst natural disasters in modern history—it killed as many as half a million people. The rescue efforts fell pathetically short and aggravated the misery. Once again, the crushed inhabitants of East Pakistan felt the Punjabis had betrayed the Bengalis during a time of tribulation.

YAHYA'S ELECTIONS

Yahya Khan is the only military dictator in Pakistan's history who actually kept his promise of early democratic elections. More than any liberal democratic instincts, Yahya was driven by the expectation that political power would be legitimized in the hands of a West Pakistani politician, Bhutto. This would give the army continuing influence on the polity. However, the free polls of December 1970 produced an unexpected thumping majority for Mujib. His Awami League won 160 of the 162 seats in East Pakistan, giving it an absolute majority in the house of 300. Bhutto's PPP won just 81 of the 138 seats in the west. A shocked Bhutto refused to accept the results and pressed Yahya to reject Mujib's claim to form the government, suggesting that a hint of force would take care of the Bengalis.

For India, the outcome of the 1970 election seemed a good augury. B. K. Acharya, the high commissioner, received an assessment from the then deputy high commissioner in Dacca, K. C. Sen Gupta, that an Awami League government in Islamabad 'would be genuinely democratic and would increasingly desist from military confrontations against India'.[9]

This assessment was widely shared by Indian policymakers, but concerns were also flagged about Pakistan's military build-up and whether the army would allow this democratic outcome to find expression on the ground.

In December 1970, B. K. Acharya expressed a view that soon came to be widely accepted in New Delhi. While recognizing the possibility of the secession of Pakistan's eastern wing, he argued that 'majority control of the central Pakistan Government by the East Pakistanis seems to be our only hope of achieving India's policy objectives towards Pakistan and for overcoming the stone-wall resistance of West Pakistan'[10]. Moreover, a secessionist East Bengal, he was concerned, might demand integration with West Bengal for a 'United Bengal' and might pass under the control of pro-Chinese Marxists. Such developments would further complicate India's defence and strategic challenges. While such a fear seemed exaggerated, for people of Acharya's generation, the 1947 proposal for an independent undivided Bengal launched jointly by Suhrawardy, Sarat Bose, and other prominent provincial politicians 'was more than a historical footnote.'[11] Foreign Secretary T. N. Kaul agreed that India should do nothing to encourage the separation of East Pakistan from West Pakistan, but added significantly that it did not lie in India's hands to stop it. Much would depend on the rulers of Pakistan on whether West Pakistan would realize the need to come to an equitable arrangement with East Pakistan.[12]

The new dynamics within Pakistan were presenting fundamental dilemmas to India's policymakers, trying to understand whether Pakistan would democratize or disintegrate. India hoped for a progressive improvement in bilateral relations with a 'new democratic Pakistan', in which the eastern wing had its rightful representation but feared it would be hard to bridge the 'vast political divide between the two disparate and distant wings' of Pakistan.[13]

External factors, reflecting a world in flux, were conspiring with internal factors in the move towards the creation of a new state. Military analyst Srinath Raghavan, for instance, has persuasively argued that three global factors of the times were shaping the destiny of the subcontinent: the play of the Cold War between the US and the USSR; the dynamics of decolonization; and the beginnings of globalization, particularly as manifested in the student protests common to the US, India, Pakistan, and Bangladesh.

EAST VS WEST

A young Indian diplomat in Islamabad, Second Secretary Deb Mukharji, watched bilateral relations sink steadily in 1971. He had 'virtually no connection with the natives' in Islamabad even though he interacted often with other diplomats. Only when Indian diplomats travelled to Karachi did they meet 'real Pakistanis'.[14] He was alarmed by the rising crescendo of the drums of war and would later reflect that he was living through the 'most cataclysmic year since 1947, in the history of the subcontinent'.[15]

At the end of January, Mukharji saw a familiar marker of plunging ties—the expulsion of several diplomats from both countries. When an Indian diplomat B. L. Joshi was given twenty-four hours to leave, he had to pack his household through the night; it was Mukharji's job to escort his expelled colleague, along with his wife and two children, to the border in the Firozpur district of Pakistan's Punjab. With unintended irony, the last Pakistani village on the crossing was named after a Hindu—Ganda Singh Wala, while the adjoining border village on the Indian side had a Muslim name—Hussain Walla. This was the primary crossing between India and Pakistan till 1986, before Attari–Wagah in Punjab became the cross point of choice. When the Indian delegation nervously reached the border to make good their exit on the late afternoon of 30 January 1971, they were surprised by the absence of hostility; in fact, the bewildered Pakistan Rangers presented them a spirited guard of honour, much to their relief and amusement. Joshi was perhaps the only diplomat in history to have been thus honoured before being booted out by his host country.[16]

Meanwhile, in New Delhi, Indian officials huddled to review the situation. Ministry of External Affairs Secretary S. K. Banerjee and High Commissioner Acharya observed in early January that the secession of Pakistan's eastern wing could occur only if it failed to secure its six-point autonomy demand through constitutional means. A basic point of contention would be powers of taxation; the army would not accept an arrangement under which it would have to depend upon subventions from the provinces for its funding. Acharya concluded that despite all reservations, Bhutto, as leader of the PPP, might accept the autonomy demand if he himself could be all-powerful in the western wing, or if each wing was allowed to go its own way. A contrarian view came from Rameshwar Nath Kao, the brilliant chief of the newly formed external intelligence agency, the Research and Analysis Wing, or R&AW. Kao repeated the R&AW assessment of 1969 that Pakistan's army would not accept autonomy in the east and Mujib would not compromise on his six-point programme. He argued that India should support the Awami League if it launched an independence movement. The Prime Minister's Office (PMO) went along with the MEA's assessment of a probable political compromise. But it was clear, in retrospect, that R&AW had assessed the situation correctly.

India's young and still callow prime minister, Indira Gandhi, was now increasingly relying on advice from her principal secretary, P. N. Haksar, whose role was less that of a mandarin advising a political leader and more that of the sage Krishna guiding the inexperienced warrior Arjuna on the battlefield. To the Americans, Haksar was Indira's chief of staff and national security adviser rolled into one, a formidable admixture of Nixon's chief of staff, Bob Haldemann, and National Security Advisor Henry Kissinger.

Haksar had been a lawyer and a friend of the Nehru family, personally recruited by Jawaharlal Nehru to the foreign office. He had spent time in unremarkable postings in Nigeria, Austria, and in Britain as deputy high commissioner before he had been catapulted into a key role in the PMO, soon becoming Indira Gandhi's key adviser and confidant. He was perhaps one of the most left-leaning of the 'mostly socialist pro-Soviet advisors'[17] of Indira Gandhi, all of whom happened to be Kashmiri Brahmins like her and came to be called the 'Kashmiri mafia'.[18] India's socialist government then was leaning more on the Soviet Union, particularly to help the country industrialize and nurture its defence industry; at this time, the government's distrust of the Americans was palpable.

Indira Gandhi faced a major challenge when, on 30 January 1971, an Indian Airlines Fokker aircraft flying from Srinagar to Jammu was hijacked and blown up in Lahore. In India, it was commonly assumed that the hijackers were Pakistani agents. Bhutto infuriated India even more by showing up at the Lahore airport for a brazenly convivial meeting with the hijackers. However, Mujib in the east quickly condemned the plane's destruction. This gave India a foretaste of the changed relationship that a Bengali-led government might have in store for bilateral relations. Soon after this spectacular act of terrorism, overflights between Pakistan's two wings were again suspended by an enraged India. For Pakistan, the difficulties in communicating and supplying soldiers to the east were mitigated in part by Sri Lanka providing transit facilities to Pakistan International Airlines (PIA). In Pakistan, conspiracy theorists continue to speculate that the hijacking was staged by India in order to engineer a debilitating overflight ban, to trigger the secession of the eastern wing from Pakistan.[19]

Diplomatic missions in both countries faced angry demonstrations in February. Deb Mukharji was also looking after security of India's diplomatic premises and had installed barbed wire on top of the chancery walls to prevent intruders from scaling them. That did not stop firebombs from being thrown into the premises in Islamabad in the first week of February. Two days later, while Mukharji was at work, his wife was hosting a bridge party at home for some spouses of diplomats. A brick crashed in through a window. Mukharji called the police and rushed back to his unprotected house. He offered sherry to the ladies to calm them down. More bricks were hurled at the house, shattering a French window. The police had arrived but did not appear to be interfering with the gathered mob. Mukharji, who possessed a licensed .405 Winchester 'designed to shoot elephants'[20] and a revolver, loaded his weapons and waited, prepared to pull the trigger. If the mob had come in, he recalled, it could have become 'seriously unpleasant'.[21] Later, the mob attacked again with firebombs and the car of another visitor, the wife of a Canadian diplomat, was set on fire in the driveway. Padma Chib, the wife of the deputy chief of mission, who was among the guests, told him, 'Deb, this is like Lahore 1947.' Pakistan media carried photographs of the blazing car, identifying the Indian diplomat as the arsonist. The narrative in the media was that some students were protesting peacefully, when Mukharji had himself set the car of his guest on fire.[22]

SPRING MADNESS

From Dacca, Deputy High Commissioner Sen Gupta was reporting to his superiors in Delhi and Islamabad that Bengali nationalism had taken root in East Pakistan. Sen Gupta believed Mujib's autonomy demands would weaken Pakistan, but the Bengali leader was open to a deal. This hope would soon be dashed.

If Yahya Khan had been guided by established democratic principles as Pakistan's head of state, he would have called upon the leader of the largest party to form the government as prime minister. He decided instead to play along with Bhutto in denying East Pakistan its due. The systemic racism of the west against the east was also at play. The West Pakistanis, in brazenly articulated notions of racial superiority, were determined not to allow the 'black bastards' close to power. Bhutto's role was becoming clearer. First Secretary K. N. Bakshi was assessing in Karachi that Bhutto had 'stonewalled the constitutional talks and secured power through slogan mongering and his not inconsiderable histrionic talents.' Bhutto was now a close collaborator with the army in keeping the Bengalis out of power. Strategic analyst K. Subrahmanyam wrote in an assessment later that Bhutto was directly responsible for 'encouraging military action against the Awami League.'[23]

Sen Gupta in Dacca was now reporting with alarm that hundreds of civilians had been killed or injured in street violence. Yahya was even suggesting that the army was above democratically elected representatives 'playing at Constitution making', leading Indian diplomats to argue that Yahya's attitude smacked of 'Latin American style despotism'.

In parallel to the violence, there was talk of a constituent assembly as well as a parliament to be formed in East Pakistan. Sen Gupta in Dacca reported admiringly about Mujib—'his constitutional method, solicitude for democratic process, discussion with West Pakistan leaders and the spirit of accommodation within the framework of his commitment is likely to create a favourable impression on President Yahya Khan and the people of West Pakistan.'[24]

Ominously, Lieutenant General Tikka Khan, the 'butcher of Balochistan', was deployed as army commander in Dacca in March, and soon took over as the military governor. Indian officials in Dacca and Islamabad were still optimistic that Yahya and Mujib would reach a power-sharing agreement. P. N. Haksar was however sceptical of a compromise. He foresaw the upcoming military challenge and ordered the Indian embassy in Moscow to find weaponry for a probable conflict with Pakistan.[25]

While the formal reporting from Indian missions was giving the impression that a deal was in the works, Indira Gandhi was not taking chances. On 2 March, she asked a team of advisers, including Haksar and R&AW chief Kao, to evaluate the option of giving arms to and recognizing the emerging state, given the inexorable march towards the creation of Bangladesh. They were asked to 'give their assessment to the PM'.[26] India's leaders were acutely conscious of the possibility that an intervention in the east could have repercussions in the west and even to the north. Going by the playbooks of both wars of the 1960s, and particularly the experience of 1965, military planners in India were wargaming scenarios of Pakistan retaliating in Kashmir or China militarily joining the fray.

Indian embassies had been activated all over the world. Diplomacy was especially focused on the United States, which was then locked in a close embrace with Pakistan. India requested the US to exert pressure on Yahya Khan to stop his crackdown. Indian ambassador Lakshmi Kant Jha told his hosts in Washington that 'nothing would be more tragic than President Yahya Khan suppressing East Bengali aspirations for autonomy by force.'[27]

India was also dealing with internal political churn. Indira Gandhi, who was the head of a coalition government at the time, called early elections to consolidate political power, perceiving an Opposition in disarray. When confronted with the slogan Indira Hatao (Remove Indira), she countered with Garibi Hatao (Eradicate Poverty.) The tactic worked superbly and Gandhi was re-elected in elections held from 1 to 10 March. Her party swept the polls with a majority of 352 out of 518 seats in the Lok Sabha, a resounding victory that boosted her confidence in dealing with the East Pakistan situation.

India was now getting more embroiled in the East Pakistan crisis. Tajuddin Ahmed, the general secretary of the Awami League, approached India's deputy high commissioner in Dacca for assistance on 5 March. He asked for political refuge for activists as well as material aid in the case of a Pakistani attack on East Bengal. Mujib's impassioned 7 March speech in Ramna urged the people to be prepared to resist force. Meanwhile, East Pakistan's administration controlled by the west soon fell apart. Second Secretary Mukarji and his colleagues in Islamabad knew matters were reaching a head when they heard nationalist songs transmitted from Dacca. With several rounds of failed political negotiations, an army crackdown appeared inevitable.

Sen Gupta met with Mujib's representative, Captain Shujat Ali, on 14 March. Ali requested that India intercept troops, ships, and aircraft sent by West Pakistan to East Pakistan, as this supply would violate Indian borders. Mujib demanded immediate responses. Sen Gupta made a swift trip to Calcutta to deliver this important message and, more importantly, to create the impression of activity to his East Bengali counterparts, as Mujib had been displeased by India's reluctance to mount a miltary intervention. Meanwhile, Sen Gupta returned to Dacca and assured Tajuddin Ahmed that India would offer all possible aid to victims in the event of an attack. It turned out that Mujib's message reached Prime Minister Indira Gandhi only on 19 March.[28]

Bhutto had also invoked the traditional Indian threat to effectively scuttle a possible east-west political deal.[29] From Islamabad, Indian diplomats were warning that hardliners were pressing Yahya, since they were 'back at their 23-year-old game of not allowing East Pakistan to exercise its majority share in the country's affairs'.[30] Bhutto's public statements were carefully ambiguous, preserving the optics of cooperation with East Bengal to ensure the West's reasonable interests, while assuring the army of its primacy in a Turkey-like political framework if he took office.

Yahya flew to Dacca on 15 March to stage negotiations, while he geared up for a crackdown. He told Tikka Khan, following his talks with Mujib, 'The bastard is not behaving. You get ready.'[31]

In Delhi, Haksar saw the moment coming. He advised Indira Gandhi to stand firm, 'We should not at this stage of development in Pakistan say anything at all placatory, but be tough within reason. This is not the time to make gestures of friendship to Pakistan. Every such gesture will bring comfort to Yahya Khan and make the position of Mujib correspondingly more difficult.' He told the prime minister that 'two and a half divisions of the Pak army are poised to decimate East Bengal.'[32] This was one week before the crackdown.

At 11.30 p.m. on 25 March, the West Pakistani army was let loose in Dacca, choking dissent and butchering civilians. Operation Searchlight was on. Officials at India's consulate in Dacca watched in horror as an exodus began, with East Pakistanis swarming to India's borders to escape the persecution.

The violent events were causing equal consternation in another consulate not far from India's—the US diplomatic mission in Dacca.

AMERICAN BLOOD

On 25 March, when the Pakistan Army launched its brutal crackdown, it shook Archer Blood, an American diplomat based in Dacca. Blood spent a sleepless night on the roof of his residence, listening to gunshots and screams. Like a war reporter, Blood started clinically relaying the horrifying story back to Washington, of thousands being shot, bombed, or burnt to death in Dacca. After his staff had visited Dacca University to get a first-hand look at the unfolding massacre, Blood cabled: 'At least two mass graves on campus. Stench terrible.'[33] But the stink was not powerful enough to get Washington, or even Islamabad, where Blood's discomfited boss was reading the telegrams, to intervene. The dynamics of the Cold War had frozen humanitarian concerns; these were realities no one wanted to face.

On 26 March, Mujib declared the independence of Bangladesh in Dacca. Yahya, now back in Islamabad, denounced Mujib and the Awami League as traitors and enemies of Pakistan. Bhutto had supported the crackdown. Mujib was arrested and flown to a jail in West Pakistan, the Awami League was banned, along with all political activity. Some leaders escaped to form a government in exile in India. Blood's team of beleaguered diplomats was overwhelmed with frustration and anger. They continued reporting the situation on the ground, expecting their reports to excite the same outrage they felt, to create a storm in Washington. But they were answered with a deafening silence.[34]

Blood decided not to pull his punches any more. He sent home a cable using stronger language and the subject line, 'Selective Genocide', reporting, 'here in Dacca we are mute and horrified witnesses to a reign of terror by the Pak military.' The report said that the military authorities were 'systematically eliminating' Awami League supporters by seeking them out in their homes and shooting them down. He gave graphic accounts of the killings of politicians, professors, and students. 'The streets are flooded with Hindus and other targeted groups trying desperately to get out of Dacca'. Blood was fearless in his recommendation. He wrote, 'full horror of Pak military atrocities will come to light sooner or later. Instead of pretending to believe Pakistan's falsehoods, we should be expressing shock at least privately to GOP, at this wave of terror directed against their own countrymen by Pak military'.[35] Blood feared that these accounts would expose his consulate and could result in Pakistan expelling him from the country. That did not come to pass.

While Blood was concerned about how his hosts would react, the greater concern was his government's studied indifference to what was going on. He had said in his cable that 'many Bengalis have sought refuge in homes of Americans, most of whom are extending shelter'.[36] He said this, aware that he was risking the wrath of his own government by putting down on paper this account of American activism.

While Washington remained cold to Blood's cables, he got a surprising endorsement from Kenneth Keating, the US ambassador in Delhi. Keating was a formidable political figure, a former republican senator from New York in his seventies, who had served in both world wars. Keating was seen as undiplomatic and unafraid to speak his mind. He had become an outspoken advocate for both India and the Bengalis, 'lending his own gravitas and respectability to the Dacca consulate's dissenters.' Keating was stirred by Blood's telegram, and shot off one of his own reinforcing the policy recommendation, urging his own government to 'promptly, publicly and prominently deplore this brutality', to 'privately lay it on line' with the Pakistani government and to unilaterally suspend all military supplies to Pakistan. He counselled his government that this was the time when principles made the best politics.[37]

ᴪ

Accounts of the atrocities in East Pakistan soon hit the American media. Keating was feeding stories of the massacres to the celebrated New York Times correspondent, Sydney Schanberg, then bureau chief for the paper in New Delhi, who also spent time in Dacca. Keating was not the only ambassador taking sides and going 'local'. The US ambassador to Pakistan, Joseph Farland, became a strong supporter of the Yahya regime. Farland was Blood's immediate superior, even though the Islamabad embassy was a thousand miles away from the Dacca consulate. Blood was wary of Farland's sympathy for Yahya; the dictator and the diplomat often drank together and went on shooting excursions.

The relationship between the Islamabad embassy and the Dacca consulate was fraught. After reading Keating's cable about selective genocide, Farland had reminded his junior, 'intervention by one country in the internal affairs of another tends to be frowned upon'. Farland was trying to rein in his officers in the eastern outpost and had cabled them that 'since we are not only human beings but also government servants, however right this indignation is not itself an adequate basis for our reaction.'[38]

Blood sent a retort to his boss, 'horror and flouting of democratic norms we have reported is objective reality and not emotionally contrived.' The US was continuing to be reluctant to even raise this issue with the Yahya regime. When Kissinger brought up the slaughter in East Pakistan, Nixon refused to say anything about it: 'I would not put out a statement praising it, but we are not going to condemn it either.'[39]

In a situation room discussion on the East Pakistan crisis in Washington, the dissenters in Dacca and Delhi were mocked. Secretary of State William Rogers said that India might be the first to recognize an independent Bangladesh, 'unless Keating beat them to the punch.'[40] The Americans were acutely aware of the fact that Pakistan's military was now at war with its own people, after being heavily armed by the United States. The explosive cable on selective genocide had not only been read anxiously by the administration but also found its way to the media through different leaks. Someone had also shared the contents of the secret reports with Democratic Senator Edward Kennedy, who was attacking Nixon and urging him to stop the killing, denouncing the use of US weaponry. Kissinger was convinced that the leak was coming from Keating, 'the trouble making ambassador in New Delhi'.

The American team at the Dacca consulate was feeling increasingly dejected by the treatment from Washington. Blood and his staffers, including Scott Butcher, the political officer, decided to risk their careers and send a 'dissent cable': this was a new device in the foreign office, a Vietnam-sparked reform meant to encourage candour by allowing diplomats to speak out confidentially against official policy. Butcher drafted a strong dissent note critical of US policy of refusing to speak out against the crushing of democracy and the slaughter of innocents. All embassy staff and the consulate signed the draft, which became the first dissent cable of the US foreign service.

On 6 April 1971, Blood transmitted the cable with the blunt subject line, 'Dissent from US policy towards East Pakistan', since considered one of the most blistering denunciations of US foreign policy ever sent by its own diplomats. It read:

> ...our government has failed to denounce the suppression of democracy. Our government has failed to denounce atrocities. Our government has failed to take forceful measures to protect its citizens while at the same time bending over backwards to placate the West Pak dominated government and to lessen likely and deservedly negative international public relations impact against them. Our government has evidenced what many will consider moral bankruptcy... we, as professional public servants express our dissent with current policy and fervently hope that a true and lasting interest here can be defined and a policy restricted in order to salvage our nation's position as a moral leader of the free world.[41]

Archer Blood and his team of twenty officials were then not aware of the 'bridge to China' project that Kissinger and Nixon had embarked upon with the help of Pakistan; this was Nixon's Cold War move to challenge the USSR with an overture to its estranged communist partner. The larger geopolitical rebalancing may have made little impact on the Dacca team's decision, given that they were driven by their visceral ground level experience. The cable gathered support among the experts of the State Department, but provoked rage at the highest levels in the White House. Kissinger was furious. Secretary of State Bill Rogers was livid. Rogers got on the phone with Kissinger to denounce 'that goddam message from my people in Dacca'. The State Department scrambled to control the damage and restrict the distribution of the cable. Kissinger did not show the document to Nixon for a couple of days, to give the State Department some time to soften its impact on the system. The concern was that the cable would soon leak to the media and embarrass the administration.[42]

Eventually, Pakistan faced nothing worse than polite concern voiced by an assistant secretary of state to its ambassador in Washington, followed by a tepid statement expressing worry and hope for a peaceful resolution. Without any serious global pushback, the bloodshed continued in Dacca.

The Blood telegram had echoes of the 'long telegram' issued in 1945 by George Kennan, another intrepid diplomat, positioned then in Moscow, who advocated the policy of containment of the Soviet Union. His cable signalled the beginning of the Cold War, which shaped US policy instincts even a quarter century later, as the White House cosied up to China, ignoring bloodshed, or pushback from a US outpost. The Blood telegram had no such lasting impact on geopolitics. But it did shake the Nixon administration, albeit briefly.

ROGUE MISSIONS

On 27 March, India took the enlightened decision to make relief available to the refugees flooding across its borders. The central government provided shelter, food, and healthcare. East Pakistan's neighbouring states were urged to implement the aid programme.[43] India had witnessed refugee surges in 1950 and 1964 when sectarian tensions rose, but the current inflow was unprecedented. The composition of the refugee groups would soon undergo an alarming change. By April, approximately 80 per cent of migrants entering India were Hindus, reversing the previous ratio of 80 Muslims to 20 Hindus.[44]

India's diplomatic efforts had become a critical element of the larger national toolkit to deal with this crisis. Envoys were exhorted in briefing cables not to be content with receiving assurances of a few tonnes of medicine or some money, but to make energetic efforts in presenting India's argument to their host governments. It even smacked of desperation: 'plug this once, twice, thrice, four times. Start from the lower rung and go up to the highest levels.'[45]

Pakistan's extraordinary brutality in its east stemmed from how Bengali nationalists were perceived—as fighters supported by the Indian state. Both the general slaughter and the specific targeting of Hindus could be attributed to West Pakistani racism that blended rivalry against India with the need to show the Bengalis their place. The irony was that Pakistan's initially misplaced conviction of collusion between Bengali rebels and Indian forces soon became a self-fulfilling prophecy. The heavy-handed strategy employed in East Pakistan generated a massive refugee crisis, providing India with an excuse to intervene in the conflict.[46]

Soon, the defections started. On 6 April, two Bengali diplomats of the Pakistan embassy in New Delhi, K. M. Shehabuddiun, second secretary, and Amjadul Haque, assistant press attaché, 'defected' to pledge their allegiance to the 'Government of the People's Republic of Bangladesh'. This opened the floodgates. Third Secretary Mohiuddin Ahmed defected from the Pakistan high commission in London and so did the vice consul of the Pakistan consulate in New York, Mahmood Ali (who became foreign minister of Bangladesh from 2013 till 2019).[47]

Pakistan's consulate in Calcutta was the most hit by the defections, while India's in Dacca had its fate sealed as well. As trust between India and Pakistan had plunged in 1971, staff strength at both consulates was cut back. Departures of personnel were being negotiated and calibrated, so that neither side had an edge. In Calcutta, on 19 April, the staff of the Pakistan deputy high commission in Calcutta dramatically switched loyalty to a nation yet to be created. The fifty-seven Bengali employees applauded as the head of the post, Hossain Ali, lowered the Pakistani flag and raised the Bangladesh movement's green, red, and gold banner. Thirty West Pakistanis were permitted to return home from this rogue mission. Pakistan retaliated by holding hostage Indian officials at the Dacca consulate, on the grounds that all their staff had been forcibly imprisoned by India. With bank accounts inaccessible, Indian officials ceased receiving salaries until an innovative solution came into play. They now received cash delivered in sacks to the Soviet embassy in Islamabad and delivered in Dacca by the Indian mission by the Soviet diplomats.

By the end of April, Pakistan asked India to shut its Dacca mission, even as it technically closed down the Pakistan deputy high commission in Calcutta. The officials of the rogue Calcutta consulate were now deemed 'anti-state elements'. Pakistan also flew down a consul from Islamabad to ask the Bengali officials if they wanted to stay in India or return home. It soon complained that India was hindering the process, while Indian authorities contended they could not force Bengalis to see the inquisitioner individually. The diplomats became virtual hostages. Policy responses were being improvised since this scenario had no precedence in international law or practice. In July, after weeks of talks under Swiss mediation, Indian officials and their families from Dacca and West Pakistani members of their Calcutta mission were sent to their respective homes—aboard planes that crossed mid-air.[48]

Despite the genocide and influx of refugees, the option of Indian military action was not on the table in April. Not everyone was advocating strategic patience. The most sophisticated argument for an early military intervention came from K. Subrahmanyam, a senior bureaucrat and expert on military matters who was the director of the Institute of Defence Studies and Analysis (IDSA). He advocated a more decisive strategy beyond just covert assistance, that could amount to a 'full-scale intervention and full-scale war with Pakistan'[49]. An advantage of early intervention would be the element of surprise. India, the argument went, could present a fait accompli to the major powers and minimize its vulnerability to China.

In a famous war council—a cabinet meeting of 25 April—Indira Gandhi ruled out the option of military intervention. Contrary to then army chief General Sam Manekshaw's narrative, embellished over several tellings across the decades, that he dissuaded her from a military adventure, Indira Gandhi was not spoiling for war. She had in fact summoned Manekshaw to the meeting so that some of her impatient and hawkish ministerial colleagues could hear for themselves the military's views on the need for some preparation and patience.[50]

COLD WAR LOVE

As has been noted, unbeknownst to Blood and his team reporting the genocide from Dacca, Nixon and Kissinger were playing a game of high geopolitical stakes, as they planned their secret opening to China. The conduit for this opening was Pakistan and more specifically its leader, Yahya Khan. The Sino–Soviet split of 1969 had only militarized disagreements that had arisen between the two communist regimes from the late 1950s. Kissinger's outreach to China at the height of the Cold War triggered an eager response, since China at the time was mulling over a 'realist' policy of engaging the superpower rival of its estranged communist ally. Pakistan as a conduit was only one of the options that the Americans had considered. France and Romania were also explored, briefly even used, but Pakistan soon became the primary channel.

Before the Pakistani elections of October 1970, Nixon had personally asked Yahya to deliver a message to China. Yahya had eagerly accepted this diplomatic assignment and met with Zhou Enlai in person during a visit to Beijing. Yahya returned with Mao's invitation to Nixon to visit Beijing. Zhou welcomed Yahya's choice as envoy since he was a head of state and a friend of China.

Kissinger had been contemplating holding a Sino–US meeting in Rawalpindi. When the massacre in East Pakistan was unfolding on 25 March 1971, the White House was considering two similar invitations from Romania and Pakistan.

The White House was also weighing substantial inputs from the 'state department and the two feuding ambassadors in New Delhi and Islamabad, as well as the renegade Consul in Dacca'.[51] Despite clear advice, Nixon and Kissinger remained committed to their broader Cold War goal. China was also crucial to the United States's ambitions to withdraw from Vietnam, where it was entangled in an impossible war. The North Vietnamese government would listen to China and Russia.

Secretary of State Rogers was playing both sides. He articulated some of the discontent among his subordinates when he informed Nixon that 'it was time to re-evaluate US policy towards Pakistan, particularly the Pakistan army's use of US-supplied military equipment', which was embarrassing for the government. Farland was still urging a non-interventionist policy posture from Islamabad, coupled with some mild criticism of Pakistan.[52]

The Pentagon wouldn't tell the White House how much American weaponry was used in East Pakistan. The fine print obfuscated the issue. After the 1965 war, Pakistan was still under a US weapons embargo. In October 1970, Nixon had created an 'exception' to the embargo and offered Pakistan a large cargo of armed personnel carriers, fighter jets, bombers, and more. Kissinger now told Nixon that Pakistan was expecting the $34 million worth of military equipment bought over the past four years, though they would likely ship half of that.

Seeing the mood in the White House, Rogers was not the one to bear only bad news. He tried to silence the dissenters in Dacca and Delhi and reported proudly to Kissinger, 'We have Keating quieted down.' In a private message to Kissinger, Farland slammed Blood and said, 'Embassy has had full-scale revolt on general issue by virtually all officers in Consulate General, Dacca, coupled with forfeiture of leadership for American community there. Dacca's reporting has been tendentious to an extreme.'[53]

Meanwhile Kissinger and Nixon were holding their ground and continuing their silence on the killings in East Pakistan: 'Thank God we didn't get into the Pakistan thing,' the president smugly concluded on 13 April. 'We are smart to stay the hell out of that'. 'Absolutely', agreed Kissinger. 'Now, State has a whole list of needling, nasty little things they want to do to West Pakistan. I don't think we should do it, Mr President.' Nixon growled, 'not a goddamn thing. I will not allow it.'[54]

On 21 April, Zhou sent a breakthrough message, using Yahya, in which the Chinese premier suggested that Kissinger, Rogers, or even Nixon himself, come to Beijing. Zhou suggested that all the arrangements could be made through the good offices of President Yahya Khan. This led the US to retire all other channels—like Bucharest, Warsaw, Paris—and focus on the Yahya channel. Kissinger and Nixon continued their policy, even though they were getting advice that 'almost all observers believe that Bangladesh will eventually become an independent entity.'[55]

Just as the Nixon administration was firming up its policy on Pakistan, Yahya relayed a message from Zhou, adding that it's the first time we've had a direct report, 'from a president, through a president, to a president.' Nixon found that phrase memorable and used it himself a few times. But it spoke to how secretive diplomacy had subverted the systemic checks and balances, crowding out professional advice.

The Nixon administration continued to hope that the Pakistan Army would regain control of the Bengali cities in the east. But the cynical geopolitical objectives needed to be balanced, to accommodate pressure from the US Congress to stop the supply of armaments. So, the US reduced arms supplies to a trickle, 'to avoid giving Yahya the impression we are cutting off military assistance', but holding the shipment of more controversial heavy arms 'in order not to provoke the Congress to force cutting off all aid.' Nixon dutifully initialled the option that Kissinger had recommended and scrawled on the margins of the note of the memo: To all hands. Don't squeeze Yahya at this time. He underlined the word don't three times.[56]

A few weeks later, Kissinger told the Pakistanis that Yahya should communicate on the China bridge only through Pakistan's ambassador to the United States, Agha Shahi, who in turn should speak only to Kissinger. He exchanged messages in complete secrecy with Pakistan's envoy, bypassing the State Department. Shahi conveyed them back to Islamabad, where they were picked up by the Chinese envoy and relayed to Beijing. The secrecy was essential because of the risk of a public backlash if the US was seen courting communist China.

Obsessed with their Cold War diplomacy, Nixon and Kissinger had failed to use critical levers available to them to stem Pakistan's genocide in its east. Kissinger had observed that, 'US economic support—multiplied by US leadership in the World Bank and associated donors—remains crucial to West Pakistan. Neither Moscow nor Peking can duplicate this assistance.'[57] China had not then emerged as an alternative donor to Pakistan. However, by rejecting the use of this leverage, Nixon and Kissinger effectively deepened the crisis and aided the demise of a united Pakistan.

IMPOTENT RAGE

Anthony Mascarenhas was a Pakistani journalist of Goan Christian descent who worked for the morning news in Karachi and was a stringer for the *Sunday Times* of London. He was one of eight Pakistani journalists taken on an officially sponsored trip to East Pakistan in late April. He was shaken to the core by what he saw. The centrefold of the *Sunday Times* on 13 June 1971 carried with his byline a single story with the headline 'Genocide'. The article had escaped the curtain of censorship drawn by the Pakistani regime and laid bare the brutalities being perpetrated on the Bengalis. Mascarenhas's 5,000-word story was a carefully crafted report of the ten days he had spent in East Pakistan. With vivid precision, he told a story of brutality, as well as grit and humanity. He wrote that the Pakistan government was 'pushing through its own final solution of the East Bengal problem and compared what was happening to the Holocaust in Europe'. The accompanying editorial—'Stop the Killing'—added that there was no escaping the terrible charge of premeditated extermination. The Bangladesh tragedy now reverberated across the world, spawning multiple other stories in the Western media.

Prime Minister Pierre Trudeau of Canada was among the first leaders to whom Yahya Khan wrote to justify his actions after the military intervention. The Canadian high commissioner in Islamabad, George Small, cabled dramatically to Ottawa that the 'Pak of Jinnah is dead', and the emergence of East Bengal was 'inevitable'. Yet, he advised an aloof and noncommittal posture. Trudeau geared up immediately to deal with the crisis. Ottawa adopted a four-pronged approach on the crisis: maintaining a neutral public posture; urging restraint in both Pakistan and India; providing humanitarian relief to East Pakistani victims; and encouraging Islamabad, softly and privately, to move towards a political solution. In practice, the last strand of his policy was so soft as to be useless. It only salved the conscience of the Liberal government led by Trudeau.[58]

The liberal Canadian newspaper, the Globe and Mail, was castigating the government and asking it to take a tougher stand to turn off aid to West Pakistan and increase assistance for the refugees. In the end, the Canadians took a bizarre position that the 'internal problem of East Pakistan will be settled sooner or later but it is inevitable that an important proportion of the ten million refugees in India will not wish to return to East Bengal.... We would suggest therefore that the world community should be prepared to assist India integrate those refugees as productive members of the economy.' It galled Indian diplomats that Canada was essentially asking India to take in 10 million refugees and ignoring Pakistan's aggression. This extraordinary posture was effectively condoning a genocide and asking India to accept the refugees simply because they were ethnically Hindu. Fortunately, the matter was not discussed in the UN General Assembly (UNGA) debate. It would have deepened India's outrage at Canada's cavalier lack of appreciation of the situation on the ground.

Sri Lanka offered to intervene in the crisis or mediate between India and Pakistan. Iran made an offer as well, as the shah of Iran was then a stalwart US ally in the Middle East and a close friend of Pakistan. Foreign Secretary T. N. Kaul flew to Iran to dissuade the Iranians from dispatching arms to Pakistan.[59]

The US was blocking out the noise about the genocide, as also any temptation to intervene in the crisis. Kissinger was indeed embarking on a mission to Asia, but he was focused more on the exciting diplomatic game between the US and Pakistan as a precursor to the US–China detente. Kissinger stopped by in India and Pakistan in July, ostensibly to address the crisis in the east. In his 6 July meeting with Indira Gandhi, Kissinger asked her how long it would be before the problem became unmanageable. Gandhi replied calmly that it was already unmanageable: 'We are just holding it together by sheer will power.' She told him of the intense domestic pressure on her, including in parliament. P. N. Haksar reinforced this message in a longer meeting with the visitor.

But Kissinger's mind was on the next leg of his tour to Pakistan and the springboard it would prove for his diplomacy in Beijing. Kissinger was next in Rawalpindi and somewhat perfunctorily advised Yahya Khan to defuse the refugee issue. Next day, feigning an upset belly, Kissinger took his famous secret flight to Beijing. It was a testimony to Kissinger's stomach for daring diplomacy that while his belly was his official alibi in this enterprise of secrecy, deception, and adventure, he actually was braving some genuine indigestion, a 'Delhi belly' he had picked up on the India leg of the tour.

'There seems to be a growing sense of inevitability of war,' Kissinger later told Secretary of State Rogers of the South Asia leg of his tour. 'Not because anybody wants it, but because they worry they will not know how to escape it.' He compared the 1971 South Asian summer to the 1914 European summer, when miscalculations had propelled Europe into World War I.[60] He was still in denial of the role the US was playing in driving the region towards that outcome.

MAO'S SMILE

In Beijing, Zhou said to Kissinger that the turmoil in East Pakistan was caused by India.[61] The Chinese were stressing this point because they felt the US had considerable leverage over India thanks to economic aid. Kissinger was however reading too much into Zhou's words, when he said: 'Please tell President Yahya Khan that if India commits aggression, we will support Pakistan.'[62]

When Kissinger reported this matter to Nixon at the White House, Nixon asked what China would do if India launched a war. Kissinger replied that he thought the Chinese would 'come in'. This loss in translation of the Chinese position was to lead Nixon and Kissinger to misjudge the Chinese moves when war broke out a few months later.

India's diplomats were reading China more accurately after the crisis erupted in March. India's chargé d'affaires in Beijing, Brajesh Mishra, was encouraging his government to mend fences with China before the Bangladesh situation drove a deeper wedge in their relationship. He was concerned that India's growing dependence on Moscow would disincentivize an improved relationship with Beijing. Mishra had good reason to stick his neck out with this advice. He had seen Mao's smile.

A year earlier, on 1 May 1970, Mishra had joined other diplomats for a routine May Day parade. What followed was an innocuous-sounding exchange with China's leader. Mishra, in a standard diplomatic line-up, shook hands with Communist Party Chairman Mao Zedong. But the Chinese leader's words were music to Mishra's sharp ears: 'We cannot keep on quarrelling like this,' Mao said through an interpreter. 'We should try and be friends again. India is a great country. Indian people are good people. We will be friends again some day.' Mishra replied, 'We are ready to do it today.' To which Mao said, 'Please convey my message of best wishes and greetings to your President and your Prime Minister.'[63] In another context, these would have been mundane pleasantries at a national day interaction between a diplomat and a head of state. But this was China, eight years after the Indo–China war of 1962 and soon after the Cultural Revolution that convulsed the communist nation. Given the bitterness of past years, here was a critical exchange that Indian diplomacy needed to decipher.

Mishra dashed off a cable to Delhi that day, describing his conversation and underlining the significance of such an expression of friendship from Mao himself. The diplomat urged handling the message with sensitivity and 'weighty consideration' of the hand of friendship from Mao. Despite Mishra's counsel for secrecy, a garbled account of the meeting was leaked to the media in India, stating that Mao had smiled at Mishra during the May Day celebrations, leading Opposition members in parliament to ask why the government had succumbed to a mere smile. The obvious insinuation was that Nehru's inexperienced daughter might be about to repeat his mistake of a decade earlier, of misreading Chinese intentions. The Chinese signal to India was nevertheless a critical factor in the calculation of India's Pakistan strategy as it unfolded in 1971. P. N. Haksar was cautious about this outreach and advised the prime minister 'not to overestimate nor underestimate' the significance of Mao's words. Mishra received instructions and an assessment from New Delhi: 'Whereas India would not be indifferent to normalising relations between India and China to the extent of exchange of ambassadors there will be no let-up in their propaganda against us. We would like to test the validity of this assessment.'[64]

When Mishra returned to Beijing on 1 June 1970, after consultations in India, he detected a subtle shift in Chinese behaviour. A slow diplomatic dance followed in meetings with his counterpart, a senior official of the Asia department, Yang Kungsu, with both sides watching each other cautiously and awaiting the first step towards normalization. Months later, when the East Pakistan crisis erupted in March 1971, China was still exploring an opening with India, even as it was attempting a conversation with the US, aided by Pakistan.

Brajesh Mishra in Beijing read the Chinese signals accurately. He recommended that India should be happy even with a relatively neutral Chinese stance in the conflict with Pakistan. As the crisis in Bangladesh worsened in July, Indira Gandhi, at Mishra's urging, wrote directly to Premier Zhou suggesting that India and China could find a true basis for durable understanding. The letter carried weight, even though China did not respond specifically to this overture. China needed to balance Pakistan's feelings. It was also watching the evolving Moscow–Delhi equation that would be capped by the Indo–Soviet Treaty of August. Unlike Nixon and Kissinger, the Chinese did not rush to emotive, unbalanced conclusions. When Kissinger eagerly assured Premier Zhou in July that Nixon would speak to Indira Gandhi in the strongest possible terms when she visited the US in November, specifically about the need for India to exercise military restraint in its dealings with Pakistan, the Chinese premier was guarded in his response: 'We will like to make a further study of this matter before telling you.'[65]

THE DRUMS OF WAR

The war had been a near certainty from the second half of 1971, as the continuing influx of refugees into India made it impossible to stanch the flow without addressing the cause for it—the Pakistan army's continuing genocide in the country's eastern wing. The matter had been escalating dangerously since late August 1971. India was by now militarily active in East Pakistan, training the Mukti Bahini armed resistance. Diplomacy had not been particularly effective in averting war. The few countries that did understand India's position were unwilling to put public pressure on Pakistan. And the country that possessed the most leverage over Pakistan—the United States—was driven to be the most energetic supporter of Yahya Khan.

By August, as India's hopes for a political solution to the crisis receded, it noted that the number of refugees cited by Pakistan, a fraction of the actual influx, was eerily close to the number of Muslims among the Bengali refugees. The implications were clear. Pakistan had no intention of allowing the Hindus to return to their homes. K. Subrahmanyam, who had advocated an early military intervention by India, weighed in again to persuasively suggest that the policy of abstention from direct involvement 'will only result in increased defence outlay for India, recurring expenditure on refugees, increased communal tension...erosion of the credibility of the Indian government and further sharply deteriorated security situation in eastern India and the likelihood of Pakistan creating trouble in Kashmir as a retaliation.' Most importantly, Subrahmanyam was arguing that India had the capacity not only to prevail in a military contest with Pakistan, but also to prevent intervention by the great powers.[66] This was an accurate assessment, as later events showed.

This time around, Subrahmanyam's views found resonance with Prime Minister Indira Gandhi. Towards the end of August 1971, she adopted a strategy of coercion towards Pakistan. By progressively increasing the military pressure on Pakistani forces in the east, she sought to convince the military regime that it would be better off seeking a negotiated settlement with Mujib than in persisting with a crackdown. In pursuit of this strategy, New Delhi stepped up its assistance to the Bengali fighters. Simultaneously,

India mounted strong diplomatic initiatives with the US, the Soviet Union, China, and the West.

Indira Gandhi was pressing all the diplomatic levers; she was not giving up on some bilateral coercion on Pakistan. She even appointed a new envoy to Pakistan to replace B. K. Acharya, who had retired in May 1971. This was a diplomat serving then as India's ambassador in Rome, Jai Kumar Atal. Meanwhile, in Islamabad, First Secretary Deb Mukharji and several of his colleagues were leaving station. Diplomatic missions in both countries were still functional, but were being pared down to minimum strength in a calibrated manner. One last and unpleasant duty Mukharji performed, as the head of chancery, before he left in August, in a 'body exchange' was to destroy the records of the mission in a furnace.[67]

BEAR HUGS

Russian influence had deepened in South Asia after the Soviet Union presided over the Tashkent Agreement of 1966 and ensured its satisfactory conclusion with some deft diplomacy. The Soviets had since then begun to seriously play a role as a peace conduit between India and Pakistan. In July 1968, Premier Alexei Kosygin wrote to Indira Gandhi, expressing hope that the two neighbours would be able to make progress in normalizing relations[68]. He had even recommended that the Indus Waters Treaty of 1960 could provide the framework for the solution of the problem posed by the Farakka Barrage, in sharing the waters of the Ganga between West Bengal and East Pakistan.

India's proactive ambassador in Moscow, D. P. Dhar, had great faith in the diplomatic heft of his hosts. He was also trusted back home—he was part of Indira Gandhi's clique of influential Kashmiri Pandit advisers. While Dhar's cables painted an optimistic picture of Soviet support for the secessionist movement in East Pakistan, and their willingness to turn the screws on West Pakistan, a more sobering portrait was presented by the Soviet envoy in New Delhi. He based his assessment on Pakistan's Foreign Secretary Sultan Khan saying that the Indian actions were being deeply resented in Pakistan and Indian fighters were infiltrating into East Pakistan to help the freedom fighters in Bengal.[69]

The Indo–Soviet Treaty was ready to be signed by July, with its famous Article IX, which called for mutual consultations in the event of an attack. India was still fighting shy of including a clause that gave the impression of an explicit military alliance. In the end, the impetus to sign the treaty came not from the Russians but from developments in the US. On 17 July, Kissinger met Indian ambassador L. K. Jha and told him that if China intervened in an India–Pakistan war, the United States would be unable to help India. Foreign Secretary T. N. Kaul sent a note to the prime minister, highlighting the US signal about potential

Chinese intervention. The note outlined the deterrence the treaty would enable against China or for any military support from the Soviets for Pakistan. National interest at this point very pointedly was privileged over the ideology of non-alignment.

It was at this stage that Indira Gandhi overcame her lingering doubts about the treaty and moved ahead to conclude it. Gandhi's instincts were right. Kissinger was to go on to actively encourage Chinese intervention, and this collusion needed to be balanced out. D. P. Dhar got the green light in Moscow to finalize negotiations. Within weeks, the foreign ministers of Russia and India, Andrei Gromyko and Sardar Swaran Singh, signed the treaty in New Delhi on 9 August 1971, signalling a decisive geopolitical shift, even as India and Pakistan hurtled inexorably towards conflict.

India's best-case scenario was now to get the benefit of Soviet support and Chinese neutrality in the case of conflict with Pakistan. Prime Minister Indira Gandhi was particularly keen not to alienate the Chinese and even entertained an idea of proposing a treaty similar to the Indo–Soviet treaty with the Chinese, before P. N. Haksar wisely talked her out of it. Haksar did not want Indira to repeat her father's error of trusting the 'inscrutable' Chinese beyond a point. India's policy nightmare was in preparing for a 'two-front situation', with China and Pakistan ganging up on it in a widening conflict. But China was reluctant to support Pakistan militarily. Part of the reluctance stemmed from its desire not to push India too far into the embrace of its now estranged communist ally, the Soviet Union.

The Soviet Union was fast becoming the most important external player in the 1971 South Asian crisis. On 6 September, Andrei Gromyko castigated the visiting foreign secretary of Pakistan Sultan Khan for the 'bloodshed and persecution' in the east. He insisted that the only solution was political and this was possible only if the Pakistan government 'stops its policy of repression and persecution. Only this will bring the refugees back, and other ways will fail'. Then came the warning: 'Please do not take any action that will oblige us to fulfil our obligations to a country with whom we have a treaty of friendship.' Gromyko then paused and switched over to English:

> 'The interpreter did not interpret me correctly. I did not use the word 'please'. I think you understand my meaning.' Sultan Khan responded to this dire warning to say that Pakistan would not take the initiative in starting hostilities but would defend itself if subject to an attack. Gromyko then advised, 'Restraint, restraint restraint! You must not yield to emotions.'[70]

Indira Gandhi arrived in Moscow on 27 September for a crucial round of consultations. She briefed the Soviets extensively. She requested them to work for a political solution, starting with Mujib's release and asked for military supplies to prepare for the contingency of war. The Soviet leaders agreed to consider these requests, but urged her to exercise restraint; that mostly translated into advice to avoid a wider war with Pakistan in the west. Indira Gandhi's visit changed the Soviet attitude to the war and persuaded them that they could trust Indira more than Yahya.

A DIPLOMATIC BLITZKRIEG

While Indira Gandhi was getting the expected support from the Soviet Union, she wanted to ensure that the rest of the world did not move to the American camp. She decided to campaign in Europe, particularly with Britain and France, veto-holding members of the United Nations Security Council. She embarked on a visit to a series of Western capitals—Brussels, Vienna, London, Paris, Bonn, Washington. This was to be her final effort for a peaceful resolution of the conflict. It would also demonstrate India's instincts to privilege a diplomatic over a military solution. Indira worked hard: interacting with host governments and engaging in public diplomacy with media, intellectuals, and artists. She gave multiple interviews; in one to the BBC, responding to a question on the moral case for the war, she likened the situation in East Pakistan to Hitler's rampage in Europe.[71]

The US leg of the tour was the toughest. On the morning of 4 November, Nixon and Indira Gandhi, flanked by Kissinger and Haksar, met at the Oval Office in the White House. Nixon and Kissinger were at that point acutely conscious of their stock with the Chinese and did not want to allow India to humiliate Pakistan and their reputation. Indira explained the Indian position at some length. The reality, she said, was that it was 'no longer realistic to expect East and West Pakistan to remain together… The crucial issue remains the future of Mujib.'[72]

The atmospherics of the meeting were not good, Nixon was wary of Indira. Nixon also had a bit of history with India. In the previous decade, he had not been particularly fond of Nehru either. He had visited the subcontinent in December 1953 on an Asian tour as vice president under Dwight Eisenhower, when he found Nehru siding with the Soviet Union. He found India's prime minister 'railing obsessively and interminably' against Pakistan and later called him 'arrogant, abrasive and suffocatingly self-righteous'. In contrast, he found Pakistan a country he would like 'to do everything for' since the Pakistanis were staunchly anti-communist and pro-American. He had been particularly impressed by one upwardly mobile General Ayub Khan, who would later become Pakistan's master. Soon after Nixon's visit, Eisenhower went ahead with the deal to provide military aid to Pakistan, which Pakistan promised would be used only to ward off communism and not to target India. The promise was, of course, broken in the next decade.

Nixon was aware of the peculiar circumstances of the South Asian conflicts of the previous decade. Nehru had asked Kennedy for help during the 1962 conflict with China; as a result, a small measure of military assistance came India's way. When Pakistan attacked India in 1965, the US was in the awkward position of providing arms to both sides, and had to soon pause that game. But this time around, geopolitical conditions were different, dictated by the Cold War. Nixon, egged on by Kissinger, had now decided to favour Pakistan's Yahya, the strongman whose suave reassurance was important to US Cold War games, even though he 'lacked the US president's complexity and keen intelligence'.[73]

In contrast, Nixon never developed a liking for Prime Minister Indira Gandhi. The Nixon tapes revealed the epithets for Mrs Gandhi the two patriarchal men deployed, like adolescent boys discussing a confusing encounter with a member of the opposite sex at a high school party. The tapes gave a transparent, if embarrassingly coarse, account of the American assessment of the meeting of 4 November. When Nixon remarked that Indira Gandhi was 'being a bitch', Kissinger observed that 'the Indians are bastards anyway. They're starting a war there.' Attempting to please his boss, Kissinger said, 'while she was a bitch, we got what we wanted too.... She will not be able to go home and say that the United States didn't give her a warm reception and therefore, in despair she's got to go to war.' Nixon famously replied, 'We really slobbered over the old witch.'[74]

The duo decided to play it cool at their meeting with Indira Gandhi the next morning, 5 November. It was, however, Gandhi who chose to remain icily aloof. She made no references to the crisis but instead quizzed Nixon about US foreign policy across the globe. A month later, Nixon told Kissinger that 'what I am concerned about, I really worry about, is whether or not I was too easy on the goddamn woman when she was here.... She was playing us. And you know the cool way she was the next day.... This woman suckered us.'

On the way back from the failed US sojourn, Indira Gandhi had equally unsuccessful meetings with smaller European countries. Belgium offered mediation in the United Nations. In response, Gandhi made her maximalist demand clear—'the only solution was for Mujib to be released and Bangladesh given its independence.'[75]

Around the same time, Pakistan's foreign minister Bhutto and foreign secretary Sultan Khan visited Beijing in early November and completely misread China's polite diplomatic noises. Bhutto later claimed to Yahya that China had assured Pakistan of its support in the event of war with India. China had, in fact, been more cautious and advised restraint. Soon after the visit, Brajesh Mishra sent an authoritative assessment of China's stance. Mishra concluded: 'China had adopted an attitude of restraint and is advising Pakistan to do the same.' It was also urging Pakistan to seek a political solution in East Pakistan. He went so far as to suggest that China wanted to keep its options open when it came to relations with India. Mishra's sources in Beijing had led him to assess that while China had assured Pakistan about the supply of arms, ammunition, and material, and of its support to Pakistan at the United Nations, 'China will not intervene in the event of war between India and Pakistan.' Indira Gandhi read Mishra's cable when in Bonn for her diplomatic outreach. Two days later, she told the West German foreign minister that she was 'not apprehensive of Chinese pressure on the borders of India, as China was occupied with its own internal problems'. Thanks to Mishra's astute diplomacy, India had assessed China correctly this time. The US and Pakistan had both misread the tea leaves.[76]

10

A SECOND PARTITION, A THIRD COUNTRY

High Commissioner Jai Kumar 'Makhi' Atal thought his first call on General Yahya Khan went off rather well, despite the dire state of ties in November 1971. Prime Minister Indira Gandhi had asked Atal to get going in his new posting in Islamabad shortly after her world tour, to draw attention to the East Pakistan crisis.

Associated with a princely family of Jaipur, Atal was also distantly related to the Nehru family. He had moved into the diplomatic service soon after Independence. He had been India's ambassador in Rome when the telegram arrived in early August: 'You have been selected as the High Commissioner to Pakistan. Join as soon as possible.' Atal was then enjoying what he thought was the last posting of an eventful career that began in 1936, when he joined the ICS. When Shekhar Dasgupta, first secretary in Rome, handed over the telegram to his ambassador and congratulated him, Atal asked his young colleague in mock wonder if the job was really worthy of felicitation. The India–Pakistan relationship was spiralling downwards. Dasgupta earnestly told his boss he was being entrusted with the job of a peacemaker at a critical stage.

It took a couple of months for Atal to get his diplomatic agrément and visa from Pakistan; he landed in Islamabad only on 11 November, for what turned out to be an ill-fated diplomatic mission. Atal also happened to be the last of the Indian envoys to claim past associations with Pakistan's leaders; Yahya was an old acquaintance from the pre-Partition days and also from the time Atal was deputy high commissioner in Pakistan in the early 1950s. In the backdrop of military action in eastern Pakistan, Atal would go on to have a few other meetings with the general in November and carry some last-minute peace proposals back and forth. Despite the tense stand-off between the two nations, Atal found time to indulge his passion for polo by getting special permission to play in Rawalpindi with the army brass. Incredibly, Yahya invited the Indian high commissioner to accompany him to inaugurate a Chinese cement plant, ostensibly to demonstrate that war was not on top of his mind. But the inauguration was ultimately cancelled. At forty days, Atal's tenure in Pakistan remains the shortest of any Indian high commissioner to Pakistan. But it was not short on adventure.

The war that Atal watched from Islamabad in 1971 marked the lowest point of the relationship between the two countries since 1947. A few weeks before Atal's arrival in Pakistan, Yahya had referred to Indira Gandhi as 'that woman'. The rude remark had peeved the Indian government, which had even lodged a protest against what was seen as Yahya's drunken outburst. When Atal casually raised this matter with Yahya, the dictator parried, 'Isn't she a woman?'

A LAST SHOT AT PEACE

Yahya did refer to Indira Gandhi more politely in an Eid message he gave Atal to carry to the Indian prime minister around 15 November. Atal was acutely conscious of, and chuffed by, his role as an instrument of wartime diplomacy. Atal had emphasized to Yahya that India was not seeking the break-up of Pakistan. He had concluded his conversation with Yahya with a discussion on the Eid letter, which, in its final form, contained some formulations suggested by the diplomat. Atal took Yahya's letter to Gandhi on 17 November. In addition to greetings for the festival of Eid coming up on 21 November, Atal carried also a secret five-point peace offer from the Pakistani president. Yahya was proposing that: India and Pakistan sign a non-aggression pact; India re-establish trade relations with East Pakistan; Nurul Amin (an elected Bengali politician opposed to Mujib) be installed as the head of a government for all Pakistan; the refugees return to East Pakistan; and a referendum be held in three years to determine whether or not East Pakistan wished to be free. The Pakistan high commissioner in Delhi was also pushing these proposals when he met Foreign Minister Swaran Singh and asked him for his views on Yahya's proposals.[1]

Indira Gandhi rejected the offer on the ground that the third and fifth points were unacceptable—the 1970 election results were valid and there was thus no need for a referendum. Atal was back in Islamabad on 25 November, with a fresh message from Mrs Gandhi that made it clear that she wanted neither war nor the partition of Pakistan. 'But Mujib must be released and the refugee problem must be settled.'[2]

On 27 November, India's cabinet formally turned down the proposals delivered by Atal after his meeting with Yahya. But upon his return to Islamabad, Atal downplayed the pushback he had received at home. While he was acutely aware that the countries were locked into a course of war, and the failure of his mission might accelerate the move towards conflict, he was seen in Delhi as having gone soft on Pakistan's dictator. On 27 November, the day India's cabinet had rejected the peace proposals, Atal told the US ambassador in Islamabad that Yahya was not an 'ogre' as made out in the Indian media and by various high officials in India. He said that 'though bound by the complexes of a military mind', Yahya was 'extremely amenable to suggestion and most desirous of ameliorating the tensions extant in the subcontinent.'[3] Atal then went on to make a dramatic proposal—he suggested a meeting between the East and West Pakistanis that could resolve the crisis.

Reporting on the meeting, the US ambassador in Islamabad, Joseph Farland, excitedly cabled an optimistic picture back home, with the Indian proposal for a meeting of a Pakistani government team with Awami League representatives in Tehran. Atal also discussed these ideas at length with Foreign Secretary Sultan Khan, on the evening of 27 November. The same evening, Farland met with Yahya to discuss Atal's proposals. Yahya said that in his opinion Atal was either 'amazingly uninformed' or was playing a 'most mischievous' role at this particularly critical time. Yahya said the former was likelier, since, in his judgement, Atal was honest in his efforts but apparently not adequately briefed. Farland agreed. Yet Yahya indicated that he was still willing to consider the substantive part of the proposal for a Tehran meeting, to avert a disastrous conflict.

A couple of days later, at the Yugoslav national day reception on 29 November, Farland had a less optimistic interaction with Atal. The US diplomat told Atal that Yahya was willing to consider the Indian proposal of a meeting in Tehran. To Farland's amazement, Atal said that this would take much too long and hence he had a new and even more dramatic idea—the immediate formation of a civilian government by Yahya in Pakistan, concomitant with the transfer of power. This government could then in turn institute conversations with the representative of Bangladesh. This left Farland's head spinning. The American cabled home his disappointment at the Indian diplomat's lack of coherence. Farland heard Atal repeat this idea at the reception to some other diplomats, who later told him that Atal may be a 'less than responsible diplomat'.

When Atal privately met the US ambassador again the next morning, 30 November, he had dropped the proposal of the previous evening, for negotiations between civilian governments, and had reverted to his original proposal of talks between the Awami League and Yahya Khan. Knowing Farland's proximity with Yahya, Atal asked him to pass on his proposals to Yahya. He cited the example of conversations on power-sharing that the British government had with Nehru before Partition and the transfer of power. He emphasized that no solution was possible without including Mujib in the mix. Despite his scepticism, Farland prepared a top-secret aide-memoire with these proposals and sent them to Yahya's attention.

Farland concluded that while Atal was probably being sincere in making these proposals for talks between the Awami League and the Government of Pakistan, it was likely that he did not have the complete backing and clear instructions of his government to either make the proposals or to deliver on them even if Pakistan agreed. Farland decided not to push the proposal with either the Pakistanis or his own government.

Atal, in his interactions with the US ambassador, projected greater optimism than he was feeling. He was possibly not in the loop where Delhi's strategic planning was concerned, but may have been used to assess the mood in Pakistan. India was by now deeply involved in military action within East Bengal, where it was continuing to train the Mukti Bahini. Even as Atal continued with his futile peace initiative, perhaps with not enough sense of the larger forces at play that had made war inevitable, Indira Gandhi had returned from a tour of the border areas to Delhi on 29 November, and rejected another floating diplomatic idea: of referring the India–Pakistan matter to the UN. She was not about to repeat the error her father made in 1948, one that was sitting heavy on Indian diplomacy. As the battle escalated in the east, Mrs Gandhi now firmly demanded the withdrawal of West Pakistan troops from East Pakistan.[4]

By the end of November, Yahya's remaining hopes for intervention by the great powers had been deflated. The only major power somewhat willing to raise this matter in the United Nations was the US. But the Soviet Union made it clear it would block any moves to summon the UN Security Council. The full-scale invasion was yet to come. On 29 November, Yahya made a tentative decision to open the western front and finally decided on this course of action the next day. The D-Day Pakistan originally chose was 2 December, but this was postponed to 3 December.

Yahya was also bracing for conflict by consolidating his hold on power. On 26 November, he had briefed Bhutto on the outline of a new Constitution designed by his experts, which would allow Yahya to remain president, supreme commander, and army commander-in-chief, as well as retain martial law powers. Four days later, on 30 November, he asked Bhutto to join a coalition government that would be headed by Nurul Amin, the old Bengali loyalist, who was one of only two non-Awami League members of the National Assembly elected from East Pakistan in 1970. Bhutto agreed to do so, provided he was designated deputy premier and foreign minister. Yahya and Bhutto struck their own power-sharing deal on the eve of the war.[5]

Despite multiple reports of Indian troops crossing over into East Pakistan, Prime Minister Indira Gandhi had refused to publicly confirm if this was true. In the last week of November, the prime minister gave the go-ahead for a full-scale attack on East Pakistan. D-Day for India had been set for 4 December.

WAR

In New Delhi, Defence Secretary K. B. Lall rushed into the operations room at the army headquarters at 5 p.m. on 3 December. Lall told General Manekshaw that the western army commander had just called to say that three Indian airfields in Punjab were under attack by Pakistani aircraft. Both the prime minister and defence minister were out of Delhi and could not immediately be contacted. Manekshaw ordered the commanders on the western front to put into effect their operational battle plans.

India's planners had been waiting for Pakistan to make the error of invasion. The prime minister's secretary, P. N. Dhar, told Ambassador D. P. Dhar of Napoleon's advice: 'Never interrupt an enemy when he is making a mistake.' D. P. Dhar was on the prime minister's plane, travelling with her from Calcutta, when the pilot informed them of the Pakistani air strikes. He appeared unsurprised and remarked, 'The fool has done exactly what I had expected.'

Indira Gandhi was received as she landed by the defence minister and driven straight to army headquarters for a briefing. Soon the war cabinet was meeting in India. It decided to declare hostilities on Pakistan and to recognize Bangladesh. The war officially began for India on the morning of 4 December 1971.

ى

High Commissioner Atal walked quietly into the chatter of a diplomatic reception in Islamabad, on 3 December, knowing it was not just another day. The briefing cables from back home were getting more alarming. Pakistan's capital was buzzing with rumours that India would attack Pakistan on 4 December, provoking a full-scale conflict in both wings. Across the border, India had definitive intelligence inputs of a planned pre-emptive air strike from West Pakistan on 3 December.

The bombing began that evening, even as Atal chatted with fellow guests at the reception—a farewell for the departing ambassador of Libya at their embassy. Some information on the start of the war even trickled into the reception.

Pakistan's attack had drawn inspiration from a war four years earlier when a pre-emptive air strike by Israel had knocked the Egyptian Air Force out of action. Pakistan's strikes, however, failed to have much impact on India's air capability, but signalled the moment their most serious military conflict formally began.

Nervous conversation at the embassy focused on the troubled border; anxious foreign diplomats tried to divine information from clueless Pakistani guests—judges, politicians, and bureaucrats. Atal overheard a Pakistani official confidently tell the Egyptian ambassador that India had attacked on the ground, so the Pakistani Air Force was taking retaliatory action. The Egyptian ambassador turned quizzically to Atal, who responded within earshot of several Pakistani guests: 'Excellency, do you think Indians are such bloody fools as to scratch on the ground and give the Pakistanis a chance to attack by air?' The Russian ambassador and some other diplomats squirmed at Atal's bravado and counselled him to leave the room, brimming as it was with Pakistani military officers. But Atal was in an expansive mood and insisted on making his views known to all he encountered.

Atal did leave the reception before it ended and had his driver take him straight to the nearby Indian chancery building. His juniors had been camping in the office for days, given the imminence of hostilities and the lockdown protocols in place. The embassy staff had been pulled in from homes spread all over Islamabad to hole up in the chancery. Atal briefly exchanged notes with his colleagues and then left for his own residence, in the F6 sector, the elite Islamabad neighbourhood favoured by diplomats, which was a fifteen-minute drive away.

Not long after he reached home, a few men in civvies walked into his unguarded residence and asked Atal to step out. He quietly obeyed. Outside on the road were three or four cars with men in military and police uniforms. Atal was ushered into a car. A man he did not recognize wordlessly slipped into the rear seat. After a short drive, Atal was taken up two flights of a tall building. He was propelled into a dark room where another man was seated at a table. Without introducing himself, his inquisitor growled: 'India has attacked us, we are at war, you are an ordinary prisoner of war. What have you to say?'

Atal guessed his diplomatic immunity meant nothing to his interrogator or even to his host government at that point. A war would lawfully have required diplomats to be repatriated or exchanged under the Vienna Convention. Taking them prisoner was, of course, illegal. But these niceties did not seem to matter at that moment. Atal remained unfazed: 'If I am a prisoner of war, I have nothing to say except that don't beat up or kill my men and don't insult and burn my flag.'

The men drove Atal back to his residence, which stood undefended on the Margalla road, with neither a garden nor compound to buffer it from aggressors. His minders ordered Atal to remain in the bedroom. The house was now surrounded by dozens of uniformed men with automatic weapons. The electricity had been shut off. It was dark. Atal's only Indian domestic helper was nowhere to be seen. His Indian chauffeur was locked up inside the garage with the diplomatic car.

Atal was effectively a prisoner of war in Pakistan, with his diplomatic status seemingly extinguished as the war began. Alone in his bedroom, Atal took stock of his situation. His electricity and telephone connections had been cut; he was incommunicado. He rushed to fill the bathtub, fearing the water supply would also go quickly. The soldiers outside were talking. Perhaps for his benefit, they said that Pakistan's air strikes had destroyed Indian airbases in Srinagar, Patiala, Delhi, and Agra; Bombay had been left burning.

This news had Atal anxious and worried, but also surprised: how could so much damage have been inflicted so quickly on India's air defences? He had a pilot's licence from Oxford and understood how aircraft operated. Sleep eluded him that night, so he sat on a chair near a window, anxiously peering out at a portion of Islamabad where he could see no lights nor hear any sound of flying aircraft. 'It was a terrible feeling,' he recalled later, 'to find oneself so completely cut off and blocked from any source of information.'

Near dawn, he heard the sound of planes flying high. He tried again to peek from the window but the guards ordered him in with pointed rifles. As a trained pilot, it was not hard for Atal to pinpoint the direction in which these planes were heading. They remained high, not landing or taking off. He was convinced they were Indian and not Pakistani aircraft, since they were flying north, not east, over Pakistani territory. This made him feel a little less depressed and a little more hopeful that India's air force had not been crippled by his host country's attack.

For three days after the war began, Atal remained a prisoner of war, under house arrest till the Red Cross took over. An official of the Red Cross came to see him on 6 December, along with Pakistan's chief of protocol. Atal was asked to sign a declaration saying that all his mission staff were alive and safe. Atal refused to sign off on the paper till he was satisfied that his staff were indeed safe. Atal insisted that his deputy, Ashok Chib, accompany him to all the venues where his colleagues were incarcerated, so that they could do a head count before signing the Red Cross form.

⸎

On 6 December, the Indian government announced its formal recognition of the government of Bangladesh. On the battlefield, India had an overwhelming advantage. A limited West Pakistani force that had descended on the east stood little chance in combating the combined might of a strengthened Indian Army and well-trained Mukti Bahini fighters. On 9 December, Lieutenant General A. A. K. Niazi, the theatre commander in the east, sent a message to Rawalpindi painting a desperate military picture: 'Situation extremely critical.... We will go on fighting and do our best.' Niazi wrote, 'Orders to own troops issued to hold on until the last man last round which may not be too long....'[6]

The same day, six days after the war began, the Swiss ambassador paid Atal a visit to inform him that Switzerland had agreed to look after India's diplomatic interests in Pakistan and that he was under Swiss protection. He handed over a Swiss flag to fly at the embassy residence. Atal flew the Swiss flag and took custody of the Indian flag that he had been zealously flying till then. Atal was then locked up in his home again, this time in better conditions than before, along with the Embassy doctor, Colonel Saksena. Here he remained incommunicado for the next two weeks. Atal painstakingly maintained a diary noting the movement of aircraft each day, hoping this data would be of some use back home. Atal kept the flag in his bedroom and finally wrapped it around himself when he carried it to India after the war was over. The flag still flies proudly on national days in Atal's residence in Jaipur, now occupied by his son.

WHITE HOUSE ILLUSIONS

Global forces had an important influence on the outcome of the war of 1971. The US had decided to tilt towards Pakistan, largely to protect their new channel and reputation with the Chinese. Nixon and Kissinger also worked themselves up to believe that India sought not only to liberate East Pakistan, but thereafter also wanted to launch a major attack on West Pakistan to incorporate into India some parts of POK.[7] This inference, based on random CIA reports, fit well into the White House preconceptions about Indira Gandhi and Yahya Khan. The larger strategic goal of fighting the Cold War was blinding the American leadership to the realities on the ground. The US took multiple measures after the hostilities began on 4 December. Nixon cut off economic aid to India, sought to remove the arms embargo on Pakistan, and tried to draw China into the fray.

Beyond the objective of challenging India and supporting Pakistan, as we have seen, the US was at this stage courting China to challenge its primary Cold War adversary—the Soviet Union. It wanted to enhance its reputation of reliability for Beijing. Kissinger and Nixon worked to bring every bit of diplomatic pressure on India. They used whatever levers they had with the Soviet Union and China. Kissinger was arguing to Nixon that it was necessary to rescue US credibility in a crisis 'where a Soviet stooge, supported with Soviet arms, is overrunning a country that is an American ally'.

The UN Security Council was ringing with calls for the cessation of hostilities and vetoes to counter them. The issue was debated in the General Assembly in a marathon session that ran late into the night of 7 December. Both India and Pakistan sent their foreign ministers for the next round of diplomatic sparring at the United Nations.

But the fate of the South Asian war was also being determined outside the UN, in some pointed diplomatic exchanges between two Cold War adversaries and Security Council members. Nixon made a clever argument to the Russians when Soviet agriculture minister Vladimir Muskievich visited Washington, 'If the Indians continue to wipe out resistance in East Pakistan and then move against West Pakistan, we then, inevitably, look to a confrontation. Because you see the Soviet Union has a treaty with India; we have one with Pakistan.' The references to a US–Pakistan treaty were significant, but a bluff. On 7 December, Kissinger had asked Pakistan's ambassador to the US to communicate with the State Department and 'invoke its mutual security treaty.' However, there was no such treaty in place. The only extant agreement, which had been signed in March 1959 under the Eisenhower administration, pertained to commitments under Pakistan's membership in the Baghdad Pact and dealt with the contingency of aggression by a communist country. Under the Kennedy administration in late 1962, the US had given an 'assurance' to Pakistan through an aide memoire, of US aid in case of an attack by India. But neither of these amounted to a defence 'treaty'.[8]

In order to complete the deception, or simply because he had not studied the details, Kissinger, in a meeting with Soviet diplomat Yuli Vorontsov on 10 December, referred to a secret protocol in the US–Pakistan agreement. This ploy succeeded in alarming the Russians. Vorontsov cabled Moscow that from Kissinger's language he could infer that this military aid involved 'moving US aircraft carriers and naval forces in general closer to the subcontinent'. He correctly assessed that the Americans were more interested in the western border between Pakistan and India and may have accepted the fact of the situation in East Pakistan being decided in favour of India.[9] The same day, Nixon instructed the largest aircraft carrier in the US Navy, the USS *Enterprise* to move from South Vietnam into the Strait of Malacca and onward to the Bay of Bengal.

Vorontsov and Maskevich sent reports which alarmed Moscow. The Soviets in turn started leaning on India. Indira Gandhi had to pull out her diplomatic weapons. She sent her trusted adviser and former ambassador to Moscow D. P. Dhar with a letter to Premier Kosygin saying 'we have no design on the territory of others nor do we have any desire to destroy Pakistan'.[10] She reiterated the demand that Pakistan withdraw forces from Bangladesh and reach a peaceful settlement. Without such a settlement, 'ten million refugees would not return to their homeland.'[11]

India was in no mood to rattle the cage in West Pakistan and open up a western front giving the Americans an excuse for intervention. Haksar had written to the Indian defence secretary K. B. Lall not to give any impression of wanting to 'detach parts of West Pakistan as well as that of Azad Kashmir'. India was repeatedly reassuring the Soviet leadership that 'we have no repeat no territorial ambitions either in West or East Pakistan. Our recognition of Bangladesh is a guarantee against any territorial ambitions in the east and our position in the West is purely defensive.'[12]

Pakistan had correctly gauged India's reluctance to open a western front. But by attacking from the west, the Pakistan Army was hoping to relieve pressure in the east, and to 'buy time for international action' to dampen the conflict. The Pakistani army's concern about an Indian invasion was accompanied ironically by an irrational 'overconfidence' in the 'innate superiority of the Muslim soldier' and an institutional myth that this human strength differential had overcome India in 1965. This was reinforced by the gendered negative view of India's leadership where Mrs Gandhi was seen as not tough enough to match the macho leaders of Pakistan.[13]

As the hostilities ramped up, India asked the Soviet Union to make a public announcement that intervention by any third parties—a reference to both US and China—could not but aggravate the situation in every way. The Soviets were reassured of India's intentions, but did not wish to make any public announcement.

Nixon and Kissinger were now on tenterhooks. The Soviet Union was not stemming the war in East Pakistan. The new geopolitics involving China was confusing them. White House chief of staff Alexander Haig interrupted an Oval Office conversation on 12 December to say that the Chinese wanted to meet urgently. Kissinger thought this was totally unprecedented and felt 'they are going to move'. Kissinger warned Nixon: 'If the Soviets move against them [the Chinese], and we don't do anything, we'll be finished.' Nixon asked, 'So what do we do if the Soviets move against them? Start lobbing nuclear weapons in, is that what you mean?' Kissinger replied, 'Well, if the Soviets move against them in these conditions and succeed, that will be the final showdown.' He added, 'If the Russians get away with facing down the Chinese and if the Indians get away with licking the Pakistanis.... We may be looking right down the gun barrel.'[14]

Nixon and Kissinger were both inaccurate and irresponsible in this reckless speculation. The Chinese had in fact sent a message to the US to the effect that they had carefully studied the options and felt that the Security Council should reconvene and push for a resolution calling for a ceasefire and mutual withdrawals. They were thus favouring diplomatic rather than military action. There was not a word about moving against India. Or a posture against the Soviet Union. Kissinger's gambit with China to check the war had failed. The Chinese had refrained from acting because they were not inclined to militarily back Pakistan, they did not want to aggravate their problems with India and push it closer to the Soviet Union. India's diplomacy was also working. Indira Gandhi had written to China the previous day seeking its understanding of India's predicament and asking Zhou to exercise his undoubted influence on Yahya to acknowledge the will of the Bengalis.[15]

With both the Russian and Chinese gambits having failed, and its appetite for direct intervention lost, the US reluctantly directed its attention to multilateral diplomacy at the United Nations. On 14 December, the Soviet leadership sent a message to Nixon that, 'we have firm assurances by the Indian leadership that India had no plans of seizing West Pakistan territory'.[16] The same day, a draft resolution came up in the Security Council, tabled by Poland, then a Soviet proxy, outlining conditions of the ceasefire.

Before the resolution came to the Security Council, Yahya Khan spoke to Bhutto on the telephone and told him that the Polish resolution looked good: 'We should accept it.' Bhutto had replied, 'I can't hear you.' When Yahya repeated himself several times Bhutto only said, 'What what?' When the phone operator in New York intervened to inform them that there was nothing wrong with the connection, Bhutto told her to 'shut up'. Clearly, Bhutto had no intention of following Yahya's instructions. Bhutto went on to make a moving speech at the Security Council meeting and closed by declaring, 'I will not be a party to the ignominious surrender of part of my country. You can take your Security Council. Here you are. I am going.' Bhutto then tore up the resolution papers with a dramatic flourish and stormed out of the meeting.[17] That spelt the end of the Polish resolution. Bhutto's decision to walk out of the UN triggered Pakistan's surrender on the battlefield and a decisive victory for India.

The war ended at 4.55 p.m. on 16 December, thirteen days after it began, when in Dacca, General Niazi unbuttoned his epaulettes, removed his revolver and handed it to Lieutenant General J. S. Arora. He then went on to sign the Instrument of Surrender. The speed and scale of the operation made the victory decisive. India held 93,000 prisoners of war.[18] The same evening, India announced a unilateral ceasefire on the western front, effective from 17 December.

The eventual outcome was influenced by chance and circumstance; it was not what the planners began with. The contingency plan drawn up by the Indian Army did not specify the capture of Dacca as the military aim, nor did the subsequent modifications to the war plan identify it as the main objective or earmark resources for each capture.[19]

Had Bhutto accepted Yahya's advice and accepted the UN resolution, Pakistani troops may not have needed to surrender. Bhutto seems to have played a larger and more clever game. Military analyst Raghavan plausibly observed:

Singed by his experiences with the military, both under Ayub and Yahya, Bhutto seems to have concluded that the new Pakistan must be built on the ash heap of the army's decisive defeat. He was not wrong. Bhutto's decision to walk out of the Security Council saved the day for India and precipitated the ceasefire, leading to a decisive and unambiguous victory for India.[20]

For the Americans, the creation of Bangladesh was a done deal and the saving of West Pakistan was the illusion of success they created. For Indira Gandhi, it was unthinkable for India to enter West Pakistan where it had no political base, as against Bangladesh, where it had political allies in Mujib and his forces.[21]

'It's the Russians working for us,' said Nixon when he met Kissinger.

'Congratulations Mr President,' said Kissinger, 'you have saved West Pakistan.' Writing their respective self-congratulatory memoirs later, both Nixon and Kissinger claimed credit for saving West Pakistan. 'By using diplomatic signals and behind the scenes pressures,' wrote Nixon, 'we had been able to save West Pakistan from the imminent threat of Indian aggression and domination.' Kissinger went a step further, 'There is no doubt in my mind, that it (the declaration of ceasefire) was a reluctant decision resulting from severe pressure which in turn grew out of American insistence, including the fleet movement.'

However, India never had West Pakistan in its sights. In February 1972, Ambassador L. K. Jha wrote to P. N. Haksar about the effort to track down the alleged cabinet source for the intelligence report on the prime minister's intention to attack Pakistan. Indira Gandhi wrote on the margins of that letter: 'At NO time have I ever made such a statement. Besides even a discussion had not taken place at any Cabinet meeting.'[22]

Clearly, Nixon and Kissinger had overplayed the importance of an intelligence source that helped them rationalize their desire to project resolve to China and the Soviet Union. The problem, concludes Raghavan, was not just deception but also self-deception:

The only practical consequence of the aggressive US posturing was to spur the Indians to capture Dacca and seal their victory—objectives that had not been on their strategic horizons when the war began. This was Nixon and Kissinger's war of illusions. In retrospect, they came across not as tough statesmen tilting toward their ally but as a picaresque pair tilting at windmills.[23]

The day the ceasefire came into effect on 17 December, India's chancery in Islamabad faced chaos—Pakistan Army guards disappeared and threatening mobs appeared on the scene. However, the situation was eventually contained, no one was injured.

Atal and all Indian personnel from Karachi and Islamabad finally made it home on 22 December on a Swissair aircraft. Atal and his 159 colleagues had left behind much of their personal possessions in Pakistan and most of their earnings in Pakistani bank accounts. These savings were not returned till a year later at miserably depreciated rates. They felt bitter about the Indian government being more generous in allowing Pakistani nationals to withdraw their money, move out of their homes and residences, and for Pakistani students to even take exams in Agra. But Atal asked his colleagues to refrain from speaking of this publicly in order not to further aggravate the post-war hostility.

The fate of the Indian team in Islamabad had been replicated in Karachi.

K. N. Bakshi, assistant high commissioner during the war, was living in Clifton at the former ambassadorial residence, a neighbour of Zulfikar Ali Bhutto. Bakshi had watched with horror the 'Rape of Bangladesh' in March and was put under house arrest along with his colleagues on 3 December, when the war began. Bakshi then spent the next few days in the chancery, sleeping on sofas and eating the 'meagre emergency rations we had kept for such a situation'. He was eventually shifted to his residence but not allowed to meet anyone, except the Swiss consul general. The officials from Karachi were then repatriated to India along with their colleagues from Islamabad, in the same Swissair flight on 22 December.

By the time India's diplomatic prisoners were released after the war, power in Pakistan had moved from Yahya to Bhutto. A weakened army had yielded power in what was effectively a civilian coup. Atal was even taken for a farewell call on Bhutto on 21 December, now the new President of Pakistan. Atal spoke from his pre-war brief, about asking for the release of Mujibur Rahman. Bhutto countered that the 93,000 prisoners India had taken from East Pakistan should be released as well. Atal softly said to him he would try. Bhutto spun this polite assurance from the departing Indian envoy—just released from house arrest—to mean that India had promised an exchange of prisoners for the leader of East Pakistan.

THREE-NATION SOLUTION
The complex interplay of global forces that precipitated the events of 1971 did not permit any simplistic conclusion about the inevitability of the birth of Bangladesh. The creation of the new nation must no doubt be located in the larger context of the rapid geopolitical realignment of the era. But human agency and human folly contributed to it, as much as global realignment.

Raghavan has credibly argued that the break-up of Pakistan can only be understood by situating these events in a wider global context and by examining the interplay between domestic, regional, and international realities. The geopolitical context of the late 1960s and early 1970s was shaped by three broad historical processes, suggests Raghavan, each poised at an interesting conjuncture. The decolonization of the European empires that had begun in the aftermath of World War II gathered pace in the late 1950s. Then there was the Cold War which had begun in Europe as an ideological and security competition between the United States and the Soviet Union, backed by their allies. By the mid-1960s, the rivalry in Europe had stabilized, but the Cold War had gone global, and its hottest locales were in the developing world. The third and incipient historical current that swirled through the period was globalization, spurred by unprecedented improvements in transport, communications, and information technology. The confluence of these three processes shaped the origins, course, and outcome of the Bangladesh crisis.[24] Against this backdrop, India's diplomacy had its finest hour. India's politicians, military leaders, and diplomats came together to craft and improvise an approach that helped India realize its internal, regional, and global objectives. Pakistan, in contrast, lost half its territory as it failed to manage its internal contradictions or its military strategy or to use the shifting geopolitical currents.

An important question to be asked is whether India's intervention early in the crisis of 1971 could have saved lives. In his first meeting with D. P. Dhar in January 1972, Mujibur Rahman asked, 'Why did India not intervene soon after the army crackdown in Bangladesh?' Such an intervention would surely have saved so much suffering and lives. Such an intervention had been proposed by K. Subrahmanyam. In retrospect, concludes Raghavan, the case for an early intervention in May 1971 seems strong. For one thing the Pakistani military deployment in the eastern wing had not yet reached the levels that it eventually would. A swift intervention may not have been as adverse as the Indian military and political leadership had assumed it could be.

11

LINE OF CONTROL

India's foreign minister Swaran Singh was the first to propose a post-war peace conference. He said in New York, on 22 December 1971, on the day Atal returned home, that he was prepared to go to Islamabad and 'we will welcome them if they want to come to Delhi'. Indira Gandhi similarly said in her statements in December and January that India was willing to hold bilateral talks to settle issues like the repatriation of the prisoners of war and the vacation of the territories occupied during the war, apart from the normalization and improvement of relations between the two countries. India said this again on 14 February 1972 to UN Secretary General Kurt Waldheim, through Samarendra Sen, now its permanent representative to the UN in New York.

India was pointedly ready for bilateral talks without any third-party mediation and without any preconditions, with the aim of achieving 'durable peace in the subcontinent'. The message was clear: it could no longer be the UN brokering the ceasefire, as in 1949, or a major power like the Soviet Union doing so, as in Tashkent in 1966. Bhutto eventually agreed to a summit meeting with Indira Gandhi that summer, to be preceded by a discussion between officials on the agenda. After three days of official-level meetings from 26 April in Murree, a hill resort in Pakistan, the two sides agreed on an agenda for a summit to be held in Simla on 27 June.

The Indian diplomatic crew that had been expelled from Pakistan was soon at headquarters in Delhi, taking the lead in crafting policy for a peace initiative, after the war they had experienced in enemy territory. Deputy High Commissioner Ashok Chib became the joint secretary or head of the Pakistan division in the Ministry of External Affairs; K. N. Bakshi who had been assistant high commissioner in Karachi was appointed his deputy. Later, Naresh Dayal, who had served in Islamabad, joined the team. This was the core group in MEA that prepared for the Simla summit. The prime minister had asked D. P. Dhar to lead the official delegation.

Dhar called Bakshi one day and asked him to take ten days off and produce a draft of what could be a possible agreement at the summit. Dhar had the experience; he had been asked by Indira Gandhi to draft and negotiate the Indo–Soviet treaty the previous year, a task he had accomplished successfully. Bakshi got down to work and produced a draft agreement that Dhar worked on. Dhar was seen by his team as a realist, a pragmatist who understood the Pakistani mindset and India's national interests. His preparations were so thorough that he had even got his team to script a possible dialogue between the prime minister and Bhutto during their first one-to-one meeting. Bakshi, with his Karachi experience, kept flagging the point that Bhutto was not trustworthy: 'We cannot depend upon him...even his mother could not fully trust him'.[1]

Bhutto arrived to a warm welcome in Simla. He had brought along some prominent members of the Opposition to Simla to signal democratic consensus in his country behind the peace move. His daughter and future prime minister, Benazir, accompanied him. The tortuous talks of five days seemed headed for failure, when Bhutto asked for a late-night farewell call on Indira Gandhi. In their one-on-one meeting, Bhutto 'convincingly argued' that given time, he would be 'able to bring public opinion in Pakistan around to accepting the Line of Control, with marginal adjustments, as the permanent international boundary'. He told her,' Aap mujh per bharosa rakhen (please trust me).' He pleaded that 'if he was seen as having yieded to pressure, the Pakistan Army, defeated though it might be, would have his head.'[2]

Indira Gandhi relented and an agreement was hammered out in the wee hours of 2 July. It underlined the principle of bilateralism, a shift away from the dependence on major powers, or the United Nations, to intervene in India–Pakistan issues. But it failed to explicitly capture Bhutto's promise to convert the LoC into an international boundary.

THE SPIRIT OF SIMLA

The Simla Agreement has been analysed threadbare over the decades and particularly on its milestone birthdays. It was mostly welcomed at that time in the two countries, even though a few critics on both sides panned it. Scholars, diplomats, and historians have judged it from various vantage points ever since.

To Kewal Singh, who was posted in Bonn in 1972, three of the pact's provisions pointed to the dawn of a new era in the subcontinent, even though his enthusiasm was 'tempered by some anxieties'.[3] These were: the decisions to end the state of confrontation and renounce the use of force to settle future disputes and differences; the promotion of commercial, cultural exchanges, and travel, to further people to people links; and the commitment to put an end to adverse propaganda to reverse the suspicion, distrust, and hatred between the countries.

Observers at the time and subsequently have compared the Simla Agreement favourably with the Tashkent Agreement that had come six years earlier. The two agreements came about in similar circumstances after the two countries had gone to war. In both cases, Pakistan had suffered serious setbacks and, in 1971, absolute defeat. Three issues confronted peacemakers on both occasions: the return of prisoners of war; the vacation of territory; and the restoration of peace and normalcy. In both cases, the belligerents decided to vacate the conquered territories and to restore normalcy in relations. In each agreement, the parties reaffirmed their allegiance to the UN charter and committed themselves to settling future differences or disputes peacefully. Both agreements placed a premium on economic, cultural, and commercial cooperation.

But there were some striking differences. First, a military dictator, Ayub Khan, had signed the Tashkent declaration in the face of total opposition from his civilian foreign minister, Bhutto. In Simla, it was Bhutto, as president of Pakistan, riding on a huge mandate from the 1970 election, who signed the agreement, after having effectively displaced a disgraced military regime that had lost half of his country's territory.

Second, the attitude of the people of Pakistan was different in the two cases. In the 1965 war, the people of West Pakistan were fed on the propaganda that Pakistan had bravely gone to liberate Kashmir and had almost succeeded. These hopes were not translated into the Tashkent Agreement. The people had eventually found out that their leaders had deceived them and that Pakistan had failed in its venture to retrieve Kashmir. The Tashkent declaration had thus met with widespread protest from January 1966 onwards, leading to Ayub's eventual downfall. In the case of the Simla Agreement, Bhutto was seen to be trying to retrieve the consequences of the reckless policies of military dictators President Ayub Khan and later President Yahya Khan. The Pakistani public now appeared to be confident that Bhutto was representing the people's voice in making the best of the situation.

Third, the Tashkent declaration had restored the status quo in terms of territory, asking troops to be withdrawn to the ceasefire positions as on 5 August 1965. In Simla however 'the Line of Control' was agreed to as the boundary that the two forces had to respect. This was effectively a rejection of the UN-supervised ceasefire line that had been considered valid for two decades.

Fourth, and most important, was the discussion on the status of Kashmir. Tashkent had seen a complete breakdown of negotiations on the Kashmir issue. The Pakistani delegation had been keen to keep the issue on the front burner while India had insisted that the matter had been settled nine years earlier in 1957, by a duly elected Kashmir constituent assembly and Kashmir was thus an integral part of India. In the final version, India had agreed to a formulation that said, 'Jammu and Kashmir was discussed and each of the sides set forth its respective position.' India had insisted that Kashmir was an integral part of India and outside powers, including the UN, had no locus standi to question it. For Ayub Khan, this one-line formulation had provided a face-saving device, even though Bhutto remained opposed to the agreement.[4]

In Simla, the talks had also broken down on the Kashmir issue. However, Bhutto retrieved the situation with some desperate diplomacy. He made the persuasive but deceptive plea that a 'sustainable solution' was not possible if he was seen to have surrendered the Pakistani position and accepted the LoC as the new international boundary. For India, an acceptance by Pakistan of the principle of a peaceful and bilateral solution to the Kashmir issue, without any outside mediation or intervention, seemed at that point a reasonable interim solution.

The Simla spirit dissipated rapidly just as the Tashkent spirit had disappeared as soon as the ink was dry. Prime Minister Indira Gandhi told Kewal Singh, who had in December 1972 returned as foreign secretary and a key adviser on Pakistan, that Bhutto had gone back on his solemn commitments. Bhutto had told Mrs Gandhi in Simla that he had himself been transformed from being a believer in confrontation against India to one who believed in cooperation as the way forward. But he had turned belligerent in his pronouncements within a year of the Simla Agreement. He had also failed to deliver on his commitment related to the recognition of Bangladesh.[5]

To many, the Simla outcome reinforced the view that India had not only won a decisive military victory, but had also exorcised the two-nation theory that had haunted the subcontinent since 1947. However, the break-up of Pakistan was not inevitable. As has been noted, it was influenced by decolonization, the Cold War, and incipient globalization interacting in ways 'far from predictable'.[6]

Over the last half century several arguments have been made that Indira Gandhi won the war but lost the peace—that she failed to use the historic opportunity presented by the victory to impose a final settlement on Kashmir. Perhaps one strong reason was that Indian leaders of the time were betting on an internal transformation of Pakistan's polity after a cathartic defeat. That was a bet that did not pay off.

P. N. Haksar had persuasively argued with Indira Gandhi about the 'Versailles effect' that led the West to conclude a peace with a Germany defeated during World War I and imposing humiliating terms that led to the rise of Nazism and World War II. Also, Gandhi felt she herself did not have the mandate of foreclosing the option of wresting POK back from Pakistan by force. The respect that India showed a defeated Pakistan laid the basis for a stable India–Pakistan relationship, but also precluded the possibility of external intervention in bilateral disputes. Most importantly, by converting the ceasefire line in Kashmir to a Line of Control that would gradually assume the characteristics of an international border, the decision-makers of the day saw prospects of an eventual settlement of the Kashmir dispute. Bhutto had then agreed that 'an agreement will emerge in the foreseeable future. It will evolve into a settlement. Let there be a line of peace; let people come and go; Let us not fight over it.'[7]

It did not quite work out that way. Bhutto rapidly retracted from his position. By 1973, he was talking of waging a 1,000-year war against India, as Pakistan's new prime minister under a new constitution.[8] By mid-1974, neither Bhutto nor Indira Gandhi had the political will or capital to forge a lasting settlement. Some historians have argued that if India had rammed through a final settlement in Kashmir, it is quite likely that the Pakistan Army would have deposed Bhutto even before it actually did.[9] More than half a century later, a robust debate still rages on both the 1971 war and the 1972 peace deal.

PRISONERS OF WAR

Indira Gandhi wrote to Bhutto on 24 January 1973 that the two sides should meet early to discuss plans to resume communications and mobility in accordance with the third clause of the Simla Agreement and to establish a durable peace. But Bhutto was weighed down by the political burden of the 93,000 captured Pakistani POWs still in Indian custody;[10] this made the normalization of relations between the two countries almost impossible.

Soon after elections in Bangladesh in March 1973, Indira sent the trusted Haksar as a special envoy, along with Foreign Secretary Kewal Singh, to explore some 'bold new initiatives' between Bangladesh and Pakistan that could eventually assist the Indian relationship. In April 1973, Pakistan and India signed a joint declaration allowing most of the Pakistani POWs to return—only 195 of them facing serious charges of war crimes remained in captivity. The Indian government was authorized to negotiate with Pakistan on behalf of Bangladesh.

In July 1973, an Indian delegation reached Rawalpindi. It comprised P. N. Haksar, P. N. Dhar, and Kewal Singh. They were pitted against the fierce Aziz Ahmed—who had by then become foreign minister—and Agha Shahi, the Pakistani foreign secretary. Tough negotiations followed on the fate of the POWs, with Pakistan strongly resisting trying some of them as war criminals. When the delegation called on Bhutto on the evening of 27 July, he was blunt in rejecting their proposal. He said, 'I simply cannot take the risk.' The trial of the POWs 'would be a point of no return...you can throw the whole lot of the POWs in the river Ganges, but I cannot agree to any of the soldiers being held back for trials.'[11] The Indian delegation left disappointed. But the deliberations resumed in New Delhi the next month.

On returning to New Delhi, Kewal Singh got on a plane with Indira Gandhi for a Commonwealth heads of government meeting in Ottawa. On arrival, she was met by scores of protestors, apparently Pakistanis, with banners condemning India for holding POWs for the past eight months.

Singh marvelled at the effectiveness of Pakistan's propaganda, which allowed the sloganeers to follow Gandhi to different cities in Canada. Before the next round of discussions in New Delhi on 18 August 1973, Pakistan reached a democratic milestone by passing a new Constitution. Pakistan's new president, Chaudhary Fazal Ilahi, called it the 'completion of political recovery and realisation of democratic ideals' in the country.[12] Bhutto was sworn in as prime minister on 14 August 1973, handing over the now ceremonial post of president to Ilahi.

In India, this was seen as a positive development, as Pakistan's democratic forces consolidated and the military kept its head down. The argument began gaining ground that a 'democratic peace' would be a reality if Pakistan continued on its path towards becoming a genuine electoral democracy. India's president and prime minister sent gushing messages, referencing the 'vigorous and responsive parliamentary system of government functioning in the countries of the subcontinent' and the prospects of a durable peace.[13] Bhutto also recognized Bangladesh in his broadcast of 14 August 1973.

The Pakistani delegation arrived in India on 18 August and after ten days of tough negotiations, arrived at an agreement, signed by P. N. Haksar and Aziz Ahmed, as a result of which the three governments agreed to the immediate and simultaneous repatriation of some 400,000 men, women, and children, who had been away from their homes for the previous twenty months—in India, Pakistan, and Bangladesh. This included 93,000 Pakistani POWs. The three-way movement of detainees was completed on 30 April 1974, with the last batch of 700 POWs crossing the Wagah checkpost into Pakistan, along with their commander, Lieutenant General A. A. K. Niazi.

With this resolution of the 1971 war mostly out of the way, the path was clear for normalizing relations. On 9 April 1974, the countries arrived at a tripartite agreement on the fate of the 195 Pakistani POWs charged with war crimes, such as crimes against humanity and genocide. They were to be returned to Pakistan. A bilateral agreement was also signed by foreign ministers Swaran Singh and Aziz Ahmed, to hold discussions quickly on the resumption of communications and travel between the two countries, working towards normalization after the 1971 war and to implement the provisions of the Simla Agreement. The date was fixed for 10 June for these discussions. But, as was becoming the new normal in India–Pakistan relations, an event took place which would again destabilize the fragile relationship.

BUDDHA'S SMILE

At 9 a.m. on 18 May 1974, All India Radio interrupted its regular program for a special announcement: 'At 0805 am this morning, India successfully conducted an underground nuclear explosion for peaceful purposes at a

carefully chosen site in western India.' An hour earlier, deep in the Thar
Desert, a group of scientists saw the earth shift and a giant mound of sand
rise up as if 'Lord Hanuman had lifted it.'[14] Indira Gandhi had verbally
ordered the test in 1972 and even her defence minister Jagjivan Ram was
not in the loop on the explosion. The big bang in the desert took place
on a festive day marking the birth of the Buddha and hence its code
name, 'Smiling Buddha'. The scientists at the site had more to smile about.
In his excitement, the father of the bomb fell down—the chairman of
India's premier nuclear research facility, the Bhabha Atomic Research
Centre (BARC), Raja Ramanna, was climbing down from the machan, a
temporary wooden viewing site rigged up in the desert, when the earth
shook violently; in the moment of his greatest triumph, he found himself
sprawled on the sands of the Thar Desert in Pokhran.[15]

Foreign Secretary Kewal Singh, one of the few people in the know of
the secret plan, had reached his workplace two hours before the Buddha
smiled. He anxiously awaited the signal from upstairs, which was to be
his cue to call in select Western ambassadors and high commissioners to
explain the party line of a 'peaceful nuclear explosion'. He got the signal
and went on to invite several ambassadors for briefings.

Delhi-based diplomats were soon reporting this narrative to sceptical
capitals. Two days after this frenetic bout of diplomacy, Kewal Singh
accompanied the prime minister and the chairman of the Atomic Energy
Commission (the apex body that decided nuclear policy), Homi Sethna, to
Pokhran, to see the site of the implosion device. India was facing strong
geopolitical headwinds; it was castigated by the United States, United
Kingdom, Japan, and Canada. Most Western countries condemned the
Indian move, except for France, which commended the 'mastery of nuclear
techniques' by India.[16] The Canadian government was the strongest in its
criticism, as it suspended all nuclear aid for India's fledgling nuclear energy
programme. Singh was deputed to explain the move to the Canadians,
who had helped India at a crucial stage of the nuclear programme—the
plutonium fuel for the bomb had been brewed in a small research reactor
called CIRUS, donated by Canada in 1956. He stopped by in the US in
August on his way to Ottawa, to meet Henry Kissinger, who later privately
apologized to Canada for publicly insinuating that Canadian negligence
had allowed India to reach weapons capability.[17]

The strongest reaction to India's nuclear test, of course, came from
Pakistan. An angry Prime Minister Bhutto called a press conference in
Lahore on 19 May to pledge that Pakistan would never submit to 'nuclear
blackmail'. He referred to the suggestion made by India of a no-war pact
during the Simla conference to say, 'now that India has begun to brandish
its nuclear sword, I declare that the question of concluding a pact simply
does not arise.'[18]

India was trying hard to allay Pakistan's fears. On 22 May, Prime Minister Indira Gandhi addressed a personal letter to Bhutto (sent through the Swiss embassy given the absence of diplomatic contacts) to assure him that India's nuclear explosion was entirely for peaceful purposes. Bhutto was scarcely persuaded. He replied angrily that India had designs to dismember Pakistan and get out of the no-war pact offer it had made earlier. He warned that India's nuclear explosion had upset the power balance between the two countries and threatened the normalization of relations.

Bhutto was whipping up sentiment within his own country, with the narrative of a dangerous, nuclear-fanged India. The nuclear explosion would weigh heavy on the bilateral relationship. On 31 May, Pakistan said it was cancelling the talks for restoration of communication and travel facilities that had been scheduled for 10 June. Bhutto stepped up the belligerence and tried to use India's new nuclear status to press the US to supply it with arms. He also made paranoid claims of a pincer move planned against Pakistan, with the simultaneous deployment of Afghan troops to its west and the concentration of Indian troops on the Sialkot border on the east. These were precursors of Pakistan's future allegations about India's attempts to squeeze Pakistan, requiring it to get strategic depth in Afghanistan.

India continued to protest against Bhutto's belligerence and insist on the peaceful nature of its nuclear programme. Minister of External Affairs Swaran Singh wrote to his Pakistani counterpart Aziz Ahmed on 15 June, pointing out that Bhutto's remarks were not only against the letter and spirit of the Simla Agreement but also 'constituted a gross interference in India's internal affairs'.

But Bhutto was not persuaded. He famously said in the Lahore's governor's house: 'We shall eat grass but have our bomb.' He was only reiterating what he said in 1965 after the Chinese explosion of 1964. Back in 1965, Bhutto's friend, Munir Ahmad Khan, had informed him of the status of India's nuclear programme. Bhutto said, 'Pakistan will fight, fight for a thousand years. If...India builds the bomb.... (Pakistan) will eat grass, even go hungry, but we will get one of our own...we have no other choice.' Bhutto remained true to this commitment towards acquiring nuclear weapons and so did his successor, Zia ul-Haq.[19]

12

LIMPING BACK

Pakistan's anger at India's nuclear test appeared to abruptly cool off as the summer ended. Aziz Ahmed replied to Swaran Singh on 10 August 1974 that talks could resume in September. Kewal Singh was back in Pakistan on 10 September and—after three days of talks with his Pakistani counterpart, Foreign Secretary Agha Shahi—signed three agreements that had remained suspended for the past three years: to resume postal, telecommunications, and travel links. They also signed an important protocol on visits by pilgrims to shrines in either country and agreed that negotiations would start to restore trade and cultural exchanges and resume air connectivity.

In late November 1974, an Indian delegation was back in Rawalpindi, this time to discuss overflights and the resumption of air links. The civil aviation talks broke down on India's insistence that Pakistan withdraw the complaint lodged with the International Civil Aviation Organization (ICAO) against India's ban on Pakistani overflights, from 4 February 1971. That was the day the Indian Airlines plane had been hijacked to Lahore and blown up with the apparent connivance of Pakistan's security agencies and to the rejoicing of the public in Lahore and elsewhere. The Government of Pakistan had also granted political asylum to the hijackers, calling them freedom fighters. India was now insisting on dealing with this issue bilaterally.

The delegation returned with this stalemate, but the return visit by Pakistan produced an agreement to lift the embargo on trade and grant mutual most favoured nation treatment. In January 1975, a follow-up agreement was signed to resume shipping links. Thus, commercial links were re-established between the countries within four years of the war.

If May 1974 was the time when Pakistan sulked, it was India's turn to be upset in February 1975. Prime Minister Bhutto visited Washington in the first week of February 1975. On 24 February, an announcement came lifting the ten-year-old embargo against supplies of arms to Pakistan and—for the sake of optics—also to India. India found the move particularly galling, given the history of US promises of the past two decades. President Eisenhower's assurances to Prime Minister Nehru in 1954—that American arms supplied to Pakistan were only to combat aggression by communism—had been belied, when those arms were used against India in the 1965 war. India was also upset at the US having given deceptive signals in recent times—when Henry Kissinger had visited New Delhi on 27 October 1974, he had praised non-alignment during a speech at the Indian Council of

World Affairs (ICWA). He seemed to be distancing himself from the 1950s posture since the days of John Foster Dulles, when this policy had been dubbed 'immoral'.[1]

Indira Gandhi made a statement on 26 February that the resumption of arms supplies to Pakistan amounted to reopening old wounds and that it would hinder the process of healing and normalization of ties between the neighbours.[2] She said that the US was falling into the trap of hyphenating Pakistan with India, which was a flawed policy. Kewal Singh personally felt that India's reaction should not have been so strong in 1975. His view reflected the frequent disagreements that politicians and diplomats had on this issue and the political hyper-sensitivity to developments related to Pakistan.

Again, February 1975 did not bring unalloyed joy to Pakistan. By a coincidence, on the day the embargo was lifted (24 February), momentous developments took place in Kashmir. Sheikh Abdullah was sworn in as the chief minister of the state, after years in the political wilderness. The new process had begun with the Indira–Sheikh accord of 1974, whereby the Kashmiri leader had dropped his hard-line plebiscite demand. Islamabad called for a general strike in Pakistan and Kashmir, evoking a strong reaction from Sheikh Abdullah. During a prayer meeting on 28 February, he said that Pakistan could not play with the future of J&K, after having committed atrocities in the part of Kashmir that it administered and having launched an orgy of violence in the state since 1947. The outburst on Kashmir provided another layer of backdrop to Pakistan's outcry about India's nuclear capability and India's outrage about US arms supplies to Pakistan.

In May 1975, elections were held in POK, rigged in favour of Bhutto's party, the ruling PPP, which led effectively to the integration of POK into Pakistan. The move by Pakistan was clearly a response to Sheikh Abdullah's installation in Kashmir, suggesting that this move had left Pakistan with no choice but to integrate POK deeper into Pakistan. Voices within Pakistan were warning about the damaging effect that this integration would have on the final solution to the disputed state of Kashmir. Bhutto, on the other hand, seemed to be working on a status quo solution that he had promised Indira Gandhi he would deliver in Simla. The move would have familiar echoes in 2021, when Gilgit Baltistan was integrated deeper into Pakistan in response to India's perceived move to irreversibly integrate J&K further after the Article 370 decision of August 2019.

It took a few months for matters to cool down enough for Kewal Singh to get permission from the PM to invite his counterpart, Agha Shahi, to India on 17 May 1975. The foreign secretary-level talks led to agreements on air links, the construction of Salal hydroelectric plant on the river Chenab in

India, and a reaffirmation of the Simla spirit. Kewal Singh again raised the issue of the non-aggression treaty to allay fears of India's nuclear capability and to end the harsh anti-India propaganda unleashed by Pakistan.

Soon, India's attention was directed inwards. On 12 June 1975, the Allahabad High Court found Indira Gandhi guilty of electoral malpractice. She was barred from holding elected office for six years. She lashed back angrily and imposed a state of Emergency on 25 June, in what became an eighteen-month interruption in India's democracy.

The bilateral contestation spilled over once again onto the international stage in October 1975, when India and Pakistan confronted each other for a claim to a UN Security Council non-permanent seat. The bitter contest arose for an Asian seat in the fifteen-member Security Council, to be available from 1976 after Iraq completed its two-year term. India had announced its candidature for the seat a couple of months earlier and conveyed this to all governments, including to Pakistan. This did not stop Pakistan from throwing its hat in the ring and lobbying for support among member nations. Foreign Secretary Kewal Singh was particularly disappointed because he thought Pakistan could have easily waited for the next Asian vacancy in 1977, instead of trying to challenge India. Singh tried to persuade his Pakistani counterpart Shahi of the futility of a public diplomatic battle but Shahi reported that Islamabad was in no mood to relent.

In the absence of agreement, India and Pakistan lobbied and slugged it out for four days with seven successive ballots, which did not produce the two-thirds majority for either candidate. The deadlock carried the danger that the Asian seat would remain vacant. Kewal Singh and India's permanent representative, Rikhi Jaipal got the approval of the government in Delhi to withdraw India's candidature. When Jaipal made the formal announcement that India had decided not to press its candidature any longer, the Pakistani permanent representative, Iqbal Akhund, rose to express his country's deep appreciation for India's decision, and said 'there is no winner or loser today', and it would be Pakistan's 'pleasure and duty to back India, fully at another Council election'. As India stepped aside for Pakistan to join the Security Council as a non-permanent member in 1976–77, Pakistan returned the favour with support for India joining the council in 1977–78.[3]

To Akhund and other Pakistani diplomats, the 'victory' at the UN was some kind of balm for the humiliation of 1971, and the 'consecration of Pakistan's reinstatement to the world community'. With India now facing democratic backsliding with Indira Gandhi's Emergency rule and in Pakistan, Bhutto's 'vigorous, leadership, and reforms', Akhund felt that 'the Indians themselves were conscious of the relative decline in India's position. On one occasion, when India's defence minister came to his home in New York for lunch, Akhund escorted him down to his car, only to find the car would not start. It had to be jumpstarted from the battery of the Pakistan mission's car. Akhund joked, 'Mr Minister, here is a practical demonstration of what we can do through peaceful coexistence'. Chavan replied with a grin, 'I know, but Pakistan likes to coexist only when India's battery is down.'[4]

THE LADDER OF PEACE

With the goodwill growing, Prime Minister Bhutto took the initiative to write a letter on 27 March 1976, telling Indira Gandhi that Pakistan was willing to withdraw its case from the ICAO. He suggested early talks between the foreign secretaries. The resulting May 1976 meetings of the foreign secretaries led to the resumption of air links and overflights and also of goods and passenger rail traffic.

Finally, in mid-1976, diplomatic relations resumed between the two countries. These had been carried out through the Swiss embassy since the 1971 war. It had taken more than five years after the war and four years after the Simla Agreement to restore air and rail links between the two countries and to normalize diplomatic relations. On 24 July, K. S. Bajpai and Syed Fida Hussain, both diplomatic veterans of the 1965 war, went across to their country missions.

It was more than five years after High Commissioner Atal had flown back to India from Islamabad in a Swissair plane that his successor Bajpai landed in the city. This was incidentally also a time when Indira Gandhi was restoring diplomatic relations with another difficult neighbour, China, after the 1962 war.

But the political trajectories of India and Pakistan were soon to diverge again. Both Gandhi and Bhutto decided at roughly the same time in January 1977 to go in for fresh elections. Bhutto needed to abide by the provisions of the 1973 Constitution, while the democrat in Gandhi had awoken, to seek the people's mandate after eighteen months of the Emergency.

Bilateral diplomacy continued. The issue of a no-war pact that had been discussed in the 1950s and 1960s came up again. Bhutto had made known his scepticism about no-war pacts. He saw these as a ruse by India to take attention away from Kashmir. One of the last major media interviews Bhutto gave was to the visiting Indian journalist Khushwant Singh, where he pointed out that a no-war pact could only be considered if it incorporated a 'self-executing mechanism for the settlement of outstanding disputes like the one provided in the Indus Basin Treaty'. Else, it 'would really mean the acceptance of the status quo in Jammu and Kashmir.'[5]

Pakistan's diplomacy was thus trying to push back the principle of bilateralism established in Simla and resume the argument that international agreements superseded bilateral ones. Bhutto's legal mind was trying to find a way out by drawing a parallel with the Indus treaty. In the midst of the election campaign, Pakistan issued an aggressive White Paper to keep the Kashmir issue simmering. It repeated the primacy of the UN resolutions and ignored Pakistan's commitment to the Simla Agreement. In his protest, Ambassador Bajpai said that 'we realize that Pakistan is in the midst of electioneering. But we do not accept the facts as presented in the White Paper.'[6]

The Indian general elections held in March 1977 led to a heavy defeat for Indira Gandhi and her Congress Party and a resounding victory for the Opposition Janata alliance led by the eighty-one-year-old Morarji Desai.

In Pakistan, Bhutto was believed to be heading for an easy win in the March 1977 elections, on the strength of his support of democratic institutions. These were only the second general elections that Pakistan was holding in the three decades of its independence, so there was much hope of Pakistan's democracy emerging strengthened. However, Bhutto decided to rig the elections, in a move that paralleled the Watergate affair a few years earlier, when US Republicans decided to distort the democratic process despite being in a comfortable electoral position.

Bhutto's embarrassingly large margin of victory failed to convince his people. An overwhelming majority of over 60 per cent of the votes for the PPP appeared to have been obtained by brazen rigging, rather than a persuasive democratic mandate. In several constituencies, votes for the PPP candidates exceeded those actually polled. In Punjab, where Bhutto faced a strong Opposition, his candidates had secured 95 per cent of the vote. To the Opposition challenge to the results, Bhutto reacted with the assured arrogance of an autocrat. He called in the army to suppress demonstrations, followed by curfew and martial law. The scenes were reminiscent not only of the last days of President Ayub Khan's reign, when Bhutto himself was leading the democratic charge against autocracy, but also reminded observers of Mrs Gandhi's weak moment in 1975 when she had imposed the Emergency.

A FRESH START

Pakistan's High Commissioner Syed Fida Hussain was one of the first diplomats to greet Atal Bihari Vajpayee, the Janata Party's new foreign minister. The genial fifty-four-year-old politician had been a rising star in India's parliament, a member since 1954. Vajpayee had imbibed several strongly democratic values in his journey in parliament and travels abroad as an MP. He had watched Nehru and Indira grow as leaders and understood the importance of realpolitik and flexibility in negotiations with adversaries. His exposure to the world was telling him that his political party, the Jan Sangh (the early avatar of the nationalist Bharatiya Janata Party founded in 1951), had to change to be accepted by the majority of Indians, as well as nations around the world. Foreign Secretary

Jagat Mehta had become a trusted and valued adviser.

Vajpayee reassured Pakistan's ambassador of the new Indian government's peaceful intentions despite his own hard-line positions in the past. Vajpayee told the envoy that the foreign policy of India had followed a pattern which was more or less based on a national consensus and his party was not going to change it. He suggested that with elections over in both countries, the time had come to pick up the old threads and to resume the normalization process.[7]

Meanwhile, across the border, Ambassador Bajpai met Bhutto in Islamabad on 26 April to present him a letter from the Indian prime minister Morarji Desai, which spoke of a positive agenda of moving from a durable to a permanent peace. Bhutto spoke enthusiastically of accelerating the normalization process and moving towards Indo–Pak trade talks and the need for a fresh approach.

On 6 June, Ambassador Hussain called on Prime Minister Desai. Desai again emphasized that there was no change in his government's policy towards Pakistan and invited Bhutto to visit India once things stabilized in his country. Desai recounted an incident from 1964, when Sheikh Abdullah had suggested to Nehru that the latter should propose to the Government of Pakistan the creation of some kind of confederation between the two countries. After hearing this proposal, Desai, who was not in government, immediately advised Nehru against it, saying that this move would be misunderstood by Pakistan. He was glad that Nehru agreed and did not make any such proposals.

Morarji Desai, conflicted on nuclear weapons because of his Gandhian beliefs, took a position that 'we have no desire to possess atomic weapons even if you produce such weapons'.[8] At the same time, he told the envoy that about ten years earlier India had been offered a nuclear umbrella by the US for giving up the option to conduct atomic tests for peaceful purposes. He had agreed with the view that India should prefer to have its own nuclear weapons, instead of coming under such an umbrella. This mixed nuclear signal would not influence Pakistan's plans.

But Pakistan soon saw a more familiar kind of regime change. With the threat of civil war imminent in Pakistan, Chief of Army Staff General Zia ul-Haq snatched power in a military coup on the morning of 5 July 1977. Bhutto was dismissed and a new dictator with a waxed moustache and toothy smile was now in power, promising early elections and stability after chaos.

When the government changed in Pakistan, Vajpayee made a statement in parliament that the army takeover in Pakistan was an internal affair of Pakistan and that India's consistent policy of non-interference in the domestic affairs of other countries would continue. A few days later, Pakistan ambassador Fida Hussain called on Vajpayee and briefed him on Pakistan's new regime. Vajpayee asked after the welfare of Bhutto. The diplomat informed the foreign minister that Pakistan's leadership, including his counterpart, Foreign Minister Aziz Ahmed, was in 'protective custody'[9]. Vajpayee observed wryly that this was exactly what his own detention had been called during India's Emergency. Hussain assured Vajpayee that the martial law government had promised to hold elections by October and hand over power to the people's representatives. He referred to the standing invitation to the Indian prime minister to visit Pakistan.

In Pakistan, Ambassador Bajpai got a chance to call on 9 July on the new dictator then designated chief martial law administrator. Zia was all charm, full of promise of holding elections within three months. Bajpai said cheekily to Zia that the bilateral relationship should be like a Hindu marriage—indissoluble. General Zia quoted Desai as having said to his envoy that politicians never want elections and generals never want wars, although both prepared constantly for these eventualities. Zia walked out to drop the ambassador to his car, pledging peace.

Vajpayee realized that both Zia in Islamabad and his envoy, Hussain, in New Delhi, were trying to downplay the significance of the military takeover. He had warmed up to the Pakistani high commissioner, and spoke to him in his poetic Urdu. But their burgeoning relationship was tragically cut short. At the end of the year, Hussain suddenly passed away after a heart attack—Vajpayee went personally to the Pakistan high commission and penned an Urdu couplet in the condolence book:

Zamana baray shouq say sunn raha tha
Tumhi so gaye dastan kahte kahte.

(The world was engrossed in your story
But you fell asleep telling it.)[10]

1977–1987: FIVE BLOODY RIVERS

13

THAWING TO DECEIVE

India's top diplomat, dapper in a dark bandhgala and thick-rimmed glasses, strode confidently to the podium of the United Nations General Assembly in New York, to deliver a fluent three-minute address. It was October 1977. The external affairs minister outlined the worldview of the new Indian government, just six-months old then, signalling a broad continuity in foreign policy. Atal Bihari Vajpayee's carefully crafted statement—the first at the UN by a non-Congress foreign minister—mostly reaffirmed traditional positions: underlining India's commitment to democracy, basic freedoms, human rights, multilateralism, support for Palestinian rights, and opposition to apartheid. 'The vision of Vasudhaiva Kutumbakum is an old one. We in India have all along believed in the concept of the world as one family,'[1] Vajpayee said, invoking civilizational values and deploying what would become a Sanskrit buzz phrase for Indian diplomats. What was also new was Vajpayee's invocation of the trauma of the recent Emergency; his wounds were fresh and personal; he had been in jail for nineteen months before the historic 1977 elections punished Indira Gandhi and catapulted the Janata government to power. India's foreign minister now vowed from the UN podium that India had closed a dark chapter that involved the trampling of democracy and human rights, and would make constitutional changes to ensure it would never tread that path again.

But its substance was not what the speech was remembered for. Vajpayee became the first foreign minister to deliver a UNGA speech in Hindi. For Vajpayee, a Hindi poet, this was a personal dream fulfilled, 'the happiest moment of my life.'[2] For many in northern India, the act became one of linguistic pride and nationalist confidence. Others panned it: Hindi was not an official language of the UN and not likely to become one.

In what was seen as a signal to Pakistan, Vajpayee said India hoped to normalize ties with all countries. The message was clearly one of continuing the 1976 process of stabilization, rather than bearing grudges for the 1971 war or the flawed Simla peace process.

The diplomacy with Pakistan began on the UN sidelines; Vajpayee had dinner with Zia's new diplomatic adviser, Pakistan's 'Secretary General' Agha Shahi. Vajpayee was his genial self that evening. He pointed out to Shahi that India had shown restraint in reacting calmly to the change in government and internal developments in Pakistan. India would be happy to have further talks on the question of Salal—a hydroelectric project on the river Chenab in Jammu and Kashmir—in March or April, after the proposed Pakistan elections. Vajpayee said talks could begin as soon as the political situation in Pakistan stabilized. In essence, India was willing to talk to Pakistan whenever it was ready.

India assessed that this was a good time to move on some practical aspects of the relationship, leaving tougher 'outstanding issues' for when the internal situation in Pakistan steadied. The pressing matters on the agenda included transit trade, the Salal project, the maritime boundary, and issues of arm supplies.

Transit issues, then, as now, remained particularly sensitive, since they required sovereignty concerns to be finessed. Transit through Pakistan would imply India's access to Iran and Afghanistan while Pakistan could gain reciprocal transit rights through India to Nepal and Bangladesh. But this implied an adversary country granting fairly untrammelled territorial access for cargo. The optics would not be politically pretty. The Salal hydroelectric project gave reason to Pakistan to invoke the dispute resolution provisions of the Indus Waters Treaty of 1960. In 1976, Pakistan had wished to take this issue to a neutral expert in terms of the treaty. India was keen to resolve the issue bilaterally, keeping up the Simla spirit. The third issue was of maritime boundary demarcation, for which India was keen, given the objective of offshore oil exploration. Another issue was of US military supplies to Pakistan. India was assessing that the military regime in Pakistan remained committed to the installation of a nuclear reprocessing plant with French know-how. But Pakistan's ambitions for nuclear weapon capability were not hidden from India, nor was India's from Pakistan. India's line on its own programme remained that it was committed to harnessing nuclear energy for peaceful purposes.

Vajpayee had received advice from MEA mandarins in October that India's attitude to Pakistan should remain one of 'patience, restraint, reasonableness and cooperation'[3], underlining the belief that there was no alternative to the peaceful and bilateral solution of problems and differences. Vajpayee was to build on this interaction with his first foray into Pakistan, in what would become a lifelong search for an elusive peace with the neighbouring nation.

A DIPLOMATIC FORAY

Behind the poker-faced Buddha-like calm, High Commissioner K. S. Bajpai was uneasy. It was a cool spring day in Islamabad in February 1978, as he waited at a military airport for a plane from India. This was no ordinary flight. It would be carrying India's external affairs minister for not just the first major bilateral political visit after the 1971 war, but the first visit by an Indian foreign minister in a dozen years, since Swaran Singh's visit of 1966. There was much that could go wrong with this goodwill visit that foreign minister Vajpayee had embarked upon. Would Vajpayee be as harsh on dictator Zia as he had been on the prime minister his government had just defeated, the autocrat Indira Gandhi?

The atmospherics before the trip had not been good. The Pakistan media had maintained a steady, troublingly hostile, and apparently orchestrated drumbeat about the new Janata government that included Vajpayee, a representative of the anti-Pakistan, right-wing Bhartiya Jana Sangh. Scarcely anything positive was being said about its senior leader and India's foreign minister, now descending upon Pakistan.

On the flight from Delhi, Vajpayee's key adviser—Foreign Secretary Jagat Mehta—was nervous too. His new boss was embarking on a critical diplomatic initiative. More worryingly, Mehta was seeing reports of major demonstrations in Pakistan that could easily drown out any positives the visit hoped to accomplish. They could even threaten security.

If Vajpayee shared his advisers' trepidation, it did not show on his boyish visage as he emerged on the tarmac from the Indian Air Force aircraft, with springy step, genial smile, and easy charm. His handshake was vigorous and friendly as he met his counterpart, Agha Shahi, who now went by the designation of adviser on foreign affairs to the martial law administrator of Pakistan. Vajpayee was keen to manage expectations and treat this as only a 'goodwill visit' that would set the stage for future dialogue. He had prepared well for this charm offensive, working assiduously on his Urdu, the poet in him transitioning from kavita to shayari, as he tried to get his pronunciation and phrases just right. Known as a master orator and an accomplished poet in Hindi, he had boned up on his Urdu to communicate better with Pakistan.

Vajpayee's quirky sense of humour did not allow him to take himself too seriously; the moment of serious diplomacy never sat too heavy on him. He had even composed a self-deprecatory poem on his new portfolio, about the poet who found himself shaking hands only to then wring them in despair:

Desh nikala mil gaya mantralaya foren;
Kootniti ke shastra hain, bain, nain aur sain;
Bain, nain aur sain, churi kaante bhi chalte;
Pehle haath milate
Phir haathon ko malte…

Pushed out of the country, to the foreign ministry
The tools of diplomacy are words, eyes, and signs;
Words, eyes, and signs; plus forks and knives;
First you shake hands,
Then wring them in repentance…[4]

Vajpayee's charm offensive during his week-long visit, directed at his counterpart, General Zia, and a host of other interlocutors, pretty much succeeded in altering Pakistan's perception of India's new government. Vajpayee's visit was not just the first by a foreign minister to Pakistan in a dozen years, it was part of the new government's outreach to the neighbourhood including both adversaries with whom India had fought wars—Pakistan and China.

General Zia admitted later that he too had been worried before the visit. The thin-skinned general was concerned about a snub from the new Indian government, given the recent coup and an elected prime minister in the lock-up, with global leaders pressing Pakistan to release Bhutto.

Vajpayee's seventy-minute call on Pakistan's dictator on 6 February 1978 went off better than expected. India's foreign minister did not press Pakistan's chief martial law administrator on the issue of Bhutto's incarceration. Bhutto had at best a mixed reputation in India—while to some, he was the democrat wronged by his country, to others he was the untrustworthy autocrat who had instigated two wars against India and then got the better of Mrs Gandhi in Simla. More importantly, the focus for the goodwill visit was on a positive, forward-looking agenda. Zia apologized for the commotion in the Pakistan media for the previous ten days and seemed to agree with Vajpayee that the obsession with solving Kashmir before anything else must go. Vajpayee cited the example of how India had made progress with Bangladesh on the tough Farakka Barrage issue for sharing the waters of the Ganga.

Zia was countering Vajpayee's charm offensive with one of his own. He kept positioning himself as the outsider, almost a peacenik. He agreed with Vajpayee that the obsession with Kashmir was misplaced. When Vajpayee said that he had considered cancelling his visit in order not to embarrass his hosts, Zia again apologized for the noise in Pakistan's media.

Zia did say that the two key issues between the countries were Kashmir and trade. But, in his perfunctory reference to Kashmir, he added that there was 'no harm in talking', but this was 'not an issue which could be solved quickly'. They went on to discuss details of economic cooperation—trade in cotton, gas, and rock salt. When Vajpayee delivered an invitation from India's prime minister for him to visit India, Zia responded with self-effacing courtier-like formality—'Daawat ki kya zaroorat thi. Ham unke khadim hain (What was the need for the invitation. We are your servants.)'[5]

Accompanied by Foreign Secretary Jagat Mehta and Ambassador K. S. Bajpai, Vajpayee also had lengthy interactions with his host and counterpart Agha Shahi. As Zia's foreign policy adviser and de facto foreign minister, the Bangalore-trained mathematician and former ICS officer was equally warm. When Vajpayee mentioned that he never thought he would visit Pakistan as foreign minister of India, Shahi presciently observed that Vajpayee—still a couple of decades away from being prime minister—was still young and 'we look forward to your further successes'. Referring to the Pakistan media speculation about an insidious Indian plot to take over the country's economy, Vajpayee clarified that there was no real proposal for the idea of an Asian common market; a South Asian free trade arrangement was still a decade away.

In his meeting with Shahi, Vajpayee admitted that he had condemned the Simla Agreement when it was signed; but he was now committed to defending this national commitment. He even referred to the informal understanding that had been reached in Simla about gradually giving the LoC the character of an international boundary. Vajpayee cautioned against Kashmir becoming an issue in Pakistan's internal politics or in Indian politics. He pointed out that in India's general elections, no bilateral issues related to Pakistan were raised: 'We kept scrupulously aloof.'[6] He suggested there was no point in even mentioning in a readout of his 'goodwill visit' that the matter was discussed and not agreed upon. The officials eventually agreed on a formulation that Kashmir was discussed, the two sides put forward their respective points of view and that the talks were held in a cordial atmosphere. Vajpayee made it a point to underline even in his public declarations that the Janata government stood by the Simla Agreement.

At a banquet in his honour, Vajpayee charmed his hosts with several Urdu couplets, compelling his flustered counterpart Shahi to rapidly translate the prepared English script of his address into stilted, Persianized Urdu. The text seemed foreign to Shahi as he stumbled through it. At home in Delhi, Vajpayee had leaned on a friend, a college professor, to polish his Urdu. Vajpayee appeared more at home in Pakistan's proudly adopted official tongue than his official hosts.

A critique of Vajpayee's visit was that he never pressed Pakistan's dictator for mercy for Bhutto. The new government of India had pointedly decided to treat this as an internal matter of Pakistan, at least in part because Bhutto had not endeared himself to India by his antipathy towards it. But Vajpayee's charm extended to his public diplomacy. As the media quoted the foreign minister's earlier comments back to him, Vajpayee disarmingly told them that he had forgotten the past and they should too.

Vajpayee was repeatedly asked by media where the Janata government stood on the Kashmir issue. Would the starting point of dialogue be the deadlock at the UN, the Tashkent declaration, or the Simla Agreement? Vajpayee consistently replied that India stood by the Simla Agreement. He even acknowledged that his party had led the move against the agreement in 1971 and also advocated nuclear weapons capability for India; but that was a minority view and he now subscribed to the Janata party view that there was no need for India to produce nuclear weapons. This disarmingly candid and easy distinction between his party's stance—and his government's view would serve Vajpayee well then and in his political future.

Vajpayee succeeded in conveying a message of fresh thinking in Delhi to facilitate the normalizing of the relationship between the two countries. He visited Taxila, the ancient Buddhist city near Islamabad, and also Lahore, where he went to the samadhi of Ranjit Singh, the Sikh leader who had ruled much of northern India in the nineteenth century. An assessment by the MEA of Vajpayee's visit summarized its three broad outcomes: emphasizing the Simla process of normalizing contacts; voicing India's commitment to a strong and stable Pakistan; and agreeing to discuss 'outstanding matters' (read the Kashmir issue) once Pakistan was more stable politically.

Vajpayee's visit had also produced a host of practical 'deliverables' which were as unexpected as they were creative: the greenlighting for India of the Salal dam project on the river Chenab in J&K; opening of consulates in Karachi and Bombay; cultural exchanges including pilgrims; resumption of cricketing contacts. While Vajpayee was in Pakistan, an Indian hockey team was playing a competitive match there. The common South Asian love for sport and particularly for hockey and cricket was clearly a point of convergence that could help bilateral diplomacy.

⁂

But in the always fraught India–Pakistan story, unforeseen events can deflate painstakingly gathered goodwill just as easily as they can reverse ill will. At a time when both sides were trying to consolidate the gains of the visit, a diplomatic storm was kicked up by Vajpayee's remarks to a North Korean visitor in Delhi—he was quoted by All India Radio as having told Pakistan during his visit in February that the UN's Kashmir resolutions were 'obsolete', since the territory was an integral part of India. The media story led to a sharp outcry in Pakistan. Ambassador Bajpai was called in for a protest in Islamabad by Foreign Secretary Shah Nawaz, even as Foreign Minister Agha Shahi was leaving for UN meetings in New York. Nawaz told Bajpai that Pakistan would issue a statement countering the version emanating from Delhi since this was a 'very sensitive issue' with Pakistan public opinion and India had brought this on itself 'by giving out (the) Foreign Minister's remarks'. Bajpai cabled home an assessment on 18 March, that the Pakistani démarche was 'part of preparations for telling us in Delhi Pakistani public opinion will not permit of advances in relations with us without movement towards Kashmir settlement'.[7]

That night, Pakistan's foreign office released Agha Shahi's statement reiterating Pakistan's carefully finessed position for its domestic constituency that the 'Simla Agreement safeguards the recognised position of either side on the J&K dispute. Bilateral talks with India on a settlement of this dispute cannot therefore in any way erode much less amount to an abandonment of Pakistan's stand on the two UNCIP resolutions of 13 August 1948 and 5 January 1949 which call for demilitarization of the state and a plebiscite to determine its future affiliation with Pakistan or with India'.[8]

More than India, Pakistan needed to continually remind its own people that Bhutto's commitment to bilateralism in Simla was conditional on a rapid solution to the Kashmir dispute, in keeping with UN resolutions. And with Bhutto no longer in charge, the UN resolutions were back in play, becoming central to the narrative.

Bajpai believed that the impending judicial verdict against Bhutto played a role in the timing of Pakistan's sharp reaction. The following week, Pakistan's Supreme Court put an end to all democratic hopes and upheld Bhutto's death sentence. This was another shameful episode for Pakistan's judiciary, matching the clean chit it had given to Ayub Khan for his decade of dictatorship, citing the doctrine of necessity.[9]

A DEMOCRAT AND A DICTATOR

Before long, India's new prime minister also ran into Pakistan's new dictator. Morarji Desai had an unscheduled and warm exchange with Zia in August 1978 in Nairobi, at the funeral of Jomo Kenyatta, the Kenyan activist and politician. The dictator was all charm again, clearly flattered by the attention he got from India's democratic leader.

On his part, Desai came from a Gandhian pacifist tradition of Indian politics; he had in general been critical of the break-up of Pakistan in 1971 and India's direct control of Sikkim in 1975. He was opposed to nuclear weapons and frowned upon the cloak and dagger games of India's intelligence agencies. His policy of silence over Zia's overthrow of Bhutto and assumption of power in Pakistan was perceived as a 'principled and detached stand'.[10] Desai was seen as breaking away from Indira Gandhi's policy, of crediting the democratically elected Bhutto with greater legitimacy in Pakistan than the dictator Zia. The Janata government was evolving its foreign policy based on 'genuine non-alignment' aimed at strengthening relations with neighbours, 'based on non-interference and respect for sovereignty'.[11] Zia was seeing this change in India's body language as an opportunity for some sweet talking, accompanied by covert moves that remained undetected by India's gullible new leaders.

14

PUNJAB AFLAME

Even as the Kashmir issue receded in in bilateral conversations, a deadly dynamic unfolded in another border state of India. In Punjab—a province Pakistan felt had been unfairly partitioned in 1947—the Akali Dal, led by Parkash Singh Badal, became an important coalition partner of the Janata Party in power at the centre. In an attempt to destabilize this coalition in Delhi, the Opposition Congress Party sought the help of extremist and secessionist elements who could challenge Badal's government in Punjab.[1] This led to the rise of radical leaders like Jarnail Singh Bhindranwale, who kept Punjab off balance with violence. The alleged political strategy was to keep the state simmering till the Congress Party returned to power and quelled the violence. The dangerous flirtation with extremist politics would continue even after Indira Gandhi's return to power at the centre in 1980, when this cynical political gambit would morph into a means of strengthening the Congress Party for the next election due in 1985.[2] Thus started the most radical phase of Punjab politics, with devastatingly violent consequences for India. The situation presented Pakistan with a unique opportunity for mischief in another border state of India. One of the tactical goals for Pakistan was to potentially create a choke point for Kashmir.

With the increasing power differential and the bitter experience of the 1971 war, Pakistan's planners seemed to adopt the view that a conventional war over Kashmir should be ruled out, at least until Pakistan added greater military muscle. Creative sub-conventional warfare options needed to be explored. The Inter-Services Intelligence's (ISI) early experiences in Afghanistan had emboldened it to try to promote an insurgency in India beyond Kashmir. Punjab now seemed ripe for the picking, where Pakistan could simply run a dagger through existing fissures in India. It decided to effectively foment and support an insurgency that would cause deep pain to India over the 1980s.

Pakistan had looked at Punjab as a covert battlefield several years earlier. The separatist idea of Khalistan—a fantasy state to be carved out of north-west India—had received early support from the ISI. Not many had heard of the concept until Dr Jagjit Singh Chauhan, a dentist and politician who had left Punjab for London, declared himself the president of Khalistan. On 12 October 1971, Chauhan placed an advertisement in the *New York Times* proclaiming the birth of Khalistan and seeking funds to propel the idea forward. This was barely two months before Bangladesh separated from Pakistan. The ad, it was widely believed in intelligence circles, was paid for by the Pakistan embassy in Washington.[3]

After Bangladesh was formed in 1971, for Pakistan's establishment, the desire for revenge for the loss of its eastern limb had been added to the core aim of reversing the 'injustice' of Kashmir going to India. Indeed, Bhutto had said at an off the record briefing, that 'Pakistan will also have a Bangladesh carved out of India, except it will be on Pakistan's border.'[4] Pakistan's deep state was looking for newer pathways to these goals.

While the larger aim was to bleed India, Pakistan's military also had an interest in creating a strategic space within India sympathetic to Pakistan. This idea of a buffer revived memories of Jinnah's initial partition claim over Punjab.[5] The tactical approach now seemed to be to work for a state that could choke India's land access to Kashmir, a chronic obsession of Pakistan's India policy. At the very least, helping Khalistanis create trouble in India was a lot cheaper and safer than conventional warfare.[6]

Chauhan later claimed in an interview to *India Today* that Bhutto had urged him to set up shop on holy ground for the Sikhs inside Pakistan, at Nankana Sahib, birthplace of Guru Nanak, the first Sikh guru. Bhutto allegedly told him in a New York hotel, 'Sardarji, you have the keys to Nankana Sahib. Come there, we will help you and make it the capital of Khalistan. Start the movement from here.' Chauhan, however, could see that Bhutto was cynically exploiting the issue to get revenge for Bangladesh.[7]

Pakistan's Punjab policy became part of the army's newer strategic doctrine covering a broad spectrum of warfare—an edge in sub-conventional warfare that India would find hard to grapple with. This would eventually be supplemented, at the other end of the spectrum, with nuclear assets at parity with India, to deter a conventional attack.

⸌

By 1979, India's post in Karachi had resumed functioning after a seven-year hiatus, with a colourful IFS officer, Mani Shankar Aiyar, as the first consul general. Aiyar was issuing visas to Sindhis at breakneck pace, as many as hundred thousand a year, generating tremendous goodwill in the process.[8] As an outcome of Vajpayee's February visit, Aiyar was in the saddle from December 1978, to occupy the long-unused office of the deputy high commission in Karachi, that itself was home till the mid-1960s to India's high commission. The Lahore-born Aiyar had proudly moved into the high commissioner's mansion in Karachi and had access to India's recreational beach cottage to boot. He would remain in Karachi until 1982 for his 'most rewarding posting abroad', to become a life-long advocate of an 'uninterrupted and uninterruptible dialogue' as a pathway to peace. In Bombay, Pakistan's new consulate did not gain the same profile; it struggled to get Jinnah's favourite property as its home.

The resumption of cricket ties, a less bloody arena of conflict for the neighbours, had been another outcome of Vajpayee's visit. In 1978–79, the Indian team led by Bishen Singh Bedi visited Pakistan and was defeated 2-0. A rakishly handsome pace bowler, Imran Khan, had ripped through India's batting in the Lahore test match. When Pakistan's cricket team paid a return visit to India in 1979–1980, it lost the test series 2-0, but Imran—a future prime minister—became a cult figure to swooning women in India, for his charm on and off the field. (When I mentioned to Imran in 2018 that he had Vajpayee to thank for his first India tour, he replied he was not aware of this history, but the goodwill he sensed during the 1970s series was far greater than in the 1980s, when much hostility had crept into the relationship.)

TROUBLE IN KABUL

Although the India–Pakistan relationship showed signs of a thaw that year, 1979 was a brutal year for much of the world. It began with turmoil in Iran, where, by February, a pro-Western autocratic monarch was replaced with an Islamic theocracy run by the ayatollahs, which deeply challenged the post-war order in West Asia. The rest of the world seemed to be in tumult too. China invaded Vietnam the same month on a punitive mission, even as India's foreign minister Vajpayee was in Beijing on a peace mission, a year after his Pakistan foray. The Chinese officially told the world they meant to teach Vietnam the same lesson they had taught India in 1962.

In March, Zia renounced Cold War Western bloc affiliations and emulated India's non-aligned stance to rebrand Pakistan for a global diplomatic debut. Pakistan officially requested India's support for its membership in the non-aligned movement.[9] Pakistan's adviser for foreign affairs wrote to the Non-aligned Movement (NAM) chair, Sri Lanka, to convey Pakistan's termination of its CENTO membership as a 'further reflection of its total solidarity with the aims and objectives of the non-aligned movement'[10], meeting the movement's criteria. Pakistan was thus formally ending its participation in a Western security alliance to join the non-aligned movement, seeking parity with India. To Zia's mind, diplomacy with India was about projecting a friendly posture while pursuing his goals covertly.

In April, the US uncovered evidence of attempts by Pakistan to develop a nuclear weapons programme at the Kahuta facility, near Islamabad. It immediately terminated economic and military aid to Pakistan, freezing a nascent deal to procure F-16 aircraft. This plunged US–Pakistan relations to a low. Pakistan slipped further into the morass when Zia executed Bhutto in April in a flimsy murder case, despite several global appeals to spare the life of the politician. Zia's martial law, as also the politics and economics of his country, was now defined by a commitment to Islamic values as the core ideology of Pakistan.

India was facing its own internal political challenge. The Janata Party experiment had begun crumbling by July, thanks mainly to infighting, with the resignation of Prime Minister Desai, making snap elections mandatory within six months.

In November, a mob torched the US embassy in Islamabad, fired up by a fake report quoting Iran's leader, Ayatollah Khomeini, that the US was behind the occupation of the Great Mosque in Mecca. Just when US–Pakistan relations had looked set to snap, Pakistan was saved by the bell that went clanging in Afghanistan; the Soviet Union made a major miscalculation there, that made Pakistan valuable again. As Soviet tanks rolled into Kabul on Christmas Eve, to begin a decade-long misadventure, Zia decided to seize the moment to make his country useful to the US. The dictator was soon playing a larger Cold War game as America's closest partner in its Afghan challenge of the Soviets.

The Soviet occupation of Afghanistan gave Pakistan a key strategic role as a frontline state in the Cold War. The US decided to jump in and lean on Pakistan again, as it had done in another Cold War episode a decade earlier when it had made an overture to China. Pakistan's soldiers and ISI handlers of the mujahideen were soon actively involved in operations within Afghanistan. Some Pakistani analysts proudly claimed that the first salvo of the end of the Cold War had been fired by the Pakistan Army. Zia was soon celebrating significant US financial aid and military supplies of $3.2 billion as a six-year package. This helped him further consolidate army control internally over the executive and to squash the little political challenge he faced. The spoils of war were adding up: Pakistan also managed to clandestinely divert home a good deal of arms and food supplies meant for the mujahideen fighting the Afghan government and the Soviet army. At the same time, Pakistan saw an influx of 3 million Afghan refugees, seriously impacting economic and cultural life, as also law and order, in the frontier districts of Pakistan.

It turned out that the Democratic US president Carter, no cold warrior like Nixon, had bought into an overstated case of a Soviet threat, prepared by hawks led by his NSA Zbigniew Brzezinski. The 'Carter Doctrine' assumed that following Afghanistan, the Soviets would strike US oil interests in the Persian Gulf. Such a plan required Moscow to believe it could overcome Afghanistan, Pakistan, and Iran en route to its objective. To ascribe this motive to Russia, the US needed to doubt not only Soviet declarations, 'but their sanity as well'.[11]

The Soviets had their delusions too, and became victims of their own paranoia. Russian strategists argued that if the Afghan prime minister Hafizullah Amin switched sides in the Cold War, like Egypt's Anwar Sadat had done in 1978, 'the Americans could use Afghanistan to aim additional missiles at the Motherland'. While the Soviets had made a grave miscalculation that would cost them and the Afghans dearly, threatening Western oil supply was 'probably the last thing on their minds'.[12]

The US, wearing its Cold War blinkers, recruited Pakistan into its corner. To defeat the Soviets, it unashamedly allied with Brzezinski's Islamist 'freedom fighters' in Afghanistan, as also a motley band of other fighters like Osama bin Laden.

More dangerously, the Cold War hawks persuaded anti-proliferation hawk Jimmy Carter to ignore Pakistan's deadly nuclear programme. The US State Department knew of Pakistan's China-supported gas centrifuge-based nuclear enrichment plant in Kahuta in January 1979, according to documents declassified in 2021.[13] After withholding funding, the Carter administration downplayed Pakistan's nuclear capability. As in 1971 under Nixon, the US avoided confronting Islamabad for fear of alienating it during a period of regional upheaval, this time the Iranian revolution and expanding Soviet power in Afghanistan. Soon after the USSR attacked Afghanistan, the US withdrew all sanctions against Pakistan. The sale of F-16 jet combat aircraft was back on the table.

US-Pakistan ties had soured in 1962 (when the US briefly supported India in the Indo–Chinese conflict, while Pakistan turned to China) and worsened in 1965 (when US weapon sales were discontinued) to look up during the 1970 US–China rapprochement and dip again as Pakistan's covert nuclear programme was detected. But after the 1979 Soviet invasion, Pakistan was back as the Cold War's 'most allied ally'[14] of the US and would remain so as long as the Soviets remained in Kabul.

ALLAH, ARMY, AMREEKA
The midterm elections of January 1980 brought back to power a chastened Indira Gandhi. She surprised Pakistan this time with her decision to continue the thaw of 1977–79. She was aware of criticism of her tough neighbourhood policy, that was being contrasted with a more friendly and prudent one rolled out by the predecessor Janata government. Also, many Indians were being won over by the smiling diplomacy of General Zia, even if most doubted his sincerity

'Kunwar' Natwar Singh replaced K. S. Bajpai as ambassador to Pakistan on 20 May. Singh, an Indian Foreign Service officer of the 1953 batch, was married into the royal family of Patiala, and had served in Indira Gandhi's secretariat (1966–71) during her formative years as PM. He was the Indian PM's pick for the job and Pakistan's dictator knew it.

When he presented credentials to Zia on 28 May, Natwar Singh was not particularly impressed by the ceremony ('not quite as spectacular, colourful and impressive as the one in Delhi'), nor by the persona of Zia (the president had power, but not personality). To Singh, Zia's 'lack of charisma was made up for by a stunning display of tahzeeb, tahammul and sharafat (politeness, patience and civility)'.[15] He was a 'master at public relations'. Singh quickly developed a strong working relationship with Zia, whom he met frequently. Pakistan's dictator, a fellow alumnus of St. Stephens college of Delhi, took to addressing the Indian envoy as 'Kunwar sahib'. Their interactions were frequent and involved some good-natured sparring. 'Zia and I frequently assaulted each other with good manners', Singh recalled, 'he was an expert at dissimulation, which he combined with a natural courtesy.' In one such exchange on Kashmir, Zia said, 'Kunwar Sahib, Kashmir is in my blood.' Singh replied, 'Sir, Kashmir is in my bone marrow.'

Before leaving for his assignment in Islamabad, Natwar Singh had called on his counterpart in India, Ambassador Sattar. Singh told Sattar that he knew what to say to people across the border, but he was wondering what not to say. Sattar gave some candid advice: 'Never say that we are the same people. We are not. If we were, then why did we part company in 1947?' Singh never overlooked that advice during his tenure.[16]

Zia's Pakistan had a new trope defining it in the 1980s—Allah, Army, Amreeka: the three pivots that determined the fate of Pakistan. The phrase captured the military dictator's hard right turn to public religiosity within the protective embrace of the US. Zia in essence had bought domestic legitimacy for his dictatorship with an alliance with the religious right and international legitimacy through an alliance with the US. With this new contract in place, Zia decided to approach India with a brand of cloyingly sugary diplomacy, while supporting a covert proxy terror campaign and accelerating a secret nuclear programme to bring force parity.

The idea of multilateral diplomacy was also gaining traction. With it came the notion that bilateral ties could be furthered under a larger South Asian umbrella. That South Asia was the least integrated region in the world was becoming clear to policymakers in India and Pakistan from the 1950s. For some in India, a regional framework could become a welcome pathway towards diluting the India–Pakistan hostility. Kewal Singh recalls that he even discussed the notion with Prime Minister Nehru, citing the example of Nordic cooperation as he accompanied the Finnish PM when ambassador to that Nordic country. Nehru was too polite to share his conviction that more than finding avenues for cooperation, Pakistan was interested in conjuring up foreign military alliances to confront India.

In 1980, Bangladesh President Ziaur Rahman, after some preliminary consultations, proposed regional cooperation between the South Asian nations, in what appeared to be an overdue initiative. South Asian efforts to establish the union were accelerated, as some of its leaders were alarmed by the regional security crisis after troops of the USSR moved into Afghanistan. The objectives were to promote among South Asian countries—including India, Pakistan and Bangladesh—the idea of collective self-reliance and accelerated economic growth keeping political differences at bay. Its proponents were promoting South Asian regional cooperation—the SAARC initiative—as a technocratic solution to create a climate of trust. The attempt was to keep out contentious areas and focus on resolving key issues of trade, industry, and technology.

But many in India and Pakistan were not convinced of the practical wisdom of the idea. A common Indian concern was that the reference to security matters in South Asia might provide an opportunity for smaller neighbours to re-internationalize bilateral issues and to collude to form an opposition against India. Pakistan assumed that the SAARC proposal might be an Indian strategy to organize the other South Asian countries against Pakistan and ensure a regional market for Indian products, further strengthening India's regional economic hegemony. To many multilateralists, it was a start that could lead to bigger regional gains in the future.

Zia was not giving up on bilateralism. He would visit India several times, seemingly unbothered by the absence of return visits, driven by a larger tactical objective to keep the eastern front quiet, while he helped the Americans on the Western front in the Cold War. He also wanted to keep India's attention away from two important covert programmes he had going: the Punjab insurgency and nuclear weapons.

While Zia had resorted to a policy of 'low intensity conflict' with India, he had seemed to successfully persuade India's prime minister Morarji Desai, that he wanted peace and reconciliation with India. Indira Gandhi, a shrewder judge of people, had her first meeting with Zia at the Commonwealth summit in Harare in April 1980. The meeting was a 'disaster'. She thought there was 'something phony' about Zia ul-Haq's profession of good intentions.[17] Zia had made some uncharitable remarks about India, reported just before the April meeting. An account of the meeting by Inder Malhotra suggests a barbed exchange: 'Madam, please do not believe everything that you read in the newspapers' was Zia's opening gambit. 'Of course not,' replied Mrs Gandhi. 'After all, aren't they calling you a democrat and me a dictator?'[18]

Zia also repaired Arab relations with his diplomatic skills. In the early 1980s, ostracized by Gulf Arabs for murdering Bhutto, he journeyed to Mecca on the 'Night of Power' in Laylat al-Qadr. He knew the Saudi king and senior Al Sauds would be present and would not deny his request to pray together on this auspicious day. This networking strategy rehabilitated him in Saudi Arabia and established a Pakistani diplomatic tradition, later followed even by Imran Khan.[19]

In 1981, Natwar Singh saw an opportunity to bring Pakistan's dictator
to India. Zia was even keen to go for the centenary of his alma mater in
Delhi. Singh recalled:

> the president was keen to come to Delhi for the Jubilee, but Mrs
> Gandhi was not keen to have him in the capital. Nevertheless, he
> telephoned Principal Rajpal on the morning of February 1, 1981. I too
> had come to attend the jubilee. Mrs Gandhi was, of course, the guest
> of honour. She spotted me, 'Representing Zia, are you?' 'No Madam, I
> am representing you.'[20]

Zia missed the centenary celebrations but invited ten students from the
college to visit Pakistan. They missed going that year, but in 1982, the
history professor of the college, Mohammad Amin, affectionately known as
Amin saab, along with college students were state guests for a week, even
as Zia placed a Pakistani Air Force plane at their service.

As Zia consolidated his position in Pakistan, he needed to defend
his brutal hanging of Bhutto in 1979 and the delay in implementing his
promise of elections for Pakistan. Zia adopted multiple ruses to perpetuate
his power. He declared a provisional Constitution in March 1981, which
precluded any challenge to his martial law in any court, and took away
fundamental rights and the rights to form political parties. Zia also retained
his position as chief of army staff, securing control over all levers of power
as head of the army and as the president.

He wanted to build a wider political alliance, which he did by an
aggressive Islamization drive and alliance with the JeI, to secure larger
social legitimacy. He promoted a right-wing coalition of Islamist and
religious forces, which later developed into the Muttahida Majlis–e–Amal,
or the United Assembly of Action (MMA) dubbed the Mullah-Military
Alliance. He strengthened his control over both the army and bureaucracy
by parachuting top army officers into the civilian bureaucracy. He set up
shariah courts to enforce Islamic tenets, thereby weakening the judiciary.
Zia was proving to be a master political manipulator who strengthened
his authoritarian rule by co-opting the religious right and eliminating or
silencing all political rivals.

On 15 September 1981, Zia revived an offer of a no-war pact with
India, reversing Bhutto's position of dismissing it as a ruse to freeze the
Kashmir issue.

Variants of such an offer had repeatedly been made by India over
the past three decades, but had been rejected by Pakistan. Even in the
1960s, India had offered a no-war pact to Pakistan and had settled the
Indus Waters dispute mostly to Pakistan's satisfaction. The conflicts of
1965 and 1971 kept this idea in abeyance. That the latest offer coincided
with a $3.2 billion military package by the US to Pakistan, which also

included the state-of-the-art F-16 fighter aircraft, made it clear that the US was prompting Pakistan to build fences with India, in their newly rediscovered security relationship. The offer was later made formally by Pakistan's foreign minister.

The gambit was met with suspicion in India. To Kewal Singh, India's position on the offer was a tactical error. India should have welcomed the no-war pact proposal as a reaffirmation of a commitment to peace and friendship with Pakistan. Eventually, Indira Gandhi went a step further and made a counter offer of a treaty of friendship and cooperation between the two countries. It was Pakistan's turn to view this offer with suspicion. The draft treaty contained clauses such as restriction on the buying of arms or to grant military bases to any foreign powers, which could not possibly be acceptable to Pakistan.[21]

Instead of quibbling on the nomenclature and making counter offers, Kewal Singh felt, accepting the no-war pact could have added to the trust level between the countries and could have opened the doors to more confidence-building measures and cooperation. Despite the distrust, the diplomats tried to work out a document. A 'flurry of aide memoires criss-crossed from Islamabad to New Delhi' while Abdus Sattar and Natwar Singh, the two ambassadors, got busy 'filling up their log-books with frantic air-dashes to their respective capitals for urgent briefings'.[22]

To seal the deal, Pakistan's foreign minister Agha Shahi showed up in New Delhi in February 1982 with a proposal of a no-war pact, incorporating the mutual reduction of armed forces and mutual inspection of nuclear installations to promote trust between the countries. But Delhi was beginning to see the pact as a ploy to win US approval for more arms that would eventually be used against India. Even the Pakistan suggestion for troop reduction was seen by the Indian government to be a gambit to extract a disproportionate concession from India.

In 1982, Zia reiterated his idea of the no-war pact to Natwar Singh. Zia was no longer concerned about the Kashmir cause getting diluted by such a commitment to peace by the neighbours. By now, the Punjab insurgency was more effective in keeping India off balance; a war was not really required to change the status quo. More importantly, Pakistan's uranium enrichment programme of 1975 was in full flow in Kahuta, near the capital, and Pakistan's planners were spooked by the prospect of any conflict leading up to Indian or Israeli or American raids to destroy the nuclear facility. Zia could not fully trust the Americans despite being consumed by their joint covert ops in Afghanistan. Singh recalls his chat with Zia: 'But what about my No-War Pact?' he again asked. I said that the government would most certainly examine this proposal seriously. Delhi was not too enthusiastic, but I did persuade Mrs Gandhi to make a mildly conciliatory reference to it in one of her public meetings.[23]

Natwar Singh's strong advocacy for him did get Zia his visit to India. Delhi reluctantly accepted only a transit halt, months after Singh was prematurely pulled out of Islamabad in March 1982. Indira Gandhi received Zia in Delhi in November 1982 for a more pressing assignment. In an hour-long meeting between the leaders, the first in India since Bhutto's sojourn to Simla a decade earlier, the two countries agreed to 'continue their search for durable peace on the sub-continent'. They agreed on another meeting in three months, on the sidelines of the non-aligned summit meeting in New Delhi (for which Natwar Singh had been pulled in as the chief coordinator). A joint statement spoke of the establishment of an Indo–Pakistani joint commission. In the next leg of his tour in Jakarta, President Zia gushed of a 'breakthrough' in his talks with PM Indira Gandhi, which would lead to the formation of a South Asian organization on the lines of the Association of South-East Asian countries (ASEAN).

Meanwhile, in January 1982, a new Indian consul general arrived in Karachi. Gopalaswami Parthasarathy, popularly known as Partha, replaced Mani Shankar Aiyar, who had made a strong impact by befriending a wide cross-section of people in Karachi. Partha continued the tradition of liberally issuing visas, often ignoring home ministry orders, to 250,000 people annually.[24]

Partha saw a Pakistan where Zia was consolidating power and benefiting from the ISI's role in the Cold War in neighbouring Afghanistan. An American diplomat explained the US proximity to Zia by drawing a parallel for Partha with what President Roosevelt had said about a Nicaraguan dictator, 'he may be an SOB. But he is *our* SOB.'[25]

Benazir Bhutto was under house arrest, and her mother, Nusrat Bhutto, had the leadership of the PPP, the party founded by her husband Zulfikar. In one dinner meeting in Karachi, Partha asked her how her husband had miscalculated in appointing his nemesis as his army chief. Nusrat replied that her husband had succumbed to Zia's flattery. Zia would 'flatter Bhutto's ego' by calling him the 'real saviour of Pakistan after the 1971 Bangladesh debacle'; he had even personally supervised the security arrangements for President Bhutto whenever he visited Multan. When Partha said he was scheduled to meet General Zia the next morning, Nusrat said, 'When you are with him, do observe his eyes, and let me know what you think.' Intrigued by her remark, Partha spent the hour-long meeting, where he was accompanying the visiting lieutenant governor of Delhi, Jagmohan, observing the dictator's eyes. Partha concluded that Zia's smile never reached his eyes. When Partha reported his observations to Nusrat, that Zia's eyes were 'cold and expressionless', she asked, 'did they not remind you of the eyes of a cobra?'

During the NAM summit in March 1983, when President Zia called on his Indian counterpart, President Zail Singh, and expressed his desire for peace with India, Singh replied with an earthy Punjabi saying: Akh bhi maare, taay ghunghat bhi kaddae (It was not possible for a woman to do two things at the same time—wink provocatively, and veil her face.)[26]

Also in 1983, India and Pakistan set up a joint commission, which, over the years, failed to fulfil its promise of cooperation in trade, communications tourism, and cultural exchanges in spite of some initial hopes. The central cause for the lack of trust and the bitter relations between the countries was Pakistan's clear hand, as India saw it, in terrorist activities in Punjab. The Punjab terrorism situation and evidence of training camps or supply of arms by Pakistan to Khalistani terrorists in Punjab made such initiatives non-starters. The confessions by captured terrorists were clearly confirming Pakistan's complicity and encouragement to the Khalistani movement.

An international conference held in Dhaka in 1983 by the Bangladesh Ministry of Foreign Affairs gave a strong push to regional integration. Seven South Asian foreign ministers, including those of India and Pakistan, adopted the declaration on SAARC and formally launched the Integrated Programme of Action (IPA) initially in five agreed areas of cooperation, namely, Agriculture; Rural Development; Telecommunications; Meteorology; and Health and Population Activities. Bangladesh had been pushing this idea in the previous three years and in 1981 had taken a concrete step to draft a working paper for discussion among the foreign secretaries of South Asian countries, who identified the five broad areas for regional cooperation. The hope was that a multilateral regional grouping, focused on economic well-being and without the political overhang of the UN, would provide a forum to dwell on areas other than the India–Pakistan hostility of three decades.

SCHADENFREUDE

At the Karachi consulate of India in the 1980s, in Zia's Pakistan, Indian diplomats[27] despaired to see that Khalistani leaders were frequent guests of Zia's government, with their provocative statements getting much play in the state-controlled media. Several Pakistanis masquerading as Sikh terrorists were known to have crossed the border to aid the militancy. In several instances, they had been killed by Indian security forces. Zia appeared firmly wedded to a policy of separatism both in J&K and in Punjab, dubbed by some as the K2 policy. The dictator's official stance was, of course, of cloying courtesy and a deep desire for friendship, accompanied by total denial of any covert operations within India.

With his over the top diplomacy, Zia would block any attempt by India to reason with him. When India dispatched Information and Broadcasting Minister H. K. L. Bhagat to Islamabad in July 1984 to address the Khalistan issue, he came back from Pakistan with plenty of assurances from Zia's government and a cow. Zia had gifted the befuddled Indian minister with a high milk-yielding Sahiwal cow since he had pre-Partition roots in the Sahiwal district of West Punjab.

Zia's regime of the mid-1980s was getting more creative in abetting Sikh militancy. Some Sikh extremists from Canada were being put up in gurdwaras in Nankana Sahib and Panja Sahib. They began attacking Indian embassy officials assigned on liaison duties to assist the jathas of pilgrims that visited these holy shrines. The Pakistan media would then gleefully report how the Sikhs had attacked Indian officials, glossing over the fact that the thugs were ISI assets. Matters became more brazen when Indian diplomats and officials were attacked during these visits. A truce was called only when a Pakistani diplomat was roughed up outside his house in Lajpat Nagar in New Delhi.

In the midst of these tensions over Punjab, on a 'scorching afternoon' in May 1984, a new Pakistani ambassador arrived in India. He was still designated 'ambassador' given that Pakistan was out of the Commonwealth in Zia's era of military dictatorship. Humayun Khan was not an India expert, but was no stranger to India, having spent his boyhood as a boarder at the Bishop Cotton School in Simla (Zia also went to school in the same city in what he called the more 'proletariat' Government School of Simla). Humayun Khan was an affable Pathan from Peshawar and had a vast network of friends in India, through connections with Hindu families of Peshawar and his undergraduate years at Trinity College, Cambridge.

Soon after the arrival of the envoy, an Indian Airlines plane was hijacked by Khalistani terrorists and forced to land in Lahore but after thirty-six hours of gruelling negotiations, the passengers returned unharmed in what Humayun Khan thought was a satisfactory resolution of the crisis. But Khan's introductory call on Prime Minister Indira Gandhi did not go off too well. The prime minister greeted the ambassador with the traditional Muslim greeting 'adab arz hai' but added with a wry smile, 'Aapke aate hi hadsa ho gaya (A mishap occurred the moment you arrived).' She cut short his attempt to highlight the cooperation between officials to resolve the crisis, to say, 'but you did not allow our people to meet the hijackers or search their luggage.' Khan was thrown off balance by the 'prime minister's directness, and even more by the long silences that followed her opening remarks'. The interview lasted seven minutes; Khan concluded that 'she was clearly a woman of few words with little time for niceties.'[28]

Pakistan was worried at the time about retaliatory action by India against its meddling in Punjab. On one occasion, when Humayun Khan led his embassy team for a cricket match at the Chelmsford Club, he was urgently called pulled aside by his defence attaché to say that he had

'information from a Grade A-one (that is, undeniable) source that India
had decided to break off diplomatic relations with Pakistan.' Khan passed
on the information to the foreign office in Islamabad; it caused a 'great
storm'. Much to his embarrassment, the report turned out to be untrue.
But the episode underscored the tensions of those troubled days.[29]

Adding to the nightmares for India's leadership were the hijacks.
Between 1980 and 1984, five Indian planes were hijacked. India's
intelligence agencies were confirming the impression that Zia's Pakistan
had given a free hand to the ISI to develop a nexus with Sikh separatists,
who mostly hijacked the Indian planes, with most of them attempting
to land in Lahore.

The Khalistani flames were fanned from overseas by radical elements
who had migrated to distant lands like the UK, Canada, and the US.
But Pakistan and its trained assets were always closer to the theatre of
action. It was needed as the staging post to light the fires. Rawalpindi
thus became the nerve centre of a globally supported insurgency that
destabilized India's Punjab of the 1980s. Weapons with clear Pakistani
fingerprints on them were flowing in from across the border to aid the
insurrection. When the crisis reached its crescendo in 1984—with an
army Operation Bluestar in the sacred Golden Temple—it led to the
assassination of Indira Gandhi.

When her Sikh bodyguards killed Indira Gandhi on 31 October 1984,
sweets were distributed in many areas of Karachi and around Pakistan.[30]
The assassination was seen as sweet justice by several Pakistanis who
resented not just her role in Punjab, but also one as the chief architects
of Pakistan's break-up in 1971.

On Indira Gandhi's death, Zia was not about to let go of the opportunity
for some funeral diplomacy. He landed in Delhi again. For Pakistan, the
most important meeting Zia had was with Rajiv Gandhi. The two met
privately for nearly an hour while the delegations waited in an anteroom.
Zia himself dictated a memo of the conversation as soon as he returned
to his hotel. It clearly indicated that the prospects for putting bilateral
relations back on track held promise.[31]

When Zia and his entourage returned to Delhi's Ashoka Hotel after
the funeral, they found that a large number of delegations were waiting
for the elevator. Not wanting to wait, with a spring in his step, Zia said
he would take the stairs. When one of his entourage tried to dissuade Zia,
saying that it was on the fifth floor, Zia said sotto voce, assuming everyone
around him was Pakistani, 'Aaj to hum paanch manzil bhi chadh jayenge
(Today, I will climb even five floors).' He was in such good spirits at the
passing of an Indian leader who seemed to have seen through his game.[32]

It appeared to many that there were karmic overtones to something that took place four years later—when Zia's plane crashed, a similar sentiment was expressed by Benazir Bhutto, this time openly, when she told the BBC, this was too good to be true.

15

AUTUMN IN KASHMIR

While India's focus in the 1980s was on dousing the flames in Punjab, many from fires lit by Pakistan, the Kashmir Valley had continued to simmer. Resentment and hostility were evident in the valley, often instigated from across the border, with pro-Pakistan slogans rising in the 1980s.

This was a continuum of a new phase of politics that had begun in J&K in 1977, when the National Conference, under Sheikh Abdullah, won a strong mandate soon after the Janata experiment started in New Delhi. Abdullah was the lion of Kashmir in his winter, now convinced that the state's future lay in cooperating with New Delhi, rather than in him spending time in prison. The Sheikh needed to counter the aggression of the Pakistan-supported militant separatist Jammu and Kashmir Liberation Front (JKLF), an outfit originally formed in the 1960s in POK and active in the Kashmir Valley from 1977. He also needed to deal with the angry youth in the state. Abdullah did both by enacting the Public Safety Act, 1978, seen in the valley as a draconian piece of legislation enabling arbitrary arrests. The PSA deepened the anger and resentment in the valley.

Abdullah died in 1982, ending half a century of tempestuous politics in the valley, that saw him in a love-hate relationship with the politicians at the centre, mainly Nehru and his daughter Indira. Soon after the Sheikh's passing, an international cricket match was played in 1983 at the Sher-i-Kashmir stadium named after Abdullah. The Indian team, which included national stars like Sunil Gavaskar and Kapil Dev, were shocked by the extraordinary hostility displayed by the young crowd which booed and jeered the Indian players and cheered every success of their West Indian opponents. They waved Pakistani flags even though Pakistan was not playing. The green flags were not new in the valley. Abdullah's term had been marked by increasing Pakistani activism and thousands of Pakistani flags appearing on 14 August, Pakistan's Independence Day, or in cricket matches.

Farooq Abdullah, Sheikh's son, won Jammu and Kashmir's mid-1983 elections. In February 1984, Farooq's National Conference faced its first major challenge when the valley faced unrest after a Kashmiri, Maqbool Bhat, was executed in Delhi. Bhat, a JKLF leader, was sentenced to death in 1968 for shooting a valley policeman. But he managed to escape to Pakistan, only to be caught again in 1976. His death sentence of 1968 was finally carried out in 1984. Bhat's hanging came days after UK-based militants of the JKLF from POK had abducted and executed a junior Indian diplomat, Ravindra Mhatre, in Birmingham, in a botched attempt at securing Bhat's release. While the killing of an Indian diplomat by Pakistan-backed militants was a huge setback to diplomacy, Bhat's hanging created a wave of anger in Kashmir, contributing to the rise of the JKLF, while stoking the idea of an armed insurgency in the Kashmir Valley.

In the spring of 1984, Indira Gandhi sent in as governor of the state a trusted trouble-shooter, Jagmohan, controversial for the part he had played as the head of the Delhi Development Authority during the Emergency (1975–77) in the bulldozing of slums in the city. Within a couple of months, Jagmohan dismissed Abdullah's government and replaced it with a leader of a rebel faction of the National Conference and son-in-law of the late Sheikh, Farooq's brother-in-law, G. M. Shah, denying Farooq's pleas for fresh elections. To some, this political drama was a surreal rerun of the 1953 political coup, with Indira Gandhi, Jagmohan, G. M. Shah, and Farooq Abdullah in the roles of Jawaharlal Nehru, Karan Singh, Bakshi Ghulam Ahmed, and Sheikh Abdullah. In the same month as the 'Srinagar coup', Mrs Gandhi sent armed forces to flush out militants from the Golden Temple in Amritsar.[1]

THE HIGHEST BATTLEFIELD

In April 1984, another India–Pakistan front opened up, this time in the upper Himalaya, north of the troubled valley, when Indian forces grabbed control of the commanding heights in the Siachen Glacier.

A cartographic error had triggered this crisis. The Siachen saga had begun in 1978 when two German explorers entered the office of Colonel Narendra 'Bull' Kumar, commandant of the High-Altitude Warfare School (HAWS) at Gulmarg. They proposed a river rafting excursion to follow up on another they had successfully completed with Kumar on the Indus in 1975. Kumar was struck by a US-published map his German friends had placed on his table while outlining their strategy. From one point, the border between India and Pakistan went on straight, as if made with a ruler, in contrast to its jagged trajectory on the rest of the map. Kumar had never seen a map with such a line in the north. This line connected grid reference NJ9842, the last northern demarcation between India and Pakistan, to the Karakoram Pass. Kumar was convinced, after reviewing historical records and treaties, including the Karachi Ceasefire Agreement of 27 July 1949, that the map was intentionally distorted and that the area beyond NJ9842 had been represented as part of Pakistan without legal or historical justification.

Kumar informed Major General M. L. Chibber, director general of military operations (DGMO), of these facts, and suggested a reconnaissance expedition to this location. A fifty-member expedition under Kumar's leadership, had soon reached the summit—the Teram Kangri II peak at 24,300 feet, on 13 October 1978. It was a historic moment because it was the first time Indian soldier-mountaineers had stood overlooking the Shaksgam Valley, an area that Pakistan had illegally ceded to China in 1963. Kumar and his team spent almost three months in the region, exploring the snowy heights and mapping routes. They returned with enough evidence of expeditions from the Pakistani side. It was Kumar who then proposed to Chibber that to counter the Pakistani line, India should draw a line joining NJ9842 with Indira Col due north, as the Saltoro Ridge formed a natural boundary between the two countries.

In fact, Pakistan had never itself conceptualized or drawn the line, going north-east from point NJ9842, which became the basis of its claim of the whole Siachen territory. Declassified records showed that a US State Department geographer Robert D. Hodgson was responsible for this 'honest cartographic mistake'. Pakistan's claim over lands north of NJ9842 and the Karakoram Pass was based on the claim that several foreign cartographers had represented this territory on their side. This assertion later was shown to be legally untenable.

It was Chibber, fortuitously the Northern Army commander in 1983–84, who planned the Indian army's high-altitude assault to take the Saltoro Ridge and Siachen Glacier. The timing of the operation had to be advanced to pre-empt the adversary, when information came in that the Pakistan Army was buying high-altitude equipment in Western capitals, to occupy the heights that summer. With Operation Meghdoot, the Indian military took control of this region by 13 April 1984.[2]

Divergent views have prevailed, at various points in time, in Indian military circles on the strategic importance of the Siachen area. Some believe that 'neither India nor Pakistan secures a strategic advantage by contesting the possession of the Saltoro range. Neither also faces a military threat to the territory it occupies in Jammu and Kashmir from over the Saltoro range...a strategic veneer is given to what is actually a political necessity for continuing the conflict.'[3]

Others insist, more plausibly, that if military collusion between Pakistan and China were to occur, this is the area where it is most likely to happen. More fundamentally, the issue is not the strategic value of Siachen, but that of territory. That is why India has been insisting on the marking of the current positions that the army holds on maps that are to be ratified by both sides. This would establish Indian territorial control along the Saltoro Ridge. On the other hand, Pakistan has been reluctant to authenticate Indian positions as it might legitimize India's 'illegal act' of violating the Simla Agreement by occupying an area that was under Pakistan's administrative control. The 'crux of the matter is that neither side is willing to make any territorial compromise'.[4] Despite the territorial logjam, resolving the

Siachen issue will become an important bilateral agenda point over the next decades, whenever the relationship reaches a stage of thaw.

ᒣ

Revenge for the Siachen surprise now became an additional driver for the Pakistan army's planning. Some army officers approached Zia with a 'Kargil plan', meant to use surprise to grab territory in the Kargil area in Ladakh, to avenge both 1971 and 1984. Zia rejected the proposal as unviable and dangerous. He had other priorities; they could be threatened by a skirmish with India. (Pakistan's next dictator, Pervez Musharraf, was not blessed with the same military acumen and would implement this disastrous plan fifteen years later.)

Zia's dream of parity with India now rested on acquiring nuclear capability. On 10 December 1984, A. Q. Khan, Pakistan's star nuclear scientist, met Zia to tell him that the nuclear bomb, fabricated with Chinese help, was ready and could be tested. Zia told him that he did not want to test just then as he was tied up with the US on the western front and did not want to jeopardize that front or risk losing US support. But Zia also did not want to challenge India; he was feeling empowered by the elimination of Indira Gandhi. It was enough for him to know that Pakistan had been able to create the nuclear capacity to challenge India's conventional military superiority, notwithstanding the Siachen setback.

Zia was also facing a few legitimacy issues at home. Midway through his reign, he had started to feel political pressure to show some semblance of a revival of democratic processes. He engineered a spurious referendum on 19 December 1984 on his Islamization policy, an effective ploy to have himself confirmed as president for another five years. He announced elections on a 'non-party basis', in effect crippling the political process. Despite these manoeuvres to eliminate opposition to his rule, the elected members of the assembly and his own prime minister Muhammad Khan Junejo started asserting democratic rights and demanded the lifting of the martial law.

In India, the young Rajiv Gandhi went on to ride a sympathy wave for a huge electoral victory for the Congress in the general election of April 1985. Even as Rajiv settled in, a new high commissioner, Shailendra Kumar Singh, took over in Islamabad, amidst rekindled hope that the India–Pakistan thaw of 1977–79 could be revived. Singh would go on to become the longest-serving Indian envoy to Pakistan, in station from 1985 to 1989, and would form a strong association with General Zia, in his attempt to avert conflict. But early in the ambassador's tenure, Rajiv, who shared his mother's scepticism of Pakistan's dictator, was in no hurry to build bridges.

Rajiv faced enormous internal security challenges early in his term.

While the familiar battleground of Kashmir was heating up, the crisis in Punjab that had claimed his mother had not quite cooled down. In fact, the tentacles of the Punjab conspiracy were going global. Air India 'Kanishka' Flight 182 was blown up over Ireland by bombs planted by Khalistani separatists in Vancouver on 23 June 1985, killing 329 people, mostly Canadians of Indian heritage. Indian intelligence had little doubt about Pakistan's role in training the men behind what was till then the world's deadliest aviation disaster.

In December 1985, Zia met Rajiv on the sidelines during the first SAARC summit in Bangladesh. This was their second encounter, after the one during Indira Gandhi's funeral the previous year. To Humayun Khan, the most important outcome of the meeting was a totally unexpected one. Rajiv casually asked Zia after a formal meeting if it would be a good idea for the two countries to enter into an agreement not to attack each other's nuclear facilities. Zia, in the throes of a covert nuclear programme, was taken aback, but quickly regained his composure to enthusiastically welcome the idea. (This accord was eventually signed in December 1988.)[5]

In Kashmir, unrest was growing through G. M. Shah's uneasy tenure of twenty-one months as chief minister. The power behind the throne remained Jagmohan, who finally dismissed the Shah government in 1986. In what was seen by many as a blow to the credibility of the democratic process in the state, Farooq Abdullah agreed to be reinstated in power in 1986, pending the 1987 assembly elections. Brazenly rigged polls brought back Farooq as chief minister, but created anger and resentment in the valley, amenable conditions for fomenting an insurgency.

The JKLF became more aggressive after the polls. It started demanding independence or integration with Pakistan. The 1987 elections in Kashmir also coincided with the peaking of the Afghan war, where Pakistan was actively engaged. Pakistan's agencies were learning lessons from the Afghan operations and drawing inspiration from the first 'Palestinian intifada' to promote a 'Kashmir movement'. A new separatist militant outfit, Hizbul Mujahideen came up with Pakistan's support, ostensibly as a reaction to the 1987 elections. A worrying feature of the new phase of militancy was that the struggle began to take on an Islamist colour, with rhetoric of the creation of an Islamic caliphate from 1987.[6]

DOWN TO BRASS TACKS

It was a military exercise that triggered a peculiar twist in Indo–Pak diplomacy in 1987. India launched Operation Brasstacks in the Thar Desert—a major war-gaming exercise that ran from November 1986 to January 1987 near Pakistan's border. Army chief General Krishnaswamy Sundarji initiated the massive air-land exercise in the Rajasthan and Gujarat sectors, ostensibly to determine whether two strike corps of the Indian Army could cover good distance by night against moderate opposition. This move rang alarm bells in Rawalpindi and Washington; the Pakistan Army put its own operational plans into unscheduled play by 'moving its offensive formations towards India's areas of vulnerabilities in Punjab and Jammu'.[7]

By mid-January 1987, the two armies were facing each other on the border, amidst rising tensions. Pakistan's ambassador Humayun Khan was summoned to the foreign office in Delhi, to be warned that India would escalate the conflict unless Pakistan withdrew its troops. In Islamabad, Indian ambassador S. K Singh was not surprised to receive a midnight summons from the foreign office, but was alarmed by what he heard. The envoy was told by Minister of State Zain Noorani, just in from an emergency meeting with President Zia, that in the event of any 'violation of Pakistan's sovereignty and territorial integrity' by India, Pakistan was capable of 'inflicting unacceptable damage'. When Singh asked Noorani whether this implied a nuclear attack, Noorani replied, 'It might be so.'[8]

The US was alarmed as well. It was now seeing Pakistan as an unreliable ally, that was being less than transparent about its nuclear weapons programme. While it accepted India's version that Operation Brasstacks was merely aimed at the 'validation of emerging operational thinking', the US looked at it as a crisis that 'had the potential to trigger a conflict as much by accident and misperception as per design'. Both Pakistan and the US had in fact overreacted to Operation Brasstacks, which was not meant to signal any intent of war. In the absence of any political directive, General Sundarji had no plan or mandate to go across the border. But both he and even more, the hawkish Minister of State for Defence Arun Singh, may have wanted to convince Rajiv Gandhi of the need to take a tougher posture on Pakistan.[9] On his part, Rajiv had no desire to escalate tension with Pakistan, but was concerned at the developments and escalating rhetoric. On one occasion, he pulled aside Natwar Singh and asked him: 'Are we going to war with Pakistan?'[10]

Although the Brasstacks crisis had resolved by January 1987, Pakistan was shaken. It found it necessary to send a strong signal to India. Journalist Kuldip Nayar was surprised to find that he had been given access, during a private visit to Lahore for a wedding, to A. Q. Khan, the father of Pakistan's nuclear bomb. Nayar cleverly baited Khan to admit that Pakistan did have the bomb. The explosive story was published in *The Guardian* of London in March 1987. Pakistan was quick to issue a denial, fearing the weight of US sanctions. But the signal had been sent to India.[11]

Whatever its motivations, Operation Brasstacks did demonstrate India's conventional force superiority against the backdrop of Pakistan's nascent nuclear capability, at a particularly sensitive time—the Punjab crisis had not stabilized and the worst of the Kashmir security crisis was to begin.

All this happened while the Cold War was still on, with Pakistan embroiled in lockstep with the US in a covert war on its western frontier. Pakistani military writings have invariably ascribed larger objectives to India's military exercise at that point. Pakistan saw, in India's muscle flexing, also an attempt to stem Pakistan's nuclear designs. Pakistan's smart diplomacy was in this narrative projected as the balm which healed the crisis.

In the midst of the tension created by Brasstacks, Rajiv Gandhi made an administrative howler, in effect publicly dismissing Foreign Secretary A. P. Venkateswaran on an issue related to Pakistan. Responding to a Pakistani journalist at a press conference, who asked him to confirm the foreign secretary's statement that the Indian PM would visit Pakistan soon, Rajiv said 'you will meet the new Foreign Secretary soon'. Rajiv faced an angry outburst from his foreign service bureaucracy. Incidentally, as I trained at the civil service academy later that year, this episode became the subject of the customary annual skit by the probationers: at a press conference, a politician is asked if he would be visiting Goa. He counters, 'Who told you that?' The journalist responds: 'Your wife, sir.' The politician's response: 'You will meet my new wife soon.'

Such incidents aside, Zia remained keen through the Brasstacks exercise to visit India to both defuse the tension and brandish Pakistan's nuclear capability. An eager student of St. Stephens College wrote to Pakistan's leader in January 1987, on behalf of an 'informal discussion group' of the college, wondering if Zia would revisit his old college some time soon. To his pleasant surprise, Zia accepted. Ambassador Humayun Khan soon came up from Pakistan House to St. Stephens College, as if for a dress rehearsal of the visit. Keen to host a president, one member of the faculty fell for the idea. But history professor Amin saab, more conscious of the tense state of political play, nixed the proposal.

Soon enough, Zia came to India in March, for his fifth unreciprocated visit, this time with the excuse of some cricket diplomacy, proudly facilitated by Ambassador S. K. Singh. The media reported that 'oblivious of the cold glares of his reticent hosts', Zia came to Jaipur, to witness the India–Pakistan test match—the only test of that series to be played in the Pink City. He 'saw some cricket and conquered the media'. Zia left, 'sadly and with mixed feelings'. And in departing said he hoped to come back and revisit 'in a much better atmosphere, the kind of atmosphere an idealist like me looks forward to'.[12]

While the public diplomacy in Jaipur was about cricket as a binding force, many Pakistani writings refer to Zia having sent a nuclear signal to India in the post-Brasstacks situation. On his return from India, Zia famously asked a journalist if he had not seen his 'six', interpreted as a nuclear threat he had issued to India's leadership.

Nevertheless, India's army leadership saw Brasstacks as a successful demonstration of India's conventional military superiority, which came close on the heels of a successful operation in Siachen. The leadership also considered consolidating the gains of Siachen. General Sundarji wanted in mid-1987 to militarily 'resolve the Siachen Glacier imbroglio once and for all.' He got plans made for an ambitious airborne operation at Khapalu, some 60 kilometres across the LoC. Code-named Operation Hammerhead, the operation's aim was to sever the Pakistani lines of communication to the Siachen Glacier. Wisely, the operation was dropped, for being impractical and risky in an increasingly nuclear environment.[13] It was never moved for political approval.

The next decade had momentous events in store. Pakistan would see the end of army rule and a shaky democratic revival; India would face tough political, economic, and internal security challenges. And, the two countries would race inexorably towards a nuclear future.

1987–1997: TROUBLE IN PARADISE

16

EXPLODING MANGOES

Ambassador Shailendra Kumar Singh was feeling good. His Independence Day reception for India's fortieth birthday bash in Islamabad had seen the arrival of a chief guest he had invited but not really expected. Pakistan's head of state, along with his foreign minister, had made a surprise appearance at the reception on 15 August 1987. The reciprocity principle would have suggested that President Zia would send an officially drafted polite greeting to his Indian counterpart, while a minister would represent the government at the embassy reception: Indira or Rajiv had not visited the Pakistan ambassador's bashes in New Delhi, nor has ministers. But Zia, like Pakistan's first dictator, Ayub Khan, relished throwing protocol to the winds to achieve larger objectives.

In Delhi, Singh's counterpart, Humayun Khan, was pleased too. Pakistan was getting high-level attention. Its ambassador was attending a special investiture ceremony in honour of a Pakistani citizen, Khan Abdul Ghaffar Khan, also known as Badshah Khan, who had fought valiantly for the freedom of united India. India's highest civilian honour, the Bharat Ratna, was going to the 'Frontier Gandhi', now ailing in a Delhi hospital. The award was received by his son, Wali Khan.

The promise of diplomacy was investing the year despite continuing concerns in India about Pakistan's proxy wars in the border states of Punjab and Kashmir, as also its growing nuclear programme. Zia's diplomatic offensive was, in retrospect, designed to play for time, blunt Indian hostility, and provide the cover for his covert battles and his secret nuclear programme.

For want of better options, India was experimenting with multilateral diplomacy under the SAARC umbrella, to see if engaging Pakistan economically could dull the hostility. On 4 November 1987, Prime Minister Rajiv Gandhi met his de jure Pakistani counterpart, Prime Minister Junejo, in Kathmandu, on the sidelines of the 3rd SAARC summit; India tried hard not to let frustrating bilateral concerns break the momentum of the gathering South Asian multilateral process. The meeting cleared the decks for talks the subsequent week in New Delhi on another deadlocked issue, the Tulbul Project, where Pakistan's strenuous objections under the Indus Treaty had stalled a project aimed at managing the water levels of the river Jhelum in J&K.

Although signs of Pakistan's march towards nuclear capability were bothering India, Rajiv decided a visit to Pakistan was in order. India's prime minister paid a ninety-minute visit to Peshawar in January 1988, to attend the funeral of Khan Abdul Gaffar Khan. Rajiv took along a high-level delegation that included his wife, Sonia; Foreign Minister Narasimha Rao; and Home Minister Buta Singh. Rajiv's diplomatic advisers, Ronen Sen and Mani Shankar Aiyar were in tow. Rajiv's decision to travel to Pakistan was 'immediate and spontaneous'. It was not based on bureaucratic advice and overturned security advice not to go.

Before leaving for Pakistan, Rajiv announced a five-day state mourning for the Frontier Gandhi. He offered the janazah prayer next to the coffin, condoled with the family, and returned to Delhi. There was no meeting with Zia, and no attempt to visit Islamabad, a calculated snub for Pakistan's dictator. This was the only visit by an Indian prime minister to Peshawar. (Nehru had visited the city in the 1940s; Manmohan Singh had attended school there.) Rajiv's visit was one of a series of gut instinct-based decisions by Indian leaders about going to Pakistan; subsequent prime ministers, like Vajpayee in 1999, and Narendra Modi in 2015, would make similar choices. One of the positives from Rajiv's visit was that it earned significant goodwill from the Afghans, particularly from Pashtuns like Gulbuddin Hekmatyar.[1] Afghanistan had continued to remain a key concern for India's policymakers. The Soviets were bleeding heavily from the Pakistan-supported Afghan resistance and were willing to negotiate a withdrawal with the West. It was in this context that Rajiv called up Zia on 25 February, and invited him for a visit to India to specially focus on Afghan developments. Zia pointed out edgily that he had visited India twice already in the recent past and countered by inviting Rajiv or his envoy to Pakistan. The two leaders finally agreed to have their foreign secretaries meet. But it was clear to India that Zia was dragging his feet since he was keen to ensure India did not get a substantive say in the Afghanistan endgame. The urgency of the Afghan crisis notwithstanding, Pakistan postponed the meeting scheduled for 1 March for a couple of months.

Despite Pakistan's concerns, some Indian diplomats, including Natwar Singh had visited Kabul, even trying to take on the role of honest brokers between the Americans and the Soviets. On 6 March 1988, Political Counsellor Arun Patwardhan, at India's embassy in Islamabad, sent a somewhat self-congratulatory assessment to Joint Secretary Satish Chandra in Delhi, arguing that big power 'recognition of quiet Indian diplomacy had served to inflame Pakistani complexes', since 'we seem to be closer to these high-level discussions than even Pakistani diplomats were allowed to be'.[2] India's diplomats in Islamabad did not seem to have a measure of how deeply the ISI and CIA were in an embrace in the covert game in Afghanistan or of the US–USSR deal being worked out in Geneva and much less of the major geopolitical shifts about to unfold in the next few years. In fact, Zia had 'adroitly sidelined India from playing a major role in Afghanistan' with the signing of the April 1988 Geneva Accords that continued US arms supplies'[3] to Pakistan. More troublingly for India, the ISI had learnt some useful lessons in Afghanistan, putting a superpower army on the backfoot. It was keen to try out this new playbook in the east.

Of the other concerns that India had to deal with at this time, the Punjab crisis was somewhat easing, as the security forces finally got the better of an insurgency that had claimed the life of a prime minister and threatened anarchy in a critical border state. But Pakistan's hand in this tragedy was now abundantly clear to India's leaders and was the central focus of bilateral diplomacy. Diplomatic exchanges on the Punjab militancy demonstrated the limitations of India's options and the height of its frustration. On 15 April 1988, India issued an aide-memoire to Pakistan, spelling out in detail the evidence of Pakistan's support to Khalistani terrorism.

> Pakistan's involvement with extremist activities directed against India continues to be a major irritant in Indo–Pak relations. India's serious concern in this matter has been conveyed to Pakistan on several occasions.... Despite assurances and denials to the contrary, there is incontrovertible evidence that Pakistan continues to aid and abet extremist activities directed against India.... Pakistan's involvement with anti-Indian secessionist activities broadly extends to:

> - Permitting its territory as sanctuary for extremist Sikh elements and a base for training and indoctrination;
> - Supply of arms and ammunition to Sikh secessionists;
> - Facilitating visits of extremists from abroad;
> - Hostile propaganda designed to inflame anti-Indian secessionist sentiments;
> - Use of Indian Jathas for instigating secessionist sentiments.[4]

This was an unusually direct message on Pakistan's abetment of the Punjab insurgency.

Rajiv Gandhi soon shared his frustrations with Pakistan with the people of India. He said to India's parliament on 20 April, that he had proposed a treaty of peace and friendship, an agreement on non-attack of nuclear facilities, discussions on new ground rules on the border, an MOU to prevent hijacking and even most favoured nation treatment for trade, but Pakistan continued to 'pursue what is very obviously a nuclear weapons program. They assume hostile postures in areas such as Siachen and allowed their territory to be used for the support, maintenance, and sanctuary of terrorists and separatists'.[5]

On 3 May, India's foreign secretary K. P. S. Menon landed in Islamabad for the postponed conversation on Afghanistan.[6] In his call on Zia, Menon raised India's concerns about Punjab, even as he discussed Afghanistan, where the Geneva peace accords were signalling hope for a bloodless resolution. Menon came away with the feeling that Pakistan would prevent Indian participation in the resolution of the Afghan crisis and was refusing to discuss any substantive aspects of the problem. Zia made all the right noises on Punjab, denying any involvement in fuelling the crisis. Zia's party line of total denial was followed down the line in the foreign office. Within a month of receiving India's specific charges, on 14 May, Pakistan responded, rejecting Indian allegations: 'India's charges are groundless and motivated and no aid or abetment has been provided by this country to any terrorist or secessionist activities directed against India.'

During the next round of Indo–Pak foreign secretary-level talks in June, India's ambassador in Islamabad, S. K. Singh, spoke up at length on the issue of Pakistan's meddling in Punjab. He pointed out that of the Muslim, Hindu, and Sikh religious pilgrims from India since the 1960s, the numbers of Hindus had remained constant over the years, but there was a greater 'interflow of Sikhs from abroad' when Indian jathas visited Pakistan. He said 'microphones and stages maintained by the Waqf authorities had been handed over to the most militant Sikhs', and huge quantities of books, videos and literature, espousing the cause of Khalistan, were available freely during the visits by Indian jathas. Singh said at the talks that he did not think that anything could be done 'till there was political will in the higher echelons of the Government to deal with these elements' and suggested that the 'dates for the visits by Indian Sikhs and foreign Sikhs could be separated'.[7]

However, Pakistan was not about to change these tactics and denied all the allegations. This despite the fact that ISI–Khalistani linkages were no longer secret. During a one-on-one meeting with Ambassador Singh, Zia conceded that a controversial US-based Khalistani secessionist, Ganga Singh Dhillon, who had been photographed embracing Zia, did visit Pakistan.[8]

At a press conference in Bonn in June 1988, Rajiv Gandhi gave vent again to his frustration in dealing with Zia's Pakistan over his tenure of the previous three years:

> Let me just say that we have made about 22 proposals to Pakistan, ranging from treaties of peace and friendship, non-attack on nuclear facilities, MOUs on air-space violation by military aircraft, direct contacts between military units so that escalation does not take place...(but) Pakistan is demonstrating two things very clearly: its intention with the nuclear weapon programme and its support to terrorists. Pakistan today is perhaps the largest supporter of terrorism on the globe and it is this that makes the difference.[9]

THE JORDAN CHANNEL

King Hussein bin Talal of Jordan, a personal friend of Rajiv Gandhi, offered to promote an initiative to bring India and Pakistan closer, using his brother crown prince Hassan's connections with President Zia. Rajiv agreed to try this idea. Zia requested Hassan to facilitate talks between the director general of the ISI, Lieutenant-General Hamid Gul, and the secretary of the R&AW, A. K. Verma, in Amman in July 1988. Rajiv handed over the project to Ronen Sen to work out the details and the two intelligence men met in Geneva and Amman. Verma summed up the outcomes of the discussion on a Siachen solution:

a) withdrawal of the Pakistani forces to the west to the ground level of the Saltoro mountains; b) giving up of Pakistani claims to territory from NJ9842 to the Karakoram pass; c) the Line of Control to run north from NJ9842 along the western ground level of Saltoro, exactly north till the Chinese border; and d) reduction of Pakistani troop strength by two divisions with some corresponding adjustments on the Indian side.[10]

The grid line was delineated on a Pakistan GHQ map and handed over by Gul to Verma, apparently with President Zia's approval. The Indian Ministry of Defence was asked to process the decision at the operational level and then bring it up for political approval.[11] The solution pencilled in by the two intelligence chiefs was a pragmatic and smart recognition of the ground realities. It could have translated into the Siachen solution and a major confidence-building step along the entire LoC. But this was not to be.

PLOTS TO KILL

Meanwhile, Zia's stock was falling precipitously within his own country. The demands for free elections grew, led by the young Benazir Bhutto and the Movement for Restoration of Democracy (MRD), which included the PPP and seven other parties. Faced with this determined opposition and the support it was receiving, Zia announced in July that elections would be held in November 1988, a decade after he took power. A faint hope grew that Zia might finally loosen his grip on power.

But India was not seeing any waning in Pakistan's covert plots. Four years after the assassination of Indira Gandhi by Punjab militants, India's intelligence uncovered a credible threat of violence directed at her son, Rajiv Gandhi. Home Minister Buta Singh told India's parliament that a plot to kill Rajiv was being hatched in Pakistan. On 9 August, Pakistan's spokesman rejected reports of any such conspiracy. The irony was to unfold eight days later, when the same parliament would declare official mourning for a death that would alter Pakistan's course.

Despite the hostility, Zia was not giving up on his special brand of diplomatic surprises. Celebrating Pakistan's 41st Independence Day on 14 August, Zia announced that Pakistan's highest civilian honour, Nishan-e-Pakistan, would go to India's former prime minister, Morarji Desai, who had in his brief tenure indulged the dictator more than Indira or her son Rajiv did, and was now a critic of the Rajiv government's approach to Pakistan. This was also seen as a riposte to the Indian diplomatic gambit of handing a civilian award to a critic of Zia, the Frontier Gandhi, a year earlier. This would also be Zia's last diplomatic gambit against India.

A FLIGHT TO DEMOCRACY
Laden with crates of mangoes, the C–130 Hercules executed a perfect take-off from Bahawalpur Airport for Rawalpindi at 3.40 in the afternoon on 17 August 1988. It was a VIP flight with seventeen passengers and thirteen crew. All was well for the first couple of minutes, but then the plane bobbed violently in the air, before plunging into the ground in a fiery ball near the Sutlej in south-eastern Punjab. Among the casualties was Zia ul-Haq, Pakistan's most powerful man of the previous eleven years.

When Ronen Sen got the intelligence signal in New Delhi's South Block, he immediately informed his boss of the dramatic death of Zia. Sen was then a joint secretary in the PMO and a trusted adviser to Rajiv Gandhi, sometimes dubbed India's de facto foreign minister. The PM asked Sen to keep close track of the situation and to keep him briefed. Sen shared news of the crash with his friend, the US ambassador in New Delhi, John Gunther Dean. The American worked the phones with Washington and soon called Sen back to convey that his friend and counterpart in Pakistan, Arnie—US ambassador Arnold Raphael—had also perished in the crash. (Dean went on to later publicly declare that the crash was no accident but an Israeli plot that had worked.)[12]

For three hours after Zia died, Pakistan was without a head of state or an army chief. While the top brass of the army and the US ambassador had been in Bahawalpur, watching a display of US M1 Abrams tanks, the deputy army chief, Aslam Beg, had jumped into a smaller aircraft, for a flight to Pakistan's capital. (Beg was later installed as the army chief, fuelling some conspiracy theories of his complicity in the crash.) Rajiv Gandhi was particularly concerned that the assassination would be the precursor of a violent coup. Indian observers were worried that the new army chief would morph into a new dictator; or that another general would replace Zia, call off the elections scheduled for November, and add a new layer of uncertainty to Pakistan's control over its secret nuclear arsenal.

From Delhi, Ronen Sen kept a careful eye on the developments. The Indian PMO decided not to make any public statements during the day for fear of worsening the situation across the border. So, although Indian intelligence listened in on the chatter in Pakistan with their newly acquired state-of-the-art gear, India waited for Pakistan to announce the news first. Pakistani official media waited till the evening to report that President Zia ul-Haq had died in the crash of Pak One.[13]

When he got over the shock of this momentous event, Ambassador S. K. Singh started planning for another round of funeral diplomacy in Islamabad: a visit to Pakistan by an Indian leader looked inevitable. Deaths of leaders had often joined the neighbours together by way of funeral diplomacy, even amidst suspicions of convenient or insincere grief. Former ambassador Natwar Singh, who had dealt with Zia closely in his years in Pakistan in 1980–82, now a minister of state in the foreign office, heard the news in South Block with concern. He quickly volunteered to go for the funeral. Natwar Singh soon joined a high-level delegation led by President Venkataraman, that included Foreign Minister Narasimha Rao and the leader of the Opposition in parliament, Atal Bihari Vajpayee. Prime Minister Rajiv Gandhi visited Pakistan's high commission to condole the death. Within three days of the crash, a high-profile funeral had been held in Islamabad, attended by several heads of state. Natwar observed that the crowd was enormous but the coffin was almost empty: it contained only Zia's spectacles, jawbone, and false teeth.[14]

Many in Pakistan assumed the moment would be reason for celebration by India's leadership just as Indira Gandhi's gory end four years earlier became a source of elation for Zia. Reports of merriment within the Indian embassy started appearing in Pakistan's media. One particular report in an Urdu weekly *Hurmat* was angrily refuted by Ambassador Singh. The embassy's press release said:

> This story is a vicious, virulent, and contemptible lie. It is well-known and was appreciated at the highest level in Pakistan that the Government of India immediately on learning of the death of the President of Pakistan declared 3-day official mourning. The President of India Shri R. Venkataraman...as also a large All-party delegation of members of Parliament, totaling about forty persons came to Islamabad for attending the funeral... Prime Minister Rajiv Gandhi cancelled his birthday celebrations....[15]

But there was no denying that Zia's sudden exit opened up diplomatic options for India. In the sudden vacuum that his death created, the prospect of handling another military dictator of Zia's ilk was a continuing concern for India's policymakers, one of dealing with a democratic leader in Pakistan more agreeable. Mercifully, Pakistan's army seemed to be in no mood to front the successor government.

That role would go to Benazir Bhutto, who was finding it hard to hide her delight. She had recently moved to Pakistan from London, inheriting the PPP that her father had founded. Benazir was eight months pregnant with her first child, later to become politician and foreign minister, Bilawal Bhutto. 'It's too good to be true,' Benazir gushed to Indian journalist Shekhar Gupta.[16] The thirty-five-year-old Benazir saw the crash as the 'wrath of God'; some divine force had claimed the dictator who had brutally executed her father and usurped power to run Pakistan unchallenged for the past eleven years. This was an Allah-sent opportunity to end the army's dominance, do well in the long-promised elections, and take Pakistan on a new trajectory.

Pakistani and American investigators came to different preliminary conclusions on the crash, respectively attributing it to sabotage and mechanical failure, causing some friction between the two allies. The cause of the explosion was never really established, adding Zia's to a long list of unexplained political deaths in Pakistan. Expectedly, several conspiracy theories swirled over the decades, pointing fingers at the usual suspects: the CIA, the Israelis, the Soviets, Zia's rivals inside the army and, of course, India. The most creative explanation however came a few years later in the form of a brilliant satirical novel by a Pakistani writer Mohammed Hanif, that described multiple assassins including the CIA and a crow deploying assorted modes of murder, including 'a case of exploding mangoes'.[17]

THE BENAZIR FACTOR

A very pregnant Benazir was already campaigning for the November elections when Zia's plane crashed. She was soon catapulted into power, even as dark rumours swirled about the CIA having engineered Zia's end to promote Benazir. After elections, in which her PPP grabbed 93 of the 205 contested seats, she was sworn in as the Islamic world's first woman prime minister on 2 December 1988.

Benazir had returned to Pakistan after an overseas education a decade earlier, a twenty-four-year-old Oxford graduate keen to join Pakistan's Foreign Service in 1977. She was traumatized by her father's 1979 hanging. Worse was to follow—she was imprisoned and then exiled, only to return in 1986. On reaching Pakistan, Benazir had dared to emphatically criticize Zia's governance, particularly for the loss of Siachen. But Benazir had been cautious not to play into Zia's hands by provoking the dictator beyond a point, conscious that he was brutal in wiping out opponents. Zia also had a history of being underestimated by his adversaries, thanks to his self-effacing, unctuous demeanour. Among those who had misjudged him, as has been noted, was Benazir's father, Zulfikar Ali Bhutto, who promoted him over the head of several other generals, believing him to be a weak and pliable yes-man.

The arrival of a democratic government led by Benazir gave the opening to Rajiv Gandhi to plan his delayed formal visit to Pakistan. Many in

India were in this hopeful moment betting on Pakistan morphing into a progressive nation under Benazir, mirroring a modern India, being shaped by another youthful leader. Rajiv wrote to his Pakistani counterpart on 2 December reflecting this heady hope, pointing out to Benazir in a personal letter that 'you and I are children of the same era' and that the 'Simla agreement signed by your father and my mother provides the basis of building together a relationship of mutual trust from 1971.' Benazir, feeling a similar empathy for Rajiv, was to repeat this formulation often.

Rajiv was confident of a new Pakistan emerging with the advent of Benazir and democratic rule. He had felt uncomfortable dealing with Zia in much the way that his grandfather Nehru was uneasy with Ayub, or his mother Indira was distrustful of Ayub, Yahya, and also Zia. Nehru's visit across the border in 1953 and his chat with the leadership had felt more natural than his interaction with Ayub in 1960. Whatever their failings, Pakistan's leaders of the early 1950s had been civilians, with half-baked aspirations to make peace with India. The democrat in Nehru had felt conflicted while dealing with Ayub. Similarly, a couple of decades later, Rajiv Gandhi's body language changed when Benazir replaced Zia; a distinct whiff of hope hung in the air.

A SAARC UMBRELLA

Rajiv Gandhi's diplomatic adviser, Ronen Sen, jumped into a BSF plane one morning in December 1988, to prepare for the visit of his boss for the SAARC summit later in the month. Sen's one-on-one meeting with Pakistan's newly minted prime minister in Karachi was going along expected lines, until they touched upon a sensitive issue. She looked at him conspiratorially and raised her finger to her lips. Benazir then conducted a part of the meeting via slips of paper, indicating that there may be bugs in the room to monitor the conversation. Sen told Benazir that while Rajiv was keen to visit Pakistan, India had grave concerns about his security and needed ironclad guarantees on this issue. If anything happened to Rajiv, this would mean war. Sen also conveyed India's concerns about Pakistan's accelerated nuclear programme, to which Benazir replied that she was out of the loop on what the army was doing on the nuclear side. She agreed, however, that an agreement on non-attack of nuclear installations would be useful.

Benazir said that dealing with India through SAARC would be easier for her than doing so bilaterally. Sen assured her that India would let her decide on the pace and scope of progress in the bilateral relationship and she should only do what she was comfortable with. Sen said that after the restoration of democracy in Pakistan, both should move ahead with a forward-looking agenda, while resolving differences on the basis of the Simla Agreement. As the meeting ended, Benazir asked Sen not to record or circulate her remarks, which were only meant for the ears of Rajiv Gandhi. The incident reflected both the paranoia of the civilian regime of the first woman prime minister of Pakistan and also the delicate relationship with India.[18]

Benazir reciprocated Rajiv's gesture of sending a special envoy, by designating her foreign affairs adviser, Iqbal Akhund, and a Pakistani Parsi confidant, Happy Minwalla, as her 'points of contact' between Rajiv's office and hers. She clearly did not trust her own foreign minister, Yaqub Khan, whom she had retained on the advice of Pakistan's president, Ghulam Ishaq Khan. Pakistan's PM was in sync with the Indian PM's attempt to use the SAARC summit to restructure the bilateral relationship.

In a fractious South Asia, regional cooperation had finally come of age after several abortive attempts, when SAARC took shape and held its first summit in Bangladesh in December 1985. SAARC also became a convenient platform for a conversation between Indian and Pakistani leaders, when a standalone bilateral summit was politically unpalatable to one or both parties. The second summit was held in Bangalore, where PM Junejo came in 1986, and the third had been held in Kathmandu in November 1987.

By the time the fourth summit was planned in Pakistan in December 1988, Zia had perished and Benazir was in charge. For India and Rajiv Gandhi, this was an important moment to test and even bolster Pakistan's fledgling democratic government.

While SAARC provided a ready platform for the two leaders to meet on 29 December, there were still many areas of friction that would have to be smoothened out. On 3 December, barely a day into her term, Benazir had publicly rejected India's no-war pact proposal, citing her father's precedent of rejecting such a pact, as Ayub's minister in 1960. She was pointedly distancing herself from Zia's diplomatic posture of 'appeasing' India. Her evolving political narrative for Pakistan involved playing up her father's role in Pakistan's history and positioning herself as the wronged child of a martyr. She claimed that the period from 1972 to 1988 had been the longest spell of peace with India. Moreover, the relationship was now one of equals, and not of Pakistan treating India as an 'elder brother'. She was contrasting herself politically with Zia's deferential diplomacy towards India. She, of course, could make no reference to the fact that Zia's smiling outreach to India was cover for massive covert operations and a secret nuclear programme.

On the last day of 1988, when Rajiv Gandhi and Benazir Bhutto met after the SAARC summit, it was, for many, the dawn of a new era: the first formal bilateral visit of an Indian leader to Pakistan in a quarter century, after Shastri's stopover in 1964 (not counting Rajiv Gandhi's trip to Peshawar for Badshah Khan's funeral). The two young leaders had detailed

EXPLODING MANGOES 213

conversations, ending in three concrete agreements: on preventing attacks on nuclear facilities; avoiding double taxation; and facilitating air transport. Positivity infused the bilateral exchange, but the leaders still made sure they aired bilateral grievances. While Rajiv spoke of India's policy of improving relations with both China and Pakistan, he pointed to three major bilateral irritants: Pakistan's nuclear programme; terrorism; and Siachen. Benazir raised the issue of Jinnah House, still not within Pakistan's grasp for its consulate in Bombay. Pakistan continued its firm denial of any meddling within India or in Afghanistan, at a time when the Cold War was coming to an end in that country. Foreign Minister Yaqub Khan insisted that Pakistan was not supporting the mujahideen to its west. It was clear to India these were both brazen lies.

Nevertheless, SAARC became a joint-family-like umbrella where the two estranged siblings would have reason to meet at the annual family dinner, dulling bilateral differences for a brief while. But India was getting increasingly exasperated by the violence it was facing in Punjab and now in Kashmir. That made good manners hard to force.

17

A THOUSAND CUTS

In 1989, the Indian security forces, as noted, were getting the better of insurgents in Punjab. Benazir Bhutto, who had in December 1988 promised Rajiv Gandhi she would put the brakes on Pakistan's proxy war, later said bitterly that she was not given enough credit for ending the Sikh insurgency.[1] Clearly, Pakistan's PM, in her innocence, believed she had helped Rajiv deal with that problem, since Pakistan's army was following her command to stop active support for Sikh insurgents. However, even as this was happening, Pakistan was gearing up to roil things up in a different Indian border state—Kashmir. The battle of a thousand cuts was about to begin.

The new phase of violence in Kashmir was also linked to wider geopolitical developments. On 15 February 1989, the last Soviet soldier crossed the bridge over the Afghan–Soviet border into Termez in Uzbekistan, ending a bloody conflict fuelled by the decade-long Soviet occupation of its southern neighbour. The USSR, then guided by Mikhail Gorbachev's perestroika, had acknowledged Afghanistan as a 'bleeding wound' and was withdrawing from an unwinnable war against a mujahideen insurgency that had succeeded only thanks to the support of the ISI in collaboration with the CIA. The Soviets had hoped that the Geneva Accords of April 1988 would ensure an orderly withdrawal and a neutral government in Kabul, helmed by Mohammad Najibullah.

Unbeknownst to Prime Minister Benazir Bhutto, Pakistan's military establishment had drawn a self-serving lesson in 1989 from the forced exit of Soviet forces from Afghanistan—that jihadis trained by the ISI could, at minimal cost, vanquish a powerful army in the neighbourhood. Pakistan's generals were persuaded that since Islamic zeal coupled with local nationalism had been successfully weaponized by the ISI to throw out the Soviets in 1989, this model could be replicated in Kashmir. Indian forces could be removed from that region, using a lethal combination of Islamist propaganda and Kashmiri nationalism, bolstered by weapons, trained militants, and tactical directions from Pakistan.

On 16 April 1989, a new high commissioner assumed office in Islamabad. With the end of the Zia era in 1988, Pakistan was back in the Commonwealth, and the envoys between India and Pakistan were back to being designated high commissioners. J. N. 'Mani' Dixit replaced S. K. Singh, who was promoted as foreign secretary in February. Before taking up his assignment, Dixit called on Rajiv a couple of times in January and February. Dixit had been India's high commissioner in Sri Lanka at a sensitive time, and had interacted closely with the prime minister when India had followed a wrong-headed and ultimately failed policy of unleashing a 'peacekeeping force' on that country during a time of upheaval. Rajiv briefed Dixit on his discussions on both Kashmir and Punjab with Benazir. On Kashmir, Rajiv told his new high commissioner that Benazir had affirmed to him that she was willing to resolve the issue in the framework of the Simla Agreement, but no details were discussed. The prime minister told Dixit he was keen to avoid an arms race in South Asia. Rajiv asked Dixit to assiduously follow up on the decisions of his December visit.[2]

Dixit soon got involved in coordinating a large number of delegations going back and forth since the beginning of the year, to discuss a range of issues, including commerce, railways, transport, and tourism, apart from security, border patrolling, and, of course, Siachen. He attended these meetings with a sense of hope in a new phase in the relationship.

Ronen Sen also visited Islamabad in the summer, as Rajiv's special envoy, to follow up on the prime minister's December 1988 visit and prepare for the next bilateral one. Sen was granted an exclusive meeting with Benazir at her official residence in Islamabad. Dixit accompanied him. In an aside to the two Indian diplomats, Benazir confided that she continued to face strong resistance from President Ghulam Ishaq Khan and army chief Aslam Beg on both India and Afghanistan policies.[3]

DIPLOMATIC HEIGHTS

When Soviet forces withdrew in the summer of 1989, Pakistan's agencies had to do little more than transfer trained global jihadis from its western to the eastern border, to fight for an old cause in Kashmir. Pakistan's political turmoil of 1988 had little impact on the army's Kashmir strategy. While Benazir thought she was in charge and could work out a modus vivendi for peace with Rajiv, Pakistan's deep state was also assessing that India had been weakened—with the political crisis of a scandal-hit, floundering Rajiv Gandhi government and an economic one of dwindling forex reserves. This seemed the right moment to launch a new tactical push in Kashmir, to catalyse a popular uprising in the valley.

The ISI's Kashmir adventure was code-named Operation Tupac, after an eighteenth-century revolutionary who led the war of liberation in Peru against Spanish rule. It was seen by India's security agencies as an elaborate plan to destabilize J&K by sponsoring an insurgency carried out through militants and through covert support to separatists. The plan was authorized by Zia in 1988, his farewell gift to India months before he perished. The programme would continue in various avatars and developed an unstoppable momentum of its own, where Pakistan's leaders, civilian or military, would sometimes press the pause button, but could never really stop the machine. The initial programme involved the creation of six separatist militant groups by the ISI, gradually relocating many mujahideen fighters freed up for battle from the Afghan theatre. The star of the stable was the Lashkar-e-Taiba (LeT), with which the ISI developed the cosiest and most enduring partnership.[4] The programme would soon morph into a low-cost, light-touch plausibly deniable scheme of pushing a stream of trained militants into India across the LoC.

North of the Kashmir Valley, the Siachen situation remained deadlocked. But for the two young prime ministers of the enemy countries, ending this mindless war in the snowy heights seemed doable. Rajiv Gandhi and Benazir Bhutto invested personal political capital and prodded their envoys to find a solution. The fifth round of defence secretary-level talks in June 1989, between Naresh Chandra and Ijlal Haider Zaidi, had been inconclusive but had brought the sides the closest to a resolution since the stand-off began in 1984. The joint statement issued after the talks promised that both sides would 'work towards a comprehensive settlement, based on redeployment of forces to reduce the chance of conflict'.[5] However, the more ambitious backchannel deal of Zia's time, to delineate the northern boundary, was not revived.

Media reports of the time reported optimistically on the deal that was about to be struck and that 'army officials from the two countries will now work out the details of redeployment'. A reality check came when Pakistan's foreign secretary Humayun Khan prematurely told the media after meeting his Indian counterpart, S. K. Singh, that the two sides had agreed to relocate to positions 'occupied at the time of the (1972) Simla Agreement'. This would have implied a literal climbdown by India. Sitting by Khan's side at the presser, in an act of diplomatic tact, India's foreign secretary did not challenge the statement.[6]

The backchannel Siachen solution had been interrupted by Zia's death. A keen observer of these dynamics argued that if the line agreed to in mid-1988 had been ratified at the intergovernmental level, it could have been a 'major political-strategic step forward', not just for peace and tranquillity, along the India–Pakistan LoC, but also in the crucial India–China border areas in eastern Ladakh. However, there was a real or feigned ignorance about such an agreement at all levels in Pakistan after Zia's passing. The Rajiv–Benazir discussions on Siachen were more limited in ambition—they did not seek agreement on demarcating the northern borders; they were about settling the issue on the basis of mutual force withdrawal from actual ground position locations (AGPLs) and establishing jointly monitored demilitarized zones (DMZs).[7]

Dixit was hopeful that the prime minister's visit on his watch would spell a breakthrough. Rajiv Gandhi's visit to Islamabad on 16 and 17 July was the first bilateral visit of an Indian leader to Pakistan in three decades, after Nehru's in 1960. Rajiv was accompanied by Sonia, Foreign Minister Narasimha Rao, and Minister of State Natwar Singh. While the visit had set expectations high, its conclusion, to Dixit, was an 'anticlimax'. Benazir seemed desperate to see some shift in India's Kashmir posture to increase her credibility domestically with the army and Islamist forces. They were accusing her of being soft on Rajiv and India. Rajiv, on his part, reminded Benazir of the discussions on the Simla Agreement, and suggested that a practical and realistic approach would serve them better than a demand for unilateral concessions. Following her father's example (of a last-minute request of Indira Gandhi to salvage the 1972 Simla Agreement), Benazir insisted on a final one-on-one meeting with Rajiv before a scheduled joint press conference that the two leaders were to address on 17 July. The unscheduled meeting delayed the press conference and was held in an adjoining room. Rajiv remained firm and articulated India's views clearly.

One concrete outcome was the setting up of a joint commission that would meet regularly. A couple of days later, on 19 July, Narasimha Rao was in Islamabad for the meeting of the bilateral joint commission. He called on PM Benazir Bhutto and discussed the glacier issue after the session with his counterpart, Sahabzada Yaqub Khan. He said he had not quite caught up on the details of the discussion on the issue between National Security Advisor Iqbal Akhund and Rajiv Gandhi's diplomatic adviser, Ronen Sen on the night of 16 July, but the Siachen situation needed to be addressed politically. Rao had got it right. No military deal was possible unless the two countries developed a basic level of political trust.

Benazir was destabilized by domestic pressures after Rajiv's visit and tried to take a tougher stand on Kashmir. Foreign Minister Yaqub Khan visited India at the end of July and made a cheeky offer to mediate between India and Sri Lanka, even as Sri Lanka refused to host the next SAARC summit unless the Indian Peacekeeping Force (IPKF) withdrew. India politely refused to countenance this politically motivated offer.

In August, a military commanders follow-up meeting on Siachen discussed the operational aspects of a possible agreement. It was clear that by now Pakistan's position had changed, as it introduced two new points. First, while they could withdraw troops to be redeployed in mutually agreed points, they would refuse to confirm these cartographically. Second, the withdrawal would be subject to the line being drawn tangentially north-eastwards to the Karakoram Ranges from NJ9842. This made it clear that the game of the Pakistan Army was now to get the Indian Army to withdraw from its strategically secure position on the glacier. The discussion had reached an impasse.

Even as they faced domestic political challenges—elections in India and civil–military tensions in Pakistan—the two leaders did meet again in

September 1989 at a non-aligned summit in Belgrade. This time, there was no headway in the meeting between the two diplomatic advisers, Ronen Sen and Iqbal Akhund. Sen made it clear to Akhund that any progress in the extension of the LoC beyond NJ9842 would have to be made after India's general elections.[8]

The line on the Siachen map that Ronen Sen, Iqbal Akhund, and the defence secretaries were debating had dramatic implications. If the line went due north, it would give the entire glacier to India; if it went north-east, Siachen would be in Pakistan. If the two sides could not decide on the line, they would need to discuss the ground positions of troops. Sen had been involved in discussions to minimize the military pain of defending the Siachen Glacier from the time Rajiv Gandhi became PM in 1985. Since neither side was politically ready, the matter had to be kicked down the road. Rajiv later revealed that he was close to a 'deal' with General Zia before his death in 1988 and subsequently came close to an agreement with Benazir in 1989. But he was not destined to untie that knot in the high Himalaya.

Rajiv was soon consumed with a bruising election campaign, fighting corruption allegations in the purchase of Bofors guns. By the end of 1989, Rajiv Gandhi's Congress government had been voted out and a coalition government sworn in on 2 December, led by former finance minister Vishwanath Pratap Singh.

The new government faced its first crisis within days, on 8 December with the kidnapping of Rubaiya Sayeed, the daughter of the home minister, Mufti Mohammed Sayeed. Pakistan's involvement in this brazen act was clear to India's security agencies. The kidnapping ended with the release of militants from Indian jails and signalled a heightened militancy in Kashmir and a weakened Indian security establishment.

To Dixit, the tenuous hopes of a new beginning came to a somewhat abrupt end in December 1989. He had several one-on-one conversations with both Benazir and Rajiv between August and December. He concluded that their 'mutual disappointment' had been inevitable, given fundamental differences in approach; the 'downward spiral' was triggered by Benazir's unrealistic expectations that India would be as accommodating as it had been in Simla in 1972, and would be willing to compromise on issues like Kashmir and Siachen. Rajiv, on the other hand, wanted to gradually create mutual trust to get to practical solutions to intractable problems. Rajiv had made it clear to his envoy that his macro-level approach to both Zia and Benazir had been to build confidence, and reduce risk in the relationship without compromising on core interests like Kashmir and Siachen.[9]

EXODUS

The Kashmir insurgency intensified in 1990, even as Pakistan denied its role and heightened its rhetoric. Benazir sent a special envoy, Abdul Sattar, to Delhi in early January. Sattar, who had been a hard-line high commissioner to India between 1978 and 1982, reported confusion and weak governance in India, with a gap between Prime Minister V. P. Singh's cautious position on Pakistan and Foreign Minister Inder Kumar Gujral's attempt to open up communications.[10]

In the valley, targeted killings of Kashmiri Hindus increased, as did a campaign of terror asking them to leave the valley. In early January, some newspapers around Srinagar started publishing messages ascribed to the terrorist group Hizbul Mujahideen, asking all Hindus to leave Kashmir immediately. Soon, posters appeared on walls asking Kashmiris to follow Islamic law and on doors of Hindu homes, asking them to leave. Masked men with Kalashnikovs were reported to be forcing people to reset their watches to Pakistan Standard Time. On 14 January, Pakistan expressed concern at the deteriorating situation in Kashmir, in what was clearly a communication offensive accompanying the terror campaign unleashed in the valley.

On 17 January, Chief Minister Farooq Abdullah resigned, protesting the appointment as governor of Jagmohan, the tough administrator sent to resume his mission in Kashmir in the wake of the Rubaiya Sayeed kidnapping. Jagmohan's appointment was meant to signal New Delhi's resolve to contain the violence. But leaders in Delhi still did not have a measure of the enormity of the assault on the valley from Pakistan. On 18 January, in an interview to *Dawn*, Foreign Minister I. K. Gujral chose to focus on fuzzier matters—his roots in Pakistan. Gujral did not touch on Kashmir as he spoke warmly of his birth on the banks of the Jhelum in Pakistan and his visit in 1982, when all of the town of Jhelum came to visit him.[11]

On the night of 18 January, a blackout hit the valley, with the apparent exception of some mosques, which broadcast violent slogans calling for the killing of Kashmiri Hindus.[12] By 19 January, thousands of Kashmiri Pandits were fleeing to Jammu, as militants appeared to have gained complete control of the valley. This departure was dubbed an exodus, the largest movement of people escaping persecution since 1971. Most analysts assess that within a few months, close to 100,000 of the valley's 140,000-strong Kashmiri Pandit community fled to Jammu, Delhi, and other areas of India and the world.[13]

On 21 January, Pakistan's foreign minister, Yaqub Khan, a scion of the princely family of Rampur in India, came to meet his Indian counterpart, I. K. Gujral. Yaqub, possibly representing the approach of the army rather than the elected PM, was aggressive and abrasive, stoutly denying any role in promoting insurgencies in India. He said that Benazir had been deeply disappointed by Rajiv's reticence on Kashmir. He implicitly threatened war if the Kashmir situation was not resolved. Gujral, visibly upset by this bluster and Yaqub's attempt to intimidate India on the Kashmir issue, was diplomatic during the day but decided to respond firmly in the evening. Gujral discussed this matter with his prime minister, V. P. Singh, who authorized him to send a clear message to Pakistan. Gujral went to a dinner hosted by High Commissioner M. Bashir Khan Babar of Pakistan for his boss, and said that he wanted a private meeting after the dinner with the foreign minister. Dixit was present at the meeting where Gujral said that Yaqub Khan's statements during the day had caused concern and resentment in the new government of India, and that such an attitude of Pakistan would only evoke firm and decisive response from India.[14] After conversing in the book-lined study in the Pakistan ambassador's house, where Jawaharlal Nehru and Liaquat Ali Khan had often met, the two foreign ministers decided to take a walk on the lawns. Several writings, including Gujral's own telling of events, suggest that Yaqub, perhaps at the behest of Pakistan's army, may also have issued a nuclear threat. 'Don't start a war now,' he said in Urdu, 'or there will be a fire that consumes our rivers, forests, mountains, everything.' Gujral responded in kind: 'I don't know what you are talking about, Yaqub sahib, lekin jin daryaon ka paani aapne piya hai, unka hee humne bhi piya hai. But remember, we've been nurtured on the waters of the same rivers as you.)'[15]

Later observers saw a pattern to Pakistan's behaviour. It started the war in August 1965 assuming that Nehru's death had left India weakened with a floundering Shastri. Now, a weak post-Rajiv Gandhi alliance led by V. P. Singh should have made India vulnerable in Kashmir and susceptible to nuclear blackmail. The sorry episode of the kidnapping of the home minister's daughter and India's weak-kneed response only reinforced the impression of an unsteady India. This pattern would be repeated in the future, despite its erroneous premise. Even when politically weak, India was institutionally strong.

Pakistan's rhetoric on Kashmir was now escalating to higher decibels, with frequent threats of war. In February, both Pakistan's newly incubated civilian politicians of the post-Zia era, Benazir Bhutto and Nawaz Sharif, were in fact competing to see who could be shriller in their rhetoric on Kashmir; such anti-India postures seemed a sure path for the civilian politicians to ingratiate themselves to the deep state, at whose pleasure they would be allowed to rule.

On 5 February, Pakistan called a 'strike' for Kashmir. This elicited compliance not just across Pakistan, but also in the Kashmir Valley. For the first time, college girls in Rawalpindi, Lahore, and POK joined in processions with men. Groups of lawyers, labourers, and students were pulled in for public meetings. A sticker on a Suzuki said: 'Time to win Kashmir'.[16]

The strike was proposed in Pakistan by Qazi Ahmad of the JeI.[17] This was the Islamist party being used by the army to prop up a young Lahore politician, Nawaz Sharif, to replace Benazir Bhutto, who was not toeing the army's line, particularly on India. 5 February would in subsequent years be packaged to become for Pakistan a 'Kashmir Solidarity Day', Youm-i-Yakjehti, ritually celebrated to this day with officially sponsored banners and events across Pakistan, and sloganeering outside the Indian high commission.

MARCHING INTO INDIA
In Islamabad, what worried Dixit most was that 'various Islam–pasand parties and groups' announced that there would be mass crossings by Pakistani civilians into the territory of Jammu and Kashmir as also into portions of northern Punjab.[18] Acting on instructions from Delhi, Dixit told Pakistan's foreign secretary, Tanvir Ahmed Khan, as well as US ambassador, Robert Oakley, that 'civilian crossings, and mass hysteria' across the LoC, and across the international frontier would be met with 'decisive responses' by the Indian armed forces. But the message was lost, the juggernaut was moving. A week after the strike call from Pakistan, violent mobs crossed the LoC twice from POK into India. On 11 February—the death anniversary of JKLF leader Maqbool Bhat—hundreds of people tried to cross the LoC in Chakothi, a crossing point in Kashmir. When Indian troops fired, they dispersed, returning later with twice the number of people. About 3,000 people crossed into the Indian side over the LoC. Initially, Indian forces used public address systems to ask the civilians to go back. But when the mobs started burning crops, wooden stakes, and pillars, security forces from India fired two bursts of Sten guns on the mob, killing about seven people. A similar crossing was attempted the same day by about a 1,000 civilians from a point north-east of Sialkot in Punjab. But with the firing in Kashmir, the civilian crossings stopped. Dixit feared Pakistan would now go back to infiltrating militants and mercenaries into India as soon as the snows melted.

Given the prevailing sentiment in her country, Benazir felt obliged to get even shriller in her anti-India rhetoric. She had emerged in public after giving birth to a baby girl, Bakhtawar, on 25 January, and wanted to reassert her political persona. She publicly repeated in March in POK, the promise her late father Bhutto had dramatically made in the 1970s[19] to fight a thousand-year war with India over Kashmir.[17] Benazir should have known that in the intervening 1980s, Zia had changed the strategic doctrine from the thousand-year war to the battle of a thousand cuts, pragmatically recognizing the military power differential and privileging

covert warfare on India's periphery. Zia, had, of course, also added nuclear
weapons to Pakistan's armoury, seeking power parity with India.

Prime Minister V. P. Singh's weak government was initially circumspect
in its response to Benazir's provocative posturing, but later responded in
kind in parliament: 'Those who threaten 1,000-year wars,' Singh said on
10 April, 'should first see if they will be able to last even 1,000 hours
of fighting.'[20] He followed up on this speech with one addressing troops
on the Rajasthan border to suggest that India was in the process of
initiating military measures against Pakistan. Predictably, Pakistan reacted
by summoning Dixit to the foreign office to explain matters. Dixit gleefully
conveyed to both the foreign office and the US ambassador that if Pakistani
'pyrotechnics' continued, it should be prepared for a military response
from India.

Later in April, Foreign Minister Gujral tried to ease the tension when
he met his counterpart Yaqub Khan again in New York. But Pakistan was
voicing its growing fears to the US, which was in turn getting worried by
the escalation in South Asia with a clear nuclear overhang. In May, US
ambassador Robert Oakley invited Dixit to his office for an urgent meeting.
He gravely produced some US satellite pictures showing an Indian Army
build-up on the Rajasthan–Sindh border, apparently threatening Pakistan's
Punjab to the south. Oakley asked Dixit if this meant that India was
preparing to attack in Punjab to reduce Pakistani violence and pressure
in Kashmir. The 1965 war story would have informed US worries. Dixit
relayed these concerns to headquarters and soon had instructions from
Cabinet Secretary Naresh Chandra to convey that India had no plans
or intention to launch any military operation against Pakistan. However,
India would certainly retaliate militarily against any violence inside J&K.
Dixit asked Oakley to convey this message also to the upper reaches of
the Pakistan Army to 'cease and desist from their adventurist inclinations'.

Oakley's messages to Rawalpindi and also to Washington resulted in
the 'Gates mission' in the summer of 1990. US deputy NSA Robert Gates
flew in to India and Pakistan on a delicate diplomatic assignment, at
a time when US policy famously hyphenated the relationship between
the two belligerent South Asian neighbours. The primary mandate of the
mission was to de-escalate the tension, given the danger of a nuclear
confrontation between the covert nuclear powers.[21] While the situation was
tense, Dixit later assessed that the danger of nuclear confrontation between
the covert nuclear powers was exaggerated. At any rate, the danger had
not reached the levels as later sensationalized in the book *Critical Mass*
by two American authors, William Burrows and Robert Windrem, which
claimed that a nuclear conflagration had been averted through smart US
diplomacy.[22] While Gates conveyed 'categorical, cautionary admonitions'
to both India and Pakistan, his trip did not, Dixit noted wryly, result in

any abatement of Pakistan-sponsored separatism in J&K.

What the Gates Mission did do was to trigger a process that led to five rounds of Indo–Pak discussions at the foreign secretary level between May 1990 and October 1991. But the underlying structural chasms in the relationship would ensure that the talks produced no substantive outcomes of note, much like the Bhutto-Swaran Singh talks that preceded the 1965 conflict.

Too much was happening in 1990 on the bilateral front, for both countries to notice the tectonic geopolitical shifts that would impact them even more. The Soviet Union was collapsing after the Afghan withdrawal as the West doubled down on the Soviets and Mikhail Gorbachev seemed only too willing to dismantle the communist empire. The unipolar moment of the United States was beginning.

This was also the period when regional geopolitics was in churn, severely impacting an India preoccupied with internal woes. In June 1990, Iraq had invaded Kuwait, suddenly bringing Western attention back to West Asia, after it had wandered away post the withdrawal of Soviet forces from Afghanistan.

Within Pakistan, Benazir was dislodged from office in August, after twenty months in power, ostensibly by the president of Pakistan, on the pretext of her indulging in nepotism and corruption. It was an open secret that the army establishment, recovering from Zia's loss, had had enough of the Benazir experiment and wanted to install Nawaz Sharif, the new puppet they had created. The army had convinced itself that Benazir had become a security risk and was spilling out national secrets to the Americans, particularly on Pakistan's nuclear programme. Elections were scheduled in October, but their outcome was never in doubt.

In September 1990, a newly appointed ISI chief, Asad Durrani, received a call from his boss, army chief Aslam Beg, with a peculiar request. Some Karachi businessmen, unhappy with Benazir's PPP, wanted to contribute to the Opposition's election campaign. Since time was short, could the ISI help ensure the money reached the right hands? The request struck Durrani as unusual, but he was eager to please his boss who had got him his new job. Durrani deployed intelligence men to collect ₹140 million from a banker and distribute the money into various accounts.

When this sordid story tumbled out into the media four years later, the by now retired General Beg said that the money had been passed on to the ISI for 'political intelligence'. Retired air marshal and PPP politician Asghar Khan filed a petition in the Supreme Court in 1996, submitting that this operation had violated his human rights at a time when he was campaigning for the PPP in 1990. Durrani later called his decision to distribute the cash the 'most imprudent move' of his career. He indicted himself when he signed an affidavit later for an internal enquiry, admitting to this transgression. He even dedicated some part of his memoir to a mea culpa explaining his actions of 1990.

Three decades later, I asked Durrani about this episode at a party in Islamabad, soon after I read his remarkable self-critical memoir.[23] Durrani was unusually forthcoming—the ISI had clear evidence, he said, that Benazir had gone too much into the arms of the US, and he was persuaded at that point that she had to go. This wasn't justification for the act, just one of the reasons.

THE ARMY'S NAWAZ

For Dixit, 1990 had been a tough year. He reflected that both India and Pakistan had in place weak coalition governments. On its part, Pakistan had kept tensions ratcheted up in J&K instead of trying to distance itself from the violence, to focus on building more important aspects of bilateral relations. The general positive push given to bilateral relations by Rajiv Gandhi went into 'slow motion' in the term of V. P. Singh's Janata Party government.

The October elections brought in Nawaz Sharif, riding on the benevolence of his army mentors. (Imran Khan told me in 2018 that Nawaz had been 'manufactured in GHQ' in 1990.) In this election, as with every subsequent democratic election in Pakistan, the army had a favourite civilian candidate it was backing. Having got a bad rap with the dictatorships of Ayub, Yahya, and Zia, the army was learning through its ISI to 'manage' Pakistan's democracy.

Even as Nawaz Sharif took over as Pakistan's prime minister in November, V. P. Singh's coalition government collapsed, to be replaced by a Congress-supported regime headed by a new prime minister, Chandra Shekhar. During Chandra Shekhar's brief tenure, India–Pakistan relations continued on a negative trajectory, even though the two prime ministers met during the SAARC summit in the Maldives on 21 and 23 November 1990. They even decided to set up direct hotlines between themselves, as also between the foreign secretaries and the DGMOs, as confidence-building measures. The hotlines were seldom used, except the one at the DGMO level, to discuss operational issues.

Despite the meeting of Chandra Shekhar and Nawaz Sharif, diplomacy on the ground remained inflamed. In November, complaints emerged of the harassment of diplomats in both countries. On 1 December, Pakistan issued a note on the continued harassment of its diplomats; India's spokesman dismissed the allegation as a 'cover-up for provocative harassment and intimidation' by Pakistan.

UTOPIAN PROPOSALS

As a difficult year ended, another equally tough one began for both countries. 1991 saw turmoil in the larger neighbourhood, as it kicked off with a war in the Persian Gulf when the US launched Operation Desert Storm on 17 January, with air attacks on Iraq and Kuwait. The Cold War had ended messily. The USSR—India's strong friend of the previous three decades—had imploded and America's unipolar global position was gathering strength. In South Asia, Sri Lanka was in ferment, its ethnic battles spilling over into India.

Around midnight of 21 May, Dixit received shocking news. Rajiv Gandhi, on the campaign trail in south India, had been brutally assassinated by Sri Lankan Tamil militants. Dixit immediately conveyed this information to Pakistan's president, Ghulam Ishaq Khan, and Prime Minister Nawaz Sharif. The president arrived the next day at the Indian high commission to sign the condolence book. Nawaz Sharif, on his part, decided to lead the Pakistani delegation to the funeral in Delhi. Benazir as the former PM came along as well.

On 24 May, Nawaz called Dixit up to say that he wanted a separate meeting in New Delhi with India's prime minister, apart from the standard courtesy call. Chandra Shekhar readily agreed and hosted a lunch on 25 May. After exchanging courtesies in the delegation-level talks, Sharif suggested that the two prime ministers have a private discussion. After the meeting, Dixit saw off the Pakistani delegation at the airport, and returned to brief his prime minister. The PM called a broader meeting the next day to review Pakistan's funeral diplomacy. The meeting of senior officials (of the ministries of external affairs, home, and defence) concluded that Pakistan's anti-India activities could be expected to continue in Kashmir, even if Nawaz Sharif might not personally be supportive of these activities.

Something was clearly still weighing on Chandra Shekhar's mind after the meeting had concluded; he asked Dixit to return the next day. On 28 May 1991, the PM revealed to Dixit that Pakistan's PM had sought the separate meeting to convey a message. Sharif had told Chandra Shekar that it was imperative to improve India–Pakistan relations and the only obstacle to this goal was the Kashmir issue. Further, the only practical solution was that both sides should move back from claiming total jurisdiction over the entire territory of the former princely state. Then came the crux—Nawaz Sharif advised Chandra Shekhar that his government should 'seriously consider' allowing a plebiscite in the valley, so that India could ultimately keep Ladakh and Jammu, while Pakistan would retain areas of POK. The valley would later accede to Pakistan. Chandra Shekhar, taken aback, had advised Sharif not to make 'impractical, utopian proposals'. With this snub, Sharif returned home to resume a hostile position on India, perhaps prodded by the army. However, Dixit assessed, the rhetoric on Kashmir gradually became less shrill.

In the general election of 1991, the Congress Party and its allies triumphed. A reluctant Narasimha Rao, pulled out of retirement, became the choice of the Congress as Rajiv's successor. Rao was sworn in as prime minister in June. The new prime minister's plate was full. External flux was aggravating political and economic instability at home. India's economy threatened to go into a tailspin, its foreign exchange reserves were perilously low, and it was in danger of defaulting on an IMF loan. And India faced some of the toughest internal security challenges since Independence.

Pakistan was not going to let this opportunity go. The Lashkar-e-Taiba, launched in Muridke, Pakistan's Punjab, in the mid-1980s, sharpened its attacks on Kashmir. So also did the terrorist group Hizbul Mujahideen that had been formed in 1989.

Rao was no stranger to the Pakistan relationship. As Rajiv Gandhi's foreign minister, he had met with Benazir in December 1988, and again in July 1989. Rao had come to the conclusion that Pakistan could not really be trusted. Soon enough, Rao had a visitor from Islamabad. Pakistan's foreign secretary Shahryar Khan, who, as noted, had been born into the royal family of Bhopal, visited India in August as Nawaz Sharif's special envoy. His mission, similar to that of Abdul Sattar in 1990, was to assess India's new government for vulnerabilities on Kashmir. He told Prime Minister Rao and Defence Minister Sharad Pawar that Pakistan would take 'definitive steps' to prevent subversion in Jammu and Kashmir originating from Pakistani territory. He promised that India would see a 'qualitative change in the situation on the ground'.[24] He recommended that both countries undertake a discussion on Kashmir, as also on other issues, to normalize relations.

Rao toyed with the idea of establishing a direct channel of communication between himself and Pakistan's leaders, learning from Rajiv Gandhi's successful deployment of Ronen Sen as a personal envoy to Benazir. He asked Shahryar, after a one-on-one meeting, to remain in touch with his private secretary, Ramu Damodaran. In an amusing mix-up, Shahryar made contact a few weeks later with Rao's principal secretary A. N. Verma, rather than with his private secretary, but the connection did not materialize as a channel.[25]

Rao was not overly impressed by Shahryar's expression of good intentions. His approach was to keep the conversation flowing, while never taking Pakistan at its word. Rao felt that one-on-one talks were critical. 'He always persisted' recalled his aide, 'despite his deep cynicism that anything can happen.'[26] Three months into his tenure as prime minister, Rao saw no reason to change the assessment he had astutely made in his years as foreign minister. 'Every time there is a change either in Pakistan or India, there is a sense of euphoria created, some new hopes are aroused,' he said in India's parliament in September, 'but subsequently, these hopes are dashed to the ground.'[27]

Rao encountered Nawaz Sharif in the fourth month of his tenure. The two met in Harare in October at a Commonwealth summit. They had a constructive chat, and would go on to meet five more times in Rao's first two years in office. Rao would converse in chaste Urdu, as 'the finest Urdu speaker in all of the Nizam's Hyderabad' clearly better linguistically than the West Punjab politician.[28]

Meanwhile, Dixit was completing his tenure in Islamabad. He bumped into former PM Benazir in October at an Islamabad embassy reception. She remarked: 'Mr Dixit, I am hearing good rumours, I believe you are going to be the next foreign secretary of India. I am glad that somebody who has lived in Pakistan and who knows Pakistan is going back to the foreign office. Despite the current difficulties, I hope that during your tenure in office, we will be able to improve our relations.' Dixit replied that while the rumours were not entirely baseless, he had no formal orders yet. In the same month, Dixit received Foreign Secretary Muchkund Dubey in Islamabad for the fifth round of foreign secretary-level talks. But Shahryar Khan's promise of a 'qualitative change' remained unfulfilled.[29]

ANOTHER TRACK TO TALK

Around the same time, at American nudging and given the gathering crisis in Kashmir, both sides had also agreed to try a new form of engagement, pulling in civil society representatives to brainstorm on ways forward. The 'Neemrana dialogue', at a fort in Rajasthan, began in October as a 'Track Two' accompaniment to the stuttering official dialogue. One of the proposals of the Gates Mission had been to promote a 'non-official dialogue' so that the two sides could communicate when official exchanges collapsed. Soon, the Neemrana dialogue series and other similar ones took off, with freewheeling discussions of contentious issues including Kashmir, nuclear proliferation, easing of visa restrictions, cultural and trade exchanges. The processes were supported by both governments, granting visas to participants on priority. The discussions rested on two fundamental principles. First, participants would maintain secrecy by not discussing the meetings with the media. Second, they would not dwell on 'history' at the meetings. Later, professionals were roped in to infuse fresh ideas, although many officials remained cynical of 'naïve meddlers and amateurs lacking the skills and information to manage sensitive issues'.[30]

As Dixit's tenure ended, Pakistan found another peg to ratchet up the rhetoric. Tension arose in the Indian town of Ayodhya on 31 October, as an excited mob bearing saffron flags damaged the disputed structure of an old mosque, the Babri Masjid. The movement for removing the mosque to make way for a temple at what was for Hindus the birthplace of Lord Rama, had become a lightning rod for communal tensions in India, and a perfect opportunity for Pakistan to walk into a non-Kashmir fissure. Pakistan's foreign office spokesman declared on 2 November that the government and the people of Pakistan were 'outraged and anguished over the desecration and damage to the Babri Mosque'.

18

FROZEN TRUST

In the middle of January 1992, a new high commissioner of India assumed office in Islamabad. Unlike his two predecessors, S. K. Singh and J. N. Dixit, who were at the apex of the bureaucratic pyramid, and had both transitioned after Islamabad to become foreign secretaries in India, Satinder Kumar Lambah was a relatively junior joint secretary-level officer posted as India's consul general in San Francisco.

Lambah had received a call from the PM Rao's secretary, Ramu Damodaran, in October 1991, saying that the PM had decided to post him to Pakistan and requesting his consent within twenty-four hours. Lambah confirmed he would go. He hosted a dinner at his residence the next evening, for Ambassador Abid Hussain visiting from Washington, but did not share this news with his boss. At the party, a house guest, veteran journalist Inder Malhotra, shocked his hosts when he raised a glass and said he hoped Islamabad would be Lambah's next destination.

Lambah was no stranger to Pakistan—he had served in Islamabad as deputy high commissioner in the early 1980s, and also in the MEA in the late 1980s as the joint secretary dealing with Pakistan. He had a deeper familiarity with Pakistan—his family came from pre-Partition Peshawar and his wife, Nilima, had distinguished lineage in pre-Partition Lahore. These old connections would give the Lambahs extraordinary access and connections within Pakistan. Rao had known Lambah as the ministry's long-time Pakistan expert, but also as someone who 'spoke the idiom' in fluent Punjabi and Urdu, and could communicate effectively across a broad spectrum of Pakistani society.

But the PM had played this choice of envoy close to his chest. When Mani Dixit became foreign secretary in December, Rao asked to be given a list of four names to choose his successor in Islamabad from. Dixit handed over the list, with Lambah featuring in it. The PM told Dixit later that he had chosen Lambah. In fact, Islamabad was the first station for which Rao had chosen an envoy to fill the top job.[1] He sent another young career officer he knew well, Ronen Sen, as ambassador to Moscow, but thinking out of the box, he chose politicians Lakshmi Mall Singhvi for London and Siddhartha Shankar Ray for the US.

Lambah's reputation preceded him in Pakistan. At a protocol line-up at the Islamabad airport in December, PM Nawaz Sharif had casually asked Acting High Commissioner Bhadrakumar when India would send the next HC. The Indian diplomat replied that Pakistan's concurrence was awaited in the case of S. K. Lambah. Sharif paused and asked, 'You mean Satinder Lambah?'[2] When the acting HC confirmed the name, Sharif said he would receive the agrément immediately. Later that evening, Foreign Secretary Shahryar Khan informed Bhadrakumar that he could consider the agrément as having been given, even though the formal communication would follow in a couple of days.

Pakistan's PM had recognized the name for good reason. When Lambah had been posted as deputy high commissioner in Pakistan (1978–82), he had been introduced to a young steel tycoon in Lahore, who became a friend. This was Nawaz Sharif. Lambah had kept in touch and even hosted Sharif in Delhi to a Chinese meal at the House of Ming, where the server had memorably spilled soup on the future prime minister's white suit.

When Lambah presented his credentials to Pakistan's president in January, he got a call from the PMO, with an invitation to join Nawaz Sharif and his wife for lunch the next day, along with his family. The prime minister discussed their past association, mostly in Punjabi. Lambah handed over a personal letter from Prime Minister Rao that read, 'This note is just to tell you that Sati Lambah, whom I am sending as our High Commissioner to Pakistan, enjoys my personal confidence.' Lambah hoped that the message from this additional gesture would be clear—that any discussions on the backchannel could be shared with him. Lambah also conveyed PM Rao's request that Pakistan change its attitude towards support to Sikh extremists in Punjab. Nawaz said he would try to do 'as much as he could'.[3] The envoy requested unfettered access to the PM. Sharif designated an official in his office to be Lambah's point of contact. This direct line to the PM would serve Lambah well.

The ISI's activism in Kashmir was, however, not abating. In February, Lambah had to contend with a threatened march by the JKLF across the LoC, carrying the risk of escalation, as in 1990. This time, the march was stopped by Pakistani forces but as many as seventeen people died in the firing and clashes. Sharif was being more careful than Benazir had been; he said that Pakistan would not allow such a crossing since 'we did not want a fourth war with India'. The JKLF attempted another crossing at the end of March, but this time Pakistani forces controlled it without loss of life.

Another tack for Pakistan, to capitalize on the unrest in the region, was to try to again bring Kashmir to international attention. Lambah reported on meetings of Pakistani envoys with a focus on the Kashmir issue. Pakistan was also raising the matter at the UN and international fora, apart from sending delegations around the world to spread a narrative of Kashmir as a global trouble spot. This policy started paying dividends. The European community passed a resolution on 12 March[4], supporting the right to self-determination in Kashmir. Soon after, the Swedish parliament expressed 'deep concern' at the human rights situation there.

BEATING DIPLOMACY

Cricket proved a unifier, when against all odds, Pakistan's team led by Imran Khan won the cricket world cup in March 1992. This was seen as a subcontinental victory, and India's president, R. Venkataraman, sent a congratulatory telegram to his Pakistani counterpart within minutes of the win. Lambah dashed off a handwritten note to Sharif, ahead of any other the prime minister received. It seemed only natural that both countries should pause hostilities and celebrate the subcontinent's cricketing triumph.

But the default position of hostility soon returned. Lambah faced a peculiar but not unfamiliar challenge early in his tenure. On 24 May, Pakistani agents grabbed an Indian diplomat outside his home. Counsellor Rajesh Mittal's father and a domestic help watched in horror as the goons roughed him up outside his residence and then whisked him away in a car, despite his diplomatic immunity. Mittal suffered seven hours of torture in captivity and was released battered and bruised after vigorous protests by Lambah and relentless pressure from India. The Pakistani action seemed to have been in retaliation for the arrest and detention of a Pakistani official in April, when he was caught red-handed meeting an Indian official whom he had subverted. The official, Arshad Ali, had been returned to Pakistan on 13 May after several weeks of detention[5]. But Pakistan had retaliated with disproportionate brutality, causing a good deal of public outrage in India. Relations hit a new low as these events played out in the media.

Even though Mittal had been declared persona non grata, and asked to leave Pakistan within forty-eight hours, his safe passage from Islamabad to the border near Lahore was not guaranteed, nor was the option of a commercial flight feasible. Mittal was a stretcher case, and Foreign Secretary Dixit offered to send an Indian Air Force plane to pick him up. Pakistan refused on the grounds that they could not permit the Indian Air Force to land in their territory. Eventually, a Border Security Force (BSF) plane picked up the injured officer. Foreign Secretary Dixit himself received the officer in Delhi and was horrified to see his condition; Mittal had to be hospitalized for months. India retaliated by expelling two Pakistani counsellors from Delhi. The two Pakistani diplomats walked normally into a commercial aircraft in Delhi but mysteriously descended from the plane in Pakistan limping and bandaged. Pakistani media reported that they had been subjected to physical abuse and violence, like the Indian diplomat was. Dixit concluded wryly that some 'mid-air arrangement' had been conjured up, to temper Indian indignation and portray equivalence to the 'diplomatic courtesies' extended to Mittal by Pakistani intelligence.[6]

Diplomats who had been respected in the first decade of Independence, and mostly spared in the second till the 1965 war, seemed no longer out of bounds for intelligence agencies, even in the absence of war. The killing of Ravindra Mhatre in 1984 and the assault on Mittal in 1992 demonstrated the edge of anger poisoning the diplomatic relationship. Something needed to be done to reverse this situation. India suggested that whenever the next foreign secretary-level talks were held, the two sides should agree on a code of conduct governing the treatment of each other's diplomats. Pakistan's Foreign Secretary Shahryar Khan agreed.

Rao had his fourth meeting with Nawaz Sharif on 14 June at the Earth Summit in Rio de Janeiro. Given the Mittal affair and the other lows in the relationship, Rao was reluctant to meet his counterpart, but was finally persuaded by Foreign Secretary Dixit to go ahead. One of the considerations was not to allow Pakistan a propaganda advantage by a refusal to engage. A positive outcome of the conversation was a decision to resume the dialogue at the level of foreign secretaries.

In July, Lambah had a chance chat, at an Islamabad gathering, with the ISI chief Lieutenant General Javid Nasir that led to a structured conversation between them at ISI headquarters. This reinforced Lambah's view that India should formally engage with the Pakistan Army as well. Lambah recommended to Delhi that India should invite the army chief of Pakistan, since India was the only key country which did not have such an engagement with Pakistan's main power centre. Lambah thought that even if Pakistan would find the optics of a visit by its army chief unacceptable, they might be softened by the gesture, leading to broader gains for India.

Shahryar Khan arrived in India in mid-August for foreign secretary-level talks with Dixit. Once both sides had stated their well-known positions on Kashmir, they sensibly moved to ideas for the future. The sixth round of talks was special for its focus on confidence-building measures; these included an agreement on the 'code of conduct' for the treatment of diplomatic and consular personnel. A key decision was to resume discussions at the level of the defence ministries and armed forces to try and address the Siachen stand-off. As part of the CBMs, India handed over a formal invitation from India's army chief for his counterpart to visit India. While Pakistan accepted the invitation 'in principle', such a visit is still to take place over three decades later.

Despite this burst of realism, Lambah remained concerned at the rising tension in the relationship, particularly after a resolution in Pakistan's National Assembly on the Ayodhya temple issue on 27 August, seen by India as interference in its internal affairs. PM Rao was sensing the decline in bilateral ties, despite his preoccupation with challenges at home. Rao instructed Lambah to discuss these matters with his Pakistani hosts. Lambah met PM Nawaz Sharif and Foreign Secretary Shahryar Khan and reported on 29 August that Pakistan had 'noted' India's strong feelings. [7]

Rao went through the motions of his fifth meeting with Nawaz Sharif on 3 September on the margins of a non-aligned summit in Jakarta. While the fact of the meeting itself was touted as a means of defusing tension, Rao said later that he considered these meetings with Sharif as 'merely cosmetic'. [8]

ICY RESOLVE

Notwithstanding the deteriorating Kashmir situation and bilateral tensions, India played along with Pakistan's enthusiasm in looking for a solution to the Siachen dispute, agreeing to resume the annual official dialogues. The resolution would involve for India a leap of faith, of giving up a military advantage, withdrawing troops, and trusting Pakistan not to breach the written agreement.

Between 2 and 6 November 1992, the sixth round of talks on the Siachen Glacier was held in New Delhi. The Indian side was again led by N. N. Vohra, the defence secretary, who had been part of four of the five rounds of talks held during 1985–89, while Rajiv Gandhi was PM. India had pressed the pause button since, given the political shifts and Pakistan's proxy war in J&K since 1990. A draft agreement was exchanged before the talks. Pakistan seemed to agree to India's demand to mark the existing positions—in India's favour—before recording demilitarization.

The world had changed between the fourth and fifth rounds, impacting negotiations with Pakistan. India's chief negotiator Vohra later recalled.

> This period witnessed momentous changes across the globe—the Iraq War, the fall of the Berlin Wall, the implosion of the USSR and the end of the Cold War... Domestically we were going through a very bad patch—fall of two successive governments within a year and a half, and a mounting economic breakdown. The end of the rupee–rouble trading agreement with the erstwhile USSR created a huge crisis with regard to the procurement of defence supplies, and the growing financial stringency made it impossible to meet the defence expenditures, particularly foreign currency payments for the procurement of munitions. [9]

Lambah came in from Islamabad for consultations on the eve of the discussions. He saw that while the ground position favoured India, policymakers were entertaining the idea of a mutually agreed pull-back, provided Pakistan did not insist on reverting to the pre-1971 ground positions, or on its own physical presence on the glacier. Pakistan was in fact only focused on containing India's presence on the glacier. But India's leaders had their doubts. When Lambah called on President R.

Venkataraman, who had been India's defence minister in 1984, the year India moved into Siachen, the president said that 'there was still blood in the snow'. Lambah reported this conversation to Prime Minister Rao, reinforcing the PM's reservations at a time when he was heading a minority government. Rao was also not happy with the reports he was hearing about Pakistan's attitude in the talks; he was beginning to seriously doubt Pakistan's intentions'[10]

But India's defence secretary felt the countries were coming closer to a deal in 1992 than in 1989. India had proposed a 'zone of disengagement', with both sides withdrawing their forward posts and base camps to given locations; the area of this zone was to be subjected to surveillance by both sides for a specified period and, thereafter, 'collaborative non-military activities' were to be allowed, including removing military waste, ecological conservation, trekking, mountaineering, and adventure sports.[11] Vohra later described India's moment of truth. After three days of 'hard discussions', when he reached PM Rao's residence at Race Course Road, Foreign Secretary J. N. Dixit was already present. He briefed Rao on the signing ceremony planned the next morning and pointed out that his Pak counterpart had already gone public about 'the successful conclusion of the talks.'[12] After a thoughtful silence, Rao said, '...do not sign the Agreement tomorrow...' and asked Vohra to 'visit Islamabad in January 1993 to commence the process ad referendum.'[13]

Rao's gut instinct proved right, the agreement was ahead of its time and assumed a level of trust in the relationship that did not then exist. Decades later, Vohra conceded that 'whatever may have been PVR's constraints or considerations when I reported to him late that winter evening, it could perhaps be said, in hindsight, that he had rare farsightedness when he stopped me from signing the agreement with Pakistan.'[14]

A MARTYRED MOSQUE

Worse was to come that year. Lambah's hopes for an upturn in the relationship on his watch were dashed on 6 December, for him 'one of the most difficult days as High Commissioner in Pakistan'. The destruction that evening by a charged mob of the Babri Masjid, the more than 400-year-old mosque in Ayodhya, plunged India into socio-religious turmoil. For Pakistan, this was an unmissable chance to wade into India's internal politics.

Lambah had to take a call on whether to make an appearance at a National Day reception of Finland later that evening. He decided to stick to his normal routine, and soon became the centre of attraction at the gathering, with multiple Pakistani guests accosting him to voice their disapproval at the demolition of the mosque. The secretary general of the Pakistan foreign office was happily directing all Pakistani journalists to the Indian high commissioner. Lambah's response to mediapersons was brief—he was extremely unhappy at what had happened, was in principle against any place of worship being a target of attack; but Indian democracy was strong enough to bear such shocks.[15]

Soon, Nawaz Sharif issued a statement expressing '[a] deep sense of shock and horror'[16] at the Ayodhya developments. In Karachi, stones were thrown at Indian residences at Shivaji Court. Lambah was summoned to the foreign office the next day to be handed over an aide-memoire, protesting the demolition, on the basis of the 'Inter-Dominion agreement of August 1947, and the Nehru-Liaquat pact of 1950'. Lambah found these references odd, since Pakistan itself had disowned the 1950 pact in 1974; in the wake of the Simla Agreement and in the immediate context of communal riots in Delhi's Sadar Bazar, Pakistan's foreign minister Aziz Ahmed had said that such issues would be treated as internal matters. Pakistan had then rejected the stake the 1950 bilateral pact gave both countries in the other's minority dealings.

But angry and violent reactions continued in Pakistan. Security became a priority for the Indian mission, even as an Indian Airlines office in Lahore was torched. Pakistan's cabinet met after Lambah's meeting to declare 8 December a day of mourning and protest. On the streets, violence grew. Minorities in Pakistan faced the (mostly orchestrated) wrath of the mobs; 120 temples were eventually demolished, apart from gurdwaras and churches.

A demand arose within ruling circles to declare the Indian high commissioner persona non grata, to express Pakistan's anger to the world. The issue was not debated publicly, since the proposal was overruled by Nawaz Sharif, pointing out that the international repercussions on Pakistan of such a move would be negative. Also, Sharif did not want Lambah's tenure to end given their personal relationship. Lambah learnt of these developments only later, when a cabinet minister confided in him.[17]

Most worryingly for Lambah, a mob attacked and ransacked the consul general's residence in Karachi. Part of the residence of Consular General Rajiv Dogra was burnt,[18] though Dogra's family managed to escape disaster by hiding in a room. Lambah was on the phone with the traumatized wife of the CG, Meenakshi, while the ransacking was ongoing. Gallingly, the house was attacked in the presence of the security services.[19]

A SAARC summit scheduled in Dhaka in December had to be postponed. Pakistan was now demanding that the 'martyred' Babri Masjid must be reconstructed exactly on the site it had stood on for more than 400 years. Pakistan also started pushing India to cut down its diplomatic operations in Karachi; the Indian consulate there was often described as a 'nest of spies', for the excellent access it had with multiple actors in Sindh society. On 29 December, India issued a statement warning that any reduction of staff in Karachi would affect the Muhajir community. On 31 December, Pakistan asked India to scale back the Karachi consulate. India protested that it needed the manpower to promote people-to-people links, to continue issuing 700 visas every day. That was precisely the problem. Pakistan icily pointed out that while there were sixty-four diplomats in Karachi, Pakistan's consulate in Mumbai housed only two diplomats and one official. Foreign Secretary Shahryar Khan, a votary for better ties with India, had instructions to ask High Commissioner Lambah to immediately cut down staff in Karachi from sixty-four to twenty. Lambah called up CG Rajiv Dogra to start the exercise.

EXPLOSIONS IN BOMBAY

The destruction of the Babri Masjid in December 1992 had given ready cause to multiple militant outfits within and without India, leading to an orgy of violence. In December 1992 and January 1993, India was convulsed by rioting across the nation with Bombay particularly affected. A commission later estimated that 900 had died and over 2,000 had been injured in the two months of violence. On 12 March 1993, Bombay was shaken by a series of 12 terrorist bombings that resulted in 257 fatalities and 1,400 injuries.[20] The bombings were engineered by the Dubai-based gangster, Dawood Ibrahim, who became a close ally of the ISI. Dawood, boss of a crime syndicate, D-Company, carried out the bombings through his henchmen Tiger Memon and Yakub Memon. Both escaped to Pakistan via Dubai.

Pakistan's motives and involvement were soon clear to Indian investigators, as some of the conspirators arrested admitted to being trained in Pakistan.[21] India also had some advance warning. Lambah had picked up information from a source and sent a report from Islamabad a fortnight before the attack, warning of impending 'disaster in Bombay'. Lambah was surprised that instead of taking action, authorities in India only wanted to know the source of the envoy's information. The news of the advance warning leaked into the media and Lambah on his next visit to Delhi expressed his 'anguish' to the prime minister on these developments.

In April, the postponed SAARC summit was held in Dhaka; Sharif and Rao had another ritual meeting but the army effectively fired Sharif soon after his return. Ostensibly, Pakistan's president, Ghulam Ishaq Khan, dismissed Nawaz Sharif on the basis of corruption charges against him and his party Islami Jamhoori Ittehad (IJI). Soon after, on 16 May, Lambah met with the caretaker prime minister, Balak Sher Mazari, who admitted to him that six members of the Memon family had arrived at Karachi on 17 March, but had thereafter disappeared.[22] India did subsequently (in September 1993) provide detailed evidence on the D-Company through a note verbale, but Pakistan, as would become the norm for terrorism cases, did little by way of investigation. Three decades later, Dawood Ibrahim continues to be a guest of the Pakistan ISI in Karachi. India's foreign minister S. Jaishankar would comment at the UN in 2023 about terrorists granted safe haven in Pakistan, that the crime syndicate responsible for the 1993 Bombay blasts was 'not just given state protection, but enjoying five-star hospitality'.[23]

Meanwhile, in Islamabad, Sharif was temporarily restored to his job on 26 May, only to be fired again, in a formula where the army chief got rid of both the president and the prime minister, announcing fresh elections in October 1993.

AN INALIENABLE PART

North of Bombay, militancy supported by Pakistan was deepening in Kashmir. The All Parties Hurriyat Conference (APHC) was formed in 1993 to raise the cause of Kashmir's self-determination. On the violent end of the spectrum, another militant group, Harkat ul-Ansar (now known as Harkat ul-Mujahideen)[24], emerged in 1993 from a combination of organizations that had been dedicated to the Afghan jihad, but now could be repurposed for Kashmir.[25]

Speaking from the ramparts of the Red Fort on 15 August, PM Narasimha Rao said that Pakistan was 'fuelling Muslim militancy and a guerrilla campaign in an integral and inalienable part of India'.[26] Pakistan's caretaker foreign minister, Abdul Sattar, decided not to let Rao's assertions go unchallenged. Sattar said that the assertions on Kashmir by the Indian prime minister amounted to 'claiming ownership of robbed goods'. India's spokesman countered that 'if India claiming Kashmir was robbery, then Pakistan's occupation of one-third of the state was nothing less than armed dacoity'.[27] Such rhetorical flourishes for public consumption became par for the course whenever Kashmir was debated by the neighbours.

As Pakistan's assiduous global campaign on Kashmir succeeded, the region became an internationally recognized hotspot, at least for the US. President Clinton referred to Kashmir in his UN address in September as 'a trouble spot where bloody ethnic religious war rages'. In October, the US assistant secretary of state, Robin Raphel, made a statement that flustered India, 'We view Kashmir as a disputed territory, and that means we do not recognise the instrument of accession as meaning that Kashmir is forevermore an integral part of India.'[28] This seemed like a shift in the considered US position that called for bilateral dialogue.

Soon after making the statement Raphel visited Pakistan. Raphel had lost her husband, the US envoy Arnold Raphel, in the plane crash that killed Zia in 1988, and was seen in India to have a soft corner for Pakistan. On the day of her arrival, US Ambassador John Monjo hosted a dinner to which Lambah was invited. Raphel requested a pre-dinner chat with the Indian high commissioner, in which she insisted that she had been misquoted. Lambah advised her to make that statement publicly, since her original statement was public too. Raphel agreed but appeared restless during the dinner. She delivered a formal speech and raised a toast to India, instead of Pakistan, needing to hastily correct herself. The slip prompted the chief guest, Pakistan's interior minister, Major General Naseerullah Babar, to joke that this was undoubtedly the doing of the Indian high commissioner, who was talking to her before she entered the dining room. By the end of 1993, after a strong pushback from India, the US line had been corrected, and Robin Raphel had back-pedalled to say that it was time to move forward on Kashmir, 'not to look at past prescriptions'.[29]

On 18 October 1993, Benazir Bhutto was back in the saddle as prime minister, having won the elections with the blessings of the army. This time around, she was eager not to repeat the mistakes that had estranged her from the army establishment. She took a tougher position on Kashmir, in step with the unrest in the valley.

GENEVA BATTLES

With Benazir getting more hawkish on Kashmir, a chill gripped the relationship. Despite the pessimism, Mani Dixit and Shahryar Khan met in Islamabad in early January 1994, for a foreign secretary-level dialogue— the seventh edition of the 1990s. India had agreed to discuss 'all issues', including Jammu and Kashmir. The Indian delegation was flown by special aircraft to Karachi, to call on Benazir, who on the day of their arrival, 5 January, was observing the 66th birth anniversary of her father, Zulfikar Ali Bhutto. Recognizing the 'basic divergence' in positions on Kashmir, the two sides agreed to make 'sincere efforts to resolve the problem'. When the Indian delegation flew back from Islamabad, Lambah learnt that Pakistani officials had told their media that there would be no further talks at the foreign secretary level 'till there were meaningful discussions on Kashmir'. Lambah passed this message onto Dixit in Delhi so he could keep this in mind while briefing media in India. A few days later, Pakistan's new foreign minister, Sardar Asif Ali, told the media in Tashkent that there was a danger of a 'fourth war in South Asia' that could go nuclear. Benazir, on her part, stepped up the verbal campaign on 23 January, saying, 'We do not want to give a wrong signal to the Kashmiris by holding meaningless talks with India.' She then prepared to take the battle to a human rights conference in Geneva that was scheduled in April. Lambah observed later that she had underestimated Narasimha Rao.

Lambah was constantly looking for newer initiatives to give Pakistan a more realistic assessment of India's thinking and its own limitations. Before the foreign secretary-level talks, he suggested to Prime Minister Rao that India should spell out its views clearly in black and white on five or six key issues. The prime minister readily approved the proposal; on 24 January, India, handed over six 'non-papers',[30] which were concrete but informal proposals on the live bilateral issues of the day: Siachen; the disputed Sir Creek estuary on the Gujarat border; the Tulbul navigation project in J&K; a draft agreement on maintenance of peace and tranquillity along the LoC; confidence-building measures; and revival of the India–Pakistan joint commission. Lambah pointed out that the package of CBMs included two critical nuclear measures: a proposal to expand the existing agreement on not attacking nuclear facilities to include population centres and economic targets; and an undertaking on no first use of nuclear capability against the other. These were significant and substantive proposals that emphasized a principle of constructive bilateralism, suggesting that the two countries could engage deeply and solve bilateral problems without recruiting third parties.

Not surprisingly, Pakistan, in its response, pushed Kashmir back on centre stage. On 9 February, Pakistan proffered two non-papers of its own: on the modalities of holding a plebiscite in J&K; and measures required to create a propitious climate for talks on the J&K dispute. On Siachen, Pakistan commented that there was no understanding in the sixth round in 1992, but only an agreement in the fifth round in 1989, and that Pakistan did not agree on any authentication of the ground positions held by the two sides in Siachen. Pakistan's message was clear: discussions should focus only on J&K.

Rao was troubled by Pakistan's new activism on Kashmir, particularly its attempt to internationalize the issue and bring it to the UN Human Rights Commission. With the internal security challenges in the state and Pakistan's successful global campaign to shape a new narrative, Rao did not like the way his minority government was being perceived in its handling of the issue, domestically and externally in the new unipolar world. Taking forward the idea of clearly stating India's position on all issues, Rao decided to take India's parliament into confidence to send a ringing domestic and international message, apart from making matters clear to Pakistan. For the first time since Independence, a resolution passed by India's parliament affirmed that POK was part of India. With masterly political finesse, Rao had the resolution adopted in both houses of Indian parliament on 22 February 1994. The text emphasized that the entire state of Jammu and Kashmir 'has been, is, and shall always be an integral part of India'. It also demanded that 'Pakistan must vacate the areas of the Indian state of Jammu and Kashmir, which they have occupied through aggression.'

To Lambah, watching events in Islamabad, the resolution responded well to Pakistan's slogan that Kashmir was the 'unfinished business of partition'. Lambah noted admiringly that Rao never bragged about this resolution because he knew the message was evident in the fact of its passing. When Pakistan protested the resolution, Lambah pointed out to his hosts that India was only responding to, and effectively acknowledging, Pakistan's position on the Kashmir issue.

Five days after the resolution claiming POK was passed in India's parliament, Pakistan tabled a resolution at the UN Human Rights Commission in Geneva through the OIC condemning India for human rights violations in J&K. This presented an opportunity to Rao to display his extraordinary diplomatic skills and those of his diplomats on the ground. Riding on the back of the parliamentary resolution asserting India's claim to the areas under Pakistan's occupation, Rao made several inspired moves, including the choice of Opposition leader Atal Bihari Vajpayee to make the Indian case at the UN.

From Islamabad, Lambah was reporting that Pakistan was choosing its delegation to Geneva with great care. It was betting on UN experts within the system rather than on political heavyweights. Iqbal Akhund, Benazir's trusted adviser, and an expert on the UN system, became the leader of Pakistan's delegation. Several multi-lateralists were roped in, including Munir Akram, later Pakistan's permanent representative to the UN in Geneva and New York, apart from India experts like Shafqat Kakakhel. A competent permanent representative in Geneva, Ahmed Kamal, coordinated the exercise. Neelam Sabherwal, India's deputy permanent representative in Geneva, reported that Pakistan's delegation had fewer generals and more foot soldiers.[31]

India seemed to be doing the opposite, packing its delegation with generals. At its peak, India's delegation had twenty to twenty-five high-level delegates for the month-long HR council meetings, arriving from Delhi, New York, and other missions. The list included Finance Minister Manmohan Singh, Opposition leader Atal Bihari Vajpayee, the BJP foreign policy chief Brajesh Mishra, minister of state Salman Khurshid, former Congress minister Natwar Singh, former J&K chief minister Farooq Abdullah, high commissioner from London L. M. Singhvi, the permanent representative to the UN in New York Hamid Ansari, and the UN team from Delhi, led by MEA Secretary Vinod Grover, and UN Division chief Prakash Shah. Fortuitously, the diplomat coordinating this exercise was India's permanent representative to the UN in Geneva, Satish Chandra, an old Pakistan hand. Chandra had his hands full, managing the prima donnas of the Indian team, his advice about not having too many bigwigs having been shot down by a nervous Delhi, keen to deploy all its strength for this mission. His Geneva team was preparing the statements and lobbying strategy for interactions with other delegations to the council in Geneva. The VIPs were interacting with other delegates, but Chandra was disappointed that they were not striking a good rapport with the other official delegates.

Chandra's team needed to selectively deploy the big guns. Finance

Minister Manmohan Singh and leader of Opposition Vajpayee would add gravitas from the podium. The mercurial Farooq Abdullah, with his histrionic talents, could be used in 'short bursts', an effective counter to the blistering attack from Prime Minister Benazir Bhutto launched from the podium.

Chandra recalled a bilateral lunch with a German delegation which he set up with Khurshid and Natwar Singh. India was relentlessly grilled on its human rights record, putting Khurshid and Chandra on the defensive. Singh remained silent, until Chandra suggested towards the end of the lunch that he should respond. After an 'inordinately lengthy pause', Natwar said he saw no reason to engage on issues related to human rights with the representatives of the nation responsible for millions of deaths with a record in the matter that was amongst the most horrific. Singh's caustic comments abruptly ended the discussion, which then moved to more neutral matters.

When Finance Minister Manmohan Singh landed in Geneva, he was told that Benazir had addressed the council from the podium with a piercing diatribe against India. Dr Singh insisted on responding himself. Since technically, this privilege was accorded not to the head of a delegation but to an 'eminent person', this meant that Singh had to be re-designated as a 'statesman' and could not lead the delegation. That also meant that India had to choose another leader for its delegation. Chandra advised the ministry that the next most senior person was the leader of the Opposition, Vajpayee, who should be designated the delegation leader. He received clearance within twenty-four hours from Delhi. Prime Minister Rao had an excellent equation with Vajpayee and had possibly planned on this approach anyway.

Chandra had experienced the dress rehearsal for this drama the previous year. When Pakistan had made a similar move at the 1993 council meeting, India had successfully countered the gambit through intense diplomacy. But as the stakes were higher in 1994, both sides had pulled out the heavy artillery. Policymakers were thinking of worst-case scenarios. A resolution passed at the UN criticizing India for its role in Kashmir, would have, regardless of the exact text, encouraged militancy in Kashmir. Its optics would have weakened the government domestically. The PMO in India was prepared to have any draft resolution watered down to a 'chairman's statement' on Kashmir. Chandra's advice however was to fight it out and not compromise in this winnable battle; to defeat any resolution in a vote.

On the eve of the debate on the resolution, India's team assessed that they would win a 'no action motion' on the resolution by a margin of 7–4, with all others abstaining in a house of fifty-three. The countries still counted in the Pakistan camp included Iran, Libya, and Syria. The position of many others remained undefined or undisclosed. This situation needed a relentless diplomatic effort in Geneva, in Delhi, and in various country capitals through India's heads of mission, to persuade member states of the council to vote in favour of India or to abstain. Iran's vote became critical in the overall scheme of things.[32]

Prime Minister Rao was closely following the Geneva story. He had been hearing disturbing reports on the uncertain levels of support for India. He called a meeting at his residence on 6 March, to take stock of the situation. Foreign Secretary Krishnan Srinivasan presented his ministry's assessment that seven countries would side with India and four with Pakistan, with the rest abstaining. But Rao was 'shaky' and looking for some alternative way out. He was worried that 'a loss in Geneva would result in his loss in Delhi'. An additional concern, as has been noted, was that a loss in Geneva, would fuel the fire and encourage militancy in Kashmir. When Srinivasan assured Rao that the numbers were on the Indian side, 'he looked dubious, but mercifully allowed matters to take their own course'.[33]

As the debate progressed in Geneva, Lambah reported from Islamabad that key members of the OIC—Indonesia, Libya, and Syria—might not finally support Pakistan. As their tally of votes of support dwindled, the Pakistani delegation sought approval from Islamabad to amend the resolution by dropping the demand of a fact-finding mission being sent to J&K. This was a familiar multilateral trick—keep diluting formulations to get broader support, to focus on the optics of a successful resolution rather than the substance. Lambah reported that this verbal request was rejected in Islamabad since any further dilution would have created more trouble for Benazir domestically.

The Iran vote was critical. Rao decided to send a special envoy to Tehran to clinch Iranian support. Foreign Minister Dinesh Singh, who was ailing by this time, volunteered to undertake this mission. Singh carried a special letter from Rao for President Akbar Hashemi Rafsanjani, who had received Rao in 1993 as the first non-Muslim leader to address the Iranian Majlis.[34] Iranian foreign minister Ali Akbar Velayati, received Singh and on learning of the purpose of his visit, suggested that he may also want to meet the Chinese foreign minister who was coincidently visiting Tehran on the same days. The Iranian president gave Singh no assurance during their meeting, but said that the matter would be carefully considered. Singh also managed to meet his Chinese counterpart for a 'positive' meeting. As Singh departed Tehran, Foreign Minister Velayati informed him that the president had instructed him to say that India's interests 'would be kept in mind'.[35]

The Iran visit, Dinesh Singh's last diplomatic foray before he passed away, had a significant impact in Geneva. Chandra had been working on the Iranian ambassador, Cyrus Nasseri. The Iranian diplomat took the floor on the final morning of discussions on 9 March and asked for a 'deferral' of the resolution, when Pakistan was still hopeful of pushing it through. This move puzzled India's representative, Prakash Shah, who asked for a procedural clarification. Brajesh Mishra, who had an inkling of the Iranian development, tapped Shah on the shoulder and asked him to accept the deferral proposal.[36]

An anxious PMO in Delhi had instructed the teams in Geneva to accept any deals to ensure that the proposed resolution did not go through. Before the afternoon session resumed, the Chinese ambassador approached the Indian delegation to say that he had been in touch with the Iranian ambassador and was going to ask Pakistan to withdraw the resolution. At another venue, India voted in favour of China as a quid pro quo. A seminar on Tibet proposed by an Indian activist George Fernandes was shelved. The Chinese noted these developments.[37]

When the session reconvened, Iqbal Akhund announced the withdrawal of the Pakistan resolution.

India's success was celebrated by a jubilant media, bolstering PM Narasimha Rao's image as a master tactician and unifier. Rao had, with his choice of Vajpayee to lead the Indian delegation, ensured non-partisan support not just for India's position on J&K, but also for his own minority government. In the annals of Indian diplomacy, this game plan for success at the UN became a story for Indian diplomats to celebrate and to learn from.

GOODBYE KARACHI

Pinak Chakravarty had replaced Rajiv Dogra as India's consul general in Karachi in September 1994. Chakravarty was presiding over a depleted mission that, as we have seen, his hosts had called a 'nest of spies'. The success of the mission's outreach, and visa policy had proven to be its undoing. Both Chakravarty and New Delhi's decision-makers had a strong suspicion that he would need to shut down the consulate in Karachi, though it had been unclear when that would happen. Chakravarty received a phone call from High Commissioner Lambah one afternoon in January 1995 saying they had ten days to close down the Karachi consulate and that all staff there had been declared persona non grata. Lambah had been summoned to the foreign office that morning and given this ultimatum. One of the reasons cited for the decision was that Pakistan's Bombay consulate had not been allotted the use of Jinnah House in Bombay. The other ostensible factor was the Pakistani allegation that India was behind the rising violence in Karachi. In reality, Pakistan wanted to get rid of the Indian diplomatic post in Karachi because it felt that India was getting more out of Karachi than Pakistan out of Bombay. High Commissioner Lambah sent political counsellor G. Parthasarathy to Karachi to help in the winding down of the post. Chakravarty locked up the Karachi consulate towards the end of January 1995, thus ending an important chapter in

India's diplomatic history in Pakistan.

Even as the formal dialogue between the countries froze with the chill in the relationship, the 'Track II' conversations between civil societies picked up steam. The Pakistan India People's Forum (PPIF) held a meeting in Delhi in February, while the ninth round of the Neemrana dialogue intensified another non-official track of exchange. Even though participants often used talking points procured from officials, the conversations broadened the base of bilateral ties.[38]

Kashmir continued to be on the boil. In May 1995, terrorists returning from Kashmir after successful attacks were glorified in Pakistan, as for instance, Mast Gul, who led the team that razed the Sufi Charar-e-Sharief shrine in Kashmir to the ground. Indian diplomats' protests were brushed off in Pakistan.

Benazir Bhutto, who thought of Narasimha Rao as a poor successor to Rajiv, decided not to attend the 8th SAARC summit in New Delhi in June 1995. She sent Pakistan's president, Farooq Leghari, instead, under the protocol excuse that the summit could have either heads of state or government. Ironically, the approach seemed to backfire on her as his participation just added to Leghari's perception of his position as a constitutionally autonomous one. He would go on to dismiss Benazir a little over a year later, in November 1996, at the prodding of the army.

Lambah's own relationship with Pakistan's prime minister was strained. After becoming prime minister, she had not met him for some time since she was suspicious of Lambah's strong association with her political rival and predecessor, Nawaz Sharif. On one occasion, Lambah raised this issue with Prime Minister Rao, even suggesting he appoint someone else as high commissioner to ensure better access to Pakistan's PM. Rao wisely dismissed the notion, pointing out, 'You are our High Commissioner, not theirs.'[39]

To Lambah's surprise, when he asked for a farewell call on the PM on the eve of his departure in July 1995, Benazir not just granted one but also hosted a lunch for him after the meeting. Lambah noted that this was the first time any Pakistan prime minister had ever hosted a meal for a departing Indian envoy. After the lunch, Benazir 'suddenly dropped a bombshell' when she asked Lambah: why don't you send the missile man to us? She was referring to Abdul Kalam, then a missile scientist, and later the president of India. Given the implicit assumption of Pakistan's claim on India's Muslim citizens, a shocked Lambah asked the PM if she was serious, because he would not report this part of the conversation back at home. He did give her a gentle lecture on Muslims in India, pointing out that they were held in high esteem, and occupied high positions in the country, unlike in her home province of Sindh, where the 'Mohajir Muslims, who came from India (were) still treated as second-class citizens.' Benazir quickly changed the subject. Lambah mentioned this conversation verbally when he called on PM Rao, who told him he had done the right thing.[40]

Lambah also had a farewell lunch in July with Nawaz Sharif, the leader of the Opposition, at his Murree house, where the top leadership of Sharif's party was in attendance. Sharif told Lambah that he would like to see him at his swearing in ceremony when he was appointed prime minister again.[41] Clearly, Nawaz knew something Lambah did not, since he would be back in the saddle within eight months of that lunch.

Satish Chandra walked in as the new high commissioner of India in Pakistan in August 1995 with bilateral relations at a low. Apart from being a Pakistan expert in the ministry, Chandra was born in Lahore, and spoke some Saraiki, the language of his parents who came from Multan, apart from Urdu and Punjabi. As an old Pakistan hand, Chandra had little illusion about the scope for reversing the downturn of relations. In the aviary of Indian diplomats serving in Pakistan, if Lambah was a dove, Chandra was a distinct hawk. The two officers were close friends, but developed different prescriptions for dealing with Pakistan.

Chandra thought not much had changed since he was last posted in Karachi on the eve of the 1971 war: 'There was the same hostility to India, the same ISI surveillance and harassment of our diplomats', he recalled in his 2023 memoir.[42] Chandra's first cable home assessed that while the military was not directly ruling the country, civilian rule was merely a façade. Frustrated by the harassment his teams faced, Chandra tried to persuade the Indian government to retaliate in equal measure, and even personally took up this matter with Prime Minister Rao. The prime minister scoffed at the idea and told his envoy that India could not stoop to any such tit-for-tat retaliation. This posture would change only in the twenty-first century.

Chandra felt the frosty relationship and the absence of a dialogue could be attributed to terrorism in Kashmir and to the fact that Pakistan had not yet reconciled itself to its diplomatic failure in Geneva and other UN fora. He sensed that there was little love lost between the two prime ministers. In fact, when Chandra, on Lambah's recommendation, suggested to Rao that he consider the possibility of meeting Benazir at the 1995 NAM summit, Rao appeared cold to the idea. On her part, Benazir later lamented that she was unable to have the same sort of cordial relationship with Rao that she had with Rajiv. Chandra assessed that part of the problem was the feudal mindset of Benazir; she identified herself more with the Nehru–Gandhi family and saw Rao as a 'commoner'.[43]

Soon after Chandra had presented his credentials to President Farooq Leghari, he got a rude reminder of the violence that had gripped Pakistan's capital in the late 1990s. One morning around 9.30 a.m., a vehicle laden with a tonne of explosives was detonated at the gate of the Egyptian embassy, just 500 yards from the Indian high commission. Around fifteen people were killed and more than eighty injured. With the intensity of the blast, some papers flew off Chandra's desk, and some glass panes cracked. The blast was directed against the Egyptian state, but underlined the reality that after the Soviets were expelled from Afghanistan, militant outfits, some of them reared by the ISI, had a free run within Pakistan, even in the bubble of Islamabad's diplomatic districts.

THE MOST FAVOURED NATION

When a new army chief, General Jahangir Karamat, took over in January 1996, High Commissioner Chandra sought an appointment with him through the ministry of foreign affairs, as was the norm in those days. The foreign office sat on the request, but Chandra bumped into the chief at an Islamabad wedding. Karamat was cordial and invited Chandra to his office. Soon, Chandra was in Rawalpindi, sitting across Pakistan's most powerful person. Karamat, perhaps Pakistan's most straightforward army chief, was correct and proper through the meeting. When Chandra invited the general to India, Karamat said that the decision would rest with Prime Minister Benazir Bhutto. He did give the high commissioner a telephone number to call if he was 'ever in any trouble'.

Benazir, in her second term, had pretty much given up on India, but allowed herself to be persuaded by the British to try an initiative to engage Narasimha Rao in some tea diplomacy. Even though India was in election mode and Rao was not about to get a second term from the Congress Party, British prime minister John Major addressed a letter to Rao, which the UK high commissioner delivered personally. The British high commission reported to London:

> Rao read the passage about Benazir Bhutto carefully twice. Then he said that... 'we had better forget about cups of tea until after the Indian elections. Such suggestions might be useful in due course, though it was difficult to drink tea in secret.' He hoped that in time he would be able to dispense with the intervention of friends and talk to Benazir Bhutto direct. He did not doubt her good intentions, but she was immature and was not mistress in her own house. There was no short-cut to summit level dialogue.[44]

The April elections in India produced a surprising result. The Bhartiya Janata Party led by Vajpayee emerged as the single largest party in parliament, leaving Indian president Shankar Dayal Sharma no choice but to invite Vajpayee to form the government. In May, Vajpayee was sworn in as prime minister of a government that lasted thirteen days, since the BJP failed to cobble together an alliance to form the government. On 1

June, Vajpayee was replaced by another PM, H. D. Deve Gowda, who had been the chief minister of the southern state of Karnataka. This shaky coalition government wanted to take no foreign policy risks even though the Pakistan policy remained in the steady hands of Foreign Minister I. K. Gujral.

The Taliban takeover in Afghanistan in September 1996 was met with jubilation in Pakistan's security apparatus, which celebrated the success of its protégés. The Afghan mujahideen, incubated and trained by Pakistan's ISI with CIA funding, had now grown up and morphed into the Taliban, to take formal control of Afghanistan. Pakistan was among the first countries to recognize the brutal regime. Pakistan was openly claiming ownership of the Taliban and the ISI was commended for that success. An Indian diplomat in Islamabad recalled that in 1996, when India was trying to locate an Indian woman who had eloped with a foreign national into Afghanistan, the ISI offered to help, but wanted Masood Azhar, then in an Indian jail, and later head of the militant outfit Jaish-e-Mohammed, to be released and sent to Pakistan as a quid pro quo.[45]

✧

Trade between India and Pakistan had always been a political matter, even though it began organically enough with trade agreements periodically signed, in 1957 and in 1975. Trade exchanges were, of course, interrupted by the wars of 1965 and 1971. Trade diplomacy began in earnest when India joined the World Trade Organization (WTO) in 1995 and then as an instrument of bilateral diplomacy decided to accord Pakistan the most favoured nation status in 1996 for a non-discriminatory trade regime, in the expectation that the act would be reciprocated and the two countries could create some positive equities through trade and its lobbies. Under WTO norms, member countries were mandated to give this status to each other on a reciprocal basis. However, Pakistan continued to block reciprocal benefits to India for fear of its markets being flooded by Indian goods, and in part since it misinterpreted in its political system the idea of a most favoured nation, pasandeeda tareen mulk, in Urdu. More crucially, official circles continued to believe that trade was more in the interest of India, and worse, a ruse to dilute the primacy of the Kashmir issue. One outcome of the MFN status was that 'there was more Indian whiskey available in Pakistani homes in Karachi than we could find here in India'.[46]

As global trade evolved, MFN treatment and its withdrawal would become political instruments over the years. For India, as its economy grew, matters of trade and transit would become a confidence-building tool when it came to its bilateral ties with Pakistan—these would also be of relevance when it came to the issue of access to Afghanistan and Central Asia. Where Pakistan's much smaller economy was concerned, enhanced trade with India could have provided significant economic benefits especially in the sectors of textiles and pharmaceuticals. The Pakistani deep state looked at the matter through another lens: it remained suspicious of growing bilateral trade and felt it was an instrument wielded by India to dilute the primacy of the core issue of Kashmir.

Benazir's government was running out of luck by the end of the year. She was also visited by personal tragedy. Tensions had grown between Benazir's brother, Murtaza, and husband, Zardari. Murtaza was killed, apparently by the police, in Karachi on 20 September. In November, President Farooq Leghari, a former associate of Benazir, dismissed her government with a midnight proclamation that depicted her administration as incompetent, corrupt, and having committed several illegal acts. Zardari, whom the establishment had portrayed as 'Mister Ten Percent', enriching himself from kickbacks on government contracts, was arrested. The president called for new elections in February 1997. The military was not walking in this time, but simply rotating its civilian puppets.

19

TALKING OF EVERYTHING

When Nawaz Sharif was elected prime minister in February 1997 with a huge (but suspect) majority, the Pakistan Army remained the dominant power centre. It had steadily increased its power and influence since the first military coup in 1958. The military exercised an unchallenged veto over most critical decisions affecting both foreign and security policy and during the era of General Zia in the 1980s expanded its reach into several areas of domestic politics as well, often pandering to religious zealots in social policy. While civilian governments in Pakistan had some transient significance, the military, the higher echelons of the civil service, and the intelligence services were unquestionably the permanent features of the deep state.

As always, a diplomatic door opened with the change in government. Prime Minister Deve Gowda felicitated Nawaz Sharif in a letter and proposed the early resumption of talks between the two countries. In his reply, Pakistan's PM proposed a foreign secretary-level meeting. Pakistan's foreign secretary, Najmuddin Shaikh, was in Delhi at the end of March, to resume the dialogue after a gap of three years.

For High Commissioner Satish Chandra in Islamabad, a key challenge was to try to resume and sustain the India–Pakistan dialogue process that had stalled during Benazir's second regime. Chandra had seen that foreign secretary-level talks had continued from the mid-1980s till early 1994, as almost a routine affair, with seven rounds taking place annually or every second year. The sixth (August 1992) and seventh (January 1994) rounds between Mani Dixit and Shahryar Khan had been particularly productive, even though they had focused excessively on Kashmir. The long hiatus in talks since then was attributed in Indian thinking to Pakistan's interest in projecting a breakdown in dialogue, so as to strengthen the case for third–party involvement in Kashmir and to internationalize the issue. From 1996 onwards, the approach finding favour in India was to try and deal with all bilateral issues in one 'composite' process. The six non-papers initiated by Lambah in 1994 provided the basis for designing this new framework for engagement.

Chandra became part of a four-month process of behind-the-scenes 'talks about talks' between the two sides. Four diplomats were involved in this conversation: foreign secretaries Salman Haider of India and Najmuddin Shaikh of Pakistan, along with high commissioners Satish Chandra and Riaz Khokhar. The foursome first met at Hyderabad House in Delhi over lunch, 'away from the glare of publicity', to discuss the modus vivendi of the reimagined dialogue. Pakistan was somewhat reluctant and insisted on three preconditions: a written agenda; a visibly higher profile for the Kashmir issue; and tying progress on any other issue with that on Kashmir. In examining the preconditions, India was inclined to be more open on discussing Kashmir, since it had in any case committed to do so bilaterally under the Simla process. A written agenda was also something India could live with, even though it deprived the process of flexibility for each meeting. While the high profile for Kashmir could also be handled 'tactically', the sticking point was Pakistan's demand of linking forward movement on any issue to Kashmir. Within these constraints, the diplomats worked constructively for a solution.

Meanwhile in April, political conditions for a dialogue became more favourable. Inder Kumar Gujral found himself promoted from foreign minister to prime minister, as India's shaky coalition went through another political convulsion. He met Nawaz Sharif in the Maldives in May 1997 for the SAARC summit. Both Punjabis born in Pakistan found a common language and hit it off.

The foreign secretaries met again in Islamabad in June. They had by now hammered out the basic framework for a composite dialogue process. An agenda of eight items was agreed to: peace and security, including confidence-building measures; Jammu and Kashmir; Siachen; Wullar bridge project/Tulbul navigation project; Sir Creek; terrorism and drug trafficking; economic and commercial cooperation; and promotion of friendly exchanges in various fields.

The diplomats set up mechanisms including working groups to address these issues 'in an integrated manner'. The first two issues were to be discussed by the foreign secretaries directly; they would also monitor and coordinate the work of all the working groups. A joint statement issued at the end of talks between the foreign secretaries spoke of discussing 'all outstanding issues of concern to both sides'[1].

India was now not overly worried about a higher profile to the Kashmir matter. It was no longer only about Pakistani demands, but clear Indian asks had been added. Guided by the 1994 parliamentary resolution, India was also asking for Pakistan to vacate the areas of Kashmir held by it, apart from bringing an end to its export of terrorism.

Gujral was personally involved in fine-tuning India's negotiation strategy. Chandra, who interacted with the prime minister regularly, found him not quite the unalloyed peacenik he was made out to be, but in fact 'clear-headed and sagacious' on Pakistan. His 'Gujral doctrine' (which called for accommodating neighbours like Bangladesh, Bhutan, the Maldives, Nepal, and Sri Lanka to the extent possible without insisting on reciprocity) did not apply to Pakistan. While Gujral was able to sustain a warm and cordial relationship with his fellow Punjabi and Pakistani counterpart, Nawaz Sharif, he was no romantic on Pakistan. As evidence, Chandra cites a couple of occasions when Gujral asked him if he should visit Pakistan; when the envoy responded in the negative, Gujral readily concurred.

The next decade held out the promise of deploying the new mechanism of a multi-track comprehensive dialogue. Jammu and Kashmir and terrorism would be discussed as also nuclear matters and a host of other festering issues. The hope was that a constructive engagement on these issues would counter Pakistan's Kashmir obsession, terrorism in the region, and five decades of distrust. This was not to be.

1997–2007: NUCLEAR GAMES

20

STRATEGIC PARITY

The 50th anniversary of Independence in August 1997 gave both
countries cause for some celebration at a time of relative truce. The
stars seemed favourably aligned for a bilateral breakthrough. Both prime
ministers appeared keen on improving ties, not least since they spoke the
same language, and had common roots in western Punjab: the forty-eight-
year-old Nawaz Sharif was born in Lahore and the seventy-eight-year-old
I. K. Gujral, a hundred miles north in Jhelum.

The Gujral–Sharif meeting in the Maldives for the SAARC summit
earlier in May had produced positive chemistry between the leaders, even
though their bureaucrats had found it hard to share the optimism. The guns
were not going silent on the LoC, violence in Kashmir had not stopped,
and officials were quibbling about operationalizing the innovative bilateral
comprehensive dialogue originated in June. Foreign secretaries Krishnan
Raghunath and Shamshad Ahmed met in Delhi on 18 September, only to
disagree on whether they would form a separate working group to discuss
the Kashmir issue or continue discussing it in parallel with other issues.

Even though the divergence in national trajectories was becoming more
apparent, some cautious optimism hung in the air. The takeaway from
the journeys of the two countries this far, for some observers, was that
while India's democracy was robust and its economy was still to reap the
benefits of reform, Pakistan's story was the obverse, with its economy less
fragile than its democracy.[1]

On 23 September, Sharif and Gujral met in New York to take their
conversation forward. While the leaders had developed an easy conviviality,
neither of them was stable enough politically to sustain the process. More
importantly, neither bureaucracy was persuaded of the wisdom of this
top-down rapprochement.

A week after the New York summit, Foreign Secretary Raghunath
summoned Ashraf Jehangir Qazi, Pakistan's new high commissioner in New
Delhi. Qazi was a suave, high-flying diplomat, born to a prominent Balochi
Hazara father and an Irish mother. He was well-connected back home
and had landed in New Delhi that year after back-to-back ambassadorial
assignments in Russia and China. In the 9 p.m. meeting in South Block,
Raghunath registered a familiar complaint—Pakistan's unprovoked artillery
firing the previous night at the LoC had caused civilian casualties on the
Indian side. This had happened, the foreign secretary reminded the envoy,
despite the prime ministers agreeing in New York to take joint steps to

stop firing at the LoC and to ask the DGMOs to work out the modalities. India had given political directions to its defence forces, following which India's DGMO spoke to his Pakistani counterpart, who said that he had received no 'instructions' to stop the shooting. High Commissioner Satish Chandra had got the same response from Pakistan's foreign office when he raised the issue. Raghunath pressed Qazi—it was really a question of straightforward implementation of a bilateral understanding. He pointed out that the New York meeting had 'again renewed the spirit and personal rapport which exist between the two prime ministers and once again indicated their desire that steps be taken to improve the relationship'[2]. Qazi said he would take this matter home and press his side. He was true to his word.

The next day, the two prime ministers spoke over the phone and reaffirmed their agreement that the guns would go silent on the LoC. But a day later, ironically on the birthday of peace apostle Mahatma Gandhi, Satish Chandra was summoned by Pakistan's foreign secretary, Shamshad Ahmad, in Islamabad, to be told of ceasefire violations by India. Unusually, the two PMs spoke again on 4 October, this time agreeing to 'ask the army commanders' to establish contact and stop the shelling. The guns did go silent, but clearly, political decisions were taking time to percolate to those manning the artillery; the episode demonstrated both the hostility between the armies at the borders and their trigger-happy instincts, half a century after Independence and a quarter century after the 1971 war.

HER MAJESTY WADES IN

Five decades after the Raj had departed the subcontinent, the British leaders were again reminded how prickly former subjects could be to about any British interference in their matters. In an amusing sideshow to the India–Pakistan relationship, Queen Elizabeth visited both countries in October, to celebrate fifty years of their Independence. During her visit, Her Majesty received a rude reminder that the two former dominions of the empire were still adversaries.

The Queen was visiting soon after Princess Diana's wrenching funeral, where British royalty was targeted for the 'inadequacy of its grief'. The Queen visited Pakistan first, and it was here that trouble started. Pakistani journalists reported that Robin Cook, the Labour foreign secretary, said in informal remarks that Britain would 'take up the issue of Kashmir with India' and even that it could help mediate the conflict. These comments sparked outrage in India. Prime Minister Gujral, who was in Egypt at the time, countered angrily. Britain was a 'third-rate power', he told a gathering of intellectuals in Cairo. Tony Blair's government scrambled to retrieve the situation. Cook said that he had been misquoted, and in response, Gujral said he had been too. 'The Queen is doing everything she can to make India like her. But so far it does not seem to be working', British media reported.[3]

The prime ministers of India and Pakistan met in New York on the sidelines of the UNGA and were soon hosted by the Queen in Edinburgh for a Commonwealth summit in October 1997. They did make some progress in clearing the path for a comprehensive dialogue between their officials. Both in New York and in Edinburgh, when Nawaz Sharif tried to widen the conversation, he seemed to be interrupted by his bureaucrats to suggest that Kashmir should not be forgotten. They stymied the attempt made by Sharif to discuss trade. Pakistan's diplomats had neatly divided issues into two boxes—trade or travel matters—of interest to India; and the Kashmir issue—Pakistan's chief concern.[4]

Nevertheless, the innovation of the eight-track comprehensive dialogue—for officials to discuss all contentious issues on an equal footing—was gradually gaining traction, as both countries demonstrated the political will to normalize the relationship. Critics of this process on both sides were however questioning its wisdom. The biggest problem for India was of equating Pakistan's terrorism with seven other factors, rather than asking for its immediate end as a prequel to engagement, particularly after a decade of proxy terror in Punjab and then in Kashmir. For Pakistan, it spelt a dilution of the core Kashmir cause.

But the Gujral doctrine of good neighbourly relations, propelled by the Gujral–Sharif bromance, did not get the chance to flower. Elections in India in February-March 1998, now gave the mandate to a coalition led by the BJP. This led to the beginning of the Vajpayee era in India, ending two years of uncertainty that saw three prime ministers and several false starts in the bilateral relationship.

As we saw, Prime Minister Vajpayee was no stranger to Pakistan, having made a successful foray to the neighbouring country in 1978 as foreign minister and having grappled with the Pakistan issue in his two-year ministerial tenure. He started his new term in March 1998—technically the second, after his thirteen-day innings in 1996—as the prime minister who would make critical security choices for India and then defend them through his brand of reconciliation domestically and engagement internationally.

Soon after Vajpayee's inauguration, the comprehensive dialogue mechanism went back into the freezer in the explosive summer of '98. Strategies, plans, diplomacy—all had to be reimagined for nuclear times.

BIG BANGS

The first blast shook the Thar Desert. It was 3.45 in the afternoon on Monday, 11 May 1998. The shock waves travelled speedily westward; the news flashed in Pakistan within minutes. High Commissioner Satish

Chandra caught them in Islamabad and braced himself for some heavy turbulence.

Chandra was not entirely surprised. A couple of years earlier, when he had dinner with Brajesh Mishra, then head of the BJP's foreign policy cell, the retired IFS officer casually mentioned to Chandra that if the BJP came to power, India would certainly go in for nuclear tests. This was made explicitly clear in the foreign policy section of the BJP election manifesto of 1998, drafted by Mishra. But Chandra also picked up, quite by accident, an advance signal of the test a couple of days before it happened. He had been in Delhi the previous week, doing the rounds on 'consultations', meeting members of the new government that had been sworn in on 19 March. One of Chandra's last calls—scheduled in South Block on a Friday—was on Mishra, now Prime Minister Vajpayee's principal secretary. Mishra appeared surprised to see Chandra in Delhi and instructed the envoy to get back to Islamabad forthwith. Chandra guessed that nuclear tests were round the corner.[5]

The Pokhran blasts were originally planned for April 1998, but India's president K. R. Narayanan was travelling to Latin America. Vajpayee, as head of the government, met the head of state on 10 May to brief him on the explosions planned for the next day. Vajpayee later told Mishra that Narayanan, a thoughtful diplomat, teared up with joy when he heard that this long-delayed step would finally be taken.[6] The blast was no easy decision for Vajpayee. He realized it was a dangerous gamble—India could face global isolation, economic sanctions, and possibly a domestic political backlash, even if it was the right choice for the country.

But Vajpayee was determined to take the nuclear leap. Soon after he was sworn in as prime minister in his thirteen-day government in 1996, Vajpayee had met with the outgoing prime minister, Narasimha Rao, and scientists Abdul Kalam, and R. Chidambaran, so that 'the smooth takeover of such a very important programme can take place'. Rao had explained the circumstances, including US pressure, which had obliged him to stay his hand. Rao had, in fact, agreed to the tests in 1995, but American satellites had picked up evidence of the activities around Pokhran and the US ambassador showed the pictures to Rao. President Clinton also spoke to him 'in strong terms' and he had buckled.[7] Rao now told Vajpayee, 'Samagri taiyar hai (the ingredients are ready). You can go ahead.' Vajpayee had then asked for the tests, but was himself compelled to reverse the decision when he realized his government would not last.[8]

On 11 May, Vajpayee had waited, tense, in a control room in No. 5, Race Course Road, a few steps away from his office in No. 7. The control room had been rigged up with a direct communications hotline to the test site in Pokhran. He was joined that afternoon by his colleagues in the Cabinet Committee on Security (CCS)—L. K. Advani, George Fernandes,

Jaswant Singh, and Yashwant Sinha. The team of officials included Principal Secretary Brajesh Mishra, Cabinet Secretary Prabhat Kumar, Foreign Secretary Krishnan Raghunath, and Vajpayee's private secretary, Shakti Sinha. The men sat wordlessly around the dining table.[9]

At exactly 3.45 p.m., the scientists in Pokhran saw a blinding flash of light on the three monitors they were watching. This told them that three devices had detonated successfully in underground shafts. A few minutes later, Abdul Kalam called the PMO control room. It was Brajesh Mishra who picked up the phone, to hear an excited Kalam say, 'Sir, we have done it.' Mishra said, 'God bless you,' and announced to the room it was a success.

The effect, recalls Sinha, was 'electric'. Joy and tears filled the room. But Vajpayee's face reflected a feeling of 'sombre responsibility'. He had argued for a nuclear test all through his political career, from right after China had tested in 1964. Although he had written poetry about the pain of Hiroshima, he had come to the conclusion that if India had to live in peace in its neighbourhood, credible nuclear deterrence was essential. He saw nuclear weapons as instruments for preventing war. Besides, both Vajpayee and Mishra saw India's destiny as a great power. The possession of nuclear weapons was a minimum entry criterion to the club of powers.

Right after the test, Jaswant Singh and Mishra jointly dictated to Shakti Sinha a statement which he typed himself. Vajpayee had wanted a short and factual statement to create a sober narrative, devoid of triumphalism. Soon, Vajpayee read out a bare press statement to hastily summoned mediapersons: 'Today at 3:45 pm, India conducted three underground nuclear tests in the Pokhran range. The tests conducted were with a fission device, a low yield device, and a thermonuclear device.... These were contained explosions, like the experiment conducted in 1974....' Unlike Indira Gandhi, in 1974, Vajpayee did not use the word 'peaceful' to describe the tests. A few years later, Vajpayee gave credit to his predecessor Congress PM Narasimha Rao: 'Rao told me that the bomb was ready. I only exploded it.'[10]

Nawaz Sharif was touring Central Asia when Foreign Secretary Shamshad Ahmad told him of the tests. The civil servant advised Sharif that he had no real choice but to order Pakistan to follow suit. It was no secret that Pakistan's covert nuclear programme initiated in the 1970s by Bhutto, and pushed along by Zia in the 1980s (credible reports suggested that Pakistan had even conducted its nuclear test in a Chinese location in 1982)[11], had reached maturity in the 1990s, with nuclear weapons ready for testing. India was expecting the Pakistan response soon. In fact, Lambah had written in 'a handing over note' in 1982, when leaving Pakistan as deputy chief of mission, that Pakistan 'conceives its nuclear program to subserve its strategic military interests, which would necessitate an explosion'.[12]

'The Indians have gone crazy', screamed Pakistani headlines after the second set of explosions of Operation Shakti on 13 May, even as Vajpayee declared the day after: 'India is now a nuclear weapon state.' Sharif cut short his visit for emergency meetings in Islamabad, where the army told him they were ready to go ahead as soon as they had the order.

US secretary of state Madeleine Albright leaked to the *New York Times* a secret letter from Vajpayee to Clinton, that pointed a finger north, to China, as the primary driver of India's decision to test. The letter said that China had conducted overt nuclear tests on India's border and that an atmosphere of distrust prevailed due to 'the unresolved border problem'. China, the letter pointed out, had helped Pakistan become a 'covert nuclear weapon state' making India a 'victim of relentless terrorism and militancy'. Mishra was furious at this breach of diplomatic faith by the Americans, in leaking a confidential communication. He was relieved that it was Deputy Secretary Strobe Talbott India was dealing with and not Albright herself.[13] China, on its part, expressed outrage at being singled out at a time of relative calm in bilateral ties.

Vajpayee explained the decision to India's parliament:

India is now a nuclear weapon state. This is a reality that cannot be denied. It is not a conferment that we seek; nor is it a status for others to grant. It is an endowment to the nation by our scientists and engineers.... Our strengthened capability adds to our sense of responsibility. We do not intend to use these weapons for aggression or for mounting threats against any country, these are weapons of self-defence, to ensure that India is not subjected to nuclear threats or coercion.[14]

But Pakistan was judging India's capacity, not intent. US president Clinton dangled an incentive package of F-16s and other goodies in front of Nawaz Sharif to persuade him not to go in for his big bang.[15] But the pressure on Sharif from the army establishment and indeed, domestic public opinion, was unbearable and it became increasingly clear that Pakistan would respond with tests of their own soon.

Satish Chandra received a peculiar message in Islamabad on 27 May at 11 p.m. Foreign Secretary Shamshad Ahmad wanted him in his office immediately. Chandra insisted it would take him at least an hour to get there. That would be a fair rejoinder, Chandra thought, for another pointless midnight summons; Pakistan's foreign secretary would now need to remain at work longer. Apart from some sadistic pleasure in keeping his interlocutor waiting past midnight, Chandra was playing for time to ensure that he could rouse a colleague and take him along. It was past one in the morning when the Indian high commissioner and his deputy, Sharat Sabharwal, landed at the foreign office. Ahmad and three or four other Pakistani officers received the Indian duo. Ahmad said that Pakistan had credible information that India was going to attack Pakistan's nuclear facilities. The attack would be mounted by F-16 aircraft stationed at the Chennai airfield. In the event of such an attack, Shamshad added darkly, he had instructions from his government to say that there would be 'massive retaliation with devastating consequences'.[16] When the high commissioner pointed out that India did not possess F-16 aircraft, Ahmad parried that the aircraft could be Israeli. Chandra asked if the foreign secretary was referring to any of the nuclear installations and facilities included in the list given by Pakistan at the beginning of every year[17], Ahmad mumbled in response that he was referring to 'other' facilities. To Chandra, the brief meeting was relatively relaxed; he sensed no 'air of tension', which should have been palpable if Pakistan was 'genuinely apprehensive of an imminent Indian attack'.

Chandra and Sabharwal went straight to the high commission to report their midnight meeting to headquarters. When he called Delhi on a secure line to discuss this démarche, Chandra took some time getting through to the foreign secretary. The diplomats in Islamabad surmised that since Pakistan did not appear to be really expecting a nuclear strike and India appeared 'extraordinarily relaxed' for a country about to launch a deadly attack on its neighbour, the threat was perhaps unreal. It turned out that the Indian foreign secretary had already been alerted to the démarche by the Indian mission in New York, since Pakistan had made identical ones to all five permanent (P5) members of the UN Security Council. The high commission team cabled in an assessment that night, correctly guessing that Pakistan was about to carry out its nuclear tests and was nervous about pre-emptive strikes on the testing site in the Chagai hills of Baluchistan. This site did not feature in the list given to India at the beginning of the year and explained Ahmad's use of the word 'other' while answering Chandra's query. Chandra had little doubt that he had heard a major nuclear threat from his host country—warning of a 'massive retaliation with devastating consequences'. Pakistan's nuclear doctrine at that point was ambiguous and would only evolve in the weeks following the tests. By the time Chandra had cabled home his report and assessment, it was already 5 a.m. He needed to de-stress. So, instead of returning home, he headed straight for the Islamabad golf course.

Not for the first time or the last, Pakistan had reacted with nuclear bluster to a non-existent threat. Sabharwal learnt years later from a retired Pakistani official, also present at the midnight meeting, that Pakistan had received reports of Israeli aircraft at the Chennai airfield, which were to be used to attack the nuclear testing site in Baluchistan. Pakistan also believed that the US was complicit in this plan to attack the testing site. The trope of an Indian, US, and Israeli collusion, a 'Hindu-Jewish-Christian' conspiracy against Pakistan, was a familiar one and would make frequent appearances in Pakistan's strategic and media discourse.[18]

Pakistan's explosive response on 28 May seemed to calm official anxiety but not public worries. Nawaz Sharif proudly announced to his people that Pakistan had conducted five nuclear tests. To further showcase the 'existential threat' and in a climate of uncertainty about India's next moves, Pakistan braced itself for strong Western sanctions. Soon, Pakistan's president imposed a state of emergency.

To Indian strategic analysts, Pakistan's tests vindicated India's position at multiple levels. Clearly, the weapons were not hastily assembled in 1998, but had been around for a decade (and several more years in the works). The opacity had now been shed. Nuclear ambiguity had given way to nuclear assertion. This was the nuclear coming out party for both countries.

Pakistan's approach was to try and defuse the situation and pre-empt any Indian or Western attack on its nuclear capability. It called for the resumption of talks with India on the very day it tested. Even after Pakistan's foreign minister announced two additional tests on 30 May, Nawaz Sharif offered talks with India in Pakistan's National Assembly on 6 June.

To many observers, the days that followed emphasized the fundamental difference between the neighbours. India was rapidly developing a reassuringly professional doctrine based on a study of the existing literature of four decades of Cold War nuclear doctrines and episodes of nuclear brinksmanship—it spoke of no first use, a ban on further testing, apart from responsible command and control. Pakistan's army had to go on the defensive: its record of proliferation and illegal acquisitions came under intense global scrutiny; it could only articulate an India-centric doctrine not precluding a first strike. Nuclear diplomacy and confidence-building measures now became an imperative, as India–Pakistan relations acquired a new dimension more troubling and dangerous than ever before. The hope among some observers was that a new era of strategic stability would finally end Pakistan's paranoia about a conventional military invasion by India, given its credible nuclear deterrence capacity. The optimistic view was that the tests by Pakistan would remove its incentive to carry on a sub-conventional proxy war or cross-border terrorism.

Brajesh Mishra later summarized a strategic vision behind India's Pokhran blasts that went past Pakistan, and even beyond China:

Since the demise of the Soviet Union and the lapse of the Indo–Soviet treaty, India found itself more or less friendless. The US was not very keen on having better relations with India. When Clinton was the President he was much more attracted to China. Narasimha Rao went to the US and met President Clinton. Nothing came out of it. So what has changed? We had to find a place for ourselves in the new global order and therefore Pokhran II happened. Pokhran II had two purposes. One was to test the nuclear devices which had been built, and the armed forces never accepted it till a lot of tests had been done. And second was to firmly establish India as nuclear weapons power and enter the new world order.[19]

India was articulating its compulsions forcefully. Pakistan's proliferation record, on the other hand, was under the scanner. Writing in 2007, a long-term Pakistan watcher Adrian Levy revealed how Abdul Qadeer Khan stole nuclear secrets to build a bomb before selling these secrets around the world. Levy also revealed how the US had ended up arming countries President George Bush had dubbed the axis of evil, by enabling Pakistan to arm itself. The US had turned a blind eye to the naked proliferation mounted by its Cold War ally.[20] Pakistan had lucked out in the 1980s, given the US dependence on General Zia during the Afghan war, just as it had benefited from Nixon's reliance on Yahya Khan during the Cold War in 1971.

India's planners had gamed the scenario of the global reaction to India's tests, confident that the sanctions 'would last no more than one year'.[21] Vajpayee decided to engage with the increasingly frantic major powers to tell India's side of the story. The dialogue with the US started by the summer. Mishra embarked on a diplomatic mission in June to explain India's position to other P5 leaders: the UK's Tony Blair, France's Jacques Chirac and then Russia's Foreign Minister Yevgeny Primakov. He got the most traction in Paris, when France expressed empathy with India's concerns. While President Boris Yeltsin's Russia was then nervous about US concerns on South Asia's nuclearization, Russia's foreign minister saw India now as a significant power. To the Russians, India had in fact gained enough heft to be a pillar of the 1999 'Primakov Doctrine' that saw Russia, China, and India as a 'strategic triangle' to counterbalance a powerful post-Cold War United States.

Both countries now needed to prepare for diplomacy in a nuclear environment. They had to learn from the experience of the major nuclear powers, develop structures, doctrines, cadres of diplomats, and military leaders who could understand and strategize on these weapons of unthinkable catastrophic potential. The unanswered question remained whether India and Pakistan would now also work out a stable truce with the 'weapons of peace' given the spectre of mutually assured destruction or whether the nuclear umbrella could be a perverse incentive for military-backed revisionism or terrorism. Within a year of the explosions, the hope of peace would be dashed as Pakistan demonstrated that it had neither abandoned military efforts for the Kashmir cause, nor terrorism.

In the years to come, as the implications of a nuclear South Asia started sinking in, both countries would develop fairly robust nuclear CBMs. They were now forever condemned to execute their diplomacy under a nuclear shadow. Additionally, Pakistan would chime in to agree whenever global leaders would periodically put the region on top of the charts as the most dangerous nuclear flashpoint in the world.

ASSUAGING UNCLE SAM

The May explosions in India had caught the Clinton administration by surprise, coming as they did decades after the almost forgotten 'peaceful' nuclear tests of 1974. Years of technology denial had followed. In a knee-jerk reaction, a flustered US chose to react with sanctions against India and an attempt to 'cap, roll back and eliminate' the nuclear programme.

The re-engagement with India started, surprisingly only months after the nuclear tests, through an extended dialogue between Vajpayee's government and the Clinton administration. Strobe Talbott, the deputy secretary of state, represented the US, while Jaswant Singh, a close friend of Vajpayee and the deputy chairman of India's Planning Commission, represented India; they began in 1998 a protracted multi-round conversation (dubbed by *India Today* as the 'longest foreplay in Indo-US history'[22]) that would continue for years. The dialogue promoted a better understanding of the strategic rationale of India's nuclear programme, as also the strong sense of nuclear restraint and responsibility of its successive civilian governments.

In fact, the Singh–Talbott dialogue became an important inflexion point in the trajectory of US–India bilateral relations of the past five decades. As we have seen, the world's oldest and the largest democracy had a chequered history of relations during the Cold War. India's professed non-alignment with a tilt towards the Soviet Union had been countered by a distinct US tilt towards Pakistan. Relations between the US and India had taken on a positive but slow 'collaborative' trajectory with the end of the Cold War in 1991, when India entered a pragmatic policy phase, based on multiple engagements with the global community.

However, to India's disappointment, US attention in the Clinton era had wandered away from South Asia in the 1990s. With the withdrawal of Soviet troops from Afghanistan, and the end of the Cold War, it was not just Afghanistan that the US took its eyes off. All of South Asia slipped off its radar, even though India—and particularly Kashmir—was suffering a terrible decade of terrorism and insurgency which ran from 1989.

The US had continued to look at India through the prism of 'hyphenated' relations with Pakistan.[23] By most accounts, US intelligence was well aware that al-Qaeda and the Taliban had taken over the training of Kashmiri militants in Afghanistan after 1997 and were promoting the jihad in Kashmir as part of their programme of global jihad.[24] This apparent indifference on the part of the US made India deeply suspicious of its sincerity when it came to resolving any South Asian problems.

In May 1998, following the nuclear tests, more American sanctions kicked in (triggered by the Glenn and Symington Amendments designed to check nuclear proliferation) for Pakistan, mirroring the ones imposed on India. The US approach of doubling down on its ally was seen by Pakistan as a particularly unkind cut. It should not have been surprised as its usefulness to the Americans had declined. The US no longer felt a strong need for a South Asian regional ally after the Soviet withdrawal from Afghanistan and the end of the Cold War. An inflexion point had come in 1990, as sanctions associated with the 'Pressler Amendment' kicked in, when the US president refused to certify that Pakistan did not have nuclear weapons. These episodes of US 'perfidy' would be invoked again by Pakistani analysts after the US withdrawal from Afghanistan in 2021, to point to the transactional US 'use and throw' Pakistan policy.

∿

While bilateral suspicions between the neighbours had risen, an impulse was also growing within the military-strategic community in Pakistan to match India's stance of being a responsible nuclear power. Some deft diplomacy set the partnership on a positive path. Again, the SAARC came to the rescue. Vajpayee and Sharif met at the SAARC summit in Colombo in July 1998, mindful this time of the burdens that came with their nuclear status. Their nuclear credentials had changed the game in terms of the power equation but also lent an immediacy to peace, not least because the global community was prodding both countries to patch up their differences. They agreed to discuss confidence-building measures and resume the composite dialogue. Both terrorism and Jammu and Kashmir could be addressed along with other more constructive issues. The two prime ministers met again in New York in September, reaffirming their commitment to meaningful dialogue. One innocuous idea tossed around at the meeting—of a bus service between Lahore and Delhi—would become the basis of the boldest diplomatic gambit between them.

∿

But the reality of continuing violence soon dampened the prospects of successful diplomacy. India's fears were confirmed when cross-border terrorism seemed to continue with greater impunity under the nuclear umbrella. Pakistan's denials were wearing thin. Even as terror attacks became more brazen, Pakistan's diplomats were attempting business as usual with the eight-track composite dialogue, denying the state's complicity in the violence. Pakistan's foreign secretary, Shamshad Ahmad, in a meeting in October 1998, dismissed India's allegations about militant outfits like the LeT, insouciantly calling them 'charitable organisations'. The denials were not fooling India. But others were still being taken in. For example, in 1998, US officials were asking Pakistani counterparts in

Islamabad about the whereabouts of al-Qaeda's Osama bin Laden, three years before he masterminded the mayhem of 9/11 in New York. While Pakistan's foreign secretary innocently promised help in tracing bin Laden, the DG of the ISI flatly denied any knowledge of the Saudi guest, already known to be an ISI asset.[25]

In October 1998, Prime Minister Nawaz Sharif rattled the army's cage. He forced the military chief, Jehangir Karamat, into early retirement, after Karamat proposed, quite reasonably, the creation of a National Security Council as an institutional means of providing more formal input from the armed forces into policy-making for a nuclear Pakistan. Karamat's removal was to prove a major blunder. The navy chief of the time, Admiral Fasih Bokhari, criticized General Karamat for resigning, implying he should have stayed on and challenged the civilians. But Karamat defended his actions as the 'right thing' to do as he had lost the confidence of a constitutionally and popularly elected prime minister.

Sharif compounded his error by picking a relatively junior general, Pervez Musharraf, to replace Karamat. The new army chief had scant respect for what he thought were weak civilian leaders such as Sharif and would end up exiling Sharif from power the next year. Musharraf was a Mujahir, one of the millions who were born in India and migrated during the Partition in 1947. He had strong views, to the point of obsession, on Pakistan's right to capture Kashmir. He had been wrenched by the 1971 dismemberment of Pakistan where he saw India as the villain. He was angry over India's pre-emptive action of 1984 in Siachen. He had yearned for the day he would be in a position to launch a military campaign across the LoC, even though such aggressive ideas had been rejected by Zia, as also by Benazir when Musharraf was DGMO. Musharraf also happened to be a commando trained in unconventional warfare; he was acutely aware that Pakistan's army had lost every conventional war and fared much better at guerrilla wars.[26] He now had a chance to implement plans he had long dreamed of; he just needed a clique of supporters within the army to execute these plans, and he was working on them by November.

As his tenure in Pakistan drew to a close, Satish Chandra closely watched this transition in Pakistan's most critical post. He soon encountered Musharraf socially, at a dinner hosted by Pakistan's former army chief Aslam Beg on 19 December, as a farewell to the Indian HC. Beg engineered a one-on-one chat, between the army chief and the diplomat. After the thirty-minute meeting in a alcove in Beg's home, Chandra cabled an assessment back home, describing Musharraf as 'ambitious, devious and virulently anti-Indian'. He wrote that Musharraf's appointment was 'bad news for the India–Pakistan relationship' and presciently suggested that Musharraf was a general who would 'not be averse to overthrowing the democratic dispensation in his country', to do what Zia had done to Bhutto.[27]

A BUS TO LAHORE AND A TRAIN OF EVENTS

More than high politics, it was sports that exercised a calming influence on the nuclear powers for a brief while. The last year of the millennium began with a cricket series when the Pakistan team toured India after twelve years, in January-February 1999. Pakistan's former foreign secretary and one-time heir to the princely state of Bhopal, Shahryar Khan, was by now the manager of the Pakistan cricket team. He experienced first-hand the exhilaration and frustration of an India–Pakistan cricket tour, with high passion playing out off the field. An angry Shiv Sena kept the matches away from the state of Maharashtra; its activists even inflicted some minor damage to the pitch at the Feroze Shah Kotla in Delhi. The series was restricted to two tests, given the charged atmosphere and the looming security threats. As if to reflect the new nuclear parity, the two-test series ended in a tie between the teams led by the Indian captain Mohammad Azharuddin and Pakistan's Wasim Akram.

A more serious people-to-people game was also in the works. Both sides had been toying with the idea of a bus service between Delhi and Lahore, since the two prime ministers met in New York for the UN General Assembly in September 1998. But the hallmark of India–Pakistan relations had been that diplomatic initiatives could abruptly be aborted, and could equally suddenly fructify. The final preparations for the visit came only weeks before the bus journey. It started with a very public invitation to Vajpayee from Nawaz Sharif, in an interview published in the *Indian Express* with Shekhar Gupta on 3 February 1999.[28] The journalist recalled that he had asked Nawaz Sharif in a light-hearted exchange in Punjabi: 'Why don't you announce the bus in the interview and invite our prime minister to Pakistan on the first bus?' Nawaz asked: 'What if I invited him and he declined?' Gupta had then reached out to Vajpayee, who seemed to like the idea. Till then, the plan most talked about was for Vajpayee to flag off the bus service and for Sharif to receive the bus in Pakistan.

Vajpayee's private secretary Shakti Sinha confirmed that the proposal for this public acceptance of a public invitation was not finding much favour with the bureaucracy. Vivek Katju, who headed the Pakistan desk as joint secretary, and was considered a hawk on Pakistan relations, called Sinha on 2 February 1999 to say that the ministry was going with an unimaginative line, where the spokesman was going to say that 'the government would give an appropriate answer as and when a formal invitation was received'.[29] Katju felt this was a matter that required the prime minister's political judgement and he was short-circuiting the system through Sinha for the prime minister to consider the invitation carefully. Sinha spoke to Vajpayee during a visit to his constituency in Lucknow. Vajpayee agreed that this gesture needed a positive not a formalistic response. Later that day, on 2 February, while answering a media question, Vajpayee said, 'I would like to have a bus ride from Delhi to Lahore.'[30] After dropping this bombshell, Vajpayee would only say that the details would be worked out between the two governments. To global observers, the visit was an indication that India and Pakistan could move on the road to sign the Comprehensive Test Ban Treaty (CTBT). Western non-proliferation lobbies had been pressing both countries to forsake further testing by signing the 1996 treaty, after which nuclear sanctions could be lifted. Pakistan had made it clear that it would do so only if India also signed the treaty.

What Vajpayee had perhaps not revealed to Shekhar Gupta or even to his private secretary was that he had been turning this idea over in his mind for several months. Foreign Minister Jaswant Singh, who was in London for some difficult conversations with the British on nuclear issues, said that Vajpayee had decided to take the inaugural bus to Lahore months ago, 'but the announcement had come only now'.[31]

The atmospherics suddenly changed, as did the tone of the commentary. This was a way for the nuclear adversaries to devise a pathway to peace. As the visit was confirmed, expectations veered on the unrealistic. Rumours surfaced that Sharif would visit Delhi for the second India–Pakistan match even before Vajpayee's trip began. That did not happen but Vajpayee did visit the Feroze Shah Kotla grounds to meet with the teams and later hosted a reception for them at his official residence.

Soon, the MEA got into the act of playing up the significance of the political decision. This would be the first visit to Pakistan by an Indian PM since Rajiv Gandhi's in 1988 and could be as significant as Nehru's tour in 1960. More positive statements started emanating from both sides, underlining the significance of the visit and its timing. The Pakistani establishment said it was a 'welcome step and would go a long way in establishing good ties with India'. The official invitation however was caught in a bureaucratic loop with one side asking for a written invitation and the other written confirmation.[32]

Days before Vajpayee's visit, India sent a new high commissioner to Pakistan—Gopalaswami Parthasarathy (Partha) who had been India's second consul general in Karachi, in Zia's Pakistan, from 1982 to 1985. With the same name as, but no relative of, the high-flying high commissioner of the 1960s, Partha had been a short-service commission army officer before he joined the foreign service. He was now moving, with mixed feelings, from a cushy assignment in Canberra to the neighbouring country. Before leaving for Islamabad, Partha called on Vajpayee. The designated envoy sensed that despite the deep misgivings about Pakistan within India, and particularly in the BJP, Vajpayee had a vision of progress and was keen to write a new chapter in bilateral relations. Partha assessed it had been Vajpayee's ambition that he could achieve in foreign policy something that even Nehru was unable to do.

Despite his own personal scepticism about prospects for improvement in ties, Partha went to Pakistan, determined to make every effort to ensure that the prime minister's visit was 'hailed as a major effort for peace and reconciliation'. In Pakistan, Partha found no let-up in hostility to India as he set to work preparing for the PM's impending visit. He had to navigate rivalries within the Pakistani establishment—the foreign secretary and his deputy, were seeing the visit from India as an unnecessary diversion from the 'core agenda' of Kashmir; they seemed determined to queer the pitch of a visit coming at the initiative of their own prime minister.[33]

The bus service that was being proposed envisaged a point-to-point service between Delhi and Lahore, a distance of 500 kilometres that would be traversed in fourteen hours. The initial idea for Vajpayee to travel the entire length of the journey was dropped in favour of his boarding the bus at Amritsar airport and travelling 37 kilometres to the Attari border, where he would be received by Nawaz Sharif. High Commissioner Parthasarathy rushed to sign the agreement on the bus service just a couple of days before the trip was to begin.

Shakti Sinha and Satish Mehta, a director in the PMO, scrambled to get together eminent persons for the bus ride. They included journalist and peace activist Kuldip Nayar, poet Javed Akhtar, actor Dev Anand, cricketer Kapil Dev, heads of Indian Chambers of Commerce like Rajesh Shah, actor–politician Shatrughan Sinha, and Punjab's chief minister Parkash Singh Badal. Sinha rued that he forgot to include Jinnah's grandson and Vajpayee's friend, Nusli Wadia, whose symbolic presence in Pakistan would have been a 'coup'. The official machinery started its preparation. Vajpayee's principal secretary, Brajesh Mishra, along with joint secretaries, Vivek Katju (heading MEA's Pakistan desk) and Rakesh Sood (heading the disarmament division), were dispatched to Islamabad in advance. A joint statement was in the works. Partha had initiated the negotiations even before the Indian delegation arrived and had suggested to his colleagues in the MEA that the ambition should be upped to work out a 'declaration'.

On 20 February, Vajpayee was on the inaugural bus, riding from Amritsar to Wagah, gambling on a 'risk for peace' that could fundamentally alter the contours of the relationship. In Amritsar, Vajpayee repeated a message of peace and friendship. The billion people of India, he said, wanted relations with Pakistan to improve, trade between the two nations to increase, and travel to be made easier. At Attari, the prime minister said his message to the people of Pakistan would be short and simple—to put aside the bitterness of the past. 'Together, let us make a new beginning.'[34]

Nawaz Sharif received Vajpayee with a warm embrace and with half his cabinet ministers in tow. The veteran Indian actor Dev Anand who stood by watching the two men hug launched into reminiscences of his move from Lahore to Mumbai and had to be gently guided away. But while the bonhomie was palpable to the delegation, the chaos on the ground gave anxious moments to the planners. Pakistan's military guard of honour ceremony at Wagah was so squeezed for space that when the guard commander lowered his weapon to convey the ritualistic acceptance of dismissal, Prime Minister Vajpayee, to his nervously watching private secretary, was well within striking distance of a Pakistani sword.[35]

The outcomes of the visit lived up to the heady hope it had generated in the final week. The symbolic significance was staggering. The countries seemed to have achieved the breakthrough their people had failed to achieve around the 25th anniversary of Independence and had sought in the 50th anniversary year. Hostile neighbours that had recently acquired nuclear power had agreed to address their territorial disagreements and to establish confidence in each other despite their nuclear weapons capability.

But the cracks within Pakistan were showing. Partha recalled that the lavish dinner hosted by Nawaz Sharif at the Lahore Fort had to be delayed, because the Lahore police was fighting running battles with protesters from the fundamentalist Jamat-e-Islami, who were trying to block the route that Vajpayee's motorcade had to take. Apart from negotiating the delegation's security, the high commissioner and his team were taking care of a giant media delegation of 300, several high-profile delegates, and negotiating teams that were hammering out agreements. Despite all the problems, the visit seemed to be breaking new ground, both in terms of optics and substance.

At the official talks, the two sides referred to their known positions, but agreed to expand contacts and interaction. At lunch after the talks, a Punjab Police band played instrumental music from Indian movies of the 1950s and 1960s, familiar tunes in Pakistan. Neither Vajpayee, nor Foreign Minister Jaswant Singh could satisfactorily answer Nawaz Sharif's questions on the tunes played. It was left to Partha, with his fondness for old Hindi musical hits, to identify the tunes for the Pakistan prime minister. Partha found that the Pakistani prime minister's wife, Kulsoom, and the governor of Sind, Lieutenant General Moinuddin Haider, shared a love for the hits of Lata Mangeshkar and Mohammed Rafi.

With the 'Lahore Declaration', the two prime ministers agreed to intensify the composite dialogue process, to address all issues including J&K. More importantly, they agreed on an MOU for nuclear times—to consult each other on nuclear postures and doctrines and to notify each other in advance of ballistic missile tests and any nuclear accidents. For India, the Lahore Declaration was also a nod to the principle of bilateralism; it reaffirmed the Simla Agreement. Vajpayee's public statements had a deep impact, even greater than the one he had made two decades earlier as a foreign minister on his maiden trip to Pakistan. He won over several Pakistanis by affirming several times that India had accepted the reality of Pakistan as an immutable geographical fact.

The most memorable outcomes came at public events on 21 February, which spotlighted the emotional connection in the relationship. At the Minar-e-Pakistan, Vajpayee made another powerful affirmation:

> I wish to assure the people of Pakistan of my country's deep desire for lasting peace and friendship. I have said it before and I will say it again that a stable, secure and prosperous Pakistan is in India's interest. Let no one in Pakistan be in any doubt of it, India sincerely wishes the people of Pakistan well.

More than the words, the symbolism silenced the fringe elements in India asking for an Akhand Bharat and those in Pakistan portraying India as an existential threat.

Later in the evening, Vajpayee played to the gallery with a theatrical flourish: 'I was told that my presence at the *minar* put my *mohar* (seal) of approval on the creation of Pakistan, but 'Pakistan does not run on my seals. It has its own seal.'[36] The optics were strong. Vajpayee was driving the message home. He continued in this vein at a reception on the lawns of the governor's house: 'One can change history, not geography. One can change friends, not neighbours.' And he then unleashed his most potent weapon, reading out from his poem, 'Jung na hone denge':

> To those who peddle shrouds, we must say
> We have seen through your game;
> you will not succeed.
> We shall not allow war.

A moved audience greeted the poetry, replete with Urdu words, with standing ovations and wet eyes.[37] A sentiment among those watching was that if Vajpayee were to stand for election from Lahore, he would sweep the polls.[38]

On his part, Sharif also struck a note of high optimism in his media remarks. He said that in the near future, Pakistan would extend the most favoured nation treatment to India, reciprocating India's act of 1996. For both leaders the meeting had been an act of some courage.

The chief ministers of both the Punjabs met separately. Parkash Singh Badal discussed with Shehbaz Sharif the upkeep of Sikh shrines. Among the issues raised was the matter of the Kartarpur corridor that led from India to the birthplace of the first Sikh guru in Pakistan. Shehbaz was more cautious and raised issues of Kashmir and bilateral trade. When Parthasarathy tried to arrange a meeting between Opposition leaders, Benazir Bhutto and Vajpayee, Sharif's government seemed reluctant to give her the stage and did not allow it to materialize. Pakistan's democracy had a long way to go before it matured, inferred the Indian high commissioner.

The next day the prime ministers met again informally, expressing mutual satisfaction at the outcomes they had achieved. It felt, recalled Sinha, like the morning after a grand subcontinental wedding.[39]

Not everyone was swayed by this friendly sentiment. Watching the proceedings disapprovingly was Pakistan's army chief Pervez Musharraf, a man who had refused to publicly salute Vajpayee and later dismissed the visit as 'hot air'. The army chief had plans to take the relationship in a different direction.

A DISCREET CHANNEL

The two prime ministers decided to nominate personal representatives for closer and more reliable communication between them. The Indian side nominated R. K. Mishra, a former journalist and a friend of Dhirubhai Ambani, who headed the Reliance conglomerate. Reliance had an additional stake in India–Pakistan peace; they were invested in a refinery in Jamnagar on the Gujarat border, within shooting distance of Pakistan. The project was vulnerable to India–Pakistan tensions. Nawaz played it safer: he nominated a former foreign secretary, Niaz Naik.

The visit of 1999 was hugely successful, if the metric is to be the optics and the hope it generated at that time. The emotional content was high—it seemed that a page had been firmly turned and a new glorious one was about to be written. It was the most innovative diplomatic move in the history of India–Pakistan relations till then. Initially it seemed that Vajpayee's instinctive gamble, on a move that would build peace and friendship in the twenty-first century between the nuclear neighbours, would pay rich dividends. This was the first of the two forays to Pakistan that Vajpayee would make in his six years as prime minister. It is tempting to believe that had the gains of Lahore not been frittered away by a bitter general, the twenty-first century relationship may have unfolded a lot more positively.

The euphoria generated by the visit began to dissipate rather quickly. High Commissioner Partha, who had been sceptical about the 'Lahore spirit', was unsurprised when Nawaz Sharif again started 'playing footsie with Sikh separatists' nurtured by Pakistan. Sharif appointed the former DG of the ISI, Lieutenant General Javed Nasir, as chair of the so-called 'Pakistan Gurdwara Prabandhak Committee', positioned to mirror the highest Sikh body in India. Nasir had earlier been fired by Sharif under US pressure, for allegedly engineering the 1993 Bombay blasts. The intelligence man was now hobnobbing openly with Khalistani extremists from Indian Punjab. The army was clearly pressing Sharif not to let up the pressure on Kashmir and Punjab, and was stepping up operations under the nuclear umbrella.

21

HEIGHTS OF TROUBLE

Vajpayee's sunny disposition during his charm offensive in Pakistan masked his political woes at home. A day before his departure for the border, on 19 February, Vajpayee had called a meeting of the National Development Council that included chief ministers of the states and was used to allocate resources between provinces. A trend of 'competitive populism', or reckless spending to gain electoral advantages, had pushed some states into bankruptcy and brought Vajpayee's government at the centre—a coalition of regional interests—under considerable strain. On the day he left for Lahore, a key ally, Om Prakash Chautala, from Haryana's Lok Dal Party, had walked out of the coalition, handing over his letter of withdrawal of support to the president of India.

Vajpayee's government fell on 17 April, where he lost his thin majority by precisely one vote in a no-confidence motion, when another key ally, this time the leader of the Tamil Nadu AIADMK Party, J. Jayalalithaa, walked out of the alliance after her stiff demands were left unmet. Mid-term elections were now to be concluded by early October, giving nearly five months to a lame duck regime; the government faced the challenge of fixing a declining economy without a convincing mandate. Reeling from bruising politics and economic challenges, Vajpayee's government was counting the decision to explode nuclear devices and the subsequent diplomatic effort around the world, and especially with Pakistan, as key achievements of its abbreviated tenure. Vajpayee had no inkling that Pakistan would soon draw his caretaker set-up into a huge national security crisis.

On 3 May 1999, a shepherd in Kashmir reported the presence of strangers in the deserted mountainous expanse of Batalik, a little village in western Ladakh within the LoC on the Indian side. An Indian patrol sent out to investigate the problem was ambushed on 5 May, four soldiers were killed and as many injured. Thus were fired the first shots of the Kargil war. Soon, India started artillery shelling to dislodge the infiltrators from the heights. Pakistan responded in kind. On 8 May, army chief Pervez Musharraf made an unannounced visit to the forward areas opposite Kargil. A day later, a munitions dump was blown up in Kargil by Pakistani artillery shelling, destroying about 5,000 tonnes of ammunition.[1]

For an Indian Army used to an active western border, the situation was still not serious enough to retaliate strongly. On 10 May, army chief General V. P. Malik proceeded on a ten-day tour of Poland and the Czech Republic; he did not consider cutting it short for what seemed like the usual infiltration and shelling in J&K. On 17 May, Principal Secretary Brajesh Mishra informed Vajpayee that cross-border developments in Kashmir might be cause for concern. He organized a briefing in the Ops room of South Block for the prime minister the next day, where DGMO N. C. Vij told the prime minister that groups of irregular mujahideen had crossed over the LoC Pakistan had tried to maintain the fiction that the infiltrators were not Pakistani troops but 'freedom fighters' for Kashmir's independence who had slipped past the LoC, unbeknownst to the Pakistan Army. The Indian army's initial estimates said that the intruders would now be evicted in a matter of days. It seemed simple enough but was not quite so.

Across the border, Nawaz Sharif came to know about the incursion around the same time as Vajpayee. But the briefing the Pakistani army gave its prime minister was much too fuzzy for him to sense anything amiss. Sharif had received three earlier briefings on Kashmir that year: on 29 January, 5 February, and 12 March. But those briefing had him obfuscated the central issue with confusing military maps and none of these referred to the specific Kargil operation. Only the briefing of 17 May touched upon the ongoing operation in Kargil. Still, no alarms rang in Sharif's non-military brain, no political red flags went up in Pakistan.[2]

When General Malik returned to India on 20 May, he rushed to review the situation before briefing Vajpayee in more detail in the Ops room.[3] HC Parthasarthy, in from Islamabad, also attended the briefing. The ex-army diplomat was appalled, as were many others, at the poor intelligence and surveillance on India's border.

On 26 May 1999, the Cabinet Committee on Security, meeting in the Ops room, authorized the use of air power after the three service chiefs agreed on operational principles. The Kargil operations were on. The HC was asked to return to Islamabad immediately, given the imminence of the air strikes.

An outraged Vajpayee called Sharif the same evening he had authorized the launch of Operation Vijay—air strikes and ground assaults to oust the invaders from the heights. He told Sharif that India was aware that the intrusion in Kargil involved the use of regular troops from the Pakistan Army. He said this was totally unacceptable and would compel India to take 'all necessary steps'. This was the first time Sharif realized that his rogue army generals had got Pakistan into a serious conflict with India.

Apart from a military counter-offensive, India also launched a diplomatic one. The Indian permanent pepresentative at the United Nations mobilized international opinion. Indian embassies were activated, particularly in Washington; the ambassador gave extensive briefings on Capitol Hill and to the media.[4]

Partha in Islamabad had served in the Indian Army and knew that air operations would be both difficult and hazardous given Vajpayee's insistence that under no circumstances, would the Indian Air Force cross the Line of Control.[5] The Indian high commissioner watched with some discomfort as the air strikes in the first few days led to the downing of two Indian MiG fighters, and the loss of a helicopter gunship. All these were caught on camera and gleefully played on loop on Pakistani television screens, causing much joy to the Pakistan establishment.

Given that there was 'every chance of matters escalating' Partha also asked his colleague, Counsellor Syed Akbaruddin to draw up a contingency plan of a lockdown: this would have involved stocking up on rations and herding all staff, then scattered in residences across Islamabad, into the chancery premises in case of a full-blown war.[6]

A PILOT DOWN

A ticklish diplomatic issue that the Indian team in Islamabad faced was the capture of an Indian air force pilot, Flight Lieutenant Kambampati Nachiketa. The pilot flew one of the first MiG-27s to strike the entrenched intruders in the heights of the Batalik Sector on 26 May 1999. The aircraft took a hit from a Pakistan Army surface to air MANPADS missile; the pilot was forced to eject. Nachiketa was initially beaten up and later taken into custody by Pakistani forces as a POW. The Geneva Conventions required POWs to be returned and Nawaz Sharif grandiosely announced that the pilot would be handed back to India. An excited Tariq Altaf, manning the India desk in Pakistan's foreign office, called up High Commissioner Parthasarathy to say that the pilot would be handed over to him. 'Smelling a rat', the high commissioner asked if the media would be present. Altaf confirmed that it would. An angry Parthasarathy retorted, 'Tariq, if you think I am going to allow you to make a media monkey of an officer of the Indian Air Force, you are sadly mistaken. There is no way I am coming to the Foreign Office if there is even one media person present anywhere in sight.'[7]

Partha took the call because he felt the world media was watching, and Pakistan was keen to create a spectacle, matching the surrender by General Niazi in 1971. The high commissioner took a calculated risk that Pakistan would be unable to hold the prisoner after making a public announcement and had not factored in the possibility that India would refuse to play along. After checking with Delhi, the HC suggested that the prisoner could be handed over to the International Red Cross authorities, who would then drive him over to the high commission without fanfare. After eight days of traumatic captivity that he said was 'difficult to be described in words', Nachiketa was repatriated to India on 3 June 1999, crossing over at the Attari border post.

A SPARSE TERRAIN

Kargil made for a tempting target for the Pakistan military. It was strategically valuable, located on the only road between the Kashmiri summer capital of Srinagar and the town of Leh in the far north-east, near the Chinese border. Since 1997, the sparse terrain had seen a pattern of relatively minor Pakistani incursions that had triggered bursts of sniper fire and occasional artillery exchanges.

By a gentlemen's agreement, Indian and Pakistani forces withdrew every year from the heights in the winter harshness and returned to man the posts in spring. The two sides had refrained from major attempts to alter the status quo during this ebb and flow of seasonal deployments. This had been the case in Siachen as also in the Kargil sector. Pakistan had now violated this agreement.

The total area of Pakistan's ingress was between 130 and 200 square kilometres. India's Operation Vijay mobilized 200,000 Indian troops. However, because of the nature of the terrain, the fighting was limited mostly to the regimental and battalion level. Pakistan's infiltration of armed intruders involved some 700 men who crossed the LoC; most of them were attached to the Pakistani army's 10 Corps. The US condemned the intrusion and went public with this information.[8]

By the end of May, the initial skirmishes had blown up into a full-fledged border conflict involving infantry assaults, artillery barrages, and other operations including attacks on ground positions by helicopter gunships. By mid-June, the fighting intensified between military units in the Kargil area. The Indian Army was paying a heavy price and suffering losses as they tried to dislodge the Pakistani fighters from strategically advantageous and well dug-in positions in the mountain heights.

By mid-June, India also began firing on targets on the Pakistani side of the LoC. US military experts were worried that India might break out of its restraint mode and cross the LoC since its tempered approach was costing it additional casualties around Kargil. After shooting down two Indian aircraft near the border, the Pakistan Army had moved its regular army troops into the Kargil area to construct bunkers on the Indian side of the line.

The conflict was initially characterized as a skirmish or a border incident. However, it was later judged to be a war launched by Pakistan with definite and clear strategic, territorial, and political motives, with premeditated planning and detailed preparation. The US confirmed the assessment that the thrust by Pakistan was a pre-planned probe mounted by the Pakistani military and intended to create a 'new' LoC more favourable to Pakistan.[9]

TALKING IT OUT

India had not shut the door to wartime bilateral diplomacy. Starting in May, Vajpayee spoke to Sharif some five times during the course of the summer conflict. With each call, it was clearer to Vajpayee that Sharif had little grasp of the war being run by his army chief. The two foreign ministers, Jaswant Singh and Sartaj Aziz, met on 12 June 1999 in New Delhi, to look for a solution. But Aziz had a brief to link withdrawal of the border intruders with a time-bound discussion on Kashmir, while for India an unconditional withdrawal was non-negotiable.

The deadlock at the FM level catalysed a robust backchannel conversation between R. K. Mishra and Pakistan's former foreign secretary, Niaz Naik. An additional impetus for the apex level communication between the two prime ministers came after Mishra (who met his counterpart some five times from mid-June) reported Sharif's dilemmas. In one of Mishra's missions, he carried tapes and transcripts of two intercepts procured by Indian intelligence—of army chief Musharraf's conversations with his chief of general staff, Lieutenant General Mohammad Aziz—to Nawaz Sharif. The tapes made it clear that the Pakistan Army was the central actor in the Kargil operation, with the 'Mujahideen' playing only a bit part. Mishra reported to Vajpayee that Sharif had turned ashen listening to the tapes.

Sharif's position seemed to be getting increasingly tenuous in June 1999. After another meeting with Mishra, Sharif seemed concerned that his own house was bugged and told his guest that they should take a walk in the garden. When Mishra reported this to Vajpayee, the latter took this as an indication that Sharif was more a 'prisoner of circumstances' than anything else'.[10] Following another visit on 25 June 1999, Mishra returned in a Pakistani special aircraft. The next day, his counterpart, Niaz Naik, reached Delhi for a meeting at the Imperial Hotel. Naik later called on Vajpayee, who asked him, 'We started the journey from Lahore. How did we reach Kargil?' Naik responded that a way needed to be found to return from Kargil to Lahore. Vajpayee said, 'Very simple. You should just withdraw.'

In Islamabad, High Commissioner Parthasarathy remained sceptical of the backchannel, and particularly of the ability of R. K. Mishra to deal with a wily diplomat like Niaz Naik. Partha felt it was 'unusual' that Mishra was not overly familiar with basics like the Simla Agreement or past negotiations between India and Pakistan. Naik claimed that Mishra had said in one of the meetings that India would agree to 'adjustments' in the LoC that would eventually lead the line to be moved to the Chenab River basin. Such an 'adjustment' would have meant that the entire Kashmir Valley would be handed over to Pakistan. Naik claimed that it was on this basis that Nawaz Sharif was proposing to visit Delhi on his way back from China in June. Mishra had vehemently denied this assertion.[11]

US COERCION

The US had been deeply concerned with the situation in South Asia since the nuclear tests. While the first US instinct was to bring both parties to the table, and to offer mediation, this was no easy task. Pakistan was steadfastly insisting that the intrusions were caused by Kashmiri freedom fighters; India, on the other hand, was suspicious of any mediation, its primary goal was to reverse the occupation of its territory by Pakistan. India was apprehensive that the US would also fall into the trap of pointed 'neutrality' adopted by some other international players. Major powers of the world as well as the United Nations tended to take the view that while Pakistan's violation of the LoC was wrong, the intrusion had occurred because India and Pakistan did not have a substantive and meaningful dialogue going on the Kashmir issue.

The US was trying to use every bit of leverage it had on Pakistan. The administration pointed out that if Prime Minister Sharif did not order a pullback, the US would hold up the $100 million International Monetary Fund loan that Pakistan needed. Sharif meanwhile visited Beijing hoping for comfort from Pakistan's 'all-weather' friend, but got none. The US embassy reported that he came home desperate.[12]

The US was unsure whether Sharif had personally ordered the infiltration above Kargil, reluctantly acquiesced in it, or had not even known about it until after it happened. But there was no question that Sharif now realized it had been a colossal blunder. Pakistan was universally seen to have precipitated the crisis, ruining the promising peace process that had begun in Lahore.

By the end of May 1999, when the situation seemed somewhat stable, the US saw an opportunity to offer its 'good offices' to look for a diplomatic solution. State Department officials Rick Inderfurth and Tom Pickering began a regular dialogue with the Indian and Pakistani ambassadors in Washington, while Secretary of State Madeleine Albright made phone calls to Prime Minister Nawaz Sharif, Jaswant Singh, and the British foreign secretary Robin Cook. The central message was to blame Pakistan for instigating the crisis, while urging India to exercise restraint and not broaden the conflict.

President Clinton became fully involved from early June, even though he was preoccupied with the resolution of the 'Kosovo crisis' in the former Yugoslavia, where NATO was executing air strikes to coerce the Serbian leader Slobodan Milošević to withdraw Yugoslav forces from Kosovo. In a turning point in US diplomacy, Clinton, on the Kargil issue discarded the traditional US posture of studied neutrality as the primary mediator and now leaned heavily on Pakistan. In letters to both prime ministers, Clinton made Pakistan's withdrawal a precondition for a settlement and the price it must pay for the US diplomatic involvement that it was seeking. Clinton also made phone calls to the two leaders in mid-June to emphasize this point. The private diplomacy soon became public as the US was reinforcing the same two-fold message (asking for Pakistani withdrawal and Indian restraint) through the media. For India, Kargil was its first 'TV war', as the conflict was being beamed live into homes across the country; the 'fair and just' US stand was playing well with public opinion in India.

In late June, President Clinton called Prime Minister Sharif to stress that the US saw Pakistan as an aggressor and rejected the fiction that the fighters were separatist guerrillas. He sent a special envoy, General Anthony Zinni, who was in charge of the US Central Command, to reinforce the message in person to Musharraf and Nawaz Sharif. Zinni warned Musharraf that India would cross the LoC if Pakistan did not pull back. Musharraf appeared unmoved by the threat.

Clearly, the US attempt at crisis management through private and public diplomacy was not gaining much traction with either side. The US had aligned itself with India's position, but Pakistan was unwilling to change the status quo unconditionally. The opportunity for replacing the strategy with coercive diplomacy came in late June, when, through the US ambassador in Islamabad, Prime Minister Sharif 'begged Clinton to come to his rescue' with a plan that would stop the fighting and set the stage for a US brokered solution to Kashmir.[13]

On 2 July 1999, Sharif phoned Clinton and pleaded for his personal intervention in South Asia. Clinton recalls in his autobiography that he agreed, with two conditions: 'first, he had to agree to withdraw his troops back across the Line of Control; and, second, I would not agree to intervene in the Kashmir dispute, especially under circumstances that appeared to reward Pakistan's wrongful incursion.'[14] Clinton then telephoned Vajpayee to report on Sharif's request and his own reply. Vajpayee expressed concern that Sharif would deceive, or worse, co-opt Clinton.

The exchanges between Strobe Talbott and Jaswant Singh became an important additional channel of communication during the crisis.[15] Talbott called Singh several times by phone in June, even as he shuttled between European capitals to deal with the Kosovo situation, to reinforce Clinton's assurance that under no circumstances would the US associate itself with any outcome that rewarded Pakistan for its violation of the LoC. Singh expressed 'muted, cautious, but unmistakable relief that this time the United States was tilting in India's direction rather than Pakistan's.'[16] National Security Advisor Sandy Berger did the same with his counterpart Brajesh Mishra.[17]

In early July, President Clinton's team was looking at diminishing options in an escalating crisis. The crisis management strategy implemented so far—asking Pakistan to revert to the status quo and pleading with India not to escalate the conflict—had not worked. Pakistan continued to plead with the US to get involved in mediating and brokering a ceasefire, consistent with its objective of 'internationalizing' the Kashmir issue. For precisely that reason, India was allergic to any kind of mediation and wanted a Pakistani withdrawal from the LoC to precede any dialogue. President Clinton's principal mediator role had worked well in the Arab-Israeli conflict and the Irish peace process and could be replicated here only if India could be persuaded to join in trilateral talks.[18] Should the US push for a trilateral summit or a three-way dialogue so that it could jump into a mediatory role? Should it continue its vigorous public and private diplomacy, offering its 'good offices' and sending across envoys in a situation where India's patience was running thin and the conflict could rapidly spiral out of control? Or should it attempt to use its leverage with Pakistan to try a policy of 'coercive diplomacy', getting Pakistan to climb down?[19]

When Nawaz Sharif called Clinton and announced he would come to Washington the next day, 4 July 1999, Clinton took a snap decision to receive him, knowing instinctively that this would be an opportunity to push for a resolution. Clinton subsequently invited Vajpayee to Washington for a face-to-face meeting with Sharif, but the Indian prime minister politely declined, citing the prevailing security situation.[20] This effectively foreclosed the mediation option and obliged the US to try a bout of coercive diplomacy. An additional layer of complexity was added by the fact that while the US was exercising coercion on Pakistan, the other key player in the game—India—was not willing to play. The US hope, bolstered by continuous multi-channel communication with India, was that since the primary objective of both India and the US coincided (unconditional Pakistani withdrawal), the outcome would be acceptable to India.

A key driver for the US security establishment to press the president to play a direct role was the genuine fear of nuclear escalation if the US diplomacy failed. The US NSA Sandy Berger told Clinton after Sharif arrived that he was heading into the 'most important and most delicate' meeting with a foreign leader of his entire presidency. The overriding objective was to induce Pakistan's withdrawal from the LoC. But another goal was to increase the chances of Sharif's political survival. If Sharif lost his job while he was in the US, he would be unable to keep his end of the bargain in Islamabad. The US objective was to find a way to provide Sharif 'just enough cover to go home and give the necessary orders to Musharraf and the military.'[21]

India's objectives were also clear to the Americans and had even been spelt out directly to Pakistan (when the Pakistan foreign minister Sartaj Aziz had visited New Delhi on 12 June 1999): Immediate vacation of the aggression; Reaffirmation of the validity of the Line of Control; Abandoning of cross-border terrorism; Dismantling the infrastructure of terrorism in

Pakistan-occupied Kashmir; Reaffirmation of the Simla Agreement and the Lahore Declaration.[22]

Strobe Talbott, who as deputy secretary of state, remained the point man for India, added a caution that even though Clinton would be meeting the prime minister of Pakistan in the 'most intense, high-stakes circumstances imaginable'[23], he must keep his Indian audience in mind. The US, he said, 'was finally making headway with India...in allaying their doubts, accumulated over 50 years, about whether the US would take their security interests properly into account, especially when push came to shove with Pakistan.' Talbott knew that India 'would scrutinise every word that came out of Blair House for evidence that the US had fallen into a trap the Pakistanis had set' for them and recommended that 'providing Sharif with political cover was fine, as long as what the US was covering was Pakistan's retreat from the mountain tops.'[24] The US planners had assessed that while key US and Indian objectives coincided, Pakistan's army had different ideas. Sharif's brief from the army was to make Pakistani withdrawal conditional to India agreeing to direct negotiations sponsored or even mediated by the US. But the US also realized Sharif was politically weak, 'fighting for his own political and physical survival'. He would therefore prioritize his own interests, 'which would not always coincide with that of the army, or even with Pakistan's national interest'.[25]

The Clinton strategy was to confront Sharif at the end of the talks with a 'good' and a 'bad' press statement: the good statement would hail him for withdrawing—or restoring the sanctity of the LoC—and the bad one would blame Pakistan for starting the crisis and the escalation sure to follow Sharif's 'failed mission to Washington.'[26]

Nawaz Sharif started the meeting by raising the 'Kashmir cause'; he pleaded with Clinton to devote more attention to the issue. If Clinton would devote to South Asia just 1 per cent of the time and energy he had put into the Middle East, Pakistan's prime minister said, there would be no problem. He argued that India was to blame for the crisis, since it had carried out an incursion of its own fifteen years earlier, in Siachen. Clinton rejected Sharif's depiction of India as an instigator of the crisis. He pointed out that the Indian prime minister had been more than flexible in going to Lahore—he had taken a 'risk for peace' (a phrase that Clinton had used to describe Yitzhak Rabin of Israel).

Clinton made his demand clear early in the talks: 'If you want me to be able to do anything with the Indians, I've got to have some leverage. Only withdrawal will bring this crisis to an end.' He also said that a Pakistani military pullback across the line had to be without any links to American diplomatic intervention in the Kashmir dispute: 'I can't publicly or privately pretend you're withdrawing in return for my agreeing to be an intermediary. The result will be war. Plus, I'll have sanctioned you having crossed the LoC. I can't let it appear that you held a gun to our head by moving across the line.'[27]

Sharif responded from his brief: 'I'm prepared to help resolve the current crisis in Kargil, but India must commit to resolve the larger issue in a specific timeframe.'[28] That translated into negotiating a settlement on Kashmir under the pressure of a Pakistani imposed, US-sanctioned deadline.

Clinton was furious: 'If I were the Indian Prime Minister, I'd never do that. I'd be crazy to do it. It would be nuclear blackmail. If you proceed with this line, I'll have no leverage with them.... I'll be stripped of all influence with the Indians. I'm not—and the Indians are not—going to let you get away with blackmail, and I'll not permit any characterisation of this meeting that suggests I'm giving in to blackmail.'[29]

Clinton quoted from John Keegan's *The First World War*, which he was then reading. He said that European generals and politicians had stumbled into a world war once military plans went into autopilot and the diplomats couldn't do anything about it. It was important not to get into a position in which India felt that because of what Pakistan had done, it had to cross the LoC itself. 'That would be very dangerous. I genuinely believe you could get into a nuclear war by accident.'[30]

Clinton said that he had just a year and a half left in office and he was committed to working with India and Pakistan.

> If you announce you're withdrawing in response to my agreeing to mediate, India will escalate before you even get home, and we will be a step closer to nuclear war. If you hold out for a date certain for the resolution of the Kashmir dispute, you would have made a terrible mistake in coming here...What I'm prepared to support, however, is a resumption and intensification of the Lahore process and a commitment on the part of the US to work hard on this.[31]

Sharif repeated that he was trying to work out a deal with India that would feature the trade-off between Pakistani withdrawal and a timetable for the resolution of the Kashmir issue. It was clear that Sharif needed a face-saver to show back home that he had achieved something beyond an unconditional surrender over Kargil.

When Clinton asked Sharif if he understood how far along his military was in preparing nuclear-armed missiles for possible use in a war against India, Sharif seemed genuinely surprised. Clinton invoked the Cuban missile crisis, which had been a formative experience for him (he was sixteen at the time). Now India and Pakistan were similarly on the edge of a precipice. It would be catastrophic if even one bomb were to be used.

At this point, President Clinton returned to the offensive.

He could see they were getting nowhere. Fearing that result, he had a statement ready to release to the press in time for the evening news shows that would lay all the blame for the crisis on Pakistan.... Having listened to Sharif's complaints against the US, he had a list of his own, and it started with terrorism. Pakistan was the principal sponsor of the Taliban, which in turn had allowed Osama Bin Laden to run his worldwide network out of Afghanistan. Clinton had asked Sharif repeatedly to cooperate in bringing Osama to justice.... Sharif had promised to do so but failed to deliver. The statement the US would make to the press would mention Pakistan's role in supporting terrorism in Afghanistan—and, through its backing of Kashmiri militants, in India as well.[32]

Clinton was by now deep in the throes of coercive diplomacy—with 'his face flushed, eyes narrowed, lips pursed, cheek muscles pulsing, fists clenched,' he said it was 'crazy enough for Sharif to have let his military violate the Line of Control, start a border war with India, and now prepare nuclear forces for action. On top of that he had put Clinton in the middle of the mess and set him up for diplomatic failure.'[33] Sharif seemed beaten. He denied he had given any orders with regard to nuclear weaponry and said he was worried for his life.

In a break in the negotiations, Clinton called Vajpayee. It was past midnight in India. Brajesh Mishra, who was by Vajpayee's side, recalled that Clinton told Vajpayee he had just broken off a meeting with Sharif and was to meet again in about half an hour. Clinton shared with Vajpayee that he was persuading Sharif that Pakistan had to withdraw from the area beyond the LoC. Vajpayee stressed that this was the least India would expect.[34]

Now that Clinton had made the maximum use of the 'bad statement' his team had prepared in advance to coerce Sharif, it was time to dangle the good one. Clinton's team cobbled together a new version of the good statement incorporating some of the Pakistani language from the paper that Sharif claimed was in play bilaterally between India and Pakistan. But the key sentence in the new document was added by the US and it focused on the primary objective of the US from the talks—'the Prime Minister has agreed to take concrete and immediate steps for the restoration of the Line of Control.'[35] The paper called for a ceasefire but only after the Pakistanis were back on their side of the line. It also reaffirmed President Clinton's long-standing plan to visit South Asia. To this draft, Sharif and the Pakistan team requested just one addition: a promise that Clinton would take a personal interest in encouraging an expeditious resumption and intensification of the bilateral efforts (that is, the Lahore process) once the sanctity of the LoC had been fully restored. This was acceptable to the US and the meeting came to a satisfying end.

The public messaging from Washington was clear. It was Pakistan that had to step back from the line. At a White House briefing shortly after the three-hour talk between Sharif and Clinton, the US said it 'has been given a clear understanding by Pakistan that there will be a withdrawal from Kargil only by those forces that had crossed the LoC from the Pakistani side and not by the Indians'.[36]

The diplomatic endgame had been reached 10,000 miles to the west of the theatre of conflict. The US had tried mediation and crisis management but had soon de-hyphenated that relationship and moved to coercive diplomacy with Pakistan. This successfully combined with Operation Vijay, with the credible use of hard power exercised by India, notwithstanding the nuclear overhang. Clinton's role in the Kargil endgame marked a tipping point. It ended the painful period since the 1998 explosions and built trust that was to serve the India–US partnership well. India spent a few more weeks to secure the hilltops and declared victory on 26 July 1999. Operation Vijay had concluded with victory.

REFLECTING ON KARGIL

In public comments on 30 July 1999, Foreign Minister Jaswant Singh said that Pakistan's 'ill-conceived misadventure' may have aimed to turn 'tactical surprise into a strategic gain by bringing about a de facto realignment of the LoC', or to 'provoke India into an escalation'. But India had decided to respond firmly without crossing the LoC, even in the face of high casualties and even when the decision to employ air power was taken. The area of conflict was thus not expanded.[37]

The discourse at the time also recognized it to be India's first televised conflict; the age of aggressive round the clock media was beginning. While Jaswant Singh belonged to the old school of conducting war and diplomacy away from the media glare, he had to reluctantly acknowledge the shape the media machine was taking 'marked by exuberant enthusiasm bordering, at times, on the reckless', to influence the conduct of warfare. Singh, a former army officer, confessed that 'this was our first experience of conflict in the TV/information age. We learnt as we went along'. Singh was also drawing lessons on how to strengthen India's military capability and to overcome its hesitations about US and global diplomacy, 'as in the present instance, we should always be ready to engage with the world...such engagement is the very substance of diplomacy. That is not any internationalization of an issue. Nor does it imply mediation or any acceptance of intermediaries.'[38]

Across the border, Pakistan's foreign office was floundering for answers, with none forthcoming from the military. It decided to take the safest position of blaming India for not resolving the Kashmir issue. Commenting on Jaswant Singh's remarks, Foreign Secretary Shamshad Ahmad urged

India to avoid using dialogue as a tactical ploy and resume meaningful talks to resolve the core issue of Kashmir, since so far, it had been India's policy to 'wriggle out of a serious dialogue' to resolve issues. 'Kargil like situation erupts,' he added lamely, 'only due to non-resolution of the core issue of Kashmir.'[39]

To later analysts in both countries, Kargil, by many metrics, was a success for India and a setback for Pakistan. The conflict demonstrated to the world the difference between a responsible nuclear power and an army-dominated autocracy prone to taking wild risks. It exposed Pakistan's fiction of irregular troops versus the regular army and showed India's determination in ejecting every intruder across the LoC. Nuclear analysts were perturbed by another reality: a year after Pakistan's nuclear tests, the Pakistani army and the state had behaved irresponsibly, risking war with a nuclear neighbour. Through the Cold War, no such action had been tried by the US and Soviet Union in each other's territory

Military tensions shot up again on 10 August 1999. A Pakistani naval aircraft, Atlantique, was downed at the border by the Indian Air Force, killing twenty personnel. Conflicting versions emerged from both sides on whether the aircraft had crossed into Indian territory. But military escalation was contained as Pakistan this time took the matter to the International Court of Justice, where the matter was eventually dismissed. To analysts, this incident pointed to the 'dangers of unintended escalation on aggressively patrolled and monitored borders'.[40]

In September, Pakistan tried to defend the army's Kargil record with another 'revelation': 'backchannel' talks had taken place both before the Kargil operation and after it. 'After the Lahore diplomacy, negotiations started and continued for at least two months till the time Prime Minister Vajpayee's government fell,' Foreign Minister Sartaj Aziz told Pakistan's parliamentary senate: 'When the Kargil operation started, India approached us to defuse the tension and this was a time when (R. K.) Mishra came here and we told him that they should hold serious negotiations on Kashmir,' he added. There was emphasis on abiding by the Simla Agreement as far as the LoC was concerned and this package was to culminate in a joint statement by the two prime ministers after Nawaz Sharif's visit to China. 'But India backed out of this package,' he said.[41]

India categorically denied this version. Brajesh Mishra said that there was no 'deal' whatsoever on resolving the Kashmir dispute and, consequently, there was no question of laying down a time frame to implement it. Moreover, there was no proposal from the Pakistani side that Nawaz Sharif should stop over in New Delhi during the Kargil conflict on his way home from China. All communications between India and Pakistan during the conflict, Mishra insisted, focused on a single issue: to get Pakistan to unconditionally withdraw its troops to its side of the

LoC as swiftly as possible.[42]

Serious Pakistani analysis of this issue later judged the Kargil misadventure to be a huge military blunder. But Army Chief Musharraf was maintaining a public line that the Kargil operation was a 'great military success'. Privately, he felt the civilians had surrendered too early. Fears had arisen that the army chief might move against the prime minister just after Kargil, but Musharraf, with his duplicity, pretended otherwise. 'Are you comfortable with the prime minister?' Pakistan's media asked him on 30 September. 'Yes', he replied, 'very comfortable.'[43] But within two weeks, Musharraf had removed Nawaz Sharif and installed himself as Pakistan's leader. The Kargil misadventure launched by a rogue army chief had claimed a civilian regime.

SEPARATE PATHS

High Commissioner Parthasarathy was preparing to leave for a National Day reception at the Spanish embassy residence on 12 October 1999 when the news on television announced that General Musharraf (who had been away on an official visit to Colombo) had been removed from office as army chief, and replaced by the ISI chief, General Ziauddin. Partha called foreign secretary, K. Raghunath, and informed him of this development, pointing out that the matter would not end with this announcement. He asked his team to fan out in the city and watch for developments. As the Indian high commissioner drove home to change for the reception, he saw army soldiers in battle gear clambering up the walls of the PTV headquarters on Constitution Avenue, from where the announcement of the firing of the army chief had come. He rushed back to the office to report that the army had arrested Nawaz Sharif and was surrounding the presidential palace. The fact that the infamous 111 brigade of 'coup makers' had moved within minutes of the announcement of the army chief's firing, suggested to the Indian diplomat that the army had made preparations for the takeover, even prior to Musharraf's departure from Colombo. Pakistan's third bloodless coup of the century was underway.[44]

The day after Sharif was ousted for the second time, Vajpayee took office as prime minister for the third time. In India, Vajpayee was again sworn in as prime minister on 13 October, heading a stronger NDA coalition of twenty-four parties with 299 seats in a 543-member house, ending a period of political instability that had continued since his thirteen-day government in 1996. Vajpayee's NDA coalition had stepped into elections in September, with the caretaker government's handling of security and the Kargil victory an important plank of the campaign.

That the trajectories of nations born on the same day, gone nuclear in the same month, and emerging from a bruising conflict at their border, were now starkly diverging, became clear to observers in the subcontinent and elsewhere. The new Indian government, with little change in its leadership, was worried by events in Pakistan—unmistakably the result of the Kargil conflict and Sharif's efforts to rein in his army. Musharraf's choice of foreign minister added to the worries: Abdul Sattar, who had been both high commissioner to India and foreign secretary in Pakistan, was hawkish on India and regarded the Simla Agreement as an 'unequal treaty imposed on a defeated nation'.[45] He was a member of the Tehreek-e-Insaf Party (PTI), ostensibly led by cricketer Imran Khan, who had founded it in 1996, under the tutelage of a hardline Islamist, former ISI chief, Hamid Gul.[46]

To make sense of Musharraf's Pakistan, HC Parthasarathy took Gul out for lunch in November. Gul, who had political ambitions, was voluble, candid, and insightful. He told Partha that Musharraf's intention was to stay in power for an indefinite period of time, but the World Bank recipes that he was adopting were no cure for the economic ills of Pakistan. When Partha asked about Afghanistan, Gul predicted, two years before 9/11, that the Taliban would not surrender or offer terrorist Osama bin Laden to the US. And 'given the strong pro-Taliban sentiments in Pakistan, no Government in this country could afford to be seen to be pressurizing or acting against the interests of the Taliban.' He failed to tell the Indian diplomat that bin Laden would soon be a guest of the Pakistan government.[47]

A TROUBLED FLIGHT

On 24 December 1999, when Prime Minister Vajpayee's plane returned from a tour within India, I clambered into the car with him for the fifteen-minute ride from the Palam Air Force station to his official residence at Race Course Road. Vajpayee was going to turn seventy-five the next day and was his usual reflective self in the car. He did not know then that the last week of the year would bring a major crisis from heights higher than Kargil.

I had joined as the prime minister's private secretary the previous month. On 1 April, I had received the orders out of the blue, when posted as first secretary in the Indian embassy in Berlin. A telex message that morning said I had been posted as the prime minister's additional private secretary and should join immediately. I initially thought it was an April Fool prank and then naively wrote to HQ that I needed a few months to finish working on a crucial project of the new Indian embassy in Berlin. Ronen Sen, then my ambassador based in Bonn, gently admonished me to say that one never said no to the PMO. As luck would have it, Vajpayee's government was defeated by one vote that month and went into caretaker mode, allowing me to leave for Delhi at my own pace. I did join as a deputy secretary in the PMO, just as the Kargil crisis was ending in early July. So, on Christmas Eve 1999, I was about to get my first lesson in crisis management in high places.

I received a message on the Special Protection Group net, from my colleague Anandrajan, the PM's other private secretary, to call him urgently. As the 'VIP carcade' sped towards RCR, I spoke to Anand and then breathlessly told the prime minister that an Indian Airlines flight from Nepal had been hijacked and had landed at Amritsar airport; the crisis management group led by the cabinet secretary was in session and (the principal secretary) Brajesh Mishra was waiting at RCR to brief the prime minister on unfolding events. The PM, seated in the front seat of the white Ambassador, said, 'Oh' and asked me if I had anything else. He stared out of the window, deep in thought. We went straight to office, and a few minutes later, a grim Mishra was briefing Vajpayee.

Pakistan's involvement in this operation became apparent to India's security experts as the hijack drama unfolded over the next few days, particularly when the hijackers demanded the plane land in Lahore. Plans had been afoot to celebrate Vajpayee's seventy-fifth birthday on a grand scale, given that he had been sworn in prime minister for the third time. These were instantly abandoned, as the Cabinet Committee on Security met continuously to take stock of the evolving situation. Flight IC-814, scheduled to fly from Kathmandu to Delhi, had finally landed in Taliban-controlled Kandahar, after a tortuous journey that took it to Amritsar, Lahore, and the UAE. A passenger Rupin Katyal, returning from his honeymoon, had been knifed to death. The hijackers brandished the blood-soaked knife before the pilot, Captain Devi Sharan, and assured him that a passenger would be killed every five minutes, unless he did their bidding.

Musharraf's Pakistan reacted defensively on 26 December with a familiar narrative—suggesting India had launched a false-flag operation. 'Since October 12 New Delhi has been trying to isolate Pakistan, beginning with its moves to seek suspension of our Commonwealth membership, its unilateral postponement of [the] SAARC summit and now perhaps, India decided to manufacture the hijacking incident,' Foreign Minister Abdul Sattar told the media. He also dusted off a thirty-year old story—the hijacking incident was 'not unlike the operation of January 30 1971 when India planned and foisted a so-called hijacking of an Indian airliner named 'Ganga' for manufacturing a pretext to deny Pakistan's rights and block overnight flights by PIA between East and West Pakistan.' He denied Indian assertions that the hijackers boarded the Indian aircraft at Kathmandu airport after disembarking from a PIA flight.[48]

For India, the hijacking was real enough. Pakistan's role was clear and exasperating. Relatives of passengers were marching in protest, a pressure group the government needed to mollify, their anxiety amplified and exaggerated by over the top electronic media reportage. Worse, despite the multiple hijacks of a decade ago, no protocols or reflexive anti-hijack measures seemed to have come into play. India's crisis managers were floundering for a coherent response.

High Commissioner Parthasarathy watched the drama from Islamabad with a sense of déjà vu. He had handled two hijackings when posted in Karachi in 1984; during one of these which terminated in Dubai, the ISI had actually provided a pistol to the hijackers at Lahore airport. Familiar with the modus operandi of the hijackers, the high commissioner predicted to Delhi that the flight would land in Lahore after Amritsar. He suspected that the Pakistanis would not be keen to let the flight stay in Lahore and it might end up in Dubai like the last time. Hoping to negotiate in Lahore, he asked the Pakistan foreign office to facilitate his trip to the city. The foreign office went through the motions of trying to transport Partha from Rawalpindi to Lahore, but told him at the airport that the hijacked flight had taken off from Lahore.

The high commission team was then contacted by Taliban representatives in Pakistan, who told them that the final destination of the aircraft would be Kandahar in Afghanistan. In his negotiations with the Taliban representatives, the high commissioner insisted that no terrorist would be released. On 28 December, he was told to step down from his role in negotiation since this was now being handled by a team from Delhi. The ISI's links with the Taliban were well-established and their connection with the hijackers was now clear to the high commission, as well as the Indian negotiating team that reached the tarmac in Kandahar. Counsellor A. R. Ghanshyam from Islamabad joined the Kandahar team and saw Urdu-speaking, apparently Pakistani, handlers guiding the Taliban. Partha soon learnt that after intense negotiations, India had agreed to release three jailed terrorists to secure the hijacked passengers and plane.

Under pressure to resolve the issue before the new millennium began, Foreign Minister Jaswant Singh informed the Cabinet Committee on Security that he would personally go to Kandahar. His act came in for criticism since the three terrorists exchanged for the passengers were on the same flight as the foreign minister. But Singh defended himself later to point out that only one aircraft could land at the airport and bring the passengers back. The final act of the drama was enacted on the last day of the millennium, 31 December 1999, when three terrorists were delivered in Kandahar in exchange for the passengers who returned safely.

To Parthasarathy, the decision to exchange terrorists for passengers, was reminiscent of the one in 1990 in the case of the kidnapping of Rubaiya Sayeed. He rued that this capitulation would tell the Pakistani establishment that India was a soft and vulnerable state.[49] As it turned out, each of the terrorists would be responsible for multiple murders in their respective Kashmir-focused terrorism careers launched with ISI support. Maulana Masood Azhar would go on to found the Jaish-e-Mohammed in 2000, responsible for spectacular acts of terror, including on India's parliament in 2001 and in Pulwama, Kashmir, in 2019; Mushtaq Ahmed Zargar was assigned to training Kashmiri terrorists in POK; Omar Sheikh was involved in plotting 9/11 in 2001 and then 'arrested' for the murder of the US reporter Daniel Pearl in 2002, only to have his death sentence reversed in seven years.[50]

The NDA government, in its new term, had faced its first major crisis with the eighth Pakistan-related hijacking, evoking unhappy memories of the series of hijackings of the 1970s and 1980s. This was yet another manifestation of terror, with a global dimension, a humanitarian situation and a media spectacle that reduced policy options. Vajpayee had mixed feelings about how the crisis had ended. When I informed him of a felicitation function to celebrate the success of the operation, led by the family of Captain Sharan, the prime minister asked me, 'But why did he not ground the plane in Amritsar?'

Vajpayee's abbreviated term of thirteen months, followed by the caretaker phase of six months had seen the Pokhran explosions, the Lahore visit, and Kargil, all connected deeply to one another. But the decision to go nuclear had redefined diplomacy between the estranged neighbours. Hopes that were revived of the nuclear-armed rivals forging a new détente with Vajpayee's bus diplomacy to Lahore had been dashed with Pakistan's aggression in Kargil; this hope plummeted further for India as the millennium ended with the traumatic hijack.

22

MILLENNIAL DIPLOMACY

Bill Clinton made his promised South Asia visit in March 2000. The highlight of his tour was five intense days in India, right after the colourful festival of Holi. But the first US presidential visit to India in twenty-two years was clouded by a terrorist massacre of thirty-five Sikh villagers in Chittisinghpura, J&K. It was a brutal reminder for Clinton, on the eve of his visit, that apart from nuclear weapons, terrorism could destabilize the region. While sharing his anguish at the tragedy, Vajpayee told Clinton that Pakistani groups were behind the massacre and asked him to press the matter in Pakistan. The visit served to develop a bond of trust between the leaders, bordering on friendship; Vajpayee thanked Clinton for his role in Kargil.

The Pakistan leg of the tour stood in stark contrast to the Indian visit; Clinton spent six hours in Islamabad, with some tough talking for Pakistan's new military dictator and a lecture on what democracy meant. Clinton's visit to Pakistan had come on the heels of a sentence of life imprisonment awarded to Nawaz Sharif by a anti-terrorism kangaroo court. Soon after the visit, Pakistan's Supreme Court once again invoked the doctrine of necessity to give Musharraf three long years for the restoration of civilian rule. The US worked hard behind the scenes to ensure Sharif did not meet Bhutto's fate of being hanged by a dictator—he was exiled instead.

In July, India sent in a new high commissioner to Musharraf's Pakistan. Vijay Kumar Nambiar was a career diplomat with expertise on China and UN matters. He had earlier served in Afghanistan in the chaotic times right after Soviet troops exited. He took over in Islamabad when ties were at a low but also when India was reconciling to a post-Kargil reality of a nuclear Pakistan with power firmly in the grip of the army.

Meanwhile, Pakistan's ambassador in Delhi, Ashraf Jehangir Qazi, had lunch with the MEA's Pakistan division chief, Vivek Katju, on a July afternoon in 2000. Qazi had for months been trying to create grounds for India to hear out the dictator he now represented. In a note, since declassified, recording their unusual chat, Katju reported, 'PHC remarked that Kargil should never have happened.' Qazi told Katju that 'Musharraf was a soldier who had never expected to assume the office which he was now holding.' Pakistan's ambassador also argued 'that the General's articulation was becoming a little more nuanced...he was now saying that while Kashmir was the core issue and had to be discussed in a major way, other issues would also be discussed'.[1]

Qazi felt he needed to jump the barrier of the MEA and develop direct contact with the BJP leadership. After establishing a relationship with George Fernandes, he decided to approach Lal Krishna Advani, the leader branded the most inflexible hawk within the BJP. To approach the Sindh-born home minister Advani, Qazi deployed his family connections with journalist Karan Thapar. The journalist drove him to Advani's home where he would secretly hobnob with the deputy prime minister 'perhaps twenty or thirty times'[2] and eventually persuade him to consider a visit by Musharraf.

The betrayal of Kargil and Pakistan-supported terrorism were on Vajpayee's mind when he paid a return visit to the US at Clinton's insistence, in September 2000. In his meetings, Vajpayee found a US system that still did not share India's deep concerns about terrorism emanating from Pakistan. Even scholars debating the grand strategy for US foreign policy in the 1990's failed to recognize the threat and displayed 'a lack of concern about terrorism.'[3] The picture, Vajpayee told his US interlocutors, looked remarkably different to countries that were victims of terror. India, for instance, had been painfully aware of the global and transborder dimension of international terrorism, with terrorist bombs reverberating through the 1980s and 1990s in the border states of Punjab and Jammu and Kashmir. Vajpayee presciently told the US Congress, a year ahead of 9/11: 'No country has faced as ferocious an attack of terrorist violence as India has over the past two decades: 21,000 were killed by foreign-sponsored terrorists in Punjab alone, 16,000 have been killed in Jammu and Kashmir…Distance offers no insulation. It should not cause complacence.'[4]

In November, a couple of months after his visit to the US, Vajpayee's government balanced his Pakistan and Kashmir policy to announce a month-long ceasefire by Indian security forces against militants in the Kashmir Valley for he holy month of Ramzan. Called the non-initiation of combat operations (NICO), this controversial move built some confidence for Kashmiri leaders. But to some security experts, it gave time to the militants to regroup to attack again.

It was an active time for India's post-Pokhran engagement with the world. The Vajpayee–Mishra duo worked on building on strategic partnerships with several emerging poles: the US, Russia, the EU, and the ASEAN; the last put into action Narasimha Rao's 'Look East' policy. A few years later, when Mishra and I sat with Vajpayee in his living room, reminiscing about those years, Mishra summarized India's approach succinctly: after our nuclear tests, we needed powerful friends to realize our greater global status. The Russians were too weak to help. The Americans were the most powerful and willing to help. Our diplomacy worked; the Americans came to our corner. And the rest of the West followed.

VAJPAYEE'S MUSINGS

India–Pakistan tensions weighed heavy on Prime Minister Vajpayee's mind as he spent the end of the year in an idyllic resort in Kerala, to muse on the state of the nation. Vajpayee's 'Musings from Kumarakom' appeared as two separate articles in select newspapers on 1 January 2001. I was with Vajpayee on that break, from 26 December to 1 January, running the personal office, sitting in on some sessions as Vajpayee discussed issues at length with speechwriter Sudheendra Kulkarni, who drafted the text. The approach was to squarely address the two major issues playing on Vajpayee's mind—the Ayodhya temple[5] and the Pakistan conundrum—since, as the article said, 'a self-confident and resilient nation does not postpone the inconvenient issues of yesterday to a distant tomorrow.'[6] So, India was willing to 'seek a lasting solution to the Kashmir problem', and was 'prepared to recommence talks with Pakistan, including at the highest level, provided Islamabad gives sufficient proof of its preparedness to create a conducive atmosphere for a meaningful dialogue.' Vajpayee was willing to get over the Kargil betrayal and deal with Pakistan's dictator, to find a solution to the terrorism problem.[7]

At one of the periodic lunches at the PM's residence in May 2001, the big three BJP leaders—Advani, Vajpayee, and Jaswant Singh—discussed Pakistan. Advani broached the idea of inviting Musharraf to India, while simultaneously intensifying counter-terror operations. Singh agreed and added a third prong of a 'diplomatic offensive' to the approach: make the global community understand the reality of Kargil and Pakistan's continuing sponsorship of terrorism. Vajpayee was game to try the experiment his two friends and most senior CCS colleagues were suggesting.[8] It would be useful, he thought, to read the mind of Pakistan's new dictator, to make him understand what the new India was about and to find an arrangement to counter terrorism.[9]

The operational approach that emerged was to experiment with the new idea of inviting Musharraf to India and to simultaneously end the ceasefire that had been declared for Ramzan and later extended for six months. India's security forces had been complaining of large-scale infiltration of trained militants into Kashmir in the absence of artillery fire, and pushing for the ceasefire to end. Across the border, Musharraf had repeatedly been offering a meeting with India's leaders 'at any time and at any place'.[10]

When the discussion was brought to the Cabinet Committee on Security in May, a couple of MEA officers, Vivek Katju and Raminder Jassal, waited in my office, adjoining the cabinet room. Jaswant Singh walked in and informed them of the 'well thought out decision' to invite Pakistan's dictator. 'Good grief,' said Jassal, reflecting the anti-Musharraf mood prevalent in the baffled foreign office. Nevertheless, the invitation to Pakistan's 'CEO' went on 23 May. India had, in essence, reversed its decision on not engaging with Pakistan until terrorism was stopped; and also linked the Kashmir issue with its Pakistan policy. Both decisions had their critics, but also supporters for another 'bold move' by Vajpayee to look for peace in a nuclear environment.

THE DICTATOR AT THE TAJ

Agra, a town in western Uttar Pradesh famous for the Taj Mahal, was designated the venue for the summit. Elections to the legislative assembly of India's most populous state were expected in a few months and the idea to showcase the state as a venue for global diplomacy had been proposed by the prime minister's politically-savvy media adviser, Ashok Tandon. I was packed off with security teams to recce the Agra hotels, including the new Oberoi property, where the Taj Mahal could provide a backdrop to the talks.

Musharraf landed in Agra in July 2001 after promoting himself as president of Pakistan, throwing out then President Rafiq Tarar, a Nawaz Sharif acolyte. Musharraf was coming on an official visit and needed to claim protocol equivalence with his host, India's president and veteran diplomat, K. R. Narayanan; else, he would not receive the guard of honour.

The media wanted the summit to play out like a high-octane cricket match, with a huge appetite for a ball-by-ball telecast. Private TV channels had started in India a decade earlier and were then seeing a mushrooming of round the clock news channels hungry for content. The first televised foreign policy show was to unfold after the first television war of Kargil and the first televised communal riots in Gujarat that were to follow. It was television that was to prove the undoing of Musharraf's diplomatic foray.

In Vajpayee's PMO, the media coverage of the visit was a hot topic. Media adviser Ashok Tandon was making the case for hourly briefings in Agra. Foreign Minister Jaswant Singh was sceptical of a 'media circus', and suggested a traditional diplomatic format—such as the ones that were in place for summits in Tashkent or Simla or Camp David—with leaders emerging with smiles and handshakes to release a brief outcome document in stilted prose. But India–Pakistan relations in the twenty-first century were a different game, and round the clock TV demanded round the clock briefings, on minutiae if not on substance. Jaswant Singh later felt the media pinch of a failed summit, but became its greatest explainer.

The question playing in Vajpayee's mind, and before the diplomats, was whether Agra could become the peace conference that transmogrified the bitterness, humiliation, and tragic loss of lives of Kargil, just like Tashkent was for the 1965 war and Simla for 1971. Could something come out of talking with the new dictator?

Apart from the formal conversations with prepared statements in the delegation-level talks, the bulk of the diplomacy took place at the apex level, with Vajpayee and Musharraf in conversation, with only their notetakers present. The entire Cabinet Committee on Security, including Advani and Jaswant Singh, waited in anterooms along with officials, as the two principals met in a banquet hall improvised as a room for summitry at the Jaypee Palace Hotel, Agra.

Towards the end of the delegation-level talks, Musharraf launched into an exposition of his plans to bring grassroots democracy to Pakistan and garrulously explained how important this was. In a break before the official lunch began, I walked up to Principal Secretary Brajesh Mishra and said that I hoped everyone got the irony of Pakistan's dictator explaining democracy to India's cabinet. Mishra laughed and said I should present my view to the cabinet myself. We walked to where Vajpayee, Advani, and other cabinet members were seated, and Mishra said to Vajpayee that his private secretary had an important observation to share. I did repeat my take to the prime minister and his cabinet colleagues. Vajpayee chuckled. He was letting Musharraf do most of the talking, he wanted to read the man.

On the second day of the summit, Musharraf met with editors of major newspapers and TV networks for a breakfast conversation. The event was filmed by NDTV, with an apparent understanding with the Pakistani embassy that the event was not to be telecast. NDTV however soon decided to telecast the entire conversation. Musharraf had let loose his hawkish position on Kashmir and equated terrorists with freedom fighters. This public telecast sounded to observers like a mid-summit report on the talks, where Pakistan's hard views were being inflicted on India, while India's positions were unclear.

In our makeshift PMO at the hotel, Brajesh Mishra and I watched the proceedings with dismay. Mishra turned to me and said that the PM needed to be informed of this development, since he was sitting in conversation with Musharraf oblivious to everything happening outside the meeting room. Mishra scribbled a few lines. I had them quickly typed up, adding a couple of sentences of my own. The note basically said that a press conference by Musharraf was being telecast, where he had repeated his hardline positions, harping on the Kashmir issue and had talked of terrorists as freedom fighters. It fell upon me to walk into the room where the two principals and the two notetakers were sitting. My arrival interrupted the conversation as both leaders looked up. Musharraf had been talking and Vajpayee was listening, apparently with great interest. I handed over the paper to the boss and said that there had been some important developments. After I left the room, Vajpayee looked at the paper and then read out from it to Musharraf, saying edgily that his behaviour was not helping the talks. *India Today* reported that the summit went downhill from the point I had handed over the note to the prime minister[11]; I was playfully accused by some colleagues of torpedoing the Agra initiative.

Advani was quite aware of the slant in the media reporting, making him the villain of the piece. The simplistic narrative emerging from the meetings, fuelled by Pakistani leaks, was that while Vajpayee and Jaswant Singh were for an understanding and OK with Pakistan's convoluted draft of the Agra joint statement (linking progress in bilateral ties to forward movement on the Kashmir issue), Advani the hawk had vetoed it since he did not want any progress with Pakistan. Later Pakistani writings tend to highlight the almost agreed upon draft.[12]

The reality was different. Jaswant Singh walked in to Vajpayee's hotel suite to show him the paper he had negotiated with his counterpart, Sattar. Vajpayee asked his other cabinet colleagues to come to the suite. Brajesh Mishra was already present. Pakistan's initial formulations linking a Kashmir settlement to other bilateral matters had been diluted, but the first operative paragraph still referred to 'progress towards settlement of (the) Jammu and Kashmir issue.' The draft ended with calling for addressing all issues 'in an integrated manner.'[13] The draft also asked for a sustained dialogue at the political level on terrorism, but made no promises of Pakistan curtailing it.[14] While the overall formulations seemed innocent enough, the draft was sending a political message that India was letting Musharraf get away lightly on the terrorism issue. Several red flags went up in the room.

Jaswant Singh recalled that the 'collective view expressed there was that without sufficient and clear emphasis on terrorism, also accepting categorically that it must cease, how could there be any significant movement on issues that are of concern or are a priority only to Pakistan? And none that are in the hierarchy of priorities for India? How can we abandon Shimla or Lahore? Or forget the reality of Kargil? I went back and reported failure to Sattar.'[15] As Jaswant Singh walked out of the room, Advani sighed and said, in English, that he would now be the 'fall guy'.

Musharraf asked for a last meeting with Vajpayee to see if he could save the failing summit. To Vajpayee, this move had echoes of Bhutto's gambit in Simla in 1972, when he had asked for a last call on Indira Gandhi, at a time when the Simla Agreement was deadlocked. Bhutto had pleaded with Gandhi and persuaded her that he would not survive if he did not carry back an agreement. Musharraf famously claimed that he bluntly told Vajpayee that there seemed to be 'someone above the two of us who had power to overrule us'. But Vajpayee 'just sat there speechless'.[13] Vajpayee had in fact let Musharraf speak and refused to cave in to the dictator's pleas. He then gently said it was too late to retrieve the situation. The meeting ended on that note. When Vajpayee walked out grimly, Advani joked he was going to send someone to check 'kya guppen lada rahen hain (what the tittle-tattle was all about).' Vajpayee would refer to this remark when he spoke later in parliament. Jaswant Singh, who was also waiting for the meeting to end, later recalled, 'I knew that a mistake was being made by our guest, for when I later asked Vajpayee what had happened, he said quietly, "nothing". He said it in Hindi, in effect to mean, "the visiting general sahib kept talking and I kept listening". This is an art at which Vajpayee, so often and so disconcertingly to the unfamiliar, specialises.'[17]

Musharraf's overreach in terms of publicly broadcasting hawkish positions on Kashmir—and his insistence on a formulation linking progress on all issues with progress on Kashmir—had led to the unravelling of the summit. Another factor was that both countries attempted to summit a mountain with little planning or even Sherpas to help them. Negotiating a joint statement at the level of the prime minister and foreign minister was not the smartest choice by Pakistan. There had been little diplomatic bargaining, no backchannel dialogue, and limited diplomatic attempts to choreograph the summit's outcomes to bridge the vast chasm in the two positions on Kashmir and terrorism.

The night of Musharraf's sudden departure saw some tense moments in the Indian camp. Global media, including Pakistani journalists, were awaiting India's position on the collapse of the talks and Musharraf's premature departure. The new external affairs spokesperson, Nirupama Rao, stepped up to ask Jaswant Singh if he would address the media. Singh said that he would not, but added dramatically in his baritone that she should make an appearance in the media room with the message: 'The caravan has left but was yet to reach its destination.'[18] Rao went in past midnight to battle a roomful of journalists baying for information. She had to go on with this woefully inadequate brief, just that Urdu phrase rendered into English about a travelling caravan. She announced that the longer press conference would be held the next day at 'a level above' hers since the leaders had not decided on this issue. The waiting media howled in protest. Rao was even jostled and heckled by Pakistani journalists. The next day, Vajpayee asked Jaswant Singh to handle the press conference, nixing Singh's gentle suggestion that Advani do it instead.

Jaswant Singh was in command of the 17 July press conference, where he repeated his analogy of the departing caravan and wordily countered the suggestion that India had not shared details with the media:

India does not believe that discussions or negotiations between two heads of government are ever or can ever be conducted in public or through the press. We abided by that impeccably. However, when we found that there was a kind of approach from the other side of engaging with the media as an additionality ... it was found necessary that for the sake of the public of India the essence of what Prime Minister Vajpayee had emphasized and said be made also known to everybody.[19]

India had officially released Vajpayee's formal opening statement at the delegation-level talks. Singh focused on themes of cross-border infiltration and firing at the LoC, as also India's attempt to take forward the 'peace process' of November 2000. He deftly parried some aggressive questions, and refused to call the summit a failure.

Since the talks seemed to have collapsed because of the divergence of views in the draft joint statement, I felt then that we could easily have brought into play the blander version, which would not mention the 'K-word' and simply say that Pakistan's president came for talks and these would continue. But it was also true that if terrorism had continued in subsequent years despite the joint statement, Musharraf's Agra visit would have felt like another betrayal. A few months later, I raised this issue in a dining table conversation with Vajpayee and Brajesh Mishra: if India had gone with a bland text to declare the summit a success and then cross-border terrorism had continued, would we not have appeared even more gullible than we did when the summit was declared a failure? Mishra agreed that would have been a worse outcome. Would Musharraf have then put a lid on cross-border terrorists? More likely, Agra would become another Lahore, where risen hope had been dashed by Kargil. Still, the invitation to Musharraf served a purpose, Vajpayee did manage to read Pakistan's loquacious dictator, and this experience would help him evolve his Pakistan policy over the next three years. The summit did not succeed, but diplomacy had worked. It had worked for both countries.

23

THE TERROR FACTOR

It would take four jet planes and a handful of fanatics on a fine September morning to position terrorism at the centre of global discourse. Before the events of 9/11 shattered the calm in 2001, terrorism in the US perception appeared to be something that happened to generic others. It now became the central policy concern of the Western world. The fact that the terrorists had been trained in Pakistan put an uncomfortable spotlight on Pakistan's role as the 'epicentre' of terrorism. The US message for Pakistan was clear, that it had to be 'either with us or with the terrorists'. Musharraf felt he had no choice but to join the US effort in Afghanistan. He explained his decision later in a self-congratulatory memoir, *In the Line of Fire*, pointing to intense American pressure on him. 'In what has to be the most undiplomatic statement ever made', Musharraf recalled, '(Richard) Armitage added to what Colin Powell had said to me and told the (ISI) director general not only that we had to decide whether we were with America or with the terrorists, but that if we chose the terrorists, then we should be prepared to be bombed back to the Stone Age.'[1]

From India, the situation looked grimmer. The country that was part of the global terrorism problem, had now been recruited to be part of the solution. To most Indian observers, the US-led action in Afghanistan, part of the 'war on terror' was predicated on the use of overwhelming force against the Taliban regime in Kabul, playing hosts to the al-Qaeda. It failed to take into account the complexity of the problem—the conflicting objectives of Pakistan and the US.

Terrorism from Pakistan continued to raise its ugly head in Kashmir. On 1 October 2001, a three-man Jaish-e-Mohammed fidayeen suicide squad rammed an explosive-laden Tata Sumo into the legislative assembly complex in Srinagar. Thirty-eight people were killed. This terror in Kashmir suggested that far from hiding from the post-9/11 US spotlight on Pakistan as a training hub for terrorists, the events in the US had inspired the militants to launch spectacular acts of suicide terror. More was to come.

12/13

Around 11.30 a.m., on 13 December 2001, a white Ambassador car with security stickers entered India's Parliament complex and parked near Gate 12. When an alert guard approached the vehicle, the driver panicked and backed into the carcade of the vice president of India. Soon, five men jumped out of the car and started firing indiscriminately. Security guards locked the gates of the Parliament building and returned fire, eventually killing all five terrorists. The media covering parliament telecast the gunbattle live. When it ended, seven soldiers and five terrorists lay dead. For India, this was a 9/11 moment; the national mood of anger and outrage matched the shock at the audacity of the terrorism plot.

The Parliament attack could have been a worse tragedy. I had a footnote to add to the tragic episode. In the PM's personal office, some important files had piled up for Vajpayee to sign off on. He was leaving for parliament from Race Course Road at about 11.10 a.m. when I saw on TV that the Lok Sabha had been adjourned due to some commotion. I jogged behind the departing carcade and asked for it to stop. I told the PM that parliament had been adjourned and was unlikely to meet that morning, so there was no point in going there. A couple of meetings at the Parliament office could be shifted, and we could take care of some urgent files at the office at Race Course Road. The PM looked at me with mock reluctance, but agreed to get to work at RCR.

While my colleague in the personal office, R. P. Singh, was discussing his files with the PM, I got a breathless call from Ravi, an official in the PM's Parliament office just after 11.40 a.m.: he was hearing gunshots, the parliament building was locked and we should not come there. It's on TV, he told me. I switched on the television and saw the breaking news story; the shootout was already playing out live on every news channel. I raced to the adjoining room to tell the PM that terrorists had opened fire in the Parliament complex and he should come see it on TV. Vajpayee, whose adult life had been dedicated to parliament, watched the horror in silent outrage before he got on the phone.

That afternoon, a group of officers from the PM's security, the SPG, came in to my office. They were convinced that the PM was the primary target of the assault and thanked me for my fortuitous morning intervention. Our obsession in the PMO on 'no pendency' had prevented the prime minister's carcade from crossing paths with the terrorists.

Five days later, Home Minister Advani would confirm that 'the terrorist assault on the very bastion of our democracy was clearly aimed at wiping out the country's top political leadership.'[2] A US official, Bruce Riedel, later wrote that in the US assessment, the operation was aimed at assassinating the PM or at the minimum holding him hostage.[3]

The day after the attack, India's foreign secretary, Chokila Iyer, summoned High Commissioner Qazi to spell out 'some of the steps that were required and were also mandated by international law'.[4] These included the arrest of the leadership of Lashkar-e-Taiba and Jaish-e-Mohammed, stopping their activities and freezing their assets. Advani also revealed in parliament that the assault 'was executed jointly by Pak-based and supported terrorist outfits, LeT and JeM, organizations known to 'derive their support and patronage from Pak ISI'. All five terrorists of the suicide squad were Pakistani nationals. An angry security establishment was rounding up their Indian associates.[5]

A week later, a frustrated government said India had 'seen no attempts on the part of Pakistan to initiate action against the organisations involved'[6]; so, it had decided to recall High Commissioner Nambiar from Islamabad. India also terminated the train and bus services between the countries.[7]

PARAKRAM

Nambiar had walked into Pakistan during the post-Kargil low in the summer of 1999. He went through a roller-coaster tenure of eighteen months in nuclear times. A year into his tenure, he saw the high of the build-up to the Agra summit and then a deep low as relations plummeted after 13 December. When Nambiar received the summons from New Delhi, they did not specify a date for his return. In the next few days in Islamabad, he went to multiple farewell receptions, including one hosted by the foreign office. On one outing to the Islamabad Golf Course for a farewell round of golf with some friends, he was photographed by the media. A mischievous and clearly planted story made the headlines, suggesting that the Indian HC was reluctant to leave Islamabad. The Pakistan desk chief in Delhi, Joint Secretary Arun Singh, called up the high commissioner and requested him to return immediately.

By the end of the month, it was clear that Pakistan was not about to help in the investigation into its assets, 'veritable arms' of the ISI, nor crackdown on the terrorism machine. Musharraf's establishment seemed to be testing India. How would India react to terrorism emanating from a nuclear Pakistan? Would the fear of escalation stay India's hand? Just as the Pakistan Army had tested India's resolve in a nuclear environment with incursions into Kashmir at Kargil a couple of years earlier, it seemed to want to test its resolve in regard to cross-border terrorism. Besides, Musharraf was now not overly concerned about US censure, as a keen, if duplicitous, soldier in the US war on terror being played out to Pakistan's west.

An angry Jaswant Singh told parliament on 27 December that 'India's serious concerns about all the ramifications of the 13th December attack on our Parliament have not been fully grasped in Pakistan' and 'attempts to dupe the international community with cosmetic half measures, non-measures, or even fictitious incidents are still being made.' He also announced decisions to halve the strength of both high commissions within forty-eight hours, particularly since 'officials of the Pakistan high commission have been involved in espionage, as well as in direct dealings with terrorist organizations. Also, the remaining Pakistani officials of the high commission would be confined to the municipal limits of Delhi; and

India's air space would close again to Pakistani overflights. He warned that these were 'minimal measures' to get Pakistan to curb terrorism and that 'India remains ready to take such further measures'.[8]

All options for 'kinetic action' were thus on the table, and indeed furiously discussed in the security establishment and in the Cabinet Committee on Security. The anger was palpable. The mood in the country, in the ruling coalition led by the BJP, and within the cabinet, was to 'do something'.

Three factors were weighing strongly on Vajpayee's mind. One, Kargil had taught him the value of post-nuclear strategic restraint. It got the West to prevail over a clearly errant and irresponsible Pakistan. The US had changed administrations, with a Republican president, George Bush in the saddle, promising to be harder than ever on terror post 9/11. Besides, the services of Clinton were still available to rally global support for India. Two, Vajpayee embodied the idea of India being a responsible nuclear power. He was retrieving global relationships; the Kargil restraint had won him the trust of the US and the West. Any hasty hot pursuit or strikes across the border would undo this work. Besides, both India and Pakistan were trying to learn about their nuclear thresholds and India had not yet made up its mind where Pakistan's threshold lay. Vajpayee was acutely aware that his decision to change India's nuclear status came with a great deal of responsibility. He had taken a call during Kargil of not crossing the LoC and this was a decision his cabinet was inclined to maintain. Three, Vajpayee was not sure it would be in India's interest to risk conflict with Pakistan on its eastern border, when the US was present on the western border and indeed promoting Indian interests by ridding Afghanistan of the Taliban regime. In one conversation with Advani, Vajpayee said he was clear in his mind that India should not for the moment risk a war while NATO troops were fighting in the region. Both nuclear responsibility and global obligations thus dictated a line of action of aggressive global diplomacy backed by a credible threat of force.

India's policy response evolved into a rapid military build-up on its western border, Operation Parakram (attack), accompanied by global diplomacy to highlight the reactivated terror infrastructure within Pakistan.

The approach yielded some early results. Pakistan came under intense Western pressure to focus on supporting the US-led action on its western border and to curb terror within. A few cosmetic arrests began. India reacted cautiously at the end of the year with a media statement acknowledging 'information about some actions...against the Lashkar-e-Tayyaba and Jaish-e-Mohammad', including some arrests and raids. 'If this information is confirmed, then it is a step forward in the correct direction. We hope that such actions against terrorist activities targeting India, including Jammu and Kashmir, would be pursued vigorously, until cross-border terrorism in our country is completely eliminated.'[9]

COERCIVE DIPLOMACY

As a new year arrived, the Pakistan factor continued to be the Vajpayee government's strong preoccupation. The prime minister had cancelled his annual year-end holiday to deal with the crisis and decided to share his views with the people. He worked with speech-writer Kulkarni on an article that hit the papers on 1 January 2002.[10] Vajpayee pointed out that the December attack had shown 'beyond a shadow of doubt that the anti-India forces in Pakistan are prepared to wreak any havoc on our soil' and that 'the outrage of December 13 has breached the limit of the nation's endurance'. Addressing the people of Pakistan, he warned presciently that these forces in Pakistan had been 'allowed to play with fire, apparently with no thought given to what this fire can do to Pakistan itself.' He took a swipe at Pakistan's new approach to its western border, observing that 'the leadership of Pakistan took a commendable decision to join the international coalition against terrorism in Afghanistan, although it meant a drastic U-turn in their policy of support to the Taliban regime.' He asked Pakistan's leaders to 'shed your anti-India mentality and take effective steps to stop cross-border terrorism.' If Pakistan took that path, India would be 'willing to walk more than half the distance to work closely with Pakistan to resolve, through dialogue, any issue, including the contentious issue of Jammu & Kashmir.' Pakistan's litmus test was to demonstrate its sincerity by responding to 'India's legitimate demands' that included handing over some terrorists who had found safe haven within Pakistan.

Pakistan decided to respond by cherry-picking the convenient parts of the article. The foreign office spokesman Aziz Khan welcomed Vajpayee's 'willingness to resume high-level talks', since Pakistan had always desired 'resolution of all issues including the core issue of Jammu and Kashmir.'[11]

On 4 January, a SAARC summit had been planned in Kathmandu. Vajpayee considered postponing the meet in view of the prevailing tensions but eventually relented, since Nepal was keen. I had made a visit to the Nepali capital in December as part of a security liaison team and had the sense that Nepal, which also hosted the SAARC secretariat, saw the summit as an opportunity to add to its regional profile and to defuse the tension.

No bilateral conversation was fixed between Vajpayee and Musharraf. At a plenary meeting held in an auditorium, Musharraf surprised Vajpayee by ending his speech with a flourish, extending a hand of friendship to India. He then walked up to Vajpayee for a handshake. This grandstanding annoyed the Indian team, Musharraf had done nothing so far to demonstrate any will to act against the terrorists. Vajpayee's speech was to come later and a public response to Musharraf had to be improvised in the next twenty minutes.

Brajesh Mishra scribbled a few sentences and asked me to walk in front of the table on the dais where the leaders were seated, rather than discreetly behind, to hand the slip to the PM. This was to signal publicly that Vajpayee would respond to Musharraf's theatrical gesture. I did exactly that and passed on the slip, relaying the principal secretary's draft to the PM. He read the draft silently and said nothing. I was carrying the speech but needed to get the PM off the high table to confer with him on where to insert the paragraph. I went up to him and requested him to take a toilet break. After the break, we sat in a corner to read the draft which I had by then written in bold, adding a few words to Mishra's hasty draft. When the PM had read the draft, I added for good measure that it was important to give that message, and we could insert the draft addition at the end. 'Theek hai,' said the PM, which meant he had approved the draft and would use it.

Towards the end of his speech supporting the SAARC process, Vajpayee said:

> I am glad that President Musharraf extended a hand of friendship to me. I have shaken his hand in your presence. Now President Musharraf must follow this gesture by not permitting any activity in Pakistan or any territory in its control today, which enables terrorists to perpetuate mindless violence in India. I say this because of our past experience. I went to Lahore with a hand of friendship. We were rewarded by aggression in Kargil and the hijacking of the Indian Airlines aircraft from Kathmandu. I invited President Musharraf to Agra. We were rewarded with the terrorist attack on the Jammu and Kashmir assembly and last month on the Parliament of India. But we would be betraying the expectations of our peoples if we did not chart out the course towards satisfying the unfulfilled promises of our common South Asian destiny.

Soon, various diplomatic interlocutors were assuring India that Musharraf had been 'persuaded' by the US to soon make a statement declaring an end to Pakistan's support to terrorism. On 8 January 2002, Home Minister L. K. Advani had reached the US, where he was similarly informed of the upcoming speech by Musharraf. The US told India it had doubled down on Pakistan, emphasizing the need for credible action, both in the context of 9/11 and the Parliament attack. The Indian system found this assurance underwhelming, since India needed verifiable action, not more words. Nevertheless, on 12 January, PM Vajpayee, EAM Jaswant Singh, and Principal Secretary Brajesh Mishra, along with a few of us, assembled to watch Musharraf's speech on television. It felt like a group watching a suspense movie which could end with any twist. In a speech that started late, Musharraf did deliver a promise on checking terrorism, but added a not unexpected Kashmir twist:

I would also like to address the international community, particularly the USA on this occasion...Pakistan will not allow its territory to be used for any terrorist activity anywhere in the world. Now you must play an active role in solving the Kashmir dispute for the sake of lasting peace and harmony in the region....[12]

Jaswant Singh responded the next day at a press conference spelling out India's expectations. But he welcomed

the now declared commitment of the Government of Pakistan not to support or permit any more the use of its territory for terrorism anywhere in the world, including in the Indian State of Jammu and Kashmir. This commitment must extend to the use of all territories under Pakistan's control today. We would assess the effectiveness of this commitment only by the concrete action taken.... The Government notes the decision of the Government of Pakistan to ban the Lashkar-e-Tayyaba and the Jaish-e-Mohammad, the two terrorist organisations involved in the December 13 attack on the India Parliament. We look forward to an effective and full implementation of this measure... lack of action against fugitives from law about whom detailed information has been provided to Pakistan on several occasions is disappointing....[13]

India was now piling on the pressure for Pakistan to act on its promises, especially the extradition of terrorists in Pakistan, including Indian citizens, 'fugitives from the law' like the Bombay blasts mastermind, Dawood Ibrahim. 'Withdrawn' high commissioner Nambiar, now based in Delhi, said in an interview that India had demanded that twenty criminals housed in Pakistan be prosecuted; fourteen of these were non-Pakistani and India demanded their extradition. He rejected Pakistan's claim it had no idea about their whereabouts: 'They have properties, relatives, associates—all that can be used to track them down. The Pakistani government must take these measures to restore its credibility....'[14]

Pakistan's deputy high commissioner, Jalil Abbas Jilani, was also called in to the Ministry of External Affairs to be reminded of the list of twenty 'fugitives from law' that had been handed over on 31 December 2001. If Pakistan was sincere in its recently declared commitment to fight against international terrorism, he was told, it must 'apprehend and hand over these persons to India.'

But the violence within Pakistan was not abating. On 23 January 2002, an American journalist reporting for the Wall Street Journal, Daniel Pearl, was kidnapped in Lahore while meeting a fake source for a story. One of Pearl's abductors was Ahmed Omar Saeed Sheikh, one of the terrorists released by India in the 1999 hijacking of an Indian Airlines aircraft. To the shock of the global community, Pearl, who was Jewish, was brutally murdered on 1 February, his beheading chillingly captured on a videotape released later by the killers. With Musharraf's Pakistan under intense US pressure to deliver justice, Sheikh, a British national of Pakistani origin, surrendered in March to his ISI handler, Brigadier Ijaz Shah. After the high-profile arrest, India's foreign office summoned Jilani, to demand that Sheikh be interrogated for information relevant to the hijacking of IC-814, as well as the recent terrorist attacks on the Srinagar Assembly building and on India's Parliament. But Sheikh was a special guest of the ISI and a precious asset who needed to be shielded at all costs, both from the US and India. (He was sentenced to death by hanging for Pearl's abduction and murder in July 2002, but his conviction for murder was overturned by a Pakistani court in April 2020.)

AN ENVOY EXPELLED

On 14 May 2002, three armed men gunned down thirty-one people, including army men and children, in Kaluchak, J&K. Again, the terrorists were shot dead and identified as Pakistanis. This bloodbath gave India reason to correct a diplomatic asymmetry and expel Pakistan's HC, Jehangir Qazi. India had after the Parliament attack five months earlier only withdrawn its own envoy, but overlooked removing Pakistan's. The next day, EAM Jaswant Singh announced that the Cabinet Committee on Security had decided to ask Pakistan to 'recall' its envoy in Delhi. Joint secretary in the Pakistan Division Arun Singh called in Qazi's deputy, Jilani, at 3 p.m., and told him Qazi had a week to leave.

Pakistan expressed disappointment at the expulsion, arguing that India's move would escalate tension between the 'two nuclear-capable rivals by hampering the communication between them.'[15] Pakistan's spokesman claimed that when India recalled its HC in December, 'we did not take a reciprocal action because we felt that our diplomatic representation at the highest level should be maintained so that all issues with India should be resolved through dialogue and through peaceful means.'[16]

When she met Qazi for a farewell call, Foreign Secretary Chokila Iyer conveyed India's message to Qazi to take back home: Pakistan's current approach towards India and its reliance on violence and terrorism is unacceptable.[17] In the week he had, Qazi himself hosted a well-attended farewell reception before he left India. Qazi also called on Deputy PM Advani, the political leader with whom he had interacted the most, when an emotional Advani even embraced him at the instance of Mrs Advani.[18]

The escalating violence was worrying the world. Would India continue to exercise restraint or would it retaliate? Nuclear concerns became serious in 2001–02. A large number of diplomats fled New Delhi as advisories were issued on the dangers of tensions escalating to nuclear levels. The ban on civilian overflights by both countries persisted. Firing continued at the LoC, the two armies were primed and ready for battle, and the Pakistan Air Force practised for war by landing fighter aircraft on the Islamabad–Lahore highway.

Global attention was riveted on the subcontinent. Western diplomats and peace negotiators came in droves to both India and Pakistan. They included the prime minister of Britain Tony Blair and several US diplomats like Richard Armitage, who told Vajpayee that the US had told Musharraf that the idea of root causes of terrorism had gone out of the window after 9/11.

WHOSE JINNAH HOUSE IS IT ANYWAY?

In July, India had a new foreign minister, Yashwant Sinha; he swapped portfolios with Jaswant Singh, who became finance minister. Sinha took over at a time of high tension with Pakistan. He had been familiar with the collapsing ties, as a member of the Cabinet Committee of Security. A ticklish issue Sinha faced was of Jinnah House, a contentious matter since 1947, with a new twist in the twenty-first century. The issue of Pakistan's claim on this property had been long settled, with the closing of the Mumbai consulate and the bungalow being treated as abandoned enemy property. But it was now a matter of the Indian government contesting an Indian citizen's claim. In Sinha's account:

> A recommendation had been made to the PM, by my predecessor Jaswant Singh, that Jinnah House in Mumbai should be returned to its 'rightful' owner—Nusli Wadia's mother Dina Wadia, daughter of Muhammad Ali Jinnah. The PM had already approved the proposal. When the file came back from the PMO to the foreign secretary, Kanwal Sibal personally brought it to me, saying it would be wrong and indefensible for us to part with the precious property.... Sibal prepared a note in which he succinctly argued why the property should not be transferred to Dina Wadia. I added my own argument on the file and we asked the PM to reconsider his earlier decision. Vajpayee promptly agreed with our revised recommendation.[19]

The house that Jinnah had hoped to return to one day was eventually taken over by the Government of India.

ﬗ

India's leaders were persuaded by October 2002 that the military stand-off with Pakistan with the massive mobilization of forces at the border, Operation Parakram, had achieved its objectives and the tactic had run its course. Following international diplomatic intervention, mainly by US president George Bush and his team, but also by the UK PM Tony Blair,

Pakistan had made the right noises on fighting terrorism. India had drawn sufficient global attention to South Asia and on the ISI's undeniable links with militant groups within Pakistan. Both countries pulled back troops from the border, reducing tensions considerably. But firing at the border continued, as did some bellicose rhetoric pointed at each other.

CASH FOR SEPARATISM

Diplomacy suffered another setback, when in February 2003, India expelled Pakistan's charge d'affaires, Jalil Abbas Jilani, for 'activities incompatible with his official status'. Jalani was detected passing cash to Kashmiri separatist Hurriyat members at a hotel and given forty-eight hours to leave the country. Predictably, Pakistan wasted no time in following suit in Islamabad, although the Indian mission indulged in no comparable practice of paying off separatists. Three days later, India's CdA, Sudhir Vyas, was asked to leave Islamabad. With both CdAs expelled, the missions were looking emaciated, with little hope of diplomacy reviving. Before he left, Vyas needed to pare down the size of the mission further, with now only a handful of staff available to man the mission.

The cross-border dynamics in J&K were shifting. Musharraf had said more than once that the territory of Pakistan would not be used for any action against India. The feeling in the Indian camp was that it would be useful to capture that assurance in a bilateral document, to make it more sustainable. But for that, relations needed to get better.

As soon as Jalani was packed off, India's Foreign Secretary Kanwal Sibal called diplomat T. C. A. Raghavan to his office. Raghavan who had worked in EAM Jaswant Singh's office, had received posting orders in 2002, having volunteered to go as CdA to Pakistan despite more glamorous options. However, the bureaucratic chain of postings had been jammed, since Sudhir Vyas was unable to relocate to his next posting. With Vyas expelled, the chain moved. Sibal instructed Raghavan to urgently take over as CdA in Islamabad. Raghavan and his Pakistani counterpart, Munawwar Bhati, received assignment visas right away.

Raghavan's briefings in Delhi offered little hope of any improvement in the relationship; most policymakers were pessimistic. But the one meeting that offered him a glimmer of hope was his last call in Delhi—on Vajpayee's principal secretary and national security advisor Brajesh Mishra. Mishra said that once Pakistan withdrew its petition from the International Civil Aviation Organization (ICAO) and overflights were allowed, the relationship might improve, culminating in the Indian prime minister visiting Pakistan for the SAARC summit in a few months. Mishra knew the mood in Pakistan through his backchannel connection with Musharraf's confidant Tariq Aziz.

Raghavan arrived in a bleak Islamabad. Aziz Ahmed Khan, in charge of South Asia at the foreign office at the time, was as pessimistic about the relationship as Raghavan's Indian colleagues. The bilateral relationship was severely disrupted. The mission had been reduced to seventeen people against a sanctioned strength, bilaterally agreed, of 110. Manning the fort were three armed-forces attachés, and a young IFS officer, Vikram Misri, apart from a few security guards and junior officials. This mirrored exactly the composition of Pakistan's embassy in Delhi. Given the level of animosity, Raghavan had the sinking feeling that he would have to close the mission and return to India in a few months.

24

A HAND OF FRIENDSHIP

A nd then, suddenly, things changed.
India's prime minister decided to disrupt the status quo. Vajpayee was acutely conscious of the need to bring peace to Jammu and Kashmir, to free it from the violence Pakistan had promoted since 1990. The Pakistan factor had become part of the politics of the state, with most political parties advocating a better relationship with the contiguous western neighbour. We were prioritizing Kashmir-focused meetings in the PMO in preparation for Vajpayee's trip there in April 2003. Vajpayee had been speaking to Pakistan experts, including former R&AW chief A. S. Dulat, now an adviser on Kashmir matters in the PMO. Vajpayee carefully read and listened to a range of opinions and recipes for healing Kashmir. Brajesh Mishra, who was continuously discussing both Kashmir and Pakistan with the PM, told me even he was not sure whether the Pakistan issue would come up in a public speech Vajpayee was about to deliver, where his healing touch was expected. Dulat, who had prepared an excellent set of reports on Kashmir, was not sure either.

Speaking extempore at a public rally in Srinagar on 18 April 2003, trusting his own political instincts, Vajpayee spoke of a poetically ambiguous approach of Insaniyat (Humanity), Jamhooriyat (Democracy), and Kashmiriyat (Kashmiri values), later widely acclaimed as the 'Vajpayee doctrine', even if not interpreted uniformly. The prime minister congratulated the people of Kashmir on the previous year's elections, where they had participated 'defying bullets' and added that he had come to share their pain and suffering. Then came the surprise: 'I once again extend a hand of friendship to Pakistan, but the hand must be extended both ways.' The next day, at a crowded press conference, Vajpayee said he was awaiting a reply from Pakistan. But terrorism needed to stop for talks to be meaningful. On 23 April, he told parliament in Delhi: 'I expressed the hope that a new beginning can take place between India and Pakistan...stopping cross-border infiltration and destruction of terrorist infrastructure can open the doors for talks. Talks can take place on all issues, including that of Jammu & Kashmir.'

Vajpayee's surprise offer led to a rapidly unfolding chain of events, including the appointment of envoys by both countries. When Brajesh Mishra came to discuss a few names of possible envoys, I was with Vajpayee in his room. Harsh Bhasin, an IFS officer, had been posted to Pakistan the previous year, but had got tired of waiting indefinitely given the deadlock in diplomatic relations. He had requested Foreign Secretary Sibal to send him to the only available slot—in Denmark. One option was to pull Bhasin back in. The PM looked at the names, heard Mishra out, thought for a while and then said, 'Nahin sahab, Menon ko bhejiye. (Send Menon.)' Shivshankar Menon, then envoy to China, was thus Vajpayee's personal choice to take forward the latest peace initiative. Menon had been a star diplomat whom Vajpayee trusted and had seen in action from his Sri Lanka and China days. I sat in on the meeting when Menon called on Vajpayee. Menon, who had not dealt with Pakistan in his career that far, asked the PM, 'Why me?' Vajpayee chuckled: 'Because you are innocent.'[1]

Even before Menon arrived in Islamabad, the situation had improved. Menon had in Beijing known Foreign Secretary Riaz Khokhar well, who was, till the previous year, Pakistan's envoy to China. Khokhar told his staff officer Shafqat Ali Khan that the 'agrèment', accepting the nomination of Menon by Pakistan, was approved at his level and should be conveyed immediately. CdA Raghavan was surprised to get the nod from the foreign office the same day he had put in the request.

The mood in Pakistan was changing. The later Musharraf was different from the early Musharraf, less impetuous, more understanding of nuances, less reflexively combative about India. A good influence on Musharraf was his friend and classmate Tariq Aziz, a level-headed and pragmatic adviser committed to India–Pakistan peace, with little patience for the games being played by the army.

India, on its part, was looking beyond Pakistan. India's post-nuclear global diplomacy was picking up, as the country emerged from relative isolation with the 1998 sanctions. Vajpayee, thoughtful and wise in the eyes of other leaders, became the global face of this new India. With Clinton's visit to India in 2000 and Vajpayee's to the US, a strong strategic partnership was being constructed with the US. The same year, Vajpayee had visited Moscow to establish a strategic partnership with an emerging Russian leader, Vladimir Putin. Apart from the US and Russia, India was looking at building ties with other poles of the emerging global order. Vajpayee's global vision had translated into a good deal of summitry with substantive outcomes: the first India–EU Summit had been held in Portugal in the summer of 2000. In 2003, Vajpayee went for a 'G8 plus' summit of rich economies, where the French invited India to Evian for a meeting format that was gradually giving way to the G20. He went in October for the first India–ASEAN Summit in Bali, as part of a 'Look East' orientation to India's foreign policy. Being boxed in by Pakistan in South Asia was not acceptable to those helming an emerging India. But it was also important to address the Pakistan question and the terrorism problem, to give greater bandwidth to diplomacy, to focus on India's global rise.

A QUIET CHANNEL

Vajpayee was now thinking seriously of a visit to Islamabad for a SAARC summit scheduled in January 2004. He needed to follow up on his hand of friendship to attempt a breakthrough that had eluded him in Lahore and Agra. On one occasion, since I was the only one around, Vajpayee asked me, thinking aloud, whom he could send to Pakistan to prepare the ground for his visit. I suggested it could be Jagat Mehta, Vajpayee's foreign secretary when he was foreign minister, who was now sending long handwritten notes to Vajpayee on an approach to Pakistan. The PM said, 'Nah, too old now to travel.' We tossed around a few other names. Finally, Vajpayee decided to go with his trusted principal secretary, Brajesh Mishra, who had earlier made a diplomatic foray into Pakistan during Kargil, and now became a messenger on the backchannel that was earlier run by Niaz Naik and R. K. Mishra.

Mishra quickly got down to work. He went across to Islamabad in May 2003, and hit it off with his newly designated counterpart, Tariq Aziz, an officer of the Pakistan Taxation Service whom Musharraf had known as a student when they were both in the Forman Christian College of Lahore. Aziz was now Musharraf's most trusted and loyal civilian aide. Mishra would go on to meet Aziz five times over the next year.

Gradually, the atmospherics began to improve. An India–Pakistan CEO forum was launched in mid-September with much fanfare, both sides believing that industry would be in a position to develop linkages that could reinforce the détente.

Musharraf and Vajpayee were to meet in New York on the sidelines of the UNGA in September, in the backdrop of a positive turn in relations helped along by an active backchannel. On the eve of the bilateral meeting, Musharraf's address at the UN on 24 September was unexpectedly brimming with the usual strong rhetoric, condemning India's suppression of the Kashmiri people. The flustered Indian camp had to devise a sharp retort, with Vajpayee accusing Pakistan of making terrorism a tool to blackmail the world.

I later asked Tariq Aziz on what went wrong, with Pakistan making such a statement at the UN at a time when the two leaders were to discuss the possibility of a SAARC summit and a breakthrough in the relationship. Aziz told me that the speech became an embarrassment for Musharraf. It was the standard draft of the foreign office with the usual references to Kashmir which no one really checked until Musharraf actually delivered it.

But the peace process was strong enough for both sides to retrieve the situation in the bilateral conversation. Mishra continued his outreach and conversations with Aziz. The breakthrough came soon enough the next month when the external affairs minister, Yashwant Sinha, made an announcement regarding the resumption of civil aviation talks to address the overflight ban in place since January 2002.

It was an odd peace when both sides had not ceased artillery firing at the border. On 25 November, this anomaly was corrected. Indian and Pakistani commanders formalized the ceasefire during a weekly teleconference. An official statement said the ceasefire deal 'included the 450-mile Line of Control, India–Pakistan boundary, and Siachen Glacier'.[2] Pakistani Prime Minister Jamali had declared a unilateral ceasefire two days earlier to commemorate Eid al-Fitr. The yearlong ceasefire on the LoC that had begun in July 2001 had only ended with hostilities. Now, after eighteen months, the guns would go silent again. The ceasefire also led to a dramatic decrease in cross-border infiltration, confirming the view of some observers in India that most of the artillery firing from Pakistan was meant to give cover to infiltrating militants.

Both countries worked hard in the run-up to Vajpayee's visit to normalize relations. Pakistan was particularly keen that the visit and the SAARC summit should go well. It was important to prepare well this time around to ensure that the bilateral process did not falter as it had done in Agra.

One day at the breakfast table, where Vajpayee would often take key decisions, Mishra conferred with Vajpayee and instructed me to invite in all previous envoys to Pakistan to give inputs to the PM. I contacted Satinder Lambah, my former ambassador in Germany, to drop in and share his views with the PM. Lambah offered his pointed advice based on years of dealing with Pakistan, Vajpayee listened patiently and I took notes. To be sure I got it right, I requested Lambah to send his advice in writing so that I could share it within the PMO. Lambah's plan included: having Pakistan strengthen the 2003 ceasefire line; ensuring it caused no harm to India, through official, or jihadi action; adhering to a code of conduct for diplomatic missions to function; and resuming economic, trade, and travel contacts.[3] India's approach was pretty much on the lines suggested by the veteran diplomat.

On 30 November, at a meeting with members of the Pakistani and Indian chapters of the Young Presidents Organization (YPO), Musharraf dramatically announced, 'As a gesture of goodwill, Pakistan will agree to the resumption of overflights with India at the talks being held in Delhi next week.'[4] He disarmingly told the Indian delegates that their flight home would be the first from Pakistan after the resumption of air links. Musharraf's unilateral offer to end the ban on Indian flights over Pakistani territory eliminated the main obstacle to resuming air services. The next day, a memorandum of understanding (MOU) was signed in New Delhi, on 1 December 2003, by the Directors General of Civil Aviation of both countries, agreeing to resume air links and overflights with effect from 1 January 2004 'on a reciprocal basis'. The aviation experts in Delhi had by resuming air links after a two-year hiatus, firmly laid the ground for Vajpayee's visit. The agreement had come a week after the guns went silent and was seen as part of a peace process pushed by the newfound political will on both sides.

Worryingly for India, the internal security situation in Pakistan deteriorated on the eve of the SAARC summit. December saw two separate attempts on Musharraf's life. On 14 December, a powerful bomb went off minutes after the president's convoy crossed a bridge in Rawalpindi; this was the third such attempt. On Christmas Day, two suicide bombers tried to assassinate him. The dictator escaped with only a cracked windshield, but the car bombs killed sixteen others.

When I travelled to Pakistan as part of the advance security and liaison team in late December, the Indian side was anxious about security for the prime minister. The visit was my first exposure to Pakistan, and it was clear that the Pakistani establishment was pulling out all the stops for Vajpayee's visit.

THE ISLAMABAD BREAKTHROUGH

The 2004 visit to Pakistan was critical for Vajpayee. He would turn eighty that year and wanted to leave behind a legacy of peace in Kashmir, and with Pakistan. General elections were due in a few months, and Vajpayee was not keen on another term personally because of his failing health, but he was willing to lead the election campaign. The visit to Pakistan was politically risky, given recent history, but this was a risk for peace he had to take. It was important for his team to prepare well and get it right. Brajesh Mishra went to Islamabad a week in advance and parked himself at the Serena Hotel. So did Pakistan's envoy in India, Aziz Ahmed Khan. HC Menon had withdrawn from the logistics and was closeted with Mishra, leaving the bandobast in the safe hands of his deputy, Raghavan. The key interlocutor for Mishra was Tariq Aziz, who was discussing matters directly with Musharraf. The script worked out by Mishra was playing out. Pakistan had allowed overflights and withdrawn a contentious case from the ICAO that alleged violations of international norms by India. Raghavan sensed something big was afoot. But he had his hands full negotiating the SAARC meeting logistics, including a ride by helicopter to a leaders' retreat, which was giving nightmares to security teams. The SAARC summit was becoming a footnote to the bigger bilateral game. Mishra and Menon, along with the MEA team, were quietly hammering out the text of a joint statement. The Pakistan foreign office was involved in negotiating the text, but the helpline to Tariq Aziz was available to Mishra to remove any roadblocks. It was used on the morning of 6 January. In a last-minute hitch, the negotiated text got stuck at a line in Pakistan's draft, which said that Pakistan's soil would not be used to support terrorism. For India, a better formulation was to refer to 'territory under Pakistan's control', which would pointedly include POK. Menon called up Tariq Aziz to explain the problem. Aziz told me later that he was with Musharraf when he got Menon's call. He got the president's approval for India's formulation 'within seconds'. Aziz then asked Riaz Khokhar in Punjabi to get it done. The backchannel work of Mishra and Aziz had paid off.

The bilateral deal at the end of a multilateral meet made global headlines. Vajpayee had achieved what was promised in Lahore but snatched away in Kargil. This was finally the peace deal for Kargil that had proved elusive in Agra. The joint statement of 6 January 2004 had been crafted to mention both terrorism and Kashmir but focus on a future roadmap.

> Both leaders welcomed the recent steps towards normalisation of relations between the two countries and expressed the hope that the positive trends set by the CBMs would be consolidated. Prime Minister Vajpayee said that in order to take forward and sustain the dialogue process, violence, hostility and terrorism must be prevented. President Musharraf reassured Prime Minister Vajpayee that he will not permit any territory under Pakistan's control to be used to support terrorism in any manner. President Musharraf emphasised that a sustained and productive dialogue addressing all issues would lead to positive results. To carry the process of normalisation forward, the president of Pakistan and the Prime Minister of India agreed to commence the process of the composite dialogue in February 2004. The two leaders are confident that the resumption of the composite dialogue will lead to peaceful settlement of all bilateral issues, including Jammu and Kashmir, to the satisfaction of both sides. The two leaders agreed that constructive dialogue would promote progress towards the common objective of peace, security and economic development for our peoples and for future generations.[5]

When Vajpayee had gone with SAARC leaders for the customary retreat, the Indian delegation reported enormous goodwill for Indians in the streets and markets of Islamabad, where many picked up pirated CDs of the latest Bollywood movies. Vajpayee's son-in-law, Ranjan Bhattacharya, was keen to get in a round of golf at the famous Islamabad Golf Club. He roped me in, along with our Pakistani host, to sneak out for a quick round of golf. At the course, we saw no other golfers. Suddenly, armed security men in battle gear appeared from behind a cluster of trees. Alarmed that there may have been an incident, Ranjan asked one of them what was going on. Assuming he was a Pakistani, the security man whispered conspiratorially: 'Vajpayee ka damaad khelne aaya hai (Vajpayee's son-in-law has shown up to play.)'

Vajpayee's diplomacy had paused the hostility, with the guns at the border silenced, terrorism reduced and a robust bilateral engagement in the works. An issue that concerned policymakers was whether these processes would endure beyond the Musharraf regime. With the rapprochement with Pakistan, India's leaders were hoping to get a peace dividend in Kashmir. A moderate faction of the Kashmiri separatist Hurriyat met Deputy PM Advani in late January for their first direct discussions with New Delhi. Vajpayee also met them briefly as a gesture of goodwill. The Hurriyat had created conditions for the talks by dropping its earlier insistence on three-way talks between India, Pakistan, and the Hurriyat. They had deferred to the government's position that separate tracks of dialogue viz India–Pakistan and Centre–Hurriyat, was a more pragmatic approach. The talks in January marked a step forward in the healing and reconciliation process in Kashmir.

NUCLEAR SCAPEGOAT

Later that month, Musharraf was hit by a fresh crisis that threatened his fragile relationship with the US, as also the domestic stability of his military regime. On 31 January, Pakistan's leader was compelled to fire his 'Science Advisor', nuclear physicist Abdul Qadeer Khan. In a choreographed move, Khan appeared on official PTV on 4 February to confess to running a 'proliferation ring' that transferred nuclear technology to Iran, North Korea, and Libya in the 1990s. Musharraf's government did not arrest Khan but launched 'security hearings' to investigate the scientist's misdeeds. On 5 February, Musharraf issued a presidential pardon to Khan. He was now placed under 'house arrest'.

Few had any doubts that the Pakistani state was complicit in smuggling technology to rogue states and that Khan was being scapegoated in the 'national interest'. Khan, who had been feted for transforming his country into the first Islamic nuclear weapons power, had come under US scrutiny after Pakistan's 1998 tests. He began to lose his domestic sheen when Musharraf, under US pressure, removed him as chief of the Kahuta nuclear lab in 2001 and made him an adviser. In 2003, the Bush administration confronted Musharraf with evidence of a nuclear proliferation network that implicated Khan. That Khan was a lone-wolf proliferator was a convenient fiction for both Musharraf and the US; if it had not been for the war on terror, Musharraf would have invited the full weight of US sanctions on his country. An embittered Khan later retracted his confession to say he had been wronged even though 'I saved the country for the first time when I made Pakistan a nuclear nation and saved it again when I confessed and took the whole blame on myself.'[6]

The episode underlined once again the different trajectories of the nuclear programmes being run by the two countries and raised questions about nuclear responsibility within Musharraf's military regime.

✓

The next month, on 13 March, it was a peacenik-like Musharraf who spoke via a satellite link to a *India Today* conclave in New Delhi. Pakistan, he said, was determined 'to take two steps forward if India takes one step' towards peace. But his message was mixed, even in his own mind, as he tried to reintroduce the centrality of Kashmir into the bilateral discourse. India and Pakistan, he said, 'must bury the past and chart a new roadmap for peace' but 'Kashmir is the central issue that awaits just and durable settlement' and there was an 'indigenous freedom struggle' being waged in Kashmir.[7] An exasperated India scolded Musharraf the next day. An MEA statement pointed out that the 6 January joint press statement had made no reference to 'any so-called central or core issue, but to addressing all bilateral issues, including Jammu and Kashmir' and that double standards in describing the violent attack on himself as terrorism, but on the J&K Assembly as a 'freedom fight' were 'clearly not tenable'.[8]

Musharraf's peace rhetoric of 'two steps forward and one back' would be often repeated by Pakistan's leaders, both civilian and military. Imran Khan used it in 2018 after he became PM and army chief General Bajwa deployed it in 2021.

✓

Pakistan became cause for a hiccup in the US–India relationship when the US declared it a major 'non-NATO ally', despite the A. Q. Khan episode. US secretary of state in the Bush administration, Colin Powell, made the announcement on 18 March in Islamabad, after visiting New Delhi. India's problem was more being kept in the dark by the US, than it bending over backwards to reward Musharraf for his Af-Pak policy. Brajesh Mishra complained sharply to his counterpart NSA Condoleezza Rice, the chief architect then of the foreign policy of President George W. Bush. Rice expressed surprise that Powell had not taken India into confidence on this issue. It was clear to Mishra that Rice and Powell were not on the same page, and that Powell might not last too long in his job. Powell, under pressure from the White House, tried to reach External Affairs Minister Yashwant Sinha to explain himself but Sinha was out campaigning and unreachable.

In an election year, it was important to publicly admonish the US, and the MEA spokesman duly did so on 20 March.

The Secretary of State was in India just two days before this statement was made in Islamabad. While he was in India, there was much emphasis on (the) India–US strategic partnership. It is disappointing that he did not share with us this decision...which has significant implications for India–US relations.[9]

Powell did connect with Sinha the next day to say his intention had not been to spring a surprise on India. The media reported this as an apology and sourced a report from the US that pointed out that Bush had offered the same status to India. The MEA spokesman clarified tersely that 'we have not given any consideration to that kind of relationship with the US.'[10]

25

ESSAYS IN MUTUAL COMPREHENSION

In May 2004, the Vajpayee-led NDA suffered a shock defeat in the general elections. The new Congress-led United Progressive Alliance (UPA) government, with Manmohan Singh as prime minister, signalled strong continuity in foreign policy. PM Singh made it a point to seek a few briefings from Mishra and met Vajpayee several times.

On the new PM's first day in office, I remained one of his private secretaries, as part of the transition team that would make way for a new one. I needed to schedule a series of congratulatory calls from world leaders and sit in on them. George W. Bush was one of the first callers (with Condoleezza Rice patched in); he assured Singh of continuing US friendship and suggested that Rice, who was working closely with him, would be the point person for the relationship.

We had Pakistan's president scheduled next. Before the call from Musharraf, after I had quickly briefed the new PM on Vajpayee's peace process, he asked me whether it was OK to quote a couple of Urdu couplets, apart from using the PMO brief. He produced a piece of paper and read out two couplets he had handwritten in Urdu. I said they sounded perfectly fine, reflected his persona, and should go down well with Musharraf.

Soon after the conversation began, in English, Manmohan Singh told Musharraf he had something to say in Urdu: 'Kuch aise bhi manzar hain tareek ki nazron mein/ lamhe ne khata ki, sadiyon ne saza payee (History has seen missteps that we have suffered for ages.). He followed it up with another one: 'Aa ki tarikyon se surkhiyan paide karen, is jameen ki bastiyon se aasman paida karen (Let's seize this moment and reach for the sky.)[1]

A bemused Musharraf listened with rapt attention as his new Indian counterpart recited couplets in Pakistan's official language. The two men agreed to work for peace.

As Manmohan Singh crafted his new foreign policy, the emphasis remained on continuity in major relationships. On Pakistan, Singh decided to take forward the Vajpayee peace initiative and the Lahore–Islamabad peace process. This was in line with the personal convictions of the prime minister who had been born in what was now Pakistan's Punjab. Singh had the advantage of having two former envoys to Pakistan in his team—National Security Advisor Mani Dixit and External Affairs Minister Natwar Singh. Both former IFS officers seemed equally convinced that a breakthrough with Musharraf's Pakistan was worth striving for.

Without wasting any time, Dixit met with Tariq Aziz in June, resuming the quiet conversations that had led Brajesh Mishra to the January document. Dixit would meet Aziz four times that year. He did not discuss any specific agreement on Kashmir, but prepared the ground for opening the LoC for travel and trade.[2]

On 23 July 2004, External Affairs Minister Natwar Singh, who had dealt extensively with Zia in the 1980s, got to call on Pakistan's latest dictator. The ninety-minute meeting took place in Musharraf's camp office at Rawalpindi. Musharraf reiterated a statement he had made the day before, that without any progress towards the settlement of the core issue of Kashmir, no headway on confidence-building measures was possible.[3] Despite Musharraf blowing hot and cold, the meetings held by former envoys Natwar Singh and Dixit created grounds for the upcoming first encounter between Manmohan Singh and Musharraf in September.

The meeting in New York between the new Indian PM and Pakistan's dictator at the height of his powers was held on the margins of the September UN General Assembly. As the talks began, Manmohan Singh assured Musharraf that he remained personally committed to the dialogue process. Both leaders emerged pleased with the hour-long conversation and, unusually, Musharraf read out the agreement their teams had worked out, saying they had 'also addressed the issue of Jammu and Kashmir and agreed that possible options for a peaceful, negotiated settlement of the issue'. They signalled continuity by adhering to the 'spirit of the Islamabad joint press statement of January 6, 2004', and 'agreed that CBMs will contribute to generating an atmosphere of trust'.[4]

Manmohan Singh added poetically that this meeting was 'an essay in mutual comprehension'[5] and that the two leaders would together write a new chapter in the history of the two countries. Musharraf presented Singh a painting of the school in Gah village (now in Pakistan), the Indian PM's birthplace, and where he had had his initial schooling. On his part Singh again recited the Urdu couplets which he had read out to Musharraf in their phone conversation.

Reacting to criticism that the latest joint statement failed to mention 'cross-border terrorism' Natwar Singh told journalists in London on 1 October that the fact that the 6 January statement was specifically mentioned at the meeting meant that terrorism was indeed discussed. He pointed out that the composite dialogue had kicked off with as many as eight meetings 'in all areas and at all levels'. Underlining the importance of economic contacts despite political hurdles, he cited China's example and said that India's trade with that country was slated to touch $10 billion that year.[6]

The competing narratives of terrorism or Kashmir as central issues continued to play. When Indian Foreign Secretary Shyam Saran arrived in Islamabad on 25 December to wrap up the eight-track composite dialogue process, he was conscious of criticism at home that the new government was falling into Pakistan's trap and not keeping the focus on terrorism. In Islamabad, however, he felt obliged to counter another critique in the Pakistani media: that India was putting a premium on confidence-building measures to sideline the Kashmir issue. Saran said while the focus of the foreign secretary-level engagement was on building mutual trust in the fields of nuclear and conventional arms and countering narcotics trafficking, India was ready for a 'serious and sustained dialogue' on Kashmir.[7] But he also reminded the media of the 'fundamental assurance' given by General Musharraf in January 2004 about not allowing Pakistani soil for anti-India activities.[8]

THE UNQUIET INDUS WATERS

Despite the bonhomie, the waters in Kashmir were not flowing quite so calmly. For the first time since the Indus Waters Treaty was signed in 1960, Pakistan invoked the dispute resolution clause of the treaty, in late 2004, taking the matter to a 'neutral expert'. Thus far, disagreements had been resolved in the bilateral Indus waters commission. As Pakistan took the matter to the World Bank, which pondered over this situation, India warned the bank that interfering in the project would be seen as an 'act unfriendly to India'. The Indus Waters Treaty came up for discussion once again in 2005 when the Baglihar project, a run-of-the-river dam on the Chenab River, was referred to a neutral expert to be appointed by the World Bank. I had just joined the World Bank group as an adviser to C. M. Vasudev, the executive director for South Asia, and this ticklish matter landed on my desk. Eventually, the Indian and Pakistani delegations made their case before a Swiss expert, Raymond Lafitte, who seemed to favour India with small technical changes. The dispute resolution clause would become the default option for Pakistan for future projects. When it came to the Kishanganga project, Pakistan decided to invoke the arbitration panel clause of the treaty and take the matter beyond a neutral expert in the hope of getting a more favourable judgement. Pakistan's security concern was that India would construct a large number of upstream projects in the western rivers, making it possible to start using these as leverage.

PEACE DIVIDEND

India's new government had kept up the frenetic pace of global engagements of the Vajpayee years. Soon after he returned with the PM from one overseas visit, India's overworked NSA, Mani Dixit, tragically passed away of a heart attack in January 2005. His departure left a huge vacuum for Manmohan Singh, who had come to rely on Dixit's strategic thinking and advice, particularly on the neighbourhood. Singh now reached out to Satinder Lambah and appointed him in the PMO to pick up where Dixit had left off in the backchannel dialogue with Pakistan.

Soon after his appointment in April, Lambah met Tariq Aziz. The two men instantly developed a strong rapport and would go on to meet eighteen times between April 2005 and August 2008, in different cities.[9] It was in these meetings that Lambah would negotiate, discuss and nearly finalize a draft agreement on the J&K issue. Lambah worked more formally than his Pakistani counterpart. He had taken the PM's permission to take along a deputy secretary in the PMO, and later the prime minister's private secretary, Jaideep Sarkar. Lambah had told the PM that this would ensure the prime minister stayed in the loop on the backchannel conversations. Aziz however 'travelled alone, rarely carried a briefcase, and often had to scribble his notes on hotel stationery'.[10]

In mid-April 2005, Musharraf arrived in New Delhi to strengthen ties with the new government and for a spot of cricket diplomacy. The visit coincided with the last One Day International cricket match between India and Pakistan, parts of which Musharraf watched, along with Manmohan Singh. In their talks, Singh and Musharraf reaffirmed past commitments and 'determined that the peace process was now irreversible'.[11] They endorsed several decisions taken by the foreign secretaries and foreign ministers to boost trade and connectivity. They agreed to add new routes and step up the frequency of bus services in Kashmir and Punjab. Trucks would be allowed to use these routes to promote trade.[12] Significantly, they also agreed that the consulates general of the two countries in Mumbai and Karachi, shut in the 1990s, would be revived.

The upbeat media coverage did not mention the backchannel that was now working on a long-term solution for the contentious Kashmir issue. But the Indian PM did drop a hint in April, when he told journalists that if the process of allowing increased interaction between the people of J&K was to continue, it would 'create a climate conducive to the final settlement' of the 'territorial dispute'.[13]

ENDORSING JINNAH

Lal Krishna Advani embarked on an emotional trip to Pakistan in June 2005, a visit he could not undertake to the land of his roots when he was India's home minister. Advani visited his old school and home in Karachi, the city where he was born in 1927. At the mausoleum of Pakistan's founder Jinnah, the BJP president wrote a glowing tribute, fairly standard fare in Pakistan's official narratives, recalling a description of Jinnah as an 'ambassador of Hindu–Muslim unity' early in his political career. 'There are many people who leave an inerasable stamp on history,' Advani wrote, 'but there are very few who actually create history. Quaid-e-Azam Mohammed Ali Jinnah was one such rare individual.'[14] Advani went on to describe Jinnah's famous 11 August 1947 speech as a 'forceful espousal of a secular state.' The reaction back home, particularly in Advani's political party, surprised the former minister for its intensity. It also illustrated the complexity of bilateral relations, the politicized past that always preyed on the present and the conflicts within Advani himself. Once an icon of the Ayodhya temple movement, Advani was conscious of his roots in Pakistan; he was a hawk on relations with Pakistan but also the man who had engineered stronger relations with Pakistan's current dictator. Advani's BJP, not yet recovered from the loss in the 2004 polls, could not stomach its president's praise of a man who had been demonized as the villain of Partition. Advani was compelled to resign as president of the BJP though he insisted he had 'no regrets'.[15] The speculation did not go away that with Vajpayee now unwell, Advani was trying to soften his image as an acceptable face to lead a future BJP-led coalition.

DISASTER DIPLOMACY
A devastating earthquake hit Pakistan on 8 October 2005, its impact felt most in the northern reaches of Kashmir under Pakistan's control. As many as 20,000 people died. The humanitarian tragedy presented an opportunity for strengthening bilateral trust and goodwill. India offered assistance; Pakistan accepted. $25 million worth of earthquake relief assistance soon reached Pakistan. The disaster gave a tantalizing glimpse of the latent goodwill that still persisted in the relationship, even if not as freely expressed as the lurking hostility.

TALKING WITH TERROR
The good times would not last. On the night of 30 April 2006, the pause in major terrorism ended. Heavily armed terrorists, suspected to be Lashkar-e-Taiba, targeted and gunned down thirty-four Hindu villagers, in serial terror strikes in the J&K districts of Doda and Udhampur. High Commissioner Shivshankar Menon was to speak about this in Lahore on 2 May. 'Despite some variations in infiltration patterns,' he reminded Pakistan, 'terrorist training, communications and support continue, waxing and waning with the seasons and the political climate.'[16]

But India was giving the Pakistani state the benefit of the doubt about its complicity, or at least it chose not to blame Pakistan until investigations provided evidence. In retrospect, the three years since Vajpayee had extended his hand of friendship to Pakistan in April 2003 had been heady years of goodwill, where cross-border infiltration had fallen, major terrorist incidents were absent, border firing was at its minimum, and the army in Pakistan was talking peace. This was when cricket was played and talks were held via multiple channels and the BJP hardliner president praised Pakistan's founder and India rushed to the aid of Pakistan in its moment of need. The period matched the one of 1977 to 1979 when Vajpayee had managed to push an agenda for peace. Another earlier parallel was

of 1958 to 1961, Ayub Khan's times, when the Indus Waters Treaty was
signed by Nehru. The period from 1972, since the Simla Agreement, to
1987, before the bloodbath in Kashmir, had been of one of relative peace
too, albeit marred by Pakistan's support to an insurgency in Punjab. The
neighbours seemed to have from 2003 found a way of building trust. But
the terrorists bred by Pakistan were now issuing a reminder that they had
not abandoned their cause.

TALKING SIACHEN

As the eight-track composite dialogue chugged along at the level of
secretaries, defence secretary-level talks were scheduled in May 2006. The
will to demilitarize the Siachen Glacier seemed stronger on both sides than
in 1989 or 1992; the two armies had even agreed on authenticating ground
positions of the troops in an 'annexure' to the proposed agreement. This
would have allowed troops 'to mutually withdraw' and be spared 'extreme
cold and unpredictable weather in inhospitable areas'. In fact, Foreign
Secretary Shyam Saran had worked out the contours of an agreement
with his Pakistani counterpart, Riaz Mohammad Khan. India had insisted
that the agreement and its annexure be signed together, explicitly stating
that the annexure (authenticating ground positions) carried the same legal
validity as the agreement itself. PM Manmohan Singh asked Saran to draft
the agreement and take key Indian stakeholders on board. Saran did both.

A crucial meeting of the CCS—the apex national security body chaired
by the PM—was to approve the draft agreement, already cleared by
the 'army and other stakeholders'. However, two men in the room had
changed their minds. When the meeting started, Saran recalled, NSA M.
K. Narayanan 'launched into a bitter offensive against the proposal, saying
that Pakistan could not be trusted, that there would be political and public
opposition to any such initiative and that India's military position in the
northern sector vis-à-vis both Pakistan and China would be compromised.'[17]
Army Chief J. J. Singh, 'who had happily gone along with the proposal in
its earlier iterations, now decided to join Narayanan in rubbishing it.'[18]
Narayanan also suggested that the Siachen issue be taken off the agenda
for India–Pakistan talks on border issues. Even though Defence Minister
Pranab Mukherjee supported demilitarization of the glacier and Home
Minister Shivraj Patil held the same view, the CCS killed the proposal.

Saran's account confirmed the prevailing view among diplomats on both
sides that agreements on Siachen, as also Sir Creek, were the 'low-hanging
fruit'[19] of the composite bilateral dialogue. But the army continued to ask
if India could 'trust Pakistan' and ensure Pakistani troops wouldn't return
to occupy positions in Siachen.

The initiative of 2006—to demilitarize the glacier, mutually withdraw
troops from the area and thereafter establish a joint monitoring team—met

the same fate as its predecessors in 1989 and 1992. The trust deficit had not yet been bridged.

Sharp differences on the Siachen stand-off within both political and military circles, made a resolution harder. On the Indian side, military commentator and former Northern Army commander, Lieutenant General Rustom Nanavatty, argued that 'the conflict is essentially over preserving territorial integrity and upholding national military pride. It is an irrational conflict in subhuman conditions with significant costs and little prospect of military solution. Its perpetuation does no credit to political and military leadership at the highest levels in both countries.'[20] He suggested that 'India's approach to a final settlement should be based on demilitarization of a limited, well-defined and mutually agreed area following a political agreement. There should be a lasting ceasefire, delimiting, demarcation, disengagement, redeployment, verification and joint monitoring and administration'.[21] In contrast, a Pakistani perspective by Omer Farooq Zain suggested never giving up: 'For Pakistan, Siachen glacier is worth the blood spilled over it, and to give it up would be nothing short of giving up its coat of arms.'[22] Indian military historian Arjun Subramaniam concluded in 2020 that 'Indian and Pakistani soldiers will continue to patrol the glacier, and the best the two countries can do at this juncture is to minimize the human price they pay by ensuring that living on the glacier is made easier.'[23]

A JOINT BATTLE?

The pain of terrorism was to hit India again in mid-2006, this time in the financial capital, Mumbai, on 11 July: a series of seven bombs ripped through the suburban railway system over a period of eleven minutes. 209 people lay dead and over 700 injured. The bombs were set off in pressure cookers on trains; the role of the Pakistan-based LeT was suspected, but India did not reflexively blame Pakistan in the absence of 'clinching' evidence.

Pakistan condoled the deaths, but Foreign Minister Khurshid Mahmud Kasuri seemed to link the terror to the lack of resolution of disputes between India and Pakistan. 'His remarks,' India retorted angrily, 'appear to suggest that Pakistan will cooperate with India against the scourge of cross-border terrorism and terrorist violence only if such so-called so disputes are resolved.'[24] But India was trying a new experiment, exhibiting its willingness to engage Pakistan in a joint anti-terrorism mechanism.

On 24 July, speaking in Nainital, PM Manmohan Singh defended himself against domestic criticism of the proposed anti-terrorism mechanism. It was designed, he said, to 'test' how Islamabad would 'fulfil its responsibility towards fighting terrorism'.[25] He insisted there was no change in the government's policy on terrorism and that Pakistan must ensure that its soil was not being used to spread terrorism in India.

Shivshankar Menon—the latest in a series of high commissioners to Pakistan who were elevated as foreign secretary—left Islamabad to take over his new assignment in New Delhi on 1 October 2006. Soon after assuming charge, he said that India would use the anti-terrorism mechanism, envisaging joint investigations with Pakistan's security agencies, to seek Pakistani action on the evidence unearthed by the police. Since the preliminary evidence suggested an ISI role in the serial train blasts, he added 'we will judge them not by their immediate reaction of verbal statements but by what they actually do about terrorism.'[26]

Satyabrata Pal succeeded Menon in Islamabad. Pal was a quiet professional, a scholar–diplomat endowed with extraordinary analytical and communication skills. He appeared dauntingly clever at Islamabad parties as he made a sophisticated case for deepening engagement. Years later, a Pakistani journalist would mention to me, only half in jest, that India had adopted a strategy of sending as envoys strong South Indian and Bengali intellectuals like Nambiar, Menon, and Pal, rather than regular Punjabi-knowing North Indian folk, only to intellectually humiliate Pakistan.

The signs of internal collapse in Pakistan had begun to show from 2006. Just as the India–Pakistan diplomatic rapprochement began to show promise, Musharraf had begun to lose his grip on a Pakistan steadily descending into violent chaos. To many observers, the snakes in the backyard, nurtured to bite the neighbours, were now turning on their masters. The charitable explanation was that Musharraf may have lost control, if not over his own ISI, then certainly over the terrorist groups that were mounting audacious attacks, as in the 1990s. To others, the instability triggered by the violence once again underlined the need for confident and stable regimes in both countries to propel any peace process. The surge in terrorism in the year seemed set to derail ties again.

A Non-Aligned Movement (NAM) Summit in Havana in September 2006 helped prevent a breakdown in ties that the recent acts of terrorism should have caused. Musharraf and Manmohan Singh met on the sidelines of the summit to reaffirm their faith in the peace process and agreed to 'put in place an India–Pakistan anti-terrorism institutional mechanism to identify and implement counter-terrorism initiatives and investigations'. They also directed their foreign secretaries to resume the composite dialogue.[27]

At the end of the year, Musharraf articulated a posture on Kashmir that was not normally seen from Pakistan in public statements. In an interview with the Indian journalist, Prannoy Roy of NDTV, Musharraf said that an 'independent Kashmir' would be unviable and unacceptable to both Pakistan and India. This did inject some degree of realism into the debate on the future of Kashmir, where Pakistan's position was to speak only of UN-supervised referenda, giving Kashmir the choice to join either India or Pakistan. Pakistan had mainly remained silent on the scenario of azadi or independence.

26

DOWN TO SEMICOLONS

On 8 January 2007, Manmohan Singh repeated his idea of soft borders to a Federation of Indian Chambers of Commerce and Industry (FICCI) business gathering; he dreamt, he said, of the day when 'one can have breakfast in Amritsar, lunch in Lahore and dinner in Kabul'. He added for good measure that industry ought to be prepared for 'fast-track economic integration in South Asia'. The next week, India's external affairs minister, Pranab Mukherjee, met some political leaders of Pakistan for an informal breakfast, where he told them that the borders were not up for negotiations, but India was prepared to discuss all ideas towards the resolution of the Kashmir issue. He said India and Pakistan must learn from Europe that had set aside differences to forge a successful economic union.[1] Mukherjee had been briefed on the quiet progress on the backchannel.

THE BACKCHANNEL

By early 2007, the tenacious engagement between Lambah and Aziz had led to broad agreement on the contours of a deal that was ready for political endorsement. Away from the spotlight, the countries had engaged in a 'serious, sustained and structured backchannel negotiation' for the first time in their history. They had a non-paper ready and had come down to 'negotiating semicolons'.[2]

Lambah saw his backchannel role as a continuation of the 'pre-negotiations' that Brajesh Mishra had initiated in 2003–04 and Dixit had continued in 2004–05, both with Tariq Aziz. Lambah reflected that the backchannel initiatives of the twenty-first century were really a continuation of different initiatives by past prime ministers for a final settlement with Pakistan on the issue of J&K. Past proposals had involved adjustments to the ceasefire line, or to the LoC and its conversion into an international boundary. But this time, the vision was to make borders irrelevant. When Lambah was appointed in 2005 as special envoy in the PMO, he saw his mandate from Manmohan Singh as a solution that did not involve redrawing borders. An important reference point to the conversations was Musharraf's 'four-point plan' for Kashmir, which the general had articulated in bits and dribbles at various points over the period 2001–06. The four-point plan involved demilitarization with cessation of military activities; self-governance in the region; a joint mechanism with representatives of India, Pakistan, and Kashmir for overseeing the self-governance; and trade and movement of people between the two parts of Kashmir.

At the same time, Manmohan Singh had famously said in Amritsar on 24 March 2006, that 'borders cannot be redrawn, but we can work towards making them irrelevant—towards making them just lines on a map'.[3] Essentially, Singh's idea was of economic integration through soft borders, much like in the European Union. Lambah had concluded that it would be 'manageable' to discuss Jammu and Kashmir with Pakistan on the basis of the four-point formula and guided by Manmohan Singh's Amritsar speech.

With the PM's permission, Lambah later laid out in a public address in Srinagar the five broad principles at the heart of the Kashmir settlement, that India had explored with Pakistan during 2005-07. These were: freezing the current territorial disposition in Kashmir; changing the nature of the LoC by allowing freer movement of goods and people across it; granting substantive and similar levels of autonomy on both sides of the LoC; creating a cross-LoC consultative mechanism to deepen cooperation on a range of issues; and reducing military forces on either side of the LoC after violence and terrorism come to an end.[4]

But Musharraf was losing control of his country by 2007 and had little room for a bold initiative with India. Manmohan Singh later revealed that India was close to an 'important breakthrough' in the talks with Musharraf, just before the general's power began to ebb.

SAMJHAUTA EXPRESS

In the early hours of 18 February, around sixty-eight people, mostly Pakistani civilians, were killed and scores more injured in a terrorist attack on the Delhi–Attari Samjhauta (reconciliation) Express train. The attack, near the Indian city of Panipat, the scene of many historical battles, was initially attributed to Pakistani terrorists but later evidence suggested the perpetrators were Indian citizens.

While India promised Pakistan full investigations into the incident, and even offered to share the findings with Pakistan, the Pakistan National Assembly passed a resolution asking for a joint investigation. This time, External Affairs Minister Pranab Mukherjee on 21 February ruled out a joint investigation, saying, 'As per the law of the land, the probe will be conducted by India and the results shared with Pakistan.' He pointed out that the basic objective of the anti-terror mechanism, scheduled to meet in Islamabad, was to both 'share and act on the information' passed on between the two nations.

Fortuitously, the first meeting of the 'anti-terrorism mechanism' was held in Islamabad on 6 March 2007, within a fortnight of the incident. It agreed to exchange specific information for 'helping investigations on either side related to terrorist acts'.[5]

Despite the growing violence, the diplomats were trying to take the composite dialogue forward. Foreign Secretary Menon cautioned against cherry-picking issues, since the process 'walks on three legs': confidence-building measures; resolution of conflicts, including the issue of Kashmir; and establishing links between the peoples to build 'mutual stakes'. He added, 'Frankly, I think the reason this process has moved forward for the last almost three years is because we have done all three things together and we have avoided getting into saying, do one first, if you do this, then we can do that.'[6]

DECLINE OF THE DICTATOR
But the dictator India had invested in was now seeing the terminal decline of his regime. On 9 March 2007, Musharraf suspended the Pakistan Supreme Court's maverick chief justice, Iftikhar Muhammad Chaudhry, and pressed corruption charges against him. Musharraf's move was the spark Pakistan's civil society needed. On 12 March, Pakistani lawyers started a campaign across Pakistan, dubbed 'judicial activism', and began boycotting all court procedures in protest against the suspension. In multiple cities, hundreds of lawyers dressed in black suits attended rallies condemning the suspension as unconstitutional. This major pushback from the fraternity of lawyers, and more generally from civil society, turned into a wider questioning of the country's military leadership. By May, protesters and Opposition parties were taking out huge rallies against Musharraf. His tenure as army chief was challenged in the courts. At the same time, Musharraf was also alienated from his own corps commanders. He had pushed them too hard against their institutional convictions on India and Kashmir, to ensure his own political survival; he was seen to be jeopardizing the interests of the army.

Another blow to Musharraf's regime came in July, this time from the religious right. The Lal Masjid administration in Islamabad, associated with the right-wing Jamia Hafsa madrasa, had from April started to encourage attacks on local video shops, alleging that they were selling pornographic films, and on massage parlours, allegedly being used as brothels. These attacks were often carried out by the madrasa's female students. In July, the authorities decided to stop the student violence by sending in the police. Mosque leaders and students fired at the police, leading to casualties on both sides. The police action at the mosque was reminiscent of other such dangerous actions at places of worship that alienate a large part of the population.

Musharraf faced two attempts on his life in July, both ironically by the Kashmir-centric Jaish-e-Mohammed. The dictator's popularity plummeted. By August, polls showed that almost two thirds of Pakistanis did not want another Musharraf term. Musharraf faced public anger for his battle with the judiciary and lawyers, the Lal Masjid action, the earlier arrest of nuclear hero A. Q. Khan, the unpopular war in the Federally Administered Tribal Area (FATA) region in north-west Pakistan, as also the scathing remarks on him by Benazir Bhutto and Nawaz Sharif. His personal image was damaged beyond repair, as in the case of Ayub Khan in the late 1960s and Yahya Khan in the early 1970s.

ᕁ

Still, the decade was ending on a relatively peaceful bilateral note as India and Pakistan celebrated their 60th anniversaries. The decade of Musharraf in Pakistan that had begun with aggression against India had ended with shifts in entrenched positions. The Vajpayee–Musharraf tango began in Agra in 2001, but was derailed by terrorism. It was some quiet diplomacy away from the public glare that had finally led to the breakthroughs for an era of relative peace from 2004. India had tried hard to do business with Pakistan's dictator, primarily through a backchannel that continued the conversation for a lasting Kashmir solution, until it was abandoned with Pakistan's internal turmoil in 2007. Pakistan also faced a backlash from the terror proxies it had created. The era of 'good and bad terrorists' had begun. Pakistan's forces were hunting down the groups who were increasingly attacking Pakistan's security forces, and protecting the 'good terrorists' who were being actively encouraged to focus their deadly talents on India.

This was an era when the two nuclear powers developed greater stakes in peace. Pakistan, under Musharraf, experimented with both Kashmir adventurism and terrorism under a nuclear umbrella. India had not made a judgement on Pakistan's nuclear threshold, nor had it found the space for an answer for the asymmetric on-and-off proxy warfare coming from Pakistan. India's tolerance of terrorism was diminishing yet was tempered by a desire to try to normalize the relationship. This would all change in the next decade, when events in Mumbai would harden India's views on terrorism forever.

2007–2017
KILLING AND CHILLING

27

REVENGE OF THE SNAKES

If the sixth decade had raised hopes of a backchannel breakthrough to untie the Kashmir knot and stabilize ties, the seventh began on a sombre note, with even those slim prospects thinning. Pakistan was convulsed by violence in 2007. The Afghan Taliban, nurtured by the ISI as a hugely successful geostrategic tool in the 1990s, had now spawned a sibling that hated Pakistan and declared war on the country. It resided in the badlands of the FATA region of north-west Pakistan (now Khyber Pakthunkhwa) and called itself the Tehrik-e-Taliban Pakistan (TTP). Ambassador Satyabrata Pal watched in dismay from the Indian chancery in Islamabad as the mayhem unfolded. Explosions rocked Pakistan, blood spilled, even the bubble of Islamabad was not safe.

Musharraf was embattled and cornered. His decade-old military regime was floundering in the face of this security challenge. The terrorists seemed to be gaining the upper hand over his forces. The judiciary and politicians in the Opposition sensed an opportunity to push back against the illegitimate military ruler. Benazir Bhutto's PPP and Nawaz Sharif's PML-N, both in exile, were not just questioning army rule, but preparing for a post-Musharraf political contest. On 14 September 2007, the military regime's deputy information minister, Tariq Azim, said that if Benazir Bhutto showed up in Pakistan, she would not be deported, but would face corruption charges. He still did not challenge Sharif's and Bhutto's right to return to Pakistan.

The exiled civilian leaders had been building on the 'charter of democracy' which they had cobbled together in London in May 2006, to try and challenge the military regime. In July 2007, Bhutto had met with Musharraf for the first time, in Dubai, to negotiate her return to Pakistan. On 17 September, Bhutto spoke from exile, accusing Musharraf and his allies of pushing Pakistan into crisis by refusing to restore democracy or to share power. Sharif returned to Pakistan that month to test the military regime, only to be arrested and taken into custody at the airport. He was sent back to Saudi Arabia. Musharraf, who had now mostly lost popular support and legitimacy, still held on to the illusion that he could reinvent himself as a politician and contest presidential elections. He had in a March 2007 interview said he intended to stay in office for another five years. He now sought a judicial stamp to these ambitions.

Some hope arose of judicial censure on the dictator when a nine-member panel of Supreme Court judges looked at six petitions (including one from the JeI, Pakistan's largest Islamic group) for disqualifying Musharraf as a presidential candidate. But on 28 September, in a majority 6-3 verdict, Judge Rana Bhagwandas's court permitted Musharraf to contest elections. Bhagwandas, from a Sindhi Rajput family, became that year the first Hindu (acting) chief of Pakistan's Supreme Court.[1]

A condition for Musharraf, the politician, to emerge was that he concede some space to the civilians. He relented, and approved a 'national reconciliation' ordinance, NRO, issued on 5 October, to drop pending corruption cases against the civilian politicians, in an attempt to restore the democratic process. The NRO granted amnesty to those facing corruption proceedings from January 1986 and October 1999, between two martial law periods. (The NRO clearly illegal and effectively a free pass to the corrupt; it was revoked by one judge later in October, and reinstated the next year, to be eventually declared unconstitutional by the Supreme Court of Pakistan in December 2009.)

The day after he signed off on the NRO, Musharraf engineered his own re-election as president. He won by a huge majority, in indirect elections on 6 October 2007. The electoral college was packed with members of the 'king's party', PML-Q, that had occupied legislatures since sham elections on Musharraf's watch in 2002. Controversially, Musharraf decided to hang on to the post of army chief, given his inability to trust his own army colleagues.

But the NRO and Musharraf's assurances paved the way for Benazir Bhutto to return home on 18 October, from eight years of exile. Bhutto was hoping to reprise her feat of 1988, of replacing a dictator. Then, she had been assisted by a providential plane crash that killed Zia. This time, fate had a crueller twist in store.

FIGHTING TERROR TOGETHER?

In the midst of the political volatility within Pakistan, and somewhat delayed by it, the second meeting of the joint terror mechanism was held in New Delhi on 22 October. The meeting came days after a terrorist blast in Ludhiana and amidst Indian concern over Pakistan's attempts to revive Sikh radicalism in Punjab. To many in India, joint efforts with Pakistan against terrorism spelt a contradiction in terms—a disastrous idea, at the very least akin to an attempt to collaborate with one thief to catch another. The idea of the mechanism, as we saw, had gained sanction at a meeting between Manmohan Singh and Musharraf in Havana in September 2006. It was basically designed as an experimental CBM; some hoped that the tactic could fruitfully engage Pakistan on the terrorism issue.

But the Jammu and Kashmir issue muddied the waters here as well. Pakistan continued to draw a distinction between terrorism in the northern state and elsewhere in India. Responding to an *Indian Express* report on the meeting that claimed that 'for first time Pak accepts Indian dossier on terror in J&K', Pakistan's foreign office dismissed the media story as baseless. The Pakistani spokesman added that the purview of the talks 'does not cover Jammu and Kashmir, which is a disputed territory, and is being discussed under the Composite Dialogue process. The scope of discussions under the Mechanism relates to the terrorist incidents in India and Pakistan.'[2]

India was quick to rebut this take, reminded Pakistan of its 'assurance of 6 January 2004 of not permitting territory in its control to be used to support terrorism in any form.' The mandate of the mechanism, an Indian statement said was 'helping investigations on either side related to terrorist acts and prevention of violence and terrorist acts in the two countries.'[3]

Pakistan wanted to treat the state of Jammu and Kashmir effectively as a third entity, apart from India and Pakistan. To Indian analysts, this was a bizarre posture: Pakistan wanted to discuss J&K, and was OK with discussing terrorism, but not with discussing terrorism in Kashmir.

DESCENT INTO CHAOS

Despite his re-election on 6 October, Musharraf was weakened by the judicial and security challenge that he faced. With his back firmly to the wall, Musharraf declared a state of emergency on 3 November 2007, suspending the Constitution to consolidate his hold on power. Chief Justice Iftikhar Chaudhry, the defiant judge who had been reinstated in July after Musharraf had suspended him in March, promptly convened a seven-member bench, which issued an interim order against the Emergency. Soon, the 111th 'coup-maker' brigade of the army entered the Supreme Court building, arrested Chaudhry, along with some sixty other judges, and detained them in their homes. Musharraf once again fired the chief justice, asked other judges to take fresh oaths of office, blocked TV channels, and cracked down on public protests. The emergency situation was justified on grounds of the threat from Islamic militancy, but it was clear that it was only the dictator's desperate bid to cling on to power.

PM Manmohan Singh watched the situation with increasing concern. He reviewed Pakistan's crisis on the evening of 3 November, along with external affairs minister Pranab Mukherjee and a few key officials. While National Security Advisor M. K. Narayanan said after the meeting that India was treating the situation as an 'internal problem of Pakistan', the official spokesman said, 'we regret the difficult times that Pakistan is passing through', adding that India hoped that 'conditions of normalcy will soon return, permitting Pakistan's transition to stability and democracy to continue'.

Under pressure to give up one of his posts, Musharraf resigned as army chief on 28 November, appointing General Ashfaq Kayani as chief of army staff. While Musharraf was still clinging to the office of president, the newly invigorated political Opposition was aggressively criticizing Musharraf's army regime; Benazir Bhutto was sharply critical of Musharraf's four-point formula on Kashmir. Musharraf was compelled to lift the Emergency on 15 December, in preparation for elections promised on 8 January 2008. But more bad news was to come.

A HOPE EXTINGUISHED

Benazir Bhutto clambered onto the rear seat of a Toyota Cruiser to stick her head out of the sunroof hatch. She waved with practised cheer to a crowd of charged supporters. It was early evening of 27 December 2007, she had just finished a stump speech at the Liaquat Bagh in Rawalpindi, as part of her comeback campaign, given the imminent end of the Musharraf era. She had made a strong pitch for support to her party to more than ten thousand people at the traditional rallying ground where Pakistan's first prime minister Liaquat Khan had been assassinated in 1951. At 5.10 p.m., a fifteen-year-old boy called Bilal, who had been fitted with a suicide jacket by his Taliban handlers, and promised paradise for what he was about to accomplish, pumped three bullets into Benazir, before blowing himself up. The young assassin had added another bloody chapter to the Bhutto dynasty's tragic saga. Benazir, it turned out, had been warned of the specific threat by no less than the DG of the ISI, Lieutenant General Nadeem Taj, just fifteen hours before being killed. But she saw no option to the path she had chosen: risking her life for the larger cause of pulling Pakistan back to normalcy.[4]

A cruel December killed the hope for stability in Pakistan that the ascendance of the civilians had stirred. Musharraf called for a three-day mourning period, even as many pointed fingers at the army for a pre-meditated murder. Did Musharraf just brutally eliminate Benazir, many asked, as Zia had erased her father three decades earlier? For many liberal Pakistanis, all hope was interred with the end of Bhutto. To some others, after Benazir's funeral on 27 December, it was her benign ghost that would run the country, with her husband Asif Zardari as proxy, a placeholder till her son and heir, Bilawal Bhutto, came of political age. At the same time, public revulsion rose against domestic militancy, as the army tried to take on the splinter group of the Taliban, the TTP.

⟋

Benazir's death saw the spontaneous eruption of grief and empathy in India. This killing of a promising leader from a political dynasty was a subcontinental tragedy, with familiar historical parallels in India. Less than two decades earlier, a young, popular former prime minister from a violence-hit political dynasty had been assassinated in India while working on a political comeback. Apart from the analogous destinies of Rajiv Gandhi and Benazir Bhutto, commentators cited the parallel loss to political violence of a parent in both cases, Indira Gandhi and Zulfikar Ali Bhutto. The *Hindustan Times* commented that the light had gone out of Pakistan, invoking a phrase used by Nehru for the assassination of Mahatma Gandhi on 1948.[5]

India's president, Pratibha Patil, said in a message that the assassination was a 'tragedy not just for Pakistan but for our entire region'. PM Manmohan Singh extolled Benazir's 'contributions to a previous moment of hope in India–Pakistan relations, and her intent to break India–Pakistan relations out of the sterile patterns of the past,' adding that 'the sub-continent has lost an outstanding leader who worked for democracy and reconciliation in her country'.[6]

India was increasingly worried about Pakistan's implosion. Apart from fears of a takeover in Pakistan by mullahs, in a situation akin to the Taliban capture of power in Afghanistan in the 1990s, New Delhi was concerned about the physical safety of its Islamabad mission. An intelligence report in January 2008 warned of a suicide bomber planning to target the Indian high commission in Islamabad. The threat came from a banned militant group, called Tehreek Nifaz-e-Shariat Mohammadi, meaning 'movement for the enforcement of Prophet Mohammad's Islamic laws'. The group specialized in suicide missions, had been running a parallel government in Pakistan's Swat district, and now wanted to demonstrate its reach in Islamabad. High Commissioner Satyabrata Pal asked for extra security from the Pakistan government for the mission.[7]

∿

To many Pakistanis, Benazir's assassination signalled the victory of darker forces over both the military and civilian politicians; militant groups had now got emboldened, with the writ of the state challenged all over Pakistan. The killing demoralized the nation, but led to a strong sympathy wave for Benazir's PPP, which emerged as the single largest party when the postponed general elections were finally held on 18 February 2008. With Musharraf still president, the two largest parties—the PPP now led by Benazir's widower, Asif Zardari; and the PML-N, helmed by Nawaz Sharif—cobbled together a coalition to work under the dictator.

Taking credit for the elections, Musharraf said an 'era of democracy' had begun in Pakistan and that he had now put the country 'on the track of development and progress'. Since Zardari had not contested the elections, the PPP, on 22 March, named a former parliament speaker, a political lightweight, Yousaf Raza Gilani, to lead the coalition government as prime minister.

∿

As Satyabrata Pal watched the bewildering politics in his host country, an attack came dangerously close to home on a Monday afternoon. Around 12.10 p.m. on 2 June, a man drove a speeding Toyota Corolla with diplomatic registration plates into Islamabad's F6 sector, passing in front of India House and the entrance of the Danish embassy located next door, to stop at the parking lot in front of the embassy complex. Seconds later, the vehicle exploded, killing six and wounding several others. The residences of the Dutch ambassador and the Australian defence attaché, located nearby, were damaged. Windowpanes were shattered in Ambassador Pal's home. Both Pal, who happened to be home, and his wife, got cuts from the glass that shattered. The target this time was the Danish embassy, the explosion a reprisal for cartoons published in a Danish newspaper insulting the Prophet of Islam.

Another blast, specifically targeted at India, came in the middle of the year. This bombing took place not in Islamabad, but ripped through the heart of Kabul. In the morning office rush hour, on 7 July, a suicide bomber drove a heavy vehicle packed with explosives towards the gate of the Indian embassy, where he detonated his load. The blast outside the embassy killed fifty-eight people and wounded 141, mostly Afghan visa seekers. It destroyed two embassy vehicles entering the compound.

In Delhi, Malti, a teacher in Sanskriti School, got a call that morning, saying that the media was reporting an explosion near the Indian embassy in Kabul. Malti's first reaction was that such explosions were pretty much routine for Kabul, but nevertheless rang up her husband, Venkat Rao, press counsellor at the Kabul mission, to check if he was OK. The phone rang, but Venkat did not answer. It was only later that Malti learnt that her worst fears had come true: Rao was in the car that was blown up that day, his mobile phone intact as it was flung far by the explosion.[8] Soon, Foreign Minister Pranab Mukherjee announced that among others, India had lost two diplomats, Counsellor Venkat Rao and Brigadier Rajesh Mehta, the military attaché. Mukherjee said two Indian security guards and an Afghan national who worked at the embassy were also killed.

The needle of suspicion initially pointed towards the Taliban, which had been attacking the Kabul regime in a wave of suicide attacks across the country, since the US had moved in seven years earlier. However, evidence soon emerged of Pakistani involvement from Indian, Afghan, and US intelligence agencies. Taliban sources started saying they would never mount an attack where the majority of those killed were Afghan civilians. The Afghan government said the attack was the work of 'regional influences'; Afghanistan expert Ahmed Rashid told *Al Jazeera* that the Kabul government was implicitly linking Pakistan to the attack. Pakistan's agencies had been worried about India's growing profile in Afghanistan, and particularly the collaboration between Indian and Afghan security agencies. Pakistan's paranoia about being squeezed on both borders by Indian influence might have instigated it to take desperate and violent measures.

Rangeen Spanta, the Afghan foreign minister, visited the Indian embassy in Kabul soon after the attack in a show of support; his spokesman said that the 'enemies of Afghanistan and India's relationship' were behind the attacks. Rao's killing, the first of a diplomat in Pakistan-related violence since Ravindra Mhatre's abduction and death in London in 1984, was a grim reminder that when Pakistan gave free run to violence, Indian diplomats were unsafe not just in Islamabad, but everywhere.

⌣

The peace process somehow survived the near fatal blow of the Kabul bombing. It was once again summit diplomacy that kept communication channels open. A SAARC summit in August 2008 in Colombo opened up the possibility of a bilateral conversation. Musharraf himself was fighting for his political survival and sent his PM instead. The meeting between prime ministers Manmohan Singh and Yousaf Raza Gilani on the sidelines of the Colombo summit barely thawed the frosty relationship between the neighbours—India remained angered and frustrated by the unrelenting terrorism directed against it by Pakistan.

Soon after the summit, on 7 August, Zardari and Sharif joined hands to force Musharraf to step down. The two politicians announced they were filing a 'charge sheet' to compel Musharraf to resign, and would impeach him through a parliamentary process in case he refused. Musharraf refused to be dislodged, and the charge sheet was made public, listing all Musharraf's violations of law: his seizure of power in 1999, accompanied by the imprisonment and exile of Sharif; the Emergency of 2007; and his role in the US-led 'war on terror'.

With the possibility of impeachment now real, Musharraf announced his resignation on 18 August. The Musharraf era thus ended with a bloodless transition, despite the sharpening violence within Pakistan. But Musharraf's exit was not unique. Each of Pakistan's previous three major dictators had been eased out of power, with no trial of their illegal regimes. Zia had, of course, been killed at the height of his powers, but his regime had faced no trial. None had been imprisoned, unlike their civilian counterparts.

On the following day, Musharraf defended his rule in an hour-long televised speech. Public opinion was hardly persuaded: a poll conducted a day after his resignation showed that 63 per cent Pakistanis welcomed Musharraf's decision to step down while only 15 per cent were unhappy with it. Three months later, on 23 November, Pakistan's dictator of a decade would leave for exile in London, his safe passage negotiated by the army. Musharraf would go, holding on to his political ambition to one day return to his country to contest elections.

Asif Ali Zardari succeeded Musharraf as president on 9 September, with Afghanistan's president Hamid Karzai present at his inauguration. Apart from signalling continuity in the US-led war on terror, Zardari tried to consolidate the PPP's hold on power. But the structural primacy of the army was embedded in Pakistan's polity. Zardari's regime over the next four years would struggle to shake off the grip of the post-Musharraf army.

Hours after Zardari made his first speech to Pakistan's parliament, terrorists issued a reminder that they could now strike at will in Pakistan's capital. On the night of 20 September, a truck laden with explosives was detonated in front of Islamabad's prestigious Marriott Hotel, killing some fifty-four people and injuring over 266. Among those killed were five foreign nationals. (The al-Qaeda–TTP masterminds of the attack were later reported killed by a US drone attack in eastern Afghanistan in 2017.)

Despite the violence at home, Zardari made it to New York for the UNGA. On the sidelines, he held his first meeting on 24 September 2008 with India's PM, Manmohan Singh, who told him that the peace process had come 'under strain in recent months'. Zardari reiterated that Pakistan 'stands by its commitments of January 2004' and agreed that the 'forces that have tried to derail the peace process must be defeated'.

Pakistan's army was worried about a few other things. Despite Pakistan's collaboration with the US in Afghanistan, the US was going ahead with the India–US nuclear deal, which carved out a strong exception for India from the non-proliferation protocols then in force, apart from unlocking dual use technologies for India's use. The US Congress approved the deal on 1 October. None was envisaged for Pakistan. The nuclear deal, seen as a watershed in US–India relations, completed a process initiated in 2005 by Bush and Manmohan Singh, lifting a three-decade US moratorium on nuclear trade with India. It was signed by External Affairs Minister Pranab Mukherjee with his counterpart, Condoleezza Rice, on 10 October.

Zardari, innocent of nuclear matters, saw himself and his wife as victims of terrorism; he was not sticking to his talking points on India. In October 2008, he faced criticism in Pakistan's media for calling out 'terrorists' in Kashmir, given their official characterization as 'Kashmiri nationalists'. In November, Zardari told an Indian newspaper that Pakistan was for closer economic ties with India and would not be the first to use nuclear weapons. He had clearly spoken without the army's approval. Pakistan walked back the declaration, asserting that it had not moved to a 'no first use' nuclear posture.[9]

28

MASSACRE IN MUMBAI

W hen the shooting began in Mumbai, just after 9 p.m. on 26
November, High Commissioner Satyabrata Pal was in Delhi for the
visit of Shah Mahmood Qureshi, Pakistan's new foreign minister. Qureshi
himself was giving a pre-dinner media interview to CNN-IBN's Suhasini
Haider at Pakistan House, the residence of Pakistan's high commissioner,
Shahid Malik, when the news of the terror attacks broke on the evening of
26/11. The interview was never aired.

Qureshi should normally have been dining with his host, but India's
EAM, Pranab Mukherjee, had decided not to host a dinner for him, only
a high tea. As the visit was being planned, Malik had joked that he would
take his minister to Wimpy for a meal, since India was not hosting a
formal dinner. Malik eventually did host an official dinner at his residence
for both delegations; National Security Advisor Shivshankar Menon and
High Commissioner Satyabrata Pal were among those present. The Indian
minister seemed to have had a premonition about things to come; he
could have been caught in the awkward position of breaking bread with
a Pakistani minister as Pakistani terrorists sprayed bullets in Mumbai.
Mukherjee had, however, agreed to have lunch with Qureshi the next
day in Chandigarh; they had been invited for a round table discussion
on India–Pakistan agricultural cooperation, by the Centre for Research in
Rural and Industrial Development. The centre, headed by Rashpal Malhotra,
where Manmohan Singh was one of the founders, also worked on bringing
the 'two Punjabs' closer.

The talks earlier that day at Hyderabad House had gone off well.
Mukherjee had announced to spirited applause at the post-meeting press
conference that cricketing ties between the countries would resume. In
the car ride back to his hotel, Qureshi exulted over the day's proceedings
and told Malik that they were going through perhaps the best period in
bilateral relations. He had spoken too soon, the good times would last
about three hours.[1]

After the engagements with Qureshi, Mukherjee left Hyderabad House
that evening for his office in South Block. At around 9 p.m., his staff
alerted him to breaking news on TV, of unfolding violence in Mumbai.
Mukherjee watched the news in South Block, 'shocked to see the audacity
and scale of the attack', and returned home only around midnight 'but
could hardly take my eyes off the TV'.[2] Millions of Indians were up
watching in horror, as the terror attacks played out live on television

screens through the night. The body count mounted, as smoke and fire billowed from the rooms of Mumbai's landmark hotels—the Taj Mahal Palace and the Oberoi, and other targeted buildings. The day was later dubbed 26/11, echoing the trauma of New York's 9/11 seven years earlier.

The next morning, Mukherjee cancelled his visit to Chandigarh, but Qureshi decided to proceed with his scheduled programme to Jaipur, Ajmer, and Chandigarh. The siege of the hotels continued, as security forces tried to neutralize the ten Lashkar-e-Taiba terrorists. Meanwhile Pakistan's foreign minister was still holding meetings in India.

A bizarre twist to the crisis diplomacy came when President Asif Zardari received a 'threatening call' from someone he thought was India's EAM, Mukherjee. It turned out the hoax caller, who also tried to threaten Pranab Mukherjee and US leaders, was Omar Sheikh, the murderer of Daniel Pearl who had been released in the 1999 hijack drama and who was now lodged in a jail in Pakistan. He had managed to fool Zardari and hoped to con a few other world leaders or at least to alleviate some boredom in the Hyderabad jail.[3]

President Zardari called PM Manmohan Singh on the morning of 27 November to condemn the attacks and surprisingly, promised to send the DG of the ISI, Shuja Pasha, to help in the investigation.[4] On the evening of 27 November, just before Qureshi addressed a group of journalists at the Women's Press Club in New Delhi, Shahid Malik's phone buzzed. It was Pakistan's army chief, Kayani. The Pakistani diplomat was given the delicate job of relaying the army chief's instructions to his foreign minister to walk back the rash offer made by his president. This was an announcement Qureshi made early in his presser—the visit of the Pakistani intelligence chief was not imminent.

During the media meet, Malik received another call. This time, it was the office of India's external affairs minister, demanding that Qureshi be pulled out of whatever he was doing for an urgent conversation. When Qureshi came on the line, Mukherjee sounded furious. He read out a 'speaking note' prepared by Foreign Secretary Menon, concluding: 'Mr Minister, no purpose will be served by your continuing to stay in India in these circumstances. I advise you to leave immediately. My official aircraft is available to take you back home whenever you find convenient. But it would be desirable if a decision is taken as quickly as possible.'[5]

T. C. A. Raghavan, then heading the Pakistan desk at MEA, was woken up at 4 a.m. the next morning to be told that a Pakistan Air Force aircraft was on its way to Delhi to take the minister home. He had an hour to organize the flight clearances. India's foreign minister had just politely expelled his counterpart in the throes of an official visit. Both the ignorance and the irrelevance of Pakistan's civilian leadership was clear to India, but the gesture was important. Since he was already in Delhi, Pal did not need to be 'recalled,' or even called in for consultations. The expulsion of High Commissioner Shahid Malik was not considered necessary; this time, India had effectively expelled Pakistan's foreign minister. Mukherjee recalled later:

> As usual, Pakistan was in denial mode and some Pakistani leaders maintained that the terrorists were non-state actors. My response was sharp and strong. When asked by the media, I asserted 'non-state actors do not come from heaven. They are located in the territory of a particular country.' In this case, we had evidence that the terrorists came from Karachi port. They were dropped in mid-sea with a smaller vessel. They captured an Indian fishing vessel, killed the crew, and finally killed the pilot, upon reaching Mumbai coast.[6]

But asking Pakistan's minister to leave India was not retribution enough. As the attacks played out live on TV channels, 175 people lay dead, including nine terrorists and a few foreign citizens—Israeli, American, British. The impact on the national psyche was deep. The anger was mounting and the national mood was to 'do something'. Even though the complicity of the Pakistan state had not been established, the Opposition BJP blamed the UPA government for its soft stance on Pakistan. A pained Prime Minister Manmohan Singh addressed the nation on 27 November: 'We will take up strongly with our neighbours that the use of their territory for launching attacks on us will not be tolerated, and that there would be a cost if suitable measures are not taken by them.'[7]

While India's Pakistan policy has largely been run by prime ministers, Pranab Mukherjee, with his heft in the cabinet of Manmohan Singh, was an exception. He was detailing neighbourhood policy, even though he would consult with the PM frequently. In one meeting, in the wake of the Mumbai attacks, as Foreign Secretary Menon, High Commissioner Pal, and Joint Secretary Raghavan sat across the table in his South Block room, he asked his advisers what should be done. After a brief silence, Menon said India could target the LeT headquarters in Muridke with a cruise missile. Visibly startled, Mukherjee paused to clean his glasses, then thanked the officers to signal that the meeting was over.

Menon later confirmed that he had for a while argued for 'immediate visible retaliation of some sort, either against the LeT in Muridke, in Pakistan's Punjab province, or their camps in Pakistan-occupied Kashmir, or against the ISI, which was clearly complicit.' But 'on sober reflection and in hindsight', he was convinced that restraint was the right choice.

While the public debate on policy choices was angry, with an overwhelming sense that India's reaction to Mumbai fell short, experts were trying to bring out the nuances of India's policy considerations. Menon argued that the choice was made to use restraint and diplomacy at that point for multiple reasons, including the fact that a new civilian leadership had taken over in Pakistan which had nothing to do with the planning or execution of the attacks. Also, India could take the high moral ground and put global pressure on Pakistan to clamp down on its terrorist activities. Perhaps a key factor informing India's restraint was also the civil nuclear deal arrived at with the US, after a great deal of diplomatic manoeuvring. The deal could be jeopardized if India went into a full-scale war with Pakistan in a nuclear environment. India's preoccupation with other geopolitical priorities, like the global economic crisis, stayed its hand in dealing with the terrorism problem in a firmer way.

In his 2016 book, Menon noted presciently that the policy would change with the next major terror attack:

> All the same, should another such attack be mounted from Pakistan, with or without visible support from the ISI or the Pakistan Army, it would be virtually impossible for any government of India to make the same choice again. Pakistan's prevarications in bringing the perpetrators to justice and its continued use of terrorism as an instrument of state policy after 26/11 have ensured this. In fact, I personally consider some public retribution and a military response inevitable. The circumstances of November 2008 no longer exist and are unlikely to be replicated in the future.[8]

The policy dilemma was not new. A fierce debate had taken place in 2001 after the brazen attacks on India's Parliament and would be reprised several times in the next decade after each act of terror; the response, however, would now be of a different order. In 2001, India had responded to the terror attack with Operation Parakram, a credible threat of conventional force, while the nuclear threshold was still being debated. The then NSA, Brajesh Mishra, had later argued that this was a one-off response pattern that could not be credibly repeated. In 2008, the countries were already a decade into being nuclear, with doctrines and systems in place; this was arguably a time when India could have found this space to give a 'sub-conventional' response to Pakistan through a military operation. Another former NSA, Menon, had later assessed that the posture of restraint of 2008 would not be effective if repeated in the future. The debate continues to this day on whether India's restraint gave the wrong message to the terrorists and their backers after Mumbai, about India's high threshold of tolerance for terror. An attack then on Muridke, the headquarters of the LeT, may not have resulted in huge operational success, but could have been an important signal to Pakistan and the world of India's resolve.

In case India had reacted in 2008 the way it did in 2016 or 2019, with a surgical or air strike, a strong Indian response would have entered the security calculus of Pakistan and served as a disincentive for the Pakistan army's support of India-focused militant groups. A decisive strike on a terrorist base like Muridke could have acted as an effective deterrent for the attacks India would face for a decade.

ᔓ

In 2008, it was clear that Mumbai had caused a churn within Pakistan. While the complicity in the attack of the top echelons of the army could not be proven, and the civilian leadership was definitely unaware of the planning for these events, it was clear that the ISI was actively conniving with the militant groups that had mounted the attack. In many ways, the Mumbai attacks did a great deal of damage to Pakistan's own reputation. Together with its training of the 9/11 hijackers, and the shelter given to Osama bin Laden that would be outed three years later, Mumbai reinforced Pakistan's reputation as the epicentre of global terrorism—there was now no question that the country was deploying terrorists and lying about it.

Asif Ali Zardari's arrival on the political scene had seemed to usher in a new rather less uncivil line on India, but this soft line seemed personal to him and served only to highlight the weakness of Pakistan's civilian leaders. As we have seen, Zardari had mentioned 'no first use' and had immediately been chastised by the Pakistan establishment for tampering with a foundational nuclear doctrine. The 2008 nuclear deal between India and the US along with the NSG waiver had been another critical moment of disappointment for Pakistan in 2008 in its quest for nuclear parity. Pakistan felt left out and cheated once again: its role in Afghanistan, it felt, was not properly acknowledged, much less rewarded.

Within Pakistan, most analysts recognized that the civilians had nothing to do with the Mumbai attacks. So far as the Pakistan Army was concerned, the post-Musharraf army led by General Kayani was also assisting the US in fighting a full-scale battle against terrorists to the west. The TTP, and some elements in the army may have taken a bet that India would not react with force while the Pakistan Army was colluding with the US. To HC Pal, assessing the domestic convolutions within Pakistan, the army's role in encouraging the Mumbai attacks was undeniable:

Under General Kayani, there has been a clear and very obvious shift in the use to which skirmishes at the LoC are being put. Sending infiltrators into Jammu and Kashmir is of secondary importance; the primary objective is to create incidents that would nip in the bud any attempt to make peace. In 2008, every public statement by Asif Zardari, proclaiming his intention to make peace was followed by an attack on a soft Indian target. When raids on Indian soldiers at the LoC did not work, our Embassy in Kabul was attacked, which did derail the process for several months. When the leaders nevertheless met in New York in the autumn and decided to resume the process, Pakistan's Inter-Services Intelligence (ISI) went further with Mumbai, attacking it on the evening that its Foreign Minister arrived in Delhi for talks.[9]

⟋

The Mumbai attack soon crowded out all other bilateral issues between India and Pakistan, as it became the defining event of the decade for India and damaged the bilateral relationship in ways that were to become clear only in the coming years. The Musharraf four-point formula on Kashmir was not being discussed any more, even though the records of discussion had been shared with the army. Kayani appeared to have distanced himself from the backchannel initiatives. Husain Haqqani, the Pakistani ambassador in the US who came in for consultations in Islamabad in 2008, tried to look for the files but could not lay his hands on them. He was told the whole matter had been a personal initiative of Musharraf and no files were available.

The peace process that Manmohan Singh was continuing from Vajpayee's last year, which Lambah had pursued on the backchannels, had proved resilient enough to withstand a severe shock of terrorism: the 2006 Mumbai train blasts. It also survived the Kabul blasts on the Indian embassy of July 2008. But it was overwhelmed by the shock of the Mumbai attacks. The peace process that had continued robustly from 2003 to 2006 was now clearly at a standstill. The central political assurance of 2004 that Musharraf had given to Vajpayee, to end terrorism from Pakistani soil, now lay in tatters. Mumbai's trauma redefined the decade as one when India became more vulnerable to terrorism, but failed to quickly develop a credible strategy to deal with the issue.

Despite the surge in uncontrolled violence, Satyabrata Pal remained persuaded of the need for continuous engagement with Pakistan. He was a dove in the aviary of Indo–Pak engagement. His counterpart in Delhi, Shahid Malik, was also known as a peacenik. It was therefore ironic that the biggest terrorist blow on the bilateral relationship in the twenty-first century took place during the tenures of these two diplomats. Arguably, the presence of civilian 'engagers' on both sides hastened the diplomatic recovery, even if the trauma of the attack irretrievably damaged the trust.

High Commissioner Pal was arguing for continuing dialogue, making a sophisticated argument for sympathizing with Pakistan's predicament:

> Pakistanis feel that the world now sees them as mendicants with suicide belts on...Gandhi would have urged India to be generous for pity's sake, but also in its self-interest, as he did when he went on his

last fast, just months after the first war with Pakistan, to urge India to give Pakistan the 550 million that were its due... Since then, we have become more Chanakya's disciples than Gandhi's, but of the seven ways of dealing with neighbours the *Arthashastra* offered—samman, upeksha, bheda, maya, indrajala, danda and dana—(honour, overlook, divide, bribe, entrap, punish and pity). We have tried the first six, without much luck either. So, perhaps the time has come for us to marry Gandhi and Chanakya and try on Pakistan a selfish altruism, our dana, not a gift that can be turned against us, but a determined, hard-headed generosity that we can turn to our advantage.[10]

But it was not selfish altruism that Indian policymakers needed to be deployed any longer.

Pal was conflating an engagement with Zardari as one with Pakistan's foreign policy establishment. The message, however, needed to go directly to the army. India had failed to unambiguously impress upon Pakistan the unacceptable cost of terrorism. Public opinion dictated that they search for that elusive answer to cross-border terror, in the domain of what security analysts saw as sub-conventional warfare. India needed to inflict a cost for terrorism on the Pakistan establishment factoring in hardening public opinion and lowering thresholds of tolerance to terror attacks.

Another terror attack from Pakistan-based terrorist groups would inevitably come. It would need a different response. The policy would be given newer names from 2016—no talks with terror. Offensive defence. Surgical strikes. With the benefit of hindsight, it does appear, as I have said earlier, that if India had executed surgical or air strikes after Mumbai, these would have made for strong disincentives for later attacks by Pakistan in Pathankot, Uri, and Pulwama. It would not have just punished the civilian government of Zardari, but also the deep state.

For the world at large, the terrorism in South Asia seemed to be an aberration in the twenty-first century. The US engagement in Afghanistan had plateaued into a stalemate. Global leaders were fully occupied with the global financial crisis, which began with the fall of Lehman Brothers in 2008; geoeconomics seem to be triumphing over geopolitics. It was a time for the G20 to step up as the premier global economic forum to try to save the world; India was a member and its economist leader, Manmohan Singh, the star. Regressive violent developments in South Asia were distracting the world from that agenda. And Pakistan was to blame.

Within Pakistan, the Mumbai attacks had exacerbated civil–military tension. The Zardari regime was deeply embarrassed, and initially denied any links between the perpetrators and Pakistan. Ajmal Kasab, the lone living terrorist arrested by India, was not accepted as a Pakistani citizen; his family, when journalists unearthed them in Pakistan's south Punjab, was whisked away into the custody of the ISI. But the government soon succumbed to global pressure and raided the Lashkar-e-Taiba's hideout on 7 December.

29

DIPLOMATIC DOODLES

In March 2009, President Zardari challenged another institution that had been responsible for ridding the country of Musharraf. He angered the judiciary by postponing the reinstatement of Iftikhar Chaudhry, the maverick chief justice Musharraf had fired. This gave his political rival Nawaz Sharif the opportunity to join another lawyers' movement leading to a 'Long March' that forced the restoration of Chaudhry, along with other suspended judges, on 22 March. (Chaudhry would go on to complete his tenure in December 2013.)

In April, another veteran Pakistan hand, Sharat Sabharwal, landed in Islamabad as Indian high commissioner. Sabharwal, who had been the deputy HC in the 1990s, arrived at a time when policymakers in Delhi were worried about his safety, and that of the Indian mission in Islamabad, given the impunity with which the Taliban seem to be striking within Pakistan's capital. More broadly, Delhi was worried about the larger implications for India of the lawlessness within Pakistan. The fact that the Taliban 'had consolidated their power in the Swat valley, barely 200 kilometres from Islamabad, raised the spectre of them coming to control the nuclear-armed Pakistani state'.[1] The high commissioner walked into an Islamabad that looked like a garrison town with visible security barriers and armed personnel, his residence was a 'veritable fortress'. Three security barriers guarded the road to his home in the F6 sector. The height of the boundary wall of India House had been raised. It was surrounded by Hesco and Texas barriers, with concertina wire running along its perimeter and security cameras looking nervously in all directions. This did not come as a surprise to the HC, given the Marriot Hotel bombing of 2007, and the attack on the neighbouring Danish embassy the previous year.[2]

Yet, Sabharwal, saw some 'silver linings' on the bilateral front, 'feeble' indicators of a possible turn in the relationship compared to his previous tenure in the 1990s. He saw an increasingly vocal constituency questioning the use of terrorism; an information revolution that had reduced the dependence on state media; an increasing tendency to question the post-Musharraf army; a judiciary capable of pushback; and widespread awareness of the growing gap between its power and international standing, and that of India.[3]

Sabharwal tried to pursue the Mumbai investigations. He encountered a good deal of rhetoric about Pakistan's attempts to stamp out 'non-state actors' but very little forward movement. On the civilian side, he saw

Pakistan keen to resume a structured dialogue with India and found that the civilian leaders did have some breathing room, but were still wary of each other. When Sabharwal called on Nawaz Sharif in May 2009, the former PM appeared bitter with the PPP, but was not inclined to rock the boat too hard for fear of playing into the army's hands. In fact, the reluctance of both the PPP and PML-N to collaborate with the army against each other gave them greater democratic space. The army on its part reacted to the challenge by promoting a third force—Imran Khan's Pakistan Tehreek-e-Insaf (PTI), the movement for the restoration of justice.

After Manmohan Singh got a second term in the Indian elections from May 2009, the bilateral engagement increased. In June, Zardari met Singh for the first time since the Mumbai attacks, at a Shanghai Cooperation Organisation (SCO) summit in Yekaterinburg, Russia. The meeting took place against the backdrop of the release from prison of the Mumbai attacks mastermind, Hafiz Saeed. The UN-designated terrorist had defiantly emerged in public view after a nominal house arrest. Singh pointedly told Zardari after a handshake in front of the assembled media that Pakistan's territory must not be used for terrorism.

The two leaders met again in Egypt on the sidelines of a NAM summit. But the national appetite was low in India for the conciliatory 'joint' document with Pakistan issued so soon after Mumbai. The Sharm El Sheikh agreement of July 2009 came in for scathing criticism from the Opposition BJP, for allowing the mention of Balochistan, interpreted as conceding equivalence between Pakistan's covert activity over the decades in Kashmir and India's recent alleged operations within Pakistan. The agreement was also panned in Pakistan—the Balochistan reference was seen as a concession to India and an invitation to interfere in Pakistan's internal matters. Former HC and Foreign Secretary Menon, who negotiated the document, reflected later on the dynamics and found the critique within India illogical: 'If Pakistan wished to discuss its internal affairs in Balochistan with India, even if it was to accuse India of meddling, why should Indian diplomats shy away from a discussion?' he asked. He argued while speaking to parliamentarians that 'while we might be accused of bad drafting, there was nothing wrong with the policy behind the attempt at Sharm El Sheikh'.[4]

Menon later recalled that

> in the resulting media cacophony, only the first part of the sentence was picked up; my statement was portrayed as an attempt to shield the government from blame, and the policy arguments were ignored... In retrospect, it may be that it was premature to resume dialogue with Pakistan nine months after the Mumbai attack. One problem was the general impression in India that while Pakistan had much to gain by way of international respectability from a dialogue, India

did not. But that was a time when a new government in India and a positively inclined civilian government in Pakistan could have made a difference, if domestic politics had not intervened. To me, Sharm El-Sheikh was another opportunity squandered in the long list of missed half chances in India–Pakistan relations. Too often in India the debate on Pakistan policy is reduced to a series of meaningless shibboleths or false opposites—to talk or not to talk, for instance.[5]

In the politically polarized debate, critics were buying neither the 'bad drafting' theory nor the 'good policy' one, and were attributing base motives to Manmohan Singh of being overly soft on the land of his birth. More fundamentally, as Menon discovered by hindsight, it was too soon after Mumbai to have any kind of joint statement with Pakistan, which would need trust and a congruence of views.

Given the prevailing mood in India, former foreign minister Jaswant Singh's book, *Jinnah: India-Partition-Independence,* on the partition of India and Jinnah's role in it, which was released in August, plunged the author into controversy over some positive references to Jinnah. Over six decades after Independence, the mention of Partition's primary protagonist was still an ideologically loaded proposition in India. Jaswant Singh was expelled from his party for violating party discipline, ironically by a committee chaired by L. K. Advani, who, as has been noted earlier, himself had been compelled to resign as BJP president in 2005, when he praised Jinnah during a sentimental trip to Pakistan.

On 10 September, High Commissioner Sharat Sabharwal hosted the Indian high commission's traditional iftar at an Islamabad hotel. Unusually, the British high commissioner told Sabharwal that he might receive a high-ranking guest from the ISI that evening. A few minutes before the event was to start, the Indian HC received confirmation that the DG of the ISI would show up. Lieutenant General Ahmed Shuja Pasha landed up in a black sherwani and made small talk with the high commissioner at the head table. It was clearly a message to suggest that the military was on board for the rapprochement with India and to show a benign side of the ISI (the ISI's seeming desire to build bridges was in part due to its struggles with the US). The ISI chief's presence at an event hosted by the Indian high commissioner made it to the front pages of Pakistani newspapers with one daily gushingly describing the development as a 'milestone' in the history of Indo–Pak ties.

In October 2009, the US Congress passed the Kerry Lugar Bill, which became a flashpoint between the civilian Government of Pakistan and the army. The bill made security assistance to Pakistan contingent on good nuclear behaviour, action to combat terrorist groups, and on ensuring that the security forces of Pakistan were not subverting the political or judicial processes in the country. The Pakistan Army reacted angrily to the last element, over the 'national security implications' of requiring US certification over its role in Pakistan's polity. Sabharwal assessed that the army suspected President Zardari of having engineered the provisions of this bill through its ambassador in the US, Hussain Haqqani. This led to rumours in Islamabad that the army would sack the Zardari government and replace him with a technocratic one, a not unfamiliar fear through all the years of civilian rule in the country.[6]

By 2010, the bilateral relationship was hobbling back from the pain of 2008. Manmohan Singh had begun to engage with Zardari. Diplomacy veered towards discussing issues beyond security, like trade, even as Pakistan contemplated reciprocating the MFN status that it had received from India in 1996.

Even as governments cautiously tried to engage with each other ferment arose within civil society on both sides of the border. The Arab Spring that began stirring in 2010, destabilizing regimes in West Asia through spontaneous popular movements, gave inspiration to Pakistan's support for the movement in Kashmir, to revive the conditions created by the political and militant movements of the 1980s. In India, a state government led by Omar Abdullah, grandson of Sheikh Abdullah, had come to power in Jammu and Kashmir from the end of 2008, with the support of the Congress Party at the centre. To some commentators, the summer of 2010 that saw an uprising of young men pelting stones marked 'a new generation of resistance' in Kashmir. Security agencies often saw Pakistan's hand behind the stone-throwers, as an ecosystem emerged of young stone pelters, who would suddenly appear as 'overground supporters' whenever 'underground' militants were cornered by security forces or during funerals of slain militants. Some tough summers were coming up in Kashmir with a huge increase in stone pelting cases.

However, despite all that was going on, so far as Indian diplomacy was concerned, post Mumbai, terrorism remained the central theme of bilateral conversation. It was increasingly an Indian condition that negotiations with Pakistan could not go on while terrorism continued to seep across the border; linking incidents of terrorism with 'progress on the Jammu and Kashmir' issue was unacceptable to India. But the ISI continued to deploy the made-for-India proxies for terror within Kashmir. It also tried to repurpose the militant groups waging the war within, to focus their wrath on India. The chief of the infamous Taliban faction TTP revealed a feeler he got from the ISI in 2011. The former TTP commander, Ehsanullah Ehsan, who escaped from a safe house operated by the Pakistan Army in 2021, revealed, including in a piece for the *Sunday Guardian* from an undisclosed location, how the ISI had approached him when in North Waziristan to lead a hit squad of his cadres to target 'enemies' including Pashtun freedom activists, Indian and US forces.[7]

A GUEST OF THE PAKISTAN STATE

On 2 May 2011, shortly after 1 a.m. local time, a US military special operations unit executed America's most wanted man. The 9/11 mastermind, Osama bin Laden, was sniffed out in a military township in Abbottabad, Pakistan. Reports later emerged that a former Pakistani intelligence officer had provided the tip-off to the US embassy in August 2010, following which the US recruited a Pakistani doctor, Shakil Afridi, to run a fake vaccination programme, which enabled the US to get blood samples of bin Laden's children to confirm his presence at the safe house.

The episode embarrassed the Pakistan Army and presented it with two dilemmas. The first hard choice was whether they should admit to complicity or to incompetence—of harbouring America's most wanted man on Pakistani soil while pretending to hunt for him; or being unaware of his presence in a safe house in a Pakistani garrison town. The second dilemma was whether to admit to prior knowledge of the US operation and therefore complicity; or to ignorance and a failure to detect the ingress of American aircraft, therefore incompetence. The army chose to claim incompetence on both counts. There were few takers for the first claim; most observers were persuaded that Pakistan was complicit in providing a safe haven for bin Laden, but had been incompetent in detecting the US operation to rescue him. Sharat Sabharwal surmised that Pakistani radars failed to pick up the US helicopters that flew in from Afghan bases that morning, since they were all directed eastward towards India.[8]

But the shamefaced army still needed to display outrage, so a joint session of Pakistan's parliament was made to pass a resolution condemning American violation of Pakistani sovereignty. It failed though to hold its army accountable for harbouring bin Laden as its guest. The CIA director, Leon Panetta, confirmed that no information on the US operation was shared with Pakistan, but investigative journalist Seymour Hersh later claimed that the army leadership had been taken into confidence. Sabharwal would not rule out some senior members of the Pakistan Army having played a private game in facilitating the US action.[9]

Even as fears rose in Pakistan of a cornered army resorting to a familiar tactic of mounting a coup to dismiss the civilian government, the aftershocks of the bin Laden operation continued to claim victims. In October 2009, Sabharwal watched fascinated as 'Memogate' unfolded. A global hedge fund manager of Pakistani origin, Mansoor Ijaz, claimed in an article in the *Financial Times*[10] that he had passed on a one-page unsigned memorandum from President Zardari to Mike Mullen, the chairman of the US Joint Chiefs of Staff committee, that spoke of a 'unique window of opportunity' for Pakistani civilians to 'gain the upper hand over the army and intelligence directorate due to their complicity in the UBL (bin Laden) matter.' It called upon the US administration to send a 'strong, urgent and direct message to General Kayani and General Pasha' to 'end their brinkmanship aimed at bringing down the civilian apparatus'. In return, the president would order an enquiry into the harbouring of bin Laden, and would help in handing over to the US other al-Qaeda operatives—including Ayman al-Zawahiri, Mullah Omar, and Sirajuddin Haqqani—and allow US forces to capture them on Pakistani soil. Also, the document promised, a new security dispensation in Pakistan would cooperate with the Indian government 'on bringing all perpetrators of Pakistani origin to account for the 2008 Mumbai attacks, whether outside government or inside any part of the government, including its intelligence agencies. This includes handing over those against whom sufficient evidence exists of guilt to the Indian security services.'

Zardari and Haqqani immediately denied their involvement in the matter. But the army was accusing both of treason. Zardari was forced to replace Haqqani as ambassador. The president of Pakistan himself suffered a nervous breakdown, for the treatment of which he headed to Dubai. Mullen was later reported to say that he did not take the memo seriously. Both the army and the civilian government lost public credibility with this episode. The matter only served, Sabharwal noted, to put more army pressure on the civilian leadership. Sensing a political opportunity, Nawaz Sharif went to the Supreme Court in November 2011, asking for a thorough probe into the memo matter. Sharif subsequently regretted his action, speaking to journalists in March 2018, since the matter had only served to give the army a handle to corner the civilians.[11]

TALKING TRADE

On 8 April 2012, President Zardari, along with his son Bilawal Zardari Bhutto, the president of the PPP, visited Dargah Sharif in Ajmer, India, on a pilgrimage, a 'private visit'. The duo also met with the Indian PM Manmohan Singh. Behind the religious diplomacy was an attempt to revive the peace process that had been interrupted by the Mumbai attacks, particularly since Zardari's term was coming to an end in the shadow of the attacks, despite his party's and his own personal agenda to improve relations with India. Manmohan Singh's government reciprocated the sentiment, this time by pushing along the dialogue process, already on since 2011, by rechristening the 'composite' dialogue as a 'resumed' dialogue process.

Soon after, in June 2012, the thirteenth (and last) round of talks on the Siachen Glacier took place in Rawalpindi. The talks focused on the demilitarization of the Siachen Glacier, but the Indian precondition remained acceptance of the Actual Ground Position Line (AGPL). For India, the AGPL lay along the Saltoro Range west of the Siachen Glacier, where the Indian Army held most of the heights; Pakistan needed to accept ground positions on maps and 'sign on the dotted line before any kind of disengagement takes place.' But the defence secretary-level talks proved to be another stalemate, with the countries not coming any closer than they had thrice in the past: in the fifth round of talks (1989) when they discussed redeployment of forces; in the sixth round (1992) when Narasimha Rao had refused political clearance for an agreement all but signed; and the tenth round (2006), when a draft agreement was drawn up for a phased, mutual withdrawal and joint monitoring of a demilitarized zone at Siachen—the Indian cabinet refused permission on that occasion. Once again, arguments for withdrawals to prevent mounting peacetime casualties in the harsh mountain conditions were pitted against those pointing to the absence of trust. 'Pakistan has violated every written agreement and verbal commitment since 1947. Why does our Prime Minister want to close his eyes to hard facts and trust Pakistan blindly?' asked an army analyst. 'What are the guarantees that Pakistan will not occupy the heights vacated by India?[12]

A more tangible fruit of the dialogue process was a liberalized visa regime agreed upon by the two countries in September 2012. Sporting ties resumed as well, after a gap of five years, with a tour by a Pakistan cricket team to India from 25 December 2012 to 6 January 2013. At the same time, tensions rose on the LoC, with increased firing signalling that the Pakistan Army might not be on board in the process of normalization.

The most significant initiative was the resumed dialogue on trade, even as it was continuously threatened by the firing at the border and worries about the next terrorist attack. Trade relations between India and Pakistan had always been conducted in the shadow of the volatile political relationship. The trade agreement of 1957, with an MFN-like clause, had lapsed in 1963. It had been followed by another MFN-based agreement in 1975, that had itself expired in 1978. India had accorded formal MFN status to Pakistan in 1996, soon after joining the WTO in 1995, but this gesture had not so far been reciprocated. Trade discussions had featured prominently in the commerce secretary dialogues, as part of the 'composite dialogue' process from 2004 to 2008, but the process crashed after the Mumbai attacks. When Sabharwal took over as high commissioner in Pakistan in 2009, trade was based on a positive list of 2,000 items and stood at about $2 billion with another $5 billion flowing in through third countries like the UAE. Sabharwal sensed a strong appetite for increasing trade with India in Pakistan's business community as he went about the country, speaking to chambers of commerce.

At a meeting of commerce secretaries in 2011, Pakistan's high commissioner to India, Shahid Malik, told Sabharwal that the two foreign offices needed to control the process of trade liberalization closely. Sabharwal saw this as a sign of the foreign office bureaucracy trying to scuttle the process, thanks to their traditional positions of seeing trade as a distraction to the central political issue of Kashmir. Nevertheless, India pursued the trade agenda with enthusiasm.

Indian commerce minister Anand Sharma led a business delegation of 100 businessmen to Lahore, Karachi, and Islamabad in February 2012. Pakistan was planning to transition from the 'positive list' of items permitted for trade to a 'negative list' of only those forbidden. This significant move was to be announced during the Indian visit. However, the Government of Pakistan lost its political nerve, even as Sharma attended a business event in Karachi, and 'deferred' the move. When Sharma expressed his displeasure, and even walked out of a dinner, Pakistan promised to make amends before the end of that month. Pakistan's cabinet did later approve the transition to a liberal resume of a negative list of 1,209 items, which could not be imported from India. A separate trade and travel gate opened at the Attari border in April 2012, and was inaugurated with fanfare in the presence of the chief ministers of the two Punjabs and commerce ministers.

The two sides moved towards the last mile of trade liberalization with another meeting of the commerce secretaries in September 2012. The joint statement issued at the end of the meet noted that India had reduced its 'sensitive' list, applicable to Pakistan, to 614 tariff lines, while Pakistan pared its own list to 936 products that could not be imported from Pakistan. Clearly, Pakistani politicians, particularly in Punjab, were seeing this as a move that would go down well with the electorate in the upcoming elections in May 2013. Sabharwal pushed the agenda forward till he retired in June 2013.

NAWAZ RETURNS

In May 2013, Nawaz Sharif, carrying some uneasy memories of his two aborted terms of the 1990s, comfortably won the general elections held that year, to become PM again, fourteen long years after Musharraf had displaced him in a coup. For his first term as Pakistan's democratic leader in the twenty-first century, Sharif had cashed in on the growing unpopularity of Zardari, and trumped Imran Khan, who was beginning to emerge as the favourite candidate of the army. The most significant achievement of the Zardari government, tripped up continuously by civil–military tensions, was that it had managed to complete a full parliamentary term in the post-Musharraf era, although it was routed in a relatively free democratic election. Khan at that point had only half-hearted support from the establishment, with some former army luminaries guiding his campaign. The strategic decision to decisively back Imran Khan as a 'third force' would be taken only later, to destabilize the Sharif regime.

As Sabharwal left Islamabad after completing his tenure in June, he was replaced by T. C. A. Raghavan, another Pakistan veteran. Raghavan's earlier tenure in 2003–06, as deputy high commissioner, was mostly spent under Musharraf's military reign, at a time when the bilateral relationship was on an extraordinary high. He was now starting his tenure in a democratic Pakistan, almost at the same time as Nawaz Sharif, a politician known to favour a stronger relationship with India.

The prime minister's past relationship with his own military had been troubled. Even before Sharif was sworn in, the Pakistan Army was getting suspicious of foreigners. The *New York Times* journalist Declan Walsh, who had been covering Pakistan for a decade, was abruptly expelled from the country, after being served notice by police who arrived at his Islamabad residence at night. He was given seventy-two hours to leave and asked to sign his own expulsion order.

Walsh was not the only one under scrutiny. Soon, another outspoken foreigner, American South Asia scholar Christine Fair, was expelled from Pakistan after being declared persona non grata. Fair was accused by the Pakistani government of double standards, partisanship towards India, and for pursuing contacts with dissident leaders from Balochistan, a link which 'raises serious questions if her interest in Pakistan is merely academic'.[13]

30

DELHI DURBAR

On 3 January 2014, Prime Minister Manmohan Singh revealed that India and Pakistan had been 'on the verge of a historic deal on Jammu and Kashmir'[1], and at one time in his tenure, it appeared that an 'important breakthrough was in sight'. He attributed the failure to get there to Musharraf's exit from power. Singh was reflecting on his legacy at a press conference, having decided not to contest elections any longer. He added wistfully that he hoped to go to Pakistan, the land of his birth, even before elections in May 2014. Singh's former minister, Natwar Singh recalled in his memoirs that each time Manmohan Singh wanted to visit Pakistan, 'an anti-Indian incident took place'[2]. The frequent acts of terrorism, the resulting strong national sentiment against the neighbour, and Musharraf's political demise, all conspired against Singh from triumphantly visiting the land of his birth and returning with a peace deal to solve a sixty-year-old problem.

In Pakistan, some commentators had been offering gratuitous advice on an itinerary for Singh: it should involve a visit to the birthplace of Guru Nanak, Nankana Sahib near Lahore, Panja Sahib near Rawalpindi, the shrine believed to have an imprint of Guru Nanak's hand, where 'apart from India–Pakistan peace, Dr Singh needs to pray hard to minimise the embarrassment that awaits his party in the April-May 2014 general elections in India'. Dr Singh, a *Dawn* commentator suggested, must also 'visit Gurudwara Dera Baba Nanak at Kartarpur in Sialkot. This gurudwara is just three kilometres from the Indian border at Jammu. Dr Singh could persuade Pakistan to create a visa-free zone for Sikh pilgrims to visit Kartarpur Sahib when they like'. And he could also visit the village of his birth, Gah in district Chakwal, and meet his old schoolmates.

As Manmohan Singh prepared to leave office, Nawaz Sharif was pressing ahead firmly with the trade agenda. Pakistan had even decided to accord MFN status to India, in a cabinet meeting held in March 2014. The MFN clause now had a more politically palatable name—NDMA (non-discriminatory market access). But India was already in election mode. A new Pakistani high commissioner took over in New Delhi in March and the issue landed on his table. Abdul Basit recounted the events in his 2021 memoir, *Hostility: A Diplomat's Diary on Pakistan-India Relations*:

> Our Commerce Minister, Khurram Dastagir Khan, had visited New Delhi in January and it was decided that Pakistan would extend the

NDMA to India soon. For this purpose, his Indian counterpart, Anand Sharma, was very keen to visit Pakistan at the earliest, that is, prior to general elections that were being held in several phases in April/May 2014. While the dates for his visit to Pakistan were being worked out, I was approached by a person...who claimed to be a close friend of both Mohan Bhagwat, Chief of RSS, and the BJP's prime ministerial candidate Narendra Modi. I invited him for lunch on 1 April... He contended that granting NDMA to the outgoing Congress government would be wasteful. Islamabad should defer the matter. Since the BJP would most likely form the next government, it would make eminent sense to oblige the incoming set-up. This would help make a good beginning...I finally wrote to Islamabad that postponing the NDMA would be wise as the Congress party was in deep water and in no position to win for a third consecutive time.[3]

The decision on the NDMA was thus deferred.[4]

In May 2014, the Indian correspondent for *The Hindu* in Pakistan, Meena Menon, was expelled, mostly for writing about Balochistan. She, along with Snehesh Alex Philip of the Press Trust of India, the only two Indian journalists in Pakistan then, were told by the Pakistan's Information Ministry that their visas would not be renewed and that they would need to leave Pakistan within a week. The two Indian journalists had been in Pakistan for less than a year, and were given no reason for the decision. Their predecessors had spent more than six years each in Islamabad but had left Pakistan after being denied visa extensions in July 2013. The journalists owed their presence in Pakistan to a bilateral agreement of the late 1970s that allowed each country to post two journalists in the other. This had been an important confidence-building measure that gave both peoples a lens to see one another. But too much reality was puncturing specially synthesized official narratives. The people would now need to rely on social media and WhatsApp forwards to have a real measure of one another.

In India, Lambah spoke publicly for the first time (in his 'personal capacity') in Srinagar of a 'possible outline of a solution' of the Kashmir issue, in May 2014. His talk was a guarded public airing of the four-point Kashmir peace plan.[5] That this public lecture came towards the end of Manmohan Singh's ten-year prime-ministerial tenure indicated that for both the PM and Satinder Lambah, this was a legacy issue: a carefully nurtured secret initiative that had to be tested for the possible interest it would hold for the next Indian government. Lambah had displayed extraordinary patience and tenacity in taking the idea forward with multiple interlocutors in Pakistan. After hammering out a near agreement with his Pakistani counterpart Tariq Aziz in 2007, Lambah had seen it freeze with the political implosion in Pakistan. He had however continued sporadic low-key conversations on this quiet channel with President Zardari's representative Riaz Mohammad Khan (two meetings: in 2009 and 2012) and Nawaz Sharif's nominee Shahryar Khan (six meetings in 2013 and 2014). In Pakistan however, there was little clarity on whether the army supported or endorsed the plan after Musharraf's departure.[6]

The arrival on the scene of Prime Minister Narendra Modi of the Bharatiya Janata Party, after winning a thumping majority in the 2014 election in India, aroused, in equal parts worry, scepticism, and fear in Islamabad, given his record of tough talk on Pakistan. Yet, defying expectations, like Vajpayee had done on several occasions in his tenures, Modi reached out to the Pakistan leadership early in his term. In fact, even before he was sworn in. The new National Democratic Alliance (NDA) government, led by the BJP, reached out to Nawaz Sharif and invited him for Modi's swearing-in ceremony, along with other SAARC leaders.

When High Commissioner Raghavan got a call from Foreign Secretary Sujata Singh to check if PM Nawaz Sharif would attend the oath-taking ceremony, he asked her if she was sure Pakistan's PM was on the guest list.[7] Sharif had always shown a willingness to accept invitations from India. But even before the official acceptance arrived, Sharif had conveyed his willingness to attend, through a more informal channel. Speculation arose on that channel: was it steel tycoon Sajjan Jindal or a leader of the Bohra community or a non-resident Indian that was the messenger? But one thing was clear, the men in uniform had not been asked—an offended Pakistan Army that felt entitled to determine India policy claimed it had not been consulted before Sharif's visit to India.

To some in Pakistan, the presence of Nawaz Sharif in Delhi for the inauguration of a new Indian regime evoked unwelcome imagery of an emperor ascending the throne in Delhi and those in peripheral kingdoms attending the event, laden with gifts. For many in Pakistan's establishment, Sharif had walked into a trap set up by a new Indian government. Asad Durrani told me in Islamabad later that it had been a 'foolish' error. Multiple media stories plugging this viewpoint appeared in Pakistan's media. Clearly, accepting the invitation had been an instinctive judgement of the civilian leadership that did not have the blessings of the military establishment.

Satinder Lambah was one of the experts invited to brief the prime minister designate on the eve of his meeting with Nawaz Sharif. Lambah strongly endorsed the decision to invite Pakistan's leader and pointed out that Sharif was coming to India more than two decades after his last visit, for Rajiv Gandhi's funeral.[8]

Despite the scepticism in Pakistan and the concerns of his high commissioner, Abdul Basit, Nawaz Sharif received a cordial reception from India's new government, followed by a friendly and future-focused conversation with Modi. The new Indian PM sent Sharif a particularly warm letter after the visit, saying that he was

> delighted and honoured by your participation in the ceremony for the swearing in of the new government. Your presence and that of other leaders from our region not only added a special sheen to the event, but (was) also a celebration of the strength of democracy in our region.... I was also encouraged by our discussions on our bilateral relations and the convergence in our views, especially on the fact that a relationship between India and Pakistan defined by peace, friendship and cooperation would unleash enormous opportunities for our youth, secure a more prosperous future for our people and accelerate progress across our region. I look forward therefore to working closely with you and your Government in an atmosphere free from confrontation and violence in order to chart a new course in our bilateral relations.... I thank you once again for the sari that you sent for my mother, a gesture that she has deeply appreciated.[9]

Lambah later met PM Modi again to brief him on his backchannel talks. After his last conversation on the subject with the PMO in 2014, Lambah realized that both sides were looking at newer solutions, but concluded optimistically that 'the principles and the text of the draft agreement are still there to be taken up, whenever the two sides feel the need to resume the process. Or, they can start afresh with new guidelines and parameters, but with the same objective—to seek permanent peace between two neighbours.'[10]

PM Modi would go on to deepen his relationship with PM Nawaz Sharif, with five more meetings in the next eighteen months: on the margins of multilateral events, in Ufa, Kathmandu, New York, Paris, and even in Lahore.

While Pakistan's army chief, Raheel Sharif, on the job since 2013, kept a wary eye on the personal communication between Nawaz Sharif and Modi, he had a domestic implosion to worry about. Angered by the US presence in Afghanistan, and Pakistan's support for it, the TTP launched a fresh offensive within Pakistan. An attack on 8 June on the Jinnah International Airport in Karachi, for which the TTP and the Islamic Movement of Uzbekistan (IMU) claimed responsibility, led to much hand-wringing in the military establishment. The answer came in the shape of Zarb-e-Azb (a sword strike) from 15 June 2014—decisive strikes on militant groups by the Pakistan Army in North Waziristan, along the Pakistan–Afghanistan border.

Pakistan's top diplomat in Delhi decided to add his voice to the army's in pushing against his prime minister's attempts at rapprochement. High Commissioner Abdul Basit had been unhappy about the tone of his prime minister's visit to India in May and decided to do his bit to sabotage what he thought was a misguided peace initiative. He pointedly and publicly invited leaders of the Kashmiri separatist Hurriyat to the Pakistan high commission in August 2014, just when India was preparing to send Foreign Secretary Sujata Singh to Islamabad to follow up on the Modi–Nawaz meeting. India called off the talks between the foreign secretaries over the provocation.

Basit seemed to revel in his role of playing the spoiler. He defiantly outlined his mea culpa in his memoirs published in India, and spoke of it volubly to the Indian media:

> As the top Pakistan diplomat in New Delhi at the time when both Prime Minister Nawaz Sharif and Prime Minister Narendra Modi had made a very encouraging start with their first meeting in New Delhi on 27 May 2014, I do share some, if not total, responsibility for the later developments on the diplomatic front...Some even suggested that I was working at the behest of the Pakistan establishment and worked in close coordination with them rather than pursuing the peaceful aspirations of the civilian leadership...I somewhat crossed my mandate by displaying excessive zeal on Kashmir...For instance, I should have avoided meeting the Kashmiri leadership which led to the cancellation of India's foreign secretary's scheduled visit to Pakistan in August 2014.[11]

Basit was scathing in his criticism of Nawaz Sharif: 'His approach was to make unilateral concessions in the hope that Mr Modi would reciprocate' and he 'weakened our principled position on Jammu and Kashmir in particular'. Sharif, he judged, 'had an emotional attachment to India and Indians, which at times went beyond his stature as the prime minister.' He was particularly disapproving of Sharif's visit to the home of an Indian friend—'his visit to Sajjan Jindal's residence while he was in New Delhi was not really required...the way he received so many journalists... was again not required...he did not seek a meeting with the Hurriyat leadership...he was all out to oblige everyone, and that, to me, was not the right thing to do'.[12]

On 16 December 2014, six armed men affiliated with the TTP opened fire on the Army Public School in Peshawar killing 149 people including 132 schoolchildren. The bloody massacre executed by foreign terrorists including from Russian Chechnya, had echoes of a similar one in Beslan, Russia, in 2004. It pointed to a global dimension of terrorism visiting

Pakistan. The horrific images of children lying dead saw an outpouring of grief and solidarity in India. Prime Minister Modi condemned the attack, calling it 'a senseless act of unspeakable brutality that has claimed lives of the most innocent of human beings, young children in their school'.[13] A hashtag #IndiaWithPakistan trended on Twitter; the Lok Sabha, as also schools across India, observed a two-minute silence for the victims. Most felt that Pakistan's crackdown on terrorism after this outrage would be uncompromising. A shocked Pakistan had doubled down on its anti-terror campaign in the north-west and rolled out a 'National Action Plan' to counter terrorism. But the good terrorists, those nurtured by the ISI for action in Afghanistan and Kashmir, remained protected. The attack worried India's diplomatic establishment. India took a call to declare Islamabad a non-school station, withdrawing all children of staff from school in the city.

A WEDDING IN LAHORE

Modi would go on to encounter Nawaz Sharif on five separate occasions, as previously noted, including in July 2015, for the Ufa SCO in Russia, when Sharif was roundly criticized in Pakistan for allowing an agreement that did not mention Pakistan's Kashmir cause. Ufa was seen by some as a drafting exercise on the opposite end of the spectrum as the 2009 joint statement in Sharm El Sheikh between Manmohan Singh and Gilani, mirroring the criticism that the government of the day faced—of acquiescing in an asymmetric document that favoured the adversary.

A year after New Delhi cancelled the foreign secretary-level talks with Pakistan for inviting separatists before the talks, Abdul Basit again decided to test India's patience by inviting the Hurriyat leaders to the Pakistan high commission, this time for a meeting with Sartaj Aziz on 23 August 2015, the day the NSA-level talks between the two countries were slated. Aziz, who had been Nawaz Sharif's NSA since May 2013, was to be received by NSA Ajit Doval for a follow-up conversation on security after the Ufa dialogue. Pakistan complained of India setting up 'preconditions for talks' while India said it would be 'inappropriate' for the visitor to also meet with the Hurriyat separatist movement while in the Indian capital. The talks were cancelled amidst familiar rhetoric from Pakistan that 'no dialogue could take place between the two countries until New Delhi agreed to discuss the Kashmir issue with Islamabad'.

In September 2015, speaking at the UN General Assembly, Pakistan's prime minister, Nawaz Sharif put forward his own four-point proposal on Kashmir, a more flexible variation of Musharraf's. It envisaged: one, complete ceasefire by India and Pakistan along the LoC; two, reaffirmation by both sides that they will not resort to the threat or use of force under any circumstances; three, demilitarization of Kashmir; and four, an unconditional withdrawal by both sides from the Siachen Glacier, the world's highest battleground. To Indian analysts, the proposal was a non-starter, because it did not address the issue of terrorism, seemed to give terrorists a free pass to enter a demilitarized Kashmir, and asked India to vacate Siachen so that it could cancel the strategic advantage India had from the heights giving Pakistan a chance to occupy them some time in the future. Like Zia's no-war pact and Musharraf's four-point formula, Sharif's proposal did not address India's central concern of the day—putting an end to the proxy war and terrorism emanating from Pakistan.

The 'comprehensive' dialogue, a rebranding of the composite dialogue of the 1990s, was meant to continue after External Affairs Minister Sushma Swaraj visited Pakistan in early December 2015, for a 'Heart of Asia' conference on Afghanistan. Despite the hiccups, the conditions seemed right for another breakthrough in the relationship, with the 'composite' dialogue that had been altered to 'resumed' dialogue, now mutating into a 'comprehensive' dialogue.

An even more ambitious diplomatic gambit was to play out that month. On Christmas day in 2015, High Commissioner Raghavan, in his last week of active duty before he retired at the end of the month, was surprised by a call at 8 a.m. from Foreign Secretary S. Jaishankar, saying he better get ready to receive the Indian prime minister in Islamabad. When Raghavan asked if Nawaz Sharif would really be in Islamabad to receive his guest that day, the foreign secretary rang back to clarify that the two leaders had agreed to meet in Lahore in a few hours. By 10 a.m., Raghavan was on the road to Lahore. Since he would not be in time to receive his PM at the airport, he directly reached the Sharif residence in Raiwind, on Lahore's outskirts.

Modi later revealed[14] that he had called up from Kabul only to greet Sharif on his birthday that day, but the prime minister of Pakistan had insisted that he should drop in to Lahore en route home to attend his granddaughter's wedding that afternoon. Modi then called his cabinet colleague, External Affairs Minister Sushma Swaraj, who had visited Pakistan earlier that month, for her advice, adding that he was inclined towards accepting the invitation. She said she would have no objection to such a visit and asked the PM to take that call. Modi took a spontaneous decision to drop in on Sharif, on his way to Delhi, where he was committed to visiting the ailing Atal Bihari Vajpayee on the former PM's ninety-first birthday.

Again, demonstrating the instincts several Indian prime ministers before him had displayed when they wanted to break the mould and take the relationship forward, PM Modi went to Lahore to visit his Pakistani counterpart. The visit had India's security agencies on edge and Pakistan's military establishment in shock. India's PM agreed to jump into a Pakistani army helicopter from the airport to meet his counterpart.

Modi's instinctive judgement call was akin to Vajpayee's, when he took a bus to Lahore in 1999. Both times it was a ringing statement to the people of Pakistan and the world that Indian leaders were willing to take risks for peace. In Pakistan, Raheel Sharif's army sulked at this intrusion, just as Musharraf's had done in 1999. The India policy monopoly that the army assumed it held, had been defied by Sharif. But, as it turned out, both recent choices by Sharif—of visiting India and of inviting India's new leader—had not gone down well with Pakistan's army.

'Gatecrashing,' said former ISI chief Durrani to me in Islamabad, when I talked up that visit three years later, as an example of a huge risk for peace. I was puzzled by this reaction, but it was fairly representative of the Pak army's take on Sharif's India policy. It was as if Sharif had thrown a party and invited a neighbour only the uniformed men were entitled to deal with, both in the case of the invitation to Vajpayee in 1999 and to Modi in 2015. A Pakistani military analyst, whom I discussed this reaction with later, labelled Durrani a super hawk masquerading as a dove on the Track II circuit.

As far as Pakistan policy was concerned, the Modi government's approach in the first twenty months, from May 2014 to December 2015, paralleled Vajpayee's approach to Pakistan during his tenure, from March 1998 till April 1999. Both times, India's prime minister led intense, hopeful diplomatic engagement, culminating in a visit to Nawaz Sharif in Lahore. And each time, hope was belied.

Within a few days of the Indian PM's visit on 25 December 2015, High Commissioner Raghavan hung up his boots and left Islamabad on a note of high hope for the relationship. But a day after the envoy's departure, the trajectory of bilateral relations changed again: a terrorist attack shook Pathankot in Indian Punjab on the second day of the New Year. Twenty Indian soldiers lay dead.

STRIKING SURGICALLY

Raghavan's successor in Islamabad, Gautam Bambawale, had been preparing for his new job with upbeat briefings in Delhi in December 2015, picking up a picture of a relationship poised for a breakthrough. But in 2016, he had to contend with the aftermath of the Pathankot terrorist attack, even before he reached Islamabad. While Bambawale's brief was initially to retrieve the relationship from its post-Pathankot low, a tough summer followed in Kashmir in 2016 in his tenure. Kashmir had been overrun by new-age militants like Burhan Wani that summer. Even Bollywood movies had started to portray a glamorized Kashmir cause taken up by new-age militants, with movies like *Haider* (2014), based on *Curfewed Night*, the memoir of Kashmiri journalist, Basharat Peer. External

Affairs Minister Sushma Swaraj later said in India's parliament that even more than Pathankot, it was the Burhan Wani summer in Kashmir and Nawaz Sharif's praise for the terrorist that soured bilateral ties.[15]

On 18 September 2016, matters reached a head. Four armed men sneaked into an Indian Army brigade headquarters camp near the border town of Uri (J&K) and shot dead nineteen Indian soldiers; dozens of others were injured. The attackers, later identified as belonging to the Pakistan-based Jaish-e-Mohammed, had carried out one of the deadliest attacks on security forces in Kashmir in two decades, at a time when the leaders of the two countries were looking for diplomatic solutions. Public opinion in India was inflamed by this brutal attack by a designated terrorist organization, seen as the ISI's then weapon of choice for Kashmir, after the LeT faced the heat after the Mumbai attacks. The attack seemed designed to promote greater instability in Kashmir, with the valley already convulsed that summer by extensive violent unrest. Forces on both sides of the border went on high alert as India weighed its options.

An immediate diplomatic fallout was the cancellation of a SAARC summit planned for November in Islamabad, where PM Nawaz Sharif was hoping to receive PM Modi. India told SAARC chair Nepal that 'increasing cross-border terrorist attacks in the region and growing interference in the internal affairs of Member States by one country have created an environment that is not conducive to the successful holding of the 19th SAARC Summit.'[16] Pakistan's foreign office called the withdrawal 'unfortunate', but posted a defiant rejoinder that it was 'India that has been perpetrating and financing terrorism in Pakistan'.

India's response came on 28 September, eleven days after the Uri attack, in the shape of 'surgical strikes' on launch pads used by militants in POK. India's DGMO Lieutenant General Ranbir Singh announced that India had conducted a 'pre-emptive strike' against 'terrorist teams' preparing to 'carry out infiltration and conduct terrorist strikes inside Jammu and Kashmir and in various metros in other states'.[17]

Indian Army soldiers had returned after killing terrorists and without encountering Pakistani armed forces. Even as fears of escalation grew, Pakistan surprisingly denied any incursion. Reports appeared in the Indian media of dozens of militants killed in launch pads. More than the actual operation, the key message of the Uri surgical strikes was that India had publicly declared it had crossed the LoC in hot pursuit of terrorists. This was a significant assertion and marked a shift in policy. It was clear that retaliation against major terrorist attacks would now become the norm, as against the strategic restraint displayed after earlier ones. In strategic terms, the signal to Pakistan and to the world was that India was willing to escalate conflict in the sub-conventional space to deal with cross-border terrorism.

After the Uri events, bilateral relations took a plunge, snapping even cultural connections. Sensing strong public hostility, the Indian movie industry decided to 'ban all Pakistani actors, actresses and technicians working in India'. The TV entertainment channel Zindagi stopped airing popular Pakistani soaps. Predictably, Pakistan responded in October with a blanket ban on 'all Indian television and radio programming'. The Board of Control for Cricket in India (BCCI) ruled out reviving bilateral cricket ties with Pakistan and asked the International Cricket Council (ICC) to separate India and Pakistan cricket teams in international matches. India's participation in an international badminton series in Islamabad in October was called off.

With the surgical strikes, the Indian high commission went into 'lockdown' in Islamabad, fearing escalation and hostility. Both Indian and Pakistani media and strategic circles debated India's new posture. India had stayed its hand in 2001 against terrorism in the aftermath of the Parliament attack, by trying coercive diplomacy. Again in 2008, India did not take punitive military action, but tried restraint and global diplomacy. It was only after 2016 that India began to fine-tune 'surgical' instruments to deal with the terrorism challenge. Pakistan tried to promote the myth that any conventional action by India could lead to a threat to peace and stability (read nuclear escalation). However, in the past few years, India has demonstrated that the space existed for a sub-conventional response to terrorism.

Meanwhile, the domestic politics of Pakistan had taken a new turn. Pakistan's army was questioning Nawaz Sharif's India policy and now seemed to be backing Imran Khan more firmly. It was looking for pathways to dislodge Sharif and replace him with Khan.

THE *DAWN* LEAKS

Soon after the Uri attacks, the US ambassador in Pakistan met with PM Nawaz Sharif and handed over a file to him. It had, among other nuggets, information of the ISI's complicity in planning the Uri attacks. Sharif was dismayed. This additional evidence fuelled his resolve to confront his army, which was running down his government's reputation. He summoned two meetings: a political 'all parties' conference' to dwell on the issue, and a meeting at the PMO, where civilian leaders were invited, together with the military brass. Foreign Secretary Aizaz Ahmad Chaudhry gave a 'separate, exclusive presentation' in the second meeting, chaired by the PM himself, to a small group of civilian and military officials. The military team was led by the ISI Director General Rizwan Akhtar.

The presentation at the meeting spoke of a 'recent diplomatic outreach by Pakistan', which revealed that 'Pakistan faces diplomatic isolation and that the government's talking points have been met with indifference in major world capitals'. On the US, Chaudhry said that 'relations have deteriorated', and on India, 'completion of the Pathankot investigation and some visible action against Jaish-e-Mohammed were the principal demands'. Then, 'to a hushed but surprised room', Chaudhry suggested that China had indicated a 'preference for a change in course by Pakistan' and questioned the logic of repeatedly 'putting on technical hold a UN ban on Jaish-e-Mohammed leader Masood Azhar.' When General Akhtar asked what steps could be taken to prevent the drift towards isolation, Chaudhry suggested that action could be taken on principal international demands for 'action against Masood Azhar and the Jaish-e-Mohammed; Hafiz Saeed and the Lashkar-e-Taiba; and the Haqqani network'[18].

More unusual than the issues discussed at the meeting was the fact that a blow-by-blow account, based on 'sources', found its way to the front page of *Dawn*, on 6 October, in a story with the byline of the brilliant young journalist Cyril Almeida. The sensational 'Exclusive' was headlined: 'Act against militants or face international isolation, civilians tell military'.[19] The impact of the story on Pakistan's polity, and on civil–military, was explosive. Soon, the focus shifted from the substance of the meeting, to accusations of treason against those who had leaked this information; army-leaning journalists called it 'Dawngate'. Nawaz Sharif came under intense pressure from the army; his daughter, Maryam, who held no government post, was rumoured to be behind the leak. When the controversy refused to die down, Sharif was forced to fire two of his closest aides, Minister of Information Pervaiz Rashid and Special Assistant Tariq Fatemi.

An angry and embarrassed army saw this as the tipping point; a civilian was rocking the boat and publicly questioning a carefully considered 'security policy' of deploying militants in the neighbourhood. The time had come to remove Nawaz Sharif. The army started playing up allegations of treason against a prime minister who had dared to question a core national interest.

The internal dynamics of the army were also in play—Army chief Raheel Sharif's three-year term was ending in November and he was in no mood to relinquish charge. His own predecessor Kayani had spent six years in power and that seemed par for the course for army chiefs, unless they wanted to run the country more directly. Raheel Sharif's successor, Qamar Javed Bajwa, claimed seven years later that 'there was nothing in the *Dawn* leaks,' and that Raheel had tried to exploit the incident to seek another three-year extension for himself. Bajwa said that the '*Dawn* leaks' posed no threat to national security. The former PM had told Bajwa that Raheel kept requesting a three-year extension, whenever he met him along with former chief of ISI, Rizwan Akhtar. But the two generals were in competition themselves: 'In front of General Raheel, General Rizwan always insisted on a three-year extension for the army chief. But in private, he only asked for a one-year extension because he saw himself as the next army chief after General Raheel,' Bajwa quoted Nawaz Sharif as saying.[20] Nawaz Sharif soon announced the appointment of Qamar Bajwa as the chief of army staff. Sharif, who had been twice ousted already as prime minister by his army chiefs, was awarded a high grade by media pundits for making the right choice this time round. While Bajwa was the fourth by seniority, and superseded two generals to the top job (the most senior general, Zubair Hayat, picked up the notionally more senior appointment as the chairman Joint Chiefs of Staff Committee), he was rumoured to hold strong pro-democracy views and favour a low-key style. Bajwa took over his new assignment on 29 November 2016.

While the army under Bajwa did not pursue treason charges against Nawaz Sharif for the *Dawn* leaks, it continued to pursue corruption charges based on the 'Panama papers', published in global media in early 2016, that uncovered links between the Sharif family and offshore companies. The papers made for a juicy global financial scandal, detailing more than 200,000 offshore entities and their connections to global plutocrats. The Panama allegations were pursued by the then favourite politician of the army, Imran Khan, who had filed a petition with the Supreme Court, seeking Sharif's disqualification as prime minister and as a member of the National Assembly of Pakistan. Khan was soon encouraged to 'lockdown' Islamabad with an extended protest sit-in, until Sharif 'resigned or presented himself for accountability'.

Even as all this was rumbling on, the primary challenge for the new army chief came from the terrorists striking within Pakistan. In February 2017, General Bajwa unveiled Operation Radd-ul-Fasaad (Elimination of Strife), a military operation to support police in countering militant groups active within Pakistan. The operation aimed to double down on the gains of Operation Zarb-e-Azb which had been launched in 2014, and to also present a picture of decisive action to US forces embroiled in Afghanistan.

Nawaz Sharif appeared cornered by the army. In an order on 20 April, the Supreme Court castigated Sharif, with two of the five judges asking for his disqualification. The court, however, formed a joint investigation team (JIT) to probe the matter further. The judiciary was under enormous pressure to indict Sharif.

It later turned out that the judges hearing the case were being blackmailed or under severe pressure from the deep state.[21] A leaked audio recording of a conversation of former Pakistani chief justice Saqib Nisar emerged in 2021, sensationally disclosed by Maryam Nawaz at a press meet. It revealed he had passed on clear instructions to sentence Sharif. '[Military] institutions have asked to do so. Whether it is fair or not, it has to be done,' Nisar was heard saying. For good measure, Nisar added 'Even though there are no cases against Maryam Nawaz, she would still have to be punished.' The judge involved in the sentencing, Arshad Malik, was removed from office.[22]

Army chief Bajwa claimed later that he had persuaded Nawaz Sharif to resign earlier in 2017 in the wake of the Supreme Court's judgements on 'Panamagate', but his daughter Maryam prevailed on him to drop the idea and fight it out.[23]

On 28 July 2017, a five-member bench of the Supreme Court of Pakistan disqualified Nawaz Sharif from holding public office for life in the Panama papers case. In the end, Sharif's party claimed, he was ousted for not revealing a couple of payments and on the tenuous grounds of not being sadiq and ameen, truthful and righteous. Sharif's removal from office by the Supreme Court, in what several observers felt was a 'judicial coup', where the judiciary had acted again as a handmaiden of the army in easing out a civilian leader.

⌣

With the exit of Nawaz Sharif as PM, even the feeble efforts to find peace with India tapered off. As India and Pakistan completed seventy years of their independence, their relationship had reached another low. India was consolidating its strong economic progress, with the Pakistan relationship reduced to one of managing borders and terrorism. Within Pakistan, a new army chief was finding his feet, with Nawaz Sharif dispatched for the third time without completing his term. In the US, Donald Trump had come to power and Pakistan was under intense US pressure to end its support to the Taliban, to facilitate Trump's electoral promise of a rapid US exit from Afghanistan. China's role in the region was rising through the China–Pakistan Economic Corridor (CPEC), a promise of up to $64 billion of investment in the Pakistan leg of the global Belt and Road Initiative (BRI), the Chinese gambit for global influence. While a weakened civilian leadership under a Sharif loyalist, Shahid Khaqan Abbasi, tried gamely to run the Pakistan government, the army's writ ran large. Pakistan was now focused on a possible second democratic transition after 2013: an election in the coming months for which the army was grooming for the top job a new leader, Imran Khan, in a new experiment to run a 'hybrid' regime. The India relationship and much of Pakistan's governance was on hold in anticipation of elections in 2018.

2017–2023: TOUGH TALKING

31

LIES, DECEIT, AND DIPLOMACY

In the summer of 2017, as India and Pakistan prepared to turn seventy, I had little inkling that my own path would connect directly with the clashing destiny of the neighbours. In fact, I read about it in the news. A news story in the *Hindustan Times*[1] spoke casually of whispers about various diplomatic postings. A line in the piece said I was being considered for the Pakistan assignment. I was then India's envoy in Poland, basking in a late European summer that July. I dismissed the story as random speculation by a beat journalist picking up South Block corridor gossip. Until another media story appeared, slotting me in for the same assignment, quoting official sources with greater confidence. This was unusual. I had months to go to end my tenure in Poland. Pakistan was not listed as a possible posting option for envoys in administrative circulars. I had not asked or lobbied to be sent there. Most importantly, nobody had called or asked me. Surely, it couldn't be true. Colleagues in Delhi were not letting on any inside information. I called a couple of friends in the ministry who had also been mentioned in the media reports. They claimed equal mystification.

As I walked in the precincts of the beautiful Krakow Castle one July afternoon, my cellphone buzzed. It was a colleague, Shilpak Ambule, from the office of the foreign secretary.

'Sir, you're being considered for the western neighbour. We need your consent.'

'So the news wasn't wrong. It's of course a great honour. But I hope they know...I'm more of a Europe and Russia hand.'

They knew that. But I'd been picked nevertheless. It was final. Asking me was a formality.

The vacancy in Pakistan had arisen since our ambassador in Beijing, Vijay Gokhale, was being moved to Delhi in order to take over as foreign secretary a few months down the line; the HC in Pakistan, Gautam Bambawale, a China expert, was being sent off to replace him. I later discovered that my appointment was born of a conversation between Foreign Secretary Jaishankar and External Affairs Minister Sushma Swaraj, and then later between the EAM and PM.

MISSION PAKISTAN

On a cool December morning in 2017, I crossed the white line separating Attari from Wagah, the Indian Punjab from the Pakistani one. That border was, of course, a segment of what Cyril Radcliffe had traced on a map with a blue pencil in 1947, sundering the destinies of two new-born nations whose people had for centuries inhabited a common space. Seven decades after the two countries were born, crossing the Zero Point still felt surreal, familiar yet different, like being sucked into another dimension while still at home.

As I stepped over the thick white chalk—after handshakes with BSF officers, our 'first line of defence'—to salutes by the Pakistan Rangers, I felt a mix of excited anticipation and concern of the days to come. The central questions that buzzed in my head, in this low phase in the bilateral relationship, was the one that had been asked by many of my predecessors. Did we have the capacity or the bandwidth to create a future substantially different from the past? Could I play a role in that process?

The next morning, I was sitting in Islamabad's diplomatic enclave, on a chair that had been occupied by stalwarts I'd admired growing up in the Foreign Service, ranging from K. S. Bajpai to J. N. Dixit to Satinder Lambah to Satyabrata Pal. In South Block's scheme of things, I was a bit of an interloper in Pakistan. I hadn't ever been posted there, I hadn't manned the Pakistan desk at any level, I hadn't really 'dealt' with Pakistan directly at any stage in my career. For that matter, I had no 'neighbourhood experience'. I was part of the MEA's 'Russian mafia', speaking the language and having dealt with the USSR and Russia for chunks of my career. But I was familiar with the Indo–Pak relationship, particularly from my days in the Vajpayee PMO earlier in the century; I had more than a few Pakistan stories to tell, of the hits and misses of visits and summits.

I arrived in a Pakistan where army chief Bajwa was quietly consolidating power, while hesitatingly contemplating some change. He had been appointed to his new role for a three-year term in November 2016 by Nawaz Sharif, who, as noted, had plucked him out of a seniority list as the least bad option. Sharif had a history of misjudging army chiefs. He had been twice bitten: twice deposed by army chiefs he appointed. This time would be no different.

Bajwa, a tall, square-jawed Punjabi Jat had dreamt of being a cricketer, but ended up in the next best Pakistani profession, the army. He had developed a soft spot for Pakistan's cricketing hero, Imran Khan. He had now bought into the Pakistan army's ongoing 'project Imran', to create a third political force as an alternative to the PPP and PML-N. The previous two elections of 2008 and 2013 had largely been free, since his army backers had not been too proactive in propelling Imran Khan to the victory podium. This needed to be corrected. Sharif had been successfully removed and Khan needed to be crowned victor in the 2018 elections.

When I walked into Pakistan, the overall bilateral climate was of a troubled, prickly relationship. My brief was to work with the foreign office and official civilian interlocutors to gradually build trust to take us further up the path of resolving the bigger issues when the time was right. Our focus was on baby steps: humanitarian efforts, and quiet conversations that could build trust, rather than on leaps of faith, as had often been attempted in the past, mostly with sorry outcomes. In my briefing conversations in Delhi, the issue of engaging the army in Pakistan did come up. My mandate was to deploy 'local creativity' to engage with everyone who mattered and to convey India's point of view.

A WHITE HOUSE TROLL

> The United States has foolishly given Pakistan more than 33 billion dollars in aid over the last 15 years, and they have given us nothing but lies & deceit, thinking of our leaders as fools. They give safe haven to the terrorists we hunt in Afghanistan, with little help. No more![2]

This tweet was not from your regular Pakistan-baiting troll. US president Donald Trump's early morning rant was less than 140 characters long but powerful enough to kick up a storm in Islamabad. The peculiar diplomatic message on New Year's Day 2018 came on the back of continuing tension between Washington and Islamabad that had flared up in August 2017 when the US commander-in-chief announced his administration's national security strategy for Afghanistan. Trump had warned Pakistan against support for fighters finding safe havens along the Afghan border: 'We can no longer be silent about Pakistan's safe havens for terrorist organizations, the Taliban and other groups that pose a threat to the region and beyond… we have been paying Pakistan billions and billions of dollars at the same time they are housing the very terrorists that we are fighting. But that will have to change, and that will change immediately.' [3]

After smarting for a few hours that New Year's Day, Pakistan rustled up a retaliatory tweet, from the handle of Defence Minister Khurram Dastgir Khan:

> Pak as anti-terror ally has given free to US: land & air communication, military bases & intel cooperation that decimated Al-Qaeda over last 16 years, but they have given us nothing but invective & mistrust. They overlook cross-border safe havens of terrorists who murder Pakistanis.[4]

At 9 p.m., Pakistani foreign secretary Tehmina Janjua summoned US ambassador to Pakistan, David Hale, to give formal vent to Pakistan's outrage. Media reports amplified Pakistan's hurt pride.

But Trump's trolling of Pakistan had won him several admirers in Islamabad's diplomatic circles. It was refreshingly blunt. The blow from the US made it to the front pages in India, as also in Afghanistan, where it was seen as a vindication of what both countries had been alleging for long.

'The Trump administration decision has abundantly vindicated India's stand...as far as the role of Pakistan is concerned in perpetrating terrorism,' said Jitendra Singh, Indian minister in the PMO. Some media speculated that Trump may also have been influenced by a quip by PM Modi the previous year, that the US had given so much for so little.

Former Afghan president Hamid Karzai tweeted a dig from Kabul at both Pakistan and the US:

> President (Trump's) tweet on Pakistan's duplicitous position over the past 15 years is vindication that the war on terror is not in bombing Afghan villages and homes but in the sanctuaries beyond Afghanistan.
> I welcome today's clarity in President Trump's remarks.

Pakistan's damage control efforts did manage to dredge up some support from iron brother China: 'Pakistan has made...(an) outstanding contribution to the global cause of counter terrorism. The international community should acknowledge that,' said Chinese foreign ministry spokesman Geng Shuang, hinting that, unlike for the US, Pakistan was an 'all weather partner' for China.[5]

For Pakistan, this was yet again proof of the capriciousness of the US as a partner and, worse, its increasing tendency to 'speak India's language'. Foreign Secretary Janjua was even quoted as wondering what Trump was doing tweeting at 4 a.m. Soon, a conspiracy theory gained currency that the tweet was engineered by Pakistan's former envoy to Washington, Hussain Haqqani, a known hawk on the relationship, advocating greater accountability from the Pakistan Army.

In India, the celebration of this US epiphany was tempered with the realization that the anger was directed against Pakistan's proxy battles against US interests in Afghanistan, not India's interests in Kashmir.

WORDS MATTER

Within weeks of my arrival, I received an invitation to the Karachi Litfest, held every February, from Ameena Saiyid, a prominent civil society and literary activist. I accepted gladly. It would give me an early opportunity to see the fabled Sindhi city. Another attraction was the clutch of Indian writers who were going to converge on Karachi; they were mostly vetted by the powers that be and expected to be friendly, or at the minimum, not critical of their hosts. The organizers had risked censure from the establishment in inviting me to address the opening session. I was expected not to abuse the hospitality. The aim was also to set the tone of my outreach to civil society over the next months. I debated between touching on only safely literary matters, or dipping into more troubled aspects of the political relationship. I eventually spoke of both—our common love for literature and our common hopes of the future.

Our engagement has never been easy. Recent times have been troubled for the India–Pakistan relationship, but I do believe that we can imagine a future substantially different from the past. Writing and literature can shine the light, free thinkers often show us the way when politics becomes complex and unmanageable. We hope to see the relationship between our countries improve, we hope that we can help create an atmosphere free of violence and terror, in which we could approach each other and have a calm conversation. We could continue in mistrust and suspicion or imagine an alternate universe. We could take the high road to peace, to fight our common enemies, which are poverty, illiteracy and disease, and certainly not each other. As our democracies strengthen, we see similar aspirations in our young, with two in three Indians and Pakistanis under thirty-five. The instincts of our elected leaders are also similar: to promote peace and development, without the distractions of conflict and violence. I do hope we move to such a future.

The brief remarks got two effusive rounds of ovation. This puzzled me. This was hardly a path-breaking vision. Leaders had referred it to in the past, it echoed Vajpayee's offer to Musharraf, to take the high road to peace. It was what PM Modi had written in his first letter to PM Sharif. It was perhaps the kind of thing a diplomat would say when starting a tenure in difficult terrain. But that evening in *Dawn*, this remark became the first of top ten quotes for the festival. A distinguished older man came up to me later and said, 'Aap dushman desh se hain, phir bhi aapko sabse zyada taaliyan mili (You represent the enemy, yet you got the most applause.)' A former Pakistani civil servant asked me with some sarcasm if there was a change in government in India—was I representing some new one?

The episode told me two things: one, the default expectation in 2017 was of hostility or at least lack of warmth from India—any new diplomat speaking for the BJP-led government was expected to be aggressive, if not hostile. And two, anything positive that I would publicly say in Pakistan would only come as a welcome surprise to audiences, given the state of play of the relationship.

It was an early lesson.

I had my public diplomacy brief from the top. In a conversation that I had before my departure, with Prime Minister Modi, I had asked him what his message would be to the people of Pakistan. He unhesitatingly said that I should convey clearly that India had always stood for peace and expected the same in return.

Building on peace with the peace constituencies, such that they were, became an important part of our diplomatic outreach in Pakistan. It was important to balance the message of a tough posture coming from political and military quarters with a diplomatic position that India would be open for dialogue, should certain basic conditions be met.

DIPLOMATIC HARASSMENT

On the evening of 15 February 2018, three black sedans screeched to a halt just across from the new high commission residential complex of India in the diplomatic quarter of Islamabad. A dozen men got out of the car and walked into the diplomatic property that was under construction, lightly guarded by a hired Pakistani agency. The leader of the group, who emerged from a black vehicle with darkened windows, walked to the edge of the Indian property and directed the local service providers to get out. He then ordered out the contractor's men at the Indian high commission across the street and said that he wanted to see no Pakistani employees working there. He announced dramatically that some Pashtuns were being hidden in the Indian high commission campus. This was the time the nascent Pakhtun Tahaffuz Movement (PTM) was gaining ground in Pakistan. Both the PTM and India could at once be discredited if some Pashtuns could be planted and then 'discovered' on the Indian premises. I got a report on this incident in the night just as I heading out to host a visiting Indian delegation in the Margalla Hills. [6]

I asked to see Pakistan's foreign secretary the next morning and made a strong démarche to her about this unacceptable invasion into India's diplomatic property, and harassment of our service providers. We were concerned, I said, that the move was a gambit to shut down the Indian high commission. It would invite retaliation in India and we would needlessly aggravate an already troubled relationship. The foreign secretary was puzzled by the development and said that she would try to correct the situation. Her surprise was not feigned, we thought; the ISI would not have informed the foreign office of its little adventure.

The threat of 'assured retaliation' seemed to have some effect as the number of incidents started to taper off.[7] The problem here had always remained the fundamental asymmetry in the operations of diplomatic entities, since Pakistan's agencies treated diplomacy as an extension of some kind of proxy war. They felt they should launch small tactical operations against the Indian diplomatic representation rather than allow diplomats to do what they were supposed to do—meet people and have conversations. The oldest trick in the game known to the ISI is the classic honey trap, which they tried to set up in abundant measure against staffers of the Indian high commission. A handful of staff needed to be sent back after they were aggressively pursued.

Another asymmetry was in play: Indian diplomats were having to deal with ruffians—goons of intelligence agencies—while attempting diplomacy. The situation for Pakistan's diplomats in India was more comfortable. Over the years, as we saw, Pakistan had become known to be a difficult station for Indian diplomats given the intrusive surveillance, and the aggressive interrogation of guests who dared to walk into the homes of Indian officials.

The stories of Indian diplomats being harassed in Pakistan were legion, not matched by the stories of the treatment being meted out to Pakistani diplomats in Delhi. Successive generations of Indian diplomats posted in Pakistan had such tales to tell. For instance, in 1999, at the height of the Kargil conflict, High Commissioner Parthasarathy and his wife went through a 'harrowing experience' of consoling the sobbing wife of an Indian official after her husband had been dragged out of his house and kidnapped by 'ISI goons'. Partha recalled that a young colleague of his in Islamabad observed after the incident that it was strange that while Pakistani diplomats in Delhi were 'feted and hosted', their Indian counterparts in Islamabad were 'booted and roasted'.[8]

While, for years together, there has been talk of Pakistan's agencies acting much more brutally than their Indian counterparts, what now helped temper the behaviour of Pakistan's agencies was the 'assurance' of reciprocal action. This marked a shift in India's posture. When High Commissioner Satish Chandra had, in the 1990s, gingerly suggested reciprocity to Prime Minister Narasimha Rao, the PM had shot down the idea on the grounds that India could not stoop to that level.[9]

We felt this situation had to change. The stakeholder most critical to a satisfactory resolution of this situation would be my counterpart in New Delhi. When I discovered in March 2018 that the Pakistani high commissioner to India, Sohail Mahmood, was in Islamabad on a visit, I requested a meeting with Foreign Secretary Tehmina Janjua and High Commissioner Mahmood, so that we could jointly discuss the futility of these actions by intelligence agencies. It was bad diplomacy, I suggested, if diplomats themselves became the story. I pointed out in these meetings that we only needed to reiterate that we would abide by the Vienna Convention. Mahmood dug out the 1993 agreement on treatment of diplomats, which had become necessary after a particularly nasty round of violence against diplomats in the early 1990s. If we expressed adherence to these documents, we would probably be much better off. Mahmood pushed for a deal, equally worried about the path we were taking.

At the best of times, an Indian diplomat is never lonely in Pakistan. You are followed everywhere. You are watched closely. Your pictures are clicked with cellphones by swarms of men in salwar–kameez. You could be harassed in multiple ways; among other things, cellphone cameras could come within inches of your face at public events.

Yet, Indian diplomats had over the years also made many close friends. Pakistan touches Indian diplomats in a variety of ways—you could become a peacenik, you could become a hawk, but you're seldom left in the middle.

Very few preserve their neutrality. A retired Pakistani foreign secretary told me that on the Track II circuit, several former hawks, freed of their talking points, became doves fluttering for peace.

Curiously, the Indians were not the only diplomats targeted for special treatment in Pakistan. The US ambassador in Islamabad told me that he was having a similar set of issues with Pakistan, though it did not descend into physical harassment. The US had decided to cut reciprocal access to travel for Pakistani diplomats, who were now in a bizarre situation where they could not travel beyond the boundaries of Washington DC without permission. This was mirroring the position of US diplomats who could not travel out of Islamabad. Similarly, Pakistani diplomats in Delhi needed permission to visit the twin towns of Noida and Gurugram from Delhi.

The harassment drama was being played out in March 2018 amidst screaming headlines whipping up sentiment in both countries. We were attempting quiet diplomacy to negotiate an end to the harassment. We were discussing also construction projects to expand high commission operations in both countries. The attempt was to work out a deal to ease the harassment of diplomats and encourage projects, or at least not obstruct them. Despite the larger tensions in ties, we had soon hammered out an understanding. After months, we had a document that said 'India and Pakistan' and 'agreed' in the same sentence. 'India and Pakistan have mutually agreed to resolve matters related to the treatment of diplomats and diplomatic premises, in line with the 1992 'Code of Conduct for the treatment of diplomatic/consular personnel in India and Pakistan,' the MEA statement said on 31 March 2018.

A similar one was issued by the Pakistan foreign office the same day. The code provided for the 'smooth and unhindered functioning' of diplomats. The code also asked the two countries not to resort to 'intrusive and aggressive surveillance' and actions such as 'verbal and physical harassment', or disconnection of phone lines. India had shot off sixteen diplomatic notes to Pakistan since February listing instances of 'harassment and 'intimidation'. On its part, the Pakistan high commission in Delhi had claimed twenty-six instances of intimidation of its diplomats since 7 March. The diplomacy had worked to calm things down. For the moment.

The high commission's residential complex, where the trouble had started, was being prepared to be inaugurated during a possible high-level visit from India. We had been goading the contractors to work on it to meet repeatedly broken deadlines. The land had been acquired as early as in 1962, the foundation stone laid by PM Vajpayee during his 2004 visit, but the project execution had started only in 2009. It was to be completed in 2012, but was only half ready in 2018. On 2 April, I hurriedly inaugurated the complex myself, to underline the point that it was part of the diplomatic premises of India as much as the Pakistan high commission was in New Delhi. We soon had it going. Eventually, all of India's staff moved into the complex, giving them a higher level of protection within Islamabad's diplomatic security zone.

The harassment truce was no guarantee sporadic incidents would not recur; the restrictions to diplomatic activity remained unrelenting, particularly in my meetings with sensitive groups. On 14 April, we went to the holy Panja Sahib gurdwara to greet 1,700 Sikh pilgrims who had come for their annual pilgrimage, covered under the 1974 bilateral agreement. Halfway to the destination, I was asked to turn back, because of a 'charged atmosphere' among the 2,500 Sikhs gathered there, due to some objectionable scenes in a movie, *Nanak Shah Fakir*, that had been released in India.[10] I decided to test my boundaries and tried again on 22 June. Despite obtaining permission from the Pakistani foreign office, I was turned back again.[11] The reason given was that some overseas Sikhs, mainly from Canada, were objecting to any Indian government presence, so my security could not be guaranteed. This was not entirely convincing, since the overseas visitors from the UK and Canada were known to be under the sway of the ISI. On another occasion, I was blocked when I tried to visit the Bohra community in Karachi, again on grounds of ensuring my security. It was not easy getting out of Islamabad's diplomatic bubble.

Moreover, guests coming to the homes of Indian diplomats in Pakistan were still being aggressively questioned about their visits and on details of discussions in the diplomatic gatherings. A Pakistani minister I had once invited home was abused when he refused to give his visiting card to the ISI surveillance team. A well-connected guest leaving my residence once screamed at the minders to do something better with their lives; he got a call from a higher up in the agency the next day, asking him to let the boys do their job. Despite all this, the situation had improved after the two countries had decided that the harassment of diplomats needed to be toned down.

THE BAJWA DOCTRINE
In early 2018, a 'Bajwa doctrine' was unveiled, designed to reveal the worldview of Pakistan's most powerful man. It was based on some articles released by the army's PR machine, the Inter Services Public Relations (ISPR), reinforced by Bajwa's off the record interaction with a number of senior journalists.

This was par for the course. Several Pakistani army chiefs in the past had aired branded doctrines publicly within a couple of years of starting their innings, as much strategic communication for the general public as a message to the civilians on who was in charge of policy. History told us that in every army chief's tenure, there comes a decisive moment when, after consolidating power, he tries to leave a legacy. This turning point sometimes came in the shape of a coup (Musharraf, Ayub, Zia). Or a major speech or policy statement outlining some kind of vision (Kayani, Raheel Sharif, Bajwa). Often, the ISPR would frame a 'doctrine' to define an army chief's imprint.

For Bajwa's coming out party, he was presented by the ISPR to Pakistani media anchors for a background briefing. It turned out to be an informal, wide-ranging chat. The ISPR tried to position this doctrine as one focused on security, speaking of clearing Pakistan of terrorists and expressing concern about the relationship with the US in the wake of Trump's rude tweet about Pakistan's lies and deceit. Bajwa also disseminated his message through friendly media articles that attempted to paint a picture of a soldier with novel, progressive views, a visionary expounding on issues like terrorism, international affairs, (particularly Afghanistan, India, and the US), even financial management and democracy. The key elements of the doctrine related to issues of governance and the Pakistan army's support to the democracy project. At the same time, Bajwa expressed opposition to the eighteenth constitutional amendment's[12] devolution of power to the states, comparing it to the devolution demanded by East Pakistan, which broke up the country in 1971.

Some friendly sections of the media profiled Bajwa flatteringly, even comparing him to a Roman emperor. This was especially true of one version, suspected to have been planted by the ISPR with the liberal Jang media group's veteran and maverick writer Suhail Warraich. Bajwa, the narrative went, was a cut above his two predecessors: he was not 'unpredictable and deep thinking' like the 'philosophical' Kayani, nor 'stiff necked and robotic' like the 'showman' Raheel Sharif. He was more a pragmatist—a model soldier, a patient and rational thinker 'like Musharraf'.[13]

The doctrine quite randomly predicted a rapprochement with India in three years, since there could be no war between 'two neighbouring nuclear countries' and because the 'extremist Modi regime' within two to three years 'due to its growing economy' would realize the need for a peace dialogue with Pakistan. It also spoke of peace with Afghanistan. The strategy to counter terror included an element of 'mainstreaming' of terrorists and radicals (even inviting them to fight elections), giving a glimmer of hope that Pakistan would be willing to tackle the groups the ISI had created for proxy terror against India. In that sense, it took forward the Kayani doctrine of strengthening the fight against terrorism, rejecting 'the old idea of distinguishing between good or bad Taliban' and adding that militant groups needed to be 'de-weaponised and mainstreamed' like in Ireland. But the groups in Pakistan were expected to be deweaponized with no credible effort to have them first deradicalized. I did share my concern with some Western diplomats discussing these issues with Bajwa—the mainstreaming of the radicals could lead to radicalizing the mainstream.

Dawn was not wholly impressed by Bajwa's briefing and gently chided the army for overstepping its boundaries pointing out that 'economic policy, centre-province relations and governance matters...are civilian domains'; howsoever desirable, improvements in these 'must flow through constitutional channels.'[14] The Bajwa doctrine faced another criticism from within Pakistan—it was not tough enough on the Kashmir cause.

What the doctrine left unsaid was Bajwa's (and, by extension, the Pakistani army's) belief in political engineering with the hybrid government project, that involved ejecting the elected PM, Nawaz Sharif, in 2017 and bringing in the 'selected' Imran Khan in 2018. The doctrine would add more elements as Bajwa would grow on the job—like a stronger posture against domestic terrorism, a professed political neutrality, and a longer tenure for Bajwa to rule Pakistan.

CONNECTING WITH THE ARMY
After the doctrine was aired, almost on cue, the military invited me along with some of my colleagues, including the deputy high commissioner, J. P. Singh, and the defence attachés, to the Pakistan Day parade on 23 March. This was a courtesy extended to India after several years. Yaum-e-Pakistan, or Pakistan Resolution Day, was a national holiday in Pakistan, commemorating the Lahore Resolution passed on 23 March 1940 (with the Muslim League's call for the creation of separate Muslim homelands as 'independent states' in India) but also celebrating the first short-lived Constitution of 1956, which technically graduated Pakistan from dominion to republic.

On a blazing hot day in Islamabad, we attended the army's Pakistan Day parade, gazing at the marching contingents. We found our faces, squinting in the sun, in every Pakistani newspaper and channel the next morning. The invitation was variously interpreted as a peace gesture and a warning to India, depending on the editorial inclination of the publication. I was amused to find myself the subject of a lengthy and angry enquiry by an Indian TV channel, wondering why we would not boycott a Pakistani parade. That diplomats in both countries routinely attended National Day parades and functions was not an argument the channel was willing to countenance. While we were happy to play along with Pakistan's invites, the bottom line for India was interpreting the situation on the ground, rather than the gestures.

It was clear to us in the summer of 2018 that the army was not keen to take direct control of power, despite having removed Nawaz Sharif from the scene. It was apparent that there was something deeper afoot for the upcoming federal elections. The army was now building Imran Khan and creating conditions for his victory. It had the makings of a 'non-coup coup', with the army prepping a 'hybrid' regime, where it would not only not take over the reins of power, it would not need to.

We decided to initiate conversations with the army to sensitize them to India's concerns on violence and terrorism. The communication needed to be away from any spotlight. I had no mandate to meet Bajwa, even if he were willing to meet me. But I could be creative and communicate with Pakistan's most powerful man through people close to him.

We made it clear to the army that India no longer had the patience for words and the 'no talks with terror policy' was a fact. The position could change if Pakistan could show some sincerity in tackling terrorism against India. One basic metric of this would be a fall in the verifiable cross-border infiltration numbers. Another test would be whether Pakistan could hand over those responsible for past terrorist attacks on India. This process could begin with the twenty-six Indian citizens we knew were being given safe haven by Pakistan.

Bajwa conveyed Pakistan's sincere desire to end terrorism, but signalled in mid-2018 that we would continue this conversation once the new government was in place in Islamabad. This demonstrated confidence that the government put in place would be on the 'same page' as the army. However, it was Pakistan's assessment that India would find it hard to have any conversation until the election of a new government in India in May 2019. The window, the army was guessing in 2018, would only open in the second half of 2019, after Indian elections, when the political rhetoric would have dampened.

In retrospect, while the Pakistan Army was making a reasonably smart assessment, it was in 2018 not factoring in a few black swan events that would change the shape of the next year—the Pulwama terrorist attack, the Balakot response, and the Article 370 decision by India. It would appear that Bajwa modestly spoke of a window of opportunity between Indian elections until his date of retirement in November 2019, in which he would work for a lasting peace.

THE BLEEDING BORDER

The guns at the LoC in Jammu and Kashmir had rarely fallen silent since the relationship dipped in 2016. But as the holy month of Ramzan began on 16 May 2018, both armies announced they had agreed on a ceasefire. The most plausible explanation of the motive for a quiet border was the Pakistan army's preoccupation with its western border and with domestic elections; the two DGMOs spoke on that day and issued simultaneous statements announcing the start of a ceasefire at the LoC. This was followed by a more sustained one announced on 29 May. This was a border truce after a long gap and the question was whether it would hold. Both countries celebrated this minor outbreak of peace; analysts debated if it would lead to some bigger breakthroughs as Pakistan awaited the election of 2018 and India prepared for those of 2019.

The May ceasefire was accompanied by some other positives—a team of Indian journalists got visas to visit Pakistan. An Indian counter-terrorism team showed up in Pakistan for an SCO Regional Anti-Terrorist Structure (RATS) meet; it was not lost on observers that India and Pakistan were discussing jointly countering terrorism, albeit under a regional plurilateral structure. A Track II Neemrana dialogue group in Islamabad had been followed by a Pakistani Coast Guard team visit to India. The bilateral and multilateral security mechanisms seemed to be gingerly engaging, as Pakistan moved to an interim caretaker arrangement in preparation for elections in July. The *Indian Express* front-paged my interview mentioning signs of positivity.[15] The paper was also linking India's internal truce in Kashmir with the external ceasefire.

The optimism had to be laced with caution. Several ceasefire announcements had taken place in the past, only to be observed in the breach. Both countries were still technically committed to the 2003 ceasefire, which had been repeatedly violated after holding in the initial years.

A few days before Eid on 14 June, I received a call at 2 a.m. from my political interlocutor with the Pakistan Army. Pakistan was seeing some worrying activity, he told me sombrely, on the Indian side of the LoC, and was concerned that India was planning some misadventure in Pakistani territory. Using this channel for operational military issues was not the norm; such issues would normally be discussed at the level of the military through the hotlines of the DGMOs. It was unusual for the Pakistan Army to be raising this matter at the diplomatic level directly with the Indian high commissioner. When I asked the caller if the military had used their standard channels, he told me that he had a specific request from the ISI chief to raise this matter at my level, given the seriousness of the situation. I assured him that India had no plans or reasons to attack Pakistan that morning, but would nevertheless check. I woke up my colleague and defence attaché, Brigadier Sanjay Vishwas Rao, a veteran of Kashmir operations, who circled back after checking with military teams in Delhi that Pakistani observers may have been spooked by some standard movements. I called back my interlocutor, up for his sehri meal before the Ramzan fast began, and asked him to advise his friends in the ISI to relax and catch up on sleep.

The peacetime dynamics of India's engagement with Pakistan at the LoC (which accounts for almost a fourth—776 kilometres—of the 3,323-kilometre-long land border) had always been peculiar. A low-grade war that played out at the LoC, almost through my entire tenure, was propelled by its own internal logic, not fully controlled by the political leadership. LoC actions had been delegated to the military, very deliberately in India, to deal with the issue of terrorism and automatically in Pakistan, where the army was the final arbiter even of the political and strategic implications of actions at the border.[16]

Indian academic and commentator Happymon Jacob argued that the militaries on both sides violated the 2003 ceasefire agreement because of 'auxiliary factors', beyond foreign and security policy. These stemmed from a subjective interpretation by the two armies of each other's behaviour and for the desire for a 'perfect symmetry of firing'. Jacob based his conclusions on research, interviews, and crunching data on ceasefire violations since 2003.[17] What had changed by 2018 was that India's behaviour was now less predictable. What used to be a 'comfort posting' for the Pakistan Army on the eastern front, only meant to drive in irregulars and proxy warriors into India, became a sleepless one where the Pakistan military needed to be alert to firing from the Indian side. This was no longer a rest and recreation posting for the Pakistani military.[18] India's army chief, General Bipin Rawat, told me that this paradigm shift was causing Pakistan to pay a lot of attention to the LoC.

A peculiar public dynamic accompanied casualties on the border. Pakistan normally called the Indian deputy high commissioner or any available diplomat and handed over a public protest note for any civilian death. But killings of military personnel at the border were seldom acknowledged, even during conflicts, because this diluted the impression of the strength of the Pakistan Army and the notion of victory during conflict.

A CHANGING KASHMIR

It was special to visit Kashmir from Pakistan. I went up to the valley in June 2018, when, after a conference of heads of missions, I chose, for an official refresher visit, Kashmir, the land of my birth, rather than Uttar Pradesh, the land of my ancestors. Governor's Rule had just been imposed in the state and a group of us heads of mission had the opportunity to have extensive interactions with the state's civil and military leadership. These convinced us that Kashmir could be healed if it went a few years in absence of terrorist violence. The extent of radicalization instigated by outfits from across the border had been disturbing; as we have seen, the summer of 2016, also known as the 'Burhan Wani summer' (after one of the young social media-savvy, Kalashnikov-wielding militants), had been particularly rough and violent. Security forces had followed an approach to deal firmly with the violence, and then rapidly moved to the healing stage. The mood on the ground seemed sullen, but there were many voices arguing that violence needed to be stopped, before we could move to a new chapter in the history of Kashmir.

HUMANITARIAN DIPLOMACY

In the summer of 2018, I got a call from Manvinder Singh, the member of parliament from Barmer, a border desert district in Rajasthan. He told me that a poor family from Rajasthan had crossed to Pakistan for a wedding, where Reshma, an elder of the family, had passed away on a Sunday. The family wanted to return to India with the body via the same border crossing but the weekly train was not due till Friday, five long days away. There was no way to keep the body refrigerated. Travel for the whole day north to Punjab and to the Attari–Wagah border was not feasible, because the ambulance was not refrigerated. The request was a desperate one. Could the Munnabao border be opened to allow this body to be brought into India by road over the rail-only crossing on a priority basis? This seemed a tall order in the best of times, but particularly hard given the overall climate of the relationship. Nevertheless, we decided as an experiment to test the system.

The Thar Link Express weekly service had started in 2006, connecting Karachi and Khokrapar (Pakistan's Sindh) to a Zero Point border station, and then to Munnabao (Rajasthan's Barmer) and Jodhpur, a distance of 381 kilometres, covered in seven hours. It had been a welcome new connection between the people of the region and had worked well for years. (It would eventually be cancelled by Pakistan on 9 August 2019.) We wrote to the foreign office and also connected with some NGOs on both sides to see if they could assist with the request to move the body. We needed to get the customs and immigration folks, who came only once a week, to reach the border points for this transaction to take place smoothly. As if by a miracle, the humanitarian dimension of this poor family's drama triggered the right emotions in all the right quarters and the crossing was opened for a day on a Tuesday for the family to pass.

This episode told us that there was enough latent goodwill in the relationship to help out each other's citizens caught on the wrong side of the border. We continued to focus on citizens in distress. Visas for medical cases became a case in point. We issued these liberally after verifying details by calling up the doctors and checking the status of each case. Each medical visa produced enormous goodwill for India.

Most importantly, when the rest of the relationship was paused, we decided to build trust by continuing with the humanitarian agenda. External Affairs Minister Sushma Swaraj, with her instincts for a people-centric approach to neighbourhood diplomacy, asked me to work on the issues of prisoners. We identified three categories of the most vulnerable among the imprisoned—people with mental health problems, seniors, and women. We discovered a corresponding appetite for extending humanitarian assistance to Pakistani prisoners in Indian jails. This process clipped along even during difficult times.

Another category of humanitarian cases was that of imprisoned Indian fishermen who ended up in Pakistani waters and Pakistani custody. These poor fisherfolk defied the maritime border in their pursuit of the lal pari or red snapper. They would be housed in Karachi jails and it would usually take about six months to identify them, verify their nationality, and have them returned to India.

Many such humanitarian rescue acts caught the popular imagination when they made it to the media, particularly when cross-border love was at play. In May 2017, an Indian citizen, Uzma Ahmad, had knocked on the gates of the Indian high commission in Islamabad, pleading for help, since she had been abducted by a Pakistani citizen, Tahir Ali, whom she had met in Malaysia. She had travelled to his home in the Taliban-infested badlands of Buner district in KP, only to discover that Ali was already married with four children from a previous marriage. She was drugged, married at gunpoint, and sexually assaulted, but managed to talk her way to the high commission, where she got refuge. EAM Sushma Swaraj took personal charge of the case and Deputy HC J. P. Singh delivered her to India after a brief legal battle and a midnight run to the Wagah–Attari border.

In late 2018, some NGOs activated journalists on both sides to ask for the release of a young and very sick Indian prisoner in Karachi, who had wandered to the other side some months ago. Veteran Pakistani journalist Hamid Mir raised the profile of the case as he posed this case as a question to Pakistan's foreign minister Shah Mahmood Qureshi, saying he hoped the boy would be released. He eventually was.

On another occasion, I received a report that a married Punjabi Hindu woman from a well-connected family in India had eloped or had been kidnapped and taken to Pakistan. The family of this woman insisted that she was being held hostage by a Pakistani citizen, who had even got her a visa. We had this informally investigated through Pakistani agencies and discovered that the explanation was less complicated; the woman went of her own volition after falling in love with the Pakistani man whom she had met on social media. The challenge was to break this assessment to the family.

Blind love also drove Hamid Ansari, the software engineer from Mumbai who decided to make an entry from Afghanistan into Peshawar to meet his online flame. He was promptly nabbed and labelled a terrorist. His mother raised the alarm and after much lobbying, he was released from jail after six long years, only when it was clear to Pakistani agencies that he was only courting trouble for himself, not wreaking destruction on the Pakistani state.

32

NAYA PAKISTAN, OLD TRICKS

By July, 'Project Imran' seemed unstoppable. It was clear that Imran Khan was the army's chosen one for the elections scheduled on 25 July 2018. The stories of 'pre-election engineering' by the military establishment made this quite clear. Army chief Bajwa was firmly supporting the project that had picked up steam from 2008, under the army chiefs who succeeded Musharraf—General Kayani (and particularly his DGs of the ISI, Lieutenant General Ahmed Shuja Pasha and Lieutenant General Zaheer ul Islam), and Bajwa's predecessor, General Raheel Sharif.

One impediment to this project had been the prime minister elected in 2013, Nawaz Sharif, who had now been neatly unseated. To seal matters, Sharif was barred from politics when he was sentenced to ten years in prison in July (for owning unaccounted properties in London) and arrested, along with daughter Maryam and son-in-law, Safdar Awan.

Imran Khan's ride to power was far from smooth; he gained in popularity through mammoth election rallies resounding with populist rhetoric about tabdeeli—change—and creating a 'naya Pakistan'. But he seemed embattled as his adversaries ran a bruising smear campaign against him in the election year. Ugly details emerged of his personal life, as a London-based ex-wife, Reham Khan, joined the campaign, with a tell-all book presenting salacious details of his love for sex and cocaine; the text was gleefully circulated by Pakistan's elites in WhatsApp chat groups, with the juiciest portions helpfully highlighted in yellow. Islamabad's rumour mills also buzzed with gossip about Imran Khan's third wife, the fully veiled, burqa-clad Bushra Bibi, also known as Pinki Pirni, a Sufi spiritual preacher and faith healer from south Punjab. Khan, it was alleged, had married the pirni early in 2018, because of her prediction that their betrothal would win him the prime minister's job. The pirni and her djinns were believed to be furiously at work against Khan's enemies, and even some former associates with bad energy, to pave the way for his political success.

As we watched the drama at the high commission, we were able to confidently assess that Imran Khan was a frontrunner in Pakistan's power play, even though the 'minus Nawaz' PML-N was fighting hard. On election night, the electronic transmission system inexplicably collapsed, allowing for some onsite ballot box stuffing. The PTI captured the most seats in the National Assembly but fell short of a majority. The party subsequently formed a coalition government with several smaller parties and independents propelled by mysterious forces to join the government.

The verdict was fractured in the provinces: the PTI remained dominant in Khyber Pakhtunkhwa; the PPP-retained Sindh, and the military establishment-backed Balochistan Awami Party (BAP) emerged as the largest in Balochistan. In Punjab, the result was a hung parliament with the PML-N reaffirming its traditional dominance; but several independent MPs joined the PTI, gifting it the government. Naya Pakistan now had a PTI-led coalition at the centre, along with governments in three of the four major provinces.

THE HYBRID REGIME

When the coalition's numbers seemed assured, one of the first global leaders to call Imran Khan was Narendra Modi. India's leader congratulated Khan on 30 July on his PTI emerging as the largest political party in the 25 July polls. He also expressed the hope that 'democracy will take deeper roots' in Pakistan and spoke of a 'vision of peace and development in the entire neighbourhood'[1]. Khan spoke of his own desire to improve ties.

The call was my cue to renew my efforts to meet with Pakistan's PM-designate. The meeting had technically been in the works for a while. We had been in touch with Imran Khan's team for several months, but had not pursued the request in election season. I did meet Khan at an annual iftar he hosted in June as a fund collection drive for his cancer hospital and found myself seated next to him thanks to a common friend. But that had been an occasion for pleasantries and a chat on cricket, not any substantive discussion on political ties. He did tell me then that he thought Virat Kohli, the Indian cricket captain, was an even greater player than Sachin Tendulkar, because Kohli was helping India win matches against greater odds.

I had been in touch with the BCCI and had procured cricket bats signed by the Indian cricket team led by Virat Kohli, which I hoped to present to some cricket lovers in Pakistan. I had been intending to present one of these bats to Imran Khan earlier in the year, but the vicissitudes of the bilateral relationship and the election schedule did not allow us to meet. Post-elections, despite the conversation with India's PM, we were not sure if Khan and his team would like the optics of meeting early with the Indian high commissioner. (He had already met some Western and West Asian envoys.)

A rumour soon circulated in Islamabad that Khan was planning to 'do a Modi' and invite all South Asian leaders for his inauguration, including Prime Minister Modi. However, the fact that he led a coalition government meant that there was not enough time between proving his parliamentary majority and the swearing-in, to mount a SAARC 'festival' or even a neighbourhood mela with his South Asian peers in attendance.

My meeting with Khan came through suddenly, after we connected with a key associate of his, Naeemul Haq. Khan's friends were in a euphoric mood; it was the season to believe in Khan as the man with the Midas touch. The loyalist coterie was arguing that the breath of fresh air that Khan had brought to cricket and to the Shaukat Khanum hospitals (charitable multi-speciality hospitals driven by Khan, named after his late mother) would now have a magical impact on the governance of Pakistan.

On 10 August, I called on Imran Khan at his scenic Bani Gala residence on top of an Islamabad hillock. He was by then sure to be sworn in PM, and had begun meeting diplomats. Deputy HC J. P. Singh and I walked into a beehive of activity, prepared to be bundled out after a brief courtesy meeting. We were surprised to find Khan accompanied by the entire top PTI leadership, including Shah Mahmood Qureshi and Shirin Mazhari, both expected to find ministerial berths. This presented me an opportunity to have a substantive, even if brief, conversation on bilateral ties with Khan and his advisers; I wanted to sensitize the team to India's concerns at a time when they may not have thought through their India policy too carefully.

When I congratulated Khan on his victory, he disarmingly—and, as it turned out, presciently—said that he wished his party had got 20 more seats in parliament for a more decisive mandate. India, he added, had learnt the art of running coalitions and perhaps a complex country like India needed such coalitions, but Pakistan needed stronger governments at this stage. He expressed some unhappiness at the way the Indian media had portrayed him and his victory. (He was clearly referring to some stories, particularly on electronic media, describing him as a fundamentalist 'Taliban Khan'.) I reassured him that several of his friends had also taken to public fora in India to defend his leadership qualities and the narrative was not all negative.

Khan said he was particularly disappointed that he was being called an army puppet. He said he was perhaps the only democrat in Pakistan's history and wished to bring genuine democracy to Pakistan. The only exception was possibly Zulfikar Ali Bhutto, but he too had served as a minister under Ayub's military dictatorship. He argued that it was ironic that Nawaz Sharif was being characterized as a democrat since Sharif had been 'manufactured in Rawalpindi'. He would later repeat this narrative in public and, in his delusional way, probably believed it.

Khan said that he had multiple friends in India and was keen that we normalized our relationship. He felt that in the past, several Pakistani diplomats he worked closely with [former FM Khurshid Mahmud Kasuri was known to be an early supporter of Khan] had told him that we were close to a solution on the Kashmir issue. He said the dialogue should continue in a sustained way and not be interrupted, no matter what happened.

I pointed out that it was hard to continue a dialogue when we had to deal with terror attacks like the one in Mumbai. He nodded, 'that's true', and looked towards future foreign minister Qureshi, pointing out that Qureshi had been in India on the day of the Mumbai attacks, even though, he added with a grin, he could not be blamed for having caused them. I offered that if only we could stamp out cross-border infiltration and terrorism, we could normalize our relationship and take it forward. Shirin Mazhari, a known India hawk on social media, interrupted the conversation at this stage to say that Pakistan had its own problems about India's attacks in places like Balochistan. Khan, in turn, interrupted her and went on to say that it was important to work on each other's problems. Pakistan, he added, had issues with India's military presence in Kashmir. He argued that the presence of the military in urban settings alienated people and was bound to lead to violence. He had seen it in the province of Khyber Pakhtunkhwa, where the PTM movement had been born of the popular grievances against the Pakistan army's presence. This was a bold statement to an Indian diplomat, coming from someone who was to be Pakistan's next prime minister.

We talked cricket in the end and I presented him with an autographed cricket bat. That became the viral image of the meeting and the signal of some kind of rapprochement. Most seasoned observers were however cynical, because bilateral relations had been littered through history with positive gestures that did not necessarily translate into better ties. A new prime minister and a new elected government had always led to some hope of new beginnings. This was particularly true of Imran Khan's government, because it was famously on the same page as the army and was presumably going to make moves on India in consultation with the army, as against the two previous governments, which had seen their friendly overtures towards India vetoed by the army.

Khan's friends and supporters seemed desperate to believe in his superhuman qualities. They said that Khan carried no baggage of corruption and was only driven by good intentions to help Pakistanis; he was determined to make peace with the country's neighbours in order to achieve these objectives. The naive belief that Khan's goodness would change the reality of Pakistan's governance was often touching and even infectious. His supporters argued that the two dynasties, the Sharifs and Bhuttos that had looted Pakistan for decades were finally defeated and a viable alternative had emerged for the Pakistani people. Some commentators were privately arguing that while Khan was getting a leg up from the establishment, he would soon become his own person and would do what was good for Pakistan rather than what was good for Pakistan's army. Reinforcing this view, some army officers were arguing that Khan was too temperamental to be controlled by the army for long and might become dangerously destabilizing if he went rogue. These Cassandras would be proven right four years later.

Soon after he was sworn in, Imran Khan invited his primary mentor, army chief Bajwa, over for dinner at his residence. It was just the four of them: Khan and his wife, Bushra Bibi; and Bajwa with his wife, Ayesha. The fully veiled first lady ate nothing at the dining table, even when the general politely asked her to have something. In keeping with the traditional cultural practice, the two men sat in the living room for a post-dinner chat, while Ayesha Bajwa was led away to the women's quarters for an exclusive meal with Mrs Khan. On the way back in the car, Ayesha seemed shaken. She said to her husband in Urdu that he should save his prime minister if he still could. She refused, he said later, to explain herself.[2]

A CORRIDOR OF FAITH

Imran Khan was sworn in as PM on 18 August 2018, on that day a story hit the headlines in India that Pakistan had agreed to a long-standing request from India to open a special corridor for Sikh pilgrims by 2019. It was also the day another story from Islamabad grabbed eyeballs— of an embrace between Army Chief Qamar Bajwa and Punjab MLA Navjot Singh Sidhu. In the presidential palace Awan-e-Sadr, where Khan was sworn in, two of his buddies were present to applaud the event: his roommate in Oxford, Vikram Mehta, and his fellow cricket commentator, Navjot Singh Sidhu. Two other cricketing mates—Sunil Gavaskar and Kapil Dev—were also invited but could not make it that day.

An air of hope hung in the hall that morning, with PTI supporters suggesting that Khan would rescue Pakistan from its multiple crises and take it to a happier place. I could not speak at length to Sidhu at the ceremony, since his Pakistani minders were close by and he was in any case surrounded by selfie-seekers.

I invited Sidhu and Mehta to drop in at the high commission for a chat that morning. They came in directly from a meeting Khan had with his former Pakistani cricket team-mates, where the former cricketers had spoken to Khan with brutal frankness. By the time my guests came in, footage of the 'Sidhu hug' was making ripples in India; Sidhu's political foes were already accusing him of treason, in embracing the head of an army that had killed Indian soldiers at the border.

Sidhu revealed that Bajwa had mentioned to him that Pakistan had decided to open the Kartarpur corridor for Indian pilgrims to make it to Kartarpur Sahib, where the founder of Sikhism, Guru Nanak, had spent the last eighteen years of his life. This would be timed as a gesture from Pakistan for the 550th anniversary of Guru Nanak. Delighted by the news, Sidhu had spontaneously thanked his fellow Jat with a hug, a Punjabi jhappi.

The Kartarpur story was not a recent one. The gurdwara was renovated in the 1920s by the maharaja of Patiala, grandfather of Captain Amarinder Singh, at a cost of a million rupees. As luck would have it, when the Radcliffe Line was drawn, Kartarpur fell on the Pakistani side of the border since it was 4 kilometres east of the Ravi River. Over a period of time, Indian pilgrims had expressed a desire to walk into Kartarpur, which was in Pakistani Punjab's Narowal district, only 4 kilometres from the border with India. Yet Kartarpur Sahib was not listed as one of the pilgrimage sites when the 1974 protocol was signed, even when it was periodically amended, but it was very much a site that pilgrims started to visit—by taking a circuitous route around the Attari–Wagah border.

In 1999, when Vajpayee took the bus to Pakistan, he was accompanied by Parkash Singh Badal, the chief minister of Punjab. Badal had also articulated this longstanding Sikh demand for easier access to Kartarpur.

Now, the Pakistan Army had overnight decided to accept the longstanding Indian demand. Even more curious was the way in which the decision was conveyed to India—there had been no official communication between the two governments, this was a Pakistan Army chief softly whispering the proposal to an Indian Sikh politician on a private visit.

I gently suggested to Sidhu that he might want to correct the negative perceptions in the Indian media about his interaction with the chief of the Pakistan Army and explain the context publicly. His response was: 'Dunia vich subse vada rog, ki kende nain mere baare mein log (The biggest affliction in the world is to care about what people say about you)'.

We initially assumed this was a polite talking point that the army had prepared for their chief, to speak of pleasant matters to a politician from Indian Punjab. However, it soon became clear that this was a more serious proposal that would be welcomed by millions in India, even if it was part of a larger tactical game plan that the army was developing to gain greater influence in Indian Punjab.

I soon visited Kartarpur, given the very real possibility of a corridor opening up. The gurdwara was in the Narowal district of Pakistan's Punjab, just across from Gurdaspur in Indian Punjab. Driving into Narowal, we caught the Airtel signal and knew that the Indian border was close by. I was deeply impressed by the fertile landscape and the humble dwellings that surrounded the shrine and could easily imagine why Guru Nanak would have chosen such a peaceful spot in his final years.

Analysts wondered in India why Pakistan's army should abruptly spearhead this generous gesture towards India. Aside from the altruism, Pakistan was hoping to gain some leverage, through the corridor, in India's border state of Punjab. Some strategic influence in Punjab and some sway over Sikh sentiment could be tactically useful for Pakistan in future scenarios of fanning separatist sentiment. India's policy planners were mindful of

Pakistan's thinking behind the Kartarpur move, but confident that it was in overall terms, a welcome project. India had decided not to be overwhelmed by the security risks posed by the corridor but to welcome the opportunity, given that it was based on India's own request and represented the strong sentiment of the people of Punjab. At one level, it showed to me the successful working of Indian democracy, where the sentiments of a sizeable population of Punjab were privileged over security concerns through a political judgement by India's leadership.

It turned out that Pakistan's army had started work on the corridor soon after Imran Khan's inauguration in August. A few weeks later, Pakistan made a formal proposal to India, to work jointly on the project. India quickly agreed in principle. A divine hand seemed to be guiding both countries to do the right thing for the people. The decision in India was to move on the corridor with speed and to lay its foundation on the Indian side, in time for the start of the celebrations of the 550th anniversary of Guru Nanak coming up in November 2018. The celebratory year itself was coming at a sensitive time, six months before India's general election scheduled for May 2019. In India, the political judgement was to factor in security concerns without being overwhelmed by them. In my public remarks, I began calling Kartarpur a corridor of faith and a corridor for peace.

Pakistan soon announced that PM Imran Khan would himself lay the foundation of the corridor in a ceremony in November 2018. Speculation grew that Pakistan would want to invite PM Modi to the inauguration and that he could even accept. But if the Indian prime minister arrived, Pakistani strategists feared, all the political credit for the corridor might go to him, defeating several Pakistani objectives. Finally, Pakistan balanced these considerations to invite, for the foundation ceremony, India's foreign minister Sushma Swaraj, Punjab chief minister Amarinder Singh, and Punjab Congress MLA Navjot Singh Sidhu. India decided to field, instead of Sushma Swaraj, the two Sikh ministers in the NDA government, Hardeep Singh Puri of the BJP and Harsimrat Kaur Badal, a member of the Akali Dal, a coalition ally party at the centre.

Foreign Minister Qureshi seemed to give away Pakistan's thinking in a speech during the PTI government's hundred-day celebrations in November, when he said that Pakistan had thrown a 'googly' at India and made an offer that India could not refuse. India, he implied, was being forced to send two of its ministers to the inaugural despite its reluctance to do so. Punjab chief minister Captain Amarinder Singh chose not to travel for the ceremony, voicing objections as a former soldier against Pakistan's behaviour at the border. But his maverick party colleague Sidhu did arrive once again. I received ministers Hardeep Puri and Harsimrat Kaur at Wagah and, after some debate, we accepted the Pakistani offer of taking a chopper to Kartarpur to save time. The Pakistan high commissioner Sohail Mahmood accompanied us.

Defying all expectations, the corridor project across the river Ravi went speedily ahead on both sides. This was one of the highlights of my tenure in Pakistan. In other areas, the way forward was rockier.

TALKING OF TERROR

Bilateral conversations on terrorism in Pakistan became as dividing and sensitive as those on Kashmir. In July 2018, I was invited to speak at a panel discussion at an 'ideas conclave' organized by the Jinnah Institute in Islamabad, a think tank where 'serious conversation' was encouraged by Sherry Rehman, its president. The panel included Ayesha Jalal, a well-known Pakistani historian, and Nasim Zehra Malik, a journalist, apart from Lieutenant General Azif Janjua, a former NSA. The invitation was to speak on the 'eastern question', which of course was a geographical euphemism for India. I spoke of the 'western question' for India, the beleaguered relationship with Pakistan. I spoke of the difficulties in the relationship since 2016 and argued that the story of the twenty-first century was one of hope in the relationship dashed by acts of terror. I pointed out that bilateral ties, after showing some promise with a new government in India in 2014, had plunged in 2016 because of terrorism in Kashmir. I argued that there was hope to revive the relationship with the election of a new government in Pakistan. I traced the historical pattern of terrorism in India and suggested that containing terror was the magic bullet to pull the relationship out of trouble and onto a path of normalcy. This take was never seriously countered by the other panelists, although they did speak of Pakistan's territorial and other grievances.

On another occasion, the National Defence University of Pakistan invited me for a lecture on the bilateral relationship. We debated at the high commission on whether to confine my speech for an army audience to non-controversial areas like the small steps required to build trust or the long-term peace dividends that were possible if we made the right choices today. After much debate, we decided in favour of putting some hard facts before the audience. My presentation argued that India's instincts were primarily economic and India's relationship with its neighbours was focused on providing security for the Indian economy to grow and for preserving the economic gains already made. I explained to my audience that in the current century, the sensitivity of our policymakers to acts of terrorism appeared to have determined their choices on dialogue and détente. We decided to put some of this down on slides and show them to the young Pakistani military men and their guests who included foreigners.[3] We put together the actual numbers of the cross-border infiltrations over the years. In presenting the narrative, I paused on this slide and emphasized that if this number fell to zero, the sky was the limit when it came to India's relationship with Pakistan.

The feedback we received from the participants was positive. Some said the speech had made them revise their views of the relationship, some foreign participants at the NDU reported that even the Pakistani participants had expressed surprise that they had never experienced such a discussion in their public or private discourse.

But the speech did not go down too well with the authorities; it had too much reality and not enough diplomacy. As a result, I was not invited again to talk on India–Pakistan relations to either the military or civilian bureaucracy. A couple of my speaking engagements were mysteriously cancelled in Lahore and even in Karachi, citing scheduling issues. I was in any case not doing media interviews, which often lapsed into hostile inquisitions. Still, in private conversations, I kept trying to paint a real portrait of India's concerns.

It soon became clear to us that we needed to have these conversations directly with the army and with those diplomats who were having regular exchanges with the army on these issues. Our engagement with all elements of Naya Pakistan (Imran Khan's), the old (army, ISI, MOFA) and beyond (civil society, diplomats) came under the rubric of 'normal diplomatic activity'. In a relationship where formal dialogue was absent, the high commission became the primary vehicle of communication with Pakistan's establishment and people. We were soon having candid conversations with multiple players that were willing to talk.

Under the broad policy direction of 'no talks with terror', no structured dialogue with Pakistan was on in this period. India had signalled repeatedly that its formal interactions with the Pakistanis would be kept to the bare minimum until Pakistan renounced terrorism in word and in deed. But the informal diplomatic conversations at the level of the high commissions never stopped. They were supplemented by weekly operational conversations between the two militaries (DGMOs) which mainly focused on managing borders, and by scattered global conversations between intelligence agencies in different world capitals. This web of interaction was something that all those dealing with Pakistan were more or less aware of. But during my time in Islamabad, I was visiting India almost every month to share information and assessments, so that policymakers at home got a feel of developments on the ground.

In the big picture, the Pakistan Army was at once India's key interlocutor and primary adversary. Analysts in India pointed out that the Pakistan Army had three separate verticals to deal with three different domains: the Strategic Plans Division (SPD) for nuclear weapons; the DGMO for conventional warfare; and the Inter Services Intelligence (ISI) to run proxy wars, leveraging armed militants through its directorates. The ISI also controlled the information warfare. What distinguished the Pakistani army from normal armed forces was its robust engagement in a fourth domain—to keep the domestic situation favourable for the army. So, the fourth vertical, again run by the ISI, was its political arm. In 2018, it had added a new tool in the fourth vertical—Imran Khan. This was the essence of Naya Pakistan—a 'hybrid' regime with a prime minister under the army's control.

Another strategic objective of the Pakistani army was increasingly worrying Indian planners and analysts: its eagerness to gang up on India along with China. 'Interoperability' with the Chinese was a key goal. The Pakistani and Chinese armies had equipment and military exercises in common, doctrines in common, and an adversary in common.

A Western military delegation once told us that the ISI chief had admitted to them that they were using covert proxy means of dealing with India, because all intelligence agencies did that, particularly in our tough neighbourhood. Such a talking point would have been anathema for the foreign office, which had a party line of stout denial.

On the lighter side, during my time in Islamabad, no conversation with Imran Khan's friends or foes was complete without being peppered with some salacious gossip on the goings-on in Bani Gala, where Khan lived with his third wife. Tales of a break-up with his wife and her departure for Lahore were often followed by assertions that he would not ever leave his soulmate. Stories would often emerge of the excessive use of white powder, djinns that were fed red meat on the rooftop each day, several of the prime minister's inner circle friends being banished to the provincial Punjab, and Khan, like a schoolboy, being caught 'sexting' with his young lady ministers leading to sharp domestic strife.

QUIET CHATS

Over the next few months, we did maintain discreet contacts with Team Imran although I had no further substantive conversations directly with him. This was beyond the formal dialogue we continued to have with the foreign secretary and the India team at the foreign office, who remained our primary formal interlocutors, as indeed they had been for successive high commissioners over the decades. I got to meet several of Imran Khan's friends, some ministers in his cabinet, and was able to have discreet, deniable conversations with them.

One such interlocutor, a close friend of Khan's, disarmingly honest and committed to peace with India, was the one with whom I had several late-night conversations. Naeemul Haque was a passionate politician from Sindh, and had been one of the founder-members of the PTI. Ironically for a peacenik, Haque had slapped a minister of the previous government on live television and thrown water on another occasion at a Sindh politician, much to the entertainment of TV audiences and watchers of viral clips. He was formally a special assistant to the PM without portfolio, but worked on several issues with Imran Khan, particularly on Afghanistan and India. I discussed with Haque the possibility of peace, after we got past the prevailing troubled times. He understood the emphasis India placed on terrorism, on the destructive impact of cross-border infiltration. He was also keen that the consulate in Karachi would reopen one day. He had no romantic view on the Mumbai consulate and felt that Pakistan should not insist on reclaiming Jinnah House but rent suitable property and open the corresponding consulate. Haque would meet me intermittently, because he was in chemotherapy for blood cancer. (Sadly, he passed away in 2019.)

It was useful to continue conversations on a discreet and informal basis with Imran Khan's team, and simultaneously with the army, because it gave us the sense of where their positions converged or diverged. It became increasingly clear to us that Khan's team was mostly not in the loop on India matters and blissfully ignorant of establishment thinking. This was the experience of several diplomats who found the foreign office frustratingly behind the curve while Rawalpindi and the army teams were often refreshingly candid in admitting what Pakistan was up to. In contrast, the foreign office was great at making a virtue of spinning out army-approved talking points in mostly less than creative ways.

India cancelled the conversation between the two foreign ministers at the UN in September 2018, in response to a surge in attacks in Kashmir. Immediately after this news broke, I got a call from Tariq Aziz, the veteran of the backchannel and former Musharraf aide. I invited him to India House for a quiet conversation over dinner. Aziz, avuncular and old worldly, remained a strong advocate for peace with India. He was keen to work with me to do his bit for peace. He told me he had spent a couple of hours with army chief, Bajwa, the previous night, discussing, in particular, the India question. He had a few messages to convey to me. He had reminded Bajwa of how cross-border terrorism had been controlled in 2004 with the January joint statement between Vajpayee and Musharraf. He said both he and Bajwa were concerned about the latest setback to the relationship, the recently cancelled meeting between the two foreign ministers in New York and were keen to calm things down.

My interlocutor said he was convinced Bajwa genuinely wanted peace with India, 'more than any army chief in the past' and had said so multiple times. In his assessment, the army was willing to put a stop to cross-border infiltration. DG ISI Naveed Mukhtar was to retire in October and would be replaced by another general more aligned to Bajwa's thinking. (In October 2018, Lieutenant General Asim Munir took over as DG ISI.) This would be an opportunity to try and work things out. The Kashmir desk in the agency would be overhauled and cross-border infiltration would gradually come down.

Aziz was sending a specific peace message to India, suggesting that the Pakistan Army would make all efforts to stop cross-border infiltration and requesting the start of some kind of political dialogue. I told him I would happily carry such an encouraging message of peace to India but pointed out that words had little meaning for India these days, we needed to see action on the ground. I explained India's concerns at length—that we needed to see infiltration numbers fall, that we needed some action on extremists in safe havens as a demonstration of good faith.

I had argued that India would be ready for a conversation of some kind whenever the infiltration numbers went down. Aziz sighed and told me that it was always the 'Kashmir files' that were pulled out, whenever we spoke of a breakthrough.

My meeting with Aziz took place around the time we had opened channels of communication with the ISI, which had begun assuring us that cross-border terrorism and cross-border infiltration would end. We said we would wait for the numbers before we could make a judgement.

TALKING OF GANDHI

For the launch of Mahatma Gandhi's 150th birth anniversary celebrations on 2 October 2018, EAM Minister Sushma Swaraj, on PM Modi's suggestion, promoted a quirky idea of inviting singers from all across the world to render their version of 'Vaishnav jan', Gandhi's favourite bhajan, in Gujarati. All heads of missions were advised to explore finding global artists who would be willing to be part of this project. This presented us with a quandary in Pakistan. When the relationship was plunging low, would we even find a Pakistani artist willing to stick out their neck and sing a song for India? After much deliberation, we decided to approach Shafqat Amanat Ali, a singer popular on both sides of the border. Ali had sung for us for the Republic Day of 2018, soon after my arrival in Pakistan, where I had decided to add some oomph to our reception by inviting an iconic Pakistani singer for a brief performance.

Ali sounded nervous when we approached him for the project. We assured him that this was a global and apolitical attempt to celebrate Gandhi's legacy of humanitarian peace and nothing more. To our great relief, Ali agreed to try to sing the bhajan even though he knew no Gujarati. When we received the WhatsApp forward of Ali's version, I was astounded at the quality and depth of his performance. Ali is from the Patiala Gharana (ninth generation), and already had a huge following in India for his prowess in folk and Sufi music. He'd become a bigger star on both sides of the border and particularly in Pakistan, after his foray into Bollywood, having sung superhits like 'Mitwa'. Clearly, while he knew no Gujarati, Ali had put his soul into an extraordinary rendition.

We released this tribute to Mahatma Gandhi at a special ceremony on 2 October, where we invited a number of Pakistanis and diplomats. This song floored the audience. The invited Pakistani 'Gandhians' included the Pashtun leader of the Awami National Party, Afrasiab Khattak, whose party was linked to Gandhi's friend, Khan Abdul Ghaffar Khan.

Ali's rendition of the Gandhi bhajan got a good deal of traction on social media and was, at that time, not really censored. (Ali's fears came true soon enough. Payback time for the singer came on the first anniversary of the Article 370 revocation in August 2020. Ali produced and released an ISPR video, wearing black, on the atrocities against Kashmiris in India, with grim music and deathly greys. This potentially damaged his future Bollywood career.)[4]

MUSICAL DIPLOMACY

With traditional diplomacy stalled, we were looking for options to speak a common cultural language to engage with Pakistan's elites. For Dussehra, Diwali, and several other festivals, music became an idiom of our celebrations in Pakistan. My few attempts to get troupes from the Indian Council of Cultural Relations, or chefs for culinary diplomacy fell through, as soon as it became clear that that even if India agreed to send any such group, they would never get visas from Pakistan.

With Bollywood in Mumbai the epicentre of the regional entertainment industry, Pakistani artistes had used it as a launch pad when times were good. But the cinema connection had in recent times been severed. The Pakistani icon Fawad Khan had starred in a Bollywood movie in 2016. The Shiv Sena had stalled the release. 'When I shot my film *Ae Dil Hai Mushkil* last year (2015),' producer Karan Johar said, the 'climate was completely different.' The film was allowed a release only after Johar swore: 'I will not engage with talent from the neighbouring country given the circumstances.'[5] Cultural diplomacy had been squeezed out from 2016, the summer of violence in Kashmir.

The next best thing for us in Islamabad was to invite to our social events upcoming Pakistani artists, who were mostly of the same level of musical competence as their Indian counterparts, and underlined the cultural intimacy between our countries. Since the big names of Lahore would perhaps be nervous to walk into the Indian high commission, we decided to scout for newer talent who would play music familiar to both Indians and Pakistanis, and with their lower profiles not necessarily come to the notice of or upset Pakistani minders. On one occasion, our high commission's dentist Dr Abrar brought along a friend who regaled the audience with Mohammed Rafi and Kishore Kumar songs. For another event, a young singer from Lahore belted out songs and ghazals where both Indian and Pakistani guests were mouthing the lyrics. Pakistani music always touched special chords with the audiences at India House in Islamabad, because it was essentially subcontinental music. I would invariably introduce the artist, mentioning that while the relationship did not permit the exchange of cultural troupes, we did inhabit the same cultural space and could enjoy the same music.

It was this paradox that generations of Indian diplomats had experienced in Pakistan. The strong hostility and difficult conversations of the day would often melt away in the evenings, when layers of animosity would peel away and reveal people sharing a unique cultural intimacy.

33

PULWAMA

On Valentine's Day in February 2019, a convoy of buses carrying paramilitary personnel snaked its way from Jammu to Srinagar on National Highway 44. Just short of Lethapora, a little town in Pulwama district, a loud explosion drowned out the quiet hum of the cavalcade. It was 3.15 p.m. A bloodied Kashmir once again became the central focus of India's attention and of the bilateral relationship.

When we saw the first ticker reports of this explosion at the Indian high commission in Islamabad, we assumed we were seeing one more of those terrible terrorist attacks in the violence-ridden state, with perhaps a handful injured or dead. As the story developed, and news started trickling in of a large number of deaths of Central Reserve Police Force (CRPF) personnel, it became clear that this was bigger than the standard grenade attack that we had got used to in Kashmir. We watched alarmed as reports confirmed that some forty security men had perished in the explosion.

Soon, a video emerged of the Jaish-e-Mohammed claiming credit for the explosion, but attributing it to a local Kashmiri youth. The chief of the outfit, Maulana Masood Azhar, was known to reside in Bahawalpur, in Pakistan's south Punjab, in the protective embrace of the ISI. Chatter soon emerged of celebrations and distribution of sweets by Azhar and his Jaish henchmen, making it abundantly clear where the attack had been planned.

This attack went against the grain of the overall relationship that had seemed headed into positive territory. We hadn't expected a major breakthrough but no major quarrel either, a sort of 'unpeace', as a new government settled down in Pakistan and as India got absorbed deeper into an election campaign.

But this was big, the biggest terror attack since the one in Uri in 2016, the worst during my tenure in Pakistan. We stayed in office late, bracing ourselves for the diplomatic tremors of the explosion. In Pakistan, matters seemed superficially calm. The media reporting was factual, and PM Imran Khan was preoccupied with the visit of the Saudi crown prince Mohammed bin Salman (MBS) whom he was personally driving around Islamabad.

An emergency cabinet meeting was held the next morning in New Delhi. Foreign Secretary Vijay Gokhale called me minutes after it ended. My orders were to report immediately for consultations in New Delhi—if possible, by that night. The Pakistan high commissioner had been called in for a sharp démarche in South Block, pointing out that the killing of forty personnel had the clear imprint of a group protected by Pakistan. I had instructions not to be available for any démarche by the Pakistani side.

Speaking after the meeting, Finance Minister Arun Jaitley reflected public anger when he said they will ensure that 'those who have committed and actively supported this heinous act are made to pay a heavy price'. Jaitley added that the MEA would launch 'all possible diplomatic steps that have to be taken to ensure complete isolation of Pakistan'.[1] Home Minister Rajnath Singh reached Srinagar and PM Modi declared the 'sacrifices of our brave security personnel shall not go in vain'.[2] The condemnation had been accompanied by immediate steps to halt trade. India withdrew the most favoured nation trading partner status given to Pakistan in 1996.

Amidst the flurry of activity at the high commission the day after, we tried to assess why a terror outfit would have carried out such an attack, or the ISI allowed such a bloody blow in Kashmir. There could have been several motives. The ISI could have made the not unfamiliar assumption that the valley was smouldering with anger and a terror attack attributed to an indigenous movement could ensure both international reaction and local support for the Kashmiri struggle. An attack could weaken the ruling BJP in the upcoming general elections, assuming that India would have limited resolve to retaliate. Pakistan may have learnt the wrong lessons from Afghanistan—some radical elements were already crowing that one strategic asset, the Taliban, had brought the US to its knees in Afghanistan; similarly, the Jaish might have thought it could wear out and defeat the Indian 'occupation forces' in Kashmir. The powers that be in Pakistan may have calculated that as India had committed itself to improving relations with Pakistan through the Kartarpur corridor, it would perhaps be reluctant to retaliate for an act of terrorism. There was also the traditional trope that the India threat towards Pakistan would assure the beleaguered Pakistan Army some extra budgetary support, if India retaliated after the attack. Or perhaps the Pakistan Army might have wanted to embarrass a civilian government (albeit one supported by it) foolish enough to contemplate better relations with India.

On the record, and for public consumption, the discourse within Pakistan was one of denial and injured innocence. Why would Pakistan at this point invite trouble when they had enough trouble with the FATF[3] breathing down their backs and a Saudi prince visiting? It was a knee-jerk reaction on India's part to blame Pakistan. This was the work of a local Kashmiri freedom fighter. The army-leaning media was soon suggesting that India had launched a 'false-flag operation' to frame Pakistan, possibly to bring Pakistan into its election narrative, so that a subsequent military exchange would benefit the ruling dispensation.[4]

Even as I asked for my tickets to be booked for New Delhi on 15 February, I received the expected summons from the foreign secretary of Pakistan, Tehmina Janjua, to show up for an 'important meeting'.

The latest diplomatic game had begun.

I sent a response that I would not be available for a conversation since I was en route for consultations in India; my deputy and acting high commissioner, Gaurav Ahluwalia, was available for any conversation.

This did not go down too well with the foreign office. They knew only too well, from the watchers outside my office, that I was still ensconced in the chancery. I left work immediately. I would pick up a bag from home and reach the airport early, to be firmly not available to my hosts for a démarche. I asked my deputy to do the honours at the foreign office, and jumped on a flight to Dubai.

TERROR DIPLOMACY

Sleepless from overnight flights the next morning, I reached South Block for a series of meetings, trying my best to sidestep media stakeouts. To the amusement of my colleagues, I was thirty minutes late for my first meeting. I had forgotten to switch from Pakistani to Indian time.

In Delhi, after meeting with various agencies, I had revised some of my initial assessments. Pulwama was in all likelihood a small operation gone out of control, where the suicide bomber lucked out in getting an unprotected target in a convoy of vehicles. The general assessment of several security experts was that this was an operation that had become bigger than was originally planned: even Pakistan's agencies had been caught flat-footed by the Pulwama action—some said, they were internally trying to blame the Jaish for overstepping the brief and not executing it professionally enough. Investigations would confirm a year later that it was a meticulously planned operation of the JeM that had met with unexpected success.

When I got to South Block, walking past a battery of cameras, I joined meetings discussing options. Particularly diplomatic options. The steps taken by the Cabinet Committee on Security had included withdrawal of the most favoured nation treatment, a customs duty of 200 percent on Pakistani goods (that would effectively end imports), and a halt to trade at the Wagah border. But this was just the beginning.

A host of other ideas were mooted, to scale down our engagement with Pakistan. Stop the Samjhauta Express, stop the Lahore bus service, defer the BSF border talks, defer the Kartarpur corridor talks. And then there were the familiar proposals being bandied about in policy debates and by pundits writing in the media. Stop issuing visas. Stop honouring SAARC visas. Cease cross-LoC trade. Disallow travel of Indians to Pakistan. Suspend flights between the countries. How hard it was to build trust, I thought. And how easy to break it. All the confidence-building measures planned, negotiated, and implemented over years in this difficult relationship, could be slashed off on a yellow notepad in minutes.

South Block was in crisis management mode and I was part of the crisis team, trying to guess Pakistan's next moves. I was in constant touch with my team in Islamabad that was led by Gaurav Ahluwalia who was reporting continuously on internal developments within Pakistan.

An intense phase of diplomacy began, for sharing India's outrage with the world. Foreign Secretary Vijay Gokhale's day included briefings for envoys of twenty-five countries—including the UN P5—the US, UK, China, Russia, and France—on 15 February, to talk of the role of the Jaish in the attack and on the use of terrorism as an instrument of Pakistan's state policy. Apart from the P5, Gokhale met diplomats of key countries in Europe and Asia, such as Germany, South Korea, Japan, and Australia. Indian envoys were being asked to repeat these messages in global capitals. Countries from across the globe were condemning the incident and sharing India's outrage.

Pakistan was soon reacting to this diplomatic offensive. The foreign office had summoned India's acting high commissioner in Islamabad to reject 'baseless allegations made by India'. Prime Minister Imran Khan waited a few days before reacting, using the army's talking points of stout denial of any Pakistani involvement. In an address on 19 February, he claimed: 'This is Naya Pakistan.... If you have any actionable intelligence that a Pakistani is involved, give it to us. I guarantee you that we will take action...'[5]

In South Block, we had drafted a comprehensive response, aimed at Pakistan, but also reminding the world that it was 'a well-known fact that Jaish-e-Mohammad and its leader Masood Azhar are based in Pakistan'. Also, proof had been provided to Pakistan on the Mumbai attacks, but 'the case has not progressed for the last more than 10 years'. The international community was well acquainted with the fact, India said, 'that Pakistan is the nerve center of terrorism.' The MEA statement also called out the insinuation that 'India's response to the terrorist attack is determined by the forthcoming General Election. India rejects this false allegation. India's democracy is a model for the world which Pakistan would never understand.'[6]

As the Saudi crown prince and prime minister MBS travelled from Pakistan to India on 21 February, PM Modi shared India's anguish with him. He added publicly that punishing terrorists and their supporters was important and that Saudi Arabia and India 'have shared views about this.'

India decided to prepare a dossier of evidence on how Pakistan and the JeM were complicit in the terrorist attack in Pulwama. UN diplomacy was activated, based on the dossier, through four of the UN Security Council members, i.e., the P5 minus China. France was prepared to propose a UN resolution to corner the JeM and Pakistan. Both the UN and the EU were being approached to designate Azhar a terrorist, already so designated by the US in 2001. Even Pakistan had in the past indicted Azhar when the pressure had become unbearable in the Musharraf years; Azhar had technically been detained for a year in 2002. India was now also advocating Financial Action Task Force (FATF)-like stiff anti-terror financing conditions on Pakistan at the IMF, where Imran Khan's government was negotiating a critical loan to save its sinking economy.

India suggested to Japan that it might consider postponing the visit by Foreign Minister Qureshi, or if he did show up, highlighting the terrorism issue. Qureshi eventually had to cancel his Tokyo trip. The idea was to work towards calling out Pakistan globally as a terrorist sponsor, rather than just 'isolating' it, as was the initial rhetoric. Indian diplomats were suggesting to countries engaging with Pakistan to put the issue of terrorism on top of the agenda. On the Indus Water Treaty, while the familiar instinct was to abrogate it, the decision that was finally taken was that no data would be given to Pakistan beyond the treaty requirements. Forty-eight agreements were now being examined for possible suspension. Proposed confidence-building talks between the BSF and Coast Guard were called off.

Pakistan's military establishment seemed jittery about the impending Indian action. They decided on some nominal moves against the JeM to fend off the pressure. They were worried Azhar would be picked up or targeted by an Indian or US agency. He had been moved from Bahawalpur to Islamabad, deeper into the protective embrace of the Pak ISI.

I continued my briefings of the CCS and called separately on each of its members, including the PM and the NSA; each seemed keen to hear my assessments at this time, particularly my perspectives on Pakistan's internal conditions. I did share an assessment with the political leadership that the diplomatic space for manoeuvre was limited and that other options needed to be considered, particularly in the context of the surgical strikes of 2016. Pakistan was bracing itself for such action by India but did not know when and in what shape it would come. The PM asked me when I was scheduled to leave for Islamabad; I told him it would be in a week or so. He listened to me attentively, asked questions, but did not let on what India was contemplating by way of a response to the terror attack.

India's security analysts had been pointing out that the Jaish had become the preferred 'sword arm' of the army, instead of the LeT, in the years following the 2008 Mumbai attacks. The degree of damage that the Pulwama operation had inflicted was unexpected for the Pakistan Army. An assessment I heard was that Bajwa may not have known about the specific operation, but it could have been cleared by the DG ISI.

India's army chief General Bipin Rawat told me that the retaliatory attack that India was planning would be much bigger than the surgical strikes of 2016 and it was coming soon enough. I decided not to share this information in the other part of South Block, thinking it best that the diplomatic planning went ahead without specific knowledge of 'kinetic' operations. Rawat agreed with the assessment that his Pakistani counterpart, Bajwa, was broadly interested in peace with India, but often let the ISI set the broad directions of policy. He felt that the Pakistani corps commanders were not too happy with the Bajwa doctrine, since it seemed to be diluting traditional postures and that affected morale.

In Kashmir, a crackdown had begun on local terrorists. More than eighty 'overground supporters' of the Jaish had been arrested. Home Minister Rajnath Singh had travelled to Jammu and Kashmir. The protocols of road movements of security personnel were being looked at very carefully. The investigation of the Pulwama terror case had been handed over to the National Investigation Agency (NIA). Dossiers were under preparation on Adil Dhar and on Kamran (an alias for Abdul Rasheed Ghazi, the Pakistani national believed to be the mastermind behind the Pulwama attack; Ghazi was killed in an army operation on 18 February 2019) and the idea was to share these with the MEA for onward transmission to friendly countries looking for evidence. On the political side, an all-party meeting had been called and had passed a resolution.

India's diplomatic outreach had intensified. The P4 (P5 minus China) led by France was approaching the UN sanctions committee once again for the listing of Azhar.[7] India was in touch with the fifteen members of the 'terror sanctions committee' which happened to be composed of the fifteen UNSC members. Pakistan's global credibility was falling again.

India was also revisiting the proposed CCIT, the UN's deadlocked Comprehensive Convention on International Terrorism, to see if its diplomacy could move the needle on that ponderous process that remained deadlocked because of its inability to settle on a common definition of terrorism. The Unlawful Activities Prevention Act (UAPA) ordinance was also discussed to give it teeth for sanctions against individuals and particularly their travel and asset freezes.

But neither the bilateral nor global diplomatic measures would be enough. The matter had gone beyond the pale of diplomacy, of words. It was time for action. A cost had to be imposed on the Pakistan establishment for allowing the Pulwama attack. It was increasingly clear that India had rolled out measures that were only a faint expression of its outrage at the death of forty soldiers. Much more needed to be done to give a direct message to the terrorists and to the Pakistan Army. Also, the world was sharing India's outrage at this fresh act of terrorism and would support India for any legitimate and proportionate response.

The next CCS member I briefed was Finance Minister Arun Jaitley—whose health was slipping, but whose mind remained sharp. In my long chat with the minister I knew well from earlier times, Jaitley asked why Imran Khan the cricketer was unable to deliver better and prevent this madness from continuing. He agreed with me that my presence in Pakistan would be useful in adding persuasion to everything else we were doing for Pakistan to change its behaviour. I called on Home Minister Rajnath Singh right after his visit to Kashmir. He shared his assessment of a security establishment angered by yet another act of terror. We discussed a long-term approach to persuade Pakistan to change its behaviour.

The last of the CCS members I caught up with, on 25 February, was EAM Sushma Swaraj. I briefed her on developments within Pakistan and on my conversations with the prime minister, the NSA, and her other CCS colleagues, on the palpable anger in the security establishment. We discussed the long press conference of the ISPR, which revealed the mind of Pakistan's military.

On 22 February, DG ISPR Ghafoor had given a rambling, somewhat comical press conference, brazenly recrafting history as he went along. He blamed India for imposing wars on Pakistan in 1948, 1965, and 1971; and for capturing territory in 1984. He had skipped any reference to the 1999 Kargil conflict but argued that all terror incidents—Mumbai, Pathankot, Pulwama—had been staged by India to distract attention from Pakistan's growth. Pakistan, he insisted, was not isolated. He ended on a high note of military bluster: 'We will never be surprised by you...we will dominate the escalation ladder...don't mess with Pakistan...we can respond to a full-spectrum threat.'[8]

I also reminded EAM Swaraj of the presence of a high-profile Pakistani citizen in India: this was Ramesh Vankwani, a Hindu member of parliament and rights activist from Pakistan, who was positioning himself as a possible mediator in India–Pakistan affairs. Vankwani had arrived as part of India's global 'Kumbh diplomacy' for the Prayagraj ardh Kumbh[9], that was on from mid-January to early March, with some 50 million people converging on the banks of the Ganga for the 'world's largest peaceful gathering'. India had invited representatives from some 188 countries, including Pakistan, which had nominated the genial politician from Sindh, who had posed for pictures with PM Modi and EAM Swaraj in the midst of the bilateral tensions. Vankwani was among the guests the PM had addressed at the Kumbh global participation event on 23 February, where Modi spoke of the 'Kumbh of democracy' that was about to start—the forthcoming general election in India.

I repeated to the external affairs minister two broad assessments I had shared with the political leadership. The first was that India's diplomatic options in dealing with a terrorist attack of this nature were limited. The second, that while our diplomatic strategy to expose Pakistan's connection with this terrorist act had been successful, Pakistan would not be globally 'isolated' but must be globally identified as a perpetrator of unacceptable levels of terrorism. She gave me the impression that some tough action was round the corner, after which, I should expect the role of diplomacy to expand. I would need to return to Pakistan to resume conversations at that end.

Meanwhile, Pakistan, under strong global pressure, was showing frenetic activity in Punjab, particulary in Bahawalpur, where the government was pointedly taking over madrasas and facilities of the Jaish.

India's strong diplomatic offensive was continuing on 25 February, ten days after Pulwama. On the agenda was the designation of Masood Azhar as a terrorist by the UN sanctions committee and in the EU 'autonomous terror list'. The first to receive the Pulwama dossier was the French ambassador, in recognition of France's strong support. India was requesting the listing at the UN, based on the evidence in the dossier. The NSA had already spoken to his French counterpart. The EU ambassador was called in for discussions on the procedure for the listing of Azhar as a terrorist and similarly designating select individuals and entities. Members of the FATF were being sensitized, given that the body now had more teeth to put Pakistan on grey and black lists to ensure compliance. I had managed to persuade my colleagues to share this dossier, as an experiment, with Pakistan as well, to test the resolve of 'Naya Pakistan' in tackling the snakes in its backyard.

AIR STRIKES
I woke up early in Delhi on 26 February, to social media chatter about bombs being dropped by India in Pakistan. One of my colleagues in Islamabad had picked up a tweet by the DG ISPR at 5.35 a.m. that said that an Indian fighter plane had dropped a bomb after entering Pakistani airspace.

It was going to be a long day.

I followed the action on Twitter, and the speculation on our media channels, before making it to South Block for our morning crisis meeting. The meeting was called off, so I sat with the foreign secretary in his corner room as he prepared for the cabinet meeting at 9.30 a.m.

The public speculation mounted. The cabinet meeting dragged on as the stories on national and international media got wilder. We were finally told that the foreign secretary would make a statement. He read it out to the media at 11.30 a.m, some six hours after the news first broke, giving enough time for multiple fanciful narratives to float into the public realm.

In an intelligence-led operation in the early hours of today, India struck the biggest training camp of JeM in Balakot. In this operation, a very large number of JeM terrorists, trainers, senior commanders and groups of jihadis who were being trained for fidayeen action were eliminated...this non-military pre-emptive action was specifically targeted at the JeM camp...We expect that Pakistan lives up to its

public commitment and takes follow up actions to dismantle all JeM
and other camps and hold the terrorists accountable for the actions.[10]

Pakistan's denial came quickly. It 'strongly rejected' India's claim of
targeting a terrorist camp even as it vowed to respond at a time and place
of its choosing to this 'uncalled for aggression'. The significance of the
operation that morning was not lost on Pakistan. While Pakistan's army
had flatly denied that any surgical strikes had taken place in 2016, the air
strikes of 2019 were not deniable. The Pakistan Air Force was embarrassed
that it could not even scramble an air defence against the Indian warplanes
that had intruded deep into Pakistan's territory, and struck 50 kilometres
from the LoC in the province of Khyber Pakhtunkhwa, not far from
Abbottabad where the al-Qaeda chief Osama bin Laden was killed by
US airborne forces. This was the first time since 1971 that Indian fighter
aircraft had crossed over the international border to drop bombs. The
panic was rising. At a special meeting of the National Security Committee,
PM Imran Khan asked the armed forces and the people of Pakistan to
remain 'prepared for all eventualities'.

Reports later confirmed that twelve French-made Mirages of the Indian
Air Force took off from multiple air bases, crossed over into Pakistani
air space, and carried out the attacks. At around 3.30 a.m., the aircraft
dropped five 'Spice 2000' bombs, out of which four penetrated the rooftops
of the building in which more than 300 terrorists were housed. The IAF
jets returned to their bases unchallenged, spending all of four minutes in
Pakistani airspace. Later in the day, I met with the new DGMO in South
Block for a pre-scheduled appointment. He was one of the handful of
people in the know of the operation at Balakot. He was also the designated
point for 'mil-mil' army-level coordination and for working the hotline
between the two armies established in 2003. He or his deputy, the DMO, a
brigadier, would have a chat every Tuesday with their Pakistani counterpart.
We discussed the significance of the operation. He pointed out that the
coordination between the DGMOs would continue; a call was scheduled
later that night, since 26 February happened to be a Tuesday.

The strikes also unleashed frenetic political and diplomatic activity
in both countries. An all-party meeting was called by the government to
share details of the morning's operation. EAM Sushma Swaraj called me
later that afternoon to ask about the morale of our team in Islamabad.

'How's the josh?'

'High, ma'am!'

This was a nod to the movie Uri: The Surgical Strike, a slick thriller
based on the events following the Uri terror attack of 2016. In a comical
twist, Swaraj had been under the impression that I was already back in
Islamabad. I was, in fact, still in Delhi, but in constant touch with our

team in Islamabad. Her office called back to ask me to join her team for an all-party meeting scheduled that evening. The meeting, chaired by Swaraj and attended by the home and finance ministers, was a follow-up to another such meeting that Home Minister Rajnath Singh had chaired on 16 February to brief all political parties on the Pulwama attack.

The EAM told the political party leaders that the morning operation was a pre-emptive move in the context of what had happened in Pulwama on 14 February. On the global diplomatic effort, the EAM revealed that she had been in touch with US secretary of state, Mike Pompeo, apart from her counterparts from Afghanistan, Singapore, as also Russia and China, during the week.[11]

The EAM asked me to respond to a question from an Opposition leader on how Pakistan could be expected to react to the air strike. I described the goings-on in Pakistan during the day and the meeting of the nuclear command authority. This was signalling by Pakistan, but the nuclear sabre-rattling was only a distraction. I said it was hard to predict how soon a 'response' would come but it would inevitably come, to give the army and the people of Pakistan a notion of a 'fitting response', if not of victory.

In Pakistan, the mood was of anger giving way to panic. It was comparable in many ways to the situation after India had exploded the nuclear device in May 1998. To most serious observers, it was a question of when, and not if, Pakistan would retaliate, to give its army and its people a notion of victory—this had been of great importance to Pakistan through various skirmishes and battles with India. The DG ISPR had pointedly mentioned in his press conference that Pakistan would escalate the conflict and 'surprise' India. The meeting of Pakistan's nuclear command authority and the nuclear sabre-rattling was not lost in the din, even though Ghafoor repeated that to even talk of nuclear weapons was 'insane'. It was the same old attempt to demonstrate that the nuclear threshold was lower than it actually was.

In Islamabad, India received another démarche from Pakistan's acting foreign secretary, alleging that India had violated Pakistan's sovereignty and territorial integrity. Pakistan was also asking for 'actionable intelligence' from India on the Pulwama attack and on the alleged involvement of Pakistani nationals. No terrorist camps existed, they insisted, at the location that was attacked by the Indian Air Force. No further violation of Pakistan's territory would be tolerated. The peace process had been jeopardized by India. The Pakistan propaganda machine went a step further to allege that India's actions were part of electioneering by the current government and Pakistan was being dragged in for electoral gains.

Bilaterally, India reiterated the need to take credible and urgent action against the JeM and asked Pakistan to avoid ceasefire violations in the spirit of the 2003 agreement. India said that the meeting of the nuclear command authority in Pakistan was an act of provocation, not behaviour expected of a country that claimed to be a responsible nuclear power. India asked for additional armed guards for its high commission in Pakistan. Staff was asked to remain in the bubble of the diplomatic conclave.

On the morning of Wednesday, 27 February, I joined a defence–foreign office coordination meeting between the DGMO and the foreign secretary, reviewing the reaction from Pakistan on the border after the Balakot air strikes. It was clear that Pakistan's 'precautionary deployment' posture before the Balakot air strikes had moved by the evening of Tuesday, 26 February, to an aggressive one on the Line of Control. Pakistan was firing along the LoC south of the Pir Panjal range and the Indian side was watching their behaviour in a defensive posture. At around 5 a.m., on Wednesday, 27 February, Pakistan had escalated artillery fire across the border at the Uri sector of the LoC. It was soon obvious that the border fire was only a diversion.

At around 9.30 a.m., on 27 February, five Pakistani aircraft, of a 'package' of twenty-four, crossed over to a depth of around 4 kilometres across the LoC, through the Nowshera and Poonch sectors. They dropped their munitions near military targets (Krishna Ghati, Hamirpur, Gambhir, and at the Narayan ammunition dump). They also tried to mount an incursion into Rajasthan, around Anupgarh, possibly a decoy, but the Indian Air Force scrambled warplanes in pursuit and the Pakistan Air Force did no damage.

Early reports suggested that India had lost an aircraft in the melee and so had Pakistan. India's official statement finally came around 3.15 p.m., after the Indian Air Force had done a proper stocktaking exercise. It revealed that some twenty-four Pakistani aircraft had come in, were engaged by Indian aircraft, including a MiG-21 bison, which had targeted a Pakistani F-16, but was itself hit in the operation. India was confirming that the Pakistan Air Force had violated the LoC and entered Indian airspace. While Pakistani airspace had been shut since the Balakot air strikes, India shut its airspace for several hours after the air skirmish, but reopened it later in the day, signalling an end to air hostilities.

The fog of war was made denser by multiple 'expert' comments and visuals on social media. A host of claims, denials, and allegations flew thick and fast. Eyewitnesses on the ground and Pakistan's military spokesman initially claimed that two planes had been shot down and three pilots were spotted descending with parachutes. By some accounts, a Pakistani pilot downed in his own territory was fatally wounded by locals mistaking him for an Indian pilot. Pakistan stoutly denied the claim that any US-supplied F-16 aircraft were used in the operation, much less downed. Indian officials rejected Pakistani claims of shooting down a Russia-made

Su-30MKI. But there was no denying the significance of India's strategic paradigm shift—of using hard power for pre-emptive or punitive strikes against terrorists sheltered by Pakistan.

ABHINANDAN

Wing Commander Abhinandan Varthaman flew the MiG-21 bison that was part of the air defence sortie scrambled to intercept Pakistani aircraft on the morning of 27 February. In the ensuing aerial dogfight, his aircraft was struck by a missile and crashed, but Varthaman safely ejected, to descend into a village in Pakistan-occupied Kashmir, some 7 kilometres from the LoC. Varthaman was initially captured and assaulted by locals before army soldiers took him into custody. Soon, Varthaman became for the Indian public both a symbol of heroism—having engaged an enemy aircraft—and the human cost of the skirmish. He also became the lightning rod for the diplomatic action of the next few days and its primary focus.

India's demands for Pakistan were clear. Pakistan had retaliated against India's pre-emptive counterterrorism action. It had responded by attacking military targets. It had captured an Indian pilot and violated the Geneva Conventions. India would expect the pilot not to come to any harm. Pakistan should exercise restraint and responsibility; any provocation along the LoC would not be tolerated.

India had activated multiple diplomatic channels to deal with the crisis. Pakistan on its part was trying to drag the matter to the UN, as an issue that threatened regional peace and stability. Foreign Secretary Vijay Gokhale in Delhi had emphasized to the US and UK that any attempt by Pakistan to escalate the situation further or to cause harm to Varthaman would lead to an escalation by India; raising this issue at the UNSC instead of resolving the issue of terror could also lead to an escalated response from India. Other channels were in play to send similar messages to countries with influence over Pakistan, particularly the UAE and Saudi Arabia.

The US ambassador to India, Ken Juster, and UK envoy, Dominic Asquith, worked with their counterparts in Islamabad, Paul Jones, and Tom Drew, to impress upon Pakistani interlocutors that India was serious. Frenetic diplomatic action was unfolding in Pakistan. India's hard messages were being conveyed both in the diplomatic bubble of Islamabad and at general headquarters, Rawalpindi. The diplomats of the P5 in particular had been called in by the foreign office 'thrice in rapid succession' after 26 February, most of the time separately. To the diplomats, Pakistan appeared genuinely spooked by the prospects of an escalation in the conflict. At the same time, Pakistani officials, as also ISI officers, were insisting that they had no direct role in the Pulwama attack. It had been claimed by the JeM, which was based in Pakistan, but had no connection with the army or with Bajwa personally.[12]

Pakistan's public and private talking points included the default position that the Pulwama attacker was a local Kashmiri, the video of the JeM owning responsibility was suspect, the weapons shown in the video were not Pakistani, and that the flag displayed in the video did not belong to the JeM. There was 'considerable pushback' by the US, UK, and France to the Pakistani narrative, in their discussions with the DG ISI Asim Munir and Foreign Secretary Tehmina Janjua. They pointed out to Pakistan that its narrative was weak. One, the JeM had already undeniably claimed responsibility for Pulwama. Two, the Jaish chief Masood Azhar was undeniably in Pakistani territory. Three, the video of the claim may have been edited, but did not suggest the Jaish did not claim the attack. Four, the markings on the weapons did not matter, since any sort of weapons could be bought, even within the arms markets of Pakistan. Five, the flag of Jaish may not be the original one but could have belonged to some splinter group.

The Western diplomats were pointing out in private conversations that the connection between Pakistan and the terror attack was obvious. Pakistan also tried to make the argument that this may have been a 'false-flag operation' connected to Indian elections. The British high commissioner and the US ambassador both advised their interlocutors to not even go down that route. This was a familiar denial practised by Pakistan through this century, whether it was for 9/11 or Mumbai or Pathankot or Uri, and was no longer credible.

At 4 p.m. on 27 February, the day after India's air strikes at Balakot, the US, UK, and French ambassadors were closeted at the US embassy in Islamabad to discuss the crisis. During their consultations, their offices called to say that the foreign office was requesting them to show up for yet another meeting with the Pakistan foreign secretary at 5 p.m. While the conference was in progress, and they were discussing India's asks, Foreign Secretary Janjua paused the conversation at 5.45 p.m. to read out a message she had just received from the army, saying that nine missiles from India had been pointed towards Pakistan, to be launched any time that day. Also, India's navy had taken on an aggressive, threatening posture. The foreign secretary requested the envoys to report this intelligence to their capitals and ask India not to escalate the situation. The diplomats promptly reported these developments, leading to a flurry of diplomatic activity in Islamabad, P5 capitals, and in New Delhi that night. One of them recommended to her that Pakistan should convey its concerns directly to India. (A P5 diplomat later reconstructed these events for my benefit.)

Later in the evening, the DG for South Asia, Mohammad Faisal, summoned India's acting high commissioner, Ahluwalia, for a démarche. After condemning the 'unprovoked ceasefire violations by the Indian occupation forces along the Line of Control' a ruffled Faisal said that

Pakistan had credible information on nine missiles India had prepared to launch into Pakistani territory. India was asked to desist, since this was an unprecedented act of aggression and an action tantamount to open war. While Pakistan's media reported the démarche on ceasefire violations by India, the story of the potential missile launch was held back that night but released in a background briefing by ISPR on 4 March, with some embellishments. Several media reports appeared in March, detailing the conversations around the missiles between India and Pakistan and through global interlocutors.[13]

At around midnight I got a call in Delhi from Pakistani high commissioner Sohail Mahmood, now in Islamabad, who said that PM Imran Khan was keen to talk to Prime Minister Modi. I checked upstairs and responded that our prime minister was not available at this hour but in case Imran Khan had any urgent message to convey he could, of course, convey it to me. I got no call back that night.

The US and UK envoys in Delhi got back overnight to India's foreign secretary to claim that Pakistan was now ready to de-escalate the situation, to act on India's dossier, and to seriously address the issue of terrorism. Pakistan's PM would himself make these announcements and the pilot would be returned to India the next day. India's coercive diplomacy had been effective, India's expectations of Pakistan and of the world had been clear, backed by a credible resolve to escalate the crisis. Prime Minister Modi would later say in a campaign speech that, 'Fortunately, Pakistan announced that the pilot would be sent back to India. Else, it would have been *qatal ki raat*, a night of bloodshed.'[14]

The US secretary of state Mike Pompeo later made a dramatic claim in his memoirs that 'the Indian minister' had told him that Pakistan might escalate the conflict into a nuclear one. He wrote he was awakened to speak with his Indian counterpart who 'believed the Pakistanis had begun to prepare their nuclear weapons for a strike.' He said the Indian side informed him that New Delhi 'was contemplating its own escalation.' After the call, Pompeo and NSA John Bolton contacted the Pakistani side. 'I reached the actual leader of Pakistan, General [Qamar] Bajwa, with whom I had engaged many times. I told him what the Indians had told me. He said it wasn't true...he [Bajwa] believed the Indians were preparing their nuclear weapons for deployment. It took us a few hours—and remarkably good work by our teams on the ground in New Delhi and Islamabad—to convince each side that the other was not preparing for nuclear war.'[15] But Pompeo seemed to have overstated the case, both of fears of escalation of the conflict and of the US role in defusing it.

In Pakistan, the Indian threat of action was taken seriously. Foreign Minister Qureshi spoke at a closed-door session of parliament to explain Pakistan's decision to release the Indian pilot. A Pakistani MP later revealed in parliament: 'In the case of Abhinandan, I remember Shah Mahmood Qureshi was in that meeting which the prime minister [Imran Khan] refused to attend and the chief of army staff joined us—his [Qureshi's] legs were shaking and there was sweat on his brow.'[16]

Imran Khan's promised 'peace speech' started hesitatingly. The address in Pakistan's parliament was telecast live in India on the afternoon of 28 February. Khan apparently spoke extempore, as Foreign Secretary Gokhale and I sat in front of a TV in his chamber, making notes. Khan referred to the 'tragedy of Pulwama' and said that Pakistan was ready to investigate this incident. He did assure the world that the soil of Pakistan would not be used by terrorists to launch an attack against any other country. This promise checked a box, but it was a familiar refrain that had been sung, also under pressure, by Musharraf in 2002. Khan also said that Pakistan was ready for dialogue. Pakistan, he complained, had received the Pulwama dossier only after India had taken action in Balakot. Instead, India should have given the dossier first and waited for Pakistan to take action before attacking.

Pakistan had shown restraint, Khan insisted. When India's planes attacked Pakistan at 3.30 a.m., the Pakistan leadership waited to assess the damage and then decided to attack India, which they did successfully, without causing any damage. Khan said he had tried to call Modi on the night of 27 February in the interest of peace, 'not out of weakness'. Foreign Minister Qureshi had also tried to call his counterpart to discuss the issue. Khan ended with a flourish. Pakistan, he said, did not want to share the fate of Bahadur Shah Zafar, the last Mughal, who capitulated before the British, but its hero was Tipu Sultan, who defied them till the death. His message to the Indian PM was that India should not force Pakistan into war. Pakistan would then be forced to respond to Indian missiles and the situation could escalate to dangerous levels.

As Imran Khan sat down in parliament, Gokhale and I looked at each other in disappointment. Pakistan's prime minister had said nothing about the pilot, or about specific action against Jaish terrorists. Before we could start making calls to confer on this speech, we got the breaking news that Khan had said that he would return Abhinandan Varthaman, the IAF pilot, as a peace gesture. Khan had in fact resumed his speech after sitting down when he was prompted to deliver a part of his speech that he had forgotten—that the pilot would be released as a 'peace gesture'. I later learnt from a source in Islamabad that the army brass had been exasperated that day because Khan had forgotten his lines and spoken extempore on this crucial issue. He had to be nudged by Qureshi into making the key announcement.

Meanwhile, Foreign Minister Qureshi said publicly that Pakistan was ready to talk about terrorism and was prepared to examine India's dossier.

He told CNN and BBC that the JeM head Masood Azhar was in Pakistan but very sick. This fact, well known to India and shared with the world, had to be roundly denied by the military spokesman soon after, because of the official Pakistani line that (just as in the case of al-Qaeda leader Osama bin Laden) Pakistan had no clue where the Jaish chief was.

But India was not assuming the situation had been completely defused until Abhinandan Varthaman actually returned home. On 1 March, India's Cabinet Committee on Security met again, to make public some firm decisions. India's approach was focused—press for the return of the pilot, continue the pressure on Pakistan on dismantling the terror network, and work on the listing of Masood Azhar as a terrorist by the Security Council before mid-March.

We got working on the modalities of the return of Varthaman the next day. We decided to ask Pakistan not to make a media spectacle of the return of the pilot. We said that he could be returned through the international Red Cross like other pilots before him, most recently Flight Lieutenant Nachiketa, who was downed, as we saw, during the Kargil operations in 1999 and repatriated after eight days in Pakistani custody.[17] Varthaman would need to be returned following prisoner of war protocol. We were willing to send an Indian Air Force aircraft to pick him up but Pakistan refused permission; the optics of an Indian Air Force plane landing in Islamabad after all that had happened over the previous three days, was, of course, not acceptable to Pakistan.

Pakistan agreed to hand over Varthaman at Wagah between 2 p.m. and 5 p.m. on 1 March. We activated a team in Islamabad, led by the air attaché, Group Captain Joy Kurien, to go to Wagah to pick up the pilot who, we heard, would be transported from Islamabad to Lahore. For Kurien, who had been stationed in Islamabad for three years and was about to return to India, it was a special joy for his last official task to be one to escort his colleague from Pakistan to India.

India decided to call off the border ceremony at Wagah on that day and said that the prisoner should be returned in compliance with Geneva Conventions. A representative of the Indian Air Force would receive the wing commander according to protocol norms. India issued a statement expressing satisfaction that a worthy son of India was returning.

I was continuously on the phone with colleagues in Islamabad monitoring Varthaman's release, as was the entire Indian media. We had word that the pilot had been taken to Lahore. I told Defence Minister Nirmala Sitharaman when she called me that the ISI was possibly making multiple propoganda videos in some Lahore studio starring the Indian pilot, and would release Varthaman before the day was over. But only when they had the perfect take. As it turned out, the pilot was finally produced at Wagah at around 9 p.m. and was handed over to the Indian side.

Our overall approach had been to go by standard global protocols on these matters and to avoid a media circus. But the public narrative had been frenzied on Pulwama, Balakot, and Varthaman. What was missing was a deeper analysis of Indo–Pak relations and India's shifting security paradigms. Pakistan maintained the line that it had returned the pilot 'as a goodwill gesture aimed at de-escalating rising tensions with India.' The IAF simply said it was 'happy to have Abhinandan back'.

REVIVING DIPLOMACY

The events of February had moved rapidly, with many operational details still blurred; commentators were asking penetrating questions and demanding answers. Why was the government not producing evidence of those killed in the Balakot operation? If India had intelligence inputs about the Balakot terror camps preparing terrorists to be let loose on India for attacks, why did it not have such inputs for Pulwama? A media article[18] had suggested that only seven people knew about the Balakot operation—the PM, NSA, the IB and R&AW chiefs, and the three service chiefs: was this true? Did international pressure work and did global powers play middlemen to mediate for the release of the wing commander? In an election season, the questions had to be credibly answered, even if they were not particularly relevant to the big picture.

In internal meetings in South Block, a senior security official pointed out that the objective of the mission was to destroy terrorists, not to photograph them. The army chief pointed out that India had not released details of operations even when forces had crossed the LoC for the surgical strikes. Details could be sensitive, they could at times compromise sources or operations or tactics. Yet, some strategic communication was essential. India's military and diplomatic strategy had worked in concert to deal with a national crisis; the defence establishment would gradually share what it could in the media.

The diplomacy of the time had necessarily to be more transparent since multiple countries were involved. Multiple global partners had played their roles, and India had seen strong global sympathy for and in alignment with its positions. Several countries had offered to send special envoys over to the subcontinent but this was no longer necessary. Even China, not to be left behind, had suggested that it could send its deputy minister to both countries to seek de-escalation. India had politely declined the offer.

The action now shifted to the UN. India continued making demarches to the fifteen UN Security Council members, including the ten non-permanent members, all of them in the terror sanctions committee. They all held a persuasive Pulwama dossier in their hands. The case was clear. India had only conducted a counterterrorism strike on non-military terrorist targets; Pakistan had escalated this situation twenty-four hours later; Pakistan was now peddling news of 'credible intelligence' about India's escalation even before it had taken place; this was a counter-terrorism issue and not a 'peace and security' issue which needed to be debated at the UN; and the listing of Masood Azhar as a terrorist was the issue the Security Council should be focusing on.

Bilaterally with Pakistan, India was underlining expectations of immediate credible and verifiable action to dismantle the terrorist infrastructure and to deal with terrorists. India had not closed its channels of communication. The DGMOs hotline was open and so were the high commissions in India and Pakistan. In media briefings, Foreign Secretary Gokhale was also pointing out that Pakistan had issued a notice to airmen, 'NOTAM' closing its airspace, while India had quickly opened its airspace to normalize the situation.

With the dust settling on Pulwama, Balakot, and with the return of Varthaman, the political temperature had come down in India. By 5 March, we seemed to be getting into the de-escalation phase. The CCS felt that it would be in India's best interest to have its high commissioner back in Pakistan, a nod to moving to the next phase of diplomacy. I reached Islamabad via Dubai on 10 March, twenty-two days after I left in the wake of Pulwama. India was willing to give old-fashioned diplomacy another chance.

India had signalled to Pakistan through its acting high commissioner that I would be back in Islamabad that weekend. Pakistan responded by sending its own high commissioner back to Delhi. At that point, Sohail Mahmood was already the front runner to take over as the Pakistani foreign secretary, since Tehmina Janjua was to retire the next month. His interaction with the Pakistani leadership through the Pulwama and Balakot crisis had apparently strengthened his candidature, as also his credentials as a quiet and competent diplomat with the most recent experience in handling the key India relationship.

The media interpreted the coordinated return of the diplomats as evidence of a thaw in diplomatic relations between the two countries. The most serious military exchange between the countries since Kargil had thus run its course in less than a month from a Pakistani proxy attack, to a military response from India, a counter from Pakistan, and an Indian diplomatic move to press Pakistan for credible action against terrorism. This, with India having achieved a strategic and military objective and Pakistan having claimed a notion of victory for its domestic audience.

What this episode, from Pulwama to my return to Islamabad, told me was that the recovery time from an India–Pakistan crisis, triggered by terrorism, could be as short as three weeks as long as escalatory steps were accompanied by a de-escalation impulse on both sides. We had seen the first attack by Indian aircraft across the international border since 1971.

We had seen Pakistan's response. We had seen a move towards normalizing ties even if no peace conference or peace pact had followed this exchange to give the matter closure.

In terms of the 'escalation dynamics' of the conflict (as determined by a theoretical conflict escalation ladder favoured by some nuclear experts[19]), the first rung of the escalation ladder was Pulwama, a terrorist action whether state-sponsored or otherwise. Only as a response to such action did the situation escalate to the next rung of the ladder with India's air strikes, still a military operation in the sub-conventional space. A response to Pakistan's action after Balakot by India could have led to a further escalation, experts argued, that could lead the countries over the conventional threshold. While Pakistan tried to speak of false-flag operations, it was trying to create insurance policies: to question global diplomatic acquiescence in India's response to the first-rung terrorist attack, which, in the case of Balakot, did not invite any international censure.

My mandate in Pakistan in March 2019 was to meet diplomatic and other interlocutors to explain India's post-Balakot posture and expectations for the future. I was still not to seek meetings with either Khan or Qureshi or Bajwa, to avoid these being mischaracterized as a formally resumed dialogue. But I was free to hold quiet chats with other players.

Hectic diplomacy followed over the next few days. India had signalled the intention to seal the Kartarpur agreement and Pakistan was all set to send its team to India in mid-March for talks. I had been recommending that the conversation take place as an official and technical discussion, away from the spotlight of the capital, at newly renovated facilities at Attari on the border, to signal a desire to do business without indicating any deeper political reconciliation for the moment. This is eventually what we did when the Pakistan team arrived in India for joint secretary-level talks at Attari on 1 April.

More privately, Pakistan was beginning to signal a serious intention to address the core issue of terrorism, rather than repeating its line about the centrality of the Kashmir issue. Both countries had therefore run the course of military actions for the moment, even though the sporadic firing at the LoC continued at its own momentum. India was willing to move towards a phase of diplomatic normality with a focus on a conversation on terrorism. Pakistan seemed willing to play ball.

THE PULWAMA DOSSIER

The Pulwama dossier was a unique document. It enhanced the credibility of India's claim of Pakistan's role in the attack. While the full National Investigation Agency (NIA) charge sheet would take eighteen painstaking months to construct and present to the courts[20], the early evidence was clear. Forty people had been killed in an explosive attack, the Jaish had claimed responsibility, the Jaish leader and headquarters were in Pakistan. A credible narration of these details with the names of Jaish operatives and the last known locations of terror camps was what India had put in the dossier and even shared with Pakistan. The dossier listed some ninety active JeM members. It also gave coordinates of about twenty JeM camps.

A Western envoy close to Pakistan's army told me on my return to Islamabad that he was optimistic that India's actions had triggered a rethink by the Pakistan Army. Bajwa now appeared to have been persuaded that the cost to benefit ratio of deploying proxy terror was no longer in Pakistan's favour. What was even more encouraging was that the civilian and army leadership were still on the same page. In the past, such friction with India had often strained the civil–military equation. We had, for instance, seen Nawaz Sharif's stock with the army sink after Kargil and after the surgical strikes in Uri on both occasions, the elected PM had lost his job.

One strong external impulse that was playing on Pakistan's mind was the FATF and its staying hand, which was compelling the country to change its behaviour on terrorism. Pakistan was added to the Paris-based UN body's inglorious 'grey list', and subjected to 'increased monitoring' from June 2018 onwards. It had been struggling to shake off this intense global scrutiny of its state support to militant groups; the post-Pulwama global spotlight was not helping, particularly since FATF conditionalities were finding their way into the IMF economic rescue package it was negotiating. The Pulwama dossier that India had shared widely was also something of a game changer, since India had so openly shared evidence with Pakistan and the world. Moreover, Pakistan was actually claiming to be acting on it, not, as in the past, dismissing it offhand. Bajwa was telling Western diplomats that the hard action against the 'Barelvi' extremist political formation, TLP (Tehreek-e-Labaik, known for its violent street protests against changes to the blasphemy law) showed that if an organization acted against the national interest, then Pakistan would push back. The same would be the case with Jaish. What Pakistan needed was support on the FATF front.

A theory that soon emerged in Islamabad was that some 190 people from 'proscribed organizations' that Pakistan claimed to have arrested in March were militants killed in the Balakot action; Pakistan was trying to account for them in some way. The arrests on 7 and 21 March were simply reported with no documentation or videos, and the numbers seemed to match those quoted by an Italian journalist Francesca Marino who filed a story on 8 March claiming that 170 terrorists died in India's air strikes.[21]

On the Indian side, a colleague from one of the agencies expressed some cynicism to me about sharing details with Pakistan; each time a dossier was passed on to Pakistan, it used it as briefing material for its ISI handlers to explain to the terrorists what not to do in the future. This was spoken only half in jest.

Meanwhile, the Pakistan Army was telling some Western confidants that this was another 'APS moment' for the army in dealing with non-state actors, referring to the killing of 145 children in the Army Public School of Peshawar back in 2015 that had traumatized the army. This was an opportunity for Bajwa's army to reclaim the 'monopoly of force' with the state and to disarm the terrorists, even the Kashmir-focused ones like JeM believed to be 'good', as distinct from the 'bad' Pakistan-targeting TTP. The situation paralleled the 'good Taliban, bad Taliban' debate of the early 2000s, a constant gripe of Pakistan's partners in the global war on terror initiated in 2001.

A key issue was the mainstreaming and disarming of radical groups. The Pakistan Army was engaging with the UK and quoting the Irish example of mainstreaming militants. The UK was explaining that the analogy was not necessarily close, since a disarming and deradicalizing process was essential before mainstreaming could begin. Some Pakistani commentators were pointing to the Saudi model of deradicalization: to arrest the militants, re-train them, 'explain' to them that the monopoly on violence lay with the state and then release them into society. But the Pakistan case was different—state structures had created armed militant groups and trained them for 'jihad'. It was not easy to undo this mess.

On his part, Bajwa was claiming that the push against terror was serious. The army was citing multiple data points: the arrest of 154 Jaish militants, which meant the top leadership of Jaish and also of LeT 'reincarnates'— Jamat ul dawa (JUD) and Falah-e Insaniyat Foundation (FIF); there was a new 'top-down' impetus against some groups, with Khan and Bajwa firmly on the 'same page' on this issue. The JUD had been forced to mainstream its 'ambulance service', thus separating the charity arm from the militant wing of the organization. The Pakistan Army was now working closely with the Interior Ministry to work on this issue of deradicalization, implying a strong civil–military consensus on the moves.

Bajwa explained to various interlocutors the difficulties of dismantling organizations like JeM. He argued that small and incremental steps needed to be taken. The radicalization had been taking place over the previous thirty years. So deradicalization would take at least a few months. The militant elements could be dismantled, but how did one take over the charitable parts of militant organizations?

Based on my briefings in Delhi, we embarked on multiple conversations in Islamabad with Pakistani influencers and diplomats. Our counter-terror diplomacy was focused. We did some blunt speaking. There were broadly ten messages that we shared with Pakistani and foreign interlocutors.

One, India's threshold of tolerance of terrorism had come down. India was now determined to take swift, surgical, and resolute action against the terrorists. India had no quarrel with the people of Pakistan and was not even directly targeting Pakistan's army. Two, India was encouraged by the reiteration by Prime Minister Imran Khan and Foreign Minister Qureshi in Pakistan's parliament and to CNN and the BBC that the territory of Pakistan would not be used for any act of terrorism against its neighbours. But we wanted to see these promises translated into action. Three, India was willing to work with Pakistan to ensure there was sustained, credible, and verifiable action against terrorism. We would encourage Pakistan's government and army to take more than cosmetic action against terrorists to win back India's confidence and that of the world community. Four, we would ask Pakistan to proscribe Jaish, Lashkar, and Hizbul. The leaders should be locked up, disarmed, banned from travel, and their assets frozen. Five, India was willing to discuss modalities for an informal dialogue with Pakistan on terrorism and ways of tackling it. Six, for the army and civilian leadership, for Bajwa and Khan, I was carrying a clear message that we could use this opportunity to move ahead and tackle what for Pakistan were good terrorists. Seven, we were willing to work on the humanitarian front to build trust. We were willing to work on the exchange of prisoners and on the Kartarpur project which had popular support in India, particularly in Punjab. Eight, India was requesting the support of the global community when it came to tackling the menace of terrorism, since it was clear the kind of danger it was putting the world into. Nine, the world community needed to deploy the FATF to do what it was designed to do—counter the financing of terror and demanding that Pakistan commit clearly to timelines to stop funding terrorist outfits. Ten, we deeply appreciated the role of several partners including the US, UK, Saudi Arabia, and the UAE, who had helped defuse the tension.

Armed with this brief, I started a period of intense diplomacy in Islamabad, talking to people close to Imran Khan and Bajwa while continuing conversations with the foreign office. The talks with the MOFA were more on the 'humanitarian agenda' because the foreign office followed a party line of stout denial on terrorism. It had failed to create for itself the space to engage on this issue. On 12 March, I met with Foreign Secretary Janjua for a candid chat on the month gone by. I discussed the dossier we had handed over. Since we were back from the brink, I suggested, we needed to continue the diplomacy. Action on the dossier in Pakistan would be a good confidence-building measure for India. The foreign office was not taking any chances. They continued to deny any role in Pulwama by any agency from Pakistan. But the party line had changed. Pakistan was informing us it was taking action against terror under its own National Action Plan (NAP) of 2014, and not due to any Indian pressure. The imminent Indian election had a part to play in focusing the mind of the Pakistani establishment. I was beginning to perceive more attentive engagement because the Pakistan establishment had by now assessed that I was a spokesman of an Indian government that would return to power with a firmer mandate to deal decisively with Pakistan and terrorism.

The coalescing of multiple factors—India's focused diplomatic effort after the air strikes, the Pulwama dossier, FATF and global pressure— was having a telling effect on Pakistan. In March 2019, an ordinance amended Pakistan's antiterrorism act to ban the groups that were already proscribed under the UNSC sanctions, i.e., FIF and JUD, both front outfits of the Mumbai attack mastermind Hafiz Sayeed's LeT. Pakistan's National Counter-Terrorism Authority (NACTA) had earlier put seventy organizations on its watchlist. The ordinance banning them had lapsed in October 2018. The JUD had gone to the Lahore High Court in October 2018 and had succeeded in overturning the ban on its activities. The script seemed familiar—this was the usual pre-FATF meeting illusion of activity. But many in Pakistan were insisting that the army was shifting its approach to terrorism.

Some analysts, like Abdul Basit, Pakistan's former high commissioner to India, were more critical of the new global narrative, arguing that the Pulwama–Balakot episode had shown that the international community was keener to de-escalate the tension between the two countries rather than focus on the 'root cause' of Kashmir. Once again, Pakistan's echo chamber of readily churned out narratives tried to switch off global voices. But, this time around, not even Pakistan's loyal friends in the OIC were buying the weakly proffered and oft-repeated hypothesis that the root cause of Kashmir triggered the latest violence. All data was reaffirming the reputation that Pakistan's deep state had earned for the country—of a terror-exporting nation.

The weekly conversations between the DGMOs were continuing. Pakistan had been told in mid-April that if terrorist infiltration stopped, firing at the border would stop. The Indian Army had reminded Pakistan's Army about the mutually agreed moratorium on artillery fire and the use of special forces on the border. The only ongoing official conversation between India and Pakistan, apart from the one we were having at the diplomatic level, was the one between the two militaries. The DGMOs were talking regularly and India had made its substantive position clear. When Pakistan claimed that it was taking action on the western border, India's suggestion was to take similar action against terrorists and militants on its eastern border. India had pointed out that some forty Indian nationals including of the 'D company', who were known terrorists, had been given safe sanctuary on Pakistan's territory.

Somewhere in mid-April, Pakistan summoned Western diplomats to the foreign office again, alleging imminent Indian attacks against it. Curiously, it even put this episode in the public domain.[22] The diplomats were assessing that Pakistan was genuinely spooked and jumpy. It perhaps also saw crying wolf as a means of pre-emption, an insurance policy against an Indian punitive attack. In case of an incident, it would have the advantage of suggesting to the West that South Asia was a dangerous flashpoint. The international community was however not even raising these issues with India, dismissing them as alarmist rhetoric and arguing that India was much too busy with its election to be involved with such gambits.

My interlocutor with the ISI was reporting a more receptive attitude for India's concerns. The message from DG ISI Asim Munir was clear—Pakistan was working on a project to finish militancy, there would be no more terror incidents in Jammu and Kashmir, there would be no cross-border infiltration. But it was hard to act on the Indian asks in the prevailing climate of inflamed Pakistani public opinion. High-profile actions, like arresting Masood Azhar or Hafiz Sayeed, were therefore ruled out.

The ISI had made a clear assessment that the BJP would return to power in India's elections. Pakistan would be prepared for a dialogue, to participate in the swearing-in of the new prime minister, and to send Imran Khan for a meeting at the SCO summit in June with India's new prime minister. The ISI was rejecting for the moment India's demand to hand over Indian fugitives. This was a big ask and not quite feasible for the moment, when even the listing of Masood Azhar as a terrorist was being blocked.

On JeM chief Azhar, while fourteen of the fifteen sanctions committee member countries of the Security Council were on board to have him listed, the Chinese were the holdout, trying to 'persuade' Pakistan to give its consent, in effect giving a veto to Pakistan. From 2009, there had been four attempts to put Azhar on the UN counter-terrorism sanctions list, all of which saw blocks by China, citing 'lack of evidence'. China had again moved to protect Azhar in October 2016 when it blocked India's appeal but famously asked Pakistan to get its act in order.[23] China also blocked the post-Pulwama moves to get Azhar banned in February and March.

Three permanent UNSC members (P3)—the US, UK, and France—were pressing Pakistan to talk to their Chinese friends to unblock the listing. Pakistan was again overplaying its hand and placing an unreasonable condition to acquiesce in the listing—that there should be no further listing of any individual, especially in relationship to Kashmir, at least for the rest of the year. This was a bizarre demand that the Chinese seemed to be relaying unthinkingly; the rest of the P5 members were shaking their heads in disbelief. How could there be political quotas on the listing of terrorists? Pakistan, some in its media were warning, was 'testing its friends'.[24]

In the midst of this debate, I had a frank chat with the Chinese ambassador Yao Jing, along with his deputy Zhao Lijian, who later went on to become a 'wolf warrior' anti-West spokesman of the Chinese foreign ministry. (Zhao incidentally departed from Pakistan on the same day that I left for Delhi, the end of my abbreviated tenure coinciding with his longer one. To my amusement, he told me at the airport lounge that the Pakistan establishment would miss me.) The Chinese ambassador hinted at frustration at Pakistan's tall asks of guarantees against any further listing of Pakistan's citizens. China seemed to be playing for time to deal with this issue but seemed also to be pressing Pakistan to relent. China lifted the technical hold only on 1 May, when Masood Azhar was finally listed as a global terrorist by the UNSC's al-Qaeda and Taliban Sanctions Committee. Islamabad tried to play this development as a Pakistani decision, but still kept Azhar hidden from public view.

BAJWA'S CT DOCTRINE

Bajwa, due to end his tenure in November, seemed to be caught, in the summer of 2019, between legacy and extension. He was claiming he would leave at the appointed hour when his term ended in November, but this seemed to be some 'virtue signalling'. Almost all of Pakistan's army chiefs have indulged in some 'political management' in the months leading up to the end of their first terms and Bajwa was no exception. But Bajwa had also set up some long term goals. He seemed prepared to add to his doctrine an element of having stamped out terrorism from Pakistan.

A new kind of Bajwa doctrine was emerging. By early April, Bajwa's confidants were claiming a distinctly different tone at the GHQ. The word had got around that the army was trying to create 'political space' to deal with the Jaish militants, to avoid a blowback by right-wing forces. Bajwa was arguing that he would take action in a series of sequential steps. The first action would be on the Indian dossier. It would be followed by wider arrests of both the LeT and the JeM, more madrasas would be taken over, and the authorities would not let the militants regroup.

Bajwa, we learnt, was speaking the same language within the army, with his senior commanders and at limited conferences. Most Western interlocutors were coming away convinced that the army was beginning to change, at least at the top. Bajwa was openly questioning a forty-year-old doctrine that he had seen in play from the time he was a young cadet and which now needed to change because it was not working. He was saying clearly that Pakistan's assets had become liabilities and the time had come to insist that the use of force should be the monopoly of the state. This point was not being conceded publicly, nor by the foreign office, which tended to be behind the curve and balk at the prospect of any public admission of past errors.

The DG ISI appeared to be taking an even harder line on domestic terrorism compared to Bajwa in his conversations with Western diplomats. DG Munir said that a few misdirected men were threatening the reputation of 200 million Pakistanis by their actions. He said that Pakistan was taking serious action against the militants and it was not facing much resistance, even though militant groups were splintering and merging into other groups.

The 'good terrorists' were however still getting a free pass. The ISI was taking a harder line on Kashmir and fudging the issue of whether it would use proxy groups to fuel conflict in Kashmir. It would often justify its actions to diplomats by alleging that India was using its own proxy groups within Pakistan.

Nevertheless, it was unquestionable that Pakistan's action against terrorist groups was gaining momentum. At the very least, Pakistan's public and diplomatic proclamations were gaining pace as Pakistan took the trouble to brief all diplomats (except India) repeatedly on the action it was taking against militants. While the official line was that all the action was based upon Pakistan's own National Action Plan (NAP) against terrorism, more private briefings to Western diplomats were quoting the Indian dossier and saying that Pakistan had detained fifty-six of the fifty-seven individuals listed in that document. Two hundred of the 'most egregious' madrasas had been taken over. Pakistan would now try the militants in civilian and military courts to lead up to a process of demobilization and the decommissioning of weapons. This was part of the professed doctrine of retaining monopoly of force with the state. While 'kinetic action' would be taken against the JeM, the JUD, and and other militant groups with large charitable wings, would be taken over more gently.

To the British, Pakistan was claiming it was following the Northern Ireland model. Both the British and the Americans had argued that Pakistan was dealing with hardcore terrorists and needed a different approach. The counter from Pakistan was that they were not dealing with five or six terrorists but a hundred thousand and needed a more gradual approach to demobilize them. Pakistan's army was claiming to confidants that its approach to the militants was marked by much ambiguity, learning from the TLP experience. It was meeting with surprisingly little resistance as it rounded up these militants. A few of the Jaish cadres were splintering and joining up with the Tehreek-i-Taliban Afghanistan (TTA) and TTP.

Pakistan had claimed to have eliminated more than 17,600 terrorists. of the militant organizations in counter-terror operations from 2001 till February 2018, and cleared over 46,000 kilometres of land of terrorists, mainly in the badlands of the former FATA, in numbers publicly announced in February 2018, after Trump's tweet of 1 January 2018.[25] From India's viewpoint, the real problem was the camps in the heart of Pakistan, in Punjab's Bahawalpur, and in Balakot, which were providing state protection to the India-directed groups like JeM and LeT.

India was also pressing its global partners to insist on direct action against the JeM and LeT and on punishing the guilty for previous acts of terrorism, like Pathankot 2016, Mumbai 2008, Parliament 2001, and the earlier Mumbai 1993 and 1996 blasts. A prominent Pakistani think tanker relayed the message to me from the army that it was important to mainstream and re-educate the militants. You could not quite jail 300,000 people from the LeT in the same way as Pakistan had managed to deal with the smaller number of the TLP.

ٮ

Global opinion was supporting India's position. Ashley Tellis, the US security analyst, prepared a comprehensive assessment of the post-Pulwama situation to argue that the focus must continue to be on Pakistan's terrorism, that India should not fall for Pakistan's 'nuclear coercion' and that the new paradigm of India's response should be 'ambiguous'. He saw the US role as positive, with Secretary of State Pompeo having recognized India's right to self-defence and asked Pakistan to focus its attention on countering terrorism.[26]

A Pakistani acquaintance, close to both the army and the civilian regime, assured me that 1,800 JeM members would be arrested as both Imran Khan and the army were determined to act against the JeM. However, unlike the TLP, the JeM carried arms and they were not easy to wish away or to neutralize. When we argued that the Pakistan Army had the capacity to make the bad guys disappear as they did in the FATA region and with the TLP not long ago, we were told that the JeM was different.

Varying characteristics of the various terrorist organizations, and the need to find an appropriate way of dealing with them, was only one aspect of what Bajwa was dealing with. He was also up against a deeper systemic problem. As Christine Fair has argued, the ethos and the strategic culture of the Pakistan Army favoured 'persistent revisionism'.[27] Pakistan's own narrative was that India was implacably opposed to its existence and the Pakistan Army was thus obsessed with strategic depth despite all its professions otherwise. The temptation was to keep doing 'jihad under an expanding nuclear umbrella',[28] to continue to use non-state actors with an attempt not to cross India's retaliation threshold.

Yet, two significant new trends accelerated forward on Bajwa's watch, which required Pakistan to rethink older strategies. The first was that the western border of Pakistan was now more troubled, with the Afghan regime confronting the Taliban and the TTP directly attacking Pakistan's forces. The second was that on the eastern front the ideological fervour of the 'Kashmir cause' had been toned down, with a post-Balakot pause in Pakistani support to militants. This implied a new direction to security policy. It did seem that Pakistan's army would see the balance of advantage in pressing the pause button on Kashmir-directed militancy.[29]

A former Pakistan high commissioner, active on the Track II circuit, told me that Pakistan was now willing to talk on all issues with India, including terrorism and trade/business. The Pakistan establishment was perhaps trying to change the narrative on identifying discussions on both terrorism and trade as perfidious Indian attempts to take attention away from the core issue of Kashmir. A signal to the Track II circuit would normally imply that Pakistan would test the waters for having a similar conversation through normal official channels as well. The reality on the ground seemed to substantiate the Pakistani claims that they were making a genuine effort to curb militant activity. The infiltration numbers from Pakistan into India were showing only twenty-three cross-border bids in 2019 compared to 300 in 2018, and 400 in 2017.[30]

In the bigger picture, three decades of terrorism had an important impact on bilateral diplomacy—it increased the political risk for India of high-level engagement with Pakistan. India's instincts were now to factor in the risk that dialogue with Pakistan may result in an immediate significant terrorist attack by Pakistan-based militants; this had happened to Vajpayee's Lahore initiative with Kargil and to Modi's with Pathankot.[31]

Also, despite its historical concerns about internationalization of disagreements with Pakistan, India was now not averse to taking the terror issue to global fora like the FATF and the UNSC sanctions committee for the listing of Masood Azhar and others. This was part of a policy of 'measured flexibility'[32], to take forward bilateral disputes to specialized global bodies like the International Court of Justice (for the captured Indian citizen Kulbhushan Jadhav) or the World Bank (for the Indus Waters Treaty), or the ICAO (for airspace closure matters) while sticking to the principle of bilateralism to address the Kashmir issue.

34

KASHMIRIYAT

In the spring of 2019, the world's biggest dance of democracy was underway in India. As the dust settled on the February events, we received requests in April for visas for Pakistani journalists to cover the elections. I was all for sending Pakistani media in for the journalists to see the scale and efficiency of India's electoral process. The concern in India was that the coverage was unlikely to be balanced and objective. It was too soon after the events of February to expect unbiased reports in Pakistan's press. The visas finally did not come through.

By mid-April, diplomatic conversations in Islamabad were veering back to the prospects of peace in a post-election scenario in India, as prophesied by the Bajwa doctrine. Pakistan's establishment had by now assessed that a BJP-led coalition would return to power. Policymakers in the country were debating what that would mean for bilateral ties. I had been pointing out to most interlocutors that India's threshold of tolerance for terrorism had lowered and would remain low, no matter which political dispensation came to power. It would be advisable for Pakistan to approach any new government in India with both the assurance and the evidence of some concrete action against terrorism. That would be the biggest confidence-building measure and could give reason for a new Indian government to turn a new page in the relationship.

We were telling our interlocutors that Pakistan could do this in obvious ways—by turning off the tap and switching off cross-border infiltration completely, by taking some high-profile action against terrorists like Masood Azhar and the dozens of Indian terrorists enjoying sanctuary in Pakistan, by counter-terrorism action that was credible, verifiable and irreversible, and, most importantly, by ensuring that there would be no violence in India that would disrupt Indian elections. This was a key concern on the Indian side.

Given that the February events were still fresh in the public mind, national security, terrorism, Pakistan, Pulwama, and Balakot were constant themes in India's electoral discourse. 'We want to tread the path of friendship but a lot depends on Pakistan's response. I reiterate that only talks can resolve all the issues,' PM Modi said in a media interview in Varanasi on 27 April, while campaigning in his constituency, adding that that 'only Atal Bihari Vajpayeeji's formula can work for Jammu and Kashmir.' He vowed to follow Vajpayee's doctrine of 'Insaniyat, Jamhuriyat and Kashmiriyat' but with a caveat not to let the state be 'emotionally blackmailed by a handful of families.'[1]

I made a quick trip to India at the end of April to sense the policy mood in election season. The mammoth exercise was on from 11 April to 19 May. The results were to be declared on 23 May. I got an opportunity to meet with key non-political players in a relaxed mood, to brainstorm on options on the next steps with Pakistan. The key issues on which we needed decisions were—whether there would be at the inauguration of the new government a reprise of the 2014 invitation to SAARC countries? Was it time to consider inviting Pakistan?

In my meetings with a range of interlocutors in Delhi, we discussed Pakistan's internal situation, its dealing with the issue of terrorism post-Pulwama and Balakot, its IMF loan antics and its approach to the upcoming FATF plenary meeting in June.

An SCO foreign ministers meeting was scheduled in Bishkek, Kyrgyzstan, on 22 May, as the Central Asian country held the rotational chair of the regional body. The question arose if India's foreign minister Sushma Swaraj would participate, and if she did, would she meet Pakistan's foreign minister Qureshi? The SCO heads of state summit was scheduled in Bishkek later in June, soon after the new Indian government was sworn in. Would the new Indian PM attend the summit and could that lead to an encounter with PM Imran Khan?

EAM Sushma Swaraj, struck by a kidney ailment and in need of regular dialysis by now, was being brave; she was effusive in my last chat with her. She had already announced her retirement from electoral politics and was widely expected to transition to a less taxing, possibly gubernatorial, role after the elections. India granted a meeting with the minister to the departing Pakistani HC and foreign secretary designate Sohail Mahmood, so that he could carry a direct message to the Pakistan leadership. She contemplated an approach to have a 'shishtachar ki bhent', a courtesy meeting, with Qureshi, depending on the situation on the ground and with no prior announcements, learning from the experience of the non-meeting in New York in September. She told me in jest that Qureshi's whole attitude was bitter and he perhaps needed some sweets to change his style. She gave the same message to Mahmood, which, given its directness, I doubted would be accurately conveyed to Qureshi.

The decision on a meeting between the prime ministers would need to await the actual election results that would be clear by the end of May.

Pakistan's new foreign secretary Sohail Mahmood was fresh from his New Delhi posting when I met him in Islamabad in early May. I emphasized the central message of India's lowered threshold of terrorism. He insisted that Pakistan was taking firm action under its own national plan against terrorism. He had reverted in his new job to the default position that if there was no corresponding movement on resolving the Kashmir issue, it would be difficult for Pakistan to move ahead on any of the other agenda items.

But analysts in Pakistan were speculating that an inauguration of Modi 2.0 might see a reprise of 2014 and an invitation to SAARC leaders. Imran Khan, the guess was, could then go to Delhi on a peace initiative, trying to erase the memories of the February events. The Pulwama–Balakot shock may have caused the army to rethink its use of terror proxies. But this was only a tentative pause button that was being pressed. Thirty years of addiction to the proxy war strategy could not end overnight. All action on curbing the militants, as we later learnt, was reversible.

India's overarching policy direction of 'no talks with terror' remained in place and the central ask of Pakistan remained that it would need to take credible and irreversible action against terrorism. In this broad framework, we started diplomacy in Islamabad within the rubric of 'normal diplomatic activity'. This was a focus on activism on the terrorism question on multiple tracks—engagement with the foreign office, and with foreign diplomats. But also more discreet chats with Imran Khan's camp and particularly with the army. This was a moment of some change in Pakistan and the conversations began to get more candid and pointed.

Some members of Khan's team were pointing out that India's sharp electoral rhetoric targeting Pakistan was upsetting Khan. This could poison bilateral relations. Khan, I was told, had decided to stay clear of the 'Khalistan 2020 referendum', a global propaganda move by separatists demanding a separate Sikh homeland, which had several ISI-supported activists within Pakistan. It was clear to us that while Khan's intentions may have been noble, the ISI would not easily withdraw its covert support for the idea. Khan had said in an interview to *The Economist* that the 'Kashmir exception' for terrorism would go. He had repeated this formulation to the BBC on 11 April.[2] He said this would be the end of militants including Jaish; Pakistan was dismantling the terrorist infrastructure, dismantling the militant groups 'in the first serious effort'. This was positioned as a major concession to India.

Meanwhile, the deep state was dusting up old narratives to say that India had been launching false-flag operations to besmirch Pakistan's reputation and Pulwama was the latest example. Pakistan was, on the other hand, cracking down on militants under its new counter-terrorism policy—about 8,000 militants had been proscribed. The move came with an eye on the FATF process; the government claimed that the militants faced travel bans, asset freezes, and arms embargos. Later in July, Imran Khan was to blurt out that Pakistan hosted about 40,000 armed militants in its territory, who still needed to be disarmed.

Bajwa was also hinting at an overhaul of the ISI and its new leadership so that it became a more effective instrument to address domestic security issues. Diplomats were assessing that the military-PTI project was threatened by the floundering economic project even though the political opposition was too weak to take advantage of the situation.

Pakistan's airspace had remained closed for Indian aircraft after India's air strikes. To test Pakistan, we requested special permission for EAM Sushma Swaraj's aircraft to go through to Bishkek and got it soon enough. Swaraj and Qureshi met in Bishkek on 22 May for a friendly exchange of greetings. She did tell him that his language was harsh, 'kadva bolte hain', and that he needed some sweets to keep his bitterness in check. He praised her sari and she complimented him on his sherwani. This conversation took place in a lounge where foreign ministers waited before a SCO plenary session, a day before the Indian election results were to be announced. A Pakistani photographer sneaked in to shoot a few photos which were happily supplied to the Pakistani media to depict a pleasant chat between ministers. Qureshi attempted to turn this courtesy encounter into a story about a substantive meeting and a thaw in the relationship.

JASHN-E-JAMOORIYAT
On the eve of the Indian elections, we decided to risk some public diplomacy at the high commission, despite a fairly hostile climate in Pakistan's media against India. We agreed to an interview focused on Indian elections with a young Urdu online channel. The journalist who had approached us agreed on the election-oriented format of the interview, but her editor apparently did not. As the camera started rolling and the pro forma question on Indian elections was out of the way, the familiar 'hard' questions breathlessly rolled out, about 'warmongering' by Indian media, India's 'proxy terror' against Pakistan from Afghanistan and Iran, India's 'false claims' on Pulwama and Balakot. This surprise turn to an 'election special' had me batting defensively and trying to steer the chat to positive subjects. Clearly, the young journalist had succumbed to editorial pressure to tease out a juicy controversy by trying to trip up an Indian diplomat.

Soon afterwards, we invited a group of Pakistani journalists, think tankers, and diplomats to watch the Indian election results unfold live on television in the high commission's auditorium. I tried to supplement the assessments of the TV talking heads with a big-picture analysis of Indian democracy at work. The question that hung in the air was the impact on Pakistan of the new government in Delhi. The upcoming overwhelming majority for the ruling BJP became clear early in the counting. Soon, some of our Pakistani guests were taking all the credit for this turn of events, arguing that the election was won by the BJP thanks to India's post-Pulwama actions against Pakistan.

The more thoughtful journalists were soon debating the nuances of the results over wine, samosas and pizzas. The election results on 23 May were variously interpreted—to some, the ruling party in India had won a sweeping mandate in an election, an apparent endorsement for tougher positions on terrorism and by extension, Pakistan, accompanied by a harder posture on the Kashmir issue. To others, it was a glimmer of hope of post-election rapprochement, as we had seen in 2014.

The latter view seemed to find favour in Pakistan's official circles—that the tough pre-election rhetoric and action would be replaced by more conciliatory positions from India. Imran Khan tweeted his congratulations to PM Modi and made a phone call on 26 May. It appeared, at least to some columnists, that Pakistan was hoping to make a new beginning with India and be forgiven transgressions like Pulwama. Khan had earlier publicly assessed that ties between the two countries could improve if Modi returned to power. Perhaps if the BJP wins, Khan said, 'some kind of settlement in Kashmir could be reached'.[3] Now, in their first telephonic conversation after the Balakot air strikes, Modi had told Khan that 'creating trust and an environment free of violence and terrorism was essential for fostering peace and prosperity in the region'.[4]

A rare positive report that appeared in Pakistani media assessed that 'Modicare' rather than Balakot was a key reason for the BJP victory. It said that Modi's healthcare programme covered 500 million people and provided them health insurance that won him hearts and votes.

When the new Indian government was sworn in on 30 May, Pakistan did not have an invitation for the ceremony. The decision in Delhi was to invite BIMSTEC (a regional South Asian grouping that did not include Pakistan) leaders rather than those of SAARC, as was done in 2014. Imran Khan tweeted his felicitations after the oath-taking ceremony on 30 May, despite not being invited to the party. After India's re-elected PM had thanked Khan in a tweet, media speculation began in Pakistan about a possible breakthrough meeting in Bishkek. The two leaders would soon spend some time under the same roof during an SCO summit.

THE IFTAR SIEGE

Each year, in the fasting month of Ramzan, we hosted an iftar dinner at Islamabad's spiffy Hotel Serena, where we would invite the movers and shakers of Pakistan, as well as common folk we were in touch with. This was an event for which invitations were coveted by Pakistani society, particularly by the media, because a large number of Pakistani dignitaries and the entire diplomatic corps would attend, giving much potential for gossip and breaking news.

Indian envoys in Pakistan had traditionally hosted the iftar each year but it had been discontinued when ties soured in the late 1990s. The iftar tradition had been revived in 2004 by three officers of the high commission—Political Counsellor Sibi George, Embassy Doctor Dr Qureshi, and Head of Chancery Pal. The hosts of the event, who happened to be, in Bollywood *Amar Akbar Anthony* fashion, Christian, Muslim, and Hindu, pooled their representational grants to host an event at the Islamabad Club. Over time, the idea regained momentum and the annual Indian iftar continued in Islamabad, weathering all manner of adverse events. And so, I hosted one with over 500 guests in 2018.

In 2019, we planned to hold the event again, scheduling it on 1 June, despite the negativity in the relationship. We sent out over 1,000 invitations, expecting as many as 500 guests to show up. However, I had an inkling that this year would be different. Pakistan was bitter about their National Day having been boycotted by a large number of Indians on 23 March. Some Pakistanis now reported that they had received phone calls warning them not to visit the Indian high commission. Our invitations were mailed using a local courier service and we had reason to believe that our watchers were intercepting the invitation cards. We were not sure how far they would go to prevent guests from coming to this iftar celebration. But the extent and severity of the action by the Pakistani agencies surprised us.

On the evening of the reception, Pakistani agencies launched what looked like a military operation against the Serena, the fanciest hotel in Islamabad, built by the Aga Khan, where our event was being held. Security personnel laid siege to all the entrances. Forklifts were in attendance to lift any defiant cars and to fling them aside. Barriers had been set up. Some foreign diplomats were allowed in, but Pakistani guests were told that the event was cancelled and entry was forbidden. Bizarre scenes unfolded, of guests who had been fasting all day arriving for the iftar and arguing with the plainclothes operatives. A former DG of the ISPR, former high commissioners to India, and former ministers were turned away. The irony was not lost on us. In order to spite India, Pakistan's agencies had decided to cut their own noses, to harass hundreds of their own elite citizens who were trying to arrive for an evening of goodwill. I spoke that evening to the few Pakistanis and the diplomats who had managed to penetrate the siege and publicly apologized for the harassment they had faced. The irony was that the bulk of the spite directed at India was borne by Pakistani citizens.

∽

A few days later in June, I received a phone call in Islamabad at two in the morning. My caller was a contact close to the ISI and I assumed he was calling me simply because he was up late like most folks in Islamabad awaiting the sehri meal in the month of Ramzan. The call had a more serious purpose, it was to tip me off with a specific input about al-Qaeda planning an attack in Kashmir. On 23 May, a terrorist, Zakir Musa, had been killed in the town of Tral in Kashmir's now famous Pulwama district.

Musa, whose funeral drew a horde of over 10,000 mourners, had been an associate of slain terrorist Burhan Wani, but had split from the Kashmir-focused militant group, Hizbul Mujahideen to declare his allegiance to al-Qaeda in 2017.[5] Al-Qaeda was apparently about to avenge Musa's killing.

I asked if this information had been conveyed through the normal military channels, the DGMO hotline. I was told it might have been, but that the ISI leadership was keen to escalate the information to my level so that I could convey this to India. At this point Asim Munir was the DG of the ISI. I passed on this information to India, concerned this was some kind of game.

It turned out that this was a genuine enough tip-off when an attack was indeed attempted close to the predicted time and place. This was an unusual input that Pakistan seemed to be giving to India. One theory about why the high commission was used as a channel was that the ISI was taking no chances and wanted no repeat of Pulwama; it wanted to make it clear at a political level it was not involved with the revenge attack being planned, but was only giving India a friendly tip-off with a piece of intercepted intelligence. Another surmise was that General Bajwa, the army chief, through the ISI, was trying to improve the atmospherics in the relationship in the run-up to the Bishkek summit of 14 June, hoping that Pakistan's sincerity about trying to better relations would register on the Indian side. Perhaps coincidentally, a day before the attack, the ISI chief, Asim Munir, lost his job.

Munir was replaced overnight as DG of the ISI by Faiz Hameed, a three-star general who had been famously named by Nawaz Sharif as the army man who was responsible for giving cash to TLP militants during an anti-blasphemy protest, the Faislabad sit-in. He was someone Bajwa appeared to trust, and Imran Khan was familiar with, as the political fixer within the ISI. Hameed's forte was political manipulation within, rather than strategic games with neighbours.

Rumours were afloat of an angry moment with Imran Khan insisting that Munir, who had been appointed spy chief on Khan's watch only eight months earlier, should be removed that very day. Bajwa, whose extension file needed to be signed by Khan, reluctantly agreed to humour the angry PM. Talk began in Islamabad's gossip circles of a litany of lapses by the short-lived departing DG—he had not shared information on Pulwama; not warned his bosses about Balakot; had goofed up on a few domestic political operations, like a hatchet job against Justice Qazi Faez Isa, an upright Balochi judge who was challenging the writ of the army and would later become Pakistan's Chief Justice.[6] When I asked my interlocutor if the change had anything to do with India and Pulwama, he flatly denied this theory and told me it was a sensitive internal matter and he could not share details of that time, but 'Khan Munir se bahut gussa hua (Khan was mad at Munir)'. The real reason for Munir's axing would only tumble out into the public domain in 2022. Asim Munir, the revelation went, had dared put the scope on First Lady Bushra Begum and warned PM Imran Khan about corruption in his household.[7]

TALKING PEACE

Imran Khan's friend, Naeemul Haque, invited me to his home late one night in June 2019 to share some thoughts after India's elections. Despite his battle with cancer and continuing chemotherapy, Haque at that point was deeply involved in the Pak–Afghan relationship. Haque felt the 'Afghan model' of Khan's diplomacy could be applied to India—Khan's short meeting with President Ghani in Mecca on 1 June on the sidelines of an OIC meeting had gone off well. Haque was convinced that his friend could have a similar meeting with Modi and convince him of his sincerity. He would be willing to give some persuasive answers to the Indians on the question of terrorism and how he intended to stamp it out in Pakistan. The opportunity would present itself in a few days in Bishkek on 14 June and all it required was a brief handshake and conversation. Khan would be happy to spend just five or ten minutes with Modi in a one-on-one meeting—that's all it would take to persuade the Indian prime minister of his sincerity. He would hope to get a positive response to starting a dialogue that could perhaps kick off with a meeting of the foreign secretaries but should be rapidly escalated to a personal structured meeting between the political leaders. If the Indian prime minister chose to discuss the issue of 'violent extremism', Khan could give a reassuring response on Pakistan's action so far and its vision of the future. This could open doors for flights, trade, transit. Haque also believed that we could move towards opening our consulates in Mumbai and Karachi; he felt Pakistan should not insist on getting back Jinnah House.

Haque's optimism was infectious, as much as his faith in Khan's abilities was touching. I said that I would pass on these ideas to Delhi, but this was a meeting perhaps too soon after Pulwama–Balakot and much too soon after Indian elections for us to hope for a breakthrough. We might perhaps need to wait for decisions on the spot in Bishkek on the nature of the meeting and whether it could go beyond the courtesies. Most importantly, India had not been convinced that elements in the Pakistani system would not try to sabotage any fresh peace initiative with a new terror initiative. The previous month, the meeting between the two foreign ministers was also a courtesy chat in a waiting lounge. It was a better model than what we had experienced in New York the previous year on the UNGA sidelines, of the ministers studiously avoiding each other.

Clearly, Haque's naive assessment was that India might forgive and forget Pakistan's transgressions and terrorist attacks once Indian elections were over and perhaps even make peace overtures to Pakistan. But India was not in a mood to humour Pakistan without significant movement on terrorism. In an election fought in the wake of Pulwama–Balakot, the electoral mandate was one requiring a tough posture on terror. In the phone call between the prime ministers, PM Modi had asked PM Khan for action on the fugitives that were present in Pakistan.

I was sure Haque had not run these ideas past Rawalpindi. Even if he had, Pakistan had wrongly assessed the Indian national mood which India's political leadership needed to respect. The policy of 'no talks with terror' could not be reversed overnight and Pakistan needed to build trust, showing some demonstrable results on the ground.

The media had been abuzz with speculation on whether Modi and Khan would meet in Bishkek or steer clear of each other. India did not seek a meeting, and the Pakistan foreign office did not make any formal request. A range of options were available under the rubric of a 'courtesy meeting' between the prime ministers on 14 June. The two leaders did not mingle in the more visible settings of the SCO family portrait or the leaders' dinner. As it happened, there was no structured bilateral engagement in Bishkek, but the two prime ministers did exchange courtesies in the 'leaders' lounge', one of the anterooms. Khan, Pakistani media claimed, had congratulated Modi on his big win in the election.

I met Haque again in the end of June and we continued our candid conversations. We agreed that Bishkek in mid-June had perhaps been too early for a meaningful conversation to take place between leaders and that action on the ground was necessary to build trust. Pakistan by now had a list of India's demands in terms of visible action against Indian fugitives living in safe sanctuaries in Pakistan and against JeM and LeT on whom we had requested irreversible action. I had also suggested action against a prominent Khalistani activist in Lahore. Haque had already taken up the issue with Punjab governor Sarwar in my presence.

⌣

I arrived in Delhi in July 2019 for another round of consultations, to brief our side on the post-Pulwama Pakistan, and to get a sense of where we were after the Bishkek 'courtesies'.

Before I travelled to India, I had met with Foreign Secretary Sohail Mahmood for a stock-taking exercise. Mahmood told me that Pakistan continued to believe in the need of structured and sustained dialogue with India. It was Foreign Minister Qureshi's view that Pakistan would not be pleading for such a dialogue, but would give enough time to India to come to the table. Pakistan was willing to take forward the 'stalled' initiative of Kartarpur and had acted with restraint. It would be keen that India's position became 'less inflexible', India's media became less strident, so that diplomacy got a chance. I pointed out that India would need to see some tangible action taken on terrorism before we could think of a dialogue. Clearly, the foreign office was behind the curve in reimagining the relationship, compared to the political class or even the military.

In India, domestic public opinion had still not settled. The anger over Pulwama lingered both in political and popular perception and the distrust of Pakistan continued. It did appear that a major and visible change of heart in Pakistan would be required to change the narrative in India. Any attempt to reconcile politically could easily be derailed by another act of terrorism, which would not be acceptable to any government, regardless of whether it was in election mode or not. India was moving ahead cautiously with Pakistan. The Kartarpur initiative had a clear political impetus to continue, but India would be circumspect about any sudden détente with Pakistan without first building a certain level of trust.

I found the various arms of our government eager to understand what was happening in Pakistan. I got to have substantive conversations on the state of play with our security establishment, diplomatic establishment, and also the political leadership. The highlights of the visit were meetings with the re-elected prime minister, the reappointed NSA, and the freshly minted external affairs minister, S. Jaishankar. I had been particularly keen to meet Jaishankar, who, as foreign secretary, had sent me to Pakistan and was now elevated to a more critical role. I wanted to share some perspectives and get his take on the relationship.

I also briefed NSA Ajit Doval and Prime Minister Narendra Modi on internal developments and prospects in Pakistan, particularly the fragile state of the Pakistan economy and the finalization of the IMF loan to the beleaguered country. I tried to draw a roadmap of the next six months—the possible meeting of Imran Khan with President Donald Trump in the US, the possibility of a meeting between the two prime ministers in September at the UNGA, the possible invitation to the PM to visit Kartarpur for the corridor opening in November, and the FATF plenary meeting in October where Pakistan's blacklisting issue would be discussed.

My conversation with Jaishankar revealed his clear, realistic take on the Pakistan conundrum. I told him that Pakistan was not too happy about him calling it not a 'normal neighbour' in a recent interview. He said in mock surprise that was the politest expression he could use.[8] We agreed that India's Pakistan policy needed to meet three objectives simultaneously—of managing the bilateral relationship, managing global influences, and managing the domestic narrative.

My advice to the leadership was that India's Pakistan and Kashmir policy could and should work on separate tracks. We should do what was right for Kashmir and not be overly concerned about Pakistan's reaction. I had argued that Pakistan was at its weakest and would not risk any military misadventure over Kashmir, even though it might escalate the rhetoric.

While I had an inkling of the imminent action on Kashmir, I did not know of the specific time frame. My takeaway mandate from my consultations was to keep pressing on the counterterrorism agenda and the Kartarpur corridor opening.

PAKISTAN'S SINKING ECONOMY

One of the issues I had briefed our policymakers on was Pakistan's economic crisis. After more than nine months of stalling and self-delusionary populism, Imran Khan's government had finalized a deal with the IMF. On 3 July, the IMF approved its 23rd bailout package for Pakistan, a $6 billion, 39-month extended fund facility (EFF) arrangement, envisaging immediate disbursement of about $1 billion. The programme was optimistically expected to unlock from Pakistan's international partners around $38 billion over the programme period. All this when GDP growth was limping below 3 per cent.

Economic trouble had been brewing for the ruling dispensation with early signs of economic tension, particularly in April 2019, when Imran Khan was forced to effect a mini reshuffle of his cabinet, firing an old friend, Asad Umar. Cricket analogies had been legion—the captain was only changing his top-order team for better performance in the next game. Finance Minister Umar was eased out because he was unable to comprehend the complexity of his job or the inescapability of bailouts, given years of economic mismanagement. The IMF teams had been frustrated by his intransigence. An international economist, Hafeez Sheikh (who had run a mutual fund in Dubai), replaced him, even though the IMF was not too pleased with Sheikh's handling of an earlier bailout programme of 2010, which remained incomplete when Pakistan did not fulfil IMF conditions. This time around, he had asked for a freer hand in handling the IMF and steering the economy.

But the malaise ran deeper, it was more structural and long-term. Experts were saying that the IMF's injection of funds was too little too late. Pakistan's economy was seeing the cumulative impact of decades of mismanagement and the absence of economic reform. Several experts had pointed to it. The World Bank had released a report in 2019[9] mentioning an annual cost of 'elite capture' at about $8 billion. It repeated the argument made earlier by Pakistani economists—that four influential groups had captured the Pakistan economy: civil servants, landowners, industrialists, and the military. It even went so far as to say that the military's security-centric policies were a tool to extract state resources. Pakistan's 23rd trip to the IMF was being likened to an addiction for which the country refused long-term treatment but landed up every few years for a quick fix.

A CORRIDOR OF DEBT

Pakistan now needed $50 billion over two years because of unsustainable fiscal and external deficits. The only FDI Pakistan was getting was from China, directed to the China Pakistan Economic Corridor (CPEC), which was stalling with only about $24 billion invested in completed projects, far short of the promised $64 billion.

While the corridor of faith at Kartarpur hummed with activity, Pakistan's key ally, China, was losing faith in its own corridor, the CPEC, flagship of the global BRI. A CPEC authority was being created to manage this flagship project of the BRI that had considerable strategic significance for both Pakistan and China. This would later be headed by General Asim Bajwa, caught out for vast corruption and a global 'pizza' empire, allegedly funded by skimming funds meant for the project. China was insisting on security guarantees and arguing that Pakistan needed to improve its relations with Afghanistan, the US, and even with India, to create security for the corridor to be built. Sporadic stories were appearing in the Pakistan media asking if the CPEC was dead or only recycling older projects, with China investing only a third of the targeted $64 billion.

Chinese embassy sources were expressing frustration to us in July about getting projects done with Khan's government. I also learnt that Khan had told the Chinese that they should support Pakistan since the US had decided to support India against China. President Xi Jinping apparently responded sharply to Imran Khan for this simplistic geopolitical assessment and declared that China would not be propping up Pakistan against India. He had advised Khan that it was the US that could help Pakistan in its India relationship and it would be in Pakistan's interest to make up with the US as well as with Afghanistan.

*

In July 2019 we were still trying to work on the small steps to build trust to push the counterterrorism agenda. Bajwa, I learnt, had acknowledged that he had been overly optimistic in assuming that India would move ahead quickly to repair relations after elections.

I met with Naeemul Haque for his usual blunt take. On the new DG of the ISI, he said that he had heard mixed reviews of his competence. He felt that both Khan and Bajwa were willing to work hard and sincerely on repairing the relationship with India, but their attention was then focused on working out the US visit of Khan. Haque promised me that there would be serious consideration of our ask of taking action against some or all of the Indian fugitives, but this would take time.

One step towards building trust was to open the closed airspace. Pakistan was losing more in revenue, lost flights and lost routes than it was gaining by making India pay for avoiding overflights. A media report in early July suggested that while India had lost $78 million as a cost of airspace closure for four Indian airlines, Pakistan had lost $100 million from 26 February till early July.[10] Technically, Pakistan could not single out Indian commercial airlines, so it had effectively shut down the eastern routes to Pakistan of British Airways, United Airlines, and Thai Airways flights.

Wilting under Western pressure on airspace closure, Pakistan had begun to tell the Britons and the Americans that they would open the airspace if India did it too. This was a specious argument, because India had already unilaterally opened its airspace on 31 May. It was only incumbent on Indian ATCs to warn West-bound traffic that Pakistani airspace was closed. I was tasked with negotiating with the foreign office to have the airspace opened. We were not easily going to give Pakistan a face-saving formula of issuing a joint statement that said that both sides had agreed to open their airspace. We argued that India had not closed its airspace at all and would have no problem resuming air activity that Pakistan had shut. Pakistan finally opened its airspace to incoming flights from the east on the eve of Imran Khan's visit to the US on 16 July 2019.

KHAN IN AMERICA

Pakistan had strong hopes for Khan's visit to the US. Army chief Bajwa was to accompany Khan, since the army felt it was important to retrieve that relationship given that a dependence on China alone would not serve Pakistan well. For many analysts, the army's ability to game the US had been a characteristic of the US-Pakistan relationship for decades.

I shared with the US envoy in Islamabad, during one of our chats, India's expectations and red lines for the visit. The US, we thought, should ask for the following: credible and verifiable action against cross-border terrorism, on Pakistan's western, as well as eastern, border; Pakistan to extradite to India the thirty-five fugitives (especially the twenty-six Indian nationals) under Pakistani protection; greater regional stability by removing restrictions in trade and transit between India and Afghanistan; and action on past terrorist cases and investigations like Mumbai (where six US citizens were also slain) and Pathankot.

When Imran Khan reached the US, his conversation with Trump made headlines with the US president's offer to mediate on Kashmir. When India issued a sharp response, saying it had not asked the US to mediate, Trump rapidly walked back his offer, clarifying that he would only intervene if asked by both sides, which was the traditional US position.[11]

Meanwhile, the US and Pakistan were continuing discussions on the FATF. Pakistan was claiming that it was implementing all the obligations outlined by the 1267 sanctions committee. It was expressing frustration at the lack of acknowledgement of its heroic efforts in fighting terrorism. It was arguing that the legal and evidentiary requirements of Pakistan courts were high. This was a familiar argument to stonewall the arrests of militants. The US was not buying this and continued to seek a commitment from Pakistan on fighting terrorism. At this time, besides the US, the others involved with the FATF process were turning up the heat on Pakistan.

The Asia–Pacific Group of the FATF met in the US in June. We were watching, along with other diplomats in Islamabad, as Pakistan twisted and turned, trying to avoid getting scorched by the heat that was being brought to bear on it. Internally, Pakistan's actions against terrorists were being carried out under Punjab's Maintenance of Public Order (MPO) ordinance rather than under the more robust Antiterrorism Act (ATA) of 1997. We were concerned that the terrorists who were being rounded up would be held under protective detentions rather than punitive ones, where the militants would be sent to ISI safehouses as guests of the army to create the optics of action. We were told that 66 organizations and 7,600 individuals had been proscribed but the problem was that concrete data was simply not available on arrests made, assets frozen, and funds confiscated.

Nevertheless, the FATF became an effective instrument to influence Pakistan's behaviour. Both army and civilian leaders were saying in private conversations that the FATF was a blessing in disguise for Pakistan, compelling it to change its habits.[12]

DIPLOMATIC BATCHMATES
A week before my expulsion from Islamabad, I invited Moin ul Haque, Pakistan's high commissioner-designate for Delhi for a quiet meal, where I briefed him on what I saw as the challenges of his role and the opportunities they presented for peace. I sensitized him to India's sensitivities to terror. I was not making any special gesture, but only reflecting the diplomatic nicety afforded me by Moin's predecessor Sohail Mahmood, when he hosted a lunch for me in Delhi. Mahmood modestly told me he was in turn only repaying the generous hospitality of India's HC, Gautam Bambawale, who had hosted him in Islamabad.

I wished Moin ul Haque a successful tenure that was to start the next week. We discovered we were notional batchmates, both having joined our respective foreign services the same year in 1987. Haque had gushed with considerable excitement about his forthcoming stint in Delhi. It was by far, he said, the greatest honour of his career to have been nominated to go to India, since it was the most important head of mission assignment a Pakistani diplomat could hope for. I tried to give him pointers for a meaningful tenure and for the strong allies he could make in Delhi in our common quest for normalizing this relationship.

My farewell meal for the Pakistani diplomat turned out to be his for me, since I would leave Islamabad within ten days of that meeting. Haque's Delhi posting remained stillborn, a farewell to his India hopes. In the event, both of us had soft landings in our next assignments. I was in Canada within a few months. Haque continued his sojourn in Paris and landed finally in China almost a year later.

A SURPRISE IN KASHMIR

A puzzled Pakistan had begun to watch India closely in August. It was tracking the situation in Kashmir, with increasing concern at the build-up of troops, but still without a fix on the impending changes.

The diplomacy in Pakistan reflected this confusion. A Western diplomat revealed to me that he received a call from army chief Bajwa on Saturday, 3 August. Bajwa expressed worry at the escalation of firing on the LoC. He pointed to the dangers of a miscalculation by either side. He said Pakistan was concerned that there would be some constitutional changes that would impact Kashmir, that troop movement into Kashmir was rocking the boat, threatening regional stability. He also brought out the familiar trope of the Afghan border—while Pakistan was engaged in managing its western border at a sensitive time, India was escalating the situation in Kashmir. This made it harder for Pakistan to deal with the counterterrorism agenda that the West expected of it. Even if there was no dialogue, India's activities were creating a problem. Clearly, Pakistan was even in early August more worried about military activity by India across the LoC.

Foreign Secretary Sohail Mahmood similarly complained to Western diplomats about escalation on the LoC, the paramilitary build-up, the warning to Amarnath pilgrims to leave Kashmir, and the talk of constitutional changes on the status of the state. The cumulative effect, he said, would be that any violent acts would be blamed on Pakistan and may involve an attack across the border by India. Foreign Minister Qureshi wrote a letter to the UN articulating these fears to the world.

On 5 August, India's parliament revoked Article 370. Jammu and Kashmir's special status was now extinguished and it became a union territory, at a par with others in the Indian union. Home Minister Amit Shah said in parliament that the revocation of Article 370 was meant to bring an end to the bloodshed and violence in Kashmir. With 41,000 lives lost in Kashmir, he asked, should we wait to lose 10,000 more before we changed the status quo?

When Pakistan's policy establishment recovered from the shock of India's announcement, it felt obliged to take a series of short-term measures to assuage the public opinion within the country that it had itself whipped up. Among the measures being envisaged was a ban on trade, raising diplomatic decibel levels globally, and, of course, asking India to withdraw its high commissioner. In retrospect, many in Pakistan thought their country could have managed the situation better, limiting its reaction to a strong protest note and some moderately angry diplomatic and political rhetoric. But Imran Khan's inexperienced government did not have the capacity to think its moves through or calibrate its reaction to the event.

Pakistan's media was full of alarmist rhetoric. In the absence of a clear line from the official PR machinery, multiple lines of action were being advocated, everything from military action to isolating India globally, by raising the matter at the UN. Tribal militia 'Kabalis' from Khyber Pakhtunkhwa announced plans to march into Kashmir, in a move reminiscent of 1947 and 1965. The implications of this move chilled Pakistan's establishment for the reputational damage it could cause Pakistan, and even more, for a military escalation with a powerful India. 2019 was not 1947. Imran Khan had to intervene and say that such actions would be anti-Pakistan.

Pakistan's best hope was that there would be a violent pushback on the Article 370 move within Kashmir. Any bloodshed there would give Pakistan the basis to raise the issue in international fora from a 'peace and security' and also a 'human rights' perspective. Mounting a terror attack, as in Pulwama, was now ruled out by the establishment. Any jihadi action would invite an assured and currently unacceptable reaction from India. The internal jihadis in Pakistan could not defy the establishment and still go to India. The immediate use of non-state actors was ruled out thanks to Pakistan's NAP and commitments made to the international community under the FATF. The Opposition was already critical of Khan and reminding him that he had said that Modi would be good for resolving the Kashmir issue if he was re-elected.

Much confusion arose about the Simla Agreement, which the Pakistan media was saying India had abrogated. In the same breath, Pakistani commentators were rejecting the Simla Agreement and harking back to the UN resolutions. While the abrogation of Article 370 was being roundly criticized as amounting to annexation, the military spokesman tweeted a view that Article 370 was itself flawed and had been rejected by Pakistan in the 1950s.

Pakistan media commentators[13] were beginning to point to the lack of viable options. Pakistan was militarily weak and could not attack India. Diplomatic options were limited. Trump's mediation offer could be revived, but the US would certainly favour India.

In the days I was in Pakistan after the Article 370 move, I also met with US assistant secretary of state Alice Wells, the point person for India and Pakistan policy, at the residence of the US envoy Paul Jones. She was there to discuss the FATF issue. She assured me that Trump's offer for mediation was an off-the-cuff remark that was later qualified to reconfirm that there was no change in the US position and that mediation would be considered only if both parties would request it.

After I was 'withdrawn' from Islamabad on 10 August, Pakistan escalated the rhetoric further. The floundering responses and overreaction had surprised policymakers in New Delhi. Angry statements were expected from across the border, but what India was facing bordered on hysteria.

MANAGING THE HYPE

India had anticipated some shrill rhetoric and Pakistan taking this issue to the global fora. If Pakistan had done just that and chosen to talk to India at a later stage, it would have promoted its own cause. However, this rhetoric would escalate uncontrollably and become so personal against India's leadership that Imran Khan effectively shut that door. When I asked some Pakistani interlocutors later why this was happening, I was told that Khan had run away with the talking points and was taking them too much to heart. The army had been quiet on this issue and not shut the door entirely. Army chief Bajwa, some suggested, had taken a back seat with his extension file in play for November 2019; the inexperienced Khan was handling the crisis without the army's guiding hand.

For me personally, the action shifted to Delhi. I had hoped to take a few days off to take a breather after the frenetic action of Islamabad. However, in my first meeting with Foreign Secretary Vijay Gokhale, it became clear that we were in crisis management mode at the MEA and that I was willy-nilly part of that team. I wasn't complaining. This was important, several diplomatic fronts were open. We were keeping a firm eye on the UN and knew that this game would continue for the next few days and weeks. The UN Security Council would get into session in September, as would the Human Rights Council in Geneva soon after. We could expect Pakistan to escalate its shrill rhetoric. Indian diplomacy needed to step up and defend both these positions.

Simultaneously, within Pakistan, the jihadi groups were now active. The United Jehad Council (an organization formed in 1994 by the army to coordinate the activities of various Kashmir-focused militant outfits) had given directives to all groups to start mobilizing their cadres. India's security agencies spotted increased activity at the launch pads along the LoC. Clearly, the Kashmir files had been dusted off and were back in circulation. The path of least resistance of the Pakistani establishment was the default option, the low-cost option, of getting the jihadi groups working. Bajwa's deradicalization process was sent into deep freeze.

Pakistan was internally debating whether to give the status of 'interim province' to both parts of Pakistan-occupied Kashmir (what it called 'Azad Jammu' and 'Gilgit Baltistan' by Pakistan). While the former had the de jure character within Pakistan of an independent state, the latter was a federally administered territory with a governor and chief minister. All of POK was technically UN-administered awaiting a plebiscite to determine its future. These provinces had been given the legal character in Pakistan of independent states, technically pending a plebiscite to determine which way they would go.

Simultaneously, an internal narrative was triggered of an imminent false-flag operation from India: an act of terrorism for which Pakistan would be blamed. The propaganda machine was back in high gear, Pakistani diplomats were being asked to write articles on Kashmir for the global media.

With Pakistan's counter-terror campaign paused, the 'good terrorists' were also back in business. The JeM and LeT had stepped up their recruitment drives. Training camps were being reactivated and arms were now funnelled to the jihadists.

But India had learnt lessons from several bitter summers of terrorist violence in Kashmir when the security forces seemed to lose control of the valley. This time a pre-emptive security counter-terrorism grid and counter-infiltration grid had been put in place in J&K to ensure that bloodshed was minimized and Pakistani militants were contained.

Pakistan was debating approaching the UNGA for a resolution to take the matter to the International Court of Justice (ICJ), if not for any substantive gains, then for its propaganda value. The information campaign was getting shriller. PM Imran Khan was calling India's PM a 'fascist' and deploying all social media assets for a new war against 'Hindutva'.[14]

The UN Security Council in New York would not respond to Pakistan's representations because it was not seeing a peace and security issue. Nevertheless, on Pakistan's prodding, the Chinese brought up the issue of Kashmir at an informal meeting of the UNSC. The gambit ended with no formal statement or even a press note. Pakistan decided to make diplomatic capital of the process regardless of the absence of outcomes. It even set up a press conference through its permanent representative in New York, Maleeha Lodhi, claiming that the issue of Kashmir was taken up at the UNSC after decades. For its domestic audience, Pakistan was playing up the meeting as a diplomatic success. The Chinese ambassador also made himself available to the press. India's permanent representative, Syed Akbaruddin, was obliged to counter the statements and point out that Pakistan was not even in the room when the discussion took place. When this matter was raised in Beijing, the explanation given was that the Chinese PR was new and inexperienced and did not quite know the procedures.

Bilateral relations had dipped and Pakistan's best hope was that the

Article 370 move would be deeply unpopular in Kashmir, even if it could not engineer violence by Kashmir-focused militants. One more promising venue was presenting itself to Pakistan to try to internationalize the issue— at the Human Rights Council in Geneva.

KASHMIR GOES TO GENEVA

The Human Rights Council in Geneva was scheduled to hold its regular sessions from late September. Pakistan had decided to focus its attention there, hoping to do better than its past failed attempt to stir up the issue in 1994.[15]

EAM Jaishankar decided to send me to Geneva to make India's case. So, less than a month after my abrupt departure from Islamabad, I found myself in the salubrious surroundings of the Hotel Kempinski in Geneva, overlooking Lake Geneva and Mont Blanc. But this was no holiday. The upcoming HRC session needed careful preparation. We were spending hours gaming every scenario that could play out in the coming weeks.

Pakistan was making an all-out diplomatic effort. Its themes included dressing up the issue as a regional peace and security crisis at the UNSC in New York, and as a human rights crisis in Kashmir for its UNHRC narrative. In Geneva, Pakistan was keen on getting some visibility on the Kashmir issue through three process options—an urgent debate, a special resolution or a joint statement. Each option required procedural support from some of the forty-five member states of the HRC.

India had started some diplomacy at the EU level, approaching individual members of the European Parliament that were contemplating a Pakistan-inspired resolution on Kashmir. Indian diplomacy was also focused on chats with OIC members. The conversation with the UAE and Saudi Arabia was particularly critical; PM Modi happened to visit the UAE at this time and had reiterated India's request for support at the HRC. India needed to ensure there was no OIC statement, no call for a referendum on Article 370, and no country specific resolution against India. At the OIC, the secretarial work had been virtually 'outsourced' to Pakistan, with Pakistani officials managing the paperwork for resolutions. No voting among members or majority approval was required at the OIC for passing resolutions on issues like Kashmir and Palestine. In Geneva's Human Rights Commission, the threshold for passing resolutions was higher, but the OIC and EU were important constituent groupings within the HRC. While the OIC had a strength of 15 of the 47 members, the EU had 11 members. Each group tended to think if not vote en bloc.

The mission to Geneva was welcome for me personally for another reason. In 1994, as we saw,[16] Atal Bihari Vajpayee had been deputed as Opposition leader to go to Geneva to fight a similar diplomatic battle with Pakistan. When I worked in his office, I had often heard Vajpayee extol this unique show of political bipartisanship by Narasimha Rao. He spoke also about India's success in blocking Pakistan's resolution. We needed to do this again and my mandate was to do some quiet diplomacy with not just the forty-seven members but with all the major delegations in Geneva. We had a credible narrative to offer, in contrast to Pakistan's overhyped brief, and India's standing with most member countries was at a different level compared to a quarter century earlier.

Pakistan often expresses disappointment and surprise that its narrative on Kashmir does not find traction in the world. This narrative is mostly developed in the echo chamber of a controlled domestic environment where both the originator of the story and its consumers start believing it. It is normally the same domestic version, with some minor tweaking, that is trotted out for international audiences. The Kashmir narrative, hastily drawn up by ISPR, was now ready for international use.

At the OIC, Pakistan was trying to make the latest Kashmir issue a common cause for the Muslim ummah. The Kashmir matter had been agitated in the OIC several times in the past, invoked in the same breath as Palestine, a symbol of the oppression of the Muslim. At the UNSC, it was dressed up as a threat to regional peace and security in South Asia. At the UNHRC in Geneva, it was positioned as a human rights problem. In their public diplomacy, Pakistan's missions were being pressed to have articles published, particularly in liberal newspapers like the *New York Times* and *Washington Post* through Pakistan's PR agencies and lobbyists. Elements of the Kashmiri diaspora were being deployed with prepared talking points and arresting visuals of those injured.

We decided to keep India's account in Geneva more balanced, rather than defiantly insistent on this being an internal matter and everything being near normal. The central thrust of India's case was that while the situation in the valley was not how India wanted it to be, the status quo could not have continued. Over 40,000 lives had been lost in Kashmir and $40 billion had been spent on Kashmir, ten times more per capita than the national average. Business as usual was no longer tenable. The Article 370 move aimed to correct a historical wrong that had been allowed to persist for too long.

India's diplomacy had faced the last such challenge perhaps in 1998, when global pressure was brought to bear on India after the nuclear tests. The difference was that three of the five P5 countries were then against India; France had been the P5 holdout, Russia had been ambivalent. Even Japan had gone after India, as global public opinion had veered against the country. In 1998, the UNSC had passed a resolution censuring India for the nuclear tests.

This time, the P5 countries, even China, were not ganging up on India. In the twenty days since the Article 370 decisions, the UNSC had held closed door consultations which had come to naught. The UNHRC was being activated for possible resolutions. Several national parliaments were being approached, apart from the EU Parliament. Of course, the driving force behind this effort was Pakistan, which was trying desperately to trigger overseas reactions.

Indian diplomacy's challenge was to globally counter this narrative and prevent any outcomes that unfairly censured India. In the event, what went most in India's favour was the negation on the ground of Pakistan's prediction that rivers of blood would soon be flowing in Kashmir. This had to be conveyed to the world through some effective diplomacy.

The Kashmir case we were making went somewhat like this. No 'special deal' had been put in place with the princely state of Kashmir at Partition. The Instrument of Accession that was signed in that period of history was the same as the one signed with all other princely states. The Constituent Assembly had given premiers of the 560 states a platform and an opportunity to make their views known. Eventually Kashmir became the only state that had the requirement of endorsement of central laws by its own state-level Constituent Assembly. While the federal constitution was being written, Kashmir was facing an extraordinary situation in two ways—it was under attack by tribal militia from Pakistan. More importantly, it was the site of the first India–Pakistan war that ended only in 1949. In this context, Article 370 came as a temporary and transient provision. Clearly, seventy years was a long enough shelf life for a transient provision.

On the constitutional issue of whether the manner in which the state assembly was dissolved was correct, the matter was before the courts. Essentially, the exercise was of repealing a temporary provision in India's Constitution. Each of the 560 states changed their borders and states were reorganized in India multiple times since 1956. Even before 5 August, Kashmir was a troubled land. There was a climate of separatism, of terrorism fuelled by cross-border ingresses, of discrimination, and of lack of development.

India's attempt was to address the problem at its root, not at the impact point. We needed to end the discriminatory climate where 106 central laws did not apply to Jammu and Kashmir, including progressive ones on socio-economic issues like domestic violence and inheritance laws.

1989 had been a watershed moment for Jammu and Kashmir. This was the year when terrorism started, just as the war was ending in Afghanistan. The politics of the state changed with terrorism and a stronger proxy presence of Pakistan in the valley. From that year, Kashmir's assembly did not implement central legislation. From 1989 to 2017, the implementation of central laws in Jammu and Kashmir had ceased. The last law that had been adopted by the assembly was the anti-defection law of 1989. The next law that could be applied in Kashmir was the Goods and Services

ANGER MANAGEMENT

Tax of 2017, that was aimed at bringing India under the umbrella of a single tax system.

In these three decades, the progressive integration of Jammu and Kashmir into the national mainstream was halted. Pakistan, through its political and militant proxies, had begun to play an outsized role in this part of India. The political parties active in Kashmir had played a somewhat dubious role in gaming the centre's concerns for narrow interests, and not for the good of the people. It was clear after the bloodshed of 2016 and in 2017 that the status quo in Kashmir was unacceptable. Business as usual was not an option given the strong deterioration in the overall climate.

⌁

Meanwhile, the situation on the ground in Kashmir, after the dismantling of Article 370, gave some reason for cautious optimism. There had been no loss of life for days. There was no curfew in Kashmir except for the imposition of Section 144 preventing the assembly of more than five people. The shutdown in communications was critical to prevent Pakistan-based terrorists from attacking and as long as it was temporary it was a defensible position in human rights fora. Overall, the situation was improving by the day, the police in crowd control measures had used no live ammunition, and there had been no fatalities. The detention of political leaders had been effected as a law-and-order measure and was clearly a temporary situation. We were being told that of the 196 police districts in Kashmir, 136 were peaceful and 10 faced moderate violence. In the valley, there were reports of shock but also of relief that there was no major bloodshed. The sense was of wait and watch.

A stronger argument was about borders. The borders of J&K had not been constant. Pakistan itself had reorganized the areas under its control multiple times in decades. The 1927 order of ownership of property and domicile had been revised in POK in 1974. Some voices in Pakistan were heard about further consolidating their hold on POK. Pakistan had ceded territory to China, which had not only built a highway in Aksai Chin but also taken control of the Shaksgam Valley in the trans-Karokaram area to build the Karokaram Highway. The CPEC projects in the northern 'Gilgit Baltistan' area of POK also amounted to illegally ceding of territory to China.

Pakistan's case of citing early UNSC resolutions was also a weak one. Resolutions 39 and 47 (of 21 April 1948) on Kashmir clearly laid out a sequential three-step procedure for a solution. This included Pakistan removing all its nationals from Jammu and Kashmir followed by India progressively reducing its forces to minimal levels, followed by a plebiscite. From India's point of view, these matters had been debated, discussed, and disputed for decades, but had been overtaken by the 1972 Simla Agreement and the Lahore Declaration of 1999. The Simla Agreement specifically referred to the bilateral settlement of all issues.

While Pakistan was trying to take its familiar arguments to the UN bodies, along with a set of dramatic exaggerations about 8 million Kashmiris locked up like animals in a prison, suffering like Palestinians in Gaza, they were using a different tack with Muslim OIC member countries. A new narrative was being added to the mix about the current dispensation in India being anti-Muslim and looking for ethnic cleansing in Kashmir. We were in our response pointing towards our commitment to the Constitution and the intent of the new amendment to bring good governance and development to Kashmir. It was not about changing demographics.

⌣

I landed in Geneva on 22 August and walked in the next morning to the office of the permanent representative of India to the UN, Rajiv Chander, an old friend and Moscow hand. Many of the international delegates were returning from holiday that week, in time for the plenary session of the HR Council starting on 11 September. We decided to meet all forty-seven delegations at the UNHRC, except Pakistan, although I was tempted to ask for a conversation with familiar faces from across the border. In Geneva, the OIC and EU tended to think like blocs, even if they did not always vote en bloc, and therefore, these were the two crucial groups we needed to speak to. My mandate was for some old-fashioned diplomacy in exposing delegations to India's point of view and offering perspectives on the Kashmir issue, briefing them on Pakistan's intentions and requesting support in blocking Pakistan's propoganda games.

Pakistan's diplomats, well-versed in the intricacies of multilateral diplomacy, had an unenviable brief. They had two disadvantages to deal with. The first was an overly militant anti-India brief which had not found much traction anywhere outside Pakistan. The diplomats would clearly be forced to spew out those fallacious claims about the status of Kashmir since they were coming from the top. Second, they had to contend simultaneously with a situation on the ground that did not match their narrative of mayhem in J&K. Pakistan had fielded former Foreign Secretary Tehmina Janjua, an old hand at the Geneva game, while foreign secretary Qureshi was expected to speak at the plenary session. Janjua had been my chief interlocutor in Pakistan as foreign secretary and I had a sound working relationship with her, despite having had several difficult conversations. I knew she would stick to the talking points but would not take any impetuous decisions to subvert procedures at the HRC.

To fine-tune our strategy, we brainstormed with veteran multilateral diplomats in the UN bureaucracy on the lessons of the past. From the 1994 experience, we knew we needed to prepare for multiple scenarios. Veteran

UN diplomat A. Gopinathan confirmed to us that in 1994, if Iran had not persuaded Pakistan to withdraw the 'resolution', India would have faced a close vote. We also needed to make a realistic tabulation of support. In case a resolution was moved, we would not engage in discussions on text. However, draft amendments would be kept ready just in case. We also met with the human rights commissioner, Michelle Bachelet of Chile, and got a chance to brief her at length, armed with maps of Kashmir, explaining both India's and Pakistan's point of view and giving a picture of the current ground realities. We decided to acknowledge transparently that the detention of leaders, as also the communication blockade for maintaining a security grid were essential measures, but not desirable. These measures were temporary and would be reversed soon. This was in stark contrast to Pakistan's alarmist narrative about rivers of blood flowing in Kashmir, unmarked graves, and 8 million people herded in an open-air prison like animals.

In our narrative, which evolved after listening to our Geneva interlocutors, we rebutted each of the arguments the diplomats were hearing from Pakistan's teams. It helped us that delegates were hearing both points of view and could contrast the conversations.

Secretary (East) Vijay Thakur led our delegation to the opening plenary session and delivered a strong statement defending India's position. This was the first global statement we issued after 5 August and it was again a huge contrast to the vitriol that came out of Foreign Minister Qureshi. As the session unfolded, only two countries mentioned Kashmir in their plenary statements. This was all reassuring.

Mid-campaign, we realized that both the EU and OIC were divided on the J&K issue, and were unlikely to vote as blocs. Most countries were reluctant to take sides, especially given our strong demarches.

The three mechanisms available at the forum to Pakistan, to highlight the Kashmir issue, were a special session, an urgent debate or a resolution. Soon, Pakistan had given up hope on calling a special session, the strongest mechanism offered by the HRC, since that would need to be triggered by support of at least one-third of the member states (16); more importantly, for an 'outcome' of the session, Pakistan would need a simple majority of those present and voting (24).

For a request for an 'urgent debate' to be admitted, a minimum support from 24 nations (simple majority) was required. But the 'urgency', of a grave crisis, had to be established. A resolution could be introduced, but had to pass with a majority of those present and voting. Most delegations were rejecting the idea of an urgent debate because the council in session already provided a forum for such conversations. In any case, India was likely to win any vote to block an 'urgent debate' or a resolution.

It was clear that Pakistan did not have the required majority for a resolution either. Pakistan's reluctance to invoke these mechanisms or to call for a 'resolution' also stemmed from the fact that a failure during voting would be a bigger embarrassment. Pakistan did not want a reprise of 1994 when it withdrew a request for a resolution, because it did not have the numbers; the resolution would have failed.

Pakistan was now informally circulating drafts of clever resolutions that did not really criticize anyone but asked for an early resolution of the issue peacefully. But this was to the UN diplomats a familiar multilateral gambit—produce the mildest text to give it a chance of being approved by the largest number of members. It was clearly not something that the world community would buy.

Based on India's global diplomacy during the course of the month-long Human Rights Commission meeting, we had assessed that a resolution, if brought to vote, would get over 10 votes for India and under 5 for Pakistan. Any substantive or procedural vote would not go in Pakistan's favour. Pakistan's UN team had come to similar conclusions and decided to spare itself the embarrassment of a defeat in the vote. It did not move any resolution.

India's global equities were strong, we realized, and so was its case on Kashmir. India had come a long way from its diplomatic vulnerabilities of the 1990s. The friendships in West Asia, with OIC countries, and the understanding in the larger West had ensured that no unfair resolution could be passed against India, simply because Pakistan felt aggrieved and made allegations.

Geneva 2019 had ended with even greater success than Geneva 1994. Pakistan realized that there was little international traction for its version of what was happening in India, much less any resolution on Kashmir. India's diplomacy had come together in Geneva, New Delhi, and in multiple global capitals to stymie the attempt to create a narrative of a bleeding Kashmir. In fact, the occasion provided an opportunity for India to explain clearly to the world the measures it was taking to normalize a wounded part of its country. India's focus now had to be within. As Vajpayee had advised the country in 1994, when basking in the glory of a diplomatic victory: 'Let us now use this reprieve to clean up our act in Kashmir or there will be a Geneva every few months.'[17]

THE CORRIDOR OF FAITH

The Kartarpur agreement was finally signed by India and Pakistan before its November 2019 deadline and the approaching birth anniversary of Guru Nanak. The process went off surprisingly smoothly both on the diplomatic table and on the ground in Punjab. Miraculously, the project had survived the diplomatic crises of Pulwama, Balakot, and the August animosity over Article 370. All other people-to-people links had been paused. A few sticking points had remained in the talks; a twenty-dollar fee that Pakistan was imposing and India was opposing; visas for Indian-heritage holders of Overseas Citizens of India (OCI) cards; whether passports would be done away with as a condition for entry. India had stoutly opposed Pakistan's attempts to allow only Sikh pilgrims from India, but insisted the corridor should be open to Indians of all faiths. Both countries eventually agreed to allow visa free travel for Indian passport holders and OCI card holders seven days a week. They expected about 5,000 pilgrims to visit the Kartarpur Sahib Gurudwara each day. This appeared to be a reasonable guess, given that the holiest Sikh shrine in Amritsar, the Golden Temple, hosted more than a 100,000 visitors daily.

In my public comments, I had called Kartarpur the corridor of faith. As if steered by a divine hand, the process had chugged along in a landscape littered with trouble. As it happened, India was confident that the security risks of this gambit could be plugged and the corridor seen as a gift to the people of Punjab, along with a host of other measures, for a grand celebration of the 550th anniversary of Guru Nanak.

The corridor was inaugurated in November 2019. It had been built rapidly in India and at a furious pace in Pakistan by the army's Frontier Works Organisation (FWO.) A turbaned Prime Minister Modi inaugurated a huge terminal in India on 19 November and flagged off the first group of yatris to go across. PM Imran Khan inaugurated the Pakistani facilities and welcomed the special Indian delegation with a rambling speech about Pakistan opening up the Sikh Mecca and Medina. As noted earlier, the delegation included Punjab CM Amarinder Singh, and two Sikh central ministers, Hardeep Singh Puri and Harsimrat Kaur, Navjot Sidhu, and various leaders from Punjab.

Even after the inauguration, Pakistan painted a narrative of the birth and resting place of Guru Nanak at Nankana Sahib in Lahore and Kartarpur Sahib in Narowal being for Sikhs like Mecca and Medina for the Muslim faith. To security analysts, the Kartarpur initiative was also Pakistan's strategic attempt to shift the centre of gravity of Sikhism from eastern Punjab to its west. Tourism promotion and goodwill were the ostensible reasons. Why did Pakistan, some cynics asked, not promote Buddhist heritage with the same fervour? Because it had an interest in Khalistan not Buddhistan.[18]

But the Kartarpur project became a case study of a successful people-to-people and confidence-building project at a time of diplomatic stress and security suspicions between adversarial neighbours. If 2019 had not seen the shocks of Pulwama and Pakistan's overreaction on Article 370, India's prime minister could well have walked across to Kartarpur to meet his Pakistani counterpart. More importantly, for many pilgrims who would reach the holy lands through the corridor, it did not matter why the border was opened, it was simply a blessing, gratefully accepted, from the first Sikh guru, 550 years after he was born.

POLYCRISIS

With an acting high commissioner manning the Indian mission in Islamabad, I technically remained the Indian high commissioner to Pakistan till February 2020, even when on 'temporary duty' in Delhi. Bilateral relations remained deadlocked, with neither side in a rush to repair ties. India was still exhibiting 'strategic patience' with Pakistan, when I left Delhi in March, on an assignment as high commissioner of India in Canada.

In late 2020, a year after Kashmir's special status was extinguished, India revived quiet conversations with the Pakistan Army. The first fruit of the engagement came when a ceasefire was suddenly announced on the LoC by both sides on 25 February 2021. For six years before that date, the ceasefire of 2003 had been frequently violated. India was now busy on the northern front with China, Pakistan using up its military bandwidth on its western front. The ceasefire suited both sides, but it had needed quiet diplomacy to get to that point.

On 15 August 2021, as the 75th year of Independence began for India and Pakistan, the Taliban seized power in Kabul, after running an insurgency for two decades. The US-backed Afghan government led by Ashraf Ghani shockingly dissipated in a blink, the Afghan national army surrendered in one afternoon. As US troops withdrew from Afghanistan, America's longest war came to a chaotic end. Civil war loomed and the security situation in the city deteriorated, as the US evacuated all personnel. Most countries, including India, shuttered embassies and left. But Pakistan stayed. It seemed to rejoice in the arrival of the Taliban regime. PM Imran Khan suggested that Afghanistan had broken the 'shackles of slavery'. And the DG ISI Faiz Hameed visited Kabul soon after the departure of the US forces, to have tea with the Taliban, in a public assertion of ownership of the regime.

But Hameed's proximity to his civilian boss Imran Khan precipitated an internal crisis for Pakistan. The hybrid Khan–Bajwa regime in Islamabad had begun to unravel by the end of 2021, reinforcing India's view that business would need to be done through quiet channels to the army. As the Pakistani army turned 'neutral', Khan floundered. His government fell in a parliamentary no-confidence vote, held past midnight on 10 April 2022. A new coalition regime of the Sharifs and Bhuttos emerged from the political debris, again enabled by the army, with Shehbaz Sharif as prime minister and Bilawal Bhutto as finance minister. Pakistan's shaky new coalition did not seem to have the power to make any major departure in the India policy, with Imran Khan snapping at their heels.

Pakistan's attention had by now turned firmly inward, as it fell deeper into the vortex of multiple crises—the cumulative impact of the faulty choices and misgovernance of past decades. The pain of an economic meltdown had been worsened by political confrontations, severe security challenges, and devastating floods in 2022 that submerged a third of the country. Even as Asim Munir asserted himself as army chief, the legacy of his predecessor, General Qamar Bajwa, was debated on both sides of the border. Bajwa had spent six years in power, effectively ousting two elected prime ministers. He had not been averse to seeking a third term for himself in 2022, but dropped the idea when the political situation spiralled out of control.

The 'Bajwa doctrine' needed to be updated. It initially spelt out a strategic reset towards a 'normal' Pakistan, at peace with its neighbours. It later spoke of the primacy of geo-economics, which meant that the army was deeply worried that the economic crisis would damage its capacities and hence Pakistan's security and foreign policy. Bajwa also claimed a move towards a 'neutral' or 'apolitical' army. In describing his legacy, Bajwa had made sporadic attempts to rein in terrorism and make peace with India, but had seemed to give up abruptly on these objectives, when his relations with Khan soured in 2021.

The passing of former dictator Pervez Musharraf in February 2023, brought attention within Pakistan to another army chief's dubious legacy. When Musharraf breathed his last in Dubai, the former dictator was perhaps unaware of the complex crisis that gripped his country fifteen years after he left power. Musharraf's own contribution to Pakistan's misery was monumental; the four (military-overseen) civilian governments since had been unable to reverse the damage inflicted by him and his uniformed predecessors. The reign of Pakistan's last dictator was assessed mostly negatively in Pakistan—he was forced into exile as a fugitive in treason and murder cases, including the killing of Benazir Bhutto and later even sentenced to death. He received little applause for engineering the Kargil conflict or for the coup of 1999. But for India, he had somewhat redeemed himself by his later attempts at stemming terrorism and by the backchannel efforts on his watch to forge an agreement with India sealing the territorial status quo on Kashmir.

In 2023, after consolidating some power, Pakistan's new army chief, Asim Munir grappled with a collapsing economy and a major security challenge from the western periphery. Pakistan's quest for strategic depth in Afghanistan was denied by the Taliban as it gave sanctuary to the anti-Pakistan TTP. Effectively, Pakistan's Afghan policy which had been carefully crafted with extremist proxies was not starting to unravel. With little success in managing the economic and security challenges, Pakistan's army focused on the easier task of directing the country's politics. The army began to dismantle Imran Khan's PTI; Khan himself was tossed into jail in August 2023, like Nawaz Sharif had been in 2017. With the return from exile in London of Nawaz Sharif in October 2023, the army's Project Imran was replaced by the latest edition of Project Nawaz, grooming the three-time PM for another shot at power in 2024. As Pakistan began to make an uncertain journey towards elections with a caretaker government, the paths of the two countries seemed to diverge more than ever.

While India grew in heft, powered by the world's fastest-growing large economy, Pakistan seemed to have reverted to familiar army-dominated structures to address its debilitating polycrisis. And the differential between the two countries in terms of comprehensive national power seemed even more pronounced. Young observers within Pakistan were fervently hoping that the crisis would help Pakistan move towards becoming a 'normal' country. Even if their futures look decidedly different, and even if relations are troubled, India and Pakistan will be unable to shake off a common history and geography.

The next twenty-five years, till the centenary of Independence, hold both promise and peril for bilateral ties. The countries could find newer pathways, or tread old ones that had brought them so often to conflict or its brink. To pick the right path, it is important to look back deep, hard, and often at the journey thus far, to avoid the grievous mistakes of the past. A reimagined Pakistan and a reimagined relationship between the two sibling nations is critical to bringing coherence and prosperity to South Asia. In the conclusion that follows this chapter, I look at some ways in which the bilateral relationship might be reimagined.

As this book went to press, the diplomatic relationship remained downgraded and my successor in Islamabad had not yet been appointed. I look forward to this situation being corrected, just as I hope the two neighbours will find better ways to manage this troubled relationship. I do not wish to remain listed as the last Indian high commissioner to Pakistan.

Conclusion

HISTORY'S AMBIGUOUS LESSONS

In dissecting relationships between nations, especially those between hostile neighbours, a fair occupation for scholars and analysts is to tease out patterns from history. The past is after all prologue to the present and shines a light on the future. But parsing a troubled past can be tricky. Interpreting the antagonism between neighbours is even more so because the variables at play tend to be multiple and complex, while we tend to favour convenient, univariate explanations.

This temptation particularly afflicts those observing India–Pakistan relations, where opposite lessons are often drawn on either side of the border, and where experts abound but seldom agree. The lessons within borders also tend to be debatable, contentious, and all too often, motivated and self-serving.

What does the story of the diplomatic relationship between India and Pakistan tell us? We have seen that across the decades, both practitioners and observers have drawn conflicting lessons. They have made varying policy prescriptions for the future, not just depending on what side of the border they are on, but also on their ideological predilections within borders.

Nevertheless, the broad messages from the past are critical to determining our approaches to the future. Are these two neighbours destined to fight? Is it inevitable that the ties should periodically snap? Can we drive around the potholes? Can the few happy episodes of the past provide some pointers for a policy that could guide us to peace? Can India and Pakistan erase the past and become like today's Germany and France? Or will they remain uneasy rivals like North Korea and South Korea?

More than three quarters of a century after their birth, India and Pakistan have failed to develop, jointly or separately, a viable model for dealing with each other. Their interaction and diplomacy of the past years, as we have seen, has been angry, turbulent, troubled.

Not that diplomats have not engaged in finding solutions. For the practitioners of the art, it would be crucial not just to revisit the past but also to avoid repeating the mistakes of their predecessors.

Looking back at the end of seven decades of diplomacy, one former Indian envoy to Pakistan reflected on the words of a predecessor, who was himself looking back at three decades. Natwar Singh offered a cryptic assessment in 1980, that the future of India–Pakistan relations lay in the past. These remarks came when Singh was beginning his tenure as ambassador in Islamabad in 1980, just as the Zia era was beginning to take shape. The burden of history, of Partition, of territorial and identity issues, was real and immediate then. T. C. A. Raghavan echoed Singh's remark, in the seventh decade. And diplomats going about their business in both countries carry this burden to this day. Singh's weary wisdom suggested at once that the current diplomats were prisoners of a past created by their predecessors, at the bidding of political masters. And that they were mostly condemned to repeat history.

But the past is not always the best predictor of the future. We know that all too well in the age of global disruptions, when black swan events have hit us all too often. The 2008 financial meltdown and the 2020 pandemic had little historical precedence, just as Europe's post-war integration and German unification in the 1990s had no close parallels or precursors.

So, what do the years of our story since Independence tell us?

One, security matters. The Indo–Pak relationship has been heavily 'securitized', not just by four major conflicts, but also by all the minor ones that unfolded every day. Pakistan's unsettled quest for an identity that drove India–Pakistan diplomacy at Partition is still relevant in informing its approach to its larger neighbour. The relative importance of the themes of ideology, territory, and security may have ebbed and risen in their influence on the bilateral relationship. But in the twenty-first century, the quest for security became the key driver of diplomacy between the countries. Pakistan's continued obsession with the India threat and India's lowered tolerance of terrorism ensured that bilateral diplomacy will keep security issues at the centre of the grand strategy that the two countries define and deploy to deal with each other.

Both countries accept that security is their dominant concern. With the army in Pakistan having primary control on India policy, India's security establishment now plays a greater role in determining the shape of Pakistan policy and diplomacy, albeit under the guidance of elected leaders. For many in India, Pakistan is to be seen as a key internal security threat through its proxy wars in Jammu and Kashmir primarily, but also in Punjab. For Pakistan, the growing military strength of a rising India, the vast power differential, the widening economic gap, are all cause for concern and indeed key drivers of policy and diplomacy.

Terrorism in the last three decades has derailed détente processes. Many in India believe that Pakistan is now to be approached with the policy of 'active defence' to counter terrorism. To some, India's Pakistan policy for the moment should be a counterterrorism policy rather than a neighbourly foreign policy. Acts of terror over the decades, particularly in the twenty-first century, have set the dialogue back by years and are often timed to derail major meetings between the countries. Frequently, the terrorist would wield the veto. But the distinction between a Pakistan-based terrorist and the Pakistani state is no longer a valid one for India.

After the Simla Agreement was signed, in July 1972, former high commissioner Shivshankar Menon observed in 2016 the two countries fell into a 'repetitive pattern or dance' of engagement and disruption. But when breakthroughs seemed near, 'there is a big disruption, most often a terrorist incident or attack, and then negotiators start the cycle all over again, first tentatively and then a little more surely.' This pattern has continuously frustrated Indian policymakers.

For India, the strategic restraint exercised during Kargil in 1999 and after the Parliament attack of 2001 has now been replaced by a sophisticated counterterror and active defence policy. A credible counter-factual to ponder over is that if the air strikes on Pakistan had taken place in 1999 after Kargil, if Uri and Balakot-like actions had been executed by India, and had been factored into Pakistan's security calculus, the attacks of 2001 and 2008 could perhaps have been prevented. Strategic restraint was vital for India after turning nuclear in 1998, not just for security reasons but also for its international reputation. Arguably, such restraint was unnecessary after the Mumbai 2008 attacks. A Balakot-like strike after Mumbai could have prevented more attacks subsequently. Going further back, if India had found an effective military response to the proxy war of the 1980s that inflamed Punjab, it could conceivably have prevented the conflagration of the 1990s in Jammu and Kashmir; if India had placed a heavy and unacceptable cost on the Pakistan Army in response to the terror of the 1990s in Kashmir, it could have created a deterrent for the terrorism that mounted from the turn of the century.

Two, leadership matters. In India's case the buck has always stopped with the elected prime minister—from Nehru to Modi and every PM in between. They have been personally responsible for Pakistan policy, for judgements that led to war or peace. For Pakistan, these decisions lay with the army, with varying degrees of consultation with civilian regimes. We need the coincidence of strong governments on both sides to make peace diplomacy effective, to ensure that any significant breakthroughs are sustainable. It was in an era of relative political stability and confidence that Nehru could go to Ayub Khan in 1960 to sign the Indus Waters Treaty. Conversely, Rajiv Gandhi's attempt at peace with Benazir Bhutto could not be sustained beyond 1989 because her regime was unstable, tripped up by an army deeply suspicious of her. Vajpayee's visit in 1999 and Modi's foray in 2015 were goodwill visits by confident Indian leaders, but came at a time when Pakistan was not strong enough, when the civilian leader in both cases Nawaz Sharif was at odds with the army. Just like it took a Nixon to go to China, a Republican to make tactical friends with the dreaded communists, it has taken politicians from a muscular political party, the BJP, to tango with Pakistan's army. Any peace initiative, most observers now agree, would need to be actively owned by the BJP in India and the army in Pakistan, irrespective of the political components of the governments of the day.

Changes in government provide occasion to attempt changes in policy. Vajpayee defied conventional wisdom on the Pakistan file several times in his career. In 1978, he visited Pakistan when it was concerned about the Janata regime's attitude to Pakistan. In 1999, he defied expectations again by making the bus trip to Lahore. Modi's visit to Lahore in 2015 was similarly unexpected, as was the initiative to invite Nawaz Sharif for the oath-taking of the new Indian government in May 2014. Modi, in fact, pointed out in public remarks that Sharif's visit to India in 2014 and his own return visit to Lahore in 2015, demonstrated India's sincere desire for dialogue; these engagements made it easier to explain subsequent tough actions against terrorists to the world.

The flawed choices of the past by Pakistan's leaders, both army and civilian, have at critical moments altered the trajectory of ties. The flaw in Jinnah's foundational two-nation theory was exposed within a quarter century of Pakistan's birth. The creation of Bangladesh confirmed that Jinnah erred in assuming that a common religion could erase identity markers like language and ethnicity, and even geography and history. The endorsement by Pakistan's founders of Akbar Khan's scheme to send raiders into Kashmir in 1947 led to an avoidable war, adding to the trauma of Partition. Similarly, Ayub Khan's failed attempt to grab Kashmir in 1965 with Operation Gibraltar soured a relationship that was headed into positive territory. Yahya Khan made a terrible choice in 1970, of disrespecting an electoral verdict of 1970 favouring Mujib, which led to the dismemberment of Pakistan. In 1999, Musharraf's Kargil misadventure negated the benefits of the boldest peace initiative from India—Vajpayee's bus ride to Lahore. Similarly, allowing terrorists into Pathankot was a choice of Pakistan's army leaders that derailed the diplomacy of 2014–15. An inexperienced Imran Khan's overreaction to the August 2019 moves by India reduced the space for détente. On its part, India perhaps paid a price as its leaders failed to craft an effective response to Pakistan's terrorism.

Three, diplomacy matters. We saw across the decades that while overall national policy postures emerged organically from national objectives, the diplomats of the day could often influence events through their actions. In the 1960s, Rajeshwar Dayal managed to persuade Nehru to give Ayub Khan a chance, despite Nehru's instinctive suspicion of the dictator. Natwar Singh became an advocate for Zia in the 1980s despite Mrs Gandhi's aversion to him. Pakistan's envoy Jehangir Qazi, through his quiet diplomacy with Advani, managed to get the Agra Summit of 2001 in place giving Musharraf a chance to make his case. Leaders were often putting a personal stamp to the diplomacy. Nehru was himself his foreign minister and India's chief diplomat of the 1950s, Vajpayee's diplomatic forays into Pakistan defined India's sincerity and balanced approach. Zia was perhaps the most consummate diplomat for Pakistan who tried to sweet-talk India while running a nuclear programme and a jihad in Punjab, modelled after the Afghan jihad that he successfully ran for the Americans. Diplomacy, conducted at whatever level, has unquestionably shaped the trajectory of ties.

To some observers, Indo–Pak diplomacy has mostly focused on conflict management rather than conflict resolution. Diplomats have engaged in fighting fires, managing the furies, rather than in looking for long-term sustainable solutions for good neighbourliness. The nature of diplomacy has also changed. Personal intimacy between leaders and diplomats in India and Pakistan defined their interaction till the 1970s. In later times, it was more the professionals pitted against one another, even if the innate South Asian cultural affinity often came into play. Overall, the space has shrunk for quiet diplomacy, for the traditional and classic secret conversations, away from the public glare. In the age of social media scrutiny, a lot needs to be shared in real time; quiet diplomatic manoeuvres are rare, not least because they are harder to pull off. More importantly, the public postures of populist politicians reduce the space further. Imran Khan and his government's demand to reverse India's move on Article 370 as a precondition for a conversation with India painted Pakistan into a corner. The age of the jhappi pappi diplomacy between Punjabis or North Indians has also gone, with each country needing to treat the other as foreign. Rikhi Jaipal, a diplomat dealing with Pakistan in the 1970s, would famously identify himself as a 'Madrasi' who spoke no Punjabi in dealing with his Pakistani counterparts.

Four, global forces matter. Major powers have started playing a larger role, as global geopolitics itself has entered a period of churn, particularly in the twenty-first century. 'Great' powers pursuing their global interest impinge on the relationship in various ways. At their creation, it was British national interest that determined the fate of India and Pakistan. Subsequently it was the US and Russia fighting the Cold War, which made them choose partners who could further their cause. The Chinese made no secret of befriending the adversary's adversary.

The Cold War between the US and the Soviet Union has thawed into a new one in the twenty-first century with Ukraine as its primary theatre between Russia and the larger West. It runs in parallel with the new contestation between the US and China as also the West Asian conflagration that derails peace processes in the region. For some scholars, the new era is one of South Asia seeing a resumption of hard power geopolitics as the US withdraws from the region, China becomes more belligerent, India's tolerance of terrorism diminishes, and Pakistan's economy nosedives. The

US withdrawal from Afghanistan in 2021, and its robust contest with China has deepened Pakistan's dependence on China, as also India's concerns of a two-front collusion and military challenge. For military experts, the power differential between India and Pakistan has widened, and will continue to do so, leaving Pakistan more dependent on alliances and more vulnerable to the seduction of sub-conventional means to challenge India.

Five, multilateral institutions play a role. Aside from the major powers, the UN has tried since its inception to help sort out the Indo–Pak territorial issue, just as the World Bank successfully mediated the waters. The bilateralism of diplomacy between the countries is supplemented by a nod to specialized multilaterals. They play a role, not just in contests over territorial boundaries and minorities or in the traditional UN bodies like the UNSC and HRC. After being wary of 'internationalizing' the Kashmir issue for what it saw as decades of propaganda, India has shown greater confidence and flexibility in approaching the International Court of Justice to discuss imprisoned citizens; FATF for terror; ICAO for aviation disputes; or the World Bank again to amend the Indus Waters Treaty. Traditional multilateral instruments like the IMF and newer ones like the FATF have now put Pakistan under intense scrutiny and forced it to modify its behaviour in various ways.

Six, people matter. Popular opinion, particularly in Pakistan, was mostly shaped in the early decades by official narratives amplified by the media. Vajpayee's visit to Lahore in 1999 seemed to create an emotive positivity among the people that was not acceptable to the Pakistani state. The period which began with Vajpayee's visit in 2004, and accelerated in the Manmohan Singh years, saw people not having to pay for cabs when they visited for cricket in the golden period of 2004 to 2006. But popular goodwill is often overestimated; it is easily poisoned by state narratives. The newer phenomenon of social media run by young 'influencers' has allowed a large section of young people in Pakistan to express themselves fairly independently and their young audiences to consume opinions they never had access to earlier. While social media can be a toxic multiplier of hostility and fake narratives, it also democratizes the expression of opinion, removing the monopoly on information with a propogandist state. Cross-border connections between young influencers in the virtual space gives an indication of times to come.

Seven, the territorial disagreement will never really go away, but can be put on the back burner. The hardened positions on Kashmir make an explicit territorial compromise impossible. Any solutions will have to work around this issue. In the 1970s, bilateralism was accepted as the guiding principle for engagement on the Kashmir question. In the 1990s, India reiterated its claim on POK, the western and northern parts of the erstwhile princely state occupied by Pakistan. In this century, both countries tried to make borders 'irrelevant' and accept the LoC as a de facto reality. But the heightened terrorism in Kashmir has hardened India's position. What is required by both is a process of negotiation about borders while continuing conversations on other tracks. Army chief Bajwa's reported proposal of a twenty-year freeze to territorial disputes offers hope for a modus vivendi.[1]

Eight, Pakistan's structure matters. The structural issue of the domination of Pakistan's army is perhaps the single largest challenge to bilateral diplomacy, as indeed to Pakistan's economic survival. Even though, arguably, the Pakistan Army under Bajwa struggled to change and redefine its role in Pakistan, any conflict brings it back to the default position, which to India is of continuing the proxy war. The military will continue to be Pakistan's most important political institution that will continue to matter even if it goes 'neutral' or apolitical. Pakistan's garrison state may adopt a different form, say, the pre-Erdoğan Turkish model (of withdrawing to the barracks but emerging if the civilians don't deliver) or the Thai model (of a military dominated elite overseeing elected civilian politicians) but the essential architecture will be military-led. Pakistan's democracy with fifteen years of civilian faces in the front office at the time of writing, is holding but the institutions continue to be weak, subverted by the deep state.

Populist civilian leaders like Imran Khan are no guarantors of improved relations with India, nor can such leaders pull off feats like Erdoğan did, of bottling up the Turkish army. From India's point of view, while civilian leaders of the past, like Nawaz Sharif, had defied the army to improve ties with India, they could also exhibit behaviour like Imran Khan, picking up the convenient prop of right-wing religious ideology, new narratives of 'Islamophobia', backed by the revival of a distrust for India and the deployment of extreme rhetoric. While civilian leaders could potentially derail peace initiatives or equally lead them, no such initiative would be sustainable without a buy-in by the army.

While the structural reality of Pakistan's security state is accepted by analysts, the other structural fact of its Islamic state is often overstated in assessing bilateral tensions with India. These cannot be framed in religious terms as a contest between an Islamic state with a predominantly Hindu neighbour. India's excellent ties with Islamic West Asian countries, and with Bangladesh, challenge any religion-based hypothesis. With Bangladesh, a predominantly Muslim neighbour with 170 million people, India has over five decades, resolved water and land boundary disputes. It now has a trade level of over $18 million, multiple weekly flights, lines of credit of over $8 billion, and a robust exchange of high-level visits. Indo–Bangladesh ties, not without irritants, can serve as a model for future Indo–Pak ties.

Nine, the economic aspects of the relationship matter less. For India, a conversation on trade is more a confidence-building measure, an element of foreign policy, rather than a plank of an economic blueprint designed to promote prosperity in the region. Successive prime ministers in India have articulated the exalted objective of jointly or separately addressing the challenge of bringing prosperity to the poor. Vajpayee said this in letters to Nawaz Sharif and Musharraf and Modi said it to Sharif, as also to Imran Khan in his congratulatory calls. India's 'no talks with terror' policy has a corollary for some—of no trade with terror. In Pakistan, in contrast, trade links were traditionally regarded as a ploy by India to distract bilateral attention from the core Kashmir issue. But with Pakistan's economic downturn, serious voices—particularly in Pakistan's pharmaceutical and textile sectors—have asked for trade and connectivity with India as part of efforts to improve ties with India.

Trade can thus be both a CBM and a low-hanging fruit for a diplomatic revival. Analysts feel that Pakistan's army no longer sees trade with India as a dilution of the Kashmir cause but a means to longer-term security benefits.[2] The previous serious attempts to normalize trade in 2011–12 were questioned by 'vested economic interests (such as the agriculture, automobile, and pharmaceutical lobbies)', not the army. Since the army now pushes for geo-economics in the context of an economic collapse, it would be more amenable to trading with the traditional enemy.

In a more fundamental sense, Pakistan's India policy has cost it its economy. An exaggerated India threat led to a bloated role of the army in domestic power structures, foreign, and security policy. But perhaps most corrosive was the army's role in the domestic economy. The current economic collapse was triggered in part through the army's choices: its capture of the economy through Military Inc., the proxy terror wars in India and Afghanistan that damaged Pakistan's global reputation. Also, Pakistan can no longer benefit from monetizing its strategic location, the geopolitical rents seem to have dried up, particularly after the US exit from Afghanistan. Even the Chinese seem wary of further infusions of capital, with CPEC funds drying up. A reimagined Pakistan would perhaps need to reinvent its India policy. That would be true geo-economics.

Ten, minority issues continue to matter. The highly emotive issue of the treatment of minorities continues to inform contemporary diplomacy and ties. Aggression against minorities in Pakistan is a cause for concern in India; but the Hindu and Sikh minorities within Pakistan are now microscopic. And with barely a voice within Pakistan. Minority relations within India come up for major comment in Pakistan for an existential reason. It is important for the Pakistan state to tell its people that despite their myriad problems, contrasted with India's rise and prosperity, they are the more fortunate ones to live in a Muslim homeland compared to India's over 200 million Muslims. Identity issues of religion continue to define the politics in both countries to varying degrees and therefore continue to matter in their diplomacy.

While these issues, ranging from security to leadership to diplomacy to minorities, have mattered to define the trajectory of ties, longer-term relations have become more resilient to shocks. Curiously, the cycles of engagement and hostility have become shorter, particularly in the fast-paced twenty-first century. The pattern of interest to policymakers should be of micro-cycles within the cycles. The traditional view of the India–Pakistan engagement has been that it is cyclical, with periods of peace and dialogue alternating with war or conflict or high hostility. Even in times of 'unpeace', within extended periods of hostility or absence of dialogue, there have been some positive moments. India and Pakistan signed an agreement on travel for pilgrims in 1974, when they had no diplomatic engagement or missions. In recent times, the Kartarpur corridor came up in 2019, despite the animosity of Pulwama, Balakot, and the dismantling of Article 370. A ceasefire was accomplished in 2021, despite the absence of high commissioners or a structured dialogue. Periods of recovery from conflict have shortened in the current century. It took five years to resume missions after the 1971 war, but I was back in office as high commissioner in Islamabad within three weeks of the Balakot strikes.

Even in periods of a fraught diplomatic relationship, feelers have quietly been sent across the border for improving ties at the worst of times. Changes in government, absent disruptive events or violence, give that brief opening. And sometimes so do less happy occasions like funerals of leaders or natural disasters like earthquakes and pandemics, provided the countervailing forces are not overwhelming.

Some years become seminal, profoundly impacting the relationship. Shifting alliances between the major powers, particularly the US–China dalliance, impacted the 1971 India–Pakistan war. 1979 saw a global churn, with events like the Iran revolution and the Soviet invasion of Afghanistan, a backdrop to the India–Pakistan thaw of 1979–80. In 1989, we saw the end of the Cold War, as also the Rajiv–Benazir thaw: 1998 was when the countries went overtly nuclear. 2001 was the year of the Musharraf Agra summit, it was also the year of 9/11 and the Parliament attack in India which changed security paradigms for both the US and India. 2012 was the year when Osama bin Laden was found, eroding US trust in Pakistan. And 2019 was when Pulwama, Balakot, and the abrogation of Article 370 were bunched together. This tells us that larger global forces, more than human agency—diplomatic or political, seem to be at play at some critical junctures, impacting the bilateral relationship in unpredictable ways. These can provide headwinds or tailwinds to diplomacy depending on how they play out.

To create a future substantively different from the past, we need to learn from that history, not repeat its mistakes; to manage the anger and create new pathways. For that, we need strong and wise leaders aided by smart diplomacy.

SHOOTING FOR A CENTURY?

As much as looking back to reflect on how two neighbours got into this troubled, angry, often fratricidal relationship, we need more perhaps to look ahead and see how they could head to a better place. Can we create a future different from the past? Will centennial Pakistan and centennial India continue to be adversaries with the same degree of mutual hostility as now, or can the future bring normalcy, if not bonhomie? Will 2047 bring greater wisdom with smarter technologies and newer aspirations for close to two billion people inhabiting the countries then?

In a volatile relationship, predicting events in distant decades is a risky game, as much astrology as futurology. This has not stopped analysts and scholars from trying to divine the future. And that's where our gaze must now turn.

The eminent South Asia expert Stephen Cohen had argued a decade ago that Pakistan and India could be 'shooting for a century', embroiled in worse hostility in 2047 than at present. Cohen had painted a picture of 'conditional pessimism' arguing that neither country had demonstrated any interest in resolving issues.[3] On the fringes of the mainstream discourse are the outlandish fantasies that sometimes confuse analysts—an Islamic conquest of India with Ghazwa-e-Hind, or an Akhand Bharat stretching west to Afghanistan as an undivided cultural space.

Some experts have argued that India should not worry about territory (Kashmir) since it would be the third largest economy by GDP by 2050 and therefore its grand strategy should go beyond territory to a more comprehensive projection of national power. This was a 'net assessment' based on strategic analysis.[4] Others have argued that India has no long-term vision in place with respect to Pakistan, since it lacks a coherent grand strategy to manage Pakistan's animosity, making it the most dangerous bilateral relationship India has.[5] This is more an indictment of Pakistan, which thanks to army predominance, thinks more tactically than strategically.

POLICY CHOICES

If policymakers have agency, what would be the optimal policy path to fix this broken relationship? That question leads to more fundamental ones. How do practitioners look at policy? Is it determined by political realities or is it something that organically evolves on the ground? While diplomats implement foreign policy determined by a political leadership, they never seem to lack views on what that policy should be.

Indian high commissioners in Pakistan have made their opinions well known, certainly quite articulately internally, but also often enough in the public domain. While they seem to broadly agree on the diagnosis of the problem, they have offered varying prescriptions across the decades. India's first HC in Pakistan, Sri Prakasa, had famously offered Nehru a radical solution for a 'neutral' Kashmir, with common Indian and Pakistani citizenship.[6] Many of his successors had proffered their views as well. Given the propensity of the media to classify those pronouncing on policy as 'doves' or 'hawks', Pakistan's former foreign minister Khurshid Kasuri defensively classified himself as 'neither hawk nor dove'. But when Natwar Singh, his Indian counterpart was asked to define himself, he shot back, 'We are running foreign policy here, not an aviary.'[7] The advice from practitioners on the way forward has nevertheless covered the entire range of the dove–hawk spectrum.

Satinder Lambah, the Indian diplomat born in pre-Partition west Punjab, who led the backchannel talks for a modus vivendi on Kashmir, wrote in his 2023 book[8], published posthumously, that India and Pakistan needed 'purposeful engagement directed towards attainment of realistic outcomes'. This way forward could be achieved through a 'mutually agreed template for an overall understanding on managing the Kashmir issue'. This was the basis of the backchannel understanding of giving the LoC the 'characteristics of a permanent border', with an end to violence, a demilitarized region and porous borders. All this required 'engagement', a globally accepted essential tool of diplomacy resorted to by all 'inimical countries' in history. India could defend itself against hostility from Pakistan, Lambah felt, but instability in Pakistan could have unanticipated consequences for India and thus engaging with the neighbour was essential.

Another (Lahore-born) Indian diplomat, Mani Shankar Aiyar, argued that contact between the peoples of the two countries was key to the diplomacy, and the reason to have an 'uninterrupted and uninterruptible' dialogue. Aiyar felt that 'sustaining distrust between the governments' was easier than the patient building of trust between people. Former high commissioner Mani Dixit gently chided Aiyar for propagating an excessively optimistic 'Pollyanna view' since 'tough stands and tough action, not treacly sentimentality, is what the professionals believe, counts in diplomacy'.[9] In his last week as consul general in Karachi in 1981, Aiyar sent his assessment to the government, since declassified, advising a three-pronged peace initiative and goodwill blitz to deal with Zia's Pakistan[10], that included strong people-to-people connections, an 'interlocking web' of relationships in diverse spheres, and persistent bilateralism that would make Pakistan resist the temptation of becoming part of 'global strategic entities'.

Yet another pre-Partition Punjab-born Indian high commissioner, Satish Chandra, came to a different set of policy prescriptions. Chandra felt Kashmir was a symptom of the persistent hostility of Pakistan towards India, not its cause. Chandra, who finished his tenure in 1998, recommended in a monograph, a 'punitive policy', based on a vigorous diplomatic campaign to project Pakistan as a terrorist state; an act of Indian parliament declaring it as one; pursuing global sanctions against the terrorist state; renegotiating the Indus Water Treaty to get a fairer share of the Indus waters and linking its continuation with Pakistan's action against terrorism; exploiting Pakistan's fault lines in Balochistan, Khyber Pakhtunkhwa, Sindh, and POK, the way Pakistan did in India; covert action and focused strikes like Balakot against terrorist elements; targeting the crumbling Pakistan economy for further damage rather than assisting it; and better relationships with Pakistan's neighbours, Afghanistan, and Iran, to corner the country. Chandra advocated sustained adherence to this 'get tough policy', given the Indian tendency to periodically lapse into sentimentality.[11]

Between the hawks and the doves is a more centrist view, that India needs to be pragmatic in 'managing' the difficult relationship. India's high commissioner to Pakistan till 2013, Sharat Sabharwal argued[12] that the way forward lay in the twin tracks of 'countering and containing' those threatening India's security and engaging the 'constructive constituency'. His message to Pakistan was to stop terror and promote trade; and for India to include Pakistan in a more regional approach to 'co-prosperity', thus engaging its constructive constituencies.

While Pakistan has tended to engage with the Indian government of the day, India's policymakers need to be mindful of multiple strands within Pakistan. Former high commissioner Shivshankar Menon argued that India 'must deal with several Pakistans' and 'run several Pakistan policies simultaneously, engaging civil society, business, and civilian politicians and containing or answering what the ISI and others attempt'. This complex environment invites accusations of inconsistent policy 'because we are engaging in several policies and policy modes simultaneously—talking, doing business, and attempting to counter cross-border terrorism from Pakistan, all at the same time.' Several practitioners, including Menon, have warned that 'thanks to Pakistan's secular decline into irrelevance, Indian motives to address India–Pakistan issues are diminishing,' with Pakistan 'increasingly becoming a single-issue country in Indian discourse, and that issue is the zero-sum one of security.'[13]

Another layer of complexity to policy choices came after both countries became declared nuclear powers in 1998. Nuclear escalation had to be factored in by policymakers in any conflict situation. Also, the threshold for political intervention by external powers was lowered. Nuclear weapons, Menon argued, 'changed the interstate dimension of conflict in South Asia... lowered the nuclear threshold and therefore diminished the likelihood of large-scale conventional war.' The Kargil War of 1999 was a surprise exception early in the subcontinent's nuclear journey and that too 'was brought about by General Musharraf and his small coterie by stealth as a closely held secret within the Pakistan Army.' More importantly, one of the few things 'both Pakistani and Indian establishments are agreed on is that nuclear weapons have stabilized the subcontinent.'[14]

Former HC Sharat Sabharwal agrees that while the nuclear dimension has not completely ruled out the use of conventional military power by India to inflict pain on Pakistan, it has 'placed a serious limitation on India's ability to coerce Pakistan's military into altering its behaviour.'[15] For the militaries, a nuclear environment meant the need to fashion newer doctrines to get the better of each other. While India's undeclared 'Cold Start' doctrine (swift, short, shallow thrusts into Pakistani territory by integrated battle groups) is sought to be countered by Pakistan's 'full spectrum deterrence' (tactical nuclear weapons to deter the ingress of an enemy army), these are tactics for the conventional realm of conflict. The Balakot air strikes of 2019 demonstrated room in the sub-conventional domain for an escalation, but the diplomatic implications were that the impulses for de-escalating a crisis would be strong, particularly with the rapid intervention by external powers.[16]

To several diplomatic observers (and practitioners like Sabharwal) India's policy approach should go beyond security, factoring in multiple strands including the nuclear environment. Bilateral relations thus can only be 'managed' rather than significantly altered in the foreseeable future, particularly given Pakistan's structural dynamics.

In my view, while a structured dialogue with Pakistan would have to be calibrated with actions on its terrorism ecosystem, a sustained engagement with the Pakistan Army, through quiet or direct channels, is critical, given the reality that the army would be the primary determinant of Pakistan's India policy over the next decade. India would need to inflict disproportionate costs on the army's interests for every bit of terror mounted from Pakistan's soil. And, whenever democratic regimes are in power, India will need to triangulate all understanding with civilian regimes, to confirm that the deep state and the army establishment are on board. In other words, to be sustainable, Pakistani civilian initiatives would need to be verifiably approved by the army, formally or informally. Even if it works the other way round in India or in other normal polities.

In the snakes and ladders board game of India's engagement with Pakistan, the snakes have been not just the major conflicts, but also major terrorist incidents which have set back the diplomacy by years. 1965, 1971, and Kargil were setbacks, but so were the different attacks in Mumbai (1993, 2006, 2008) or Delhi (2001) or Pathankot (2015) or Pulwama (2019). Other minor snakes have been smaller actions or terrorist incidents, firing on the border or ugly rhetoric against Indian leaders. The ladders, on the other hand, have been periods of relative terrorism-free peace; and elections, bringing new regimes attempting fresh thinking or geopolitical pressures on Pakistan. Arguably, while strong Indian governments have looked for ways to bring about neighbourly peace, Pakistan has looked to forge peace only when it was weak, hoping to fight another day. What Indian needs is a structurally normal Pakistan, one that does not support terror and looks to gain from, and not always compete with, a larger neighbour.

GRAND STRATEGIES

To many security analysts, both India and Pakistan have been bereft of grand national strategies of dealing with one another. Both countries have been guilty of short-term measures to deal with crises rather than attempting broader visions of dealing with this critical adversarial relationship.

Pakistan in 2021 articulated a strategy of the primacy of geo-economics, that to many was an acknowledgement, at least on paper, of the failure of earlier approaches and a recognition of being faced with a collapsing economy. This nod to the shift from geopolitics to geo-economics seems to be a cry from within the power structure, to reform and locate the India factor in a broader vision of reform. To some in India, it was an acknowledgement that the Pakistani grand vision of jihadism that had prevailed since the 1980s had failed.

India has been experimenting with a broader plan to alter Pakistan's behaviour, based on a rising power differential and a strategic neglect of Pakistan. As the countries head towards a century of Independence, India is veering towards a Pakistan strategy based on 'active defence', which would need a sophisticated counter-terrorism strategy accompanied by a diplomatic strategy of calibrated engagement. This has to be located within a broader vision of an India on the path of rapid economic growth, aided by strong global partnerships and a calm neighbourhood.

The two grand strategies of the neighbours are often at odds. In a military sense, Pakistan has not been able to fulfil its grand strategy objectives of parity with India or revisionism in Kashmir on either end of the military spectrum, through nuclear weapons or jihadism. With its professed policy of geo-economics as the key to saving Pakistan, it tries to emulate India's vision of getting to the centennial year through an economic pathway of sustained growth. But security is a pre-condition in both visions.

GAMING 2047

How will the future decades unfold?

Scenarios of the medium to long term not only provide opportunities for scholars to hypothesize, but are important pegs for policymakers to wargame different approaches. We could perhaps look at three broad scenarios when we peer at August 2047, when India and Pakistan celebrate their hundredth anniversary. These could be: business as usual; conditional optimism; and conditional pessimism.

The first scenario would imply a continuation of the tension with periodic episodes of working towards normalcy. This would basically mean that India and Pakistan would continue in an unsteady equilibrium of low-level tension, an 'unpeace' not leading to any major breakthrough but with a risk of eruptions of conflict.

The second scenario, with poor diplomatic and policy choices, or structural failures within Pakistan, would see the two countries move along the path of aggravating tension with significant risks of further conflict or worse, nuclear Armageddon. This could be triggered by acts of terrorism, unilateral attempts to change the territorial status quo, possibly by Pakistan in collusion with China. Within the pessimistic scenario would be the possibility that Pakistan fails to 'normalize', or even ceases to exist as we know it. A Pakistan that breaks up into four or five parts would be looking inward at its own woes and may drop its hostility to India. But, some analysts worry, in a scenario where Sindh, Balochistan, and Khyber Pakhtunkhwa break away from a Punjabi rump, that Punjab with nuclear weapons may be an even bigger threat for India. Even worse would be a situation of some nukes falling into the hands of terrorist tanzeem or a rogue army splinter. In another possibility of extreme economic collapse, Pakistan could send millions of refugees India's way across the borders; fences and troops may not be able to hold back the flow and India would need to deal with a humanitarian crisis.

In the third scenario, India would hope that Pakistan hastens its journey to 'reimagined' and corrected structures and move towards becoming a 'normal' state that does not rely on proxy terror to achieve irredentist ambitions. In this scenario, India would continue to move towards improving relations as part of a larger strategy of preparing to share prosperity in its South Asian neighbourhood, as it moves to claim its position as a global leader and the third largest global economy. Both states would need to realize that the long-term interest of bringing safety and prosperity for their peoples would lie in moving from a securitized hostile relationship to a normalized neighbourly, if not friendly, one. The flexibility and creativity that the two countries adopt can take them towards a future of becoming more trusting neighbours. The diplomacy would need to move from anger management to interest management, to bring prosperity to 2 billion inhabitants of a common South Asian homeland.

Epilogue

A NORMAL KASHMIR

I gazed at the stunning colours of tulips in full bloom, more than a million of them, swaying gently in the breeze. It was a spectacular setting in the heart of the Kashmir Valley, in the spring of 2023. As the happy buzz of thousands of tourists, many of them locals, filled the air, it was hard not to be filled with a sense of hope for the future of this land.

This was Ground Zero of the India–Pakistan contestation, the coveted land that became the reason for bloodshed and broken ties. It had been five years since my last visit, and four after the constitutional changes that had shifted the paradigm in the valley and ended my tenure in Pakistan. I could sense that much had changed since; the infiltration numbers, the incidents of terrorism and violence, had all gone down, cautious optimism hung in the air, an almost desperate hope that we would see normalcy, the end of three decades of grief and pain. Srinagar now had a new multiplex cinema. A shiny new mall was coming up. Foreign investment was poised to come in. The road and tourism infrastructure was being furiously upgraded, as in many other cities in India, to prepare for an onslaught of foreign tourists and delegates—Srinagar was one of the host cities for a global event in the summer, a G20 meet on tourism.

The sense that the agony of Kashmir might be slowly easing held a personal resonance for me. It was the land of my birth.

I was born in Srinagar in a summer long ago, a few months before a brutal war to the north. It was a cold winter that year; the Dal Lake had frozen over. The next winter was even colder, with jeeps running on the frozen Dal Lake, and I was one of the kids playing with snowballs. But the prevailing mood had turned ominous. Suddenly, one day, the rumours went, the hair of the Holy Prophet, a revered relic of the Hazratbal Mosque, had been stolen. This led to agitation and riots. The Regal Theatre was burnt down.

Prime Minister Nehru was obliged to address the nation on the radio and urge Kashmiris to remain calm. My father was then working with All India Radio, which innocently broadcast a Kashmiri song of celebration, 'Chakri'. Soon a group of protesters with black flags marched up shouting slogans against the radio station, which had desecrated the mourning over the loss of the holy relic. The team at the radio station did some quick thinking and hurriedly assembled a black flag, which they flew on the roof of the radio station to express solidarity with the protesters. Five days later, the ninth day after its disconcerting disappearance, the holy relic mysteriously reappeared, found in a bottle floating on the Jhelum. My family left Srinagar when I was three. I had always wanted to go back, but managed to make it to my birthplace only in the new century, when the violence ebbed somewhat.

Less than a hundred miles west of Srinagar lay the fabled hill town of Murree. It was Pakistan's hill resort favoured by the British; it lay on the other side of the LoC from India, on the eastern edge of Pakistan's Punjab. The Indian high commission traditionally rented a property in Murree in the fond hope that staff of the high commission could go across there to decompress from the tensions of Islamabad. I got there in July 2018, along with a high commission team, after badgering the foreign office for official permission. We were allowed to stay in a hotel, but could not visit our rented holiday home.

Murree also held some personal meaning for me. It had to do with a summer years before Independence. For a shy twelve-year-old in pigtails, the summer of '42 was special. The girl had just moved to Lahore a year earlier from Delhi. Pakistan's birth was still five years away; the Muslim League's 'independent countries' resolution of Lahore was just two years old. The girl hadn't heard of this idea of a new country to be carved out of India. What she did catch was the steady drumbeat of freedom from the British yoke and the war the British empire was fighting, with the help of Indian soldiers, in distant lands. Her father, a civil servant from the colonial audit and accounts service, was packed off to Lahore on an assignment, possibly related to procuring supplies for the British war effort. She was in Lahore when the Quit India movement began in August 1942, when noisy protestors marched in jaloos, shouting slogans demanding Bharat Chhodo.

My mother, who this girl later would become, recalled these events fondly and vividly in her ninetieth year, when I was stationed in Pakistan. My grandfather, she told us, loved travelling. And the family holiday in the summer of '42 took them to Murree. My mother remembered being struck by Murree's charm, especially the fancy cottages belonging to maharajas of princely states like the Kapurthala, and those housing British officers escaping the heat and dust of the Punjab plains.

Destiny had sent me seventy-five years after that summer to represent India in Islamabad. As I had walked into Pakistan, I carried this sliver of history, this little bit of family baggage, along with the heavier burden of subcontinental history. Amidst all the debate on war and peace, terrorism and Kashmir, diplomacy and discord, I reminded myself of the steps my mother and her family had taken all those decades ago, of a South Asian space more connected than it is today. I wondered if the borders of the future could be more open and welcoming.

I thought of all this as I stood in the valley of Kashmir amidst the tulips and I allowed myself the cautious hope that the day would come before long when the confidence of Kashmiris would be restored, when soldiers would not be required to guard every nook, when the borders could be opened up once again without the fear of terrorists and bloodshed. If newer generations reject the flawed choices of the past, such a future does seem possible.

ACKNOWLEDGEMENTS

I had little idea that writing a book requires such a high degree of consistent effort and discipline. This one started as a Covid project, with social distancing suddenly giving me space to read deeply and reflect on the India–Pakistan story. In researching and writing this story over four years, I have accumulated several debts.

The triumvirate of Prime Minister Modi, the late External Affairs minister Sushma Swaraj, and then foreign secretary S. Jaishankar packed me off to a diplomatic adventure in Pakistan in 2017. I am filled with gratitude for the trust they reposed in me to represent India in Pakistan in challenging times. I also feel indebted to the late prime minister, Atal Bihari Vajpayee, in whose office, from 1999 to 2004, I got a ringside view of the shaping of India's Pakistan policy, of the vision of a twenty-first century India, and of counterintuitive policy choices at critical times. Vajpayee's closest counsel, the late Brajesh Mishra, a consummate strategist, became my guide and mentor.

I am grateful to my twenty-four predecessors, the Indian heads of mission to Pakistan, most of whom told their stories and recorded their experiences in Pakistan. I could immerse myself in their times, revel in their stories, and walk in their shoes. I gained unique perspectives from the accounts of Sri Prakasa, Rajeshwar Dayal, Kewal Singh, Natwar Singh, and J. N. Dixit. I hugely benefited from a crop of more recent books, supplemented by several insightful conversations with their authors: the late Satinder Lambah, Satish Chandra, Shivshankar Menon, Sharat Sabharwal and T. C. A. Raghavan. These former diplomats, gave me generously of their time to speak about their experiences in Pakistan. Natwar Singh gave me a flavour of Zia's early days in the 1980s. Sati Lambah became a mentor, explaining to me the intricacies of Pakistan in the 1990s. He also armed me with some diplomatic hacks, including to never discuss Kashmir in Pakistan after 6 p.m. Satish Chandra's autobiography came just in time for me to gain insights into the late 1990s; he read early drafts and gave me valuable feedback. Raghavan took the time to critically read the manuscript and discuss Pakistan over several rounds of golf.

I also benefited hugely from conversations with Sharat Sabharwal, Deb Mukharji, Pinak Chakravarti, Ronen Sen, Ramu Damodaran, Asoke Mukherji, Mani Shankar Aiyar, Sudhir Vyas, Rajeev Dogra, Vivek Katju, Rakesh Sood, A. S. Dulat, and many others who shared insights and anecdotes. I wish to especially thank Ajay Atal, son of J. K. Atal, Indira Gandhi's wartime ambassador to Pakistan in 1971, who generously shared his late father's papers and memories of 1971.

I salute Avtar Singh Bhasin for his efforts in creating the monumental documentary study on Indo-Pakistan relations till 2007. I learnt much from some excellent scholarship on South Asia, particularly the works of Ian Talbot, Ayesha Jalal, Tilak Devasher, Srinath Raghavan, Ramachandra Guha, Chandrashekhar Dasgupta, Gary Bass, and Happymon Jacob. Several journalists and academics shared perspectives to deepen my understanding of Pakistan, including Jyoti Malhotra, Suhasini Haider, Sushant Sareen, and Shalini Chawla. Valuable feedback on early drafts came from Roli Asthana, Ravi Rajan, Suresh Shankar, and Shivam Shekhawat at ORF.

My team in Islamabad during my tenure in Islamabad made light of challenging times and helped me decipher Pakistan. I am grateful particularly to J. P. Singh, Gaurav Ahluwalia, Avinash Singh, Akhilesh Singh, Vipul Dev, Shubham Singh, and colleagues from the forces—military attaché, Sanjay P. Vishwasrao; naval attachés Amit Gurbaxani and Peter Varghese; and air attachés, Joy Kurien and Manu Midha. Numerous colleagues at headquarters supported my innings across the border, particularly Foreign Secretary Vijay Gokhale and Joint Secretary Deepak Mittal.

Across the border, many Pakistani diplomats and friends shared insights. My thanks to Shahid Malik, Hussain Haqqani, Ayesha Siddiqua, Raoof Hasan, Fakir Aijazuddin, Khurshid Kasuri, Aziz Khan, Asad Kazmi, Zulfi Haider, Nilofer Qazi, and Zainab Khan. Many others will have to remain unnamed.

I was contemplating trying my hand at fiction, but publishing guru David Davidar persuaded me in August 2019 to tell the stranger-than-fiction story of India–Pakistan diplomacy. David spurred me to write this book, guiding me not just with brilliant editorial suggestions but also by shaping my words into a coherent account. Aienla Ozukum at Aleph proved to be a superb, eagle-eyed editor, ably assisted by Amrin Naaz.

I am grateful to my late uncle, the writer in the family and Hindi poet, Raj Narayan Bisaria, who brought out his last book past the age of ninety, and constantly goaded me to write about my experiences. Finally, this book would not have seen the light of day without my closest friend, companion, wife, and partner-in-crime in Pakistan, Bharati Chaturvedi. Also an early reader, she morphed into a fierce in-house critic and brutal editor, indulging my anti-social writing behaviour, while pushing me to complete this project.

INDIAN HIGH COMMISSIONERS/AMBASSADORS
POSTED IN PAKISTAN FROM 1947–2020

HC Sri Prakasa (1947–49)
HC Sita Ram (1949–51)
HC Mohan Singh Mehta (1952–55)
HC C. C. Desai (1955–58)
HC Rajeshwar Dayal (1958–62)
HC G. Parthasarathi (1962–65)
HC Kewal Singh (1965–66)
HC S. Sen (1968–69)
HC B. K. Acharya (1969–71)
HC Jai Kumar Atal (1971)
Amb. K. S. Bajpai (1976–80)
Amb. Natwar Singh (1980–82)
Amb. K. D. Sharma (1982–85)
Amb. S. K. Singh (1985–89)
HC J. N. Dixit (1989–91)
HC Satinder Kumar Bajpai (1992–95)
HC Satish Chandra (1995–98)
HC Gopalaswami Parthasarathy (1999–2000)
HC Vijay K. Nambiar (2000–01)
HC Shivshankar Menon (2003–06)
HC Satyabrata Pal (2006–09)
HC Sharat Sabharwal (2009–13)
HC T. C. A. Raghavan (2013–15)
HC Gautam Bambawale (2015–17)
HC Ajay Bisaria (2017–20)

PAKISTANI HIGH COMMISSIONERS/AMBASSADORS
POSTED IN INDIA FROM 1947–2020

HC Zahid Hussain (1947–48)
HC Khawaja Shahabuddin (1948–48)
HC Muhammad Ismail (1948–52)
HC Raja Ghazanfar Ali Khan (1953–56)
HC Mian Ziauddin (1957–58)
HC A. K. Brohi (1959–61)
HC Agha Hilaly (1961–63)
HC M. Arshad Hussain (1963–68)
HC Sajjad Hyder (June 1968–71)
Amb. Syed Fida Hussain (1976–78)
Amb. Abdul Sattar (1978–82)
Amb. Riaz Paracha (1982–83)
Amb. M. Humayun Khan (1984–88)
Amb. Niaz A. Naik (1988–89)
HC M. Bashir Khan Babar (1989–90)
HC Abdul Sattar (1990–92)
HC Riaz H. Khokhar (1992–97)
HC Ashraf Jehangir Qazi (1997–2002)
HC Aziz Ahmad Khan (2003–06)
HC Shahid Malik (2006 –12)
HC Salman Bashir (2012–14)
HC Abdul Basit (2014–17)
HC Sohail Mahmood (2017–19)

INDIAN PRIME MINISTERS & FOREIGN MINISTERS FROM 1947–2023

PRIME MINISTERS

Jawaharlal Nehru (1947–64)
Gulzari Lal Nanda (1964)
Lal Bahadur Shastri (1964–66)

Gulzari Lal Nanda (1966)
Indira Gandhi (1966–77)

Morarji Desai (1977–79)
Charan Singh (1979–80)
Indira Gandhi (1980–84)

Rajiv Gandhi (1984–89)

V. P. Singh (1989–90)

Chandra Shekhar (1990–91)

P. V. Narasimha Rao (1991–96)

Atal Bihari Vajpayee (1996)

H. D. Deve Gowda (1996–97)
I. K. Gujral (1997–98)
Atal Bihari Vajpayee (1998–2004)

Manmohan Singh (2004–14)

Narendra Modi (2014–to present)

FOREIGN MINISTERS

Jawaharlal Nehru (1947–64)
Gulzari Lal Nanda (1964–64)
Lal Bahadur Shastri (1964)
Swaran Singh (1964–66)
Swaran Singh (1966)
M. C. Chagla (1966–67)
Indira Gandhi (1967–69)
Dinesh Singh (1969–70)
Swaran Singh (1970–74)
Yashwantrao Chavan (1974–77)
Atal Bihari Vajpayee (1977–79)
Shyam Nandan Prasad Mishra (1979–80)
P. V. Narasimha Rao (1980–84)
Indira Gandhi (1984–84)
Rajiv Gandhi (1984–85)
Bali Ram Bhagat (1985–86)
P. Shiv Shankar (1986)
N. D. Tiwari (1986–87)
Rajiv Gandhi (1987–88)
P. V. Narasimha Rao (1988–89)
V. P. Singh (1989–89)
I. K. Gujral (1989–90)
Chandra Shekhar (1990–90)
Vidya Charan Shukla (1990–91)
Chandra Shekhar (1991)
Madhavsinh Solanki (1991–92)
P. V. Narasimha Rao (1992–93)
Dinesh Singh (1993–95)
Pranab Mukherjee (1995–96)
Atal Bihari Vajpayee (1996)
Sikander Bakht (1996)
I. K. Gujral (1996–97)
I. K. Gujral (1997–98)
Atal Bihari Vajpayee (1998)
Jaswant Singh (1998–2002)
Yashwant Sinha (2002–04)
K. Natwar Singh (2004–05)
Manmohan Singh (2005–06)
Pranab Mukherjee (2006–09)
S. M. Krishna (2009–12)
Salman Khurshid (2012–14)
Sushma Swaraj (2014–19)
S. Jaishankar (2019–to present)

PAKISTANI HEADS OF STATE/PRIME MINISTERS & FOREIGN MINISTERS FROM 1947–2023

HEADS OF STATE/PRIME MINISTERS

Mohammed Ali Jinnah (Governor General 1947–48)
Liaquat Ali Khan (PM: 1947–51)
Khawaja Nazimuddin (GG: 1948–51, PM: 1951–53)
Ghulam Mohammad (GG: 1953–55)
Iskander Mirza (GG: 1955–56) (President: 1956–58)
Muhammad Ali Bogra (PM: 1953–55)
Chaudhary Muhammad Ali (PM: 1955–56)
Huseyn Shaheed Suhrawardy (PM:1956 –57)
Ibrahim Ismail Chaundrigar (PM: 1957)
Malik Feroz Khan Noon (PM: 1957–58)
Ayub Khan (President: 1958–62, 1962–69)

Sharifuddin Pirzada (1966–68)

Yahya Khan (President:1969–71)
Noor ul-Amin (PM: 1971)
Zulfikar Ali Bhutto (President: 1971–73)
Fazal Ilahi Chaudhry (President: 1973–78)
Zulfikar Ali Bhutto (PM: 1973–77)
Zia ul-Haq (President: 1978–88)

Muhammad Khan Junejo (PM: 1985–88)
Benazir Bhutto (PM: 1988–90)
Ghulam Ishaq Khan (President: 1988–93)
Ghulam Mustafa Khan Jatoi (Caretaker PM: 1990–90)
Nawaz Sharif (PM: 1990–93)
Balakh Sher Mazari (Caretaker PM: 1993–93)
Nawaz Sharif (PM: 1993)
Farooq Leghari (1993)
Moin Qureshi (Caretaker PM: 1993)
Wasim Sajjad (Acting President: 1993)
Benazir Bhutto (PM: 1993–96)
Malik Meraj Khalid (Caretaker PM: 1996–97)
Farooq Leghari (President: 1993–97)
Nawaz Sharif (PM: 1997–99)
Wasim Sajjad (Acting President: 1997–98)
Rafiq Tarar (President: 1998–2001)
Pervez Musharraf (President: 2001–08)
Mir Zafarullah Khan Jamali (PM: 2002–04)
Chaudhary Shujaat Hussain (PM: 2004–04)
Shaukat Aziz (PM: 2004–07)
Muhammad Mian Soomro (Caretaker PM: 2007–08)
Muhammad Mian Soomro (Acting President: 2008)
Asif Ali Zardari (President: 2008–13)
Syed Yousaf Raza Gillani (PM: 2008–12)
Raja Parvaiz Ashraf (PM: 2012–13)
Mir Hazar Khan Khoso (Caretaker PM: 2013)
Nawaz Sharif (PM: 2013–17)
Shahid Khaqan Abbasi (PM: 2017–18)
Mamnoon Hussain (President: 2013–18)
Nasir ul-Mulk (Caretaker PM: 2018)
Imran Khan (PM: 2018–22)
Arif Alvi (President: 2018–incumbent)
Shehbaz Sharif (PM: 2022–23)
Anwaar ul-Haq Kakar (PM: 2023–to present)

FOREIGN MINISTERS

Mohammad Zafarullah Khan (1947–54)

Muhammad Ali Bogra (1954–55)
Hamidul Haq Chowdhury (1955–56)

Malik Feroz Khan Noon (1956–58)

Muhammad Ali Bogra (1962–63)
Zulfikar Ali Bhutto (1963–66)

Arshad Hussain (1968–69)
Yahya Khan (1969–71)

Zulfikar Ali Bhutto (1971–77)

Aziz Ahmed (1977)
Agha Shahi (1978–82)
Yaqub Khan (1982–87)
Yaqub Khan (1988–91)

Abdul Sattar (1993)

Aseef Ahmad Ali (1993–96)
Yaqub Khan (Caretaker) (1996–97)

Gohar Ayub (1997–98)
Sartaj Aziz (1998–99)
Abdul Sattar (1999–2002)

Khurshid Mahmud Kasuri (2002–07)

Inam ul-Haq (2007–08)

Shah Mahmood Qureshi (2008–11)
Hina Rabbani Khar (2011–13)

Nawaz Sharif (2013–17)
Khawaja Muhammad Asif (2017–18)
Khurram Dastagir Khan (2018)
Abdullah Hussain Haroon (Caretaker) (2018)
Shah Mahmood Qureshi (2018–22)

Bilawal Bhutto Zardari (2022–to present)

NOTES

PROLOGUE: THE EXIT

1 Pakistan Foreign Office statement, 8 August 2019, <https://mofa.gov.pk/transcript-of-the-press-briefing-by-spokesperson-on-thursday-8th-august-2019-2/>; Imtiaz Ahmad, 'Pakistan asks India to 'halt and reverse' its J-K move on Article 370', *Hindustan Times*, 10 June 2020; Asad Hashim, 'Pakistan summons Indian envoy on Kashmir, reaches out to allies', *Al Jazeera*, 5 August 2019.

2 Article 370 of the Indian Constitution of 1950 gave special status to the former princely state of Jammu and Kashmir, allowing it to function as a state of the union of India, initially with a separate Constitution and state flag; later with significant autonomy in internal administration.

3 'Parliament unanimously passes resolution condemning India's 'unilateral move' on Kashmir', *Dawn*, 7 August 2019.

4 Pakistan Foreign Office statement, 8 August 2019.

5 MEA India spokesman, Ministry of External Affairs, Media Center, 'On Pakistan's Unilateral Decision in respect of Bilateral Relations with India', 8 August 2019, <https://www.mea.gov.in/press-releases.htm?dtl/31722/On_Pakistans_Unilateral_Decision_in_respect_of_Bilateral_Relations_with_India>.

6 'Pakistan orders tit-for-tat expulsions', *CNN*, 8 February 2003; Rajeev Sharma, 'India expels Pak diplomat Islamabad retaliates with tit-for-tat', *Tribune News Service*, 9 February 2003.

INTRODUCTION: A QUEST FOR IDENTITY

1 The two-nation theory was a concept that was born of religious nationalism and advocated separate homelands for Indian Muslims and Indian Hindus within a decolonized British India. It asserted that Muslims and Hindus were two separate nations, with their own customs, traditions, and ways of life.

2 Tilak Devasher, *The Pashtuns: A Contested History*, Gurugram: HarperCollins India, 2022.

3 Husain Haqqani, *Reimagining Pakistan: Transforming a Dysfunctional Nuclear State*, Gurugram: HarperCollins India, 2018.

4 Christophe Jaffrelot (ed.), *Pakistan: Nationalism Without a Nation?*, London: Zed Books, 2002.

5 See, for instance, Venkat Dhulipala, *Creating a New Medina: State Power, Islam, and the Quest for Pakistan in Late Colonial North India*, Cambridge University Press, 2015.

6 Haqqani, *Reimagining Pakistan*.

7 Ibid.

8 Shashi Tharoor, *The Battle of Belonging: On Nationalism, Patriotism, and What it Means to be Indian*, New Delhi: Aleph Book Company, 2020.

9 Graham Allison, 'The Great Rivalry: China vs. the U.S. in the 21st Century', Paper, Belfer Center for Science and International Affairs, Harvard Kennedy School, 7 December 7 2021.

10 Since the Treaty of Westphalia in 1648.

SECTION 1: 1947–1957: BUILDING STATES
1. MIDNIGHT'S NATIONS

1 Jawaharlal Nehru, 'Tryst with Destiny', Speech, 15 August 1947, <https://www.youtube.com/watch?v=2Cudc5Mhlcc>.

2 Sri Prakasa, *Pakistan: Birth and Last Days of Jinnah*, Meerut: Meenakshi Prakashan, 1965.

3 Prabhash K. Dutta, 'Why Pakistan celebrates Independence Day on August 14 a day before India does', *India Today*,15 August 2020.

4 Ayesha Jalal, *The Sole Spokesman: Jinnah, the Muslim League and the Demand for Pakistan*, Cambridge: Cambridge University Press, 1985.

5 Prakasa, *Pakistan*.

6 Ibid.

7 Ibid., p. 9.

8 Pallavi Raghavan, *Animosity at Bay: An Alternative History of the India–Pakistan Relationship, 1947-1952*, Gurugram: HarperCollins India, 2020.

9 Ibid.

10 Prakasa, *Pakistan*.

11 Ibid.

12 Ibid., p. 11.
13 Ayesha Jalal, *The Struggle for Pakistan*, Cambridge: Harvard University Press, 2014.
14 Salman Rushdie in his book *Shame*, described Pakistan as 'that country divided into two Wings a thousand miles apart, that fantasic bird of a place, two Wings without a body, sundered by the land-mass of its greatest foe, joined by nothing but God...'; The geographical contours of Pakistan did not entirely match its conception by Choudhry Rahmat Ali, an activist, who in 1933 first defined it (originally as 'Pakstan' which in Urdu meant the land of the pure) in a pamphlet 'Now or Never'. Rahmat Ali had put together the acronym 'from the names of all our homelands' viz Panjab, Afghania, Kashmir, Sindh, and Baluchistan. He also proposed the name 'Banglastan' for the Muslim areas of Bengal and 'Osmanistan' for Hyderabad State, as well as a political federation between the three.
15 Prakasa, *Pakistan*.
16 In 1974, Pakistan's parliament adopted a law declaring Ahmadis to be non-Muslims, allegedly because of religious beliefs at variance with the tenets of Islam; the country's constitution was amended to define a Muslim 'as a person who believes in the finality of the Prophet Muhammad'.
17 Ramachandra Guha, *India After Gandhi*, HarperCollins, 2007, pp. 30-32.
18 Kuldip Nayar, *Scoop!: Inside Stories from The Partition to the Present*, Gurugram: HarperCollins India, 2006.
19 Ibid., p. 213.
20 Narendra Singh Sarila, *The Shadow of the Great Game: The Untold Story of India's Partition*, Gurugram: HarperCollins India, 2009
21 Ibid., p. 17.
22 Ibid.
23 Ibid.
24 Ibid.
25 Ibid.
26 Ibid, p. 18.
27 Chandrashekhar Dasgupta, *War and Diplomacy in Kashmir,1947-48*, New Delhi: SAGE Publications India, 2002.
28 Ibid., p. 19.
29 Sarila, *The Shadow of the Great Game*, p. 25.
30 Ibid., p. 413.
31 Ibid., p. 16.
32 Raghavan, *Animosity at Bay*.
33 Shahryar M. Khan, *The Begums of Bhopal: A History of the Princely State of Bhopal*, London: I. B. Tauris, 2002.
34 Sumantra Bose, *Kashmir at the Crossroads: Inside a 21-st Century Conflict*, New Haven/ London: Yale University Press, 2021, p. 3.
35 Sandeep Bamzai, *Princestan: How Nehru, Patel and Mountbatten Made India*, New Delhi: Rupa Publications, 2020.
36 Ibid, p. 11.
37 Prakasa, *Pakistan*.
38 Ibid.
39 Ibid., p. 6.
40 Sarila, *The Shadow of the Great Game*, p.94.
41 Ibid.
42 Kewal Singh, *Partition and Aftermath: Memoirs of an Ambassador*, New Delhi: Vikas Publishing, p. 87.
43 K. S. Bajpai, 'Oral History', Indian Foreign Affairs Journal, Vol. 1, No. 3. http://www.associationdiplomats.org/publications/ifaj/Vol1/1.3/1.3-OralHistory-KSBajpai-The_Evolution_of_the_Indian_Foreign_Service_Establishment.pdf.
44 Prakasa, *Pakistan*.
45 Ibid.
46 Ibid.
47 Ibid.
48 Ibid.
49 Ibid., p. 62.

2. PARTITION PAINS

1 Tilak Devasher, *Pakistan: Courting the Abyss*, Gurugram: HarperCollins, 2016, p. 28.
2 Ian Talbot, *Pakistan: A Modern History*, London: C. Hurst & Co., 1999, p. 101.
3 Ibid.

4   Ishtiaq Ahmed, *Jinnah: His Successes, Failures, Role in History*, New Delhi: Viking, 2020.
5   Ibid.
6   The Majithas were an extended family of Sikhs that originated from the region of Majitha, near Amritsar in Punjab.
7   Talbot, *Pakistan.*
8   Prakasa, *Pakistan.*
9   Guha, *India After Gandhi*, p. 31.
10 Prakasa, *Pakistan.*
11 Ibid.
12 Ibid.
13 Ibid.
14 Ibid., p. 82.
15 Ibid,. p. 80.
16 Ibid., p. 27.
17 Ibid.
18 The statue was vandalized and broken during riots in Karachi around 1950. It was deposited in pieces with the Indian Consulate in the city three decades later, in 1981. It now stands restored and greets visitors at the Indian High Commission in Islamabad.
19 Prakasa, *Pakistan.*
20 Ibid., p. 105.
21 Ibid.
22 Ibid, p. 118.
23 Devasher. *Pakistan: Courting the Abyss.*
24 Dhulipala, *Creating a New Medina*; Ishtiaq Ahmed, *Jinnah.*
25 In this telling, Jinnah would have only tactically conceded the Cabinet Mission plan that called for an undivided India with a loose confederation of provinces classified as 'largely Hindu', 'mainly Muslim' and 'the princely states'. An early biography of Jinnah by Stanley Wolpert, named *Jinnah of Pakistan*, had made a similar argument. Wolpert had in fact admiringly made the argument, which became a familiar quote in the state narrative of Pakistan: 'Few individuals significantly alter the course of history. Fewer still modify the map of the world. Hardly anyone can be credited with creating a nation-state. Mohammad Ali Jinnah did all three.'
26 Yasmin Khan, *The Great Partition: The Making of India and Pakistan*, New Haven, Yale University Press, 2007, p. 10.
27 Anam Zakaria, *The Footprints of Partition*, Gurugram: HarperCollins India, 2015.
28 Yasmin Khan, *The Great Partition.*
29 Dhulipala argued with *Creating a New Medina* that Partition was more an idea of Muslim elites of UP, than of the Muslim-majority provinces, that it was more Aligarh than Lahore driving the argument in the twentieth century. Similarly, political scientist Ishtiaq Ahmed has argued in his 2021 tome *Jinnah* that Pakistan's founding father was firmly wedded to the two-nation theory and the idea of a separate Muslim homeland. His occasionally expressed liberal views may have been aberration or expediency given the nature of his audiences.
30 Some writers have argued that even if Jinnah knew of the Pakistan he was creating, he did not articulate the plan well enough. Recent scholarship, like that of Nisid Hajari in *Midnight's Furies*, argues that while Gandhi and Nehru were prolific and transparent and left vast reams of works and views at different times in their life, Jinnah was more of a mystery and did not write a book or share a larger vision. The writing around Jinnah's central views is largely speculative. The Cabinet Mission plan was the crucial last-ditch effort by the British for a loose confederation that Jinnah had agreed to. However, Nehru and the Congress leadership favoured a strong Centre and a strong state. Several contemporary writers have chipped in, emphasising their own takes on the partition story. M. J. Akbar has argued that the politics of separation of 1906 became the language of partition later. The seeds of partition were in fact sown in 1739, with Nadir Shah invading India at the end of the Moghul reign. The idea was reinforced for the British in 1857. Jinnah had in 1906 opposed separate electorates. He had worked for communal harmony. It was at this point that the idea of separation was truly born.
31 Kewal Singh, *Partition and Aftermath*, p. 129.

3. THE KASHMIR CONUNDRUM
1   Akbar Khan, *Raiders in Kashmir*, Srinagar: Rebus Publishing House, 1975.
2   Husain Haqqani, *Reimagining Pakistan;* Pakistan had in fact inherited 17 percent of the population, 19 percent of GDP, but 33 percent of the armed forces of independent India. The British Indian army's northern HQ in Rawalpindi became the powerful GHQ of Pakistan's army. Pakistan thus had to create a threat to

match the military machine it inherited.

3   Akbar Khan, *Raiders.*
4   Dasgupta, *War and Diplomacy*, p. 38.
5   Ibid.
6   Ibid., p. 200.
7   Ibid., p. 201.
8   Ibid.
9   Ibid., p.203.
10 Ibid., p. 206.
11 Abdul Sattar, *Pakistan's Foreign Policy 1947-2019: A Concise History*, Karachi: OUP Pakistan, 2011.
12 Dasgupta, *War and Diplomacy*, p. 210.
13 Ibid, p. 28.
14 Ibid, p. 29.
15 Ibid.
16 Arjun Subramaniam, *India's Wars: A Military History, 1947-1971*, Gurugram: HarperCollins India, 2016; Guha, *India after Gandhi*, p. 51.
17 Avtar Singh Bhasin, *India–Pakistan Relations 1947-2007: A Documentary Study*, New Delhi: Geetika Publishers, 2012, p. 2.
18 Ibid., p. 208.
19 Ibid., p. 128.
20 Ibid., p. 90.
21 Talbot, *Pakistan*, p.118.
22 Ibid., p. 119.

4. DECOUPLING

1   Fortnightly report from M.K. Kirpalani, Deputy High Commissioner for India in Lahore, 17 September 1948, File No. 8-15/48-Pak I, NAI, cited by Pallavi Raghavan in *Animosity at Bay: An Alternative History of the India–Pakistan Relationship.*
2   Ibid.
3   Raghavan, *Animosity at Bay.*
4   Ibid.
5   Ibid.
6   Kewal Singh, *Partition and Aftermath*, p. 100.
7   Raghavan, *Animosity at Bay.*
8   Ibid.
9   Vinay Sitapati, *Jugalbandi: The BJP Before Modi*, Gurugram: Penguin Random House, 2020.
10 Prakasa, *Pakistan*, p. 83.
11 Ishtiaq Ahmed, *Jinnah.*
12 Prakasa, *Pakistan.*
13 Raghavan, *Animosity at Bay.*
14 Talbot, *Pakistan*, p. 137.

5. THE FORMATIVE FIFTIES

1   Guha, *Indian After Gandhi.*
2   Ibid., p. 134.
3   Raghavan, *Animosity at Bay.*
4   'Pakistan Incited Riots, Says Nehru; India Leader Says Anti-Hindu Propaganda in East Bengal Led to Migration of 24,600', *New York Times*, 24 February 1950.
5   Proceedings of the inter-dominion Conference on 18th April 1948 at Writers Building, Calcutta'; File No. F. 8-15/48-Pak I; MEA, Pak I Branch; NAI, cited by Pallavi Raghavan in *Animosity at Bay: An Alternative History of the India–Pakistan Relationship.*
6   Ibid.
7   Raghavan, *Animosity at Bay.*
8   Ibid.
9   T. C. A. Raghavan, *The People Next Door*, Gurugram: HarperCollins India, 2018.
10 Ibid.
11 Raghavan, *Animosity at Bay*; Also: During the early 1950s, the question of migration and refugees represented a substantial threat to the political stability of both governments. As refugees and migrants streamed in in uncontrollable numbers in search of rehabilitation, employment and security, the issue also became politically charged, which could be hurled between the central and provincial governments in India

and Pakistan as accusations of incompetence, corruption, and neglect.
12 Raghavan, *Animosity at Bay.*
13 Ishtiaq Ahmed, *Jinnah.*
14 Talbot, *Pakistan*, p. 139.
15 Ibid., p. 136.
16 Ibid., p. 143.
17 Tharoor, *Battle of Belonging.*
18 Devasher, *Pakistan: Courting the Abyss*, p. 108.
19 Ibid., p. 167.
20 Raghavan, *People Next Door.*
21 Kewal Singh, *Partition and Aftermath*, p. 101.
22 Ibid.
23 Raghavan, *People Next Door*, p. 50.
24 Ibid., p. 51.
25 Kewal Singh, *Partition and Aftermath*, p.104.
26 Nirupama Rao, *The Fractured Himalaya: India Tibet China 1949-62*, Gurugram: Penguin India, 2022, pp. 166-168.
27 Bose, *Kashmir at the Crossroads.*
28 Kewal Singh, *Partition and Aftermath,* p. 106.
29 Ibid.
30 Sattar, *Pakistan's Foreign Policy.*
31 Ibid., p. 108.
32 Natwar Singh, *One Life Is Not Enough*, New Delhi: Rupa Publications India, 2021, p. 121.
33 Ibid., p. 32.
34 Ibid., p.188.
35 Sattar, *Pakistan's Foreign Policy*, p. 29.
36 Raghavan, *Animosity at Bay.*

SECTION 2. 1957–1967: DICTATORS AND DEMOCRATS
6. THE GARRISON STATE

1 Talbot, *Pakistan*, p. 146.
2 Muhammad Ayub Khan, *Friends not Masters, A Political Autobiography*, New York: Oxford University Press, 1967.
3 Ibid., p. 74.
4 Rajeshwar Dayal, *A Life in our Times*, Hyderabad: Orient BlackSwan, 1998, p. 257.
5 Ibid., p. 263.
6 Ibid., p. 268
7 Sattar, *Pakistan's Foreign Policy*, p. 59.
8 Ibid., p. 79.
9 Kewal Singh, *Partition and Aftermath.*
10 Ayub Khan, *Friends not Masters.*
11 Ibid.
12 Ishtiaq Ahmed, *The Pakistan Garrison State: Origins, Evolution, Consequences (1947-2011)*, OUP *Pakistan*, 2013; Harold Lasswell, 'The Garrison State', *American Journal of Sociology*, Vol. 46, No. 4, January 1941, pp. 455–468.
13 Kewal Singh, *Partition and Aftermath.*
14 Dayal, *A Life in Our Times*, p. 258.
15 Ibid., p. 279.
16 Ibid., p. 140.
17 Author's conversation with Khurshid Mahmud Kasuri, the former Foreign Minister of Pakistan.
18 Sharat Sabharwal, *India's Pakistan Conundrum*, Routledge, pp. 167-173.
19 Raghavan, *Animosity at Bay.*
20 Ibid.
21 Ibid.
22 Brahma Chellaney, 'Dragon's water weapon against India', *DNA*, 11 September 2018.
23 K.V. Padmanabhan, 'How the Indus Treaty was signed', *The Hindu*, 28 September 2016.
24 Dayal, *A Life in Our Times*, p. 318.
25 Ibid., p. 301.
26 K.V. Padmanabhan, 'How the Indus Treaty was signed'.
27 Ayub Khan, *Friends not Masters.*

28　P. Raman, 'When Opposition asked... PM Nehru answered the questions on China in Parliament', *Indian Express*, 15 November 2020.
29　Kewal Singh, *Partition and Aftermath*, p. 163.
30　P. Raman, 'When Opposition asked'.
31　Kewal Singh. *Partition and Aftermath*.
32　For a detailed account on the India-China border talks, see Nirupama Rao's *The Fractured Himalaya*.
33　Sattar, *Pakistan's Foreign Policy*, p. 86.
34　Rao, *The Fractured Himalaya*.
35　Sattar, *Pakistan's Foreign Policy*.
36　Ibid., p. 86.
37　Ibid., p. 93.
38　Prasar Bharati Archives, 'Jawaharlal Nehru's last TV Interview - May 1964', YouTube, 14 May 2019.

7. DIALOGUES OF THE DEAF

1　Kewal Singh, *Partition and Aftermath*, page 143.
2　Sattar, *Pakistan's Foreign Policy*, p. 89.
3　Ibid., p. 90.
4　Kewal Singh, *Partition and Aftermath*, p.143.
5　Ibid., p. 153.
6　Ibid.
7　'When Atal Bihari Vajpayee delivered emotional speech after Jawahar Lal Nehru's death', *Economic Times*, 17 August, 2018.
8　K. Shankar Bajpai, 'Tashkent syndrome', *Indian Express*, 9 January 2016.
9　Sumantra Bose, *Kashmir at the Crossroads*, pp. 41-43.
10　Kewal Singh, *Partition and Aftermath*.

8. A GRAB AT KASHMIR

1　Kewal Singh, *Partition and Aftermath*.
2　Sattar, *Pakistan's Foreign Policy*.
3　Kewal Singh, *Partition and Aftermath*, p. 160.
4　Ibid.
5　'Golden Jubilee Commemoration of Indo–Pak War, 1965 is a Befitting Tribute to Gallantry & Sacrifice of our Soldiers - Vice President', Press Information Bureau
6　Sattar, *Pakistan's Foreign Policy*, p. 106.
7　Ibid.
8　Kewal Singh, *Partition and Aftermath*, p.166.
9　Ibid., 169-172.
10　Ibid., p. 173.
11　Sattar, *Pakistan's Foreign Policy*
12　Ibid., p. 113.
13　Kewal Singh, *Partition and Aftermath*.
14　Ibid.
15　Ibid.
16　Ibid.
17　Ibid., p.186.
18　Sattar, *Pakistan's Foreign Policy, p.* 118.
19　Ayub Khan, *Friends Not Masters*.
20　Ibid., p. 117.
21　K. Shankar Bajpai, '1965, the forgetting', *Indian Express*, 9 September 2015.
22　Kewal Singh, *Partition and Aftermath*, p.189
23　Ibid., p. 191.
24　Bajpai, '1965, the forgetting'.
25　The writer, a former ambassador to Pakistan, China, the US and secretary, MEA, was political officer in the Indian High Commission in Karachi, 1962-65, and secretary to the Indian delegation to Tashkent, 1966.
26　Kewal Singh, *Partition and Aftermath*, p. 223.
27　Debora Ann Shea, *Escape from Pakistan: The Untold Story of Jack Shea*, Gurugram: Penguin Books, 2021.

SECTION 3. 1967–1977: A SUBCONTINENT REDRAWN
9. JOI BANGLA

1 Ishtiaq Ahmed, *Jinnah*
2 Srinath Raghavan, *1971: A Global History of the Creation of Bangladesh*, Harvard University Press, 2013; Chandrashekhar Dasgupta, *India and the Bangladesh Liberation War*, New Delhi: Juggernaut, 2021.
3 Kewal Singh, *Partition and Aftermath*.
4 Mahbub ul Haq, 'System is to blame for the 22 wealthy families', *London Times*, 22 March 1973.
5 Srinath Raghavan, *1971: A Global History of the Creation of Bangladesh*.
6 Kewal Singh, *Partition and Aftermath*, p. 262.
7 Ibid.
8 Ibid.
9 Dasgupta, *India and the Bangladesh Liberation War*.
10 Ibid.
11 Ibid.
12 Srinath Raghavan, *1971: A Global History of the Creation of Bangladesh*.
13 Dasgupta, *India and the Bangladesh Liberation War*.
14 Deb Mukharji interviewed by the author, New Delhi, July 2023.
15 Deb Mukharji, 'For Indian Diplomats in Pakistan, the Run up To the 1971 War Was a Very Tense Time', *The Wire*, 26 March 2021.
16 Deb Mukharji interviewed by the author.
17 Srinath Raghavan, *1971: A Global History of the Creation of Bangladesh*.
18 Rukun Advani, 'A Little Outside the Ring', *The Telegraph*, 8 February 2002.
19 Srinath Raghavan, *1971: A Global History of the Creation of Bangladesh*.
20 Deb Mukharji interviewed by the author.
21 Ibid.
22 Ibid.
23 Srinath Raghavan, *1971: A Global History of the Creation of Bangladesh*.
24 Ibid.
25 Ibid.
26 Ibid.
27 Gary Bass, *The Blood Telegram: Nixon, Kissinger, and a Forgotten Genocide*, New York: Penguin Random House, 2013, p. 48.
28 Srinath Raghavan, *1971: A Global History of the Creation of Bangladesh*, p. 55.
29 Bass, *Blood Telegram*, p. 46.
30 Ibid.
31 Srinath Raghavan, *1971: A Global History of the Creation of Bangladesh*, p. 47.
32 Ibid., p. 49; Dasgupta, *India and the Bangladesh Liberation War*, p. 33.
33 Bass, *Blood Telegram*.
34 Ibid., p.58.
35 Ibid.
36 Ibid.
37 Ibid., p. 61.
38 Ibid.
39 Ibid., p. 64.
40 Ibid., p. 66.
41 Ibid.
42 Ibid.
43 Ibid., p. 75.
44 Ibid., p. 76
45 Ibid., p. 79.
46 Ahsan I. Butt, *Secession and Security: Explaining State Strategy against Separatists*, Ithaca: Cornell University Press, 2017.
47 'Role of MOFA in Liberation War', Ministry of Foreign Affairs, Bangladesh,,< https://mofa.gov.bd/site/page/3164add5-f0b4-432e-99e3-342057675660/nolink/Former--Advisers>.
48 Deb Mukharji, 'For Indian Diplomats in Pakistan'.
49 Srinath Raghavan, *1971: A Global History of the Creation of Bangladesh*.
50 Ibid., p. Page 70.
51 Bass, *Blood Telegram*.
52 Ibid., p. 105.
53 Ibid., p. 106.
54 Ibid., p. 107.

55 Ibid., p. 114.
56 Ibid., p. 116.
57 Ibid., p. 100.
58 Ibid., p. 173.
59 Ibid., p. 178.
60 Srinath Raghavan, *1971: A Global History of the Creation of Bangladesh*, p. 104.
61 Ibid., p. 198.
62 Ibid; Bass, *Blood Telegram.*
63 Srinath Raghavan, *1971: A Global History of the Creation of Bangladesh.*
64 Ibid., p. 196.
65 Ibid.
66 Ibid., p. 209.
67 Deb Mukharji interviewed by the author.
68 Srinath Raghavan, *1971: A Global History of the Creation of Bangladesh.*
69 Ibid., p. 117.
70 Ibid., p. 224.
71 Ibid., p. 227.
72 Bass, *Blood Telegram*, p. 228; Srinath Raghavan, *1971: A Global History of the Creation of Bangladesh.*
73 Bass, *Blood Telegram*, p. 5; Srinath Raghavan, *1971: A Global History of the Creation of Bangladesh.*
74 Ibid.
75 Srinath Raghavan, *1971: A Global History of the Creation of Bangladesh*, p. 228.
76 Ibid., p. 204.

10. A SECOND PARTITION, A THIRD COUNTRY
1   Bhasin, *India–Pakistan Relations*, p. 1620.
2   'Foreign Relations of The United States, 1969–1976, Volume Xi, South Asia Crisis, 1971', Office of the Historia, Washington, 29 November 1971.
3   'Yahya is not an ogre', *Dawn*, 24 January 2017.
4   Sydney H. Schanberg, 'Mrs. Gandhi Bids Pakistan Remove Forces From East', *New York Times*, 30 November 1971.
5   Srinath Raghavan, *1971: A Global History of the Creation of Bangladesh.*
6   Ibid.
7   Ibid.
8   Ibid., p. 250.
9   Ibid., p. 251.
10 Ibid.
11 Ibid., p. 255.
12 Ibid., p. 233.
13 Ibid., p. 256.
14 Ibid.
15 Ibid., p. 258.
16 Ibid.
17 Ibid., p. 261.
18 Baqir Sajjad Syed, 'Army has resolved to shun politics, assures Bajwa', *Dawn*, 24 November 2022.
19 Srinath Raghavan, *1971: A Global History of the Creation of Bangladesh*, p. 262.
20 Ibid., p. 261.
21 Ibid., p. 262.
22 Ibid., p. 262.
23 Ibid., p. 263.
24 Ibid., p. 8.

11. LINE OF CONTROL
1   K. N. Bakshi, 'Simla Agreement: From Military Victory to a Diplomatic Defeat? (1972)', *Indian Foreign Affairs Journal*, Vol. 2, No. 3, 2007, p. 105-119.
2   Humayun Khan and G. Parthasarathy, *Diplomatic Divide*, New Delhi: Roli Books, 2004, p 44.
3   Kewal Singh, *Partition and Aftermath*, p. 313.
4   Ibid., p. 315.
5   Ibid., pp. 317-318.
6   Srinath Raghavan, *1971: A Global History of the Creation of Bangladesh*, p. 265.
7   Ibid., p. 268.

8   Kewal Singh, *Partition and Aftermath*, p. 317.
9   Srinath Raghavan, *1971: A Global History of the Creation of Bangladesh*.
10 Ibid., p. 267.
11 Kewal Singh, *Partition and Aftermath*.
12 Ibid, p. 333.
13 Ibid., p. 334.
14 Raj Chengappa, *Weapons of Peace: The Secret Story of India's Quest to Be a Nuclear Power*, Gurugram: HarperCollins India, 2001.
15 Ibid., p. 201.
16 Ibid.
17 Kewal Singh, *Partition and Aftermath*, p. 340.
18 Ibid. p. 345.
19 Ibid.

12. LIMPING BACK
1   Kewal Singh, *Partition and Aftermath*, p. 349.
2   Ibid., pp. 350-51.
3   Kewal Singh, *Partition and Aftermath*, pp. 357-361.
4   T. C. A. Raghavan, *People Next Door*, p. 130.
5   Bhasin, *India–Pakistan Relations*, p. 2,533.
6   Ibid., p. 2,513.
7   Ibid., p. 2,361.
8   Bhasin, *India–Pakistan Relations*.
9   Ibid.
10 Raghavan, *People Next Door*, p 138.

SECTION 4. 1977–1987: FIVE BLOODY RIVERS
13. THAWING TO DECEIVE
1   Prasar Bharati Archives, '1977 - Then Foreign Minister Atal Bihari Vajpayee as 1st Indian leader to address UNGA in Hindi', Speech, YouTube, 24 October 2021.
2   Sagarika Ghose, *Atal Bihari Vajpayee: India's Most Loved Prime Minister*, New Delhi: Juggernaut Books, 2021, p. 158.
3   Bhasin, *India–Pakistan Relations*.
4   Ghose, *Atal Bihari Vajpayee*, p. 155.
5   Bhasin, *India–Pakistan Relations*.
6   Ibid., p. 2,410.
7   Ibid., p. 2,425.
8   Ibid., p. 2,581.
9   Ibid., p. 2,580.
10 J. N. Dixit, *India–Pakistan in War and Peace*, Routledge, 2002, p. 120.
11 Ibid., p. 121.

14. PUNJAB AFLAME
1   G. B. S. Sidhu, *The Khalistan Conspiracy*, Gurugram: HarperCollins India, 2020.
2   Ibid.
3   Terry Milewski, *Blood for Blood*, Gurugram: HarperCollins India, 2021.
4   Ibid., p. 23.
5   Ibid.
6   Ibid.
7   Ibid.
8   Mani Shankar Aiyar and Indian Foreign Affairs Journal, 'The (Hi)Story of One Lakh Visas', Indian Foreign Affairs Journal, vol. 5, no. 4, 2010.
9   Bhasin, *India–Pakistan Relations*, p. 2623.
10 Ibid.
11 Srinath Raghavan, *1971: A Global History of the Creation of Bangladesh*.
12 John Lamberton Harper, *The Cold War*, Oxford University Press, 2011.
13 Yashwant Raj, 'US knew of Pak N-plan but did not act: Declassified documents' Hindustan Times, 30 August 2021.
14 Mohammad Islam, 'Pakistan-Us New Connection: An Evaluation', *Pakistan Horizon*, Vol. 36, No. 2, 1983,

494   ANGER MANAGEMENT

pp. 31–44. JSTOR, <http://www.jstor.org/stable/41394188>.

15 Natwar Singh, *One Life Is Not Enough*, p. 189.

16 Ibid., p. 188.

17 Khan and Parthasarathy, *Diplomatic Divide*, p. 88; Bhasin, *India–Pakistan Relations*.

18 TCA Raghavan, *People Next Door*, p. 159.

19 Mahesh Sachdev, 'Pakistan, Saudi Arabia and the Night of Power, *Hindustan Times*, 13 May 2021

20 K Natwar Singh, '*Profiles & Letters*', *Sterling Publishers, 1997*.

21 Kewal Singh, *Partition and Aftermath*, p. 394.

22 Dilip Bobb, 'Pakistan President Zia's no-war pact offer to India described as a 'sucker punch', India Today, 15 February 1982

23 Natwar Singh, *One Life Is Not Enough*.

24 Khan and Parthasarathy, *Diplomatic Divide, p.* 89.

25 Ibid, p. 91.

26 TCA Raghavan, *People Next Door*, p. 166.

27 Prabhu Dayal, *Karachi Halwa*, Gurugram: Zorba Books, 2015, p. 83.

28 Khan and Parthasarathy, *Diplomatic Divide, p.* 17.

29 Ibid., p. 24.

30 Dayal, *Karachi Halwa*, p. 86.

31 Khan and Parthasarathy, *Diplomatic Divide*, p. 27.

32 Dayal, *Karachi Halwa*.

15. AUTUMN IN KASHMIR

1 Sumantra Bose, *Kashmir at the Crossroads: Inside a 21-st Century Conflict*, p. 51-60.

2 Arjun Subramaniam, *Full Spectrum: India's Wars, 1972-2020*, Noida: HarperCollins India, 2020.

3 V. R. Raghavan, *Siachen: Conflict Without End*, New Delhi: Viking, 2002.

4 Lt. Gen. D. S. Hooda, 'Many good reasons to demilitarise Siachen. But India–Pakistan ties too torn to allow it', *The Print*, 17 January 2022.

5 Khan and Parthasarathy, *Diplomatic Divide, p.* 40.

6 Ibid.

7 Subramaniam, *Full Spectrum*.

8 Inderjit Bhadwar, Dilip Bobb, 'When Indian and Pakistani forces positioned themselves along J&K and Punjab borders', *India Today*, 15 February 1987.

9 Subramaniam, *Full Spectrum*.

10 Natwar Singh, *One Life Is Not Enough*.

11 Ibid.

12 Ramindar Singh, 'Pakistan President Zia-ul-Haq comes to Jaipur, sees some cricket and conquers the media', *India Today*, 15 March 1987.

13 Subramaniam, *Full Spectrum*.

SECTION 5. 1987-1997: TROUBLE IN PARADISE

16. EXPLODING MANGOES

1 S. K. Lambah, *In Pursuit of Peace: India–Pakistan Relations Under Six Prime Ministers*, Gurugram: Penguin Viking, 2023; Ronen Sen told the author via a telephonic conversation, 2022.

2 Bhasin, *India–Pakistan Relations*.

3 Lambah, *In Pursuit of Peace*, p. 78.

4 Bhasin, *India–Pakistan Relations*, p. 3,095.

5 Lambah, *In Pursuit of Peace*, p. 77.

6 Bhasin, *India–Pakistan Relations*.

7 Ibid.

8 Ibid., p. 3,095.

9 Ibid.

10 Lambah, *In Pursuit of Peace*.

11 Ibid., p. 79.

12 Kallol Bhattacharjee, *The Great Game in Afghanistan: Rajiv Gandhi, General Zia and the Unending War*, Noida: HarperCollins, 2017; Declan Walsh, 'Ex-US diplomat blames Israel for Pakistani dictator's death', *The Guardian*, 5 December 2005; Ronen Sen to the author.

13 Kallol Bhattacharjee, *The Great Game in Afghanistan*.

14 Natwar Singh, *One Life Is Not Enough*.

15 Bhasin, *India–Pakistan Relations*, p. 3,322.

16 Shekhar Gupta, 'Biggest problem is that Zia perpetuated his rule by fragmenting the nation: Benazir Bhutto', *India Today*, 15 September 1988.
17 Mohammed Hanif, *Case of Exploding Mangoes*, Knopf Doubleday Publishing Group, 2008.
18 Lambah, *In Pursuit of Peace*, pp. 80-81, Ronen Sen to the author.

17. A THOUSAND CUTS
1   Prabhu Dayal, *Karachi Halwa.*
2   Dixit, *India–Pakistan in War and Peace.*
3   Lambah, *In Pursuit of Peace*, p. 81.
4   C. Christine Fair, *In Their Own Words: Understanding Lashkar-e-Tayyaba*, New Delhi: Oxford University Press, 2018.
5   Kewal Singh, *Partition and Aftermath.*
6   Ramindar Singh, 'Redeployment of forces at Siachen glacier to be worked out between India, Pak', *India Today*, 15 July 1989.
7   Lambah, *In Pursuit of Peace*, p. 79.
8   Ibid., p. 82.
9   Dixit, *India–Pakistan in War and Peace.*
10 Ibid.
11 Bhasin, *India–Pakistan Relations.*
12 Bose, *Kashmir at the Crossroads.*
13 Ibid.
14 Dixit, *India–Pakistan in War and Peace.*
15 Shekhar Gupta, 'Modi shouldn't trivialise nuclear weapons. His Diwali taunt at Pakistan is loose talk', *The Print*, 23 April 2019.
16 Madhu Jain, 'Nobody wants war but political compulsions restrict the options', India Today, 28 February 1990.
17 'Karachi stands with Kashmir in solidarity', *The News International*, 6 February 2018.
18 Dixit, *India–Pakistan in War and Peace.*
19 Shekhar Gupta, 'By using the Kashmir card Benazir Bhutto is playing with fire', *India Today*, 31 May 1990.
20 Shekhar Gupta, 'How Indian armed forces can defeat Pakistan in less than a week', *The Print*, 1 February 2020.
21 Sushant Singh, '25 yrs after Gates Mission, 3 stories and one mystery', *Indian Express*, 21 May 2015.
22 William Burrows, *Critical Mass: The Dangerous Race for Superweapons in a Fragmenting World*, New York: Simon & Schuster, 1994.
23 Asad Durrani, *Pakistan Adrift: Navigating Troubled Waters*, Context, 2018.
24 Lambah, *In Pursuit of Peace.*
25 Ibid., p. 85.
26 Vinay Sitapati, *Half-Lion: How P.V. Narasimha Rao Transformed India*, Gurugram: Penguin Random House, 2016.
27 Ibid.
28 Ibid.
29 Dixit, *India–Pakistan in War and Peace.*
30 Dalia Dassa Kaye. 'Regional Security Dialogues in South Asia',' Talking to the Enemy: Track Two Diplomacy in the Middle East and South Asia', RAND Corporation, 2007, pp. 75–104.

18. FROZEN TRUST
1   Dixit, *India–Pakistan in War and Peace.*
2   Lambah, *In Pursuit of Peace.*
3   Ibid.
4   Ibid.
5   Dixit, *India–Pakistan in War and Peace.*
6   Ibid.
7   Bhasin, *India–Pakistan Relations.*
8   Dixit, *India–Pakistan in War and Peace.*
9   Sanjaya Baru (ed.), *P.V. Narasimha Rao: Architect of India's Reforms,* Issued by the Government of Telangana on the occasion of the centenary year of former Prime Minister PV Narasimha Rao, 2021
10 Lambah, *In Pursuit of Peace*, p. 103.
11 Baru (ed.), *P.V. Narasimha Rao.*
12 Sitapati, *Half-Lion.*
13 Baru (ed.), *P.V. Narasimha Rao.*

14 Ibid.
15 Lambah, *In Pursuit of Peace.*
16 Ibid.
17 Ibid., p.109.
18 Rajiv Dogra interviewed by the author, 2022.
19 A previous resident of that diplomatic residence, Prabhu Dayal reflected later that seemed to have picked up the curse of the Bhutto house that was across the street from it. Zulfikar Bhutto, the man who built the house, was hanged in April 1979; his younger son died in mysterious circumstances in July 1986. Soon, his elder son Murtaza would be killed in a police encounter near the house in 1996, and of course his eldest child, Benazir, would be assassinated in 2007; Prabhu Dayal observes that power in Pakistan often came to be soaked in so much blood.
20 'How the 1993 blasts changed Mumbai forever', *BBC*, 30 July 2015.
21 On 9 March 1993, three days before the bombings took place, a small-time criminal from the Behrampada slum in Northeast Mumbai named Gul Noor Mohammad Sheikh (Gullu) was detained at the Nag Pada police station. A participant in the communal riots that had rocked Bombay the previous year, Gullu was also one of the 19 men handpicked by Tiger Memon, whose office was burnt in the riots. Tiger was a silver smuggler and chief mastermind of the bombings, for training in the use of guns and bomb-making. Gullu had been sent to Pakistan via Dubai on 19 February 1993 and upon completion of his training returned to Mumbai on 4 March. In his absence, the police had detained Gullu's brothers to encourage him to surrender, which he did. He confessed to his role in the riots, his training in Pakistan, and a conspiracy underway to bomb major locations around the city, including the Bombay Stock Exchange, Sahar International Airport and the Sena Bhavan. However, his conspiracy claim was dismissed by the police as a "mere bluff". The arrest of Gul Mohammed spurred Tiger Memon to advance the date of the bombings which had originally been planned to coincide with the Shiv Jayanti celebrations in April 1993.
22 Lambah, *In Pursuit of Peace.*
23 'Crime Syndicate Responsible for 1993 Mumbai Blasts Given State Protection, Enjoying 5-star Hospitality: Jaishankar', *News18*, 12 January 2021.
24 'Harkat ul-Ansar', South Asia Terrorism Portal.
25 Sattar, *Pakistan's Foreign Policy, p.* 43.
26 Lambah, *In Pursuit of Peace.*
27 Ibid., p. 115.
28 Ibid.
29 Ibid., p. 94.
30 Ibid.
31 Ibid., p.124.
32 Satish Chandra, *A Life Well Spent*, New Delhi: Rupa Publications India, 2023.
33 Sitapati, *Half-Lion.*
34 Lambah, *In Pursuit of Peace.*
35 Ibid., pp. 125–27.
36 Ibid.
37 Ibid.
38 Ibid., p.140.
39 Ibid.
40 Ibid., p. 149.
41 Ibid., p. 153.
42 Chandra, *A Life Well Spent.*
43 Ibid., p. 176.
44 Prasun Sonwalkar, 'When Narasimha Rao rejected Benazir's 'tea diplomacy' in London', *Hindustan Times,* 2 January 2020.
45 Sabharwal, *India's Pakistan Conundrum*, p. 115.
46 Prabhu Dayal, *Karachi Halwa.*

19. TALKING OF EVERYTHING
1   Chandra, *A Life Well Spent*, p. 192.

SECTION 6. 1997–2007: NUCLEAR GAMES
20. STRATEGIC PARITY
1   Hussain Haqqani, 'The Legacy of Partition', *Wall Street Journal*, 15 August 1997.
2   Bhasin, *India–Pakistan Relations.*

3   Peter Popham, 'Royal visit hits India's raw nerve', *The Independent,* 13 October, 1997.
4   Sabharwal, *India's Pakistan Conundrum.*
5   Chandra, *A Life Well Spent*, pp. 196-197.
6   'The Insiders: Interview with Brajesh Mishra', *NewsX,* < https://dai.ly/x738ghn>.
7   Natwar Singh, *One Life Is Not Enough*, p. 294.
8   Sitapati, *Half Lion.*
9   Shakti Sinha, *Vajpayee: The Years That Changed India*, Gurugram: Penguin Random House India, p. 100.
10 Sitapati, *Half Lion.*
11 Sabharwal, *India's Pakistan Conundrum*, p. 180.
12 Lambah, *In Pursuit of Peace*, p. 135.
13 'The Insiders: Interview with Brajesh Mishra', *NewsX;* Sinha, *Vajpayee*, p.105.
14 'Pm Calls For N-Weapon Convention', *Business Standard*, 28 May 1998.
15 Omar Farooq Khan, 'Bill Clinton offered $5 billion to not conduct nuclear test in 1998: Nawaz Sharif', *Times of India*, 20 July 2017.
16 Sabharwal, *India's Pakistan Conundrum.*
17 Under the bilateral agreement active since 1992, prohibiting attacks against the nuclear installations of each other.
18 Chandra, *A Life Well Spent*, pp. 197-198; Sabharwal, *India's Pakistan Conundrum*, p.181.
19 Brajesh Mishra, 'Annual Krishnaswamy Memorial Lecture by Shri Brajesh Mishra', < http://www.globalindiafoundation.org/Speech_Brajesh_Mishra%51B%5D.pdf>.
20 Adrian Levy and Cathy Scott, *Deception: Pakistan, the United States, and the Global Nuclear Weapons Conspiracy,* Atlantic Books, 2008.
21 'The Insiders: Interview with Brajesh Mishra', *NewsX.*
22 'A look at the zeroes of 1998', *India Today*, 4 January 1999
23 Jaswant Singh, *A Call to Honour: In Service of Emergent India*, New Delhi: Rupa Publications, 2006, p. 283.
24 Ahmed Rashid, *Descent into Chaos: The US and the disaster in Pakistan, Afghanistan, and Central Asia*, London: Penguin Books, 2009, p. 277.
25 Sabharwal, *India's Pakistan Conundrum*, p. 115-116.
26 J. N. Dixit, *India's Foreign Policy, 1947-2003*, New Delhi: Picus Books, 2003, p. 452.
27 Khan and Parthasarathy, *Diplomatic Divide, p.* 116.
28 Celia W. Dugger, 'Indian Leader Accepts Pakistani Offer to Take a Ride to Lahore', *New York Times*, 4 February 1999.
29 Sinha, *Vajpayee*, p. 222.
30 Ibid.
31 Jaswant Singh, *A Call to Honour.*
32 Ibid., p. 226.
33 Khan and Parthasarathy, *Diplomatic Divide, pp.* 106-135.
34 Sinha, *Vajpayee*, p. 239.
35 Ibid., p. 240.
36 Ibid.
37 Ibid, p. 245.
38 Ibid.
39 Ibid., p. 247.

21. HEIGHTS OF TROUBLE

1   Jaswant Singh, *A Call to Honour*, p. 202.
2   Naseem Zehra, *From Kargil to the Coup: Events that Shook Pakistan*, Lahore: Sang-e-Meel Publications, 2018. Arjun Subramaniam, Full Spectrum: India's Wars, Gurugram: HarperCollins India, 2020.
3   V. P. Malik, *Kargil: From Surprise To Victory*, Noida: HarperCollins, 2020; Sinha, *Vajpayee.*
4   Dixit, *India's Foreign Policy, 1947-2003*, p. 461.
5   Sinha, *Vajpayee;* Khan and Parthasarathy, *Diplomatic Divide*, p. 119.
6   Khan and Parthasarathy, *Diplomatic Divide,* p. 119.
7   Ibid.
8   Bruce Riedel, 'American Diplomacy and the 1999 Kargil Summit at Blair House', Policy Paper Series, Center for Advanced Studies of India, p. 4.
9   Strobe Talbott, Engaging India: Diplomacy, Democracy and the Bomb, Viking, 2004, p. 157.
10 Sinha, *Vajpayee*, pp. 300-302.
11 Khan and Parthasarathy, *Diplomatic Divide,* p. 121.
12 Talbott, Engaging India, p. 159.

13 Ibid.
14 Bill Clinton, *My Life*, New York: Random House, 2004, p. 864.
15 Talbott, *Engaging India*, p. 158.
16 Ibid., p 158.
17 Ibid., p. 160.
18 Ibid.
19 Ibid.
20 Jaswant Singh, *A Call to Honour*, p. 226.
21 Talbott, *Engaging India*, p. 162.
22 Ibid.
23 Ibid.
24 Ibid., p. 163
25 Ibid., p. 161
26 Ibid.
27 Ibid.
28 Ibid.
29 Ibid.
30 Ibid.
31 Ibid.
32 Ibid.
33 Ibid.
34 Ibid.
35 Bhasin, *India–Pakistan Relations*.
36 Ibid.
37 Ibid.
38 Ibid.
39 Ibid.
40 Subramaniam, *Full Spectrum*.
41 Bhasin, *India–Pakistan Relations*.
42 Raj Chengappa, 'Controversy over secret negotiations during Kargil war begins to hurt Vajpayee and Sharif', *India Today*, 27 September 1999.
43 Bhasin, *India–Pakistan Relations*.
44 Khan and Parthasarathy, *Diplomatic Divide*, p. 123.
45 Ibid, p. 82.
46 Ibid, p. 124.
47 Bhasin, *India–Pakistan Relations*
48 Ibid.
49 Khan and Parthasarathy, *Diplomatic Divide*, p. 130.
50 Ibid.

22. MILLENNIAL DIPLOMACY

1 Bhasin, *India–Pakistan Relations*.
2 Karan Thapar, *Devil's Advocate: The Untold Story*, HarperCollins India, 2018; L. K. Advani, *My Country, My Life*, Rupa Publications, 2008.
3 A. K. Cronin, *Attacking Terrorism, Elements of a Grand Strategy*. Georgetown University Press, 2004.
4 U.S. Government Publishing Office, 'Address by His Excellency, Atal Bihari Vajpayee, Prime Minister of India', Congressional Record (Bound Edition), Volume 146, Part 13, 2000.
5 The temple planned on the site of the razed Babri Masjid structure.
6 Atal Bihari Vajpayee, 'Musings From Kumarakom', *Outlook* (reproduced), 3 February 2022.
7 Ibid.
8 Karan Thapar, *Devil's Advocate*.
9 L. K. Advani, *My Country, My Life*.
10 B. Muralidhar Reddy, 'The message from Musharraf', *Frontline,* 9 June 2001.
11 Prabhu Chawla, 'Indo–Pak Summit in Agra turns out to be a PR disaster for India', *India Today*, 31 December 2001.
12 Sattar, *Pakistan's Foreign Policy*.
13 Ibid., p. 377.
14 Ibid.
15 Jaswant Singh, *A Call to Honour,* p. 258.
16 Pervez Musharraf, *In the Line of Fire: A Memoir*, ⊠ Free Press, 2008.

NOTES 499

17 Jaswant Singh, *A Call to Honour*, p. 259.
18 Bhasin, *India–Pakistan Relations*.
19 Ibid.

23. THE TERROR FACTOR
1 Musharraf, *In the Line of Fire*.
2 L.K. Advani, 'Aimed To Wipe Out The Entire Political Leadership Of India', *Outlook*, 3 February 2022; *Lok Sabha Debates*, 19 December 2001, p. 305.
3 Riedel, *American Diplomacy and the 1999 Kargil Summit at Blair House*.
4 Jawed Naqvi, 'Delhi blames Lashkar for attack: India wants militants' arrest', *Dawn*, 15 December 2001.
5 'Statement made by Shri L.K. Advani, Union Home Minister on Tuesday, the 18th December, 2001 In Lok Sabha in Connection with the terrorist attack on Parliament House', Media Center, Ministry of External Affairs, Government of India, 18 December 2001.
6 Bhasin, *India–Pakistan Relations*.
7 Ewan McAskill, 'New Delhi recalls its man in Islamabad', *The Guardian*, 22 December 2001.
8 Bhasin, *India–Pakistan Relations*.
9 'Text of the Statement made by the External Affairs Minister, Shri Jaswant Singh', Media Center, Ministry of External Affairs, Government of India, December 27, 2001.
10 Atal Bihari Vajpayee, 'Full text of Vajpayee's New Year message', *Times of India*, 1 January 2002.
11 Bhasin, *India–Pakistan Relations*.
12 'Pakistan's leader comes down hard on extremists', *CNN*, 12 January 2002.
13 Bhasin, *India–Pakistan Relations*.
14 'Nambiar's Total Recall', *Times of India*, New Delhi, 31 January 2002.
15 Bhasin, *India–Pakistan Relations*.
16 Ibid
17 Ibid.
18 Karan Thapar, *Devil's Advocate*.
19 Yashwant Sinha, *Relentless: An Autobiography*, New Delhi: Bloomsbury, 2019.

24. A HAND OF FRIENDSHIP
1 ShivshankarMenon, *Choices: Inside the Making of Indian Foreign Policy*, Gurugram: Penguin Random House India, 2016; Vinay Sitapati, *Jugalbandi.*.
2 Bhasin, *India–Pakistan Relations*.
3 Lambah, *In Pursuit of Peace*, p. 207.
4 K.J.M. Varma, 'Pak to lift ban on Indian overflights', *Tribune*, 1 December 2003; 'Musharraf offers resumption of overflights: Four-step approach on Kashmir proposed', *Dawn*, 1 December 2003.
5 Jaswant Singh, *A Call to Honour*.
6 'Abdul Qadeer Khan: Nuclear hero in Pakistan, villain to the West', *AlJazeera*, 10 October 2021.
7 Bhasin, *India–Pakistan Relations*.
8 Ibid.
9 Ibid.
10 Ibid.

25. ESSAYS IN MUTUAL COMPREHENSION
1 'PM turns philosophical', *The Tribune*, 24 September 2004.
2 Lambah, *In Pursuit of Peace*, p. 294.
3 Bhasin, *India–Pakistan Relations*.
4 Ibid.
5 'PM, Pervez address Kashmir issue', *The Tribune*, 24 September 2004.
6 Bhasin, *India–Pakistan Relations*.
7 Ibid.
8 Ibid.
9 Lambah, *In Pursuit of Peace*.
10 Steve Coll, 'The Back Channel', *New Yorker*, 22 February 2009.
11 Bhasin, *India–Pakistan Relations*.
12 They also agreed to operationalise additional routes including that between Poonch and Rawalakot. They called for an early start of the bus service between Amritsar and Lahore and to religious places such as Nankana Sahib. They agreed to re-establish the Khokhrapar-Munnabao rail route in the Rajasthan desert by 1 January 2006.

13 On way to Jakarta to participate in the Bandung Golden Jubilee conference, Prime Minister told the journalists (22 April 2005) accompanying him on board the special aircraft.
14 Advani, *My Country, My Life*
15 Ibid.
16 Bhasin, *India–Pakistan Relations*
17 Shyam Saran, H*ow India Sees the World: Kautilya to the 21st Century*, Juggernaut, 2018.
18 Ibid.
19 Ibid.
20 Subramaniam, *Full Spectrum*
21 Ibid.
22 Ibid.
23 Ibid.
24 Bhasin, *India–Pakistan Relations*
25 Ibid.
26 Ibid.
27 Ibid.

26. DOWN TO SEMICOLONS

1 Bhasin, *India–Pakistan Relations.*
2 Lambah *In Pursuit of Peace*, p.320.
3 A. G. Noorani, 'A step closer to consensus', *Frontline*, 15 December 2006.
4 Lambah, *In Pursuit of Peace,* p. 310.
5 Bhasin, *India–Pakistan Relations.*
6 Ibid.

SECTION 7. 2007–2017: KILLING AND CHILLING

27. REVENGE OF THE SNAKES

1 'Justice (r) Rana Bhagwandas passes away'. *The News International,* 23 February 2015.
2 Bhasin, *India–Pakistan Relations.*
3 Ibid.
4 Owen Bennett-Jones, *The Bhutto Dynasty: The Struggle for Power in Pakistan*, New Haven: Yale University Press, 2020.
5 'HT Edit: The light goes out', Hindustan Times, 27 December 2007.
6 Bhasin, *India–Pakistan Relations.*
7 Saurabh Shukla, 'Dangerous designs', *India Today*, 12 January 2008.
8 Author's conversation with Malti Rao, New Delhi, September 2023.
9 Sabharwal, *India's Pakistan Conundrum*, p. 179.

28. MASSACRE IN MUMBAI

1 Shahid Malik interviewed by the author, October 2023.
2 Pranab Mukherjee, *The Coalition Years: 1996-2012*, New Delhi: Rupa Publications, 2017, p. 117.
3 'Jailed militant's hoax calls drove India, Pakistan to brink of war', *Dawn, 26 November* 2009.
4 Salman Masood, 'Chief of Pakistan intelligence to visit India to help in investigation', *New York Times*, 28 October 2008.
5 Mukherjee, *The Coalition Years.*, p. 118.
6 Ibid.
7 'TEXT - Prime Minister's statement on Mumbai attack', *Reuters*, 27 November 2008.
8 Menon, *Choices.*
9 Satyabrata Pal, 'Dialogue is the only option', *The Hindu*, 2 September 2013.
10 Satyabrata Pal, 'Engaging Pakistan', *India Quarterly*, Volume 65, No. 4, 2009.

29. DIPLOMATIC DOODLES

1 Sabharwal, *India's Pakistan Conundrum*, p 119.
2 Ibid.
3 Ibid.
4 Menon, *Choices.*
5 Ibid.
6 Sabharwal, *India's Pakistan Conundrum*, p. 47.

7   Ehsanullah Ehsan, 'Pak military wanted me to lead its hit squad: Ex Taliban commander' *Sunday Guardian*, 3 July 2021.
8   Sabharwal, *India's Pakistan Conundrum*.
9   Ibid.
10 Farhan Bokhari and James Fontanella-Khan, 'Pakistan envoy accused over "Memogate"', *Financial Times*, 12 June 2012.
11 Sabharwal, *India's Pakistan Conundrum*, p. 49.
12 Shiv Aroor and Gaurav C. Sawant, 'Siachen demilitarisation: Could PM gift away to Pakistan what Army has won?', *India Today*, 14 May 2012.
13 'US professor's anti-Pak agenda?', *The News International*, 7 February 2016.

30. DELHI DURBAR

1   'PM hopes of visiting Pakistan in coming months', *Times of India*, 3 January 2014.
2   Natwar Singh, *One Life is Not Enough*.
3   Abdul Basit, *Hostility: A Diplomat's Diary on Pakistan-India Relations*, Gurugram: HarperCollins India, 2021.
4   Sabharwal, *India's Pakistan Conundrum*, pp. 136–40.
5   Ibid, p. 307
6   Ibid, p. 293-298
7   T. C. A. Raghavan interviewed by the author in 2022.
8   Lambah, *In Pursuit of Peace*.
9   'Prime Minister Narendra Modi`s letter to Nawaz Sharif - Full Text', *Zee News*, 13 June 2014.
10 Lambah, *In Pursuit of Peace*, p. 314-315.
11 Basit, *Hostility*.
12 Basit, *Hostility*; 'Full Text: Abdul Basit on Nawaz Sharif 'Pandering' to India and Being Sidelined By Pak PM', *The Wire*, 26 March 2021.
13 'Modi: Peshawar attack a senseless act of unspeakable brutality', *Hindu Businessline*, 16 December 2014.
14 'Unfortunate that Uri happened, but my Pak visit created a positive vibe for India: PM Modi on Nawaz Sharif meeting', *India TV*, 4 May 2019; India TV, 'I went to Lahore out of goodwill because Nawaz Sharif had come to my swearing-in, says PM Modi', YouTube, 4 May 2019.
15 Shubhajit Roy and Anand Mishra, 'Nawaz Sharif's praise for Burhan Wani soured relations with Pakistan: Sushma Swaraj', *Indian Express*, 4 August 2017.
16 'India pulls out of Saarc summit in Pak', *Deccan Herald*, 28 September 2016.
17 'Kashmir attack: India 'launches strikes against militants"', *BBC*, 30 September 2016.
18 Cyril Almeida, 'Exclusive: Act against militants or face international isolation, civilians tell military', *Dawn*, 6 October 2016.
19 Ibid.
20 'Predecessor used 'Dawn leaks' to get extension, claims Gen Bajwa,' *Dawn*, 30 March 2023.
21 'Pakistan sacks judge accused of 'blackmail' in ex-PM Sharif case', *AlJazeera*, 12 July 2019.
22 Ibid.
23 'Pakistan's ex-Army chief Bajwa claims his predecessor sought 3-year extension: Report', *Economic Times*, 30 March 2023.

SECTION 8. 2017-2023: TOUGH TALKING
31. LIES, DECEIT, AND DIPLOMACY

1   Jayanth Jacob, 'New Indian envoy for China could be delayed', *Hindustan Times*, 30 June 2017.
2   Donald Trump (@realDonaldTrump), X.com, 1 January 2018, <https://twitter.com/realDonaldTrump/status/947802588174577664>.
3   'Donald Trump warns Pakistan against providing safe havens to terrorists: Full text of his speech', *Indian Express*, 22 August 2017.
4   Pak Defence—PMLN (@PakDefencePMLN), X.com, 1 January 2018, <https://twitter.com/PakDefencePMLN/status/947843255286353921>.
5   PTI, 'China defends Pakistan after Trump tweet', *The Hindu*, 2 January 2018.
6   'After Indian Diplomats Complain of Harassment, Pakistan Protests Unfair Treatment of Its Officials', *The Wire, 11 March 2018*.
7   Ibid.
8   'G. Parthasarathy, 'Booted and roasted' during Indo–Pak chill', *Times of India*, 25 January 2003.
9   Chandra, *A Life Well Spent*, p. 174.
10 'Pakistan prevents Sikh pilgrims from meeting Indian High Commissioner and staff', Media Center, Ministry

of External Affairs, Government of India, 15 April 2018.

11 'India lodges strong protest at denial of access to the Indian High Commissioner and consular officials of the Indian High Commission to the visiting Indian pilgrims', Media Center, Ministry of External Affairs, Government of India, 23 June 2018.

12 The Constitution (Eighteenth Amendment) Act, 2010, passed after Musharraf's political demise, overhauled Pakistan's 1973 constitution to promote devolution and federalism and to deter further army coups. It altered about a third of Pakistan's Constitution and was periodically criticised by the army for devolving too much power and resources away from the centre.

13 Suhail Warraich, 'The Bajwa Doctrine: from chauvinism to realism', *The News International*, 18 March 2018.

14 'The "Bajwa doctrine"', *Dawn*, 25 March 2018.

15 Sushant Singh, 'In bilateral chill, small steps towards thaw, says Indian envoy to Pakistan Ajay Bisaria', *Indian Express*, 22 May 2018.

16 The situation on the LOC stood in stark contrast to the one on the Chinese border (LAC) that had been one of relative peace and tranquillity, with not a shot having been fired and not a life having been lost for four decades.

17 Happymon Jacob, *Line on Fire: Ceasefire Violations and India–Pakistan Escalation Dynamics*, New Delhi: Oxford University Press, 2019.

18 For his book, *The Line of Control: Travelling with the Indian and Pakistani Armies*, a professor at Jawaharlal Nehru University, Happymon Jacob, travelled on both sides of the LOC and got to be embedded, in a sense, with both armies.

32. NAYA PAKISTAN, OLD TRICKS

1 'Congratulating Imran Khan, Modi hopes democracy will take deeper roots in Pakistan', *The Hindu*, July 30 2018.

2 After returning in 2019, General Bajwa spoke informally to several journalists. Several stories appeared in Pakistan's media including reports by journalists Javed Choudhry and Shahid Maitla. See also: 'IHC issues notices to Gen (r) Bajwa, Gen (r) Faiz Hameed for 'misrepresenting events', *Daily Pakistan*, 9 October 2023; Hamid Mir, 'Dirty game: Untold story of Imran Khan and Gen Bajwa's love-hate relationship | OPINION', *India Today*, 1 August 2023.

3 The South Asia Portal hosts credible data and assessments on terrorist incidents and infiltration in Jammu and Kashmir, <https://www.satp.org/datasheet-terrorist-attack/fatalities/india-jammukashmir>.

4 'Pakistani singer Shafqat Amanat Ali stokes controversy with Kashmir song', *WION*, 3 August 2020.

5 'Won't engage with talent from neighbouring country in future: Karan Johar', *Hindustan Times*, 19 October 2016.

33. PULWAMA

1 'India Withdraws Most Favoured Nation Status To Pakistan After Pulwama Attack', *India Today*, 15 February 2019.

2 'PM Modi Condemns Pulwama Blood Bath, Says Sacrifice Will Not Go In Vain', India Today, *India Today*, 16 February 2019

3 Financial Action Task Force (FATF), the global inter-governmental watchdog for terror financing, had put Pakistan on its 'list of jurisdictions under increased monitoring', or 'Grey List', in 2018, impacting funding for Pakistan's economy. The country managed to get off the grey list only in October 2022.

4 Sabtain Ahmed Dar, 'Pulwama Attack: Another Indian "False Flag" to frame Pakistan', *Global Village Space*, 15 February 2019.

5 'Pakistan will address actionable evidence if shared by Delhi, PM Khan tells India after Pulwama attack', *Dawn*, 19 February 2019.

6 'India's response to remarks by Prime Minister of Pakistan on the Pulwama Terrorist Attack', Media Center, Ministry of External Affairs, Government of India, 19 February 2019.

7 The United Nations Security Council Resolution 1267 adopted in 1999, creating a sanctions regime of travel bans, arms embargos and asset freezes for individuals and entities associated with Al-Qaida, Taliban, and others. It saw decade-long diplomatic efforts led by India and supported by its friends at the UNSC, to list Jaish-e-Mohammad founder Maulana Azhar.

8 'DG ISPR reiterates "talks, not war" proposal to India, distances Pakistan from Pulwama', *Dawn*, 22 February 2019.

9 The Kumbh, a religious gathering associated with Hinduism, is held every six years in the city of Prayagraj, at the confluence of the Ganga, Yamuna, and the mythical Saraswati River.

10 'Statement by Foreign Secretary on 26 February 2019 on the Strike on JeM training camp at Balakot, Media Center, Ministry of External Affairs, Government of India, 26 February 2019.

11 Sunetra Choudhury, Jimmy Jacob (ed.), 'Opposition Backs Air Strike At All-Party Meet, But Warns Against Anti-Kashmiri "Jingoism"', *NDTV*, 26 February 2019.
12 In the author's conversations with western diplomats, particularly with the P5, later pieced together the Pakistan end of the diplomacy that accompanied their reaction to the Balakot air strikes.
13 Shishir Gupta, Rezaul H Laskar and Yashwant Raj, 'India, Pakistan came close to firing missiles at each other on February 27', *Hindustan Times*, 23 March 2019; Sanjeev Miglani, Drazen Jorgic, 'India, Pakistan threatened to unleash missiles at each other: sources', *Reuters*, 17 March 2019.
14 'PM: Pakistan returned Abhi or it would've seen 'qatal ki raat', *Times of India*, 22 April 2019.
15 Mike Pompeo, *Never Give an Inch: Fighting for the America I Love*, New York: Broadside Books, 2023.
16 'Foreign minister Qureshi's legs were shaking as he said India could attack over Abhinandan: Pakistani MP', *Hindustan Times*, 29 October 2019.
17 Details in Section 6, Chapter 21.
18 Shishir Gupta, 'Only seven people knew of the timing of air strike on Balakot', *Hindustan Times*, 15 June 2020.
19 The 'ladder of escalation', conceptualized by American strategist Herman Kahn, in his book *On Escalation* (1965) Kahn controversially presented a 'generalised (or abstract) scenario' made up of 44 'rungs' that the world might climb to pass from crisis to Armageddon.
20 In August 2020, the NIA filed a charge sheet with 'irrefutable evidence—technical, material and circumstantial—on Pakistan's role in the attack.' It charged the JeM chief Masood Azhar and eighteen others in the Pulwama attack, citing details like chats, calls details of terrorists. In September 2020, an NIA court declared Masood Azhar, his two brothers—Rouf Asgar and Ammar Alvi—and three others as absconders in the case. It revealed that the JeM called off another planned attack due to the global scrutiny following the Balakot air strikes.
21 Francesca Marino, 'As many as 170 JeM terrorists killed in Balakot airstrike: Italian journalist', *India Today*, 8 March 2019.
22 'Pakistan accuses India of plotting fresh military attack, *BBC*, 8 April 2019.
23 Cyril Almeida, 'Exclusive: Act against militants or face international isolation, civilians tell military', *Dawn*, 6 October 2016.
24 'Masood Azhar ban, *Dawn*, 3 May 2019
25 'Pakistan kills over 17,600 militants in counter-terrorism ops: Foreign Office', *Indian Express*, 2 February 2018.
26 Ashley J. Tellis, 'View: Pakistan will not change, India has to prepare better', Economic Times, 25 February 2019.
27 C. Christine Fair, *Fighting to the End: The Pakistan Army's Way of War*, New York: Oxford University Press, 2014; Fair, *In Their Own Words*.
28 Ibid.
29 Sarral Sharma, 'The new Pakistan army chief faces an uphill task of ensuring stability ', *Observer Research Foundation*, 22 December 2022.
30 'Infiltration in Jammu and Kashmir (J&K) 2001 – 2019*', *South Asia Terrorism Portal*.
31 Sabharwal, *India's Pakistan Conundrum*.
32 T. C. A., 'Guest Column | Kartarpur: The context of a Corridor', *India Today*, 5 August 2019.

34. KASHMIRIYAT

1 'Vajpayee formula of insaniyat, kashmiriyat & jamhooriyat is the only way for J&K: PM Modi', *India Today*, 27 April 2019.
2 'Pakistan PM Khan: Kashmir issue 'cannot keep boiling', *BBC*, 10 April 2019.
3 PTI, 'Pakistan PM sees better chance of peace talks with India if Modi's BJP wins election', *Economic Times*, 10 April 2019.
4 Kallol Bhattacherjee and Mehmal Sarfraz, 'Pakistan PM Imran Khan calls up PM Modi, expresses desire to work together', *The Hindu*, 26 May 2019.
5 'Zakir Musa: Thousands mourn India's 'most wanted' militant', *BBC*, 24 May 2019.
6 Shishir Gupta, 'Pak army tries to corner Supreme Court's tough judge. It is worried about 2023', *Hindustan Times*, 3 August 2020; Hasnaat Malik, 'No proof Justice Isa's wife, children are his dependents: SC', *The Express Tribune*, 28 October 2019.
7 PTI, 'Imran Khan sacked Gen. Munir as ISI chief for raising his wife's corruption PM Sharif', *The Week*, 22 May 2023.
8 PTI, 'Pakistan's large-scale terrorism industry prevents it from behaving like normal neighbour: S Jaishankar', *India Today*, 26 June 2019.
9 The report was called Pakistan@100, trying to create a long-term vision for where Pakistan should be headed.
10 'Pakistani airspace closure after Balakot strike cost Islamabad Rs 688 crore', *Business Today*, 3 July 2019.

11 'Trump's Kashmir 'mediation' claim: MEA S Jaishankar says "no such request has been made by PM Modi to US Prez"', *Times Now*, 23 July 2019.
12 'Pak court sentences JuD chief Hafiz Saeed to over 15 years in jail in one more terror financing case', *Hindustan Times*, 24 December 2020; In December 2020, JUD chief Hafiz Saeed would be sentenced for a collective imprisonment of more than twenty years on terror financing charges in four cases, a move analysts knew was an attempt by Pakistan to wriggle out of the FATF's grey list. Three other JUD workers were sentenced under Pakistan's Anti-Terrorism Act, 1997, but the most wanted man for India and the US remained Saeed, already in jail since 2017, was a UN designated terrorist with a USD 10 million bounty on his head as a 'Specially Designated Global Terrorist' of the US. To Indian security analysts, all it meant was that the seventy-year-old ISI asset would be kept in a safer safe house, away from the public glare.
13 Mohammad Khan, 'Post-370 options?', *Dawn*, 11 August 2019.
14 'Pakistan and India trade angry accusations at the UNGA', *AlJazeera*, 25 September 2021.
15 Details in Section 5, Chapter 18.
16 Ibid.
17 Shekhar Gupta, 'India shows the world it means business on Kashmir issue at Geneva meet', *India Today*, 31 March 1994; Geeta Mohan, 'Pakistan misses deadline to file resolution on Kashmir in UNHRC', *India Today*, 20 September 2019.
18 Sushant Sareen, 'The corridor is a trap that Pakistan has set for India | Opinion, *Hindustan Times*, 11 November 2019.

CONCLUSION: HISTORY'S AMBIGUOUS LESSONS

1 Ershad Mahmud, 'Freezing Kashmir', *The News International*, 22 January 2023.
2 Sanjay Kathuria, 'Pakistan's Missing Market', *Foreign Policy*, 5 October 2023.
3 Stephen P. Cohen, *Shooting for a Century: The India–Pakistan Conundrum*, Washington: Brookings Institution, 2013.
4 Admiral Raja Menon and Rajiv Kumar, *The Long View from Delhi: To Define the Indian Grand Strategy for Foreign Policy*, New Delhi: Academic Foundation, 2009.
5 Rahul Shewakarmani, 'Does India have a Grand Strategy?', Report on former US Ambassador to India Robert Blackwill's lecture, Gateway House: Indian Council on Global Relations, 27 September 2010.
6 Prakasa, *Pakistan*.
7 Mani Shankar Aiyar, 'A Friend And A Gentleman', *Outlook*, 5 February 2022.
8 Lambah, *In Pursuit of Peace*.
9 Mani Shankar Aiyar, *Memoirs of a Maverick: The First Fifty Years (1941-1991)*, New Delhi: Juggernaut Books, 2023 p. 232.
10 Mani Shankar Aiyar, *Pakistan Papers*, New Delhi: UBS Publishers' Distributors, 1994, p. 38.
11 Chandra, *A Life Well Spent*.
12 Sabharwal, *India's Pakistan Conundrum*, p. 219.
13 Menon, *Choices*.
14 Ibid.
15 Sabharwal, *India's Pakistan Conundrum*.
16 Sabharwal, *India's Pakistan Conundrum*; Ashley J. Tellis, *Striking Asymmetries: Nuclear Transitions in Southern Asia*, Washington, DC: Carnegie Endowment for International Peace, 2022.

BIBLIOGRAPHY

Ahmed, Ishtiaq, *Jinnah: His Successes, Failures, Role in History*, London: Penguin Viking, 2020.
———*The Pakistan Garrison State: Origins, Evolution, Consequences (1947-2011)*, Karachi: OUP Pakistan, 2013.
Aiyar, Mani Shankar, *Memoirs of a Maverick: The First Fifty Years (1941-1991)*, New Delhi: Juggernaut Books, 2023.
———*Pakistan Papers*, New Delhi: UBS Publishers' Distributors, 1994.
Ayub Khan, Muhammad, *Friends not Masters: A Political Autobiography*, New York: Oxford University Press, 1967.
Bakhsh, Ilahi, *With the Quaid-e-Azam During His Last Days*, Karachi: OUP Pakistan, 2012.
Bamzai, Sandeep, *Princestan: How Nehru, Patel and Mountbatten Made India*, New Delhi, Rupa Publications, 2020.
Basit, Abdul, *Hostility: A Diplomat's Diary on Pakistan-India Relations*, Gurugram: HarperCollins India, 2021.
Bass, Gary, *The Blood Telegram: Nixon, Kissinger, and a Forgotten Genocide*, New York: Penguin Random House, 2013.
Bennett-Jones, Owen, *The Bhutto Dynasty: The Struggle for Power in Pakistan*, New Haven: Yale University Press, 2020.
Bhasin, Avtar Singh, *India–Pakistan Relations 1947-2007: A Documentary Study*, New Delhi: Geetika Publishers, 2012.
Bhattacharjee, Kallol, *The Great Game in Afghanistan: Rajiv Gandhi, General Zia and the Unending War*, Noida: HarperCollins, 2017.
Bose, Sumantra, *Kashmir at the Crossroads: Inside a 21st Century Conflict*, New Haven/ London: Yale University Press, 2021.
Burrows, William, *Critical Mass: The Dangerous Race for Superweapons in a Fragmenting World*, New York: Simon & Schuster, 1994.
Butt, Ahsan I., *Secession and Security: Explaining State Strategy against Separatists*, Ithaca: Cornell University Press, 2017
Chandra, Satish, *A Life Well Spent*, New Delhi, Rupa Publications India, 2023.
Chengappa, Raj, *Weapons of Peace: The Secret Story of India's Quest to Be a Nuclear Power*, Gurugram: HarperCollins India, 2001.
Clinton, Bill, *My Life*, New York: Random House, 2004.
Cohen, S. P., *Shooting for a Century: The India–Pakistan Conundrum*, Washington: Brookings Institution, 2013.
Dasgupta, Chandrashekhar, *War and Diplomacy in Kashmir,1947-48*, New Delhi: SAGE Publications India, 2002.
———*India and the Bangladesh Liberation War: The Definitive Story*, New Delhi: Juggernaut Books, 2021
Dayal, Prabhu, *Karachi Halwa*, Gurugram: Zorba Books, 2015.
Dayal, Rajeshwar, *A Life in our Times*, Hyderabad: Orient BlackSwan, 1998.
Devasher, Tilak, *Pakistan: Courting the Abyss*, Gurugram, HarperCollins, 2016.
———*The Pashtuns: A Contested History*, Gurugram, HarperCollins India, 2022.
Dhulipala, Venkat, *Creating a New Medina: State Power, Islam, and the Quest for Pakistan in Late Colonial North India*, Cambridge University Press, 2015.
Dixit, J. N., *India's Foreign Policy, 1947-2003*, New Delhi: Picus, 2003
———*India–Pakistan in War and Peace*, New Delhi: Routledge, 2002.
Durrani, Asad, *Pakistan Adrift: Navigating Troubled Waters*, New Delhi: Context, 2018.
Ganguly, Swagoto (intro.), *Destined to Fight?:India and Pakistan 1990-2017*, New Delhi: Times Group Books, Bennett Coleman & Co. Ltd, 2017.
Ghose, Sagarika, *Atal Bihari Vajpayee: India's Most Loved Prime Minister*, New Delhi, Juggernaut Books, 2021.
Guha, Ramachandra, *India After Gandhi*, New Delhi: Picador, 2007.
Hanif, Mohammed, *Case of Exploding Mangoes*, New York: Knopf Doubleday Publishing Group, 2008.
Haqqani, Husain, *Reimagining Pakistan: Transforming a Dysfunctional Nuclear State*, Gurugram: HarperCollins India, 2018.
Harper, John Lamberton, *The Cold War*, Oxford: Oxford University Press, 2011.
Hajari, Nisid, *Midnight's Furies*, Gurugram: Penguin, 2016.
Jacob, Happymon, *The Line of Control: Travelling with the Indian and Pakistan Armies*, Gurugram: Viking, 2018.
Jaffrelot, Christophe (ed.), *Pakistan: Nationalism Without a Nation?*, London: Zed Books, 2002.
———*Pakistan at the Crossroads: Domestic Dynamics and External Pressures*, Gurugram: Vintage, 2016.
Jaishankar, S., *The India Way: Strategies for an Uncertain World*, Noida: HarperColllins India, 2020
Jalal, Ayesha, *The Sole Spokesman: Jinnah, the Muslim League and the Demand for Pakistan*, Cambridge: Cambridge University Press, 1985.

Jalal, Ayesha, *The Struggle for Pakistan*, Cambridge: Harvard University Press, 2014.

Kathuria, Sanjay (ed.), *A Glass Half Full: The Promise of Regional Trade in South Asia*, South Asia Development Forum, Washington: World Bank, 2018.

Khan, Akbar, *Raiders in Kashmir*, Srinagar: Rebus Publishing House, 1975.

Khan, Humayun, and Parthasarathy, G., *Diplomatic Divide*, New Delhi: Lotus Collection, 2004.

Khan, Shahryar M., *The Begums of Bhopal: A History of the Princely State of Bhopal*, New Delhi: Viva Books Private Limited, 2004.

Khan, Yasmin, *The Great Partition: The Making of India and Pakistan*, New Haven, Yale University Press, 2007.

Lambah, S. K., *In Pursuit of Peace: India-Pakistan Relations Under Six Prime Ministers*, Gurugram: Viking, 2023.

Levy, Adrian, and Scott-Clark, Cathy, *Deception: Pakistan, the United States, and the Global Nuclear Weapons Conspiracy*, New Delhi: Atlantic Books, 2008.

——*Spy Stories*, New Delhi: Juggernaut Boks, 2021.

Menon, Shivshankar, Choices: Inside the Making of Indian Foreign Policy, Gurugram, Penguin Random House India, 2016.

Milewski, Terry, Blood for Blood, Noida: HarperCollins India, 2021.

Nayar, Kuldip, *Scoop! : Inside Stories from The Partition To The Present*, Noida: HarperCollins India, 2006.

Pandita, Rahul, *The Lover Boy of Bahawalpur: How the Pulwama Case was Cracked*, New Delhi: Juggernaut Books, 2021.

Pompeo, Mike, *Never Give an Inch: Fighting for the America I Love*, New York: Broadside Books, 2023.

Prakasa, Sri, *Pakistan: Birth and Last Days of Jinnah*, Meerut, Meenakshi Prakashan, 1965.

Raghavan, Pallavi, *Animosity at Bay: An Alternative History of the India–Pakistan Relationship*, 1947-1952, Gurugram, HarperCollins India, 2020.

Raghavan, Srinath, *1971: A Global History of the Creation of Bangladesh*, Cambridge: Harvard University Press, 2013.

Raghavan, T. C. A., *The People Next Door*, Gurugram, HarperCollins India, 2018.

Raghavan, V. R., *Siachen: Conflict Without End*, New Delhi: Viking, 2002.

Rashid, Ahmed, *Descent into Chaos: The US and the disaster in Pakistan, Afghanistan, and Central Asia*, London: Penguin Books, 2009.

Rushdie, Salman, *Shame*, New York: Knopf, 1983.

Sabharwal, Sharat, *India's Pakistan Conundrum*, New Delhi: Routledge, 2022.

Sarila, Narendra Singh, *The Shadow of the Great Game: The Untold Story of India's Partition*, Noida: HarperCollins India, 2009.

Sattar, Abdul, *Pakistan's Foreign Policy 1947-2019: A Concise History*, Karachi: OUP Pakistan, 2011.

Shea, Debora Ann, *Escape from Pakistan: The Untold Story of Jack Shea*, Gurugram: Penguin Enterprise, 2021.

Sidhu, G. B. S., *The Khalistan Conspiracy*, Noida: HarperCollins, 2020.

Singh, Jaswant, *A Call to Honour: In Service of Emergent India*, New Delhi: Rupa Publications, 2006.

Singh, Kewal, *Partition and Aftermath: Memoirs of an Ambassador*, New Delhi: Vikas Pub. House, 1991.

Singh, K. Natwar, *One Life Is Not Enough*, New Delhi, Rupa Publications India, 2021.

——*'Profiles & Letters'*, New Delhi: Sterling Publishers, 1997.

Sinha, Shakti, *Vajpayee: The Years That Changed India*, Gurugram, Penguin Random House India, 2020.

Sinha, Yashwant, *Relentless: An Autobiography*, New Delhi: Bloomsbury, 2019.

Sitapati, Vinay, *Half-Lion: How P.V. Narasimha Rao Transformed India*, Gurugram, Penguin Random House, 2016.

——*Jugalbandi: The BJP Before Modi*, Gurugram, Penguin Random House, 2020.

Subramaniam, Arjun, *India's Wars: A Military History, 1947-1971*, Gurugram: HarperCollins India, 2016.

Subramaniam, Arjun, *Full Spectrum: India's Wars, 1972-2020*, Noida: HarperCollins India, 2020.

Talbot, Ian, *Pakistan: A Modern History*, London: C. Hurst & Co., 1999.

Talbott, Strobe, *Engaging India: Diplomacy, Democracy and the Bomb*, Gurugram: Viking, 2004.

Tellis, Ashley J., *Striking Asymmetries: Nuclear Transitions in Southern Asia*, Washington: Carnegie Endowment for International Peace, 2022.

Tharoor, Shashi, *The Battle of Belonging: On Nationalism, Patriotism, and What it Means to be Indian*, New Delhi, Aleph Book Company, 2020.

Walsh, Declan, *The Nine Lives od Pakistan: Dispatches from a Divided Nation*, London: Bloomsbury Publishing, 2020.

Zakaria, Anam, *Between the Great Divide: A Journey into Pakistan-administered Kashmir*, Noida: HarperCollins India, 2018.

——*The Footprints of Partition: Narratives of Four Generations of Pakistanis and Indians*, Noida: HarperCollins India, 2015.

INDEX

National Democratic Alliance (NDA), 362
  defeat in the general elections, 319
  handling of Pakistan-related hijacking, 290
  Vajpayee-led, 319
national identity, xvii, xviii
National Investigation Agency (NIA), India,
  410, 423
Nawaz, Maryam, 371
Naya Pakistan, 391, 399–400, 412
Nayar, Kuldip, 10, 197, 269
Nazimuddin, Khawaja, 56

necessity, doctrine of, 177
Neemrana dialogue, 227
Nehru–Ayub summit, 78
Nehru, Jawaharlal, 3, 7, 26, 28, 52, 68, 119,
  220
  concerns over Sino–Pakistan axis, 79
  differences with Pakistan over conduct of
    plebiscite in Kashmir, 57
  dismissal and arrest of Sheikh Abdullah, 57
  meeting with Ayub, 78
  meeting with Mohammad Ali Bogra, 57
  nationalization of the armed forces, 12
  oath in the Constituent Assembly, 11
  'Panchsheel' principles, 59, 80
  policy of non-alignment, 55, 57, 59
  resolving of the border issue of land enclaves
    in Bengal, 76
  role on the Suez crisis, 55
  seeking of US assistance against Chinese
    aggression, 81
  Soviet affair, 59–61
  taking of the Kashmir issue to the UN, 34
  'tryst with destiny', 5
  visit to Karachi, 74, 76
Nehru–Liaquat Pact (1950) 46, 53, 107, 235

Niazi, A. A. K., 146, 150, 159
Niazi, General, 275
Nimitz, Chester W., 58
Nisar, Saqib, 371
Nishtar, Abdur Rab, 7
Nixon administration, 129
Nixon, Richard, 125, 128, 137–8
  meeting with
    Vladimir Muskievich, 147
  military aid to Pakistan, 129
  policy on Pakistan, 129
  silence on the killings in East Pakistan, 129
  tilt towards Pakistan during 1971 War, 147
'no first use' nuclear posture, 342
Non-Aligned Movement (NAM), 180, 326
  summit in March 1983, 187
non-alignment, concept of, 56

non-initiation of combat operations (NICO),
  292
Noon, Feroz Khan, 67, 70, 76
Noorani, Zain, 197
North Atlantic Treaty Organization (NATO),
  58
no-war pact, idea of, 44, 46
'no-war' peace deal, xxvii
nuclear accidents, 270
nuclear diplomacy, 262–3
nuclear reprocessing plant, 172
nuclear test
  Buddha's Smile, 159–61
  by India
    in 1974, 264
    in 1998, 257–64
  Operation Shakti (1998), 259
  by Pakistan (1998), 262, 285, 316
  Pokhran blasts, 258
nuclear umbrella, 263, 272
Nye, Archibald, 40

Oakley, Robert, 221, 222
Omar, Mullah, 356
Operation 'Bluestar' (1984), 190
Operation Brasstacks (1987), 196–9
Operation Desert Storm (1991), 225
Operation Gibraltar (1965), 90, 465
Operation Grand Slam, 92
Operation Gulmarg, 32
Operation Hammerhead (1987), 199
Operation Meghdoot (1984), 194
Operation Nusrat, 90
Operation Parakram (2001–2002), 301–2,
  307, 346
Operation Polo, 38
Operation Radd-ul-Fasaad (Elimination of
  Strife, 2017), 371
Operation Searchlight (1971), 122
Operation Shakti (1998), 259
Operation Tupac (1988), 215
Operation Vijay (1999), 274, 276, 284
Operation Zarb-e-Azb (2014), 371
Organisation of Islamic countries (OIC), 115
overflights, bans on, 49
Overseas Citizens of India (OCI) cards, 458

P5 countries, 417, 452
Padmanabhan, K. V., 76, 78
Pakhtun Tahaffuz Movement (PTM), 380
Pakistan
  abetment of the Punjab insurgency, 205
  action against terrorist groups, 430
  Afghan policy, 460

Printed in the USA
CPSIA information can be obtained
at www.ICGtesting.com
CBHW021941090824
12962CB00030B/269/J